PSYCHO-PATHOLOGY

and

SOCIETY

McGRAW-HILL BOOK COMPANY
NEW YORK
ST. LOUIS
SAN FRANCISCO
AUCKLAND
DÜSSELDORF
JOHANNESBURG
KUALA LUMPUR
LONDON
MEXICO
MONTREAL
NEW DELHI
PANAMA
PARIS
SÃO PAULO
SINGAPORE
SYDNEY
TOKYO
TORONTO

PSYCHO-PATHOLOGY
and SOCIETY

Peter E. Nathan

THE GRADUATE SCHOOL

RUTGERS UNIVERSITY

Sandra L. Harris

DOUGLASS COLLEGE

RUTGERS UNIVERSITY

PSYCHOPATHOLOGY AND SOCIETY

234567890MURM798765

This book was set in Times Roman by
John C. Meyer & Son. The editors were
John Hendry, Susan Gamer, and Mary Barnett;
the designer was Hermann Strohbach;
the production supervisor was Leroy A. Young.
The photo editors were Roberta Guerette and
John Hendry. The drawings were done by
Vantage Art, Inc.
The printer was The Murray Printing Company.

Acknowledgments for quoted material and
illustrations begin on page 525.

Cover: "Inferno," the right panel of the triptych
"Garden of Earthly Delights," by Hieronymous
Bosch; original in the Prado, Madrid, Spain
(Art Reference Bureau)

LIBRARY OF CONGRESS CATALOGING IN
PUBLICATION DATA

Nathan, Peter E.
    Psychopathology and society.

    1. Social psychiatry.   2. Psychology,
Pathological.   I. Harris, Sandra L., joint author.
II. Title [DNLM: 1. Psychopathology.
2. Socioeconomic factors.   WM100 N2743p]
RC455.N37   616.8′9′07   74-12147
ISBN 0-07-046046-9

For Esther and Arthur Baker
and Felice and William Harris

Contents

CHAPTER SEVENTEEN
The organic
brain disorders

Preface

Psychopathology is as much a part of the American scene as Saturday night television, major league baseball, protest demonstrations, barbeques, presidential nominating conventions, or rush-hour traffic jams. But for too many years students of abnormal psychology studied abnormal behavior by reading about the bizarre behavior of "back ward" patients in isolated mental hospitals or by studying the memoirs of psychologists and psychiatrists whose lives, as well as those of their patients, also seemed remote from present-day reality. But in truth psychopathology is very much with all of us. Even if we ourselves have not had serious emotional or adjustment problems, it is almost certain that some of our closest friends, relatives, employers, colleagues, or fellow students have experienced mental disorder in one of its many forms. With this near-certainty in mind, we have written this book to present the facts (and some of the theories) of abnormal behavior in present-day society—without trying, on the one hand, to diminish the tragedy of severe psychopathology or, on the other, to magnify the mystery of mental disorder by making it unrealistically distant from ordinary experience.

We have tried to illustrate the varieties of psychopathology as compellingly as we could—by presenting what we know of the lives of people we have read about as well as the lives of people we have known professionally. We hope this approach will give our readers a sense of the immediate personal impact of psychopathology as well as an idea of the context within which psychopathology actually occurs. These case histories, which open each chapter and sometimes fall within a chapter, are written largely from a social learning perspective—as is the rest of the book. We think that psychopathology viewed from this perspective is more understandable and less mysterious than when conceived of in other ways. The social learning viewpoint also permits us to integrate what is known about the etiology, treatment, and descriptive characteristics of the mental disorders within a consistently data-based framework—a framework we believe is essential for an objective overview of matters best treated objectively. We recognize, however, that there are other legitimate and fruitful ways to look at psychopathology. For this reason we have tried to present these other views fairly. But we do have a distinct point of view, and the reader must be alert for unintentional biases that may have crept into our writing.

The book's title, *Psychopathology and Society,* does, however, reflect an intentional bias that runs through the text. That title emphasizes our conviction that society and psychopathology influence each other crucially in ways that are rarely recognized or fully acknowledged. Often the interaction plays itself out obscurely; those who affect society and in turn are affected by it usually escape notice in the newspapers and history books. But sometimes the interaction is noticeable, dramatic, and—we believe—at least partly traceable. We consider, for example, the impact that Lee Harvey Oswald's psychosis, Fyodor Dostoevsky's depression, and Rudolf Hess's paranoia had on society. We also deal with the important role society played in the development of Malcolm X's antisocial behavior (as well as his later reconstructive behavior), Anne Frank's understandable (and indeed "normal") apprehensions, and Piri Thomas's drug dependency. Psychopathology *and* society: In our view the words are inextricably bound together.

As in all undertakings of this kind, many others have been involved. Norman Garmezy and Frederick Kanfer read the entire manuscript and made extraordinarily helpful comments. Seymour Axelrod, Cyril Franks, Joseph Masling, Stanley Messer, and Bruce Snyder read portions of the manuscript and made many useful comments and criticisms. Our McGraw-Hill editors, John Hendry and Mary Barnett, made our words communicate sense and logic beyond our fondest hopes, Roberta Guerette provided much of the pictorial material. Barbara Honig, Louise Clempner, and Gloria Kurkowski typed the manuscript, doing so with consistent good cheer in the face of the authors' sometimes unreasonable demands. Our clients and patients, sharing with us their pain and their progress, made much of the firsthand case material in the book possible; for reasons of privacy they remain anonymous. Our students in abnormal psychology classes at Douglass College, Rutgers University, taught us a great deal about presenting this kind of material with the blend of scholarship, humanity, and seriousness it demands. We hope that lesson has carried over into the writing of this book.

David, Anne, Laura, Mark, and Florence were very patient throughout.

An instructor's manual is available to teachers of the course.

Peter E. Nathan
Sandra L. Harris

PSYCHO-
PATHOLOGY
and
SOCIETY

CHAPTER ONE
The question of normality

Daniel Paul Schreber ● Malcolm Little ● Normality and
normal behavior ● Abnormality and psychopathology

DANIEL PAUL
SCHREBER:
FAILURE
OF PERSON

Dr. Daniel Paul Schreber was born in 1842 to an influential Leipzig
family. His father, Dr. Daniel Gottlob Morita Schreber, was a physician on the faculty of Leipzig University. He was also an unorthodox
social reformer who tried to bring happiness and health to the German masses by promoting physical culture and organic gardening.
Schreber's mother was a gentle, quiet person, who raised her two
girls and two boys in the comfortable and secure setting of upper-
middle-class Leipzig.

It was during the serene years before the Franco-Prussian War of
the 1870s that Daniel Paul grew up. He remembered his childhood
as a happy one. He felt especially close to his mother, somewhat
more distant from his father. In his memoirs he spoke little of his
feelings for his brothers and sisters, so it is hard to be sure about those
relationships. In adulthood he had a long and, as far as is known,
happy marriage; the only disappointment was that there were no
children. He died in 1911 (four years after the death of his wife) at
the age of 69.

Dr. Daniel Paul Schreber twice suffered from "nervous illness," as
he called it. The first time was in the autumn of 1884, when he was
42. In his own description, the symptoms consisted of "severe hypochondriasis without any incidents bordering on the supernatural."
In other words, he had imaginary physical ailments, but no psychotic
symptoms like delusions or hallucinations. One of his imaginary ailments was loss of weight; he developed the false idea that he was
wasting away.

For this psychological disturbance Schreber spent six months in
the hospital. (Nowadays the same symptoms would not be considered serious enough to require hospitalization.) By the end of
1885, he regarded himself as fully recovered and returned to his work
as judge of the country court in Leipzig. He held that position until
1893, when he was asked to become president of the panel of judges
on the court of appeals at Dresden. For a man of 51 (relatively

Denkwürdigkeiten

eines

Nervenkranken

nebst Nachträgen

und einem Anhang über die Frage:

„Unter welchen Voraussetzungen darf eine für geistes-
krank erachtete Person gegen ihren erklärten Willen
in einer Heilanstalt festgehalten werden?"

von

Dr. jur. Daniel Paul Schreber,
Senatspräsident beim Kgl. Oberlandesgericht Dresden a. D.

Oswald Mutze in Leipzig.
1903.

Title page from Daniel Paul
Schreber's *Memoirs.*
(Schreber, 1903)

1

young, as high-court judges go) it was a great honor, and he accepted with enthusiasm.

But Daniel Paul Schreber served on the court of appeals for only six weeks before he became ill again, this time more seriously. In the middle of November 1893 he was admitted to the psychiatric clinic of the University of Leipzig. In June 1894 he was sent to a private sanatorium near Dresden, and two weeks later he was transferred to nearby Sonnenschein (Sunshine) State Hospital. He stayed there for almost nine years, during which he wrote *Memoirs of My Nervous Illness* (1955)—the source of all the information we have about him.

In this book Schreber described his psychosis in minute detail. Psychiatrists who have read it give his illness various labels: paraphrenia, paranoia, dementia praecox, schizophrenia, paranoid schizophrenia, and severe anxiety neurosis. During his years in Sonnenschein, Schreber wrote, he was at one time or another "negativistic, withdrawn, mute . . . immobile for long periods, impulsive." He repeatedly attempted suicide, was "massively hallucinated and deluded about his own body and his surroundings, suffered from unbearable insomnia" (sleeplessness), and was "tortured by compulsive acting and obsessive thinking." He devotes long sections of the memoirs to descriptions of his fantasies about changes in the shape, size, and function of his genitals. He called these imagined changes the process of "unmanning," which he gave a central place in his intricate delusional system. Because Schreber was able to remember so clearly and describe so vividly a prolonged, severe, and complex

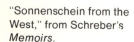

"Sonnenschein from the West," from Schreber's *Memoirs*.

psychosis, the memoirs have been used as a source book on schizophrenia by teachers, researchers, and students. We will refer to them repeatedly in this book.

One researcher who made a close study of Schreber's memoirs was Sigmund Freud, founder of the psychoanalytic movement and the most influential psychologist of the twentieth century. Freud and Schreber never met, but Freud based his theory of paranoid schizophrenia on *Memoirs of My Nervous Illness*. Like many of Freud's other theories, it has had a profound impact on modern conceptions of psychopathology—an impact which will be evaluated in Chapter 7.

MALCOLM LITTLE: FAILURE OF SOCIETY

Malcolm Little was born in 1925 in Omaha, Nebraska, to the Reverend and Mrs. Earl Little. Mr. Little, a traveling Baptist minister and volunteer organizer for Marcus Garvey's Universal Negro Improvement Association, was poor, uneducated, and black. He was a passionate apostle for the cause of black justice—a cause with few black followers in 1925. Malcolm Little's mother, Louise Little, born in the British West Indies to a black mother and white father, was a gentle person whose emotional instability powerfully affected Malcolm's life. It was from his mother that he inherited the light skin and reddish hair that he ultimately grew to hate. Malcolm had two older brothers, an older sister, and a younger sister. He also had two half brothers and a half sister—his father's older children from an earlier marriage.

Among Malcolm's earliest memories were fierce arguments between his father and mother. They usually centered on his father's emotional insensitivity and lack of ambition, and usually ended in violence. His father was gruff and impatient with Malcolm's brothers and sisters, and occasionally beat the older ones "almost savagely if they broke any of his rules." But apparently he never hit Malcolm, who as an adult concluded: "Anti-white as my father was, he was subconsciously so afflicted with the white man's brainwashing of Negroes that he inclined to favor the light ones, and I was his lightest child" (Malcolm X, 1966, pp. 61–62). Another of Malcolm's lasting memories was of hunger, apparently an almost perpetual state in the Little household.

But Malcolm Little's sharpest early memory was of the death of his father. The body, cut almost in half, its skull smashed, was discovered late one evening lying across streetcar tracks in downtown Lansing, Michigan, where the family was living. Malcolm was 6 years old. Though no one knew for sure, most people thought that his father had been killed by white vigilantes for his civil rights "agitating." Malcolm's reaction to his father's death, as he recalled it later, was surprisingly fatalistic—almost detached—perhaps because of his mixed feelings about a father who beat his wife and children. In any event, Malcolm remembered, "We children adjusted more easily than our mother did. We couldn't see, as clearly as she did, the trials that lay ahead. . . . So there we were. My mother was thirty-four years old now, with no husband, no provider or protector, to take care of her eight children" (p. 11).

Though his mother managed to hold the family together and keep it fed for three years, Malcolm became more and more impatient with himself and with his lot in life. His hatred grew toward the unknown white men who had supposedly murdered his father—and toward the white welfare bureaucrats who felt that they knew better than his mother what was right for her family. Doubtless his hostility increased as he saw his mother, worn by her responsibilities, becoming less and less able to cope with them. He wrote later: "We children watched our anchor giving way. It was something terrible that you couldn't get your hands on yet you couldn't get away from. It was a sensing that something bad was going to happen" (p. 9).

And it did happen: his mother was committed to a state hospital when Malcolm was 9 years old. Though the impact on him must have been profound, it was only when he was an adult that he placed the blame: "I truly believe that if ever a state social agency destroyed a family, it destroyed ours. We wanted and tried to stay together. Our home didn't have to be destroyed. But the Welfare, the courts, and their doctor, gave us the one-two-three punch. . . . I have rarely talked to anyone about my mother, for I believe that I am capable of killing a person, without hesitation, who happened to make the wrong kind of remark" (p. 22).

Paradoxically, Malcolm's life became much more stable and secure in the years following his mother's hospitalization and the breakup of the family. He lived with relatives and then with foster parents in Lansing, went to junior high school, began to do well in his classes, and became a good athlete. He made friends for the first time in his life, and for the first time he even had enough to eat. Despite his newfound security, however, Malcolm chose to leave Lansing when he graduated from the eighth grade. He elected to sample the unknown urban joys and sorrows of Boston, where he could live with his father's oldest daughter, Ella.

His decision to leave the place where he had been happy for the first time in his life was not an easy one. It was made much easier, though, by the thoughtless advice of Mr. Ostrowski, his eighth-grade English teacher. The two were talking about careers, and when Mal-

(Grove Press)

4

colm said that he hoped to become a lawyer, Mr. Ostrowski called it an unrealistic ambition. Later Malcolm described his reaction: "I realized that whatever I wasn't, I *was* smarter than nearly all of those white kids. But apparently I was still not intelligent enough, in their eyes, to become whatever I wanted to be. . . . It was then that I began to change—inside" (p. 37). And shortly afterwards he went to Boston.

One of the case histories this book will draw on is the story of Malcolm's years in Boston and New York—as small-time hustler, then as big-time criminal, drug addict, pimp, alcoholic, numbers runner, and robber. His term in prison—the beginning of his transformation from criminal to leader of a renascent people—will also be examined. Those years were crucial ones for Malcolm Little who, shortly after his release from prison, renounced his father's name and assumed the title by which the world now knows him—Malcolm X.

Normality and normal behavior

What is normal behavior? Through the ages men have disagreed on what is and what it is not. The generation gap that divides American society on issues like sex, drugs, and civil disobedience shows that our age is no closer to the answer than earlier ones. Two studies by psychologists have provided evidence that normal people disagree sharply over what is "normal" (Dohrenwend & Chin-Shong, 1967; Yamamoto & Dizney, 1967). And other studies of the same issue have turned up some fairly consistent differences between laymen and mental health professionals: In general, professionals apply the label of mental illness to many kinds of deviant behavior. But laymen usually call a person mentally ill only when his behavior is strikingly odd—that is, when the deviations are extreme (Sarbin & Mancuso, 1970).

It is between professional and professional, however, that the disagreements over normality and abnormality are most heated. What do the two words really mean? This chapter presents some of the contrasting definitions which scholars and scientists have proposed, and men

have lived by, through the ages. To help you see the implications of the different approaches, we will try to fit the facts about Daniel Paul Schreber and Malcolm X to each in turn. The lives of these two men illustrate some of the aggravating problems associated with the simple words *normality* and *abnormality*.

Models, theories, and the scientific method

The three views of normality and the six views of abnormality discussed in the following sections are *models*—another word for theories. The scientist formulates models or theories in order to generalize his observations from the particular instance to the general instance, from a few observations to many observations. The main purpose of a model is to help the scientist make *predictions*. If his predictions come true, he knows that the model is an accurate picture of something in the real world—that it correctly explains a phenomenon. A model of behavior, for example, can help scientists predict an individual's future behavior if it accurately identifies the causes of his past behavior. Or the same model might be used to predict the behavior of a group if it has successfully explained the behavior of a few persons in the group.

When a scientist sets out to create a model, he often starts by proposing a number of models, all of them unproved. Then he tests them against particular aspects of the subject he is investigating. As he accumulates more and more precise information about the subject, he eliminates the models that turn out to be inaccurate until he finds the one that best—most validly—explains his observations. The validation process thus follows a regular pattern, called the *scientific method:*

1 The scientist hypothesizes (proposes) a series of models, using as his starting point the information that already exists about his subject.
2 He makes predictions on the basis of each model.
3 He accumulates additional data (mostly observations and measurements) and checks his predictions against these data. He tries to gather enough information to either accept or reject the assumptions that underlie each model.
4 He sifts through his models, comparing each with the other. He adjusts, combines, or replaces them as often as the data require, until he arrives at the model which leads to the best predictions about his subject.

The resulting model is the most accurate, most generalized approximation of the real world that the scientist can derive. But when scientists everywhere are working on a complex subject, they often produce a number of confusingly different models. Some of these may complement one another, in the sense that each can be used to make predictions about a different aspect of the subject. This is the case with several of the models described here. In the future, scientists may be able to use them as building blocks in constructing larger models, until at last someone arrives at a single model which adequately maps the great dim territories of normality and abnormality. But as you will see, the difficulties associated with this two-sided subject—and particularly the difficulty of measurement—have so far been too much for scientific inquiry.

Models of normality and abnormality existed, of course, long before the eighteenth and nineteenth centuries, when the scientific method evolved. The prescientific theories were developed for the same reason as the scientific ones: people needed models in order to make predictions about the crucial issues associated with normal and abnormal behavior. (For example: Will this man attack me when my back is turned? Do the stars and planets determine human behavior? Does a woman who talks to the air have magic powers to work evil?) Besides summarizing the major scientific models, the following sections review some of these early theories. They also discuss the legal model of insanity, which arose during the age of science but is not itself scientific, since it came from the courtroom rather than the laboratory.

Normality: The ideal model

The earliest recorded view of normality is in the Old Testament, where the Ten Commandments furnish as complete a description of ideal behavior as we know. Jews who failed to keep the commandments were punished. One of the punishments was mental illness: "The Lord shall smite thee with madness, and blindness, and astonishment of heart" (Deuteronomy 28:28). King Saul, who disobeyed a specific military command from God, suffered ever after from periodic depressions which the Bible refers to as "the evil spirit from the Lord."

The concept of normality developed by the Greek philosopher Plato (427 to 347 B.C.) was also an ideal one. Plato divided the human soul into two parts, the rational and the irrational. He saw the rational soul as the rightful leader; its province was the brain, and its outstanding features were immortality and divinity. The irrational soul, essentially the exact

"So Moses went down unto the people, and spake unto them."—*Exodus* 19.25 *(New York Public Library, Prints Division)*

opposite of the rational soul, was mortal. From it came all the "base emotions" man is capable of.

In Plato's ideal system, mental illness resulted when the irrational soul evaded the leadership of the rational soul. He described three kinds of madness—melancholia, dementia, and mania—all of which he thought were products of this disunion of the rational and irrational souls. These relatively sophisticated distinctions among common patterns of abnormality suggest that Plato was a sharp observer of human behavior. He also hypothesized that too much happiness, as in mania, was as much a form of mental illness as too little, as in depression. This assumption is an idealization of mental illness, because it views normality in terms of the Greek ideal of moderation in all things (Zilboorg, 1941). Plato's

rational and irrational souls bear a strong resemblance to Sigmund Freud's rational ego and irrational id. (Similarities and differences between Freud's psychoanalytic model and other historical forerunners will be reviewed in Chapter 4.)

A number of contemporary theorists have proposed ideal conceptions of mental health (among them Kubie, 1954; Shoben, 1957). The most influential modern statement of this position has come from Marie Jahoda. In an early report (1950) she speaks of the difficulties she and her colleagues encountered in a research study on community living because they could not find a usable definition of mental health. She says: "Perhaps the greatest handicap for a systematic study of the social conditions conducive to mental health is the very elusiveness of this concept. As far as we could discover, there exists no psychologically meaningful and, from the point of view of research, operationally useful description" (p. 214).

All research in ways to improve psychological functioning, whether the study focuses on groups of people or on individuals, requires an "operationally useful" definition of mental health. To be operationally useful, the definition must enable the scientist to make evaluations. In research directed at individual functioning, for example, the clinical worker must be able to measure the changes in behavior brought about by a new drug or a new form of psychotherapy before he can recommend its use.

Jahoda believed that she was able to improve the structure and functioning of an entire community. But she found that there were no valid methods for evaluating the effects of the changes she made; she would have to formulate her own operational definition. And because she was dealing with the intricacies of community dynamics, she needed a definition that would not sacrifice breadth and psychological profundity to simplicity of measurement. She proposed five criteria of positive mental health that form a contemporary ideal model of mental health or normality (1950):

1 *The absence of mental disease*—a necessary condition of mental health, but not the only standard.

2 *Normality of behavior,* judged in terms of the society's norms for behavior.

3 *Adjustment to the environment,* which requires a workable relationship between the person's needs and expectations and those of his society.

4 *Unity of personality,* an abstract concept which implies that the person can judge his own competence fairly independently of the opinions of others.

5 *Correct perception of reality,* in that the person receives and processes information accurately from the environment.

Some of the practical problems of evaluation posed by Jahoda's work can be seen more clearly when we attempt to judge the mental health of Daniel Paul Schreber and Malcolm Little by her criteria. (1) Schreber did suffer from mental disorder, in almost everyone's judgment. (2) His behavior during that illness was abnormal. (3) His adjustment to the environment was poor, though on commitment, he did make a reasonable adjustment to the special hospital environment after a period of violent opposition to some of the rules. (4) He did feel that he was able to judge his own competence; but in view of his emotional and perceptual disturbance this criterion is not significant. (5) He did not perceive reality correctly; he was massively hallucinated and continuously deluded.

Thus we *can* judge the state of Schreber's mental health on the basis of Jahoda's 1950 criteria. Comparing his condition with her five ideal norms brings out a clear pattern of deviation.

But Jahoda's criteria are less valuable when it comes to judging Malcolm X's mental health. (1) While he certainly would not have admitted to mental disorder, he was at various times an alcoholic and a drug addict, and his behavior was often antisocial. All these are "official" symptoms of mental illness. (2, 3) While his behavior was superbly adjusted to the norms of his ghetto society, it was chaotic, dangerous, and unlawful by the standards of the surrounding white society. (4) He was independent of others in judging that he functioned competently in the ghetto. (5) But we can question the accuracy of his perception of reality: specifically, the perceptions which led him to conclude that the life-style of the ghetto hustler was the only way of life for a bright young black man of his age.

To summarize: Jahoda's 1950 criteria give a mixed picture of Malcolm X's mental health, in large part because they evaluate the individual according to the widest possible social norms. In a longer statement in 1958, Jahoda altered and added to her list of criteria, perhaps in order to tap "deeper" levels of personality. These criteria put more emphasis on the individual's own sense of his adequacy, competence, and worth, and in so doing they give a more positive (and probably more accurate) indication of Malcolm Little's mental health. For by the distinctly personal, sometimes idiosyncratic standards of Little and the other black hustlers, he was self-actualized, autonomous, supercompetent, and emotionally healthy.

Unfortunately, their increased breadth and profundity make Jahoda's 1958 criteria more abstract and speculative—and thus farther removed from operational usefulness than the early ones. And this is the problem which haunts every behavioral scientist who attempts to confront central issues in mental health: Does he choose between an imprecise evaluation which aims at capturing the essence of personality, or a precise measure which hardly scratches the surface?

Normality: The statistical model

The statistical model deals with the concept of normality in quantifiable terms—terms that can be expressed in numbers. Thus the ideal and statistical models are at the opposite extremes of a continuum. Ideal models of normality are imprecise, but they attempt to encompass the total personality and so can be useful in making judgments about psychological health and adequacy of functioning. Statistical models, since they give answers about personality in number form, are the height of precision, but these answers cover fairly limited elements of the personality.

In the statistical model, what is called normality is converted to a set of test scores that reflect various aspects of normal behavior. Any person's "normality" is then measured by comparing his test scores with the "normal range" of scores made by a large group of people on the tests. These *test norms* specifying what range of scores can be considered average or normal are based upon the relative numbers of people whose scores fall within the range. Suppose that 75 percent of a large group of high school students score within a certain range on a test measuring social maturity. The students falling below that range might well be considered immature socially, while those scoring above it could be regarded as unusually mature.

One of the major strengths of the statistical approach is that it enables different behavioral scientists, holding different theoretical positions, to arrive at similar judgments about a person's normality. But as we have said, this approach has a major weakness in that it skims over important elements of personality in order to achieve reliability (measurement reproducibility) and precision (measurement accuracy). Chapter 5 will demonstrate that the advantages and disadvantages of the statistical model have vital significance for diagnosis and classification.

Today the leading spokesman for the statistical approach is Hans J. Eysenck of the University of London (1970, 1971a, 1971b). To him, normality is judged by a set of responses to several pencil-and-paper tests and to a personal history questionnaire. The questions on the tests cover a wide variety of topics. For example, they ask the person whether he has ever requested professional help for psychological problems, whether he drinks too much, whether he thinks of himself as unusually nervous or anxious, and whether he enjoys life.

The person's answers make it possible to

Hans Eysenck.

place him at a particular point on a two-dimensional measurement matrix. The matrix in Figure 1-1 defines normality as behavior on tests of neuroticism and of introversion-extraversion. The normal group in this matrix falls at the far end of the range of neuroticism scores (because the group's test answers indicated that they feel little anxiety, depression, or discomfort in dealing with other people) and in the middle of the range of introversion-extraversion scores (because their answers showed that they are neither especially shy nor strenuously outgoing). By contrast, the six patient groups in the matrix fall much farther along the neuroticism scale and on one or the other side of the introversion-extraversion dimension.

When Eysenck's system is applied to the full range of abnormal behavior, it must include another scale dimension: psychoticism (1964b). The psychoticism dimension is measured by additional questions designed to cover such factors as whether the person is socially with-

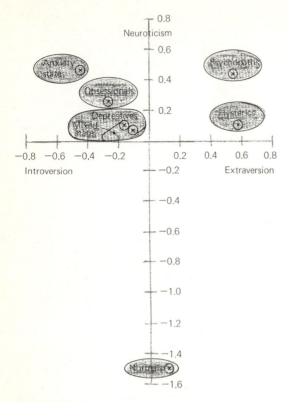

Figure 1-1. Normality, according to this two-dimensional framework or matrix proposed by Eysenck, lies midway along the introversion-extroversion scale and at the bottom of the neuroticism scale. *(Eysenck, 1960b)*

drawn, whether his thought processes are impaired, and whether he has delusions or hallucinations. This information is necessary before Schreber's behavior could be described by the Eysenckian model. On the other hand, Malcolm X's behavior could be covered by the two dimensions graphed in Figure 1-1.

Psychologists are continually developing new statistical approaches to describe behavior. As later chapters will show, many of these are efforts to differentiate more consistently between normal and abnormal responses to tests.

"You have no idea what a drag it is, living in this godforsaken place, waiting for anthropologists to turn up." *(Drawing by Handelsman; © 1970 The New Yorker Magazine, Inc.)*

Normality: The relative model

Anthropologists like to remind psychologists and other behavioral scientists that normality is a relative rather than an absolute concept. Their experiences in the field have convinced them that different cultures define normality by very different criteria. The American anthropologist Ruth Benedict, who devoted much of her life to research on cultural relativity, reached this conclusion from many field observations. As she pointed out, certain behaviors which are considered normal in our society are regarded as abnormal in others, and vice versa (1934).

As an example of behavior judged normal in our society but abnormal in others, Benedict contrasts the value that we place on ambitiousness with the repulsion felt for it by the Zuni Indians of New Mexico. In the Zuni society, "the individual with undisguised initiative and greater drive than his fellows is apt to be branded a witch and hung up by his thumbs." As examples of behaviors that are seen as abnormal in our society but normal elsewhere, Benedict cites the trance states and ascetic life-style of Indian Yogis, and the suspiciousness which dominates the lives of the Dobuans of New Guinea to an extent that we would call paranoid.

Some of Malcolm Little's behavior before he became Malcolm X can be described by the relative model. He went through periods of heavy drug use, he developed a "hustler's mentality" (of which he was very proud), and he seemed to have had sexual relations with as many women (and men) as he wanted to. All these behaviors were within the norms of his special ghetto society, though all would have set him apart if he had been a member of the white middle class. But if Little had acted from the kind of profit-minded amorality common in the executive suites of American business, he would have been out of step in the ghetto, which has its own rigid moral codes. For example, businessmen eager to make a profit have sold inferior or even dangerous products, but if Malcolm Little had peddled adulterated heroin, the ghetto code would have sanctioned his murder.

Opponents of the relative model of normality have insisted that many important forms of disordered behavior are abnormal no matter where or how they occur. They also maintain that certain kinds of normal behavior are never considered abnormal. Wegrocki, an early critic of Benedict's position, argued that the paranoid delusions of the psychotic are basically different from the "institutionalized" delusions which all members of a

To the police, the gang called the "Savage Skulls" has great potential for trouble. But to its members, this group offers the security of belonging and the satisfaction of peer recognition. Some argue that the normality or abnormality of a group's behavior depends on the function of that behavior—and it should be added that the legitimacy (or "normality") of those functions often depends on whether the judgment is being made by a member of the group or by someone outside it. *(Michael Abramson)*

tribe or society share (1939). He said that the best way to distinguish cross-cultural (universal) normality and abnormality from culture-specific (limited to one culture) normality and abnormality is to examine the *function* of the behaviors in question. If they function to maintain or promote the culture—and hence are institutionalized within the culture—they must be considered normal. This view recognizes the relativity of certain behavior patterns (say, Malcolm Little's hustling) and therefore supports a part of Benedict's position. But it broadens the criteria upon which such decisions can be made. Wegrocki's approach allows social scientists to identify almost all of Malcolm Little's behavior as normal without forcing them to say that Schreber was normal too.

Recently the trend of scholarly opinion has begun to favor culture-specific criteria for judging normality and abnormality (Ortigues et al., 1969; Pelicier, 1968). This is partly because the newly emerging countries of Africa are providing anthropologists with a broad new range of data on mental disorder in tribal and regional groups. Wegrocki's "functional" criterion for judging normality still applies to behaviors arising from African animistic religion. For example, a tribesman who believes that trees and stones are inhabited by spirits is not abnormal when these beliefs are institutionalized within his culture. What the new research does indicate is that standards of normality and abnormality vary more widely from culture to culture than was supposed.

Although the relative model of normality is not a serious evaluative or diagnostic tool like the statistical or the ideal models, it serves to remind us that behavior is always at least a partial function of the circumstances within which it takes place.

Abnormality and psychopathology

Psychopathology: The moral model

Just as the Jews of the Old Testament viewed normal behavior as an ideal way of life—a life lived in strict obedience to the Ten Commandments—they saw abnormality as the natural and inevitable consequence of deviation from God's word. That is, they thought of abnormal behavior in moral terms—as a result of sin.

The idea that mental illness is the product of sin and moral transgression has lasted almost to our own time. But its period of greatest influence came after the publication in 1487 of

Frontispiece of *Malleus Maleficarum.* (New York Public Library, Rare Books Division)

The Witches' Hammer (Malleus Maleficarum) by Johann Sprenger and Heinrich Kraemer (1970). Sprenger and Kraemer, who were Dominican Brothers, wrote their book to "prove" that an invariable relationship exists between sin and mental disease. They wanted to justify the execution of "witches," who were usually poverty-stricken, demented women. The logic of this approach to the enigma of mental illness is illustrated by their argument:

Those err who say that there is no such thing as witchcraft, but that it is purely imaginary, even although they do not believe that devils exist except in the imagination of the ignorant and vulgar, and the natural accidents which happen to a man he wrongly attributes to some supposed devil. For the imagination of some men is so vivid that they think they see actual figures and appearances which are but the reflections of their thoughts, and then these are believed to be apparitions of evil spirits or even the spectres of witches. But this is contrary to true faith, which teaches us that certain angels fell from heaven and are now devils, and we are bound to acknowledge that by their very nature they can do many wonderful things which we cannot do. And those who try to induce others to perform such evil wonders are called witches. And because infidelity in a person who has been baptized is technically called heresy, therefore such persons are plainly heretics [Sprenger & Kraemer, 1970, pp. 2–3].

Thus, says Dr. Gregory Zilboorg, a prominent historian of psychiatry, "Two monks brush aside the whole mass of psychiatric knowledge which had been so carefully collected and preserved by almost two thousand years of medical and philosophic investigation; they brush it aside almost casually and with such stunning simplicity that no room is left for argument" (1941, p. 273). The deaths of Joan of Arc, several hundred Salem women, and thousands of other women in Europe were some of the consequences of the view put forth so effectively in *Malleus Maleficarum.*

Though our society no longer burns witches, until very recently it imprisoned the insane in "hospitals" where living conditions and prospects for treatment guaranteed a living death.

Burning was not always considered necessary to exorcise devils. In this medieval picture St. Clara "treats" a psychotic young woman. *(The Bettmann Archive)*

Two contemporary authors have pointed out that our society still seems to view mental illness as a sinful act of volition. One of these men, the psychiatrist Thomas Szasz, condemns this view. The other, the psychologist O. H. Mowrer, thinks that under certain circumstances it is useful to approach mental illness as a moral issue.

Szasz, a lively and controversial critic of many traditional psychiatric practices, says: "The belief in mental illness, as something other than man's trouble in getting along with his fellow man, is the proper heir to the belief in demonology and witchcraft. Mental illness exists or is 'real' in exactly the same sense in which witches existed or were 'real'" (1960, p. 117). Thus Szasz believes that mental illness is an imaginary concept; he is convinced that what are called mental disorders are simply *problems in living* in a society as complex as ours.

Mowrer, on the other hand, claims that when the disturbed person "begins to accept his guilt and his sinfulness, the possibility of radical reformation opens up; and with this, the individual may legitimately, though not without pain and effort, pass from deep, pervasive self-rejection and self-torture to new freedom, of self-respect and peace" (1960, p. 303). That is, once the person truly believes that his disorder is his "fault," he can begin to do something about it. Of course, Szasz and Mowrer disagree as violently with each other as many behavioral scientists do with them.

Mental patients themselves sometimes speak of their disorders in morality-based terms. One study compared the attitudes of patients and nonpatients on the issue (Crumpton et al., 1967). It found that "ratings of the concept 'mental patient' are more likely to resemble ratings of 'sick person' and 'dangerous person' when made by normals, and to resemble ratings of 'criminal' and 'sinner' when made by depressed patients."

Malcolm X attributed most of his misfortunes and maladaptive behavior to a society which he considered seriously askew. By contrast, Daniel Paul Schreber, the product of an earlier age and a vastly different culture, often spoke of the possibility that his psychosis might be due to his own (imaginary) moral excesses. For example, Schreber wrote: "The talk of the voices had already become mostly an empty babel of ever recurring monotonous phrases in tiresome repetition. . . . Among these phrases are those in which I was called a *Prince of Hell* . . . 'The Prince of Hell is responsible for the loss.' . . . The phrase 'Prince of Hell' was probably meant to convey the uncanny power inimical to God that could develop from moral decay among mankind" (p. 140).

Psychopathology: The medical model

Many mental disorders are the result of temporary or permanent damage to the central nervous system—for example, cerebral aneurysm, "stroke," or brain tumor. Others are produced by infection, faulty metabolic or endocrine functioning, or poisons (including alcohol and drugs). Officially, these conditions are "disorders caused by or associated with impairment of brain tissue function" (APA, 1968, p. 5). Since they are the product of structural or functional changes in the nervous system, their treatment may involve drugs, surgery, or other physical therapies, as discussed in Chapters 11 and 17. Few people would argue that such conditions should be viewed as *medical problems* requiring medical treatment.

There are, however, many other mental disorders for which no physical or organic cause (etiology) has been found. In this group are the psychotic disorders called the schizophrenias, whose victims throughout the world occupy more hospital beds than patients with any other mental or physical complaint. Other conditions which seem to have no physical cause are the manic-depressive psychoses, the neuroses, and the personality disorders. Is it appropriate to diagnose and treat these conditions according to ideas carried over from physical medicine? Opinions are strong on both sides.

The medical model of mental illness implies (1) an organic cause, (2) certain assumptions about diagnostic methods, and (3) a certain approach to treatment strategy.

[1] The medical model for the *etiology* of a mental disorder assumes that an underlying pathological condition is causing the "disease." In physical medicine, such an underlying pathology may be an infection, tissue damage from injury, or a disorder of metabolism. The same model applied to psychopathologic conditions assumes that the basic cause of the "mental symptoms" is either tissue damage or malfunction, or an underlying "diseased" core. Examples of *tissue damage or malfunction* are the genetic theories of the etiology of manic-depressive psychosis (Chapter 8) and the metabolic theories of the etiology of schizophrenia (Chapter 7). An example of an *underlying diseased core* is the psychoanalytic theory of damage from early psychological trauma (Chapter 4). Thus psychoanalysis uses the medical model to explain "illness" even though it does

not assume that the causes of a patient's disorder are organic.

[2] The medical model for psychological *diagnosis* stems directly from medically based ideas about etiology. Doctors diagnose physical illnesses on the basis of "signs and symptoms" which they assume reflect the nature, severity, and duration of an underlying organic disorder. For this reason the doctor does not end the diagnosis by concluding that the patient has a spot on the lung, a cough, a low fever, and a feeling of weakness. He continues until he can be sure that the signs and symptoms are caused by tuberculosis, which he then treats. For the same reason, when the psychologist or psychiatrist who uses the medical model observes a patient overwhelmed with anxiety, he will "see beyond" that symptom. He will conclude that it is the sign of a more basic, deep-rooted conflict, which he will then try to treat.

[3] The medical model for psychological *treatment* follows treatment patterns in physical medicine, where the doctor aims to destroy the underlying pathological agent. Such treatment of mental disorders aims to "root out" the underlying causes of disordered behavior. Either the psychiatrist tries to alter impaired physical functioning (say, through drugs) or, as in psychoanalysis, he attempts to treat the unconscious determinants of a patient's neurosis through psychoanalytic methods.

Possibly the strongest challenge to the currently dominant position the medical model of mental illness holds in our society is the growing belief that mental disorder is only one consequence of living in the disordered and imperfect society that is twentieth-century America. Malcolm X might have chosen to explain those aspects of his character which others labeled abnormal as a *social consequence*.

By contrast, Daniel Paul Schreber's illness can be viewed clearly from the perspective of the medical model. Schreber himself thought of his disorder as having been imposed upon him by external forces, most of them beyond his control. And he felt that exorcism of these forces was necessary before he could be well again. He was convinced that the "pathologi-

cal agent" of the forces was Professor Flechsig, his psychiatrist, whom he believed was working with God to cause his hallucinations. In a way, the forces were like an infectious organism; Schreber was convinced that his "infection" had to be rooted out before he could recover.

Advantages of the medical model. In certain important ways, the medical model was a major step forward. For one thing, it took the moral responsibility for his condition away from the individual patient and placed it on circumstances over which he had no control. As a consequence this model, which began to supersede the moral model in the early 1800s, reduced the disgrace attached to the mental disorders and led to the "humanization" of conditions in mental hospitals. The medical model also encouraged empirical research and detailed, objective observation of abnormal behavior for diagnostic purposes. Finally, it raised the standing of the occupations connected with mental health, so that more and more bright, capable young people chose these careers. This was a great change from the time when the jobs in hospitals for the insane were filled by people whom no one else would hire.

Disadvantages of the medical model. But the medical model of mental disorder also has serious shortcomings. Some critics (for instance, Kanfer & Saslow, 1965; Sarbin & Mancuso, 1972) dislike it because it is responsible for the present "official" diagnostic system. (This is the *Diagnostic and Statistical Manual of Mental Disorders,* second edition, or DSM II for short; Chapter 5 will describe it.) In a carry-over from physical medicine, the system classifies patients according to the abnormal behavior they show rather than by criteria more directly relevant to treatment. Growing numbers of mental health professionals now want to base diagnosis on criteria that are connected with therapy, not etiology.

Even more important, the medical model inevitably leads to the view that hospitals and clinics are the places where the mental disorders should be treated. Yet many professionals today emphasize *primary prevention* of mental disorder in schools, at home, and in the community at large rather than treatment of neglected (and therefore more serious) conditions in hospitals. In opposition to the medical model's emphasis on hospitalization, George Albee, a clinical psychologist who was president of the American Psychological Association in 1969, has written: "Disturbed and disturbing human behavior currently is 'explained' by a conceptual model which attributes causation to 'disease' or to some form of 'illness.' The contents of the explanatory model accounting for these sorts of human deviation dictates the specific kind of institutional structure which society must support for the delivery of care or intervention" (1968, p. 317).

"On Being Sane in Insane Places." This is the title of an article by the Stanford psychologist David Rosenhan (1973). It reports a study in which he and seven other sane people applied at various times for admission to twelve psychiatric hospitals. The hospitals ranged in quality from high to low.

Rosenhan and his fellow "pseudopatients" assumed that most of the hospital admissions offices would quickly spot the hoax. To their amazement, they found that they were welcomed wherever they walked in and complained that they had been hearing voices (which said "empty," "hollow," and "thud"). Beyond giving these symptoms and falsifying their names and vocations, none of the eight pseudopatients changed their usual behavior or lied about their past history. They detailed the important events in their lives exactly as they remembered them, accurately described their relationships with people in the past and present, and spoke honestly about their pleasures and pains in life.

As soon as they were admitted to a psychiatric ward, the pseudopatients stopped pretending to have any abnormal symptoms. When they were questioned, they said that they had not heard the voices since they had been in the hospital. To pass the time they struck up conversations with other patients and the staff, looked forward to meals, watched television, read—behaved as any normal person would in a similar situation. Mainly, they were bored. For the purposes of the study they had to make running notes of their experiences, and they thought at first that the note taking would give them away. But in every case, it turned out, the ward staff paid no attention. It was only the other patients who noticed their constant writing. In some hospitals a few of the patients correctly concluded that the newcomer was a researcher instead of a fellow patient.

Thus the most unexpected finding of Rosenhan's study was that "despite their public 'show' of sanity, the pseudopatients were never detected" (p. 252). In every case but one, they were admitted to the hospital with a diagnosis of schizophrenia. The one exception was diagnosed later as schizophrenic, and all the pseudopatients were finally discharged (in 7 to 52 days) with a diagnosis of schizophrenia "in remission."

Rosenhan says that one of the primary reasons for these astonishing results is the natural tendency of doctors to call a healthy person sick when they are in doubt about a diagnosis. He believes that this practice is appropriate in medicine, where it is clearly better than calling a sick person healthy. But he considers it distinctly inappropriate in psychiatry, because psychiatric diagnoses lead to profound personal, social, and legal problems—yet do not seem to ensure effective treatment.

Rosenhan's study spotlights the professional's basic inability to distinguish the sane from the insane in psychiatric hospitals. In part this is because the hospitals themselves make normal behavior less identifiable. The "good" hospital patient is quiet, obedient, and withdrawn—behavior which is not necessarily normal in other environments. In part it is because the doctors who work in the hospitals think in terms of abnormality rather than normality. And in part it is because by definition, those who come to hospitals are sick.

The ultimate meaning of Rosenhan's study depends on who you are and where you sit.

(Jerry Cooke)

To us, the authors of this book, it means that you'd better be sure you're sick before you walk through the doors of most psychiatric hospitals.

Psychopathology: The social-consequence model

In arguing that the mental disorders are names for *problems of living* instead of illnesses, psychiatrist Thomas Szasz, the most articulate opponent of the medical model, means that abnormality is the consequence for some persons of trying to cope with our society. His critics have pointed out that the organic brain disorders (e.g., chronic alcoholism, narcotics addiction, the senile psychoses) are certainly not just "problems of living." Szasz agrees, and replies: "For those who regard mental symptoms as signs of brain disease, the concept of mental illness is unnecessary and misleading. For what they mean is that people so labeled suffer from diseases of the brain and, if that is what they mean, it would seem better for the sake of clarity to say that and not something else" (1960, p. 114).

Szasz bases his rejection of the medical model on the logical inconsistency of the arguments used to justify it. The inconsistency, he says, derives from the fact that all accepted "traditional" concepts of physical and mental illness imply "deviation from some clearly defined norm." For physical illness, this norm is the "structural and functional integrity of the human body."

For mental illness, however, Szasz sees no equivalent norm. "Whatever this norm might be," he says, "we can be certain of only one thing: namely, that it is a norm that must be stated in terms of *psychosocial, ethical,* and *legal* concepts." To Szasz the fundamental error of the medical model is its failure to recognize that while the norm for judging mental illness is a psychosocial and ethical one, its remedy is phrased inappropriately in medical terms (for example, chemotherapy, hospitalization, even psychotherapy).

Szasz concludes that this logical error places therapists in continuing conflict with themselves over the question of whose agent they are. Are they primarily in the service of "the patient, of the relatives, of the school, of the military services, of a business organization, of a court of law, and so forth?" He concludes: "It seems logically absurd to expect that [medical treatment] will help solve problems whose very existence had been defined and established on nonmedical grounds" (1960, p. 115).

Szasz defines problems in living, which others call mental illness, as man's awareness of himself, of the world about him, of the complexity of modern society, and of the irreconcilable demands society sometimes places upon its members. Furthermore, he argues strongly that each man must take responsibility for his own actions. Szasz is against any suggestion that troubled people should try to solve their problems by agreeing to live in a mental hospital, or by dropping out of society and becoming hippies. And he believes that almost every person who commits a crime, regardless of his mental status, deserves ordinary imprisonment, not hospitalization.

Szasz's arguments are often compelling. His restless pen has moved on to challenge

Psychopathology grows easily in slum settings like this. *(Bob Adelman)*

involuntary hospitalization, traditional psychiatric approaches to the drug dependencies, and the "social engineering" that psychiatrists and other mental health professionals attempt to impose on society (1968, 1970, 1972). His words inevitably generate sharp replies from fellow psychiatrists. One of his critics says: "For a decade or so, Szasz has been busily setting up psychiatric strawmen and sedulously demolishing them" (Cohen, 1973, p. 19). But given the reluctance of most established professionals to examine the validity of their methods, we believe that Szasz's continuing criticism is valuable to the profession.

Other investigators using the social-consequence model have chosen to focus directly on relationships between poverty, race, and mental illness. Robert Coles, a psychiatrist, has been one of the leaders in this movement

of social concern. As he recently pointed out, psychologists and psychiatrists have begun to recognize that mental health professionals who belong to minority groups seem to work more successfully with their own groups than "establishment" professionals do (Coles & Piers, 1969). Obviously the values of the establishment professionals may differ in important ways from those of their minority-group clients.

Behavioral scientists who subscribe to the social-consequence model are concerned with primary prevention of mental disorders. Instead of concentrating on treatment for people with serious psychopathologic conditions (which would be labeled *secondary* or *tertiary prevention*), they explore the changes that can be made and the resources that can be provided to foster healthy psychological development in the community at large (Chapter 2).

As for Malcolm Little and Daniel Paul Schreber, the relevance of the social-consequence model to Little is clear. Much of his behavior (both "normal" and "abnormal") seems a function of the demands of the black society he lived in, though these demands were imposed in part by the white society which surrounded it. The model is not as useful when applied to Schreber's case, largely because his psychotic behavior appears to have been a product of perceptual and cognitive disorders more than a reaction to society.

On the other hand, one can argue that since Schreber's hallucinations and delusions were not the result of physical illness, they must have been environmentally caused. Some theorists have emphasized just this point; they claim that schizophrenia and the other functional psychoses are products of environmental factors. But their model, as described in the following section, stresses the crucial importance of *faulty learning* rather than adverse social conditions.

Psychopathology: The behavioral model

The idea that the symptoms of psychiatric patients are learned behaviors comes from the behavioral model of mental disorder. Psychopathology, according to this model, is largely an acquired set of *maladaptive* (faulty) behaviors, not the product of physical disease or deep-seated psychological trauma. Treatment involves applying procedures derived from the principles of learning in order to modify or eliminate the maladaptive behavior and to encourage more adaptive behavior patterns.

The behavioral model arose from the work of Pavlov and Watson, experimental psychologists who laid the foundation of learning theory by their laboratory experiments during the early decades of the twentieth century. Their work in turn has been applied to clinical problems by men like Mowrer, Skinner, Wolpe, Lindsley, and Azrin. Clinical application of learning theory began in the late 1930s, with Mowrer's "bell and pad" device for bedwetters

(Mowrer & Mowrer, 1938). But the applied behavioral model did not achieve recognition as a legitimate system in its own right until the 1960s. Many of its supporters are laboratory-trained psychologists who have begun to apply laboratory-based findings to the solution of human problems. They are often outspoken in their rejection of psychoanalysis, which they consider an unproved theory rather than a body of facts established by experimentation.

Joseph Wolpe (1958, 1969), a South African psychiatrist, has developed a system of behavioral therapy called *reciprocal inhibition* that is based on classical conditioning principles. (These principles are described in Chapter 4.) From a series of animal and human experiments he concluded: "Human neuroses are

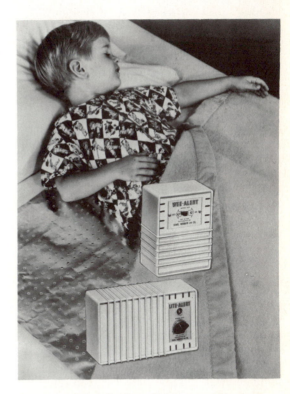

A commercial application of Mowrer and Mowrer's bell-and-pad device. "Buzzer alarm," the catalog description says, "helps keep sleeper dry and more comfortable by conditioning him to stop bedwetting." *(Sears, Roebuck & Co.)*

parallel to experimental neuroses [in animals] in . . . three features . . . : acquisition by learning, primary stimulus generalization, and elimination by unlearning" (1969, p. 9). He has satisfied himself and many others that various neurotic behaviors (including anxiety, phobic behavior, and compulsive behavior) are acquired early in life. At the time they were learned, they may have been appropriate and useful, but they are no longer so in adulthood. For example, anxiety produced in childhood by a harsh father is adaptive when it leads the child to avoid his father as much as possible. But if the person reexperiences that anxiety in adulthood as tension in the presence of other adults, it may force him to avoid social interaction. If so, it has become a learned maladaptive behavior.

Other behaviorists believe that the functional (nonorganic) psychoses are learned. Ullmann and Krasner trace the ways in which almost all symptoms of schizophrenia, including the most bizarre, are acquired by conditioning (1969). As they see it, the basic element in schizophrenic conditioning is the extinction of attention to social stimuli. The person no longer pays attention to the cues given him by others, so that his behavior is not shaped by the results he gets with it. A child like this fails to respond to parental "reinforcers" (attention, praise, a hug), because the parents have applied them wrong. Perhaps they have behaved with "consistent inconsistency," or have misused or misdirected punishment, or have acted with downright malice. The result is an individual who is no longer accessible to outside efforts at shaping his behavior.

The behavioral model of psychopathology does not help us to understand Daniel Paul Schreber's behavior very well, though it can be usefully applied to Malcolm Little's. If we try to account for Schreber's distorted perceptions, bizarre hallucinations, and disordered thinking by saying that they were the result of his parents' "consistent inconsistency," then we must explain why he was able to function so well for so long before he became psychotic. It seems clear from his memoirs that there was no sudden change in his relations with his family or friends that might have been the immediate cause of his breakdown. Nor did the hospital attendants, nurses, or doctors seem to be inadvertently reinforcing his psychotic behaviors once he was hospitalized.

Malcolm Little's behavior, by contrast, does seem to have been a function of behavioral mechanisms. Adopting the behavior of older ghetto hustlers was surely satisfying to Little, and he received reinforcement for it from the environment. Thus his maladaptive behavior was taught him by a maladaptive subsociety, within which such behavior was in fact adaptive.

As later chapters will show, the behavioral model of mental disorder has inspired new treatment approaches that seem to bring about rapid behavioral changes. In contrast, traditional methods of therapy take much longer. The behavioral approaches set out to confront maladaptive behavior in the here and now, whereas the psychoanalytic therapies pay attention to the patient's behavior only as it bears on long-past traumatic events. Because of its focus on the present, the behavioral model highlights the impact of his environment and the influence of conditioning by family and friends on an individual's development of psychopathology. This is an emphasis very much in keeping with current social movements in the United States.

The behavioral movement's greatest drawback has been the rash hopes it has aroused in so many people who are concerned with mental illness. It has given laymen an unwarranted optimism about its potential for "curing" all mental disorders. And it has given professionals an unwarranted confidence about its potential for explaining the etiology of all mental disorders. In spite of the new behaviorist treatment methods and the behaviorist insights into cause, many mental disorders remain inaccessible to "cure" by this or any other known approach.

Psychopathology: The dynamic model

The dynamic model of mental illness, developed early in this century by Sigmund Freud, is termed *psychoanalysis.* It has had a profound influence on modern conceptions of abnormality. Psychoanalysis is a dynamic theory because it hypothesizes a complex set of psychological *energy* relationships (described in Chapter 4) to explain human thinking and feeling.

The dynamic model conceives of abnormal behavior as an *interaction* between a set of inborn physiological events that begin to unfold shortly after birth and a set of crucial events occurring during the child's early years. In the first five years of life, according to Freudian theory, every child passes through three distinct stages of "psychosexual development"— the familiar oral, anal, and phallic stages. During these years, traumatic environmental events (occurrences that produce psychological injury) can interact with one or another of the stages of psychosexuality to cause lasting psychological disorder. For example, if the child is deprived of his mother's love and attention for a long period during the earliest (oral) stage, he may develop a psychosis. Or overattention from his mother during the phallic stage, when the child is troubled by a growing affection (often with sexual overtones) for her, can lead to neurosis, including anxiety and phobic behavior.

In analyzing Schreber's memoirs to arrive at a theory of functional psychosis (and in particular, a theory of paranoid schizophrenia), Freud concluded that Schreber's disorder developed "as the outcome of conflict over unconscious homosexuality" (1959f, p.10). This conflict, Freud said, arose from interaction between the demands of a very powerful, strict, successful father and the child's own developing sexual impulses. Details of this view of Schreber's psychosis are given in Chapter 7, which weighs their significance as one approach to the causes of schizophrenia.

Viewed in the context of the period when Freud lived, psychoanalysis represented a long step forward in ideas about the mental disorders. At that time—the turn of the century— the moral model still predominated, although the medical model, put forth by German psychiatrists like Kraepelin and Bleuler, was be-

Sigmund Freud. *(Culver Pictures, Inc.)*

ginning to gain influence. Unlike either the moral or the medical models, psychoanalysis did not place sole responsibility for abnormal behavior on either sinful man or diseased tissue, but assigned it to family, friends, *and* physiology. This development was helpful because it forced behavioral scientists to broaden their search for the causes of psychopathology.

But the dynamic model of mental disorder has serious shortcomings. It makes assumptions which cannot be tested. Its predictions are autocratic and narrow: according to psychoanalytic theory, for example, a person whose childhood was as chaotic and disordered as Malcolm Little's should have developed a psychosis, or at least a disabling neurosis. Behaviorists, who are the most vigorous critics of the dynamic model, also question the hypothetical genetic mechanisms (the oral, anal, and phallic stages) by which it explains a child's development. The behavioral approach, on the other hand, offers a model of abnormality that does not refer to extraenvironmental factors.

Psychopathology: The legal model

Before 1843 no generally accepted legal definition of insanity existed. Criminals whose acts may have been influenced by mental disorder were judged according to the individual models of mental illness that judge and jury brought into the courtroom with them. A plea of insanity sometimes resulted in a lighter sentence and sometimes increased the severity of punishment.

In 1843 an obviously deranged Englishman named M'Naghten committed a brutal murder. He was acquitted by reason of insanity, and Parliament asked the judges of England for a legal definition of insanity so that justice could be standardized in such cases. The *M'Naghten rules,* as they are called, continue to be the principal legal criteria of mental illness throughout the world. In essence they say that "the accused shall only be regarded as insane to the point of escaping responsibility for his criminal act, if he was laboring under such *a defect of reason, from disease of the mind, as not to know the nature and quality of the act, or if he did know it, not to know that what he was doing was wrong"* (Slater & Roth, 1969, p. 765).

Because this definition of insanity is a very narrow one which describes the mental state only of those who are most seriously disturbed, judges have tended to apply the M'Naghten rules leniently and inconsistently. Partly to correct their circumventions of the original intent of the rules, and partly to improve the consistency of justice for mentally disturbed criminals, a number of states in this country have added their own elaborations of rules. The most influential, the *Durham decision,* has come to represent a new, more modern set of legal criteria for judging mental disorder.

In 1954 the United States Court of Appeals for the District of Columbia, presided over by Judge David Bazelon, set down the Durham decision: "We conclude that a broader test [of mental competence] should be adopted. . . . It is simply that *an accused is not criminally responsible if his unlawful act was the prod-uct of mental disease or mental defect"* (*Durham v. U.S.,* 214F. 2d 862, 1954). The Durham decision, like the M'Naghten rules, has proved impossible to interpret consistently. But it has enabled the administration of criminal justice to become more humane by making the legal view of abnormality more explicit and objective.

Application of either the M'Naghten rules or the Durham decision to Malcolm Little's anti-social behavior would not have affected his sentence. By both sets of criteria his criminal behavior was not the product of mental disease. Legally Malcolm Little was sane and guilty as charged. Schreber, on the other hand, would have come under the legal protection of both definitions. That is, if he had ever been brought to trial for his attacks on attendants and the damage he did to hospital property, he would have been judged innocent by reason of insanity.

Unfortunately, the greater part of the cases which the courts must rule on are not as clear-cut as our two examples, and severe inequity results. The continuing imprecision of the legal definitions of mental disorder suggests the difficulty which lawyers and judges, although trained in making such discriminations, encounter in defining abnormality. Ethical considerations also weigh heavily when law and psychiatry meet. One authority who was trained in both psychiatry and the law recently argued that even *after* a decision has been made about a convicted criminal's mental status, three additional moral-ethical issues must be confronted. They are (1) whether the state knows what is best for the criminal or patient or both, (2) whether the state can provide appropriate facilities for the reformation of criminals or the treatment of patients, and (3) whether the state has the right to impose treatment upon a person unwilling to accept it (Stone, 1971). All three questions, which Szasz has also raised repeatedly, deserve serious consideration. Their practical aspects are only now being explored by legal experts and mental health professionals.

*200   *DANIEL M'NAGHTEN'S CASE.

1843.

Murder. Evidence. Insanity.

The House of Lords has a right to require the Judges to answer abstract questions of existing law. (a)

Notwithstanding a party accused did an act, which was in itself criminal, under the influence of insane delusion, with a view of redressing or revenging some supposed grievance or injury, or of producing some public benefit, he is nevertheless punishable if he knew at the time that he was acting contrary to law.

That if the accused was conscious that the act was one which he ought not to do ; and if the act was at the same time contrary to law, he is punishable.[1] In all cases of this kind the jurors ought to be told that every man is presumed to be sane, and to possess a sufficient degree of reason to be responsible for his crimes, until the contrary be proved to their satisfaction ; and that to establish a defence on the ground of insanity, it must be clearly proved that at the time of committing the act the party accused was labouring under such a defect of reason, from disease of the mind, as not to know the nature and quality of the act he was doing, or as not to know that what he was doing was wrong.[2]

That a party labouring under a partial delusion must be considered in the same situation, as to responsibility, as if the facts, in respect to which the delusion exists, were real.[3]

That where an accused person is supposed to be insane, a medical man, who has been present in Court and heard the evidence, may be asked, as a matter of science, whether the facts stated by the witnesses, supposing them to be true, show a state of mind incapable of distinguishing between right and wrong.[4]

The "McNaghten rules."

Summary

Through the ages people have disagreed on what is normal behavior and what is abnormal. The difficulties of making this seemingly simple distinction are illustrated by the lives of Dr. Daniel Paul Schreber and Malcolm Little, later Malcolm X. For example, can we reconcile Schreber's distinguished legal and juridical career with his intermittent bizarre delusions and massive hallucinations? And how could Malcolm X, that vibrant and constructive leader of his people, have spent the first years of his adulthood as a petty criminal, drug addict, ghetto hustler, and con man?

Mental health professionals have produced many theories, or models, of normality and abnormality. Models of behavior are created by generalizing observations from an individual to groups of similar individuals, and they are used largely for making predictions about people's future behavior. Validation of models must follow a regular pattern that is called the *scientific method*.

Three models of normality were described here. The first, which was derived from Old Testament and Greek sources, views normality as an *ideal* condition. This model considers normality to be a state of positive mental health, of truly effective individual and social functioning, rather than simply the absence of mental illness. In contrast, when normality is approached through the *statistical* model it is stated in quantifiable terms: a person's behavior is converted to a set of test scores, which must fall within a "normal range" for him or her to be considered normal. The possibility that normality might be described by a *relative* model is a fairly recent suggestion which comes from anthropology. This view is based on the premise that different cultures define normality very differently.

The chapter also described six models of abnormality. The oldest is the *moral* model, which claims that mental disorder is an inevitable product of immorality and sin. The moral theory reached its inhumane zenith in 1487 with the publication of *The Witches' Hammer,* a book written by two Dominican Brothers which argued that psychotics should be burned as witches.

The moral model of mental illness prevailed in one form or another until the end of the nineteenth century, when increasing numbers of doctors began to believe that all mental disorders are physical in origin. The *medical* model's view that abnormal behavior is the product of disease had important benefits. In particular, it removed some of the moral disgrace that had been associated with the mental disorders. It also played a major role in humanizing the treatment of patients in mental hospitals. But the medical model of mental disorder poses serious conceptual and practical problems. It has tended to restrict the search for etiological (causal) factors in psychopathology to the area of disordered bodily functioning. Its emphasis on physical disease has contributed to the unreliability of diagnosis and has fostered treatments that are based upon correction or alteration of diseased tissue.

In reaction to the medical model of mental illness men like Szasz have begun to speak out in favor of viewing psychopathology as a *social consequence*—as the result of living in a disordered society. This book agrees with them in large part. Explaining Malcolm X's behavior as a social consequence certainly makes his behavioral deviations more understandable. In a variation of the idea that society can produce mental disorder, *behavioral* theorists say that the environment is responsible. Their model views psychopathology as a set of learned maladaptive, or faulty, behaviors which a person develops because the environment reinforces them.

Sigmund Freud's model of psychopathology as a *dynamic* sequence describes mental disorder as the result of interaction between a set of inborn physiological developments (the psychosexual stages) and crucial environmental events during the child's early years. Contrasts between the behavioral and dynamic positions on diagnostic, etiologic, and treatment issues will be pointed out again and again in this book.

The final approach to psychopathology considered here was the *legal* model of abnormality. It evolved because society needs some kind of legal definition of mental disorder when the courts sit in judgment on criminal cases. The two legal definitions of psychopathology now in wide use are the M'Naghten and Durham rules. Neither is adequate to the formidable problems of administering justice to the mentally disturbed criminal.

CHAPTER TWO

Society & psychopathology: The scope of the problem

Newark ● Terezin ● Epidemiology, psychopathology, and society ● Race and psychopathology ● Sex and psychopathology ● Community psychology

NEWARK:
CHAOS IN
AN ORDERED
SOCIETY

Though the Newark riots did not explode until six weeks later, many observers think that they were ignited by the Parker-Callaghan dispute, which began at the end of May 1967. The dispute arose shortly after it was announced that City Councilman James T. Callaghan, a white man, was to be appointed secretary to the Newark board of education by Mayor Hugh J. Addonizio. The salary from this job would be added to Callaghan's income from his city council position and the $10,300 a year he made as secretary to the county purchasing agent. When Mayor Addonizio formally announced his intention to appoint Callaghan, the Newark NAACP proposed instead that the job be given to City Budget Director Wilbur Parker, New Jersey's first black CPA.

Though the dispute began during the last week in May, the board of education did not resolve it until June 26, when the board decided to retain its current secretary for another year. Commenting on the black community's reaction, James Threatt, director of the Newark Human Relations Commission, wrote: "The only issue on which I've seen Negroes get truly excited and concerned was the Parker-Callaghan dispute. For the first time, you really had a community."

Both this newly discovered sense of community and a widely recognized potential for violence among Newark's black citizens were heightened following the arrest of John W. Smith, a black cab driver, on Wednesday evening, July 12, for "careless and reckless driving." Eyewitnesses reported seeing Smith dragged, "beaten but still resisting," from a police car into the Fourth Precinct police station, located directly across the street from a virtually all-black public housing project. Sometime afterwards Smith was taken to a hospital, where he was treated for "hematoma in the left occipital-parietal

NEWARK'S MAYOR CALLS IN GUARD AS RIOTS SPREAD

11 DIE, 600 HURT IN NEWARK RIOTS; TROOPS USED TO CURB NEGROES; GOVERNOR SEES 'INSURRECTION'

UNDAY, JULY 16, 1967   60¢ beyond 50-mile 1: except Long Island. Hi

NEWARK RIOT DEATHS AT 21 AS NEGRO SNIPING WIDENS; HUGHES MAY SEEK U.S. AID

Newark Rioting Assailed By Meeting of N.A.A.C.P.

By M. S. HANDLER
Specia. to The New York Times

BOSTON, July 15—The 58th annual N.A.A.C.P. convention unanimously condemned today the riots in Newark.

A resolution prepared by 2,140 registered delegates at the Sheraton-Boston Hotel ballroom. Most of the resolutions covered civil rights in such areas as labor and industry, Roy Wilkins, executive director, education and politics.

region [of the skull] and a fracture of the right ninth rib in the axillary line"—in other words, a hard bang on the head and a broken rib.

Though police and the black community disagreed on how Smith got these injuries, both groups agreed that the Molotov cocktail which exploded against the wall of the Fourth Precinct station at 11:30 that night marked the official beginning of the Newark riots. The explosion caused little damage but brought both policemen and neighborhood residents to the front of the station house, where they exchanged racial insults. Meanwhile someone set fire to an abandoned car nearby. When additional police and firemen came to put it out, they were stoned by groups of black teenagers. More police were called to disperse the teenagers, and it was only at 4 A.M. that the streets of Newark's Fourth Precinct fell quiet.

They remained quiet through the next day, while the city administration attempted to demonstrate that the city was back to normal. City Hall referred to the previous evening's events as isolated incidents of vandalism. The administration also tried to defuse the tension in the black community by announcing that a Blue Ribbon panel would be set up to investigate the Fourth Precinct confrontation, including the circumstances of John Smith's arrest. And it announced that a black police lieutenant would be promoted to captain. But City Hall did not agree to the black community's demands that the two Fourth Precinct policemen involved in Smith's arrest be suspended. Instead, the men were transferred to administrative duties elsewhere.

Late that afternoon (Thursday, July 13), leaflets distributed in the Fourth Precinct urged: "Stop police brutality. Come out and join us at the Mass Rally, Tonight, 7:30 P.M., Fourth Precinct." About three hundred people did. The rally was held directly across the street

28

from the precinct station. An Inspector Melchior described what followed: "Again, as the night before, . . . missiles came from all directions. During the rest of the course of the night, groups of 30 to 50 young teenagers would approach in almost military formation, unleash a barrage of missiles and disperse at the approach of police officers" (New Jersey Governor's Select Commission, 1968, p. 113).

(The New York Times by Neal Boenzi)

SOLDIERS RETURN SNIPERS' GUNFIRE

Building Used by Gunman Who Had Killed a City Policeman Is Taken

Continued From Page 1, Col. 6

police headquarters tonight after standing guard in the riot area and said: "I heard what the Mayor said about it being better and I was going to come in and tell you guys that was a lot of bunk."

The private, Michael Ruane of East Orange leaned his carbine with fixed bayonet against a wall while he munched a sandwich and talked of being shot at.

"You'd see a puff of smoke from a window. We'd fire up at the window," he said.

"The guys inside would go out of the back. We'd charge

Things went from bad to worse, as recorded in the state police log: "Presently, bands of 8 to 15 people, traveling on foot and in cars, looting and starting fires. Four policemen injured, four new areas have broken out in the past fifteen minutes. There is still no organization within the Newark Police Department. All available transportation in use. The Fourth Precinct appears to be running its own show. There are no barricades. No requests for State Police assistance" (Select Commission, 1968, p. 114). Active State Police aid was requested at 1:30 Friday morning. Shortly afterwards Mayor Addonizio asked the governor to alert the New Jersey National Guard. "It's all gone, the whole town is gone!" the mayor told reporters. When they asked him where the problem was, he said, "It's all over." When they asked what had caused the riot, he said that he had no idea.

Rioting, looting, fire bombing and sniping spread through Newark's central ward on Friday and Saturday. Half of the 23 deaths and most of the 725 injuries resulting from the Newark riot occurred between

29

midnight Thursday and midnight Friday. More than half of the 1,600 arrests recorded during the five days of disorder were made during this twenty-four-hour period. Of those arrested, 85 percent were black males and 9 percent were black females.

By daybreak on Sunday, tension began to ease. On Sunday night there was much less sniping, though two men were killed by policemen returning sniper fire. On Monday all but a small residual force of state policemen and National Guardsmen left the city to its own police and residents. The riot was over. But its repercussions had not yet begun.

The Select Commission on Civil Disorder, appointed by Governor Hughes shortly after the Newark riot, issued a long report that was unexpectedly critical of the Newark city adminstration. The commission made these points:

1 The administration apparently did not know how bitter many blacks were about some of its recent actions. Besides the Parker-Callaghan dispute, the black community was enraged over city-supported plans to tear down black housing and build a medical school on the site. "The administration did not seem to understand that political support by large numbers of Negroes in past municipal elections was not a guarantee against disaffection and disappointment over specific issues of direct and deep interest to Negroes. This reflects a serious lack of communication between established authority and the black community, which is one of the prime ills of Newark" (p. 143).

2 An almost total breakdown in communication between blacks and police had occurred well before the riots started.

3 During the riots, most of the Newark Police Department's actions served to fan rather than extinguish the fires of civil disorder.

4 Incidents of police and National Guard prejudice against Negroes during the riots had been widespread. "This may have caused the use of excessive and hence unjustified force against black citizens of Newark." State police and National Guardsmen had also damaged many stores that had been marked with "soul" signs (showing black ownership). These attacks on black property resulted in "personal suffering and economic damage to innocent small businessmen and property owners who have a stake in law and order and who had not participated in any unlawful act. It embittered the Negro community as a whole at a time when the disorders had begun to ebb" (p. 144).

 The report concluded: "The evidence presented to the Commission does not support the thesis of a conspiracy or plan to initiate the Newark riot."

TEREZIN: ORDER IN A CHAOTIC SOCIETY

Terezin was named by Emperor Joseph II in 1780 for his mother, Maria Theresa. The town lies on a gentle plain that is surrounded by small hills, at the meeting of the central Bohemian rivers of Ohre and Labe, in Czechoslovakia. On very clear days the outlines of the Bohemian central mountain range appear on the distant horizon. On one side of Terezin lies the town of Litomerice; on the other, the little town of Bohusovice, terminus and frontier station for central Bohemia.

Before World War II the main landmarks of the town of Terezin were the waterworks tower and the high escarpments and deep trenches surrounding it. This fortresslike structure made Terezin look like the garrison town it actually was. Before the war it was home to 3,500 persons, mostly shopkeepers and artisans who earned their living serving the army garrison which was quartered in the town's scattered baracks.

On November 24, 1941, a transport of 342 Jewish prisoners came to Terezin. They were the vanguard of thousands more Jews and other Nazi victims who were to change the history and identity of this rural Czech town forever. The Nazis had originally planned to make Terezin only a transit camp for Jews from Bohemia and Moravia on their way east to the extermination camps of Auschwitz and Flossenburg. But Terezin actually functioned, during the forty-one-months of its existence, as many other things: a concentration camp, an enclosed community, a place where birth and death happened, a center where art, literature, and music flourished. Today Terezin stands as a monument to the Nazis' inability to prevent the oppressed from maintaining their continuity as communities and their identity as human beings. Of the 87,000 prisoners who arrived at Terezin and were then sent east, only 3,100 were known to have returned to their homes after the war.

From Bohusovice station to Terezin *(from Terezin, 1965)*

About 76,000 Jews from 151 Jewish communities in Bohemia and Moravia that the Nazis had dissolved, old and young, men and women, thousands of innocent children, were forcefully penned together in the living quarters of the small garrison town, offering just about sufficient accommodation for a population of 7,000 including the military garrison. In the course of time another 42,000 prisoners from Germany, more than 15,000 from Austria, over 1,100 from Hungary, about 4,900 from Holland and 466 from Denmark were added. What the daily regime must have been like for the prisoners may perhaps be best judged from hard documentary facts; even though Terezin was "only" a transit station on the way to the terrible extermination camps of the East, 33,430 prisoners died there from maltreatment and disease, i.e., almost a quarter of all that had been sent there. Out of that number over 15,000 died from exhaustion and starvation. [Ehrmann, 1965, p. 5]

31

These figures suggest the magnitude of the crime that was the Nazis' "final solution," because the 33,000 people who died at Terezin were less than half of 1 percent of the Jews, Slavs, Russians, Frenchmen, and others who perished in the concentration camps of Europe between 1933 and 1945.

Many more people were murdered at Auschwitz and at Buchenwald than at Terezin, but we have chosen to focus on this Czech prison camp because within its walls, an incredibly full cultural and religious life coexisted with the horror of what had come and was still to come. Terezin is an emblem of man's capacity for bringing order to chaos, of his ability to infuse life in what would seem to promise only death and destruction.

Though we might have expected depression, psychosis, and paranoia at Terezin, we are told instead of art, music, and prayer. One of Terezin's rabbis, Dr. Richard Feder, describes the religious life:

While the Nazis . . . did not explicitly permit services . . . on the other hand, they did not explicitly forbid them either. . . . During the first half of 1942, prayer houses were set up in the Terezin quarters . . . in the former barracks of a sappers' regiment and . . . in "Sudeten." . . . In the course of time many rabbis and cantors were "welcomed" to Terezin. . . . Every prayer house was allocated one rabbi and one cantor. Services at Terezin were held in the usual way. . . . The cantors sang and the rabbis preached their best, and it was not long before it was generally known where the singing and the sermon was best. Thus the prayer houses had greater or smaller attendance according to the reputation they had gained. . . . Our hardest work was to officiate at funerals [in part because] Terezin was . . . the only concentration camp where Jewish rites were observed. [Feder, 1965, pp. 53–54]

The survivors of Terezin also speak of the astounding diversity and richness of the cultural experience there. Dr. Norbert Fryd, once a prisoner at Terezin and now a historian of literature, recalls: "In the midst of war we lived in a concentration camp that was barbarously invested and barbarously kept going. . . .' But every day there was illegal education of children, every day there were theatre performances, concerts, lectures, every day news came from outside and was rapidly and dependably spread further, and every day there was tenacious confidence that nothing could subdue" (Fryd, 1965, p. 207).

Another survivor describes an "opening night" in Terezin:

The festive first night took place in the cellar of the "Sudeten" barracks. There were no plush stalls. The audience did not wear formal dress. There was no rustling of candy paper bags. No refreshments were to be had in the buffet. Applause was strictly forbidden. It was not advisable

(G. D. Hackett)

to make unnecessary noise. The closing chorus of the evening sung by the spectators, together with the performers, sounded subdued but all the more enthusiastic. It ended with the words: "Where there is a will, there is a way. Let us join hands and one day we will laugh on the ruins of the Ghetto." [Sedova, 1965, p. 219]

Here is another survivor's assessment of the cultural influence of Terezin: "We believe that neither film artists, nor writers, poets, sculptors, painters and composers have yet said their last word on the subject that offers itself with such urgency as the theme of the 'Terezin ghetto,' for its cultural heritage is inexhaustible, and the courage of its prisoners arising from their invincible optimism and will to conquer over fascism by the strength of the spirit has not yet been fully appreciated" (Iltis, 1965, p. 316).

Newark and Terezin: crucial similarities and differences

In both Newark during the summer of 1967 and Terezin between 1942 and 1945, an oppressed people struggled to express a newly renascent nationhood—by physical violence in Newark, by cultural creativity in Terezin. In both places people died. In both an "occupying force" ultimately prevailed.

In both Newark and Terezin, the struggles of the community must have had a profound impact on developing and existing psychopathology among individuals. In both places malnutrition doubtless impaired the physical and intellectual development of children. In both the "psychological climate" of fear and frustration must have had an equally devastating effect on their elders. Though we have no figures on Newark, the study of midtown Manhattan described later in this chapter suggests that the rates of serious psychopathology in the Newark ghetto before and after the riot were probably higher than in more affluent sections of the city. But in the Terezin prison camp, overt psychopathology may well have been somewhat less than it was outside the camp, for studies have shown that rates of

mental disorder tend to decrease during periods of national emergency (Kalinowsky, 1950; Winnicott, 1957).

Other differences between Newark and Terezin are related to the scope of the events in the two communities. First, the dead: 23 died in Newark, more than 33,000 in Terezin. Second, the deaths in Newark were accidental, in the sense that they were totally undesired by the city administration. But the deaths in Terezin were part of the Third Reich's "final solution" to the Jewish problem, and as such they were carefully planned and efficiently accomplished. Finally, those who died in Newark died quickly; most of those who died in Terezin had suffered for months from disease and malnutrition. Some sense of the psychological suffering endured by the prisoners of Terezin and the people all across Europe who were hunted down and persecuted by the Nazis is given by the excerpts from Anne Frank's diary that open the next chapter.

We have chosen to tell this tale of two cities because it presents two "case histories" similar to the case histories of patients who show disordered behavior. We believe that communities, like the people who live in them, can be "disordered" or "well." Some communities

There is little doubt that society played an important role in Lincoln's depression and Hitler's psychosis. Both grew up in poverty, though Lincoln's was only material whereas Hitler's was also emotional. Society's role in George III's psychosis can also be traced; his position as heir to the throne of England could not protect him from the scourge of syphilis. *(New York Public Library picture collection)*

seem able to tolerate adversity, while others seem especially vulnerable to it; some are disabled by stress, others are resistant to it.

We also suggest that the important differences in social organization and disorganization between communities (specifically, Newark and Terezin) may not be solely responsible for the eventual psychological state of their inhabitants. That is, while certain kinds of mental disorder are precipitated by environmental stress, others occur in an "ideal" environmental situation. Kings, princes, millionaires have been psychotic, whereas many others—Abraham Lincoln and Malcolm X among them—became productive, significant adults despite the adversity which surrounded their growing up.

Psychological disorder takes many forms, and has at least as many causes as forms. This chapter will consider the techniques used by behavioral scientists to discover which forms and causes are related to social and cultural factors. Our focus will be on "failures of society," as we have chosen to call persons whose psychopathology stems largely from sociocultural causes.

Epidemiology, psychopathology, and society

Epidemiology is the study of diseases and other health-related characteristics in a given population. The word comes from *epidemic,* which refers to the outbreak of communicable disease in a population group. Epidemiologists have been responsible for solving the riddle of many human diseases of viral and bacterial origin. In their work they try to answer such questions as: What is the *etiology,* or cause, of the condition? Which groups in the population are "high" and "low" risk groups? How effective are various treatment or prevention measures? What is the financial and social cost of the disease? How can public interest in treatment and prevention be aroused?

Medical epidemiology has many achievements to its credit. Two well-known examples are the discovery in the 1900s that the Anopheles mosquito carries malaria, and the triumph over polio in the 1950s through the vaccine developed by Jonas Salk.

Although the history of psychiatric epidemiology is a long one, its practical results have been less satisfactory. There are several reasons. First, reliable diagnoses for most of the psychiatric disorders do not really exist.

Yet epidemiologic studies often try to relate incidence of a particular disorder to various population characteristics (age, sex, race, etc.) —even though the diagnoses themselves are questionable. (Chapter 5 discusses this problem in greater detail.) Second, the interviewers who are hired to collect the observational data for the diagnoses are often relatively untrained in interviewing and diagnosis. This further reduces the likelihood that the study will be based on meaningful diagnostic labels. Third, differences in the quality of different surveys make it difficult to compare one with another. A survey carried out by well-trained interviewers who work within a relatively small population area might reveal a high rate of mental disorder. A survey made by less well-trained interviewers working with a large population might report a low rate of disorder. But in fact, the two populations might have very similar rates.

The fourth and perhaps most important reason why psychiatric epidemiology has had such limited success is that "carriers" of mental disorders cannot readily be isolated and quarantined. While it is possible to identify and segregate carriers of syphilis, of sickle cell anemia, and of malaria, it is not so easy to "prove" that the parents of a schizophrenic boy or the grandparents of a manic-depressive woman had a role in the patient's disorder. Nor can a health inspector disrupt their lives in order to prevent them from "infecting" others. There are simply too many instances of mental "diseases." And for the most part, they are either peculiar to the individual (as with Daniel Paul Schreber) or clearly a product of widespread social malfunction (as with Malcolm Little). Epidemiological researchers cannot identify their cause with precision or use that knowledge for preventive purposes. It is possible at reasonable cost to eradicate the Anopheles mosquito, and in areas where sickle cell anemia is prevalent, health services can offer genetic counseling (advice to prospective parents on the probability that their children might inherit a disease). But it is not possible to eradicate poverty, racial discrimination, or social and family discord at currently acceptable political, social, or economic costs.

Two basic sets of data emerge from epidemiologic survey research, whether it is medical or psychiatric: information on the *prevalence* of disorders, and information on their *incidence*. Prevalence figures tell how many persons ("index cases") within a particular population fall within a particular diagnostic category. These data are usually expressed in terms of rate per 100,000 members of the population being studied. Incidence figures tell how many persons per 100,000 become index cases within a given period of time—usually a year. The distinction between prevalence and incidence is very important in physical medicine, where many diseases last a relatively short time. But since many mental disorders last for years—even for a lifetime—the difference between prevalence and incidence is much less important in their case.

Midtown Manhattan study: A model of epidemiological research

The Midtown Manhattan Study was an eight-year (1952 to 1960) investigation of the mental health problems and resources among the 175,000 residents of a mid-Manhattan area (Srole et al., 1962). Its authors, distinguished mental health professionals, were fully aware of the pitfalls of psychiatric epidemiology. While the study was not without faults, they were outweighed by the importance of the findings and the excellence of the research design.

Early in their first report, the authors emphasized the fundamental premise which guided their work: that environmental conditions (including race, sex, age, socioeconomic status, and interpersonal factors) all have important effects on mental health—and that these effects can be measured.

Three separate data sources were tapped during the Midtown research: one set of information came from a sociological study of the community (termed the *Community Sociography Operation*), another from a survey of all residents who were psychiatric patients (the *Treatment Census Operation*), and the third

from intensive home interviews of residents (the *Home Interview Survey*). Each was designed to "get at" epidemiological data from a different perspective, so that information from each source would complement what was learned from the other two.

Community sociography. This portion of the survey treated the Midtown community as the object of an intensive case study—just as the mental health professional studies his patient's background for cues to his present behavior. It described the community in terms of separate racial, religious, and socioeconomic groups. The idea for a predominantly sociological approach to epidemiology came from earlier studies of small and large American communities by sociologists (Lynd & Lynd, 1929; Warner et al., 1941). These studies focused mainly on social grouping factors as determinants of the life-styles of community residents.

Psychiatric patient study. In this operation, two psychiatric social workers studied the files of all the hospitals, clinics, and private practitioners consulted by Midtown residents. Their aim was to measure the prevalence of *treated* mental illness among the Midtown population. They covered publicly supported mental hospitals, private psychiatric hospitals, public and private clinics, and private treatment by psychiatrists or clinical psychologists.

Home interviews. Most of the Midtown study data came from the home interview survey. This was both the study's most impressive contribution to research design and its most debatable operation. It was planned in great detail and evaluated exhaustively even while the study was underway. Ultimately, however, it proved impossible to evaluate the degree to which the carefully chosen interviewers agreed on the meaning, the validity, and the utility of the data they were collecting.

Nonetheless, the system of checks built into the study make it the best home survey of its kind so far. Midtown's authors demanded *direct* evidence of mental illness—possible

Wednesday, November 27, 196█

Scott was interviewed as part of the procedure for acceptance into the group therapy sessions being supervised by Dr. █████.

Scott reported feelings of depression, anxiety, and insecurity. His anxiety reflected his concern with being a success; he was so worried at the prospect of getting poor grades this semester (Scott is a freshman) that he was seriously considering dropping out of school until he felt more in control.

His problems seem to have developed last Spring in his senior year of high school when he developed chronic laryngitis (which, although improved, is still present) - due to overstraining his vocal cords in chorus, drama club, and as president of the student organization. Under doctor's orders, he had to stop talking. This enforced silence served to shut him off from people and bring him into closer confrontation with himself. He began to have self-doubts. Whereas he had always thought he could be a success, the loss of his voice cast doubts on this, as his vocational plans had centered on teaching or drama, both of which depend on the voice. He also began to fear that he could no longer emulate his father - a minister - whom he respects, especially for the way he talks to people.

Compounding these self-doubts was the fact that Scott's brother suffered a severe nervous breakdown last year, and was home for months at a time, out of communication with the world. Scott began to fear the same thing might happen to him.

His parents sent him to see a psychiatrist at this time. The psychiatrist put him on drug therapy and told Scott he showed neurotic, not psychotic tendencies. He also told Scott that the feelings of inferiority he was experiencing were probably there all along. Scott seemed to agree with this.

He said that until high school he had been very introverted and always studied hard, to the exclusion of having friends and fun. His parents, being very puritanical about work and sex, did not encourage Scott to go out more. He did, however, really begin to enjoy himself in high school, becoming involved in many activities and having a close girlfriend.

This year at ███████ has been a very depressing anxious one. Scott found it hard to make friends at the beginning of the year because he couldn't talk. He also found the work hard and became very anxious about finding an area in which he could succeed. Although he is getting A's, B's and C's, he wants to do better. He is also very depressed because he and his girlfriend have grown apart and he now feels inferior to her because he's been unable to adjust to ████████ whereas she's enjoying her 1st year at college.

Scott is very anxious to enter into therapy on a regular basis, to get help with his problems.

Janet █████████
Clinician

Figure 2-1. This summary of an intake interview at a college counseling center is the kind of information the Midtown study's Treatment Census Operation was based on.

only from detailed interviews—rather than inferential evidence from institutional records. For this reason, we believe that Midtown's prevalence and incidence figures are accurate.

By a design which ensured that they would be truly representative of the 175,000 residents of Midtown, 1,911 residents were selected to be interviewed. Though previous studies suggested that as many as 35 percent of this group might refuse to participate, only 13 percent did decline. The data were gathered by means of a 200-item questionnaire which guided the interviewers in their work. Interviews lasted several hours.

"How would you like me to answer that question? As a member of my ethnic group, educational class, income group, or religious category?" Interviewers and interviewees often differ in their interpretations of questions asked in epidemiological studies. *(Drawing by D. Fradon; © 1969 The New Yorker Magazine, Inc.)*

The Midtown Manhattan study: Findings and conclusions

Only the highlights from the survey of psychiatric patients and the home interviews will be reported here, and the rich insights provided by the community sociography operation will not be described at all. Students who find this discussion interesting will enjoy reading the study report itself (Srole et al., *Mental Health in the Metropolis: The Midtown Manhattan Study* 1962).

The Midtown data were gathered carefully in order to maximize their utility and enable other researchers to generalize from them. But despite this care, the findings cannot be extrapolated to any urban community other than the one from which they were drawn in the year they were drawn. Midtown's authors said: "In the long national perspective, it appears neither typical of the American scene nor unique to it. Instead, Midtown is seen to be representative in most demographic respects of the inclusive white population of Manhattan, and apparently of populations in similar high-density core residential sections found in other major American metropolitan centers" (p. 127). Today, more than ten years after the study, the last part of that statement is still only a guess. The extent to which Midtown data are representative of urban populations "in other major American metropolitan centers" has not yet been determined.

Psychopathology in Midtown. On the day of the psychiatric patient survey, 502 per 100,000 of the total Midtown population had been continuously hospitalized for more than five years. Another 788 per 100,000 were outpatients in clinics or private offices.

The home interviews assessed mental health along a six-category scale defined in Table 2-1. How the 1,660 Midtown adults who were interviewed fitted into the six categories is shown in Figure 2-2. These ratings were made by two experienced psychiatrists on the basis of the behavioral data gathered by the interviewers.

The Midtown authors combined the last three ratings of "marked," "severe," and "in-

TABLE 2-1.   CATEGORIES OF MENTAL HEALTH IN THE MIDTOWN MANHATTAN STUDY

Diagnostic category	Definition
Well	No significant symptom formation
Mild	Mild symptom formation but adequate functioning
Moderate	Moderate symptom formation with no no apparent interference in life adjustment
Marked ⎫	Moderate symptom formation with some interference in life adjustment
Severe ⎬ Impaired	Serious symptom formation, and functioning with great difficulty
Incapacitated ⎭	Serious symptom formation; functioning with great difficulty or inability to function

SOURCE: Srole et al., 1962.

capacitated" into one large symptom category which they called "impaired." As you can see in Figure 2-2, 23.4 percent of the home interview population was judged to be "impaired" in functioning. Since the sample of 1,660 interviewees was carefully chosen to be representative of the 750,000 residents of Midtown, the authors of the study could conclude that 23.4 percent of Midtown's total population was impaired in psychological functioning. If the interview survey had included Midtown's hospitalized mental patients as well as the Midtown residents who were living at home, the "mental morbidity rate" of the Midtown area would have risen from 23.4 to almost 26 percent.

Age, sex, marital status, and psychopathology. The Midtown authors took their statistical findings on psychopathology and broke them down by age, sex, and marital status. Here are some of the results.

The data for *age* showed that "mild" and "moderate" symptoms appeared in the same proportions in all age categories. But there were substantially fewer "well" residents over 30 than "well" residents between 20 and 29, and the percentage of "impaired" residents was lowest among the youngest group and highest among the oldest residents.

As for *sex,* the survey found that it was unrelated to frequency of mental disorder.

When symptoms were broken down according to *marital status,* the results showed that

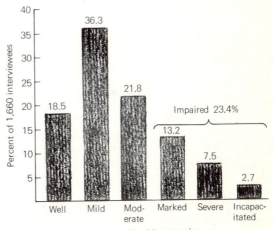

Figure 2-2. The incidence of psychopathology found in the Midtown Manhattan Study. People in the categories labeled "marked," "severe," and "incapacitated" were considered "impaired" in psychological functioning. Thus the sample data indicated that 23.4 percent, or about 175,000, of Midtown Manhattan's residents were Impaired. *(Based on Srole et al., 1962)*

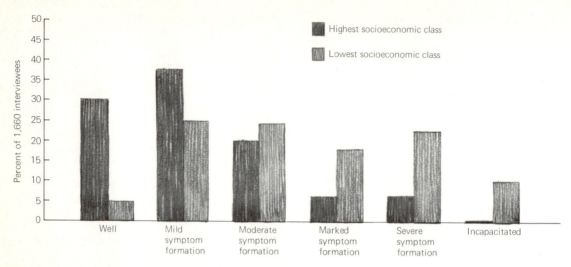

Figure 2-3. The inverse relationship between socioeconomic status and mental health, as discovered in the Midtown Manhattan Study. The lower a resident's socioeconomic status, the greater the chances that he was judged to be suffering from some degree of mental disorder. *(Based on Srole et al., 1962)*

married men were "impaired" slightly less often than married women. And single men were "impaired" significantly more often than single women.

Socioeconomic status and psychopathology. The term *socioeconomic status* (also known as SES) describes the differing values that every society places on the occupations, roles, and positions in its social and economic system. These values are expressed by differences in prestige, in pay, and in responsibilities and privileges. For example, in our society doctors and lawyers earn more money and more respect for their work than ditchdiggers and garbagemen.

The Midtown study revealed that socioeconomic status affects not just people's income, prestige, and power, but other facets of their lives too—including psychopathology.

[1] The Midtown authors divided their population into six socioeconomic status groups, from A (highest) to F (lowest). Each group contained approximately equal numbers of persons. Socioeconomic status seemed to have relatively little effect on rates of "mild"

and "moderate" psychopathology: in all six groups, between 57 and 60 percent of Midtown residents fell within these two mental disorder categories. But significantly more high socioeconomic status residents and significantly fewer low socioeconomic status residents were in the "well" category, and vice versa. Thus mental health and socioeconomic status were *inversely related* in the Midtown study. That is, the lower a resident's socioeconomic status, the greater the chances that he was suffering from some degree of mental disorder.

[2] Lower-SES residents who had mental disorders were most often treated as inpatients in public hospitals or as outpatients at public clinics. High-SES residents who needed treatment were usually inpatients in private hospitals or outpatients of private mental health professionals.

[3] The total number of psychiatric patients was 62 percent greater among high-SES residents than among low—meaning that many more high-SES residents than low were being treated for their disorders. This fact is especially dramatic in view of point 1 above—that there was a higher rate of mental disorder

among residents of low socioeconomic status. In other words, the people who most needed help—the poor—were getting the least.

National origin and psychopathology.   Among the seven major nationality groups who were represented among Midtown people, there were important differences in rates of mental disorder. For example, no immigrant Midtowners of Puerto Rican ancestry were judged free of psychopathology in the home interviews, and more than half of this group were thought to be "impaired." By contrast, 22 percent of immigrants of British ancestry and 18 percent of immigrants with German-Austrian backgrounds were considered "well," and less

than 30 percent of those groups were judged "impaired."

Conclusions.   One of the most striking and unexpected findings of the Midtown study was that fewer than 20 percent of all subjects in the home interviews were free from psychopathology. No other large-scale epidemiologic study had yielded comparably low rates of mental health. Further, more than a quarter of all Midtowners were judged to be "impaired" in mental functioning. In a sense, the second figure is even more surprising than the first, since the Midtown area was not an especially poor, low-SES, black, foreign-born, or troubled area.

It usually takes a long time to see the doctor in this outpatient clinic of a public hospital. The hospital is in a ghetto; it is overcrowded and probably understaffed. *(Ken Regan/Camera 5)*

Mental health professionals have known for some time that social class affects the ways in which they treat patients. Many psychologists and psychiatrists admit that the socioeconomic status of the patient helps determine the kind of treatment he is given. Obviously, poor people cannot afford intensive one-to-one psychotherapy. In addition, poorly educated people are not supposed to be able to deal with complex psychological issues in therapy, or to understand how talking about a problem can help alleviate it.

Midtown data add an important dimension to these earlier findings. As you have seen, they show that Midtown residents most in need of treatment—those in the lower SES categories—were much less likely to be receiving it than high-SES residents. Further, the data suggest that the treatment received by low-SES patients is probably less adequate than the treatment received by high-SES patients. This is because low-SES patients usually go to public hospitals and clinics, where overcrowding and lower professional standards often impair the quality of therapy.

However, one authority, using an argument that you might not expect, has attacked the widespread belief that patients receive inferior treatment in public facilities. In a recent (1973) article, Lorion makes this telling point: Research does *not* show that differences in kind and duration of therapy affect the results of a patient's treatment. Though eventually some experiment may be devised which proves that the differences are important, Lorion concludes that for the present, behavioral scientists must not assume that apparent bias in type of treatment necessarily results in inferior treatment results. (This conclusion is supported by studies discussed in Chapters 7 and 10 that question the ultimate utility of psychotherapy, the "treatment of choice" by most mental health professionals.)

In the predominantly middle-class area covered by the Midtown study, a wide variety of mental health resources were available. Not only were many Midtown residents able to afford private treatment, but the Manhattan area is richer in mental health resources than any other comparable urban area in the United States. So it is all the more remarkable to find the wide disparity in type and frequency of mental health services available to low- versus high-SES Midtowners. If the mental health treatment resources for Midtown's residents of lower socioeconomic status were not very good, think how much worse they must have been for Newark's Central Ward residents, most of whom were poor, black, and very low in SES. Not only were Newark's blacks, Puerto Ricans, and poor whites more likely to need mental health services than their more fortunate fellow citizens, but they were less likely than Midtown residents to find them, because very few such resources existed in Newark during the years preceding the riots (NCMHI, 1968). This lack reflected the general apathy of Newark's administration to many other deficiencies in municipal service to the Central Ward.

New Haven epidemiological study

Hollingshead and Redlich's classic study of social class and psychopathology in New Haven (1958) was the most thorough epidemiological study of mental disorder in urban America before the Midtown study. Its findings are important here for two reasons: (1) The New Haven study identified relationships between social class and mental illness similar to those revealed by the Midtown study. Therefore they confirm the general nature of these relationships. (2) The New Haven study focused on relationships between social class and adequacy of treatment, whereas the Midtown study touched on the subject only peripherally.

Most of the data in the New Haven study came from the clinical records of New Haven residents who were treated at local public hospitals, clinics, private hospitals, and the offices of private practitioners. The records of almost every New Haven patient in treatment at the time of the study (1950 and 1951) were consulted. A sociologist and a psychiatrist together evaluated each record.

As in Midtown, significantly more New

Haven residents in the lower classes than in the upper were "mentally disabled" to the extent of requiring treatment for their mental disorders. The authors of the New Haven study concluded: "Class status is a real or true factor in the prevalence of treated mental illness in this community" (Hollingshead & Redlich, 1958, p. 211).

The New Haven study also found that patients in the upper social classes are almost always treated privately, while patients in the lowest social class are almost always treated in public facilities. Choice of treatment facility, in turn, had a powerful effect on the kind of treatment offered. Upper-class neurotics and schizophrenics in New Haven received classical psychoanalysis, psychoanalytically oriented psychotherapy, or directive psychotherapy. Lower-class neurotics and schizophrenics were given organic (chemical) therapy, custodial care, or both. Although the effectiveness of psychotherapy with psychotic patients has not been proved, both professionals and the general public think it is better than organic therapy or custodial care. The New Haven data provide ample justification for the study's conclusion that, whether judged by quantity or quality, treatment received by upper-class New Haven patients was superior to that given lower-class patients.

"Hi! All power to the people, right?" Despite her good intentions, this liberal white woman betrays her insensitivity to the needs and expectations of her black guest. (Drawing by Handelsman; © 1970 The New Yorker Magazine, Inc.)

Race and psychopathology

We have looked at two studies of urban populations which show that socioeconomic status has an important influence on psychopathology in this country. Is there also a relationship between race and psychopathology? The question is a reasonable one, because in the United States racial identity does statistically (although not necessarily in the individual case) predict socioeconomic status. Blacks and American Indians are more likely than whites to be poor, unemployed, and undereducated (*Vital Statistics of the United States,* 1973). These are all important factors in determining SES.

Many militant blacks speak of the pervasive relationship between race and psychopathology in this country. In his book *Soul on Ice,* Eldridge Cleaver stresses the point that racism exacts a price from the white racist as well as the black victim: "It was long axiomatic among blacks that a black had to be twice as competent as a white in any field in order to win grudging recognition from the whites. This produced a pathological motivation in the blacks to equal or surpass the whites, and a pathological motivation in the whites to maintain a distance from the blacks. This is the rack on which black and white Americans receive their delicious torture" (1968, p. 24).

Black mental health professionals also have emphatic opinions about the psychopathological consequences of racism. Lloyd Delany, a black psychoanalyst, says: "There is a sickness in our society. White racism. It is classic pathology with the usual destructive behavior: acting out, denial of reality, projection, transference of blame, dissociation, justification. The sickness of racism runs deep in the history of this nation, and no institution in society is immune" (Delany, 1968, p. 26).

Eldridge Cleaver and Lloyd Delany both agree that the "sickness" of racism most profoundly affects the racist. Kenneth Clark, an eminent black psychologist, carries the point even farther. He sees racism as only one sign of the fact that

American society is suffering from a very serious, very severe disease. A disease which, for want of a better word, I would call moral schizophrenia. . . . We're aware of our racial conflict. That is only a single symptom. Our other symptoms include the glut of affluence, the worship of material things, the willingness to make mass expenditures for military hardware, for space exploration. And our niggardly approach to the problems of human beings. . . . What the American people have to learn is that they really can't control or destroy Negroes without destroying themselves. And whether the masses of Whites know this or not, the significant fact is that the masses of Negroes apparently do know it. They have a peculiar sort of folk wisdom that tells them that in spite of all this talk of genocide, America cannot commit genocide without at the same time committing suicide. The deprived, despised Negro has less to lose than the privileged White, you know. [Hall, 1968, pp. 19–20]

If racism in America is a symptom of "moral schizophrenia," then behavioral scientists, and psychopathologists in particular, must identify the condition and assess the extent of its consequences. Let us consider the symptom of racism as it relates to psychopathology.

The "culture of poverty" and psychopathology

Oscar Lewis, a famous anthropologist, wrote two widely read books—*The Children of San-* *chez* (1961) and *La Vida* (1966)—which describe the despair and degradation of Mexican-Americans and Puerto Ricans. He believes that it is the "culture of poverty" rather than color alone that is largely responsible for the psychopathological effects of racism on minority-group Americans. (The authors of the Midtown Manhattan study came close to this position themselves.) The following list gives some of the traits which Lewis names as belonging to the culture of poverty.

Some traits of the culture of poverty

ECONOMIC TRAITS
Unemployment and underemployment
Low wages
Child labor
No savings
Chronic shortage of cash
No food reserves in the home
Daily food purchases in small quantities
Borrowing from local moneylenders at usurious rates of interest
Secondhand clothing and furniture
Constant struggle for survival

SOCIAL AND PSYCHOLOGICAL TRAITS
Crowded quarters
No privacy
Considerable alcoholism
Violence
Violence in training children
Early initiation into sex
Abandonment of mothers and children
Mother-centered families
Authoritarianism
Daily face-to-face relations with same people
Extended strong family ties
Political apathy
Belief in sorcery and spiritualism
Cynicism about government and the church
Hatred of police
Mistrust of government and those in high position
Members attempt to integrate into a workable way of life the remnants of beliefs and customs of diverse origins
Strong feeling of marginality, helplessness, dependency

Feeling of inferiority and personal unworthiness

Little sense of history

OTHER TRAITS

Strong present-time orientation; little ability to defer gratification

Resignation and fatalism

High tolerance for psychological pathology

Marginal relationship to national institutions (social security, labor unions, banks, etc.)

Low level of education and literacy

Relatively high death rate

Lower life expectancy

Higher proportion of individuals in the younger age groups

Higher proportion of gainfully employed (because of working women and children)

[Adapted from Lewis, 1969, p. 150]

"Our landlord is a criminal," says the sheet hung from the fire escape in this Spanish-speaking neighborhood. How many of the traits of poverty are visible in this picture? *(Charles Gatewood)*

This list could also serve as a comprehensive collection of the social, economic, and personal factors that have been identified by other behavioral scientists as predictors of serious psychopathology. It suggests, as Lewis hoped it would, that poverty and powerlessness rather than race per se may play central roles in the etiology of psychopathologies like those reported in the Midtown and New Haven studies. But remember that these traits by themselves cannot be considered proof of psychopathology, though they may suggest a potential for its development.

Racial bias among psychopathologists

There has been surprisingly little research on racism and racial bias among mental health professionals. One of the first large-scale studies looked for racial differences in the diagnoses given by five psychiatrists (three white and two black) to 940 patients at a large urban mental health facility (Dorfman & Kleiner, 1962). Each clinician saw 94 black and 94 white patients. No differences that could be attributed to the race of the patient or the clinician were uncovered when separate analyses were made to identify differences in the psychiatrists' frequency of diagnoses of schizophrenia, neurosis, organic brain disorder, and personality disorder, and differences in their proposals for treatment. In other words, race was irrelevant to diagnosis or proposed treatment.

Such findings are encouraging because they suggest that many, even most, mental health professionals may be color-blind. Unfortunately, these positive early findings conflict with data from more recent research. DeHoyos and DeHoyos (1965) and Singer (1967), for example, reported that middle-class white psychiatrists record fewer symptoms for black patients than for white patients. Instead, the psychiatrists focus upon the most dramatic, unusual, and striking behaviors among blacks. As a result blacks emerge from the diagnostic process appearing more disturbed and more pathological than whites who show the same behavior. Gross and his colleagues (1969) studied the 2,279 outpatients who came to the Psychiatric Institute of the University of Maryland School of Medicine in a recent year. They report that the aberrant behavior which caused the hospitalization of white females was usually labeled "neurotic," while essentially the same behavior in black women was called "schizophrenic." Commenting on these results, Thomas and Sillen (1972) conclude: "In dealing with a white patient, the white resident tends to give a more empathic [sympathetic] diagnosis—for example, neurotic reaction—and to make a more optimistic disposition. With a black patient, he overreacts to some behaviors, pays too little attention to others. He is a prisoner of his ethnocentric attitudes, though he would no doubt be shocked to be told that he is less than objective" (pp. 64–65).

Despite the racial bias that does appear to distort the behavior of some mental health professionals, there is evidence that the usual black patient does not choose a black therapist over a white therapist (Backner, 1970; Cimbolic, 1972). However, a study by Jackson (1973) shows that blacks who identify most strongly with their African ancestry do prefer black counselors to white. (Students interested in the many factors influencing a possible relationship between race and psychopathology, by the way, should consult the *Bibliography on Racism,* published in 1972 by the National Institute of Mental Health's center for minority group mental health programs.)

Does race directly affect psychopathology?

It seems, then, that race and racism do affect the diagnostic process, at least in some settings. But we must still ask whether race directly affects psychopathology. Do blacks and other minority-group members in this country suffer psychological stress because of the racial bias to which they are exposed?

Derogatis and his colleagues concluded that *both* race and social class affected the symptoms in a group of 1,071 neurotic outpatients who were subjects of a series of clinical drug trials (1971). All patients showed neurotic symptoms involving manifest (directly observable) anxiety. Social class and severity of symptoms varied inversely with somatic (bodily) symptoms and depression: the lower the social class, the worse the symptoms. But a relationship between race and symptom was clear only in the case of one symptom, manifest hostility: blacks were less hostile than whites. Thus these data agree with the often-reported relationship between social class and psychopathology. They fail, however, to support the view that a similar relationship exists between race and psychopathology.

A recent long-term study of the comparative psychological functioning of 235 black adult males who grew up in cities and a similar group of urban whites also found no relationship between race per se and psychopathology (Robins et al., 1971). As for admission rates to public mental hospitals, they are highest among nonwhite males 35 to 44 years of age. But these rates may be largely a function of socioeconomic status rather than of race (Gullattee, 1972).

One investigator (Gynther, 1972) has reviewed the literature on differences and similarities in the performance of blacks and whites on the Minnesota Multiphasic Personality Inventory (MMPI). This is a psychological test organized as a series of scales which reflect self-reported psychopathology. Gynther says that there are some differences in test performance between blacks and whites. But on the whole, he tends to label these differences a function of culture rather than of race. For one thing, Gynther notes that of the 1,200 MMPI studies published between 1939 and 1960, only 4 included blacks as subjects. Of these 4, 3 reported that institutionalized blacks made higher scores than whites on two MMPI scales. one designed to reflect "schizophrenic" behavior and the other "manic" or hyperactive behavior. More recent MMPI studies, some of which included noninstitutionalized blacks for the first time, largely support these earlier findings, in that the racial differences in

MMPI performance which appear most often are on the same two scales.

After reviewing all available evidence, Gynther concludes that the observed differences "reflect differences in values, perceptions, and expectations that result from growing up in different cultures" (p. 395). As a consequence, "There is no satisfactory evidence to indicate that blacks' MMPI performance should be interpreted as revealing that they are less well adjusted than whites." Gynther completes his review by documenting the use to which the MMPI has been put by some administrators. They have interpreted the results in such a way as to eliminate blacks from consideration for jobs which require good judgment and good mental health—for instance, positions as policemen and hospital attendants.

We conclude that consistent differences in kind and frequency of psychopathology between comparable groups of blacks and whites have not been demonstrated. In other words, the evidence seems to show that blacks do not have higher rates of mental disorder than whites. The next question is: Why not? After all, blacks are still not granted full and equal educational and economic opportunity in our society. Consequently many blacks experience precisely the social and psychological stresses that psychologists have long believed contribute to psychopathology. Why don't groups of blacks give more evidence of mental disorder than groups of whites? There may be several answers to this question.

Black anger as a healthy response. One of the most intriguing attempts to explain black mental health in the face of white racism is the suggestion that the black man's anger in response to racism is healthy, not pathological. Two black psychiatrists, Grier and Cobbs, expressed this viewpoint in a recent book: "People bear all they can and, if required, bear even more. But if they are black in present-day America they have been asked to shoulder too much. They have had all they can stand. They will be harried no more. Turning from their tormentors, they are filled with rage" (1968, p. 94). Black rage gradually evolves into what Grier and Cobbs call "cultural paranoia" which, along with "cultural depression," "cultural masochism," and "cultural antisocialism," are seen as adaptive mechanisms which permit the black to coexist with American racism. The value of these mechanisms can be observed in blacks who have used them to develop the self-confidence to confront the system (e.g., Malcolm X, Martin Luther King, Julian Bond, Huey Newton, Angela Davis).

The "fatherless family": Myth or reality?
There is a widespread belief that the chaotic, fatherless black family is largely responsible for the social sins of blacks. Publication in 1965 of the Moynihan Report (*The Negro Family: The Case for National Action*) by the U.S. Department of Labor contributed to this view of the black family by describing it as a "tangle of pathology . . . approaching complete breakdown" and contrasting it with the strong, stable white family. But social scientists have strongly rejected the view that the black family contributes to black social disorder and psychopathology by its chaotic disorganization. Thomas and Sillen, for instance, assert that the black family may actually be a great source of support and strength for the black child who must do battle every day with a hostile environment. They write:

That black families in America face special problems goes without saying, but it is a mistake to assume that these problems have been met in the same way by all black families and all black mothers. The dilemmas of socialization in a racist society can indeed be cruel. "How Negro parents have resolved these dilemmas is a virtually untouched field of study," as Billingsley (1968) points out. "While Negro families have informally shared their experiences with one another, the startling neglect of such important areas of expressive functioning in Negro family life finds us without information which is vital to understanding not only the Negro family, but also a very rich part of the human experience."

In the absence of detailed, scientifically controlled studies, it is nothing less than racist to generalize about the "pathologic" black family and the "castrating" black mother. The tendency to parrot such stereotypes can only encourage the superstition of white superiority. [1972, pp. 99–100]

"Black self-hatred": White stereotype? Like the assumption that the black family's disorganization contributes to black failure, the popular view that racism has etched an indelible harmful mark on the "black psyche" has had a profound effect on white sterotypes about blacks. Kardiner and Ovesey's *Mark of Oppression* (1951), although well-meaning, probably contributed a great deal to the idea that discrimination permanently alters ambition, perseverance, and interpersonal trust in

(Andrew Rakoczy)

blacks. They conclude: "There is not one personality trait of the Negro the source of which cannot be traced to his difficult living conditions. There are no exceptions to this rule. The final result is a wretched internal life . . . the Negro has no possible basis for a healthy self-esteem and every incentive for self-hatred" (p. 14).

Such a hypothesis suggests that the black man, to counter unavoidable self-hatred, must behave like a white because being black is too aversive. This view, widely held during the 1950s, flies in the face of recent efforts by blacks to mobilize black self-pride, and it is challenged by empirical data from a variety of recent studies (for instance, Baughman, 1971; Getsinger et al., 1972).

Socioeconomic status: A link between race and psychopathology

Most of the research we have reviewed here encourages us to believe that race does not directly affect incidence of psychopathology in this country. But two other less encouraging facts must be noted. The first is that race does predict socioeconomic status, to the extent that blacks are much more likely than whites to be poor. Since psychopathology is high among low-SES groups, we must conclude that race and psychopathology *are* related indirectly through socioeconomic status. This means that blacks who can rise above poverty may not be psychologically marked by their beginnings, but that blacks who remain in the ghetto will suffer psychologically for their poverty just as white ghetto dwellers suffer.

Besides this indirect relation between race and psychopathology, racial prejudice may have subtle psychopathological effects that are not reflected in epidemiologic surveys. Race appears to play a role, for example, in the loneliness and alienation that black college students feel on entering a predominantly white college (Willie & Levy, 1972). It is a determining factor in the choice of the place where patients go for treatment of a mental illness (Gullattee, 1972), and in the adequacy of the treatment they receive (Halleck, 1971). Halleck expresses his views forcefully on the issue of therapy: "To many ghetto residents, it seems that the liberal psychiatrist is a forceful agent of repression. . . . They see him as an insidious agent of colonial forces whose primary purpose is to counsel or tranquilize the oppressed into a state of apathy and submissiveness" (p. 98).

Because of real or imagined injustice at the hands of the mental health establishment, blacks and other minority-group members have begun to argue for—and get— community control of neighborhood mental health facilities. It remains to be seen, however, whether community control will result in substantially improved services to the black community.

Sex and psychopathology

Being male or female affects how people "naturally" behave as well as how they learn to behave. More to the point here, a patient's sex has an influence on the diagnostic label which is applied to his or her behavioral deviations. It also affects the kind of treatment given for those deviations.

Sex-role behavior and psychopathology

The differential treatment experienced by males and females begins in childhood. More boys than girls are referred for child therapy (Gluck et al., 1964), probably in part, at least, because of the differential demands our society places upon the sexes. It is clear that the range of behavior considered appropriate and permissible for boys is narrower than that for girls. For instance, boys are trained to be aggressive—but if they are too aggressive, they are called "bullies." And boys who are not aggressive enough are "sissies." Girls who are as aggressive as boys are simply "tomboys," a label which is not especially negative. A passive girl, on the other hand, is a "little lady." Thus boys are called upon to control their behavior much more carefully than girls. Not

surprisingly, boys are most often brought to clinics for problems involving aggression. Girls are usually brought in for problems relating to withdrawal (Chesler, 1971). Society sometimes teaches its roles too well.

In adulthood, however, the tables are turned: more women than men are referred for psychological treatment (Brill and Storrow, 1960; Brown and Kosterlitz, 1964). Between 1964 and 1968, more women than men received psychiatric care on an outpatient or inpatient basis (Chesler, 1971). Phyllis Chesler, a clinical psychologist, observes that twice as many of her female patients complain of depression as her male patients. This, she feels, may be a reflection of woman's despair in trying to cope with her roles in our society—roles whose options are much narrower than the roles usually reserved for men (1971, 1972).

Many clinicians betray a sex bias in evaluating the behavior of male and female patients. Bias was illustrated in an excellent study by Broverman and her colleagues (1970). In it, 46 male and 33 female subjects—all clinicians—were given a "stereotype questionnaire" containing a number of bipolar items such as:

Very aggressive—Not at all aggressive
Doesn't hide emotions at all—Always hides emotions

One group of subjects was asked to use the bipolar items to describe an ideal person—a healthy, mature, socially competent adult— whose sex was unspecified. Two other groups were asked to describe a healthy man and a healthy woman. The results were revealing. The behaviors endorsed for the healthy male conformed closely to those set forth for the ideal person of unspecified sex; those used to describe the ideal female were quite different. Healthy women were described as "more submissive, less independent, less adventurous, more easily influenced, less aggressive, less competitive, and more excitable in minor crises" (Broverman et al., 1970, p. 5). These findings lend support to the view that clinicians, both male and female, may hold the same sex-role stereotypes as most other members of our society. Other research confirms this conclusion (Nowacki and Poe, 1973).

Society's recent concern with the liberation of women has led some people to consider the role which psychology and psychiatry play in oppressing women. Most therapists are men, while most of their patients are women. Thus therapists are in ideal positions to impose the values of a male-dominated society upon women. One of the most outspoken critics of the role of psychiatry and psychology in this regard is Phyllis Chesler. In *Women and Madness* (1972), she convincingly recounts the many ways in which women's lives are distorted both by male therapists and by female therapists with male values. Therapy for a woman, she notes with some irony, is considered most effective when she can be brought to conform to the role of wife and mother.

(Michael Abramson from Black Star)

Women's liberation movement: Agent for social change

These adverse circumstances affecting women's mental health may be changing because of the women's liberation movement. The growth of women's consciousness-raising groups, legal battles to overturn sexual discrimination in jobs, and changes in abortion laws are combining to bring about changes in society's view of the role of women. It is clear from studies like Broverman's which explore sex role stereotypes that behaviors regarded as masculine have been (and continue to be) most highly valued in our society. Based on that view, the liberated woman is one who has adopted a masculine role. However, there is now a group of women (and men) who suggest that being a liberated person need not mean that a woman has to be like a man. The notion is growing that a liberated person is free to be herself or himself with little regard for any stereotyped idea of sex-appropriate behavior.

One of the major focal points for the legislative program of the women's liberation movement has been the place of women in the working world. While poor women and single women have been relatively welcome on the lowest rungs for a long while, this acceptance has rarely extended to women who want meaningful careers and responsible positions. During the 1950s and early 1960s, as Helson points out, it was "appropriate for a *married* woman to work if her family required it, or as long as her family and children came first" (1972, p. 34). But the current changing view of this matter is that a woman's career may be as important to her as her family; a more radical view states that a career can replace the creation of a family as a legitimate goal for the liberated woman. Women who want a career are no longer a deviant minority.

The long-range social implications of these kinds of changes in women's roles are impressive. For example, if it is primarily men who make wars, then the possibility exists that a society in which women were more dominant and men felt less need to be aggressive would be a society with fewer wars. As Mednick and

"I've got an idea for a story: Gus and Ethel live on Long Island, on the North Shore. He works sixteen hours a day writing fiction. Ethel never goes out, never does anything except fix Gus sandwiches, and in the end she become a nympho-lesbo-killer-whore. Here's your sandwich." The women's liberation movement has made many women impatient with their traditional role in marriage. *(Drawing by Booth; © 1970 The New Yorker Magazine, Inc.)*

Tangri (1972) point out, if men carried an equal share of the child-rearing role, they might be less likely to send their children off to war.

Problems of population control may also be solved by the alternative roles now developing for women. As long as reproduction and nurturance are seen as the most meaningful ways in which a woman can express herself, it is unlikely that there will be a permanent solution to the overcrowding of our earth.

The changes in people's roles that are emerging from the women's liberation movement raise important questions for the student of psychopathology. If women no longer regard child rearing as their primary function, what influence will this have upon the quality of infant and child care? Will alternative family structures provide appropriate childhood experiences? Will marriage continue to have value? The answers are not immediately obvious. We all have opinions about motherhood, family, and marriage, but few of us have any data on the value of alternatives to these structures.

Community psychology

To some, a community psychologist is an activist who organizes groups of people for political confrontations like rent strikes or school protests. To others, he or she is a mental health professional who uses a wide range of standard psychological techniques in a setting which ensures that they will be available to all people, not just to the affluent. As we use the term here, community psychology involves bringing competent psychological services of many kinds to all the people in a community. Community psychology in our view not only involves traditional therapy for troubled individuals, but includes activities like going into a classroom to confer with a teacher, training policemen and prison guards in human relations, helping a group of citizens establish a suicide prevention center, and providing vocational counseling and training for the unemployed. The emphasis in community psychology should be upon the provision of necessary services to anyone who needs them.

On a hot summer day in the ghetto, this policeman is practicing community psychology. *(John Launois from Black Star)*

The community psychologist can function at several different levels. Caplan has called these primary, secondary, and tertiary prevention (1964). *Primary prevention* is the creation of an environment which prevents an individual from developing psychological disorders. It is an attempt to change communities for the better. It involves identifying the factors which facilitate healthy psychological development and ensuring that each individual is exposed to them. Thus in primary prevention, school systems are modified, poverty is attacked, conflicts between different cultural groups are resolved. But since we do not yet understand all the factors which contribute to good psychological adaptation, we do not know all the steps which must be taken to facilitate it. Nor have we done all we can to overcome the known problems. Children continue to grow up in poverty, many of our

schools continue to make education an oppressive and defeating experience, urban development still uproots established communities, and racism still pervades society. Primary prevention is not the exclusive role of the psychologist, psychiatrist, or social worker. Many others—including politicians, educators, policemen, urban planners, and architects—have important roles to play too.

Because we have not fulfilled the ideal of primary prevention, often we must fall back on *secondary prevention*. Here society must deal with individuals who have exhibited the preliminary indicators of some form of psychologically deviant behavior. The goal of secondary prevention is to minimize the intensity and duration of the deviation. The key is the early recognition of psychological problems and their prompt treatment. Here again, we are not doing as well as we could. Psychologists are hindered by their limitations as diagnosticians as well as by a lack of appropriate treatment facilities. Most communities do not have the services necessary to offer psychological treatment to all who need it. In spite of these limitations, it is often possible to make valuable contributions in the area of secondary prevention. In schools, industry, and the military, troubled people can often be identified and offered early psychological help. The effectiveness of this approach is well illustrated by the work of Cowen and his co-workers in the Rochester, New York, school system (see Chapter 15) as well as by the efforts of Beier and his colleagues to train nonprofessionals as counselors in a small community in northern California (1971).

Tertiary prevention is the last and least effective line of defense. Here, treatment is given to the individual who has developed a psychological disturbance. Its goal is often one of minimizing further damage—helping him to maintain himself within the community in spite of severe difficulties. This, unhappily, is the level at which most current mental health services function. In the best of all possible worlds, the concept of tertiary prevention would cease to have meaning.

We have decided not to write a separate chapter on community psychology, because this vital topic pervades the book. Our title—*Psychopathology and Society*—was chosen to suggest that the mental health professional's responsibility extends beyond the single individual to the entire community matrix in which he lives. Throughout the book you will find references to projects which reflect the orientation of clinical psychology toward the community.

Summary

This chapter had two major aims. The first was to consider in detail several important sociocultural factors in the etiology and treatment of psychopathology. Chief among them were socioeconomic status, race, and sex.

Data from the Midtown study suggest that socioeconomic status, or SES, affects clinical decision making about both etiology and treatment. Specifically, the Midtown survey revealed that low-SES patients were more often given schizophrenic or organic diagnoses than high-SES patients. This may mean that mental health professionals consider the behavioral deviations of poor people to be more ominous than the deviations of the well-to-do. The study also showed that the people who apparently need help most—the poor—receive less treatment and less adequate treatment for mental disorders than high-SES patients. This paradox suggests that our system of mental health care may not be achieving the goals for which many believe it was established.

A review of research on sex factors in psychopathology (derived from a smaller amount of data than the information available on SES) indicated that sex also plays a role in the labels which are given to a person's disordered behavior and in the treatment which he or she receives for it. Race, by contrast, appears to play a part only to the extent that a disproportionate number of blacks and members of other minority groups fall within the ranks of the poor. This makes them susceptible to the inferior diagnostic and treatment resources provided for the less fortunate in our society.

On the basis of these findings, we conclude that the factors of race, sex, and socioeconomic status may well account for such "failures of society" as Malcolm X and some of the nameless residents of Newark, Midtown Manhattan, and Terezin.

The second aim of the chapter was to give you a sense of the scope of the problem of mental disorder. For this purpose we included statistical data on the prevalence and incidence of psychopathology in places that have been the subject of epidemiological investigation by mental health researchers. The data indicate that mental disorder is widespread and that its rates depend to a considerable extent upon environmental factors.

We did not consider here the determinants of such "failures of person" as Daniel Paul Schreber. Though his psychopathology was doubtless influenced by family, social, and economic circumstances, his mental disorder was more clearly a function of processes which were specific to him—factors that did not stem largely from his sociocultural environment. The two chapters which follow deal with the personal variables in psychopathology: variables of psychobiology and genetics, and variables related to so-called personality factors. It is these determinants that we think contribute most to the kind of disordered behavior which can be discussed under the heading "failures of person."

CHAPTER THREE
Psychobiology, genetics, and psychopathology

Piri Thomas ● Anne Frank ● The nervous system ● The glandular system ● Biology of stress and psychopathology ● Constitution, temperament, and psychopathology ● Genetics and psychopathology ● Behavior and biological limits

PIRI THOMAS: ANGER

José didn't look at me. He decided that looking at the toilet bowl was better. "So whatta you got to find out, eh?" he said. "You're crazy, stone loco. We're Puerto Ricans, and that's different from being *moyetoes*." His voice came back very softly and his hand absentmindedly kept brushing the drying wet patch on his pants.

"That's what I've been wanting to believe all along, José," I said. "I've been hanging on to that idea even when I knew it wasn't so. But only pure white Puerto Ricans are white, and you wouldn't even believe that if you ever dug what the paddy said."

"I don't give a good shit what you say, Piri. We're Puerto Ricans, and that makes us different from black people."

I kept drying myself even though there was nothin' to dry. I was trying not to get mad. I said, "José, that's what the white man's been telling the Negro all along, that 'cause he's white he's different from the Negro; that he's better'n the Negro or anyone that's not white. That's what I've been telling myself and what I tried to tell Brew."

"Brew's that colored guy, ain't he?" José said.

"Yeah—an' like I'm saying, sure there's stone-white Puerto Ricans, like from pure Spanish way back—but it ain't us. Poppa's a Negro and, even if Momma's *blanca,* Poppa's blood carries more weight with Mr. Charlie," I said.

"Mr. Charlie, Mr. Charlie. Who the fuck is he?"

"That's the name Brew calls the paddies. Ask any true *corazon* white motherfucker what the score is," I said.

"I'm not black, no matter what you say, Piri."

I got out of the shower and sat on the edge of the tub. "Maybe not outside, José," I said. "But you're sure that way inside."

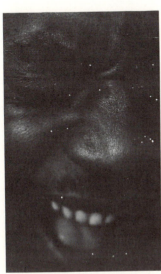

(David Margolin from Black Star)

55

"I ain't black, damn you! Look at my hair. It's almost blond. My eyes are blue, my nose is straight. My motherfuckin' lips are not like a baboon's ass. My skin is white. White, goddamit! White! Maybe Poppa's a little dark, but that's the Indian blood in him. He's got white blood in him and—"

"So what the fuck am I? Something Poppa an' Momma picked out the garbage dump?" I was jumping stink inside and I answered him like I felt it. "Look, man, better believe it, I'm one of 'you-all.' Am I your brother or ain't I?"

"Yeah, you're my brother, and James an' Sis, and we all come out of Momma an' Poppa—but we ain't Negroes. We're Puerto Ricans, an' we're white."

"Boy, you, Poppa and James sure are sold on that white kick. Poppa thinks that marrying a white woman made him white. He's wrong. It's just another nigger marrying a white woman and making her as black as him. That's the way the paddy looks at it. The Negro just stays black. Period. Dig it?"

José's face got whiter and his voice angrier at my attempt to take away his white status. He screamed out strong, "I ain't no nigger! You can be if you want to be. You can go down South and grow cotton, or pick it, or whatever the fuck they do. You can eat that cornbread or whatever shit they eat. You can bow and kiss ass and clean shit bowls. But—I—am—*white!* And you can go to hell!"

"And James is *blanco,* too?" I asked quietly.

"You're damn right."

"And Poppa?"

José flushed the toilet chain so hard it sounded as if somebody's neck had broken. "Poppa's the same as you," he said, avoiding my eyes, "Indian."

"What kinda Indian," I said bitterly. "Caribe? Or maybe Borinquen? Say, José, didn't you know the Negro made the scene in Puerto Rico way back? And when the Spanish spics ran outta Indian coolies, they brought them big blacks from you know where. Poppa's got *moyeto* blood. I got it. Sis got it. James got it. And, mah deah brudder, you-all got it! Dig it! It's with us till game time. Like I said, man, that shit-ass poison I've been living with is on its way out. It's a play-out like about me—us—being white. There ain't nobody in this fucking house can lay claim to bein' paddy exceptin' Momma, and she's never made it a mountain of fever like we have. You and James are like houses—painted white outside, and blacker'n a mother inside. An' I'm close to being like Poppa—trying to be white on both sides."

José eased by me and put his hand on the door knob.

"Where you going?" I said. "I ain't finished talking yet."

José looked at me like there was no way out. "Like I said, man, you

(David Margolin from Black Star)

can be a nigger if you want," he said, as though he were talking with a ten-ton rock on his chest. "I don't know how you come to be my brother, but I love you like one. I've busted my ass, both me and James, trying to explain to people how come you so dark and how come your hair is so curly an'—"

I couldn't help thinking, *Oh, Crutch, you were so right. We shouldn't have moved to Long Island.* I said, "You and James hadda make excuses for *me?* Like for me being *un Negrito?"* I looked at the paddy in front of me. "Who to?" I said. "Paddies?"

Lights began to jump into my head and tears blurred out that this was my brother before me. The burning came up out of me and I felt the shock run up my arm as my fists went up to the side of his head. I felt one fist hit his mouth. I wondered if I had broken any of his nice white teeth.

José fell away and bounced back with his white hands curled into fists. I felt the hate in them as his fists became a red light of exploding pain on my tender, flat nose. *Oh, God!* I tried to make the lights go away. I made myself creep up a long sinking shithole of agony and threw myself at José. The bathroom door flew open and me, naked and wet with angry sweat, and José, his mouth bleedin', crashed out of the bathroom and rolled into the living room. I heard all kinds of screaming and chairs turning over and falling lamps. I found myself on top of José. In the blurred confusion I saw his white, blood smeared face and I heard myself screaming, "You bastard! Dig it, you bastard. You're bleeding, and the blood is like anybody else's—red!" I saw an unknown face spitting blood at me. I hated it. I wanted to stay on top of this unknown what-was-it and beat him and beat him and beat him and beat him and *beat beat beat beat beat*— and feel skin smash under me and—and—and—

(Thomas, 1967, pp. 143–146)

Monday evening, 8 November, 1943

ANNE FRANK: FEAR

Dear Kitty,

If you were to read my pile of letters one after another, you would certainly be struck by the many different moods in which they are written. It annoys me that I am so dependent on the atmosphere here, but I'm certainly not the only one—we all find it the same. If I read a book that impresses me, I have to take myself firmly in hand, before I mix with other people; otherwise they would think my mind

Anne Frank in October 1942. She wrote: "This is a photo as I would wish myself to look all the time. Then I would maybe have a chance to come to Hollywood." *(Springer/Bettmann Film Archive)*

rather queer. At the moment, as you've probably noticed, I'm going through a spell of being depressed. I really couldn't tell you why it is, but I believe it's just because I'm a coward, and that's what I keep bumping up against.

This evening, while Elli was still here, there was a long, loud, penetrating ring at the door. I turned white at once, got a tummyache and heart palpitations, all from fear. At night, when I'm in bed, I see myself alone in a dungeon, without Mummy and Daddy. Sometimes I wander by the roadside or our "Secret Annexe" is on fire, or they come and take us away at night. I see everything as if it is actually taking place, and this gives me the feeling that it may all happen to me very soon! Miep often says she envies us for possessing such tranquility here. That may be true, but she is not thinking about all our fears. I simply can't imagine that the world will ever be normal for us again. I do talk about "after the war," but then it is only a castle in the air, something that will never really happen. If I think back to our old house, my girl friends, the fun at school, it is just as if another person lived it all, not me.

I see the eight of us with our "Secret Annexe" as if we were a little piece of blue heaven, surrounded by heavy black rain clouds. The round, clearly defined spot where we stand is safe, but the clouds gather more closely about us and the circle which separates us from the approaching danger circles more and more tightly. Now we are so surrounded by danger and darkness that we bump against each other, as we search desperately for a means of escape. We look down below, where people are fighting each other, we look above, where it is quiet and beautiful, and meanwhile we are cut off by the great dark mass, which will not let us go upwards, but which stands before us as an impenetrable wall, it tries to crush us, but cannot do so yet. I can only cry and implore: "Oh, if only the black circle could recede and open the way for us!"

Yours, Anne
(Frank, 1952, pp. 127–128)

Tuesday, 11 April 1944

The married couple with the torch would probably have warned the police: it was Sunday evening, Easter Sunday, no one at the office on Easter Monday, so none of us could budge until Tuesday morning. Think of it, waiting in such fear for two nights and a day! No one had anything to suggest, so we simply sat there in pitch-darkness, because Mrs. Van Daan in her fright had unintentionally turned the lamp right out; talked in whispers, and at every creak one heard "Sh! sh!"

It turned half past ten, but not a sound; Daddy and Van Daan joined us in turns. Then a quarter past eleven, a bustle and noise downstairs. Everyone's breath was audible, otherwise no one moved. Footsteps in the house, in the private office, kitchen, then . . . on our staircase. No one breathed audibly now, footsteps on our staircase, then a rattling of the swinging cupboard. This moment is indescribable. "Now we are lost!" I said, and could see us all being taken away by the Gestapo that very night. Twice they rattled at the cupboard, then there was nothing, the footsteps withdrew, we were saved so far. A shiver seemed to pass from one to another, I heard someone's teeth chattering, no one said a word.

There was not another sound in the house, but a light was burning on our landing, right in front of the cupboard. Could that be because it was a secret cupboard? Perhaps the police had forgotten the light? Would someone come back to put it out? Tongues loosened, there was no one in the house any longer, perhaps there was someone on guard outside.

Next we did three things: we went over again what we supposed had happened, we trembled with fear, and we had to go to the lavatory. The buckets were in the attic, so all we had was Peter's tin wastepaper basket. Van Daan went first, then Daddy, but Mummy was too shy to face it. Daddy brought the wastepaper basket into the room, where Margot, Mrs. Van Daan, and I gladly made use of it. Finally Mummy decided to do so too. People kept asking for paper—fortunately I had some in my pocket!

The tin smelled ghastly, everything went on in a whisper, we were tired, it was twelve o'clock. "Lie down on the floor then and sleep." Margot and I were each given a pillow and one blanket; Margot lying just near the store cupboard and I between the table legs. The smell wasn't quite so bad when one was on the floor, but still Mrs. Van Daan quietly brought some chlorine, a tea towel over the pot serving as a second expedient.

The attic where Anne Frank hid. *(Black Star)*

Talk, whispers, fear, stink, flatulation, and always someone on the pot; then try to go to sleep! However, by half past two I was so tired that I knew no more until half past three. I awoke when Mrs. Van Daan laid her head on my foot.

"For heaven's sake, give me something to put on!" I asked. I was given something, but don't ask me what—a pair of woolen knickers over my pajamas, a red jumper, and a black shirt, white oversocks and a pair of sports stockings full of holes. Then Mrs. Van Daan sat in the chair and her husband came and lay on my feet. I lay thinking till half past three, shivering the whole time, which prevented Van Daan from sleeping. I prepared myself for the return of the police, then we'd have to say that we were in hiding; they would either be good Dutch people, then we'd be saved, or N.S.B.ers, then we'd have to bribe them!

"In that case, destroy the radio," sighed Mrs. Van Daan. "Yes, in the stove!" replied her husband. "If they find us, then let them find the radio as well!"

"Then they will find Anne's diary," added Daddy. "Burn it then," suggested the most terrified member of the party. This, and when the police rattled the cupboard door, were my worst moments. "Not my diary; if my diary goes, I go with it!" But luckily Daddy didn't answer.

There is no object in recounting all the conversations that I can still remember; so much was said. I comforted Mrs. Van Daan, who was very scared. We talked about escaping and being questioned by the Gestapo, about ringing up, and being brave. (1952, pp. 215–217)

Anger, fear, and the body

Piri Thomas was a Puerto Rican who grew up in the New York City slum called Spanish Harlem. Like Malcolm X, he knew the life of the streets. And his life led him, as it did Malcolm X, to drugs. But unlike Malcolm, Thomas had a difficult problem of personal identification because he was a black Puerto Rican. In the excerpt from his book, *Down These Mean Streets,* reprinted above, Piri Thomas conveys graphically the rage—even against his whiter-skinned brother—that he must deal with again and again as he begins to consolidate his identity as a black Puerto Rican in a subculture that values whiteness.

Anne Frank was a Dutch-Jewish girl who spent two years of her early adolescence living in a "secret annexe"—a concealed apartment in a warehouse—to hide from German occupation troops during the Second World War. Like the residents of Terezin she lived in constant fear, but unlike theirs her life of fear was rarely interrupted by the joys of art or music, the pleasures of solitude, or the stimulation of new acquaintances. Throughout her years of hiding she kept a diary, which she called "Kitty" and thought of as a friend to whom she was writing letters. The excerpts presented here from *Anne Frank: The Diary of A Young Girl* chillingly illustrate Anne's terror-ridden existence.

Anger and fear are emotional responses that all of us recognize from our own lives. Like all other emotions, they are accompanied by bodily changes—physiological events. Physiological changes in bodily functioning are associated not just with universal emotions like anger, fear, and joy, but also with the emotions like severe depression, mania, and omnipresent anxiety that constitute the "core emotions" of much psychopathology. Further, while there is now general agreement that man's infinite variety of psychological states is bound up with a complex interplay of internal bodily events, many researchers also believe that science will ultimately find some types of psychopathology to be the direct result of physiological or genetic defects.

The term *psychobiology* as used in this chapter refers to the influence of psychological events upon a person's biological functioning, and to the influence of his physiological activity upon his behavior. The interplay of the two forces is perpetual; they should never be viewed as separate from one another. Along with social factors (Chapter 2) and personality factors (Chapter 4), psychobiological factors form the basis for individual behavior, both normal and deviant. Here we will explore the functioning of the human body in order to relate its functions to psychopathology.

The nervous system

The nervous system controls every move we make and every bit of awareness we experience throughout our lives. An intact and properly functioning nervous system allows us to perceive events, integrate them with previous experiences and with other incoming sensations, and then organize the whole so that we can make appropriate responses. The intricacy of this machinery is awesome.

The nervous system is composed of many billions of nerve cells. We shall concentrate here on their structure and functioning. Nerve cells, called *neurons,* are highly specialized (1) to receive information in the form of electrochemical impulses from *sensory receptors* (eyes, ears, etc.) and other *sensory neurons,* and (2) to transmit electrochemical impulses called *nerve impulses* to other neurons or to *effectors* (muscles and glands). A typical neuron inside the central nervous system consists of a *cell body,* branched extensions called *dendrites* which receive information from other cells, and an extension called the *axon* which conducts information to other cells. The point of contact between the tip of the axon of one neuron and a dendrite of another is a *synapse.* The axon tip does not quite touch the dendrite at the synapse; a tiny gap, the *synaptic cleft,* separates them. Information is transmitted from axon to dendrite by the release from the axon tip of minute amounts of chemicals, called *neurotransmitters,* which then *diffuse* (spread) across the synaptic gap and create a corresponding nerve

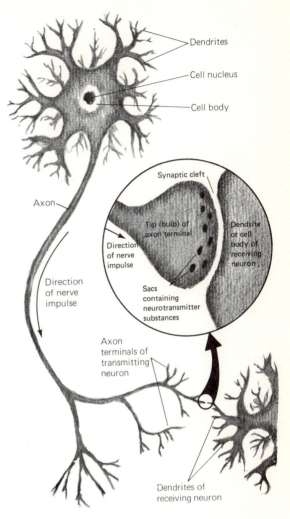

Figure 3-1. An idealized drawing of a neuron, or nerve cell. The transmission of information from an axon terminal of one neuron to a dendrite of another neuron takes place across a gap called the *synaptic cleft.* The end bulb of the axon terminal (see inset) releases chemicals called *neurotransmitter substances* into the synaptic cleft, and these substances carry the information as they spread across the gap.

impulse in the dendrite of the adjoining cell. An essentially similar process of chemical transmission occurs at the *neuroeffector junction,* where the axon makes contact with a muscle or gland cell.

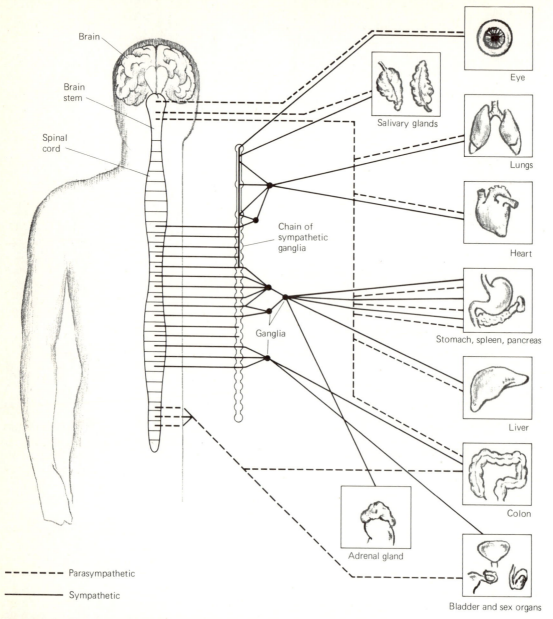

Figure 3-2. The central and autonomic nervous systems. The *central nervous system* consists of the brain and spinal cord. The *autonomic nervous system* consists of nerves and ganglia (clumps of nerve cells) that regulate the blood vessels, glands, and other internal organs. The autonomic nervous system is itself divided into the sympathetic and parasympathetic divisions. The *sympathetic division* connects the spinal cord with the various organs by means of two chains of ganglia, one on each side of the spinal cord (only one chain is shown here). The *parasympathetic division* connects the brain and lower portions of the spinal cord with its ganglia (not shown) near the organs it regulates.

Central and peripheral nervous systems

The nervous system is divided into the *central nervous system* and the *peripheral nervous system*. It is by way of the central nervous system, composed of the *brain* and the *spinal cord,* that information from internal and external sources is processed and instructions for action are sent out. The brain, the focal point of this activity, will be discussed in detail in following sections. The spinal cord serves primarily to transmit information back and forth from the brain to the peripheral nervous system. But it is also capable, independently of the brain, of integrating certain reflex (involuntary) actions. The familiar knee jerk to the doctor's rubber hammer is a good example of a reflex. Although vital to healthy bodily functioning, the spinal cord is not very important to the student of psychopathology, and so we shall say no more about it here.

The peripheral nervous system is divided into two parts. The *sensory portion* consists of neurons which carry information (via the sensory receptors) to the brain and spinal cord from the outside world and from the body organs. The *motor portion* consists of neurons which transmit nerve impulses from the brain and spinal cord in order to activate the muscles and glands.

The motor portion of the peripheral nervous system is also divided into two separate systems. The *somatic system* controls the skeletal muscles; these muscles permit voluntary behavior like walking and talking. The *autonomic nervous system* is the other division of the motor portion of the peripheral nervous system. It controls the internal organs of the body: the blood vessels, glands, heart muscle, and viscera. These functions, unlike the somatic nervous system, are generally not under voluntary control. Emotional responses are reflected in changes in autonomic functioning. For example, when a person is tense or nervous, his blood pressure, heart rate, and stomach activity change. Sometimes, as in the case of psychosomatic disorders (Chapter 14), there can be lasting damage to the body.

Consequently the autonomic nervous system is of special importance in the study of psychopathology.

The autonomic nervous system itself is subdivided: into the *sympathetic division,* which activates the body for emergency action when it is required, and the *parasympathetic division,* which conserves and stores bodily energy and attends to the body's normal "housekeeping" functions. Thus sympathetic stimulation accelerates heart rate, inhibits stomach contractions, and sends an increased supply of blood to the skeletal muscles. By contrast, parasympathetic activation facilitates the process of digestion and slows and regulates heart rate and blood vessel dilation to reduce blood pressure. Thus the two divisions of the autonomic nervous system serve opposing functions, giving the body a system of "checks and balances." If matters were not regulated in this way, a person either would become rapidly exhausted from expending energy or else would be unable to mobilize quickly for emergencies.

The brain

The brain is the most complex organ in the nervous system. It is composed of billions of densely packed nerve cells. The brain controls all the distinctly human aspects of our behavior—language, thinking, remembering, anticipating. Encased in its bony skull, the brain is organized into three main parts that differ in structure and function. These are the *forebrain,* the *midbrain,* and the *hindbrain.*

Hindbrain. In evolutionary terms, the hindbrain is the most primitive part of man's brain. The hindbrain is itself divided into three parts: the cerebellum, the pons, and the medulla. The *medulla* helps control and regulate respiration, heart action, and gastrointestinal activity. The *cerebellum* helps ensure smooth and coordinated motor activity. The *pons* connects the two halves of the cerebellum; it plays a role in eating behavior and facial expression.

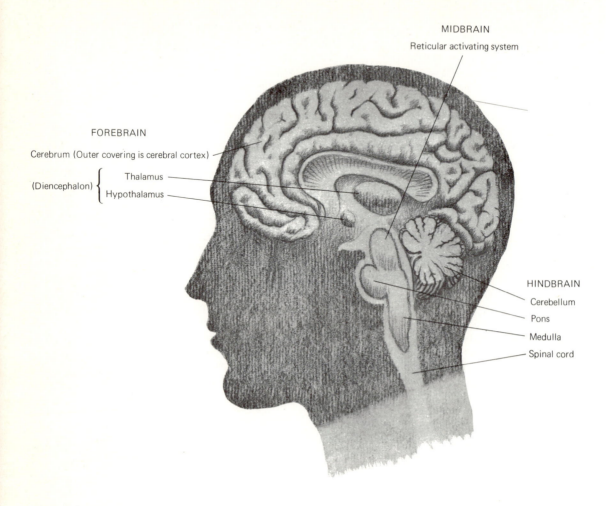

MIDBRAIN
Reticular activating system

FOREBRAIN
Cerebrum (Outer covering is cerebral cortex)
(Diencephalon) { Thalamus
Hypothalamus

HINDBRAIN
Cerebellum
Pons
Medulla
Spinal cord

Figure 3-3. Cross section of the human brain, showing its three major divisions.

Midbrain. Until recently, scientists thought that the most significant function of the midbrain was to relay visual and auditory information to higher brain centers. The discovery of the *reticular activating system* (RAS), which runs through both the hindbrain and the midbrain, has excited intense interest. The first successful study of its function was made by Moruzzi and Magoun (1949), who found that electrical stimulation of the RAS created a state of arousal in experimental animals: they behaved just as they did during periods of activation and wakefulness. More recent studies (Favale et al., 1971; Slosarska, 1969) have reported that lesions (cuts) in the reticular activating system produce a state of drowsiness in experimental animals. Thus the RAS seems to be an integral part of the brain's "waking center." It has even been suggested that some children in a profound state of withdrawal—autistic children—suffer from RAS damage (Chapter 15).

Forebrain. The forebrain is the most highly evolved, specialized, and complex part of the human brain. It gives us the capacity to speak, think, plan, and remember. It contains two parts: the diencephalon and the cerebrum.

The *diencephalon,* in turn, is composed of the thalamus and the hypothalamus. Both are important to human emotions and, for that reason, to the development and maintenance of psychopathologic states. The *thalamus,* which lies just above the midbrain, is in part a relay center transmitting impulses to higher brain centers. It also plays a role in emotional behavior and is one of the mechanisms involved in sleep. Damage to the thalamus can create apathy and forgetfulness, and in some cases causes the patient to see things that aren't there (to have hallucinations).

The role of the *hypothalamus* in behavior is even more complex than that of the thalamus. Located below the thalamus and near the pituitary gland, it fulfills a number of vital functions. These include the maintenance of proper water balance in the body, control of carbohydrate metabolism, and regulation of body temperature and blood pressure. The hypothalamus is also involved in appetite and in the wake-sleep cycle. Most important to us, electrical stimulation of specific portions of the hypothalamus produces a rage response in experimental animals (Smith, 1971; Woodworth, 1971). As soon as this electrical stimulation is terminated, the animal quiets down. This kind of behavior causes theorists to wonder whether some people who commit violent crimes might have suffered hypothalamus damage. The hypothalamus is now considered the "seat of emotions," because it is here that the varied components of emotionality appear to be organized into a coherent pattern (Morgan, 1965).

The *cerebrum,* the largest and most advanced part of the human brain, is composed of an inner core of axons and dendrites running to and from the nerve cell bodies which occupy the outer layer of the cerebrum. This outer layer is the *cerebral cortex.* It looks very much like a rumpled cloth or a

Animal research sometimes provides a vital first step in studying problems that cannot be directly investigated in human beings. *(Taylor © PUNCH 1973)*

series of ridges and valleys seen from high overhead. Known technically as *gyri* (ridges) and *fissures* (valleys), these folds in the cerebral cortex permit a great many cell bodies to be

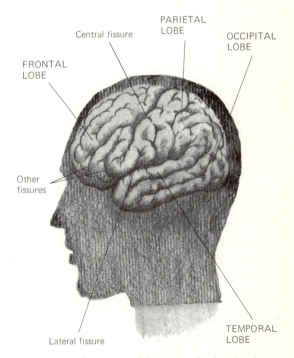

Figure 3-4. Side view of the human brain, showing major features of the cerebral cortex.

packed into a relatively small space. Thus the human brain has many more cells for processing information than the brains of lower mammals, whose cerebral cortexes are smoother.

The human cerebral cortex: Structure and functions. The human cerebral cortex performs sensory, motor, and associational functions. Its sensory function is to receive data from the sense organs and translate them into coherent and useful patterns. Its motor function is to control the movements of the body. Its most complex and most "human" function is that of association, by which reasoning, planning, fantasy, memory, creativity, and problem solving can occur. For these reasons behavioral and life scientists have long looked to the cerebral cortex for answers to the puzzle of psychopathology.

The cerebral cortex is divided into four major areas, called *lobes;* each lobe, in turn, is divided into two halves. The four halves on the left side of the cerebral cortex make up the *left hemisphere;* the four halves on the right side are the *right hemisphere.* These hemispheres are linked together by the *corpus callosum,* a band of nerve fibers which transmit information between the two halves. *Split brain research* (research done on an animal whose corpus callosum has been severed) has demonstrated that each hemisphere can carry out independent learning, memory, and perceptual functions. Neither hemisphere need be aware of what happens in the other half. An animal whose corpus callosum and other connecting fibers have been cut must learn in his right (or left) hemisphere the information which he already has available in his other hemisphere but cannot communicate without the bridge of connecting fibers (Sperry, 1968). Research done on patients suffering from a form of brain damage called epilepsy has revealed similar results. These patients, who underwent surgical destruction of the corpus callosum as treatment for their condition, have shown by their postoperative behavior that each hemisphere is independent (Gazzangia, 1970).

The *temporal lobes* of the cerebral cortex are responsible for processing visual information, for some aspects of immediate memory, and for auditory recognition. A monkey whose temporal lobes have been removed cannot recognize familiar objects, although he can make fine visual discriminations (Wilson and Miskin, 1959). The *parietal lobes* permit recognition of objects by the sense of touch. Hecaen and his colleagues reported that patients with lesions of the right parietal lobe have no awareness of their body parts (1956). A portion of the left parietal lobe is also thought to be involved in symbolic speech. The primary function of the *occipital lobes* is visual perception. The *frontal lobes* in man seem to be related to his capacity for flexible problem solving (Milner, 1964) and for abstract thinking (Goldstein, 1950).

The language areas of the brain are not in any one lobe; parts of the frontal, parietal, and temporal lobes all contribute to speech. But for most right-handed people, the speech areas of the brain are in the left hemisphere. As a result, damage to this side of the brain may produce an *aphasia*—a deficiency in understanding or communicating language. An aphasic person may find himself without words to express his feelings, or may discover that while he cannot speak the proper words, he is able to write them (or vice versa). The aphasias are discussed in detail in Chapter 16, along with other disorders of the brain.

Neurotransmitters

We noted earlier that communication across the synaptic gap separating one neuron and another, or separating a neuron and an effector (muscle or gland), is accomplished by chemicals called *neurotransmitters.* Scientists have only recently begun to explore the action of these chemicals (McGeer, 1971). The neurotransmitters, synthesized and stored within the neurons, are of central importance to the coordinated functioning of the nervous system. It is now reasonably well established, for example, that transmission of impulses within the parasympathetic and sympathetic systems is accomplished by means of the neurotransmitter *acetylcholine.* Acetylcholine is also believed to be the transmitter substance between motor neurons and the voluntary (skeletal) muscles. In the synapses between the motor neurons and the target organs of the sympathetic system, another substance, noradrenalin, is thought to be the neurotransmitter.

Within the brain and spinal cord, neurotransmission is more complex and less well understood than in the peripheral nervous system. While acetycholine is almost certainly the neurotransmitter at some synapses in the central nervous system, other neurotransmitters (notably noradrenalin, serotonin, and dopamine) are probably involved at other synapses. Thus acetycholine is found in many areas of the brain, especially the reticular activating system, while noradrenaline is found in the areas involved in regulation of the autonomic nervous system. This fact is important because there is some evidence that faulty noradrenaline metabolism is responsible for schizophrenia. Faulty metabolism of serotonin, a neurotransmitter found in high concentrations in the midbrain and hypothalamus, has also been implicated in schizophrenia. These and other metabolic theories of schizophrenia are discussed in Chapter 7.

Techniques for studying the nervous system

In recent years scientists have developed more and more sophisticated methods of measuring the activities of the nervous system. There are now five: lesion techniques, chemical methods, electrical recording, electrical stimulation, and behavioral procedures (Thompson, 1967). These methods have been used almost exclusively with animal subjects, since they involve risks of permanent neurological damage that most human beings—subjects and experimenters alike—are unwilling to take.

The *lesion* technique, which destroys nervous tissue, is the oldest method of the five. The scientist actually destroys a portion of the nervous system to observe what influence the damage has upon nervous system functioning. He can either physically remove a section of tissue or kill the cells in a specific area by using heat or electrical current.

Chemical methods utilize certain chemicals to temporarily disrupt the functioning of small parts of the brain. These methods permit examination of the chemical processes occurring in intact normal and abnormal brain tissue.

Electrical recording methods allow scientists to measure the electrical activity of the nervous system both in individual cells and in groups of cells. Electrical impulses generated within single cells are recorded with a tiny instrument called a *microelectrode,* which has a tip finer than the diameter of a cell body. A much cruder measure of the simultaneous electrical activity of many neurons is provided by *electroencephalographic* (EEG) recording. EEG records of "brain waves" have proved valuable for both clinical and research purposes.

Electrical stimulation procedures allow researchers to stimulate the brain at various points and then observe the behaviors which result. After permanently implanting electrodes, the scientist can stimulate an animal simply by "plugging him in." Electrical stimulation techniques have also been used with humans: Patients being operated upon for control of epilepsy or for the removal of brain tumors may be put under local anaesthesia so that they are awake, but not in pain. During the course of the operation the neurosurgeon may stimulate certain portions of the brain electrically to observe the patient's responses. This enables the doctor to be sure he is not removing areas of the brain which are vital to normal functioning. Information gained in these operations has also increased our understanding of how the brain works.

Many *behavioral procedures* have been developed recently to study some of the specialized functions of the central nervous system. Often these procedures involve measuring the changes in behavior which accompany or follow lesions and electrical or chemical stimulation of the brain. Much of the work follows the basic procedure developed by Olds and Milner (1954), who trained rats to press a bar in order to receive electrical stimulation in certain portions of the brain sometimes referred to as a "pleasure center." Olds and Milner found that this stimulation was so rewarding that rats would press a bar repeatedly to obtain it, just as they would to get food or water.

Measurement of autonomic activity: The polygraph. In order to study how the human nervous system functions, researchers have developed indirect techniques in which the *polygraph* (whose name comes from the Greek words for "many" and "writing") plays a major role. It uses electrical devices (transducers) to translate movement of body parts into electrical signals. The signals in turn activate pens that write on a continually moving paper chart.

The *electrocardiograph* (EKG), both a research and a clinical tool, is a component of the polygraph which measures heart activity. The *electromyograph* (EMG) measures muscle

The polygraph is much used in studying how the human nervous system functions.

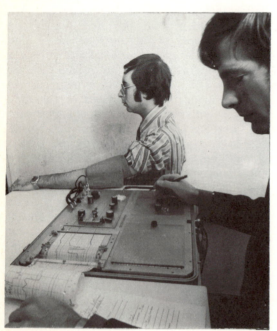

activation level. Changes in volume of blood are reflected by the *plethysmograph*. Blood pressure is recorded with the *sphygmomanometer;* this is the familiar cuff wrapped around the arm and inflated with air in routine physical checkups. The *galvanic skin response* (GSR) reflects changes in the electrical resistance of the skin which are used to measure response to stress. (Anxiety, fear, and other emotional states increase the activity of the sweat glands, and sweating reduces skin resistance to electrical flow.)

The *electroencephalograph* (EEG) is the polygraph component which records the brain's electrical activity. Electrodes attached to the scalp send this information from various parts of the brain to a machine that amplifies the voltage and records it on a moving chart. The EEG is used to measure normal brain activity as well as to diagnose abnormal forms. Human beings have different kinds of cortical activity under different conditions. For example, *alpha waves,* with a frequency between 8 and 13 cycles per second (cps), are found when a person is in a state of relaxed wakefulness. When he is very alert, his brain produces *beta waves,* with a frequency between 14 and 25 cps. Humans also show characteristic brain wave patterns when they are asleep. Deep sleep is accompanied by *delta waves*—low-frequency (0.5 to 3.5 cps) patterns. As sleep becomes lighter, these waves grow more rapid until they turn into the alpha waves of relaxed wakefulness. Although some researchers have tried to diagnose nonorganic psychopathology from EEG records, they have been unsuccessful so far. But EEG records do enable the neurologist to diagnose such organic brain disorders as epilepsy and tumors.

The glandular system

Like the nervous system, the glandular system plays a major role in regulating the body's continual adjustment to conditions both inside it and outside in the external environment. This system is composed of the *duct* or *exocrine glands* and the *ductless* or *endocrine glands.*

The duct glands, which include the tear and sweat glands, are important for health, but they contribute little to the understanding of psychopathology (except when they signal emotional states like depression and anxiety). The endocrine glands, by contrast, are intimately involved in emotionality and in psychopathology.

Hormones. The function of the endocrine glands is to produce chemicals called hormones which are released directly into the bloodstream. The blood carries them to the various "target organs." The word hormone, derived from a Greek word for "activator," refers to the fact that these chemicals trigger the functions of various glands. Different hormones regulate the activities of different organs. The release of hormones from the endocrine glands which manufacture them is caused either by other hormones or by direct nervous system stimulation. The endocrine glands include the pituitary, thyroid, and adrenal glands, the pancreas, and the ovaries and testes.

Pituitary gland. The *pituitary gland* is called the "master gland" because it controls the activities of other glands. Located at the base of the brain and connected to the hypothalamus, the pituitary gland is divided into *anterior* and *posterior* portions. The *anterior pituitary* is the more important to the student of psychopathology because a number of its endocrine secretions are directly involved in psychological behavior. *Adrenocorticotrophic hormone* (ACTH) is one of the anterior pituitary's secretions. The function of ACTH is to seek out the adrenal gland and stimulate it to secrete its own hormones.

Adrenal gland. The adrenal gland, located on the kidneys, manufactures a number of influential hormones. Among the most important are *cortisone* and *corticosterone,* essential both to body metabolism and to the control of inflammation. These adrenal gland secretions are stimulated by ACTH from the pituitary gland. Undersecretion of ACTH or damage to the

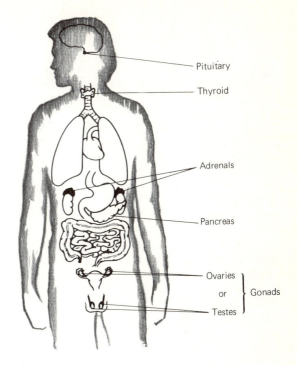

Figure 3-5. Some of the endocrine, or ductless, glands whose secretions—called *hormones*—influence behavior. The endocrine glands play a role in emotionality and thus in psychopathology.

adrenal gland causes corresponding shortages of cortisone and corticosterone. Both shortages are involved in Addison's disease, an illness characterized by faintness, a darkening of the skin pigment, and ultimately coma and even death. The adrenal gland also secretes *epinephrine* and *norepinephrine,* which are closely related chemically. These two hormones, sometimes called *adrenalin* and *noradrenalin,* appear to be intimately related to emotional responsiveness. Adrenalin has been linked to the experience of anxiety, while noradrenalin has been associated with the expression of anger (Ax, 1953; DiGiusto, Cairncross, & King, 1971).

Thyroid gland. Located in the neck on either side of the windpipe, the thyroid gland seems to function as a regulator of bodily metabolism.

(This is the process by which the body breaks food down into "building blocks.") During prenatal development, a deficiency of *thyroxin* may produce in the fetus a form of mental retardation called cretinism (Chapter 16). In adulthood, a similar deficiency can produce symptoms of depression, apathy, and lethargy. An excess of thyroid secretion is also related to psychological symptoms, including tension and irritability, as well as to physical symptoms like weakness and loss of weight.

Pancreas. This organ, which lies below the stomach, contains tissues which secrete *insulin* and *glucagon*—hormones that maintain an appropriate level of sugar in the blood. A common result of insulin deficiency is diabetes mellitus, a physical disease.

Sex glands. The *ovaries* and *testes* are, respectively, female and male sex glands. They secrete hormones which have an important influence on sexual and maternal behaviors. These secretions can also bring on psychological disorder. For example, some women regularly become irritable, tense, and depressed when several hormones are released into the blood in the days immediately preceding the onset of menstruation. Further, the arrival of menopause during middle age is accompanied by hormonal changes that may produce temporary or permanent personality changes in a woman, and sometimes may even bring on psychopathology.

Biology of stress and psychopathology

Now think of the bodily responses discussed in this chapter in terms of the anger and fear felt by Piri Thomas and Anne Frank when they were under stress. For example—

Piri Thomas: Anger

Lights began to jump in my head and tears blurred out that this was my brother before me. The burning came up out of me and I felt the shock run up my arm as my fists went to the side of his head. I felt one fist hit his mouth. . . .

I saw an unknown face spitting blood at me. I hated it. I wanted to stay on top of this unknown what-was-it and beat him and beat him and beat him and beat him and *beat beat beat beat beat*— and feel skin smash under me and—and—and—

Anne Frank: Fear

I turned white at once, got a tummyache and heart palpitations, all from fear. . . .

"Now we are lost!" I said, and could see us all being taken away by the Gestapo that very night. Twice they rattled at the cupboard, then there was nothing, the footsteps withdrew, we were saved so far. A shiver seemed to pass from one to another, I heard someone's teeth chattering, no one said a word. . . .

Next we did three things: we went over again what we supposed had happened, we trembled with fear, and we had to go to the lavatory.

We chose to put these excerpts at the beginning of the chapter because they are powerful illustrations of the relationships that exist during periods of stress between bodily changes and emotion. In the paler phrases of common talk, people often say, "He cracked under the pressure," or "She works too hard—no wonder she got an ulcer." What they are recognizing in an informal way is that everyone's normal physiological and psychological functioning suffers under stress.

Stress takes various forms. Feeling too hot or too cold, being hurt in an accident, working too hard, or agonizing over a threatening situation all create conditions of stress. In general terms, any time that the body is called upon to spend large amounts of energy to maintain itself, a person is under stress.

General adaptation syndrome

Hans Selye, a medical researcher at the University of Montreal, has spent much of his life studying the effects of stress upon bodily functioning. His descriptive theory to account for the bodily changes which accompany per-

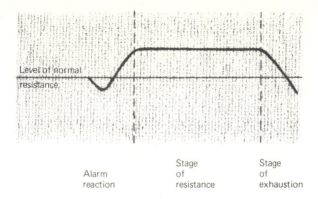

Figure 3-6. The general adaptation syndrome, or GAS. In the *alarm reaction* stage the body responds to the initial shock of the stress. During the *stage of resistance* it settles to the task of withstanding prolonged stress. But if the stress is too severe or long-continued, the body may not be able to resist it. Instead of returning to "normal," the body then enters the *stage of exhaustion*, during which it continues to weaken and may even die. *(Modified from Selye, 1956.)*

ception of, and adjustment to, stress is called the *general adaptation syndrome,* or GAS (1957). Selye describes three separate stages in the GAS: (1) The alarm reaction, (2) the stage of resistance, and (3) the stage of exhaustion. During the *alarm reaction* the body responds to stress with changes in digestive processes and an increase in secretion of corticoids from the adrenal gland. The corticoids will protect the body against further invasion at the stress site if there is actual physical damage. During the *stage of resistance,* the body recovers from the first emotional response to the stress, "settling in" for the task of resisting prolonged stress. But if the stress is sufficiently severe, prolonged, or both, the person will eventually reach the *state of exhaustion,* in which he will weaken and even die. Selye's theory is important because it provides a framework for research into the etiology of chronic physical diseases associated with chronic stress. Some of this research is discussed in Chapter 14, which also details the full range of psychosomatic disorders resulting from prolonged stress.

As an example of the general adaptation syn-drome, consider the situation of a soldier going into combat. His commander announces to the troops that they will be moving to the front in the morning. The man spends an almost sleepless, tense, and fearful night worrying about the coming day. At dawn, his assault team moves out—and almost immediately he is pinned down by machine-gun fire. After hours of hard fighting his unit drives the enemy back; a period of relative quiet follows, but he cannot sleep because of the ever-present danger of a counterattack. So all through the following night he must be awake and constantly alert. After several days like this, he is on the verge of collapse and barely able to go on fighting. His unit is finally withdrawn to the rear, where he spends several days in "R&R" (rest and recuperation).

This soldier went through a highly mobilized *alarm state* during the hours before combat. Then, during the *resistance stage,* he was able to remain alert for a rather long period. However, this alertness was biologically expensive because he finally entered the *stage of exhaustion* just before he was relieved of duty. These physiological events were related in large part to activities of his autonomic nervous system and the functioning of the pituitary and adrenal glands.

Most people do not go through combat, but many experience prolonged physical or psychological stress which can lead to harmful physical changes over time. Long-continued excessive adrenal secretions can lead to abnormal growth of the adrenal gland and are associated with high blood pressure, heart disease, and other psychosomatic disorders (Chapter 14).

Other research on human response to stress

How do behavioral scientists gather objective data on the relationships between body changes and emotion—say, in the case of emotions like Piri Thomas's anger and Anne Frank's fear? It is a difficult problem in research design, for on one hand the experimenter needs strict scientific control, while on the other he must consider ethical factors in his treatment of human beings. Yet most of these studies depend on tricking people, sometimes by frightening them. One experiment that has raised ethical questions was carried out by Berkun and his co-workers (1962). Soldiers aboard a plane on a supposedly routine training mission were told that an emergency made it necessary for them to crash-land at sea. As predicted, the men's adrenal gland secretions increased. In a study somewhat less traumatic for the subjects, Handlen (1962) showed several groups a stressful movie *(High Noon)* and other groups a relaxing film (a Walt Disney nature study). He observed an increase in adrenal gland secretions during and after the stressful film and a striking decrease in secretions after the relaxing film.

Some people can stand more stress than others without showing harmful physiological or psychological effects. In addition, different people respond to stress differently. Some soldiers "crack" in combat; others keep on fighting. An important source of these individual differences may arise from differences in the early environment. Levine and Mullins (1966)

exposed a group of young rats to a mild electric shock and compared their subsequent development with that of a group who were handled exactly the same except that they were never given shock. A third group of rats (the *control* group) was left undisturbed in the nest. The results were interesting: the undisturbed control group showed the most timidity in a strange situation, while the rats who had been shocked made faster strides in their physical development than the ones who had not. The mild stress given in infancy seems to have had a significant—and perhaps desirable—influence. The experimenters speculated that alteration of hormonal functions in infancy may have an enduring effect upon development.

Constitution, temperament, and psychopathology

Body type and temperament

Let me have men about me that are fat;
Sleek-headed men and such as sleep o'nights;
Yond Cassius has a lean and hungry look;
He thinks too much: such men are dangerous.

In this passage from *Julius Caesar* Shakespeare crystallizes into art the view that there is a relationship between body build and personality type: the lean and lank cannot be trusted, while the obese are not so likely to cause trouble. Many of us make similar assumptions —that the fat are jolly and good-natured, the slender and slight are scholarly and bookish, and the athletically built are full of energy, enthusiastic about life. Is there any truth in these ideas, or are they simply part of a cultural mythology?

William Sheldon developed an elaborate empirical approach to the study of body types (1940, 1971). Each of his thousands of experimental subjects was rated on three body-build dimensions, and attempts were then made to link these body types to psychopathology. Wittman, Sheldon, and Katz found data suggesting that the various builds were correlated with particular forms of psychopathology

(1948). The correlations were impressive, but later attempts to duplicate Sheldon's research have been less successful. One possible flaw in his research technique is that he did both the body typing and the personality typing himself, thus creating a possible source of systematic bias. When Child (1950) attempted to control for this bias, he found much smaller correlations than those reported by Sheldon, although the relationships were still significant.

In evaluating the research on relationships between body type and inborn personality, psychologists must consider a number of factors. One of the most important is the possible effect of social expectations upon behavior. To what extent is the fat man jolly because we expect him to be jolly? Perhaps the obese child who cannot run very fast or play ball very well finds that good humor is another way to win friends: in other words, he is reinforced for emitting amusing behavior. Likewise, the frail, slender child who cannot compete on the playground may turn to books as a source of pleasure and a means of maintaining self-esteem. And the large, well-built child may find a self-confident, assertive personality thrust upon him, so to speak, because his size and strength cause his smaller friends to expect him to take the lead.

Malcolm X, for example, was a tall gangling man with an impressive bearing. It would be possible to characterize him in terms of Sheldon's body types and find personality characteristics correlated with his body build (tenseness, emotional control, the "need" for solitude, willingness to be assertive when assertiveness is called for). But taking everything into account, we think it is easier to understand Malcolm X within his social and cultural context rather than on the basis of innate personality. In particular, society's reactions to him as a black man appear to have been more important to his development than inborn personality features related to body type. Then when Malcolm X asserted himself and acted as a leader, his physical size must have increased the impact of his message in a way that it probably would not if he had been small or unattractive.

Autonomic reactivity and personality

Research has linked physiology and personality in other areas besides that of body type. A person's energy level and susceptibility to stress, for example, also influence the adjustment he makes to his environment. People with high energy levels presumably need more opportunity to discharge energy than those with low levels. Hence an energetic person may be physically very active, while the individual with little energy may be more introspective and inclined to fantasy. Eysenck has also proposed certain relationships between response to stress and personality development (1960). He assumes that the child who is highly reactive to stress is more likely to develop conditioned fears and anxieties, whereas the child who is not much affected by stress may fail to learn restraints that normal levels of anxiety would teach him. Eysenck suggests that some overreactive children may develop into anxious adults, while some underreactive children may become antisocial adults.

TABLE 3-1. TEMPERAMENTAL CHARACTERISTICS OF CHILDREN

Activity level: How much does the child move around?

Rhythmicity: How well regulated are such functions as feeding and bowel movements?

Adaptability: How well does the child adapt to changes in circumstances?

Approach-withdrawal: Does the child actively approach new activities, wait passively, or avoid them?

Threshold level: How sensitive is the child to noise, heat, cold, etc.?

Intensity of reaction: Does the child indicate his pleasure and displeasure in intensive or quiet ways?

Quality of mood: Is the child more often contented or discontented?

Distractibility: Does the child focus on a task, or is he easily distracted?

Persistence and attention span: Does the child stay with a task a long time, or does he skip from thing to thing?

SOURCE: Thomas, Chess, and Birch, 1968.

In an important study of temperament and behavior disorders in children, Thomas, Chess, and Birch examined the influence which temperament has upon a child's development. They defined temperament as the "characteristic tempo, rhythmicity, adaptability, energy expenditure, mood and focus of attention of a child" (1968, p. 5). Table 3-1 presents these characteristics in more detail. The researchers studied children in 85 families from birth through childhood and concluded that temperament, although altered by experience, tends to be stable over time. The children in the study who showed some form of behavior disorder as they grew up were from the first more active than the other children, less dependable in their daily schedules, less adaptable to change, and more easily distracted. On the other hand, infants who were judged to be "easy children," with positive mood, a regular energy output, a moderate response to stimulation, and ready adaptability to change, rarely developed behavior disorders. These findings add further weight to the view that a child's inborn temperament influences his or her later development.

Genetics and psychopathology

It is hard to believe that each of us began from a single cell, from the uniting of a sperm and an ovum. But this is the fact. The total of our biological inheritance was determined at the moment when the ovum of the month encountered one of many hundreds of sperm to begin the process of human development. The process of growth from that single fertilized cell to the adult human who reads this page is an incredibly intricate one that can go wrong in many ways.

It has long been known that various portions of the genetic material inherited during reproduction can be faulty. Many behavioral scientists now believe that genetic flaws can be responsible for certain kinds of defective psychological development. Recently all psychopathology—especially the functional psychoses, the neuroses, alcoholism, and the mental retardations—has been examined from the genetic point of view. Heredity in relation to psychopathology will be a recurrent theme in this book, and to understand it you need to know a little about genetics and behavioral genetic research designs.

Chromosomes and genes

Inherited characteristics are transmitted through many thousands of *genes,* the chemical units of heredity. Genes are arranged in a specific linear order, like numbered beads on a string, along *chromosomes.* Almost every human being has 46 chromosomes in the cells of his body. They are grouped into 23 pairs of corresponding *(homologous)* chromosomes, one member of each pair having been contributed by each of the person's parents. However, when the individual matures and his testes (or ovaries) produce a *gamete* (a sperm or an egg), each of these receives only one member of each chromosomal pair. The union between egg and sperm will then bring together a full set of 46 chromosomes.

Since humans have only 23 pairs of chromosomes, why are siblings only very, very rarely genetically identical? There are two reasons.

[1] *Independent assortment.* Assume for the moment that a mature person's ovary (or testis), on producing a gamete, passes along intact one member of each pair of chromosomes that the person received from his or her parents. However, of each pair, *which* parent's chromosome goes into the gamete is a matter of chance. While the gamete might receive all of the 23 chromosomes the person received from his mother and none of those he inherited from his father, it is much more likely to receive some of each. The only requirement is that he pass on one member of each pair of homologous chromosomes. The number of different gametes that might be produced from all such combinations is 2^{23}—more than 8 million! Independent assortment, then, reduces the chance to only 1 in 8 million that two children of the same couple will both

Identical (monozygotic) twins as they appeared at different ages. *(From Kallman and Jarvik, 1959)*

inherit exactly the same chromosomes and thus be genetically identical.

[2] *Crossing over.* One chance in 8 million is a very small chance indeed—but that is not all. A second chance-determined event which occurs during the production of gametes makes even this improbability a virtual impossibility. It is that a person *doesn't* pass chromosomes *intact.* Instead, just before a gamete is produced, the members of each homologous pair of chromosomes intertwine and then separate. And the lineal arrangement of genes on the chromosomes after separation is different from that before the chromosomes intertwined. What has happened is that the intertwining chromosomes have traded sections of themselves. Equal-sized segments of each have broken off, *crossed over,* and then attached themselves to the other chromosome. Which sections cross over is deter-

mined by chance. Crossing over is the rule rather than the exception. It tremendously magnifies the number of genetically different gametes produced. A common form of retardation called Down's Syndrome (Chapter 16) is thought to be caused by chromosomal breaks or dislocations that sometimes occur during crossing over.

Identical or *monozygotic twins* are twins who developed from the same fertilized ovum or zygote. Since they develop *after* the genetic rearrangement of independent assortment and crossing over have taken place, they are truly identical in genetic makeup. They can be contrasted with fraternal or *dizygotic twins* who happen to have been conceived at the same time but who grow from two different fertilized ova. Approximately 1 percent of all children born are twins. Of this 1 percent, one set in three are identical twins. The

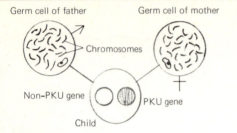

Germ cell of father   Germ cell of mother

Chromosomes

Non-PKU gene   PKU gene

Child

Each chromosome contains pairs of genes, one gene from each parent.

In this case, all of both parents' genes are for a particular characteristic—PKU retardation.

Child

The child has only PKU genes and, like his parents, has PKU.

In this case, two types of genes (PKU and non-PKU) are present, but each parent has only one type.

Child

The child has both genes. If one gene is dominant, the child will have that characteristic. Since the non-PKU gene is dominant, the child does not have PKU. He does, however, have the recessive PKU gene to transmit some day to *his* child.

Here different genes are present, and both mother and father have both types.

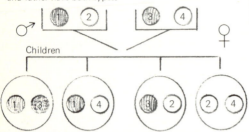

Children

In this case, neither the mother nor the father has PKU, since each has a dominant non-PKU gene as well as a recessive PKU gene. The various outcomes for their offspring are shown; the numbers designate the genes. On the average, three of the children will have the dominant non-PKU gene; one will have two recessive PKU genes and show the effects of PKU. Note that two of the three children who are symptom-free inherit the recessive gene—which has the potential of being transmitted to their own offspring someday.

identical heredities of monozygotic twins make them useful to behavioral scientists studying the effects of heredity and environment upon development.

Chromosomes can be seen under high-powered microscopes. By looking at them, scientists have sorted out the 23 pairs, assigning them numbers from 1 to 23 so that they can be identified and studied. Of the pairs, 22 are called *autosomes;* the twenty-third pair are the *sex chromosomes,* which scientists call X and Y chromosomes. Females have two X chromosomes (XX), while males have one X and one Y (XY) chromosome. Inherited characteristics which are derived from one of the sex chromosomes are said to be *sex-linked.*

Every chromosome is made up of tens of thousands of genes. The most important chemical component of the gene is *deoxyribonucleic acid* (DNA), which provides a chemical code for the proper building of enzymes and other proteins. The Watson-Crick model of the structure of DNA has become a well-known scientific model. According to it, DNA appears as a helix—a configuration that looks something like an intertwined double spiral stairway—composed of four different chemical called nucleotides. Another important chemical, *ribonucleic acid* (RNA), plays a transmitter (or "messenger," as it is sometimes called) role for the code provided by DNA. RNA takes the instructions provided by DNA and carries them throughout the cell to implement the plans drawn by the DNA structure.

Genotype and phenotype

If a person inherits the genes for blue eyes from one of his parents and the genes for brown eyes from the other parent, he will be born with brown eyes. We express this fact by saying that the genes for brown eyes are *dominant* over the genes for blue eyes. Or to put it

Figure 3-7. The inheritance of phenylketonuria (PKU), a form of mental retardation. The child who receives a PKU (recessive) gene from each parent will develop this disorder.

another way, the genes for blue eyes are *recessive*. When a person inherits one dominant and one recessive gene, he will have the characterisitc carried by the dominant gene, although his cells will contain the recessive gene too. As a result, a brown-eyed person can have blue-eyed children (that is, if his mate also possesses the genes for blue eyes, their child can inherit a gene for blue eyes from both parents). To express this difference between overt appearance and heredity, we speak of genotypes and phenotypes. *Phenotype* refers to a person's observable physical characteristics—like brown eyes. *Genotype* refers to the actual genes an individual possesses. The transmission of a recessive characteristic such as blue eyes is unimportant to the behavioral scientist, but some forms of mental retardation or psychosis are also inherited recessively. In this case two healthy people could have a sick child. These conditions will be discussed in Chapter 16.

Nonhereditary factors can also influence phenotype. Take, for example, a characteristic like physical growth. The upper limit of a person's height is set by his genotype, but his diet, the state of his health, and the medical care he receives will all determine his actual, phenotypic height. It has been suggested that a similar relationship between genotype and phenotype applies to some forms of psychopathology. People may be born with a greater or lesser tendency to psychopathology, but whether they ever actually become disturbed may depend largely upon their life experiences—that is, upon environmental influences.

Research techniques in behavioral genetics

The primary research problem facing the behavioral geneticist is to separate the influence of heredity upon behavior from that of environment. The problem is compounded by the fact that environmental factors begin operating during the prenatal period, when they are even more difficult to evaluate. For example, the mother's nutrition and health shape the baby's development while it is still inside her body. Malcolm X, Daniel Paul Schreber, you, and I—each of us came into the world complete with a full set of genetic predispositions. But how can researchers in psychopathology separate these predispositions from the social environment that each person was born into and developed within? Geneticists have developed a variety of research strategies for coping with the problem. Because the procedures vary with the mental disorder in question, we will not describe them now but later, when we explore the etiologies of the schizophrenias, the manic-depressive psychoses, alcoholism, and the sexual dysfunctions.

Behavior and biological limits

The human being, as an incredibly complex biological organism, is subject to a variety of malfunctions. They express themselves in behavioral or psychological as well as physical terms. An obvious illustration is a tumor in the brain, which can cause depression, apathy, or hallucinations as well as headaches and an unsteady gait. A defect in the production of certain hormones can cause retardation and physical malformation in the newborn. Genetic defects, while often less clear in etiology, can also produce psychological, intellectual, and physical deficits. In addition to these known causes, there remain important questions at the frontiers of research in psychopathology about the ways in which biological malfunctions relate to disorders like schizophrenia and depression. Psychological stress can also create physical problems. Changes in such things as blood pressure and stomach secretions can accompany psychological tension, and these changes may cause lasting damage to the body.

To a large extent, as discussed in Chapter 1, human behavior falls on a continuum of normality. Just as adaptive and maladaptive behavior is acquired according to the same principles of learning, so too do all of us experience the biological limits imposed by our bodies. Some of us are born stronger, have had better physical care, or are lucky enough to have avoided accidents; others may be less fortunate. Whatever our individual biology, each of us must respond to it.

What about Malcolm X and Daniel Paul Schreber in this regard? These two men fall at different points on the continuum of normality. They show different mixtures of biological, social, and psychological factors in their functioning. To understand each man, we need to evaluate all the factors in relation to each other. In reading the chapters that follow, you will rarely if ever come across cases where a single member of this triad—biology, sociology, psychology—is sufficient to explain behavior. The child who grows up in poverty and adopts a life of crime may be primarily a "failure of society." But, his physical size and temperament as well as the way his parents raised him are also crucial factors leading to his antisocial behavior. Likewise, the person with damage to his brain will doubtless suffer from the physical consequences, but how he adapts to that damage and the extent of his recovery are determined too by his personality and the opportunities society offers him for recovery. His problems may be largely due to a "failure of biology," but society and his own personality can partially counter this failure.

Summary

Emotions, including the severe depression, mania, and anxiety that occur in much psychopathology, are accompanied by physiological changes. *Psychobiology* is the study of the interplay between psychological events and the person's biological functioning.

The nervous system is made up of billions of nerve cells, or neurons, which receive and transmit information in the form of electrochemical impulses. The central nervous system is composed of the brain and spinal cord; the peripheral nervous system is divided into the sensory and motor portions.

The motor portion of the peripheral nervous system contains the somatic system, which controls the skeletal muscles, and the autonomic nervous system, which controls the internal organs of the body. These organs include the blood vessels, glands, heart muscle, and viscera. Their functions are generally not under voluntary control. The autonomic nervous system is important in the study of psychopathology because emotional responses are reflected in autonomic changes.

The brain, the most complex organ in the nervous system, is divided into the forebrain, the midbrain, and the hindbrain. The reticular activating system (RAS), which runs through the hindbrain and the midbrain, seems to be part of the brain's "waking center." Electrical stimulation of the RAS creates a state of arousal in animals; lesions in the RAS produce drowsiness.

The thalamus and the hypothalamus, located in the forebrain, both play a part in emotions. Damage to the hypothalamus can create apathy, forgetfulness, and sometimes hallucinations. Electrical stimulation of certain areas of the hypothalamus produces a rage response in animals. The hypothalamus is considered the "seat of emotions," because it appears to organize the components of emotionality into a meaningful pattern.

The human cerebral cortex, located in the cerebrum of the forebrain, performs sensory, motor, and associational functions. Association includes reasoning, planning, fantasy, memory, creativity, and problem solving. Because these are the most complex and most "human" activities of the brain, scientists have long hoped that research on the cerebral cortex will eventually solve the puzzle of mental disorder.

To study the nervous system, five methods have been developed for use with experimental animals: lesion techiques, chemical methods, electrical recording, electrical stimulation, and behavioral procedures. To study the human nervous system, researchers depend on indirect techniques such as the polygraph. This instrument records many bodily activities—including brain waves, which it measures with the electroencephalograph (EEG).

Like the nervous system, the glandular system plays a major role in regulating the body. The endocrine glands are intimately involved in emotionality and psychopathology. They produce hormones, which control the activities of various organs. The endocrine glands include the pituitary, thyroid, and adrenal glands, the pancreas, and the ovaries and testes.

Normal physiological and psychological functioning suffers when a person is under stress. The general adaptation syndrome (GAS), a model which describes bodily changes during stress, differentiates three stages: (1) the alarm reaction, (2) the stage of resistance, (3) the stage of exhaustion, which can end in death.

There is a relation between body build and temperament, but not a simple one. It involves a number of factors, including the expectations that other people have about the behavior of an individual with a certain body type. In any case, studies of temperament in children suggest that it remains stable over time.

Inherited characteristics are transmitted through thousands of genes, which are the chemical units of heredity. Some of the genes that an individual inherits can be faulty and can cause various kinds of defective psychological development. Recently all psychopathology has been restudied from the genetic point of view, with results that will be described in later chapters.

CHAPTER FOUR

Personality and psycho-pathology

Freud and Wolpe on Little Hans ● What is personality? ●
Freud's psychoanalytic theory of personality ● Mischel's
social-behavior theory of personality

FREUD:
"ANALYSIS OF
A PHOBIA IN
A FIVE-YEAR-
OLD BOY"

"In the following pages I propose to describe the course of the illness
and recovery of a very youthful patient. The case history is not,
strictly speaking, derived from my observation. It is true that I laid
down the general lines of the treatment, and that on one single occasion, when I had a conversation with the boy, I took a direct share
in it; but the treatment itself was carried out by the child's father,
and it is to him that I owe my sincerest thanks for allowing me to
publish his notes upon the case. . . . The peculiar value of this [case]
lies in the considerations which follow. When a physician treats
an adult neurotic by psycho-analysis, the process he goes through
of uncovering the psychical formations, layer by layer, eventually
enables him to frame certain hypotheses as to the patient's infantile
sexuality; and it is in the components of the latter that he believes
he has discovered the motive forces of all the neurotic symptoms
of later life. But even a psycho-analyst may confess to the wish for
a more direct and less roundabout proof of these fundamental
theorums.

The first reports of Hans date from a period when he was not quite
three years old. At that time, by means of various remarks and questions, he was showing a quite peculiarly lively interest in that portion of his body which he used to describe as his "widdler." . . . His
interest in widdlers was by no means a purely theoretical one: as
might have been expected, it impelled him to touch his member.
When he was three and half his mother found him with his hand to
his penis. She threatened him in these words: "If you do that, I shall
send for Dr. A. to cut off your widdler. And then what'll you widdle
with?" . . . This was the occasion of his acquiring the "castration
complex," the presence of which we are so often obliged to infer
in analyzing neurotics. . . .

But the great event of Hans's life was the birth of his little sister

(The Bettmann Archive)

Hanna when he was exactly three and a half. His behaviour on that occasion was noted down by his father on the spot: "At five in the morning," he writes, "labour began, and Hans's bed was moved into the next room. He woke up there at seven, and hearing his mother groaning, asked 'Why's mamma coughing?' Then, after a pause, 'The stork's coming to-day for certain.' . . .

"Hans is very jealous of the new arrival, and whenever any one praises her, says she is a lovely baby, and so on, he at once declares scornfully: 'But she hasn't got any teeth yet.' . . . Some six months later he had got over his jealousy, and his brotherly affection for the baby was only equalled by his sense of his own superiority over her. . . .

"Hans, four and a quarter. . . . It is clear that being made to widdle—having his knickers unbuttoned and his penis taken out—is a pleasurable process for Hans. On walks it is mostly his father who assists Hans in this way; and this gives the child an opportunity for the fixation of homosexual inclinations upon him. Two days ago, as I have already reported, while his mother was washing and powdering his genital region, he asked her: 'Why don't you put your finger there?' Yesterday, when I was helping Hans to do number one, he asked me for the first time to take him to the back of the house so that no one should see him. He added: 'Last year when I widdled, Berta and Olga watched me.' This meant, I think, that last year he had enjoyed being watched by the girls, but that this was no longer so. His exhibitionism has now succumbed to repression. . . .

"My dear Professor, I am sending you a little more about Hans— but this time, I am sorry to say, material for a case history. As you will see, during the last few days he has developed a nervous disorder, which had made my wife and me most uneasy. . . . No doubt the ground was prepared by sexual over-excitation due to his mother's tenderness; but I am not able to specify the actual exciting cause. He is afraid *that a horse will bite him in the street,* and this fear seems somehow to be connected with his having been frightened by a large penis. As you know from a former report, he had noticed at a very early age what large penises horses have, and at that time he inferred that as his mother was so large she must have a widdler like a horse. I cannot see what to make of it. Has he seen an exhibitionist somewhere? Or is the whole thing simply connected with his mother? It is not very pleasant for us that he should begin setting us problems so early. . . ."

The earliest accounts, dating from the first days in January of the present year (1908), run as follows: . . . "On January 7th he went to the Stadtpark with his nursemaid as usual. In the street he began to cry and asked to be taken home, saying that he wanted to 'coax'

(The Bettmann Archive)

82

(caress) with his Mummy. At home he was asked why he had refused to go any farther and had cried, but he would not say. Till the evening he was cheerful, as usual. But in the evening he grew visibly frightened; he cried and could not be separated from his mother, and wanted to 'coax' with her again. . . . On January 8th my wife decided to go out with him herself, so as to see what was wrong with him. They went to Schönbrunn, where he always likes going. Again he began to cry, did not want to start, and was frightened. In the end he did go; but was visibly frightened in the street. On the way back from Schönbrunn he said to his mother, after much internal struggling: *'I was afraid a horse would bite me.'* . . . On the same day his mother asked: 'Do you put your hand to your widdler?' and he answered: 'Yes. Every evening, when I'm in bed.' The next day, January 9th, he was warned, before his afternoon sleep, not to put his hand to his widdler. When he woke up he was asked about it, and said he had put it there for a short while all the same."

The next batch of news about Hans covers the period from March 1st to March 17th. . . . "After Hans had been enlightened [after his father had, on Freud's suggestion, told him that "this business about horses was a piece of nonsense" and that he was afraid of horses because he was so interested in their big widdlers], there followed a fairly quiet period, during which he could be induced without any particular difficulty to go for his daily walk in the Stadtpark. [But then] his fear of horses became transformed more and more into an obsession for looking at them. He said: 'I have to look at horses, and then I'm frightened.' After an attack of influenza . . . his phobia increased again so much that he could not be induced to go out, or at most on to the balcony. . . . On Sunday, March 1st, the following conversation took place on the way to the station. I was once more trying to explain to him that horses do not bite. *He:* 'But white horses bite. There's a white horse at Gmunden that bites. If you hold your finger to it it bites. . . . [Lizzi's] father was standing near the horse, and the horse turned its head round (to touch him) and he said to Lizzi: *"Don't put your finger to the white horse or it'll bite you."'* Upon this I said: 'I say, it strikes me that it isn't a horse you mean, but a widdler, that one mustn't put one's hand to.' . . .

"On March 2nd, as he again showed signs of being afraid, I said to him: 'Do you know what? This nonsense of yours . . . will get better if you go for more walks. It's so bad now because you haven't been able to go out because you were ill.' He: 'Oh no, it's so bad because I still put my hand to my widdler every night'."

That afternoon the father and son visited me during my consulting hours. I already knew the queer little chap, and with all his self-assurance he was yet so amiable that I had always been glad to see him. . . . The consultation was a short one. His father opened it by remarking that, in spite of all the pieces of enlightenment we had given Hans, his fear of horses had not diminished. . . . as I saw the two of them sitting in front of me . . . a further piece of the solution shot through my mind. . . . I then disclosed to him that he was afraid of his father, precisely because he was so fond of his mother. It must be, I told him, that he thought his father was angry with him on that account; but this was not so, his father was fond of him in spite of it, and he might admit everything to him without any fear. . . . "Does the Professor talk to God," Hans asked his father on the way home, "as he can tell all that beforehand?" I should be extraordinarily proud of this recognition out of the mouth of a child, if I had not myself provoked it by my joking boastfulness. . . . From that time forward he carried out a programme which I was able to announce to his father in advance.

"April 2nd. The *first real improvement* is to be noted. While formerly he could never be induced to go out of the street-door for very long, and always ran back into the house with every sign of fright if horses came along, this time he stayed in front of the street-door for an hour.

"On April 3rd, in the morning he came into bed with me, whereas for the last few days he had not been coming any more and had even seemed to be proud of not doing so. . . . *Hans*: 'When I'm not with you I'm frightened; when I'm not in bed with you, then I'm frightened. When I'm not frightened any more I shan't come any more.' *I*: 'So you're fond of me and you feel anxious when you're in your bed in the morning? and that's why you come in to me?' *Hans*: 'Yes, Why did you tell me I'm fond of *Mummy* and that's why I'm frightened, when I'm fond of *you?*'"

Here the little boy was displaying a really unusual degree of clarity. He was bringing to notice the fact that his love for his father was wrestling with his hostility towards him in his capacity of rival with his mother; and he was reproaching his father with not having yet drawn his attention to this interplay of forces, which was bound to end in anxiety.

"April 5th. . . . I asked Hans: 'Which horses are you actually most afraid of?' *Hans*: 'All of them.' *I*: 'That's not true.' *Hans*: 'I'm most afraid of horses with a thing on their mouths.' *I*: 'What do you mean? The piece of iron they have in their mouths?' *Hans*: 'No. They have something black on their mouths.' (He covered his mouth with his hand.) *I*: 'What? A moustache, perhaps?' *Hans* (laughing): 'Oh no!' *I*: 'Have they all got it?' *Hans*: 'No, only a few of them.' *I*: 'What is it that they've got on their mouths?' *Hans*: 'A black thing.' (I think in reality it must be the thick piece of harness that dray-horses wear over their noses.) 'And I'm most afraid of furniture-vans, too.' *I*: 'Why?' *Hans*: 'I think when furniture-horses are dragging a heavy van they'll fall down.' *I*: 'So you're not afraid with a small cart?' *Hans*: 'No. I'm not afraid with a small cart or with a post-office van. I'm most afraid too when a bus comes along.' *I*: 'Why? Because it's so big?' *Hans*: 'No. Because once a horse in a bus fell down.' *I*: 'When?' *Hans*: 'Once when I went out with Mummy in spite of my "nonsense," when I bought the waistcoat.' (This was subsequently confirmed by his mother.) *I*: 'What did you think when the horse fell down?' *Hans*: 'Now it'll always be like this. All horses in busses'll fall down.' *I*: 'In all buses?' *Hans:* 'Yes. And in furniture-vans too.'

"April 11th. This morning Hans came into our room again and was sent away, as he always has been for the last few days. Later on, he began: 'Daddy, I thought something: *I was in the bath, and then the plumber came and unscrewed it. Then he took a big borer and stuck it into my stomach.*'" Hans's father translated this phantasy as follows: "'I was in bed with Mamma. Then Papa came and drove me away. With his big penis he pushed me out of my place by Mamma.'"

"April 22nd. . . . It has been noticeable for some time that Hans's imagination was being coloured by images derived from traffic, and was advancing systematically from horses, which draw vehicles, to railways. In the same way a railway-phobia eventually becomes associated with every street-phobia. . . .

"April 24th. . . . In the afternoon we went out in front of the house. There was a visible improvement in his state. He ran after carts, and the only thing that betrayed a remaining trace of his anxiety was the fact that he did not venture away from the neighbourhood of the street-door and could not be induced to go for any considerable walk.

(The Bettmann Archive)

85

"April 25th. . . . *I*: 'Are you fond of Daddy?' *Hans*: 'Oh yes.' *I*: 'Or perhaps not.' Hans was playing with a little toy horse. At that moment the horse fell down, and Hans shouted out: 'The horse has fallen down! Look what a row it's making!' *I*: 'You're a little vexed with Daddy because Mummy's fond of him.' *Hans*: 'No.' *I*: 'Then why do you always cry whenever Mummy gives me a kiss? It's because you're jealous.' *Hans*: 'Jealous, yes.'

"April 26th. . . . The anxiety has almost completely disappeared, except that he likes to remain in the neighborhood of the house, so as to have a line of retreat in case he is frightened. . . ."

April 30th. . . . Things were moving towards a satisfactory conclusion. The little Oedipus had found a happier solution than that prescribed by destiny. Instead of putting his father out of the way, he had granted him the same happiness that he desired himself: he made him a grandfather and let him too marry his own mother. . . . In the course of the next few days Hans's mother wrote to me several times to express her joy at the little boy's recovery. [Freud, 1959a, pp. 149–155, 163, 165–166, 171–173, 184–187, 191–192, 208, 226, 230–231, 238–239]

WOLPE: CRITIQUE OF FREUD'S "ANALYSIS OF A PHOBIA"

It is our contention that Freud's view of this case is not supported by the data, either in its particulars or as a whole. The major points that he regards as demonstrated are these: (1) Hans had a sexual desire for his mother; (2) He hated and feared his father and wished to kill him; (3) Hans's sexual excitement and desire for his mother were transformed into anxiety; (4) His fear of horses was symbolic of his fear of his father; (5) The purpose of the illness was to keep near his mother; and finally, (6) His phobia disappeared because he resolved his Oedipus complex. Let us examine each of these points.

[1] That Hans derived satisfaction from his mother and enjoyed her presence we will not even attempt to dispute. But nowhere is there any evidence of his wish to copulate with her. . . .

[2] Never having expressed either fear or hatred of his father, Hans was told by Freud that he possessed these emotions. On subsequent occasions Hans denied the existence of these feelings when questioned by his father. Eventually, he said "Yes" to a statement of this kind by his father. This simple affirmative obtained after considerable pressure on the part of the father and Freud is accepted as the true state of affairs and all Hans's denials are ignored. . . .

[3] Freud's third claim is that Hans's sexual excitement and desire for his mother were transformed into anxiety. This claim is based

on the assertion [made elsewhere in Freud's writings] that "theoretical considerations require that what is today the object of a phobia must at one time in the past have been the source of a high degree of pleasure." Certainly such a transformation is not displayed by the facts presented. . . .

[4] The assertion that Hans's horse phobia symbolized a fear of his father has already been criticized. The assumed relationship between the father and the horse is unsupported and appears to have arisen as a result of the father's strange failure to believe that by the "black around their mouths" Hans meant the horses' muzzles.

[5] The fifth claim is that the purpose of Hans's phobia was to keep him near his mother. Aside from the questionable view that neurotic disturbances occur for a purpose, this interpretation fails to account for the fact that Hans experienced anxiety even when he was out walking *with his mother*.

[6] Finally, we are told that the phobia disappeared as a result of Hans's resolution of his Oedipal conflicts. As we have attempted to show, there is no adequate evidence that Hans had an Oedipus complex. . . .

There is also no satisfactory evidence that the "insights" that were incessantly brought to the boy's attention had any therapeutic value. . . . Hans's latter improvement appears to have been smooth and gradual and unaffected by the interpretations. In general, Freud infers relationships in a scientifically inadmissible manner: if the enlightenments or interpretations given to Hans are followed by behavioral improvements, then they are automatically accepted as valid. If they are not followed by improvement we are told the patient has not accepted them, and not that they are invalid. . . .

Wolpe's alternative etiology

In case it should be argued that, unsatisfactory as it is, Freud's explanation is the only available one, we shall show how Hans's phobia can be understood in terms of learning theory, in the theoretical framework provided by Wolpe (1958). . . .

In brief, phobias are regarded as conditioned anxiety (fear) reactions. Any "neutral" stimulus, simple or complex, that happens to make an impact on an individual at about the time that a fear reaction is evoked acquires the ability to evoke fear subsequently. If the fear at the original conditioning situation is of high intensity or if the conditioning is many times repeated the conditioned fear will show the persistence that is characteristic of *neurotic* fear; and there will be generalization of fear reactions to stimuli resembling the conditioned stimulus. Hans, we are told, was a sensitive child who "was never unmoved if someone wept in his presence" and long be-fore the phobia developed became "uneasy on seeing the horses in the merry-go-round being beaten." It is our contention that the incident to which Freud refers as merely the exciting cause of Hans's phobia was in fact the cause of the entire disorder. . . . The evi-dence obtained in studies on experimental neuroses in animals (e.g., Wolpe, 1958) and the studies by Watson and Rayner (1920), Jones (1924), and Woodward (1959) on phobias in children indicate that it is quite possible for one experience to induce a phobia. . . .

Just as the little boy Albert [in Watson and Rayner's classic demon-stration] reacted with anxiety not only to the original conditioned stimulus, the white rat, but to other similar stimuli such as furry ob-jects, cotton wool, and so on; Hans reacted anxiously to horses, horse-drawn buses, vans and features of horses, such as their blinkers and muzzles. In fact he showed fear of a wide range of generalized stimuli. . . .

Hans's recovery from the phobia may be explained on conditioning principles in a number of possible ways, but the actual mechanism which operated cannot be identified, since the child's father was not concerned with the kind of information that would be of interest to us. It is well known that especially in children many phobias decline and disappear over a few weeks or months. . . . But since Hans does not seem to have been greatly upset by the interpreta-tions, it is perhaps more likely that the therapy was actively help-ful, for phobic stimuli were again and again presented to the child in a variety of emotional contexts that may have inhibited the anxiety and in consequence diminished its habit strength. . . .

There is no evidence that in general, psychoanalytic conclusions are based on any better logic than that used by Freud in respect of Little Hans. Certainly no analyst has ever pointed to the failings of this account or disowned its reasoning, and it has continued to be regarded as one of the foundation stones on which psychoanalytic theory was built. [Wolpe & Rachman, 1960, pp. 143–146]

Dr. Freud, Dr. Wolpe, and Little Hans

Let us now try to reconcile Freud and Wolpe's very different analyses of the case of Little Hans. In essence, Freud believed that the child's phobias developed shortly after he un-consciously began to fear castration at the hands of his father. The castration would be inflicted in punishment of his masturbatory behavior and for his desire (again, uncon-scious) to take his father's place in his mother's bed. Contrasting with these "typical oedipal fears" were Hans's love for and dependence upon his father—conflicting feelings which generated guilt that was also a part of the child's phobia.

To accept this psychodynamic equation, grossly oversimplified and condensed here, one must accept the psychoanalytic theory's assumptions about the importance and the universality of the oedipal situation, the validity of the dynamic view of personality, and the general applicability of symbols (e.g., a biting horse equals a castrating father.) Many people do accept them, many others do not. Hans Eysenck, a prominent behavioral psychologist, is one of the dissenters. He says:

Psychoanalysis presents a rather curious dilemma to those who would evaluate it. In psychiatry it has become the leading school to such an extent that in some countries, particularly the United States, it is almost impossible to obtain a leading post, either in academic life or private practice, without having undergone a training in analysis. . . . However, there is still a hard core of unbelievers; a group of people to whom the whole story of psychoanalysis is little but a repetition of the famous fairy-tale about the Emperor's new clothes. And it is curious to note that these dissenters tend to be found mostly among those who have been trained in scientific method and who have adopted psychology as their profession. . . . We thus have the curious position that psychoanalysis is widely accepted among lay people and others untrained in psychology, ignorant of experimental methods and incapable of evaluating empirical evidence. . . . The most obvious hypothesis suggested by this state of affairs would seem to be that psychoanalysis is a myth; a set of semireligious beliefs disseminated by a group who should be regarded as prophets rather than scientists. [1963, pp. 66–67]

Though opinions on both sides are strong, the fact is that the objective data necessary to validate either Freud or Wolpe's position are not available. We, the authors, support the behavioral viewpoint, because we believe that empirical data rather than clinical observation must be the "ultimate weapon" against psychopathology. But we must point out that the behavioral explanation of Little Hans's horse phobia is not as sound as Wolpe claims.

It is true that experiments have demonstrated the permanency of "one-trial learning" and have shown that phobias can develop by behavioral mechanisms. No one, however, now knows enough of the details of Hans's case to be certain that a frightening experience with a horse actually did precipitate his phobia (as Wolpe presumes it did.)

In fact, it appears likely that Hans was never bitten by a horse—though while out walking with his mother, he did see a large bus horse fall and kick with its feet. Hans was understandably shaken, in part because he thought the horse had been killed. Can we assume that this event precipitated Hans's phobia about horses? From either the psychodynamic or the Wolpean behavioral position, we would be hard put to explain how that single experience caused the many additional maladaptive behaviors Hans developed.

Commenting on the dynamic view of this matter, Bandura says: "The Oedipal interpretation fails not only to account for the discriminative pattern of Hans's phobic behavior but also to explain satisfactorily why he was afraid of railways and locomotives as well, a phobia which probably generalized from the transport vehicle stimulus complex. The psychoanalytic interpretation would demand that the locomotive and the railway tracks were likewise symbolic representations of the castrating father and the impregnated mother" (1969, p. 13).

On the other hand, acceptance of Wolpe's explanation of the origin of Hans's phobia requires equal willingness to accept a position on faith. His account is based on assumptions about the invariable operation of a restricted set of learning mechanisms that have not yet been independently validated.

Our own view of the etiology of Little Hans's psychopathology is that we will never know it. We cannot undertake the behavioral analysis required for that purpose at long range across the years and through the medium of Freud's psychoanalytic interpretation. We can only deal with what is known about the child's psychopathology, leaving aside any speculations about etiology. The facts which are available convince us that a social-learning theory—

which takes into account the full range of learning mechanisms of which man is capable —might have been the best approach to the case of Little Hans.

What is personality?

Psychologists fail to agree on the meaning of the word *personality*. Derived from the Latin word *persona*—the theatrical mask Roman actors wore—it has been used for many different purposes. Some definitions emphasize a person's social and interpersonal skills; some stress status and prestige; some regard success in adjusting to the environment as the central element. Most definitions identify fairly enduring personal *traits* which set the individual off from others, predict his or her future behavior from past behavior, and give coherence to behavior that would otherwise be seen as random.

Recently, however, a number of theorists have questioned the so-called "trait" approach to personality. Rather than making assumptions about behavioral "predispositions" or traits, they concentrate on the circumstances under which behavior takes place. The two theories of personality discussed here represent opposing ends of this continuum. We will use the Freudian dynamic model to typify "trait theory" and Mischel and Bandura's behavioral model to stand for all "environmental" points of view.

Both adaptive and maladaptive behavior are determined by an interplay of social, biological, and psychological factors. That is, the kind of person you become—as well as the kind of maladaptive behavior you show—depends upon the social (including cultural) influences to which you are exposed, the biological equipment you have, and the thinking, feeling, sensing, and perceiving that you learn to do. Chapters 2 and 3 discussed the social and biological influences on normal and abnormal behavior. This chapter will consider the third, or psychological, factor—"personality," for want of a better word.

In these opening chapters we are trying to give some space to the determinants of normal behavior, so that we do not confuse you about the roots of normality by overemphasizing their role in pathology. But our discussion of the normal personality must be brief. Whole courses are devoted to theories of personality, whereas we will deal with it as a concept and a model rather than as a subject to explore in depth. The two contrasting approaches to personality that we have chosen to present— the dynamic or psychoanalytic model, and the behavioral or social-learning model—are crucial ones in psychology today. They will come up again and again in following chapters.

One of the most important contrasts between the two approaches is that Freud emphasizes psychopathology; the behaviorists normality. Freud's dynamic theory of personality arose from his observations of neurotic patients in his consulting room. It was first a theory of neurosis and only later a theory of the normal personality. Its history, the observations on which it was based, and its major utility all relate directly to the disordered behavior that Freud undertook to explain.

Social-learning theory, on the other hand, developed largely from studies of the normal processes of learning in animals and humans. It grew out of work by Pavlov, Skinner, Bandura, Mischel, and other learning researchers, and has only recently been extended to human psychopathology.

This difference in their origins colors the fundamental idea of humanity that each theory embodies. To the psychoanalyst, a person is born and bred with the certainty that crucial events occurring early in life will result in psychological disability. The disability may be serious or minor, curable or incurable. But to the behaviorist, a person may learn maladaptive behavior or may not. Even if he does, many behaviorists think that techniques exist (or will be discovered) to work a cure. Whether the truth is represented by the optimism of the behaviorists or the pessimism of the psychoanalysts is something we do not yet know.

Freud's psychoanalytic theory of personality

Two basic concepts: Psychic determinism and the unconscious

Of the many assumptions that psychoanalytic theory makes about human behavior, two are fundamental. The first, the *principle of psychic determinism,* assumes that in the human mind as in nature, nothing happens by chance. Every psychic event is determined by one or more events that came before it. Behavior, whether cognitive, psychomotor, or psychophysiological, can be explained.

The second fundamental psychoanalytic concept, the *principle of the unconscious,* states that mental processes exist which the individual himself is not aware of. And these unconscious mental functions have the power to influence feelings, thoughts, and actions even though they are inaccessible to conscious experience.

In Freud's *topography of the personality* there are three levels: conscious, preconscious, and unconscious. On the *conscious* level, meaning within the person's awareness, are his thoughts about current experiences as well as the thoughts, memories, and fantasies which can be brought into consciousness from the *preconscious* level by a shift of attention or environment. *Unconscious* materials are the thoughts and memories which the person cannot bring to consciousness even if he tries hard. These unconscious elements appear only during periods of free association, in dreams, after psychoanalysis, or through slips of the tongue.

Little Hans, standing before the horse which pulled his father's carriage, might have been *conscious* of the horse's size and his own fear of horses. From his *preconscious* he could have brought to awareness thoughts varying from what he had had for breakfast to how pretty his mother was. What would have remained *unconscious,* according to Freud, was his fear of mutilation at the hands of his father, his sexual attraction to his mother, and his

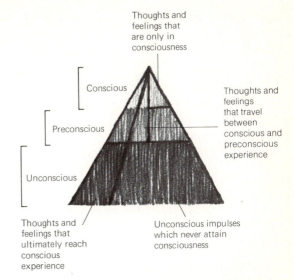

Figure 4-1. A diagram representing Freud's topography of the personality. According to Freud, conscious thoughts and feelings are only the "tip of the iceberg"; most thoughts and feelings are below the "surface" of consciousness. Some of them never become conscious and so are forever inaccessible. The process of repression may cause others to become unconscious and remain that way. Dreams, free associations, and psychoanalysis may permit some unconscious materials to enter consciousness.

feelings of guilt at having both kinds of unacceptable wishes.

Other theorists before Freud had proposed the principles of psychic determinism and of the unconscious. But Freud was the first to combine them and integrate them into a general theory of personality. Many authorities believe that his enlargement on these two principles, together with his work on dreams, were his most important and most original contributions to personality theory.

Freud's drive theory: After sex and aggression, is anything left?

If psychic determinism, the theory of the unconscious, and the analysis of dreams are Freud's most-respected contributions, his *drive theory* is certainly his most controversial. He defined drives as genetically determined behavioral predispositions which impel people to action in their search for *drive reduction, drive gratification,* or both. While these drives can be altered by influences from the environment, they exist regardless of environmental conditions. According to Freud, a person's drives can emerge with great intensity when they are not modulated by society.

Freud first evolved a drive theory in 1890. At that time he envisioned two predominant human drives which impel and determine the bulk of man's behavior: the sexual drive and the drive for self-preservation. But soon he decided that the drive for self-preservation was not so important after all. For the next 25 years he maintained that the sex drive was *the* major motive source of human behavior. In 1920, after he had seen the ravages of World War I, he added the drive for aggression. Thus Freud's amended drive theory, still endorsed today by many psychoanalysts, claims that behavior is determined by two primary drives: sex and aggression. It says that these two drives exert an influence on behavior in the form of *psychic energy.* Psychic energy associated with sexual drive is called *libido;* psychic energy associated with aggressive impulses is *aggressive energy* or *mortido.* But exactly how do these sources of energy influence behavior? Freud's explanation is one of the weakest aspects of his theory of personality. And research designed to confirm his explanation has not been particularly successful.

Stages of psychosexual development. In his attempt to trace the mechanisms by which drive energy influences behavior, Freud put forth his *theory of psychosexual development* in 1905. It was one of several statements which embroiled him in a great outpouring of Victorian controversy. It describes the development of the sexual drive from infancy to adulthood, and the Victorians objected to it because they believed that prepubertal children do not have sexual feelings. When Freud said that children do have such impulses and

attempt to gratify them in more or less open ways, he was condemned as a moral degenerate, sexual pervert, or worse. Even now many people do not believe that little children can have sexual feelings, although psychoanalysts continue to make clear that pregenital sexuality is different in important ways from postgenital, mature sexuality.

The first stage of psychosexual development, according to Freud, is the *oral stage.* It lasts from birth to about 18 months of age. The oral stage is devoted mainly to maximizing food intake. As a result, the child's mouth, lips, and tongue become the chief organs by which he or she makes contact with the environment. According to psychoanalytic theory, these organs in themselves provide pleasure—their stimulation yields pregenital sexual enjoyment. During the earliest substage of the oral period, the baby's gratification comes largely from eating; this is the *oral-receptive substage.* During a later substage he also gets pleasure from biting and aggressive behavior toward food; this is the *oral-aggressive substage.* During the oral stage the child begins to learn that he is not the center of the universe—that he cannot be fed, held, or comforted whenever he wishes, and that there are many parts of the world he cannot control. From these experiences he learns that his body has limits in terms of its potential effect on the environment.

The second stage of psychosexual development postulated by Freud is the *anal stage.* It lasts from about 1½ to 2½ years of age. The prime focus of this period is upon the elimination of waste products from the body. During the *anal-retentive substage,* the child experiences erotic pleasure from retaining feces. In the subsequent *anal-expulsive substage,* he or she obtains pleasure by learning to expel feces. Thus during the anal stage the child learns to control his own bodily processes. And in so doing he learns how to control his parents' behavior, at least in part, by the ways in which he uses his body (say, by withholding feces from a mother who expects daily bowel movements.)

From about ages 3 to 6, Freudian theory says that the genital area is the child's major source of pleasure. This is the *phallic stage* of psychoanalytic development. During it the child experiences the all-important oedipal situation (discussed in a following section). The phallic stage is characterized by concerns about power, strength, and size—all as a direct function of the oedipal situation. The child longs to possess things that symbolize power and strength, and wants to be stronger, bigger, and more powerful than the parent of the same sex.

After six or seven years of relative quiescence in pregenital sexuality—a period some psychoanalysts have called the *latency stage*—the child enters puberty and the *genital stage* of development. At this time the chief objects of pleasure become the mature genital organs.

By his theory of psychosexual development—so new and unconventional that it shocked the Victorians—Freud tied the young child's major cognitive, emotional, and physiological learning to the organs of the body on which these lessons were focused. Thus the oral, anal, and phallic stages represent successive lessons learned, successive patterns of response acquired. In recognition of this educational theme in Freud's theory of psychosexual development, Erik Erikson, a neo-Freudian theorist, outlined the "life tasks" appropriate to each stage of development: *basic trust and mistrust* are learned during the oral stage; during the anal stage a child acquires feelings of both *autonomy* (independence) and *shame and self-doubt;* and during the phallic stage he or she learns to value *initiative and success* as well as to feel *guilt over achievement* (1950).

Though concern about sexuality in young children has diminished since the Victorians first condemned Freud, controversy over his theory of the stages of psychosexual development has continued. Its critics find fault with (1) the behavioral specificity of the developmental model, with its stages and substages in which the child does this and that; (2) the notion that psychological constructs like "drive" somehow convert into units of energy like "libido" to influence behavior; and (3) the relative inaccessibility of the system to experimental validation. Consequently this theory which is at the heart of the psychoanalytic model remains an area of dispute between those who do and those who do not find psychoanalysis scientifically valid or practically useful.

Two other key concepts in the theory of psychosexual stages are fixation and regression. *Fixation* refers to psychopathologic conditions arising from an early trauma that was intense enough to cause the individual to remain *fixated* at an immature level of development. Psychosis is an example of fixation. *Regression* refers to a retreat to an earlier, less mature, more comfortable stage of development in the face of stress that rekindles memories of early trauma. Crying, loss of control of one sort or another, or dissociative (disorganized) behavior are regressions.

Freud's structural theory of personality: id, ego, superego

In still another effort to structure his complex observations of human psychological functioning, Freud divided the *psychic apparatus* into three parts: the id, the ego, and the superego (1932). At birth, he said, the infant enters its new environment as a bundle of *id functions.* These are the sexual and aggressive drives that find expression in successive organ groups (oral, anal, and phallic) as the stages of psychosexual development unfold. In other words, at birth and shortly after it the infant behaves almost entirely in response to these drives; they provide the impetus for the baby's interaction with the world.

But as that interaction continues—as the child begins to accumulate a backlog of experience with the external world—*ego functions* develop. These permit him or her to gain some active mastery over the environment. By age 3 or so, Freud believed, the ego has assumed responsibility for the many different kinds of behavior that the child has become capable of: high-level motor behavior and motor skills; sensory and perceptual processes; remembering, comparing, and thinking; affect and feeling; and reality testing.

Viewed in this way, the ego can be seen

"Double Scotches for me and my superego, and a glass of water for my id, which is driving." But according to Freudian theory, the superego is the basis of conscience whereas the id continually seeks pleasure. *(Drawing by Handelsman; © 1972 The New Yorker Magazine, Inc.)*

as a *mediator* between conflicting demands from the id (the reservoir of instinctual desires and drives) and the outside world. Later on, the ego must mediate among the id, the outside world, and a third component of the psychic apparatus, the *superego*. This is a structure that gradually emerges as children learn the rules, codes of behavior, and moral injunctions that govern society. They learn such rules largely from their parents. In fact, Freud believed, the superego ultimately comes to represent an internalized set of "parents." It takes on the responsibility of enforcing the morals and ethics of society that the real parents originally taught. Later, as the individual matures, the superego internalizes rules from outside the family as well; the parents are no longer the sole source of input.

Another word for the superego is *conscience*. Sometimes the ego must try to prevent the superego from being too harsh or repressive in its efforts to keep the individual morally in line.

Psychopathology, according to Freud, stems from crucial traumatic events occurring during the early years of life. These events affect both the child's passage through the stages of psychosexual development *and* the relative balance of id, ego, and superego. When either id or superego is too powerful, the ego cannot mediate among them and the environment—and mental disorder may result. In such a case, immediate *fixation* at, or later *regression* to, an early stage of psychosexual development may take place. It is when the ego can arbitrate successfully among the id, the superego, and the environment that the personality functioning will be essentially normal, even though imbalances may occur.

The Oedipus complex

Central to the psychoanalytic portrait of both the normal person and the disordered one is the *Oepidus complex*. It is named for the legendary Greek King Oedipus, who unwittingly killed his father and married his mother. Freud had become increasingly impressed by the number of his early patients who entertained unconscious fantasies of incest with their parent of the opposite sex. And these fantasies were combined with jealous, sometimes murderous, rage against the parent of the same sex. As early as 1900 he developed the opinion that such wishes are common among normal persons as well as neurotic ones.

Freud pointed out that the initial object of strong dependency feelings for all children is the mother. As a result, boys and girls strive for their mother's exclusive love and admiration. In doing so they also try (largely in fantasy) to do away with rivals for their mother's love—including, of course, their father and their siblings. Accompanying the fantasies is fear of retribution at the hands of those the child wishes to displace.

At this stage in the development of the oedipal situation, Freud said, boys and girls deviate in their choice of oedipal object. Boys focus their concerns about retribution on their father and on that body possession which is most valuable to boys—the penis.

The Oedipus conflict is not always dealt with in fantasy! *(Drawing by Lorenz; © 1972 The New Yorker Magazine, Inc.)*

Specifically, boys fear that their penis will be removed—that they will be castrated—because they want to displace their father in their mother's heart (and beds). Girls, on the other hand, realize that they cannot take their father's place with their mother because they do not have a penis. Becoming enraged with the mother for having permitted them to be born without one, they turn to the father as their principal love object. Experiencing these fears consciously, however, would overwhelm the child's unformed, immature ego. According to psychoanalytic theory, children therefore convert their unconscious fears of retribution into more acceptable equivalents that permit its conscious experience in disguised form. Hans, for example, became phobic toward horses, although Freud believed that the child's basic phobia was fear that he would lose his own penis.

Ultimately most boys and girls "work through" these oedipal feelings, renouncing and repressing oedipal wishes in the process. But, Freud said, residues of the experience remain in everyone and influence everyone's adult behavior toward men and women.

The ego's defense mechanisms

Traumas (chief among them the oedipal situation) occur in every young life. Accordingly, the normal ego develops a series of defensive maneuvers designed to protect itself from being overwhelmed by id or superego demands or by environmental stress. These defense mechanisms operate unconsciously and hence beyond the person's volitional control. They are most apparent in the psychoneurotic patient, who may be actually disabled by them. Some defensive maneuvers, however, are also characteristic of normal children and adults. All of us at times use some defensive techniques to avoid feeling anxious, depressed, guilty, or lonely. In fact, you will probably be able to recognize your favorite mechanism among those in the following list:

Repression: The most basic defense mechanism. Through repression, unwanted thoughts, feelings, or impulses are barred from consciousness. Repressed materials may "slip out" in dreams or slips of the tongue in everyday conversation, as well as during psychoanalytic therapy.

Suppression: The second most basic defense mechanism. Supression is the voluntary decision to forget something, to "put it out

"Probably overcompensation. After all, it *is* a foreign car." (*Drawing by J. Mirachi; © 1970 The New Yorker Magazine, Inc.*)

of mind" or out of consciousness. When we decide not to think of a particular subject, we are suppressing it. Suppression differs from repression in that suppressed materials can be recalled to consciousness more easily. Repressed memories and desires can rarely if ever be brought to consciousness voluntarily. By contrast, suppressed memories can usually be recalled if the person expends enough energy and concentration on them.

The next five defense mechanisms are the so-called "primitive" defenses most characteristic of infants, children, and psychotic patients (though normal people also use them at times).

Identification: The person becomes like something or someone else in one or several aspects of thought or behavior. "Identification with the aggressor" may be a defensive strategy; some Terezin residents, for example, became as cruel to the other prisoners as the Nazi guards were (Chapter 10).

Introjection: A kind of identification in which another person, often a parent, is symbolically taken into the ego. In this way the individual can always have the parent available. Introjection is important in the creation of the superego, when the child assimilates the parents' instructions, rewards, and punishments.

Projection: The person attributes an unwanted emotion to someone else in the effort to deny its existence in himself. Projection is common among paranoid schizophrenic patients, whose frequent attribution of homosexual intent in others is seen by psychoanalysts as a projection of their own homosexual impulses. In less intense form, the mechanism of projection is fairly common among normal people.

Displacement: The individual experiences a feeling about a person to whom it does not really apply. A father who takes out on his wife and children the anger he feels toward his boss is displacing his anger.

Denial: An unpleasant event or feeling is denied; the person simply pretends that it does not exist.

The following defense mechanisms are more mature techniques commonly employed by normal people.

Reaction Formation: Someone who is troubled by contrasting feelings (say, love and hate) excludes one of the feelings from consciousness by overemphasizing the other. Hate seems to be replaced by love, cruelty by gentleness, stubbornness by compliance. Reaction formation occurs because one of the pair of contrasting feelings is unacceptable to the ego or superego. For example, when love—and the feelings of dependency and sexuality which go with it—is more than a person can bear, hate for the loved one may be the only acceptable alternative.

Undoing: A symbolic ritual designed to ward off an unacceptable or unwanted event. For example: crossing one's fingers while telling a lie, avoiding cracks in the sidewalk, or "knocking on wood" when expressing confidence about something.

Isolation: The exclusion from consciousness of the feeling that should accompany a painful memory, thought, or experience. The person remembers the experience but does not reexperience the feeling that originally accompanied it.

Sublimation: Transformation of the psychic energy associated with unwanted sexual or aggressive drives into socially acceptable pursuits. Some psychoanalysts believe that artists and politicians are especially accomplished sublimators.

Regression: The person returns to an earlier, less mature stage of psychosexual development when confronted with a stressful or frustrating situation. Crying from frustration is a common regressive behavior. So is the changed behavior of the 4-year-old child who is suddenly confronted with a new brother or sister. Even though the child is toilet-trained and articulate, he or she may respond to the threat of the new baby by regressing to nighttime bed-wetting, daytime soiling, and baby talk—all in an effort to regain the old unchallenged position with mother.

Rationalization: After the fact, a person provides rational and logical reasons for behavior whose determinants were probably unconscious and hence irrational. Psychoanalysts would say that when a patient explains his problems with women by pointing out that he has yet to meet one who is his intellectual equal, he is probably rationalizing more primitive fears of sexuality.

Substitution: Replacement of a highly valued but psychologically unacceptable object with a less valued one which is acceptable. For example, a man might marry a woman who resembles his mother.

Dissociation: Separation from consciousness of a whole segment of behavior that is not consistent with the individual's usual personality or behavior patterns. Chapters 9 and 13 describe clinical syndromes involving massive dissociative behavior.

"Dad, I understand that Disney World has come up with some amazing technological advances and extremely interesting solutions to urban-planning problems." *(Drawing by Stevenson: © 1973 The New Yorker Magazine, Inc.)*

Mischel's social-behavior theory of personality

The contrasting model of personality that we have chosen to present—social-behavior theory—includes a variety of mechanisms of learning. These mechanisms are thought by Walter Mischel, Albert Bandura, Frederick Kanfer, and other *social-learning* theorists to be the means by which human beings acquire complex behavioral patterns. Mischel's social-behavior theory differs slightly in scope and emphasis from Bandura's social-learning theory, and both Mischel's and Bandura's theories are a little different from Kanfer's. But all these broadly based behavioral theories of personality are similar in essential ways.

In particular, all assume that (1) most human behavior is learned, (2) the laws which govern this learning are knowable and measurable, and (3) both normal and abnormal behavior is acquired by the same fundamental learning mechanisms.

Mischel draws a fundamental distinction between his social-behavior theory and trait theories, which assume the existence of identifiable traits of character that determine a person's behavior (1968, 1971, 1973). The psychoanalytic approach is a trait theory of personality. Mischel's theory bases understanding and prediction of behavior on the social and behavioral aspects of the setting in which the behavior occurs. Trait theories, on the other hand, concentrate on the person's history, genetic heritage, and underlying physiological propensities, or "psychodynamics." Mischel says: "While trait . . . theories search for consistencies in people's behavior across situations, social behavior theory seeks order and regularity in the form of general rules that relate environmental changes to behavior changes" (1968, p. 150).

The case of Little Hans will clarify this distinction between Freud's trait approach and Mischel, Kanfer, and Bandura's social-behavior models. The most troublesome events in Hans's life were his phobias. Freud emphasized the crucial importance of the oedipal situation to full understanding of Hans's phobic behavior. In doing so he removed the child's behavior from its "real-life" context and explained it by reference to a *consistent behavior pattern shared by every child that age:* the Oedipus complex. But Mischel and Bandura, who both have written analyses of Hans's phobias, *tie his behavior directly to environmental incidents:* for example, Hans saw a horse pulling a bus fall down, he observed horses turning a merry-go-round being beaten, and he felt displaced in his mother's affection by a new baby sister. As you would expect, social-learning theorists criticize Freud's view of Hans's phobias precisely because Freud "searches for consistencies in people's behavior across situations"—because he assumes that the Oedipus complex is universal. And of course, psychoanalysts criticize the social-learning approach to Hans because it deals only with "environmental changes"—horses falling down or being beaten, a sibling being born—and not intrapsychic ones.

Mischel believes that there are three basic ways in which human behavior is acquired, shaped, maintained, and if necessary, unlearned. These mechanisms of learning are the "nitty-gritty" of social-behavior theory, in that each plays at least some role in determining a person's *behavioral repertoire:*

Observational learning. This is learning by watching others.
Classical conditioning. The traditional Pavlovian learning model, in which a stimulus previously unassociated with a response eventually elicits that response.
Operant conditioning. Originally Skinner's model, this is the learning mechanism in which the reinforcing stimulus that follows the response also shapes it.

According to Mischel, the first two mechanisms—observational learning and classical conditioning—are the methods by which new behaviors are learned. The third, operant conditioning, modifies preexisting behaviors but does not teach new ones.

Observational learning

Until the early 1960s, most learning theorists believed that the classical and operant models of learning accounted for virtually all behavior. But Albert Bandura and his colleagues at Stanford then demonstrated that simply by watching other people modeling certain kinds of behavior, subjects could acquire entirely new response patterns (Bandura et al., 1961, Bandura et al., 1963, Bandura & Walters, 1963).

In one of these researchers' early studies a group of schoolchildren watched a person behaving aggressively toward a large inflated plastic doll (1961). Another group watched the same person (called the *model*) being gentle and calm with the doll. Afterwards, both groups were made to become mildly frustrated. It turned out that the children who had watched the aggressive model were themselves more aggressive than the children who had seen the passive model.

Later research by Bandura's team revealed that this "modeling" effect can occur when models are seen in movies and cartoons as well as in real life (1963). Bandura and Walters have identified some variables which influence the degree to which an observer will copy a model's behavior (1963). These include the observer's sex and age in relation to the model, the social reinforcements received just before

An example of the "modeling" effect. Top: an adult model attacks an inflated plastic doll. Middle and bottom: a boy and a girl, after watching the adult's aggressive behavior, also attack the doll. *(Bandura, Ross, & Ross, 1963)*

watching the model (that is, the observer may recently have been reinforced or punished for aggressive or submissive behavior), and the observer's history of reinforcement or punishment for learning through models.

In a series of studies by Bandura and Mischel, children were asked to select either a small reward that could be obtained immediately or a larger one that became available after a delay of one to four weeks (1965). Some of the children then watched live adult models choosing delayed rewards. As the experimenters expected, these children became more willing to select delayed rewards themselves than they had been before they watched the models. Additional experiments have demonstrated that many of the most complex actions human beings perform—cognitive, verbal, emotional, and psychomotor behaviors—can be learned, maintained, altered, and otherwise influenced by modeling (Bandura et al., 1966; Mischel & Liebert, 1966; Staub, 1965).

Observational learning clearly played an important role in the lives of Daniel Paul Schreber, Malcom X, Piri Thomas, Anne Frank, and Little Hans. Before the outbreak of his psychosis Schreber had an aloof, authoritarian, questioning approach to life which was certainly modeled after his distinguished father, whom he respected and at times feared. Malcom Little's antisocial behavior, modeled after the behavior of successful hustlers in Roxbury and Harlem, was adaptive when he had to make a life for himself in these places. And we assume that Piri Thomas's bluff and bravado, as well as Anne Frank's paradoxical mixture of docility and pluck, were learned from those around them. Even Hans, young as he was, had learned to model the behavior of others, especially his father. In fact, Freud was impressed with Hans's active efforts to be like his father, even as the child experienced anger toward him.

Observational learning and psychopathology. Research in the area of observational learning, or modeling, is beginning to move more and more in applied directions. Behavioral

scientists are trying to use the insights gained from basic research to help disturbed people. (Chapter 10 will discuss some of this work in connection with the neurotic disorders.)

In one of the excerpts which opens this chapter, the Pavlovian behaviorist Joseph Wolpe claims that Little Hans acquired his repertoire of phobic behavior through classical conditioning mechanisms. He believes that the child associated the sight of horses with frightening events which occurred at the same time. We believe that observational learning may also have played a role in this process of "symptom formation." Freud said that Hans's mother was a shy and diffident person who was herself afraid of many quite ordinary things outside the safety of her home in Vienna. It seems a safe assumption that Hans must have learned how to be fearful, even if he did not acquire his specific fear of horses, from a mother whom he revered and wished to please.

Classical conditioning

Mischel sees classical conditioning and observational learning as belonging to a single category of mechanisms involved in the *acquisition of behavior*. In both cases the subject learns new responses, sometimes to old stimuli, sometimes to new ones.

Beginnings: Pavlov and his dogs. Ivan Pavlov was professor of physiology in the Military Medical Academy of St. Petersburg between 1895 and 1924, the years when he did his major work. At first he was interested only in research on digestive secretions, for which he won a Nobel prize in 1904. Later Pavlov became fascinated by the enormous influence that environmental and psychological phenomena have on gastric and salivary secretions. In research stemming from his new interest, Pavlov found that when a dog's mouth waters in response to food, the amount of saliva depends not only on how hungry it is and what kind of food is being offered, but also on the environmental stimuli associated with the presentation of the food.

Pavlov made a variety of experiments which

established the laws of classical conditioning. His most famous experiment—the one taught to almost every first-year student in psychology—showed that repeatedly pairing a neutral stimulus with a stimulus that elicited salivation ultimately enabled the neutral stimulus itself to elicit salivation. Pavlov rang a bell immediately before presenting a small portion of meat powder to the dog. The sound of the bell ultimately acquired the capacity by itself to make the dog's mouth water, something that had previously happened only with the meat powder.

The classical conditioning paradigm. To go beyond the specifics of Pavlov's dog experiment, let us look at the essential elements of the classical conditioning paradigm, or model, which it illustrates so simply and yet so elegantly:

1 An originally neutral stimulus, the *conditioned stimulus* (the bell), occurs just before—

2 A stimulus which naturally evokes an unlearned, innate reflex response—the *unconditioned stimulus* (meat powder).

3. The reflex response to the unconditioned stimulus is called the *unconditioned response* (salivation).

4 When the conditioned and unconditioned stimuli have been paired often enough, the conditioned stimulus by itself elicits the reflex response. That response is termed the *conditioned response.*

5 The total stimulus-response reflex is the *conditioned reflex.*

Pavlov's pioneering work explored many other conditioned reflexes in addition to the meat powder-bell-salivation reflex. Since then many researchers, using a wide variety of animal species, have extended the paradigm. Among the most important of the data they have gathered are the following rules governing the acquisition, maintenance, and extinction of the conditioned reflex. These findings have turned out to be as valid for classically conditioned human behavior as for animal behavior.

[1] *Acquisition:* Conditioned reflexes are acquired gradually. How gradually one is acquired and how well it is learned depend upon many factors: whether the conditioning

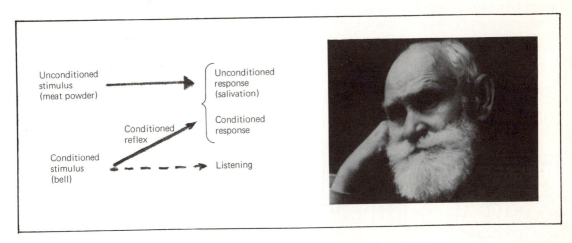

Figure 4-2. The classical conditioning paradigm. Pavlov (right) demonstrated in his experiment with dogs that if an *unconditioned stimulus* of meat powder is constantly preceded by a conditioned stimulus—say, a ringing bell—the dogs will develop a *conditioned reflex,* meaning that eventually the bell by itself will cause them to salivate. The salivation, originally an *unconditioned response,* becomes a *conditioned response* by this conditioning process.

trials are spaced out or massed, how intense the conditioned and unconditioned stimuli are, how close together the two stimuli are in time, and whether the subject's unconditioned response to the unconditioned stimulus is strong or weak (a dog will pay more attention to the pairing of a bell with meat powder when he is hungry than when he is not). Anne Frank's terror of the Gestapo, and Piri Thomas's responses of anger and fear to New York policemen, were conditioned responses that were gradually acquired over time.

[2] *Maintenance:* Though comparatively little data have been reported, the available facts suggest that conditioned reflexes are maintained at relatively high intensities for relatively long periods of time. Long after their liberation, survivors of concentration camps report reexperiencing the old feelings of fear and terror on hearing or seeing stimuli like those they learned to associate with their time of imprisonment. It is likely that Anne Frank's conditioned fear response to stimuli which she associated with the Gestapo or with her life in the "secret annexe" would never have totally disappeared if she had been permitted to live. (In fact, the fugitives in the hidden annex were discovered after two years; Anne died in a concentration camp.)

"Do you mind if I go to lunch early, Professor Pavlov? I'm hungry." *(Drawing by Burr Shafer; Copyright 1970 by Saturday Review/World, Inc.)*

[3] *Extinction:* This is the term for the process by which an acquired behavior—such as a conditioned reflex—is lost. In Pavlov's classic experiment, extinction occurred when the dog no longer salivated on hearing the bell but only on receiving the meat powder. The rate of extinction depends directly upon the timing of what are called *extinction trials.* An extinction trial involves presentation of the conditioned stimulus (the bell) in the *absence* of the unconditioned stimulus (the meat powder). The rate of extinction is measured by the rate at which the consequent conditioned response (salivation) diminishes. The more closely spaced (massed) the extinction trials are, the more rapidly extinction takes place. Piri Thomas's fear and anger responses to the police largely extinguished when he gave up drugs and crime. Policemen then became his protectors rather than his persecutors, and his fear and anger were replaced by more positive conditioned responses.

One curious fact is that after extinction trials have caused the total extinction of a conditioned reflex, the effects of extinction may subsequently vanish. As a result, the conditioned response again appears following presentation of the conditioned stimulus. This is known as *spontaneous recovery.* But successive extinction trials following spontaneous recovery will cause more and more complete extinction. Eventually a point will be reached where spontaneous recovery does not occur.

[4] *Stimulus generalization:* This element of the classical conditioning model is especially important to human behavior. In stimulus generalization a conditioned response comes to be elicited by a variety of stimuli similar to, but not the same as, the original conditioned stimulus. It is a learning mechanism that is most relevant to phobic and anxious behavior in humans, because a conditioned anxiety reflex originally elicited by one conditioned stimulus (say, an angry father, an overprotective mother) can generalize to *all* males, *all* females, or all people. In Wolpe's view, stimulus generalization is a central mechanism in the behavioral disorders (see pages 87 and 88).

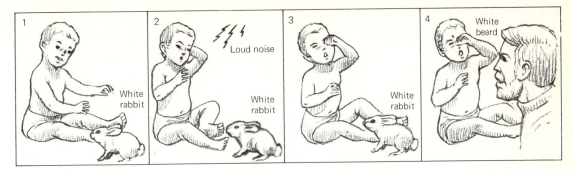

Figure 4-3. An example of stimulus generalization in fear conditioning. (1) An infant is at first unafraid of a white rabbit. (2) A loud noise (unconditioned stimulus) which startles and frightens the baby is paired with the presentation of a white rabbit. (3) Later, the infant is afraid of the white rabbit (now the conditioned stimulus) even in the absence of a loud noise. (4) He is likely to be afraid of other white furry things too, such as a beard. Many conditioned fear responses—in animals and people—are the product of stimulus generalization. *(After Watson & Rayner, 1920)*

Many of Hans's conditioned fear responses were probably products of stimulus generalization. If we assume that his early phobic behavior (specifically centering on horses) was a conditioned response to early frightening experiences with horses, we can also assume that his later phobias—to going outside his house, to trucks and buses, to railways—represented stimulus generalization. Each of the later phobic objects clearly bore some relationship to horses, the original phobic object. As a result, each came to elicit fear responses in Hans which had at first been associated only with horses.

[5] *Higher-order conditioning:* Another aspect of the classical paradigm that has special relevance to human learning is higher-order conditioning. This is the process by which a conditioned stimulus becomes in effect an unconditioned stimulus, because a "second-order" conditioned reflex has developed. If one of Pavlov's dogs, originally conditioned to salivate to a bell, then has a light paired with the bell enough times, the light by itself will come to elicit the salivation that had before been associated with the bell. With human beings, words, images, and other symbols can become conditioned stimuli for powerful emotional states that were initially associated

with real-life situations. Thus a word or phrase elicits the same emotional response which had previously been associated only with the actual circumstances. Most of us react strongly to such words as "Communist," "terrorist," or "Watergate"—as well as to other words that reawaken memories special to our own lives.

Classical conditioning and psychopathology. Researchers are still exploring the place of classical conditioning both in normal emotional behavior (Gormezano & Coleman, 1973; Kimmel, 1973) and in psychopathology. The classical conditioning paradigm has become a popular etiologic model for explaining neurotic behavior (Chapter 10), the drug dependencies and alcoholism (Chapter 11), and the psychophysiologic disorders (Chapter 14). The classical conditioning model also led to the aversive conditioning procedures that are used by some behavior therapists with alcoholics (Chapter 11), sexual deviants (Chapter 12), and autistic children (Chapter 15). In addition Wolpe reports that the model was important in his development of systematic desensitization as a major behavior therapy procedure (Chapter 10).

Operant conditioning

Beginnings: Skinner and his rats. B. F. Skinner set down the basic principles of operant conditioning in his classic book *The Behavior of Organisms* (1938). These, he said, were the rules by which behavior that did not fall within the scope of classical conditioning could be explained. Early in the book he pointed out: "There is a large body of behavior that does not seem to be elicited, in the sense in which a cinder in the eye elicits closure of the lid" (p. 19). He identified a broad range of behaviors that seem to be largely a function of their *consequences* rather than their antecedents (as in the classical conditioning paradigm). For example, pigeons quickly learn to peck colored discs when pecking brings them food. Skinner then described the basic laws by which these *operant behaviors* seem to be governed. The book was a thought-provoking mixture of carefully documented studies on the operant behavior of rats and speculative comments on the nature of man.

Skinner and operant conditioning have since had an enormous influence on academic and professional psychology, psychiatry, educa-tion, national defense, politics, and contemporary social movements. He is now American psychology's most revered living figure. His controversial role in the development of the "science of human behavior" is epitomized by his most recent book, *Beyond Freedom and Dignity* (1971). In it he faces squarely and unequivocally the practical consequences of his point of view: that people's behavior is largely determined by environmental forces over which they have little control. Naturally this position has generated fierce debate among followers and opponents of the behavioral viewpoint (Day, 1972; Mowrer, 1972).

Mischel agrees with Skinner (1954) that most human social behaviors are "voluntary, instrumental response patterns or 'operants'." As a result both men believe that an adequate explanation of behavior must specify the actual conditions which reliably produce that behavior.

The operant conditioning paradigm. The basic operant conditioning model is shown in Figure 4-4. The first term in the formula, S^D, refers to the *discriminative stimulus*. This is

Figure 4-4. The operant conditioning paradigm. Skinner (right) demonstrated that a pigeon could learn to peck repeatedly at a key (a translucent disc illuminated by a green light) to obtain food. The green key was the *discriminative stimulus*; the key peck was the *operant response*; the food was the *reinforcing stimulus*. Much human behavior is described by the operant conditioning paradigm.

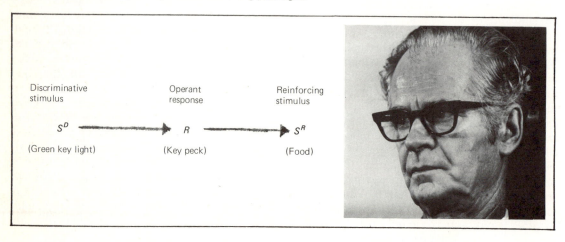

Discriminative stimulus — Operant response — Reinforcing stimulus

$$S^D \longrightarrow R \longrightarrow S^R$$

(Green key light) — (Key peck) — (Food)

something in the environment in whose presence an operant response is reinforced or rewarded. The discriminative stimulus sets the stage for the operant response, because it tells the organism what is the probability that his responses will be reinforced. In Skinner's original operant conditioning experiments, a green light behind a transparent plastic disc was a common S^D for pigeons. In the presence of that green light, the pigeons had previously received food when they pecked on the disc. Thus they could anticipate future reinforcement for future pecks when the green light was on. In real-life terms, an S^D for a boy to make a friendly approach to a girl he has just met might be her smile, her "come hither" look, or some encouraging remarks from her. Other S^Ds in the natural environment are green traffic signals ("Go") open doors ("Come in"), and firm handshakes ("Glad to meet you").

R, the second term in the operant equation, stands for the *operant response* itself. In Skinner's early animal work, this was a peck by a pigeon on the green-lighted disc (called a "pigeon key") or a press by a rat on a "rat lever." Humans, of course, have an infinite number of operant responses—ranging from a word or a phrase to a conversation, and from a nod of the head or a glint in the eye to a complex social relationship.

The final term in the operant equation, S^R, stands for the *reinforcing stimulus,* the all-important reason for responding. Skinner and his supporters maintain that the S^R determines the frequency with which the organism will give similar responses in the future. Skinner found, however, that the temporal and quantitative relationships between responses and reinforcers—between Rs and S^Rs—are more complex than he first thought. As a result he and a student, C. B. Ferster, worked out an exhaustive series of *schedules of reinforcement.* Each schedule has its own particular effect upon responding. We will describe only the four basic schedules; students interested in the variations on them should read Ferster and Skinner's *Schedules of Reinforcement* (1957) or

consult any issue of the *Journal of the Experimental Analysis of Behavior.*

[1] *Fixed-Ratio schedules (FR):* A fixed-ratio schedule is one in which the S^R follows a certain number of consecutive responses of a particular kind by the organism. The usual FR50 in an animal experiment requires the animal to make 50 consecutive responses—lever pushes or disc pecks—before it is reinforced with food. But an FR50 can also be a schedule which programs an *aversive behavior consequence,* or punishment. This means that the animal will receive a punishment (perhaps he will be given a brief electric shock, or perhaps food will be taken away from him) following those 50 responses. In the human environment, fixed-ratio schedules are "piecework" schedules. The farm laborer paid for every bushel of cucumbers he picks is paid on a fixed-ratio schedule. The harder he works, the more he earns. Free lance authors are also paid on FR schedules of reinforcement. It is a schedule whose value is taught early in life by families which stress the "work ethic."

[2] *Fixed-Interval Schedules (FI):* A fixed-interval schedule of reinforcement (or punishment) is one which requires the organism to wait for a given *interval* of time before it gives the response to be reinforced. Though the fixed interval can be measured from any observable event, the end of the previous reinforcement cycle is most commonly used. An FI2 requires the organism to wait two minutes or more after being reinforced before another response will be reinforced. Perhaps the most common human FI schedule is the salary schedule; it requires people to wait a week, two weeks, or a month before being paid. Though employees on such a reinforcement schedule work five days a week, they are paid at a regular interval, not on every day that they work. Other fixed-interval human schedules are those that are reinforced by graduation from school and those that are rewarded by job promotions based mostly upon length of service (as, for instance, in certain civil service positions).

[3] *Variable-Ratio Schedules (VR):* In a

"He always rewards good work . . ." Money, not a sugar cube, is the usual reward used to reinforce good work by employees. *(Myers © PUNCH 1971)*

PUNCH

variable-ratio schedule the *number* of responses the organism must emit in order to receive a reinforcement varies in an irregular but usually repeating fashion. In other words, though it is variable, the required number of responses clusters around an average figure. If the schedule is a VR10, the animal may emit as few as 3 responses for one reinforcement, as many as 20 for another, and so on—with an average of 10. The variable-ratio schedule is an important one for human beings, because it often typifies the relationships between parents and children. Every mother has her characteristic "threshold of frustration" beyond which her behavior changes toward her children. But the threshold is not a constant; sometimes she will punish them after one or two acts of mischief, while at other times she will let them get away with much more misbehavior before she disciplines them. Presumably every parent has an *average but variable* number of misbehaviors to which he or she responds with anger and physical abuse.

[4] *Variable-Interval Schedules (VI):* The variable-interval schedule produces the highest and most uniform rates of responding. It is also the most resistant to extinction. In a VI schedule, reinforcement is available at irregular and unpredictable *intervals,* though these cluster around an average. A VI2, for example, means that a response made after one minute may be reinforced, another made after five minutes may not be, and so on—with an average of two minutes. Human social interaction as well as maladaptive human behavior are often on VI schedules—which explains their common resistance to change or extinction. When a child's nagging and whining is usually ignored or punished but occasionally wins reinforcements of candy, affection, or attention, the child is likely to maintain that behavior for long periods of time. Or a phobic woman's fears may keep her from enjoying trips or parties, yet may secure the solicitous attention of her husband. This kind of "trade off" sometimes explains why a person keeps on with behavior that seems largely self-defeating.

Operant conditioning and psychopathology. Operant conditioning was at first concerned mainly with studying acquisition, maintenance, and extinction behavior by rats and pigeons. Experimenters in these early studies recorded the animals' behavior when faced with different discriminative stimuli, reinforcers, and schedules. Today, the operant conditioning model is used to investigate the effects of new drugs on animals (Boren, 1966; McMillan, 1973), to study animal learning processes that have relevance to human learning (Catania, 1973; Morse, 1966), to explore in animals such important human social behaviors as "mothering" and aggression (Azrin & Holz, 1966; Cherek et al., 1973; Van Hemel, 1973), and to study in humans social variables like cooperation, competition, and nurturing (Cohen, 1962; Hake et al., 1973).

More important in this book, the operant conditioning model is now seen as a prime etiologic factor in psychopathologic conditions such as schizophrenia (Chapter 7), depression (Chapter 8), the drug dependencies (Chapter 11), the psychophysiologic disorders (Chapter 14), and some of the so-called conduct disorders in children (Chapter 15). To return to Hans's disorder, we are convinced that his phobic behavior was reinforced as an operant response, largely by his mother. Though we have already noted that Hans may originally have modeled some of his phobias from a phobic mother he loved dearly, we also believe that that learning was strengthened whenever his mother commented, as Freud said she did, on how natural it was for a little child to be afraid of the things Hans feared. In other words, his mother reinforced his phobias with attention and understanding—maternal behavior that must have played an important role in the maintenance of his psychopathology.

Operant conditioners have also become increasingly important in therapy for some psychopathologic disorders. Operant technology is the basis for token economies, which are now in fashion in the treatment of chronic schizophrenia (Chapter 7), the social behavior of retarded children (Chapter 16), and the antisocial behavior of juvenile delinquents (Chapter 15). Operant approaches have also been employed to modify the behavior of neurotic patients (Chapter 10) and alcoholics (Chapter 11). Actually, Hans's father may well have used an operant strategy to modify his son's phobic behavior when he urged Hans to go with him on outings which brought the child into direct contact with some of his most feared objects. At these times Hans was in the company of a strong, protecting father who praised him whenever Hans could report that he felt little or no fear. In this way the father reinforced appropriate, nonphobic behavior in his son—and the phobic behavior ultimately disappeared.

Cognitive social-learning theory

Cognitive social-learning theory is Mischel's term for his current view of personality, put forth in a recent paper (1973). This view is designed to extend the limits of his former theory of personality by stressing the importance of *cognitive* factors—thoughts, feelings, images, memories, etc.—in social learning. Like other social-learning theorists, Mischel believes that observational learning, classical conditioning, and operant conditioning are fundamental to understanding behavior. But to understand it fully, he now says, the behavioral scientist must know more than just what has been learned or how it has been learned. Though both of these questions can be answered by reference to the three learning models, other questions relating to the subject's inner experience cannot.

The impact of Mischel's cognitive variables is to reduce significantly the behavioral scientist's assurance that a specific alteration in a person's environment or in an experimental situation will result in a predictable change in behavior. In other words, Mischel is saying that the behaviorists who have proudly pointed out that their science permits complete prediction and control of behavior have been mistaken, because they failed to recognize the importance of variables which fall outside the three models of learning. These variables are the ones Mischel terms *cognitive*.

If, somehow, Dr. Mischel were to be consulted on Hans's case today, he would probably spend a good deal of time simply following the child around and observing his behavior. Mischel would be especially interested in relating Hans's actions to their environmental context and to the basic learning mechanisms which were responsible for the boy's behavioral repertoire. But on completing such a behavioral assessment, Mischel would probably conclude that there were important determinants of the child's behavior which could not be directly observed. These are the cognitive factors—the things that Hans told himself about the situations he was in, the way he felt about them, what he had done before in similar situations, how a current situation differed even a little from past ones, and so on. Even though scientists cannot quantify these variables, Mischel insists that their importance be acknowledged, for they are *moderators* of the basic mechanisms of learning.

Mischel believes that five cognitive variables are essential to understanding behavior from the cognitive social-learning point of view. In his words, they deal "first with the individual's abilities to *construct* (generate) diverse behaviors under appropriate conditions. Next, one must consider the individual's *encoding and categorization* of events. Furthermore, a comprehensive analysis of the behavior a person performs in particular situations requires attention to his *expectancies* about outcomes, the *subjective values* of such outcomes, and his *self-regulatory systems and plans*" (Mischel, 1973, p. 265).

[1] The first of these variables, *construction competencies,* recognizes that human beings can confront new situations and solve new problems for which their previous learning has not specifically prepared them. For example, Hans must have observed his father interacting with other adults, and the child probably modeled that behavior when he interacted with adults. But of course, Hans had to adapt his behavior to fit social situations involving children or unfamiliar adults. In other words, behavior with other adults that was appropriate for Hans's father was not entirely appropriate for Hans. The son had to *modify* his social behavior, partly by using feedback on his behavior from others, partly by trial-and-error learning and problem solving, partly by thinking, planning, and projecting.

[2] By *encoding and categorization* of events, Mischel means the process by which all of us selectively attend to the most important aspects of our environment. If people could not do this, they would be overwhelmed by vast amounts of information that they could never process quickly or completely enough to decide on the appropriate behavior. In the case of Anne Frank and her family, for example, their fragile living situation required them to attend to a limited but all-important set of stimuli. A young girl on the threshold of adolescence is usually preoccupied with such things as dress, boy-girl skills, and rebellion against parental authority. But Anne's main concerns were the needs for being as quiet as possible during the day, for maintaining exquisite interpersonal sensitivity in overcrowded quarters, and perhaps most important, for keeping her psychic balance in a social climate of persecution. She had to work to hold her assurance that her ordeal as a Jew was im-

moral on society's part and did not reflect her own inadequacies or misdeeds.

[3] A person's *expectancies* about the results of his own behavior or about the results of other important variables in his environment are probably the most crucial single cognitive factor in determining his behavior. Most of you have heard about "placebo effects": placebos—meaning chemically inactive drugs or seemingly ineffective psychological treatment procedures—often turn out to be successful in treating people who believe that the placebos will help them. Similar effects due to expectancies are seen in other situations. Schreber, for example, believed that his physician was all-powerful and that this omnipotent man was "out to get him." So he readily became convinced that his real and imagined personal difficulties were the responsibility of his doctor. Malcolm X and Piri Thomas believed that the police were enemies, so the police did become enemies to be avoided or attacked. Anne Frank believed herself to be blameless for her attic imprisonment, so she continued to hope for a time when the world would be right and rational again. And Hans believed that his father loved him despite the anger and rivalry Hans felt for him, so the boy ultimately learned to deal with his disabling phobias because his father wanted him to.

[4] In his discussion of the power of expectancy to produce behavioral outcomes, Mischel notes that the *subjective stimulus values* which an individual attaches to an outcome themselves influence behavior. For example, all patients know that approval from a psychotherapist depends upon their making particular kinds of statements about themselves—usually positive ones. But the frequency with which a patient will make such a statement depends at least in part upon how much he values the therapist's approval. Hans's willingness to join his father on walks which led farther and farther from home and brought him closer and closer to horses presumably depended a great deal on the fact that the child wanted to please his father.

[5] A person's *self-regulatory systems and*

plans include the goals and performance standards he sets for himself in particular situations, as well as the consequences he imposes on himself for achieving or failing to achieve his aims. These cognitive variables permit each of us to reinforce or punish ourselves for behavior which meets or falls short of our own standards of conduct. Freud believed that some of the self-regulatory functions are performed by the superego. Mischel's idea of them is broader and less closely tied to moral issues than Freud's view of the superego. All of us have internal standards of performance by which we judge our own behavior. And all of us reward or punish ourselves when we achieve or fail to achieve our goals.

What do these five variables contribute to Mischel's view of human behavior? When they are added to the basic observational, classical, and operant models of learning, they introduce the cognitive elements which behaviorists have long been reluctant to consider. Their reluctance is based largely on the fact that cognitions cannot be directly measured

and hence cannot be directly quantified. Leaving them out of the behavioral conception of man, however, has meant that behaviorists are forced to emphasize objectively observable facts at the expense of equally important cognitions. And Mischel thinks it is important to call attention to these cognitions, identify them, and suggest research approaches to enable experimenters to measure them more precisely.

Other behavior therapists have also begun to pay serious attention to cognitive variables. Self-reinforcement, covert reinforcement and punishment, cognitive restructuring—all are cognitive behavior-change procedures that are currently being explored for use with patients. Will their inclusion in the theory and practice of behavior therapy cause behaviorists to forsake their radical empiricism—their tradition of dealing only with behaviors that can be directly measured? It is too early to suggest an answer. In our view, behaviorism does have room for the kind of variables Mischel wants to include.

Summary

Freud's psychoanalytic theory is an example of the "trait" approach to personality, which emphasizes more or less enduring personal traits that set an individual off from those around him and predict his future behavior. But other theories, like the social-learning approach of Bandura and Mischel, focus on the circumstances under which behavior takes place—the environmental context within which it occurs. The chapter used Freud's case history of little Hans—a 6-year-old boy who suffered from phobias—to illustrate the differences between psychoanalytic and social-learning theory.

Two fundamental concepts underlie psychoanalytic theory. The *principle of psychic determinism* presumes that in the mind as in nature, nothing happens by chance. The *principle of the unconscious* hypothesizes that mental processes of which the individual is not aware influence his feelings, thoughts, and actions. These processes cannot be made conscious even with a considerable expenditure of will, though they appear during free association, in dreams, through slips of the tongue, or during psychoanalysis.

Drive theory, another central psychoanalytic concept that was revised several times by Freud, assumes that behavior is determined by two primary drives: sex and aggression. They influence behavior through their psychic energy: libido in the case of sex, mortido in the case of aggression. Freud's associated theory of *psychosexual development* describes the vicissitudes of sexual drive from infancy to sexual maturity. During the oral stage, libido is focused on the organs of food intake. Stimulation of the lips, mouth, and tongue during this stage provides the child with pregenital sexual pleasure. In the anal stage, the focus is on elimination of waste products from the body, and libido is invested in those parts of the body which permit the child to expel or retain feces. In the phallic stage, the genital area provides pregenital sexual pleasure. It is in this period, Freud says, that the child participates in his family's oedipal complex, during which the roots of adult neurosis may be laid down. The crucial phallic stage is followed by the latency stage, which consists of six or seven years of relative sexual quiescence. Then comes puberty and the mature genital stage of development.

Freud believed that the individual has a psychic apparatus consisting of three parts: id, ego, and superego. At birth, the infant's psychological functioning is directed entirely by the *id,* the reservoir of sexual and aggressive drives that express themselves as the psychosexual stages unfold. But as the child accumulates experience with his external environment, *ego* functions develop. These permit high-level motor behavior; sensory and perceptual processes; remembering, comparing, and thinking; affect and feeling; and reality testing. A little later another psychic component, the *superego,* emerges as children learn from their parents the rules of behavior which govern social intercourse. This internalized representation of parental authority, also termed *conscience,* gradually takes on responsibility for enforcing the morals and ethics of society.

One of the major functions of the ego is to protect the psyche from being overwhelmed by id, superego, or environmental demands. The ego's defense mechanisms are most obvious in the behavior of neurotics, for a neurotic uses them so much that they prevent normal interaction with the environment. The two most basic ego defenses are repression and suppression. The most primitive are identification, introjection, projection, displacement, and denial. More mature defense mechanisms include reaction formation, undoing, isolation, sublimation, regression, rationalization, substitution, and dissociation.

Social-learning theory, in direct contrast with psychoanalytic theory, assumes that (1) most human behavior is learned, (2) the laws which govern this learning are knowable and measurable, and (3) both normal and abnormal behavior is acquired by the same fundamental learning mechanisms.

The three prime modes of acquisition of behavior, according to social-learning theory, are observational learning ("modeling"), classical (Pavlovian) conditioning, and operant (Skinnerian) conditioning. In *observational learning* or modeling, people can acquire new responses simply by watching someone else modeling that kind of behavior. The *classical conditioning* paradigm involves pairing a conditioned stimulus (say, a bell) with an unconditioned stimulus (meat powder) to elicit an unconditioned response (salivation). If repeated often enough, this pairing will produce a conditioned reflex, meaning that the originally neutral conditioned stimulus alone will become able to elicit the now-conditioned response. The *operant conditioning* paradigm emphasizes the organism's identification in the environment of a discriminative stimulus. This is an environmental element in whose presence an operant (free) response will be or has been reinforced. The operant paradigm assumes that an operant response is a direct function of its consequences: if a response is reinforced, its frequency will increase; if it is punished, its frequency will decrease.

Mischel's cognitive social-learning theory extends the limits of earlier social-learning theories by stressing the importance of cognitive factors—which include thoughts, feelings, images, and memories—in the process of social learning. In so doing, Mischel stresses the need to go beyond the three basic models of learning in order to explain human behavior.

CHAPTER FIVE

Problems of classification and decision making

Bill H. ● Why diagnose? ● How to diagnose? ● Efforts to systematize diagnostic procedures ● Future of psychopathologic diagnosis

**BILL H.:
THE MAN
NO ONE KNEW**

Bill H., a 36-year-old divorced white Catholic male of Irish ancestry, was admitted to the psychiatry service, Boston City Hospital, for treatment of chronic alcoholism in May 1968. During his interview he told of a twenty-year history of heavy drinking that amounted to one and often two pints of whisky a day. Hospital records showed that a year earlier, Bill had been an inpatient for two weeks because of "depression and suicidal ruminations." The records listed three other admissions, all for treatment of the physical aftereffects of prolonged drinking (gastritis, dehydration, and several head injuries). Bill—"good old Bill," as the staff called him—was a familiar face in the emergency ward, where he often showed up drunk to be treated for cuts and bruises or to be examined for possible skull fractures after he had fallen. According to police records, he had been arrested 34 times for public drunkenness and each time had served a 30- or 60-day sentence at the local "drunk farm."

The third-year psychiatric resident who admitted Bill from the emergency room to the psychiatric ward tried to interview him in depth. Though Bill was almost sober, he was alternately disoriented, distracted, irritable, and cooperative. The resident got as much family, personal, and medical history as he could and saw to it that Bill was given a thorough physical examination.

Bill told the resident that his father, then 55, had been a chronic alcoholic for as long as Bill could remember. The father had lived at home when he wasn't in the hospital, in jail, or on a spree, and had knocked Bill around. But they still saw each other from time to time and in fact, Bill said with a wry grin, had even gone on sprees together. When sober, the father worked as a clam digger; when he was drunk or in jail, his wife received welfare payments. Since clam digging had come upon bad days with the pollution of Boston harbor,

(David Krasnor/Photo Researchers Inc.)

the father now earned no more for a month of work than the state paid his wife when he was in jail.

According to Bill, his mother was an exceptionally nervous person who had a facial tic. "She looks like she's 70 and acts like she's dead." Bill had had a younger brother who died in infancy from pneumonia. He remembered little of his grandparents except that all four had been born in the "Old Country." None of them had been unusually fond of liquor, but Bill said that he had three American cousins, an Irish uncle, and an American aunt who did drink heavily.

Bill remembered his childhood as disorderly. He and his mother lived in dread of his father's bad-tempered homecomings from the bar or from jail, when he would beat both of them. As a result of the trouble at home, Bill never did very well in school. His teachers thought that he could have turned out average work if he had tried, but school was just as unpleasant as home for him and he left both as soon as he could. He worked at various menial jobs until he was 25, when he apprenticed himself to a nonunion electrician, a distant cousin. At the time of this latest hospital admission Bill considered himself an electrician even though he had not worked steadily at it for several years.

When he was 28 Bill met his wife, who was five years his junior, at the bar he hung out in after work. Their relationship developed quickly and they were married in three months. Their only child, Tim, was born after a year and a half, and the marriage itself lasted less than three years. Though his relationship with his wife was never a tranquil one, it became intolerable for Bill when he discovered shortly after Tim's birth that she had begun "sleeping around" with some of the men she had known before she married. When Bill angrily charged her with her infidelity, she told him to "take it or leave it." After a few days, he left it. He has seen his wife and son twice since the divorce, both times by accident on a downtown Boston street. He does not know where they live or, for that matter, whether she has remarried.

During the interview Bill told the psychiatric resident these additional facts:

1 For the past three weeks he had felt convinced that there were people in his home whom he could not identify. He had called the police and fire departments several times, but whenever they came the strange people disappeared.
2 Sometimes while sitting at home, Bill had intense feelings of unfamiliarity during which he could not recognize his surroundings.
3 While looking at television about two months before, he had become confused and suffered a convulsive attack, accompanied by loss of consciousness and incontinence.

114

4 Bill had been convinced at times during the past three months that he was the Boston Strangler (a notorious murderer who was terrorizing the city).

5 He had often felt lately that he knew strangers whom he passed in the street. He sometimes had the same sense of familiarity when traveling through strange towns or doing electrical work in strange houses.

6 On and off for the past six months Bill had been hearing a voice which whispered his name and made threats.

7 Several times while driving, he had lost consciousness and come to an hour or so later to find that he was still driving, though on a strange road 50 or 60 miles out of his way.

8 Having developed a pain in his chest six months ago, he collected some knives, razor blades, gauze pads, and a flashlight and planned to operate on himself if the doctors would not. (In fact he did need an operation, and it was performed shortly before this admission.)

9 For about a year Bill had had small lapses of consciousness in the middle of conversations. On recovering a moment later, he found it difficult to remember what it was he had been talking about. These attacks seemed to be coming more and more often.

10 Also for about a year he had been seeing animals (one was a white horse surrounded by a red glow) in his bedroom. He was convinced that they were real.

11 He found that whenever he ate a meal that included meat, he became dizzy and drowsy and had to lie down.

A "mental status" examination revealed that Bill was oriented in all three spheres (he knew who he was, where he was, and what time it was). He showed no overall mood or thinking disorders, related easily and well to the interviewer, and had an intact memory. During limited portions of the interview, however, he did exhibit mood and thinking disorders; he was occasionally disoriented, vague, forgetful, unemotional when emotion seemed more appropriate, and "distant" from the interviewer. It was the doctor's conclusion that this apparently random alternation between clarity and disorientation had been going on for several years.

Physically, Bill was a well-nourished, healthy looking young man. He had an enlarged liver and spleen, conspicuous spider naevi (fine red lines) over his face, chest, and neck, and a tremor in his hands— all signs of alcoholism. His other bodily systems were normal. Laboratory studies revealed some decrease in effective liver functioning, which is also typical of alcoholism. An electroencephalogram (EEG) done six months before admission, and two done at the time of admission, indicated some impairment in the right temporal lobe of

(David Margolin from Black Star)

115

his brain. (This problem had nothing to do with alcoholism: it suggested some other ailment, perhaps epilepsy.) A brain scan test for a tumor was negative.

Bill was in the hospital for three weeks. He attended group therapy sessions, saw a psychotherapist alone three times a week, and built a birdhouse and a model ship in occupational therapy, which he seemed to enjoy. When he was released from the hospital, he was given an appointment for the outpatient alcoholism clinic. But he never came; in fact, he dropped completely out of sight. No one at the hospital knows what has happened to Bill, though almost everyone has a theory.

While he was in the hospital Bill's case was taken up at the weekly conference held by the psychiatry service. The facts you have just read were discussed and evaluated by the service's assembled mental health professionals, students, and researchers. Bill himself came to the meeting for a short interview. Patients sometimes object to being made a "public spectacle" at these conferences, but Bill said later that he rather enjoyed sitting in front of so many doctors who were trying to help him. It was, as he remembered, the seventh or eighth time he had done so. The people at the meeting were supposed to come up with a diagnosis that would help Bill's therapist plan his treatment and eventual discharge. The results of the conference will be reviewed later in the chapter; for now, simply note that the group could reach no diagnostic agreement.

Although Bill's psychological, medical, and social problems might appear overwhelming, he did not see them that way. Sometimes he commented on the "streak of bad luck" he had been having, but he did not really believe that his life was much different from that of most persons he knew. And though he read about and saw on television many other people who had more material things than he, Bill never complained about his lot. In short, he had adjusted to the way things were for him. Though he was not among those of us on whom fortune smiles, in his way Bill H. was surviving.

(Richard Lawrence Stack from Black Star)

Why diagnose?

The dubious influence of the medical model

Chapter 1 pointed out that most current ideas about the etiology and treatment of psychopathology have been shaped by the medical model. As discussed there, the replacement of the moral model by the medical model around the turn of the century meant that mental disorders came to be viewed more rationally and treated more systematically. But the medical model in turn led to inflexibilities in theory and practice that have not been helpful.

In our opinion, the medical model has had an unfortunate influence on psychopathologic diagnosis. It categorizes mental disorders largely in terms of three distinguishing characteristics carried over from physical medicine: origin, course, and symptoms. The problem is that behavioral scientists cannot specify the "true" origin or predict the "usual" course of most mental disorders. Therefore they are forced to diagnose from "symptoms," meaning maladaptive, bizarre, abnormal, unsocial, or unusual behavior. Categorization from symptoms presents three equally vexing problems: (1) The word *symptom* implies the presence of an underlying diseased core, a view many behavioral scientists cannot accept. (2) Symptoms are notoriously unreliable; they may change over time, they may appear different to different observers, and they may seem different to the same observer over time. (3) Symptoms have little validity, meaning that they are not very useful in predicting the course of a patient's disorder or in helping the clinician decide what therapy to give. Of these three problems, the first concerns semantics, the second measurement, and the third function.

In physical medicine, diagnosis usually tells the physician a number of important things about the patient and his illness. It often tells what the *etiology* (cause) of the condition is (for example, tuberculosis is caused by the tubercle bacillus, and syphilis is caused by the spirochete *Treponema pallidum*). Also, it often suggests the appropriate *treatment*. (The tubercle bacillus, a hardy organism, can be destroyed by a combination of rest, surgery if required, and prolonged administration of drugs like iproniazid, streptomycin sulfate, and aminosalicylic acid. Syphilis is treated quickly and effectively with penicillin.) Further, the course—the progressive appearance of the different symptoms—of these physical disorders is predictable. Therefore diagnosis predicts what is going to happen as well as indicating the cause and treatment of the illness. While the etiology and treatment of many serious medical disorders remain unknown (as in cancer and heart disease), the diagnostic process in medicine is a tried and true procedure that has given good results over the years.

Diagnosis of the mental disorders based on symptoms has not worked nearly so well (Beck et al., 1962; Goldberg, 1968; Gough, 1971), in spite of an elaborate "official" psychiatric diagnostic system derived from the medical model. Let us take a look at it.

Diagnostic and Statistical Manual of Mental Disorders, second edition (DSM II)

The diagnostic system now used by almost every clinician in the United States has been codified in the *Diagnostic and Statistical Manual of Mental Disorders* (second edition, 1968). Published by the American Psychiatric Association, the *Diagnostic Manual* (also referred to as DSM II) was compiled by a committee appointed and funded by the APA. It is now the "official" psychiatric classification system in the United States.

DSM II divides the psychopathologic disorders into ten categories. All of them are described in detail in later chapters. Here is a brief list:

I Mental retardation (borderline, mild, moderate, severe, profound)

II Organic brain syndromes (disorders caused by or associated with impairment of brain tissue function)

    A Psychoses associated with organic brain syndromes (e.g., senile dementia, alcoholic psychosis, psychosis with epilepsy, psychosis with childbirth)

    B Nonpsychotic organic brain syndromes (OBS); for example, nonpsychotic OBS with alcohol (simple drunkenness), nonpsychotic OBS with brain tumor

III Psychoses not attributed to the physical conditions listed above in I and II (e.g., schizophrenia, the affective disorders, the paranoid states)

IV Neuroses (e.g., anxiety neurosis, phobic neurosis, depressive neurosis, obsessive-compulsive neurosis)

V   Personality disorders and certain other nonpsychotic mental disorders (e.g., paranoid personality, hysterical personality, sexual deviation, alcoholism, drug dependence)

VI   Psychophysiologic disorders (e.g., psychophysiologic respiratory disorder, psychophysiologic gastrointestinal disorder)

VII   Special symptoms (e.g., tic, disorders of sleep, enuresis)

VIII   Transient situational disturbances (adjustment reaction of childhood, adjustment reaction of adolescence, adjustment reaction of later life)

IX   Behavior disorders of childhood and adolescence (e.g., overanxious reaction of childhood, runaway reaction of adolescence)

X   Conditions without manifest psychiatric disorder and nonspecific conditions (e.g., marital maladjustment, social maladjustment, occupational maladjustment)

This list is a revision of the first *Diagnostic and Statistical Manual* (1952), which in turn evolved gradually from the work of Falret (1854), Kahlbaum (1874), Hecker (1877), and most important, Kraepelin (1896). Emil Kraepelin was a German psychiatrist who brought together the hodgepodge of clinical observations of mental patients that had accumulated through much of the nineteenth century. He based his diagnostic system—the world's first comprehensive one—on the assumption that the mental disorders are physical diseases. For that reason he applied exactly the same diagnostic criteria that were used then (and are used now) for physical diagnosis. Psychoanalytically and socially oriented psychiatrists who came after Kraepelin (like Hoch, 1912; Kretschmer, 1925; Menninger, 1952; Meyer, 1906) proposed changes in his system. But even so, it strongly influenced development of the 1952 *Diagnostic and Statistical Manual*, the first official classification system in this country. Though DSM II of 1968 contains a number of technical changes from DSM I, both editions are extensions of the basic Kraepelinian medical model.

What are the strengths of diagnosis?

Psychiatrists who value psychopathologic diagnosis—while admitting that it has shortcomings—base their arguments for it on several points. They often begin by suggesting that diagnosis, because it derives from the traditions and practices of medicine, promotes the scientific viewpoint. One of the main advantages of the scientific viewpoint is that it takes away from mental patients some of the disgrace which used to be attached to their behavior. When Bill H. has a DSM II label, everyone is more inclined to look at his alcoholism as a product of mental disease rather than a sign of moral decay.

Emil Kraepelin *(Culver Pictures, Inc.)*

Efforts at diagnostic classification also have more practical benefits. Diagnosis aids research by enabling scientists to compare different treatment strategies, to hypothesize different etiologies, and to predict different "natural" outcomes in groups of patients. And diagnosis helps the clinician bring order to an otherwise overwhelming mass of data on a patient's past and present behavior, home situation, vocational and educational history —all the facts which make up the raw material of the diagnostic process. Without some such system, each patient would be a new and different problem, and his treatment would have to develop out of trial-and-error experimentation. Seymour Kety, whose drug research programs depend upon separating patients by diagnostic groupings, has this to say in defense of diagnosis:

An unfortunate corollary of the recognized idiosyncratic aspects of personality is the rather alarming tendency today to neglect the older concepts of . . . description and classification of mental disorders. Diagnosis is undervalued and mental illness is being regarded less as a "disease" or even a "disorder" and more as a "way of life," or an individual adaptation to a unique life situation. If such were the case, of course, it would follow that what was formerly thought to be a categorical disorder is now unique for and peculiar to the individual patient. It would follow, also, that there is little sense in concerning oneself with "schizophrenia" or "anxiety neurosis." One should really speak of John Jones' Disorder or Mary Smith's Syndrome. [1961, p. 392]

Another common argument in favor of diagnosis is that diagnostic statements can function as shorthand descriptions of behavior. For example, the clinician who is asked to treat a schizophrenic patient knows some of the specifics of that patient's behavior before the two ever meet. This claim also has its dangers, for no mental disorder always looks the same, and no patient's behavior can be predicted with certainty. But it is indeed helpful to the clinician to have a diagnosis that gives him some idea of what to expect from his patient during the course of treatment.

What are the weaknesses of diagnosis?

The greatest weaknesses of diagnosis—and they may be insurmountable—are that the diagnostic process is often unreliable and, as a result, that most diagnostic labels are not useful.

The word *reliability*, in its technical, "measurement" sense, refers to the degree to which a test or other assessment procedure yields similar data each time it is used. High reliability means that the behavior being measured is stable, that the measurement instrument reflects the behavior adequately, or both. Low reliability means that the behavior in question is unstable or impermanent, that the measurement device is not a good one, or both. The reliability of procedures for measuring human height, weight, and circumference is high; the reliability of intelligence measurement is moderately high; the reliability of measures of "personality" is lower; the reliability of psychopathologic diagnosis is perhaps even lower (Beck et al., 1962; Goldberg, 1968; Gough, 1971).

Why do the traditional diagnostic procedures have such low reliability? Many explanations have been suggested. Diagnosticians themselves have frequently been blamed, for their judgments so often conflict (Chapman & Chapman, 1967, 1969, 1971). Indeed, when Bill H.'s case was discussed in the conference described at the beginning of the chapter, the 32 health professionals who attended could not agree on a diagnosis.

These clinicians ranged in age from 24 to 59 years (median age, 31) and clinical experience with psychiatric patients from 3 months to 30 years (median years of experience, 2); their professional identities included Harvard Medical School professor of psychiatry, psychiatric resident, medical resident, neurological resident, staff psychiatrist, social worker, psychiatric nurse and occupational therapist. Both sexes were included in the group. [Nathan et al., 1969, p. 10]

After Bill's medical, social, personal, and psychiatric histories were presented and Bill himself was interviewed, each conference participant filled in a diagnostic checklist (which gave 100 of the most common cues to psychopathology) and assigned Bill a diagnostic label.

Thirty observers conferred 14 different diagnostic labels; 2 observers declined to make a diagnosis. The labels were of three types: Those which labeled a purely functional condition (e.g., "paranoid schizophrenia" or "anxiety and depression in an inadequate personality"), those which named a purely organic condition (e.g., "temporal lobe epilepsy" or "temporal lobe epilepsy and chronic alcoholism") and those which combined the two (e.g., "depressive reaction and temporal lobe epilepsy"). . . . The most experienced observers were more inclined to confer an organic label on the patient's disability than were the less experienced observers. [Nathan et al., 1969, p. 12]

The literature is filled with reports like this, where clinicians could not agree on a diagnostic label for a patient's mental disorder (Gurland, 1973; McGuire, 1973). Some say that these findings are the predictable result of unclear and inexact diagnostic criteria (Nathan, 1967). Others (Welner et al., 1972) say that "traditional" diagnostic procedures depend upon symptomatic behaviors which simply do not lend themselves to precise observation (subjective experiences like depression, for example, are not really measurable). Another explanation is that mental health professionals disagree on diagnoses because of their different theoretical orientations (Sandifer, 1972).

Even standardized and objective tests do not help the clinician make more reliable diagnostic statements (Phillips & Draguns, 1971). One reason is that while tests permit *data gathering* to proceed more objectively, they do not eliminate controversy about *data analysis* (diagnostic decision making). Bill H. was given a full battery of psychological tests, including a standard measure of intelligence (the Wechsler Adult Intelligence Scale, called the WAIS), the Minnesota Multiphasic Personality Inventory (MMPI), the Rorschach Inkblot Test, and several cards from the Thematic Apperception Test (TAT). The four psychologists who examined the test results

agreed that the IQ test results indicated average intelligence. But only three considered Bill's MMPI pathological, and only two thought that the Rorschach and TAT findings were unusual. Of these two, one psychologist concluded that Bill's Rorschach responses showed schizophrenic tendencies, while the other was convinced that Bill's TAT performance was a sign of latent homosexuality.

The low reliability of diagnosis, combined with the relatively primitive state of scientific knowledge about the etiology and treatment of many psychiatric disorders, means that the diagnostic process often has little *clinical utility*. It is not consistently valuable for treatment planning, for etiologic investigation, or for predictive purposes. The diagnostic label of "chronic alcoholism" was the only one that the conference could agree upon for Bill H. And this label did not lead to a treatment plan any different from what would have been prescribed if his illness had been diagnosed as "psychopathic personality" or "neurotic depression." On the other hand, if everyone had agreed that Bill was schizophrenic (another real diagnostic possibility), he would have been given one of the phenothiazines, a family of tranquilizing drugs that have proved valuable for the schizophrenic psychoses. So in that case, the diagnostic process would have been useful. But as it was, the diagnostic label applied to Bill's condition did little to help him.

Though it would seem that unreliability and uneven utility are reasons enough to reject the current diagnostic model, other serious shortcomings have also been pointed out. For example, by itself a diagnosis can exert a profound effect on a patient's future, regardless of its objective utility. The person who is given a schizophrenic diagnosis, no matter whether it accurately reflects his behavior over a period of time, may be in trouble if his family, his employers, his school advisers, or his friends learn about it. When Bill heard that almost everyone on the wards—doctors, nurses, and patients—considered him an alcoholic, he said wryly that it meant everyone had given up on him. Probably he was right.

Burning an insane woman—a mode of "treatment" sometimes resorted to in the fifteenth and sixteenth centuries. *(The Bettmann Archive)*

How to diagnose?

Early attempts at diagnosis

Man's earliest writings on psychopathology appeared in Greece before the classical period. Among the first mental disorders they identified were the psychopathological effects of aging. Though the Greeks did not know that these effects of old age are often caused by specific physical conditions (say, cerebral arteriosclerosis, cardiovascular accidents, hypertension), their descriptions of the resulting behavior were as accurate as any clinical observations today.

The Greeks also recognized the psychopathologic consequences of alcoholism very early. It took them a little longer—until classical times—to identify and describe mania, melancholia, and paranoia, all behaviors which we now know characterize the functional (nonorganic) psychoses.

The supernatural has always played a major role in the classification and treatment of psychopathology. Long before *The Witches' Hammer*, the medieval witch-hunting book that was described in Chapter 1, it was widely believed that mental disorders were caused by demonological influences. In the fifteenth and sixteenth centuries, especially after publication of *The Witches' Hammer* in 1487, a variety of specific syndromes were diagnosed as being supernatural in origin (and were "treated" by burning at the stake). To our day a few such diagnostic terms survive: for example, *obsession* means being attacked by demons, and *alienated* means giving control of one's soul to the devil.

Origins of modern diagnosis

The founding of asylums for the insane toward the end of the eighteenth century marked the beginning of modern efforts to classify the mental disorders. Linnaeus had developed a successful taxonomy (classification system) for plants and animals, and this gave people the idea that they might do the same for the psychopathologies. Bringing together large numbers of mental patients under one roof provided doctors with an opportunity to observe their behavior over long periods of time.

Phillippe Pinel, the great French psychiatric reformer best known for breaking the chains which had literally bound institutionalized mental patients for several hundred years, was one of the first to propose a classification system. He divided the disorders into melancholia, mania without delirium, mania with delirium, dementia, and idiotism—and did so without referring to supernatural influences, hypothetical bodily structures, or presumed etiologic factors (1806). Those who came after him, notably the German psychiatrists of the nineteenth century (Griesinger, Hecker, Kahlbaum, Kraepelin), based their own classification systems on equally objective, "enlightened" criteria that were largely behavioral. They aimed for objectivity mainly because they believed that almost all the mental disorders had a physical basis, even though their etiology could not yet be traced. After all, other scientists (Alzheimer, Nissl, Wernicke, Korsakoff) were beginning to demonstrate the organic etiology of such mental disorders as general paralysis, presenile dementia, and alcoholic psychosis.

Emil Kraepelin, of course, was the man whose influence on diagnosis continues to this day. His ideas can be seen in the *Diagnostic and Statistical Manual's* view of schizophrenia as a single entity (rather than a collection of separate ones), its emphasis upon organic etiology as a prime basis for diagnosis, and its insistence that diagnoses should be made only after detailed and objective observation of behavior. Though Kraepelin might hardly recognize his own viewpoint in DSM II, most observers believe that it underlies much of the manual, especially the sections on the functional psychoses.

The neuroses, because they are less crippling and less bizarre than the functional psychoses, were not given much systematic attention until Freud produced his theory of psychoanalysis. As a result, classifications of the neuroses strongly reflect the influence of psychoanalytic theory. This influence is most apparent in the central role that such classifications assign to anxiety as *the* unifying concept of the neurotic disorders (Chapter 9).

Given the DSM II system of labels, how do mental health clinicians actually arrive at their diagnostic decisions? Until psychological tests were developed, virtually the only tools of the diagnostician were interviews and observations of patients' behavior, and such tools are still very important. They have been formalized as the *mental status examination* and the *personal history*. In addition, a detailed *physical examination* usually accompanies these interviews to determine whether the patient's psychological dysfunctions are related to physical ones.

Mental status examination. In the mental status examination, a regular feature of the diagnostic process, the clinician observes and talks to the patient. Usually he aims to assess six aspects of the patient's behavior:

[1] The patient's *general appearance and manner* suggest how closely the overall impression that he makes corresponds to his position in life, how well his facial and bodily expressions accord with his conversation in the interview, and how spontaneously he relates to the interviewer.

[2] The patient's *speech characteristics* are

important because they may show one of the abnormalities (for example, "word salading," neologisms, echolalia, and flight of ideas) which are characteristic of the functional psychoses, especially the group of schizophrenias.

[3] The level and quality of the patient's *mood* are extremely sensitive reflections of emotional disorder. The interviewer must be alert to a variety of possible moods, including sadness, depression, grief, suspicion, anxiety, fear, panic, hostility, elation, ecstasy, and tranquillity. Each can have diagnostic significance, especially when evaluated in terms of its appropriateness to circumstances. Patients who seem "flat" (expressionless) or whose mood is inappropriate are often given psychotic diagnoses—a diagnostic decision made by Bleuler more than 50 years ago.

[4] *Content of thought* can indicate both subtle and obvious thought disorders. Dynamic (psychoanalytically oriented) interviewers pay special attention to a patient's subtle thought content, both normal and abnormal, as means of assessing unconscious influences on thinking. As for the not-so-subtle disorders of thinking, the interviewer watches for hallucinations and faulty perceptions, delusions and illusions, and obsessive and phobic ideas.

[5] Assessment of the patient's *orientation, memory and learning, attention and concentration, and general information* indicate how well he is taking in, processing, and utilizing data from the environment. These functions are often impaired in acute brain disorders (e.g., intoxication and acute brain trauma). Such a patient may not know where he is, what time it is, or how he came to be where he is. On the other hand, chronic brain disorders (e.g., chronic alcoholism, senility) are often characterized by profound disorders of memory, especially recent memory. This happens to a certain extent in most old people; many of us have grandparents who cannot remember what they had for breakfast but who can talk for hours about details of their childhood.

[6] The interviewer evaluates the patient's *insight and judgment* about himself—whether he sees himself as "sick," in need of treatment, and incapable of functioning without help from others. As a general rule, patients whose behavior is grossly disordered and who do not recognize the fact are usually psychotic.

Personal history. In taking down a detailed history of the patient, the experienced interviewer aims to cover three areas, though not necessarily in any particular order. One is the patient's *chief complaint and present illness:* Why has he come for help now? When, where, and under what circumstances did his disorder develop? What are his expectations concerning treatment? The second is his *personal history,* which involves a review of each period in his life, including infancy, childhood, adolescence, and adulthood. The interviewer explores each period with him for adequacy of social, sexual, psychological, and vocational functioning. The third area is the patient's *family history.* He is asked to describe his parents and siblings, the nature of his relationships with them, and the role each plays in his current psychological turmoil.

Unreliability of traditional psychiatric procedures. Although a mental status examination and a review of the patient's personal history are still the touchstones on which diagnosis, treatment, and research are based, these methods have long aroused controversy. The dispute revolves around their subjectivity and resultant potential for unreliability. In fact, research has shown that the age, sex, race, and socioeconomic status of the patient, the examiner, or both can affect the conclusions drawn from a psychiatric examination (Edwards, 1972; Routh & King, 1972). Research has also confirmed that experienced examiners do not always reach the same diagnostic or prognostic conclusions even when supplied with the same interview or observational data (Sandifer, 1972). Furthermore, patients do not always give the same amount and kind of information to all examiners (Edelman & Snead, 1972; Perrett, 1972). These sources of unreliability in traditional psychiatric examination procedures explain why they are often not very useful. To this end, many authorities have questioned the sense of having an interview whose value is doubtful (Black, 1971; Brostoff, 1972).

Efforts to systematize diagnostic procedures

Structuring behavioral observations

In an effort to make these unstructured diagnostic procedures more reliable, researchers have developed a variety of techniques for systematizing them.

Symptom rating scales. Among the most widely used of the structured observational instruments are the IMPS (Inpatient Multidimensional Psychiatric Scale: Lorr et al., 1962; Lorr & Klett, 1966) and the WPRS (Wittenborn Psychiatric Rating Scales: Wittenborn, 1955). These tools, called *symptom rating scales,* structure judgments about a patient's degree of psychopathology in a form designed to minimize the likelihood that two different clinicians will arrive at significantly different diagnoses. Both scales were constructed following an analysis of large numbers of items that point to psychopathologic behavior. The 90 IMPS and 72 WPRS items finally chosen were those that seemed to reflect most clearly the range of psychopathology shown by most psychotic patients.

The IMPS is designed to measure ten groups of related symptoms: "excitement," "hostile belligerence," "paranoid projection," "grandiose expansiveness," "perceptual distortion," "anxious intropunitiveness," "retardation and apathy," "disorientation," "motor disturbances," and "conceptual disorganization." The WPRS divides functional psychotic behavior into nine categories: "acute anxiety," "conversion hysteria," "manic state," "depressed state," "schizophrenic excitement," "paranoid condition," "paranoid schizophrenia," "hebephrenic schizophrenic," "phobic compulsive."

This is an IMPS item intended to gauge the patient's degree of "paranoid projection":

Compared to the normal person of the same sex and age, to which degree does he:
Manifest a hostile, sullen, or morose attitude towards others by tone of voice, demeanor, or facial expression? [To be scored on a nine-point scale, ranging from 9: extremely, to 1: not at all.]
CUES: Seems to have a chip on his shoulder; slams door or bangs chair, sarcastic tone. Try not to judge on the basis of content of remarks.
[Lorr & Klett, 1966, p. 5]

This is a WPRS item intended to gauge "acute anxiety":

No complaint of subjectively experienced anxiety. Experiences at least minor feelings of anxiety. Experiences anxiety which is strong enough to make him express acutely uncomfortable feelings. Is desperately distressed by his anxiety and considers it to be intolerable.
[Clinician is to select the alternative most descriptive of his patient.]
[Wittenborn, 1955, p. 6]

The reliability of diagnoses based upon the IMPS or the WPRS appears to be higher than that of diagnoses based only upon clinical interviews (Lorr, 1968; Wittenborn, 1967). But the relative utility of these measures has not been thoroughly explored. No one has really proved that either measure is better than an interview by an experienced clinician in predicting a patient's response to psychotherapy or drug therapy—or for that matter, in anticipating an untreated patient's chances for spontaneous recovery (Phillips & Draguns, 1971).

The computer as a diagnostic tool. Some new rating scales designed specifically for computer processing have also been developed. Diagnosis by computer has two advantages: One is that *many more items,* covering a much wider range of past and present behavior, can be included in the diagnostic instrument, because the computer can process

Figure 5-1. Part of the computer-based CAPPS scale. *(Spitzer and Endicott, 1969)*

Form MS 02 (7/69)

PROBLEM APPRAISAL SCALES (PAS)*

Patient's last name	First name	M.I.	Facility	Unit

INSTRUCTIONS: Rate the patient's condition during the last two weeks. When no information is available on a dimension or when a dimension is not applicable (e.g. Social Relations With Children), the scale should be left blank.   1=none, 2=slight, 3=mild, 4=moderate, 5=severe.

::0:: ::1:: ::2:: ::3:: ::4::   ::5:: ::6:: ::7:: ::8:: ::9::

Case or consecutive number

::0:: ::1:: ::2:: ::3:: ::4::   ::5:: ::6:: ::7:: ::8:: ::9::

::0:: ::1:: ::2:: ::3:: ::4::   ::5:: ::6:: ::7:: ::8:: ::9::

::0:: ::1:: ::2:: ::3:: ::4::   ::5:: ::6:: ::7:: ::8:: ::9::

::0:: ::1:: ::2:: ::3:: ::4::   ::5:: ::6:: ::7:: ::8:: ::9::

TRANSACTION   Initial evaluation   reevaluation   partial reeval   correction   deletion

Facility code

::0:: ::1:: ::2:: ::3:: ::4::   ::5:: ::6:: ::7:: ::8:: ::9::

::0:: ::1:: ::2:: ::3:: ::4::   ::5:: ::6:: ::7:: ::8:: ::9::

::0:: ::1:: ::2:: ::3:: ::4::   ::5:: ::6:: ::7:: ::8:: ::9::

Last day of two weeks being evaluated

Jan	Feb	Mar	Apr	May	Month	Jun	Jul	Aug	Sep	Oct

::1:: ::69:: ::70:: ::71:: ::72::   Year   ::73:: ::74:: ::75::   Nov   Dec

::2:: ::3:: ::4:: ::5:: ::6::   ::7:: ::8:: ::9:: ::10:: ::11::

Day

::12:: ::13:: ::14:: ::15:: ::16::   ::17:: ::18:: ::19:: ::20:: ::21::

::22:: ::23:: ::24:: ::25:: ::26::   ::27:: ::28:: ::29:: ::30:: ::31::

PHYSICAL FUNCTION

01 Sleep problems
Too much or too little.
::1:: ::2:: ::3:: ::4:: ::5::

02 Eating problems
Too much or too little.
::1:: ::2:: ::3:: ::4:: ::5::

03 Enuresis, soiling
::1:: ::2:: ::3:: ::4:: ::5::

04 Seizures, convulsions
::1:: ::2:: ::3:: ::4:: ::5::

05 Speech articulation problem
::1:: ::2:: ::3:: ::4:: ::5::

06 Other physical problems
::1:: ::2:: ::3:: ::4:: ::5::

07 INTELLECTUAL DEVELOP.
Estimate if IQ score unavailable.

120+	110-119	86-109	68-85	below 68
super bright	average	dull	retard	

SOCIAL RELATIONS

08 With children
Impairment of expected parental role with his child(ren). Consider performance of expected tasks, comfort and satisfaction.
::1:: ::2:: ::3:: ::4:: ::5::

09 With mate, spouse
Impairment in satisfaction, comfort and performance of expected social and sexual activities with his mate or spouse (include common-law).
::1:: ::2:: ::3:: ::4:: ::5::

10 With other family
Impairment in satisfaction, comfort and performance of expected social activities with other family members (sibs, parents, cousins, in-laws).
::1:: ::2:: ::3:: ::4:: ::5::

11 With other people
Impairment in satisfaction, comfort and performance of expected social activities with other people (not in family).
::1:: ::2:: ::3:: ::4:: ::5::

SOCIAL PERFORMANCE

12 School
Impairment in performance as a student. Consider grades, work habits, missed classes. If not going to school because of psychopathology, rate 5.
::1:: ::2:: ::3:: ::4:: ::5::

13 Job
Impairment in performance of job. Include missing work, need for supervision. If not working because of psychopathology, rate 5. If retired leave blank.
::1:: ::2:: ::3:: ::4:: ::5::

14 Housekeeping
Impairment in the performance of duties associated with caring for home and family. Consider shopping, cleaning, cooking.
::1:: ::2:: ::3:: ::4:: ::5::

OTHER SIGNS AND SYMPTOMS

15 Suicidal thoughts
Suicidal thoughts or preoccupation.
::1:: ::2:: ::3:: ::4:: ::5::

16 Suicidal acts, gestures
Suicidal acts, attempts or gestures. Consider threat to life.
::1:: ::2:: ::3:: ::4:: ::5::

17 Anxiety, fears, phobias
Feelings of apprehension, worry, anxiety, nervousness, tension, fear and phobia(s).
::1:: ::2:: ::3:: ::4:: ::5::

18 Obsessions, compulsions
Unwanted recurrent thoughts, acts, or routines, the content or purpose of which he regards as senseless.
::1:: ::2:: ::3:: ::4:: ::5::

19 Depressed mood, inferiority
Feelings of sadness, depression, worthlessness, inadequacy, remorse, guilt, failure or loss.
::1:: ::2:: ::3:: ::4:: ::5::

20 Somatic concerns, hypochond.
Excessive concerns with bodily functions; preoccupation with one or more real or imagined physical complaints or disabilities.
::1:: ::2:: ::3:: ::4:: ::5::

21 Social withdrawal, isolation
Avoidance of contact or involvement with people; preference for being alone; feelings of isolation, rejection or discomfort with people.
::1:: ::2:: ::3:: ::4:: ::5::

22 Dependency, clinging
Feelings of being unable to cope without assistance, praise, or reassurance from others; clings to other people in order to get them to take care of him.
::1:: ::2:: ::3:: ::4:: ::5::

23 Grandiosity
Inflated appraisal of his worth, contacts, power or knowledge.
::1:: ::2:: ::3:: ::4:: ::5::

24 Suspicion, persecution
From mild suspiciousness to belief that he is being persecuted. Examples: distrustfulness; feels mistreated or taken advantage of; feels people stare at him.
::1:: ::2:: ::3:: ::4:: ::5::

25 Delusions
Conviction(s) in some important personal belief which is almost certainly not true.
::1:: ::2:: ::3:: ::4:: ::5::

26 Hallucinations
Hears voices or sounds; sees, feels, smells, or tastes something with no external source.
::1:: ::2:: ::3:: ::4:: ::5::

27 Anger, belligerence, negativism
Overt anger, belligerence, or negativism. Examples: evasive, argumentative, sarcastic, acts or threats of violence.
::1:: ::2:: ::3:: ::4:: ::5::

28 Assaultive acts
Actual physical violence or assault against some person.
::1:: ::2:: ::3:: ::4:: ::5::

29 Alcohol abuse
Alcohol use is excessive, causes physical symptoms, alteration in mood or behavior, or interferes with routine or duties.
::1:: ::2:: ::3:: ::4:: ::5::

30 Narcotics, other drugs
Excessive self medication, unprescribed use of narcotics, barbiturates, stimulants, or consciousness expanding substances.
::1:: ::2:: ::3:: ::4:: ::5::

31 Antisocial attitudes, acts
Lying; stealing; swindling; "conning;" encouraging breaking of rules; minor or serious illegal acts.
::1:: ::2:: ::3:: ::4:: ::5::

32 Sexual problems
Impairment in performance or satisfaction in sexual activities, homosexual or other perverse impulses or behavior.
::1:: ::2:: ::3:: ::4:: ::5::

33 Agitation, hyperactivity
Overt tension, agitation or hyperactivity. Examples: fidgeting, inability to sit still; pacing, fast speech. Do not include mere subjective restlessness or tension.
::1:: ::2:: ::3:: ::4:: ::5::

34 Disorientation, memory
Signs that he does not know where he is, the date or time of day, or who he is; impairment in memory of recent or past events.
::1:: ::2:: ::3:: ::4:: ::5::

35 Speech disorg., incoherence
Impairment in the form of speech which makes it difficult to follow or understand. Examples: speech aimless, too detailed, phrases or thoughts have little logical connection, makes no sense, rapid changes of topic so ideas are not completed.
::1:: ::2:: ::3:: ::4:: ::5::

36 Slowed up, lack of emotion
Slowing down or lack of speech or movements; lack of emotional expression or response in face, speech or gestures.
::1:: ::2:: ::3:: ::4:: ::5::

37 Daily routine, leisure time
Inability or refusal to do usual daily activities or to carry through tasks which he or others expect him to do; impairment in pleasure or ability in leisure time activities.
::1:: ::2:: ::3:: ::4:: ::5::

38 Inapprop. affect., appear., behav.
Inappropriate, odd, or strange affect, appearance or behavior.
::1:: ::2:: ::3:: ::4:: ::5::

Primary problem (Number of scale. 01 to 38. Leave blank if unknown.)
::0:: ::1:: ::2:: ::3::

::0:: ::1:: ::2:: ::3:: ::4::   ::5:: ::6:: ::7:: ::8:: ::9::

Overall severity condition or impairment
Clinicians's judgment of overall severity whether due to psychopathology or social factors or a combination of these.
::1:: ::2:: ::3:: ::4:: ::5::

Duration of condition or impairment less than Present or most recent episode showing continuous evidence of disturbance; if chronic, when a noticeable change in intensity or nature occurs.
1wk   2wk   1mo   3mo   6mo   1yr   2yr   2yr+

Signature

Date

Comments

* Developed by Robert L. Spitzer, M.D. and Jean Endicott, Ph.D., Biometrics Research, N.Y.S. Department of Mental Hygiene, with the assistance of the Multi-State Information System for Psychiatric Patients Project. Supported by N.Y.S. Department of Mental Hygiene, C29820 and NIMH Grant 14934.

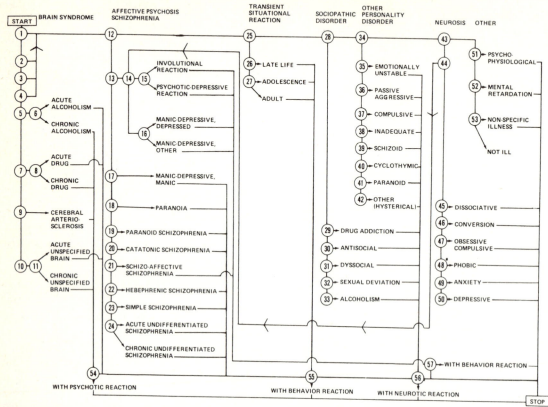

Figure 5-2. This flowchart shows that the CAPPS decision process involves a systematic consideration, one by one, of the diagnoses that would be most appropriate for a given set of pathological behaviors. *(Spitzer and Endicott, 1969, p. 15)*

great amounts of complex data very quickly. The other is that the diagnostic process is *always the same.* Human clinicians sometimes apply the rules of diagnostic decision making inconsistently; computers do only what they are told.

A part of the most comprehensive of the computer-based scales, the *Current and Past Psychopathology Scales* (CAPPS: Spitzer & Endicott, 1971), is shown in Figure 5-1. Most of the decisions required in CAPPS call for judgments along a five-point scale of severity ranging from 1 (none) to 5 (severe). Since CAPPS is tailored to computer analysis, one of these completed scales can be converted quickly to computer input data and processed to yield a reliable diagnosis. That is, with a

given set of raw data describing a patient, a computer program which has been written to process data from CAPPS will always produce the same diagnosis, thus avoiding the common problem of low diagnostic agreement among several clinicians.

The program written to process CAPPS input data is summarized in the flowchart shown in Figure 5-2. Designed to simulate the decision processes that the human clinician uses in making diagnoses, the CAPPS computer program follows a so-called logical-decision-tree model. As the figure shows, the process begins by asking whether the interviewer has given high scores to CAPPS items reflecting signs of organic brain disorder. If not, then the computer scans the cues to psychotic disorder. If these too are all negative, it scans the signs of transient situational disorders—and so on, through the sociopathic disorders, the remaining personality disorders, the neuroses, the psychophysiologic reactions, mental retardation, and finally "nonspecific illness." If all can be eliminated, the conclusion is that the patient is not mentally ill.

Although CAPPS offers a way to increase diagnostic reliability (meaning precision), does it also promise to increase diagnostic validity (meaning usefulness)? Spitzer and Endicott asked this question in 1969. To answer it they compared CAPPS computer diagnoses with diagnoses by clinicians. For each patient, four diagnoses were made: one by a rater who also completed CAPPS, two by diagnosticians

who independently examined the first rater's CAPPS records, and one by a computer program processing the CAPPS data. The results showed that computer-generated diagnoses agreed with diagnoses by the clinicians as often as the clinicians agreed with each other. This suggests that the computer program could validly predict a diagnosis produced by an experienced diagnostician.

Another computer-oriented rating scale, the *Boston City Hospital–Behavior Checklist* (BCH–BCL), was prepared by making a systems analysis of the entire diagnostic process (Nathan, 1967). Like CAPPS, the BCH–BCL was designed to increase the reliability of traditional diagnostic procedures. Unlike CAPPS, each BCH–BCL item is bipolar, re-

Figure 5-3. Portion of a flowchart showing the processes by which the most important cues to psychosis and neurosis are to be processed by the computer. *(Nathan et al., 1968.)*

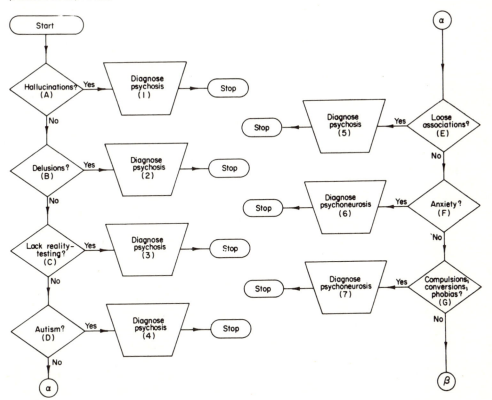

TABLE 5-1. GROUP 1: GROSS PRESENTING SYMPTOMS

Yes	Does patient:
—(1)	*HALLUCINATE?
—(2)	*Show DELUSIONS?
—(3)	*Lack REALITY TESTING?
—(4)	*Show AUTISM?
—(5)	*Show LOOSE ASSOCIATIONS?
—(6)	*Verbalize persistent ANXIETY?
—(7)	*Show COMPULSIVE, CONVERSIONAL or PHOBIC behavior?

Yes	Is patient:
—(8)	*DEPRESSED
—(8a)	**If (8):** In the ABSENCE of an APPROPRIATE RECENT EVENT or as INAPPROPRIATE RESPONSE to one?
—(8b)	**(or)** In APPROPRIATE RESPONSE to a RECENT EVENT?
—(9a)	WILLING TO ADMIT HIS ILLNESS and SUFFERING FROM IT?
—(9b)	**(or)** UNWILLING TO ADMIT ILLNESS?

Yes	Are patient's:
—(10)	EMOTIONS MORE OR LESS PRONOUNCED THAN NORMAL?
—(10a)	**If (10):** In APPROPRIATE RESPONSE to RECENT EVENTS?
—(10b)	**(or)** In the apparent ABSENCE of APPROPRIATE ENVIRONMENTAL STIMULI?
—(11)	*Symptoms producing SECONDARY GAIN which he strives to maintain?
	Continue to first relevant group.

SOURCE: Nathan, 1969.

quiring only a yes or no answer. This format was chosen to maximize the likelihood that a cue to which the interviewer answered yes would in fact characterize the patient's behavior. (A multipoint scale like that used by CAPPS enables the interviewer to take a middle course whenever he is doubtful, whereas the yes-no option forces him to answer no.) The section of the BCH BCL corresponding to the flowchart shown in Figure 5-3 is given in Table 5-1.

Both Spitzer's CAPPS and Nathan's BCH-BCL show promise in that they seem to offer much higher diagnostic reliability than traditional interview or rating scale procedures—

provided, of course, that the same diagnostic input data are used. But reliability of assessment is only the beginning of the diagnostic job. For this reason, both Nathan and Spitzer have emphasized that they believe reliability of measurement is only the beginning of diagnosis.

Psychological tests and psychodiagnosis

In addition to symptom rating scales, a great assortment of psychological tests is used in the effort to systematize and objectify psychiatric diagnosis. The entire field of clinical psychology evolved as an applied discipline because of the special training and experience it gave students in testing and personality assessment.

Many people trace the beginning of clinical psychology to the work of Alfred Binet, the French psychologist who developed a standardized test of intelligence. His aim was to differentiate between French schoolchildren who could benefit from a public school curriculum and those who needed special schooling. His test, created at the beginning of the twentieth century, was successively improved until it became what are now the Stanford-Binet Scales of Intelligence.

During the 1930s other psychologists developed the Wechsler intelligence tests for children and adults, the objective tests of personality (the MMPI, the California Psychological Inventory, and others), and the projective personality measures (the Rorschach test, the Thematic Apperception Test, and others). By the early 1940s the intelligence tests had proved their effectiveness, and it was generally agreed that the personality tests showed promise. A modest but growing number of psychologists had been trained in their use. During World War II the still-new profession of clinical psychology was given a major role in selecting, classifying, and placing hundreds of thousands of draftees. That responsibility, combined with the demand for mental health professionals who could deal with the psychological casualties of war, brought clinical psychology to its present position as one of the mental health professions.

But psychologists are now questioning the view that special training in psychological testing ought to be a major component of an education in clinical psychology (Matulef et al., 1972; McCully 1965; Thelen et al., 1968). As we will discuss shortly, many of their doubts stem from the serious reliability and validity problems the projective techniques have posed (Jackson & Wohl, 1966). Today some established clinical psychology programs are providing less training in projective testing and more in objective testing. And some new programs, as well as a few old ones, have begun to deemphasize psychodiagnostic testing altogether (Shemberg & Keeley, 1970).

This disenchantment with testing also reflects a broader effort to develop a workable alternative to DSM II. Some research studies suggest that it is valuable to therapists to have psychological reports which assign patients to the traditional DSM II "Pigeonholes" (Affleck & Strider, 1971). But many other studies indicate that therapists find these studies useless and rarely look at them (Moore et al., 1968; Olive, 1972).

Just how much do psychological tests help mental health professionals understand, evaluate, and treat mental disorder? The following sections attempt to give you an objective answer.

Intelligence tests as measures of psychopathology

Of course, the standard tests of intelligence are used largely to measure intellectual capacity for education (These tests are the Stanford-Binet Scales and the pair of Wechsler Scales: the WISC or Wechsler Intelligence Scale for Children, and the WAIS or Wechsler Adult Intelligence Scale.) (Figure 5-4 shows the WAIS summary of a college student's IQ test performance.) They have two other functions, however, which come closer to the concerns of this book. The first is documentation of severe mental retardation, which is discussed in Chapter 16. The second is that in some particulars they seem to serve as indicators of psychopathology.

Through the years, most research on the relationships between mental disorder and intellectual performance has reported three findings (Burdock & Hardesty, 1973; Rabin, 1965; Rabin & Guertin, 1951):

1 The patterning of performance on IQ tests is helpful in diagnosis (Rapaport et al., 1945; Watson, 1965). For example, when a person does much worse on IQ tasks requiring short-term memory than on tasks requiring reasoning, motor skills, and long-term memory, it may be a sign that he is disabled by anxiety. And this result can be the first indication that anxiety is a factor in his disorder, since he may not have been able to verbalize it in talking to the clinician.

2 Even before their disordered behavior is disabling enough as to call attention to itself, the behavioral problems of mental patients cause them to score lower on standard tests of intelligence than their normal siblings or peers (Lane & Albee, 1970; Miller et al., 1971).

3 Mental patients do less well on IQ tests during periods of acute turmoil than at times when they are less emotional (Hamlin & Ward, 1973).

These conclusions were recently reexamined in a carefully conceived study by Burdock and Hardesty (1973). The subjects were newly admitted patients to the New York State Psychiatric Institute. Shortly after admission, they were given an individually administered measure of psychopathology (the Structured Clinical Interview, Burdock & Hardesty, 1969) and a full-scale WAIS (Wechsler Adult Intelligence Scale). There were 148 patients: 65 men and 83 women, ranging in age from 18 to 72. They were assigned six diagnostic labels; more than 60 percent of the labels described one of the schizophrenias.

Results from this study failed to support points 2 and 3 above about IQ and psychopathology. That is, although all the patients in the sample were so disordered that they required hospitalization (most scored in the disordered range on the Structured Clinical Interview), their average WAIS score was 104.3. Since the average score of the general

WAIS RECORD FORM
Wechsler Adult Intelligence Scale

Name _Scott_ ▮▮▮
Birth Date _3_ _14_ _50_ Age _18_ Sex _M_ Marital: (S) M D W
Nat. _US_ ᴹᴼ ᴰᴬʸ ʸᴿ Color _W_ Tested by ▮▮▮
Place of Examination ▮▮▮ Date _11/27/1968_
Occupation _College Student_ Education _High School_

TABLE OF SCALED SCORE EQUIVALENTS*

RAW SCORE

Scaled Score	Information	Comprehension	Arithmetic	Similarities	Digit Span	Vocabulary	Digit Symbol	Picture Completion	Block Design	Picture Arrangement	Object Assembly	Scaled Score
19	29	27-28		26	17	78-80	87-90			36	44	19
18	28	26		25		76-77	83-86	21		35	43	18
17	27	25	18	24		74-75	79-82		48	34	42	17
16	26	24	17	23	16	71-73	76-78	20	47	33	41	16
15	25	23	16	22	15	67-70	72-75		46	32	40	15
14	23-24	22	15	21	14	63-66	69-71	19	44-45	32	40	14
13	21-22	21	14	19-20		59-62	66-68	18	42-43	30-31	38-39	13
12	19-20	20	13	17-18	13	54-58	62-65	17	39-41	28-29	36-37	12
11	17-18	19	12	15-16	12	47-53	58-61	15-16	35-38	26-27	34-35	11
10	15-16	17-18	11	13-14	11	40-46	52-57	14	31-34	23-25	31-33	10
9	13-14	15-16	10	11-12	10	32-39	47-51	12-13	28-30	20-22	28-30	9
8	11-12	14	9	9-10		26-31	41-46	10-11	25-27	18-19	25-27	8
7	9-10	12-13	7-8	7-8	9	22-25	35-40	8-9	21-24	15-17	22-24	7
6	7-8	10-11	6	5-6	8	18-21	29-34	6-7	17-20	12-14	19-21	6
5	5-6	8-9	5	4		14-17	23-28	5	13-16	9-11	15-18	5
4	4	6-7	4	3	7	11-13	18-22	4	10-12	8	11-14	4
3	3	5	3	2		10	15-17	3	6-9	7	8-10	3
2	2	4	2	1	6		13-14	2	3-5	6	5-7	2
1	1	3	1		4-5	8	12	1	2	5	3-4	1
0	0	0-2	0	0	0-3	0-7	0-11	0	0-1	0-4	0-2	0

SUMMARY

TEST	Raw Score	Scaled Score
Information	21	13
Comprehension	23	15
Arithmetic	13	12
Similarities	20	13
Digit Span	14	14
Vocabulary	68	15
Verbal Score		82
Digit Symbol	66	13
Picture Completion	20	16
Block Design	43	13
Picture Arrangement	21	9
Object Assembly	40	14
Performance Score		65
Total Score		147

VERBAL SCORE _82_ IQ _124_
PERFORMANCE SCORE _65_ IQ _120_
FULL SCALE SCORE _147_ IQ _124_

*Clinicians who wish to draw a "psychograph" on the above table may do so by connecting the subject's raw scores. The interpretation of any such profile, however, should take into account the reliabilities of the subtests and the lower reliabilities of *differences* between subtest scores.

I. INFORMATION

	SCORE 1 or 0		SCORE 1 or 0			SCORE 1 or 0
1. Flag		11. height	1	21. Senator		1
2. Ball		12. Italy	1	22. Genesis		
3. Month		13. Clothes	1	23. Temperature	170 F	0
4. Thermometer		14. Washington	1	24. Iliad		1
5. Rubber	1	15. name	1	25. Linen from	C V	0
6. Presidents	1	16. Vatican	1	26. Koran	DK	0
7. Longfellow	1	17. Paris	1	27. Faust	Homer	0
8. Weeks	1	18. Egypt	1	28. Ethnology	DK	0
9. Panama	1	19. Yeast	1	29. Apocrypha	DK	0
10. Brazil	C Am	0	20. Population	120 M	0	21

OBSERVATIONS:

Figure 5-4. This WAIS record summarizes the IQ test performance of Scott, the college student whose intake interview at a college counseling center was reproduced in Figure 2-1.

population is 100, these results refute the common view that mental patients have lower than average IQs. The study also found, contrary to expectation, that overall intellectual performance and severity of psychopathology did not correlate.

But the study did turn up some significant correlations between performance on certain WAIS subtests and degree of psychopathology. The most striking was a negative correlation between severity of psychopathology and adequacy of performance on the "similarities" subtest of the WAIS. That is, the more severe the patient's disorder, the worse his ability to think abstractly (as measured by the "similarities" subtest). This relationship between abstract thinking ability and severity of psychopathology has long been a controversial one. Discovering it in a study which failed to find other correlations between intellectual performance and psychopathology increases our conviction that the relationship is important.

We, the authors, believe that severe psychopathology does affect intellectual performance. But in view of the disparity between Burdock and Hardesty's data and the studies reported by others, we conclude that relationships between thinking ability and psychopathology take many forms. Therefore they may not be predictable from a diagnostic label or from a measure of the severity of psychopathology.

Personality tests as measures of psychopathology

As discussed in Chapter 4, *personality* is a word that means one thing to people who use it in its familiar context and something else to professionals (like Mischel, Bandura, and Freud) who use it technically. When a layman remarks that someone "has a good personality," he means that the person is easy to be with, a good companion, and a faithful friend. But when psychologists speak of personality, they are usually thinking in terms of relatively enduring belief systems, attitudes toward central moral and ethical concerns, and behavioral predispositions. Freud uses it in this sense.

David Wechsler.

Mischel and Bandura, by contrast, use it to describe "situation-specific" determinants of human behavior—those that have to do with past and present environmental variables.

In both technical uses of the word, the precise nature of relationships between personality factors and actual behavior can only be guessed at and hypothesized about. In fact, these guesses make up the sum and substance of most theories of personality. But psychologists are constantly searching for ways to base their theories on more than guesses, and in the process they have developed many formal measures of personality.

Objective and projective tests of personality. *Objective* tests of personality depend upon direct self-reports of attitudes, beliefs, feelings, and other indications of past, present, and future behavior to paint the "picture of personality." *Projective* tests of personality assess behavior by indirect or disguised means, in an effort to capture unconscious or forgotten determinants of behavior and personality. The intention of projective tests is to decrease a patient's ability to censor what he reveals of himself to others.

Bill H., whose case was described at the beginning of the chapter, was given an objective test of personality (the MMPI) and two projective tests (the Rorschach and the TAT). The MMPI required him to respond with yes or no to such questions as "Have you ever used alcohol to excess?" Because Bill was afraid that if he answered yes he would not be admitted to the hospital, he answered no. But when he kept seeing bottles, cans, and other containers of liquid in the ambiguous Rorschach inkblots, the psychologist who analyzed the test wondered whether Bill might be an alcoholic. So in this instance, Bill's projective test performance was more descriptive of one aspect of his psychopathology than his objective test performance.

For the most part, however, the few empirical studies that have compared the validities of direct (objective) and indirect (projective) tests have shown that the direct ones are superior (Kidder & Campbell, 1970; Stricker et al., 1968). In other words, the direct, objective measures have predicted behavior more accurately than indirect, projective measures. Still, most of this research used a limited range of indirect tests to predict a limited range of behaviors (Scott & Johnson, 1972). A recent series of studies was designed by Scott and Johnson to explore the objective-projective question in detail. These researchers used a number of tests and aimed to predict a variety of attitudes (political, sexual, racial, and personal), motives (achievement, affiliation, creativity, contemplation, privacy, etc.), and socially unacceptable behavior patterns (rejection of blacks and Mexican-Americans, disrespect for authority, absence of long-term goals, etc.). The measures included several direct tests and a group of indirect ones (which asked the subjects to judge the effectiveness of arguments, predict the consequences of hypothetical events, and write imaginative stories about TAT pictures). When the relative accuracy of the two kinds of tests was com-

pared, Scott and Johnson got the same results as the earlier studies: the direct measures were consistently superior to the indirect measures in predicting attitudes, beliefs, and socially unacceptable behavior patterns.

An objective test: The MMPI. As an example of an objective measure of personality and psychopathology, take the Minnesota Multiphasic Personality Inventory (MMPI). This is the most widely used of the objective measures of behavior, and it illustrates the major strengths and weaknesses of them all. Keep in mind, though, that it is only one among many. Other well-known tests include the California Psychological Inventory (Gough, 1964), the 16 Personality Factor Questionnaire (Cattell & Stice, 1957), the Eysenck Personality Inventory (Eysenck, 1957), the Guilford-Zimmerman Temperament Survey (Guilford & Zimmerman, 1949), and the Edwards Personal Preference Schedule (Edwards, 1959).

The MMPI is a self-report scale consisting of 566 statements. The subject marks each one true or false, meaning that he does or does not view the statement as descriptive of his behavior. The MMPI items were selected from a much larger group of statements drawn from psychiatric and psychological sources. The test can be scored according to ten basic psychiatric-personality scales and three "validity" scales. A subject's pattern of responding to the test items can be converted into a *profile* which shows whether his responses were deviant on any of the ten basic scales.

The scales were composed empirically: In preliminary tests the authors of the MMPI (Hathaway and McKinley) gave large numbers of potential items to over 800 psychiatric patients and more than 1,500 control (nonpatient) subjects. They compared responses by patients and nonpatients to each item in order to determine which items were sensitive both to the diagnostic differences between the psychiatric and control groups and to the finer differences among psychiatric patient groups. Here are the ten clinical scales constructed from the 566 MMPI items that were finally selected:

Scale 1. *Hypochondriasis:* Patients scoring high on this scale are overly concerned about their physical health and may have actual physical disorders which are psychological in origin.

Scale 2. *Depression:* Patients are often intensely unhappy, hopeless about the future, and lacking in self-esteem.

Scale 3. *Hysteria:* While many of these patients have physical symptoms that are psychological in origin, they are often surprisingly unconcerned about the symptoms. It is thought that they "convert" psychological turmoil into physical symptoms, some of which are quite dramatic.

Scale 4. *Psychopathic Deviate:* Patients have difficulty adjusting to society; sometimes their histories show delinquency and other antisocial behavior.

Scale 5. *Masculinity-Femininity:* Males scoring high on this scale either have "feminine" values, interests, attitudes, and styles of expression, or are well educated and therefore interested in cultural and academic topics. (Such interests were considered "feminine" by the subjects on whom the MMPI was originally validated.) The scale is of uncertain value so far as women are concerned.

Scale 6. *Paranoia:* Though they are rarely given an actual diagnosis of paranoia, these patients may be suspicious and extremely sensitive to other people's feelings about them. In some cases they may have delusions of grandeur or persecution.

Scale 7. *Psychasthenia:* Patients may show relatively unfounded fears, high levels of diffuse anxiety, feelings of guilt, and continual doubts about their adequacy in interpersonal situations.

Scale 8. *Schizophrenia:* Patients may have some degree of thought disorder and affective (mood) disturbance. They may also report unusual behavior or thoughts. They may or may not have been given a formal diagnosis of schizophrenia.

Scale 9. *Hypomania:* Patients show excessive activity, easy distractibility, elated mood, and an increased "flow of ideas."

Scale 10. *Social Introversion:* These patients are typically withdrawn, socially isolated, shy, and fearful and anxious about their relations with other people. As a result they are often unsuccessful in social situations.

One of the unique features of the MMPI is its three validity scales, which are designed to reflect the subject's test-taking attitudes. The *Lie Scale* provides a measure of his willingness to be frank in his MMPI responses. It presents 15 statements reflecting socially desirable but rather improbable behaviors (e.g., I never tell a lie; I almost never lose my temper). The *Infrequency Scale,* containing items that called forth the same answers from 90 percent of the original subjects, is designed to identify persons who answer randomly or carelessly—hence invalidly. Finally, the *Defensiveness Scale* is supposed to indicate the person's willingness or unwillingness to respond openly, frankly, and undefensively to test items.

Shortly after the MMPI came into wide use, psychologists found that it was not entirely suitable for its original purpose of clinical diagnosis. Users often reported that high scorers on particular scales seldom fitted the diagnostic categories of those scales. But psychologists then discovered that the MMPI enabled them to make useful clinical discriminations by analyzing combinations or *patterns* of scale scores. Today most of the current, empirically derived interpretative manuals for the MMPI suggest profile or pattern analysis of the test rather than interpretation from single scale peaks (Dahlstrom et al., 1972; Gilberstadt, 1970; Gilberstadt & Duker, 1965; Lanyon, 1968).

Bill H. took the MMPI shortly after he was admitted to Boston City Hospital. His profile showed significant peaks on Scales 1, 2, 4, and 7; 2 ("depression") was the highest. Gilberstadt suggests that this pattern is associated with "chronic alcoholism which may lead to delirium tremens. Anxious, tense, inferiority feelings, guilt. Severe marital conflict. Dependent on wives and mothers" (Gilberstadt, 1970, p. 25).

Many investigators have concluded that the

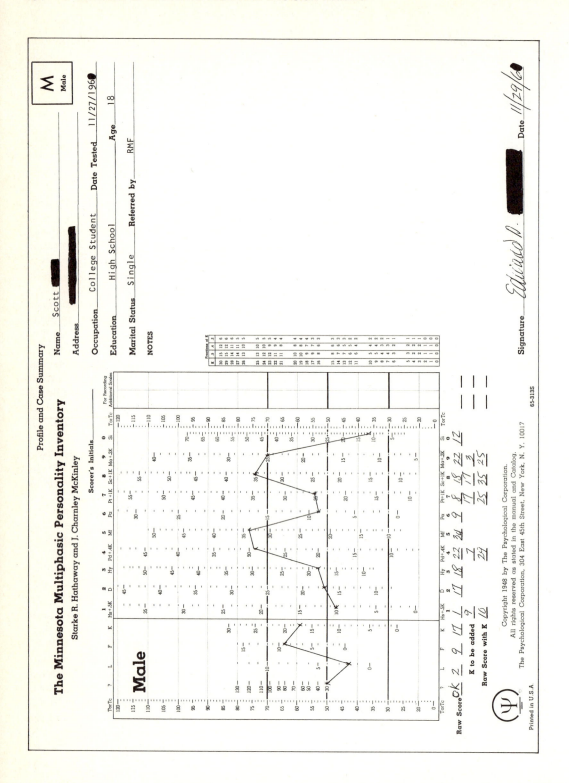

MMPI is among the most reliable of all the psychological tests (Dahlstrom, 1970; Goldberg, 1970; Meehl, 1959). *Reliability* of the MMPI means that a person taking the test at different times will give about the same answers each time, that a person scoring the test will do so accurately, and that a person interpreting MMPI profiles will do so according to the same "rules" day in and day out.

What about the MMPI's *validity?* In general, the test has proved most valuable when called upon to make gross distinctions between individuals or groups of individuals. When employed to label a given patient as either psychotic or neurotic, the MMPI is successful around 70 percent of the time (Goldberg, 1965; Meehl & Dahlstrom, 1960; Zelin, 1971). When used to identify significant behavioral differences between groups of neurotic and psychotic patients, the MMPI's acuracy rises above to 90 percent (Goldberg, 1972). The MMPI has reflected valid differences between normal and "maladjusted" college students (Kleinmuntz, 1963), between newly admitted and about-to-be-discharged psychotic patients (Graham et al., 1973), and between juvenile delinquents and nondelinquents (Follman, 1972). The MMPI has also proved helpful in personality research: it has, for example, identified differences in personality and behavior between persons who can tolerate ambiguous situations and those who cannot, and creative and uncreative persons (Diamond, 1971; Smith, 1972).

On the negative side, the MMPI has not been consistently useful in differentiating among the subtypes of schizophrenia (Young, 1972), among drug abusers with psychotic, "latent" psychotic, and nonpsychotic diagnoses (Fitzgibbons et al., 1973), or between the organic brain syndromes and other physical and psychopathological conditions (Sand, 1973). Its record has been mixed in identifying alcoholics in populations of nonpsychiatric patients, measuring response to psychotherapy, and predicting length of psychiatric hospitalization for a variety of patients (Dobbs, 1970; Garfield et al., 1971; Johnston & Cooke, 1973).

MMPI researchers have led the way in taking advantage of computer technology for diagnostic purposes. One of the pioneers was Kleinmuntz, who programmed a computer to identify maladjusted college students from their MMPI profiles (1963, 1968). Around the same time, Fowler translated MMPI scoring keys and empirically based rules for diagnostic decision making into a computer format (1967). That format, now in active commercial development by a large drug company, is said to yield reliable MMPI reports (Fowler, 1969). A sample of the automated MMPI is given in Figure 5-6. Recent studies suggest that it provides information which is at least as useful as that produced by an experienced clinician (Webb et al., 1970).

Two projective tests: The Rorschach and the TAT. The Rorschach inkblot technique and the Thematic Apperception Text (TAT) are the two most commonly used projective tests in the vast storehouse available to psychologists. Unlike the MMPI, which asks specific questions that are to be answered True or False, the Rorschach asks the subject to apply his own perceptual structure to an ambiguous stimulus. He looks at a set of random inkblots and sees people, places, or things in them. The TAT asks the subject to look at a single structured stimulus—a picture of people engaged in undefined, ambiguous behavior—and tell a story. The story may or may not stick closely to the original picture, and may or may not involve the subject himself. In both of these tests, the subject is being called upon to *project* his or her own fantasies, perceptions, and thoughts onto a stimulus that is deliberately left vague.

Hermann Rorschach, a Jungian analyst, published his *Psychodiagnostik* in 1921. His original purpose in experimenting with ten

Figure 5-5. The MMPI profile of Scott, the student whose WAIS record is given in Figure 5-4. The lines connecting the scores on the several scales (vertical rows of numbers) constitute the "profile"—a pattern that helps the clinician see how the various scores relate to one another.

ROCHE PSYCHIATRIC SERVICE INSTITUTE

MMPI REPORT

CASE NO: ███   RPSI. NO: ███
AGE 18 MALE   DEC.09,196█

        IN RESPONDING TO THE TEST ITEMS IT APPEARS THAT
THE PATIENT MADE AN EFFORT TO ANSWER TRUTHFULLY WITHOUT AT-
TEMPTING TO DENY OR EXAGGERATE.
        THIS PATIENT APPEARS TO BE CURRENTLY DEPRESSED.
HE SHOWS A PERSONALITY PATTERN WHICH IS FREQUENT AMONG PSYCH-
IATRIC PATIENTS. FEELINGS OF INADEQUACY, SEXUAL CONFLICT AND
RIGIDITY ARE ACCOMPANIED BY A LOSS OF EFFICIENCY, INITIATIVE
AND SELF-CONFIDENCE. INSOMNIA IS LIKELY TO OCCUR ALONG WITH
CHRONIC ANXIETY, FATIGUE AND TENSION. HE MAY HAVE SUICIDAL
THOUGHTS. IN THE CLINICAL PICTURE DEPRESSION IS THE DOMINANT
FEATURE. PSYCHIATRIC PATIENTS WITH THIS PATTERN ARE LIKELY
TO BE DIAGNOSED AS DEPRESSIVES, OR ANXIETY REACTIONS. THE
CHARACTERISTICS ARE RESISTANT TO CHANGE AND WILL TEND TO RE-
MAIN STABLE WITH TIME.
        THERE ARE UNUSUAL QUALITIES IN THIS PATIENT'S
THINKING WHICH MAY REPRESENT AN ORIGINAL OR ECCENTRIC ORIEN-
TATION OR PERHAPS SOME SCHIZOID TENDENCIES. FURTHER INFORMA-
TION IS REQUIRED TO MAKE THIS DETERMINATION.
        HE APPEARS TO BE A PERSON WHO REPRESSES AND DENIES
EMOTIONAL DISTRESS. WHILE HE MAY RESPOND READILY TO ADVICE
AND REASSURANCE HE IS HESITANT TO ACCEPT A PSYCHOLOGICAL EX-
PLANATION OF HIS DIFFICULTIES. IN TIMES OF PROLONGED EMO-
TIONAL STRESS, HE IS LIKELY TO DEVELOP PHYSICAL SYMPTOMS. HE
IS PARTICULARLY VULNERABLE TO PSYCHOPHYSIOLOGICAL SYMPTOMS
SUCH AS HEADACHES, TACHYCARDIA AND GASTROINTESTINAL DIS-
ORDERS.
        HE APPEARS TO BE A SOCIAL NON-CONFORMER WITH A
HISTORY OF TROUBLED INTERPERSONAL RELATIONSHIPS. HE HAS DIF-
FICULTY ACCEPTING LIMITS AND MAY EXHIBIT ASOCIAL BEHAVIOR.
HE IS ANGRY AND RESENTFUL, PARTICULARLY TOWARD PERSONS IN
AUTHORITY.
        HE SHOWS SOME CONCERN ABOUT HIS PHYSICAL HEALTH.
HE MAY OVER-REACT TO MINOR ILLNESSES, PERHAPS USING THEM AS A
MEANS OF AVOIDING DIFFICULT SITUATIONS. HE IS LIKELY TO BE
A RIGID, SOMEWHAT SELF-CENTERED PERSON.
        HE IS INCLINED TO BE OVERLY SENSITIVE TO THE RE-
SPONSES AND INTENTIONS OF THOSE AROUND HIM. HE CHRONICALLY
MISINTERPRETS THE WORDS AND ACTIONS OF OTHERS WHICH LEADS TO
DIFFICULTIES IN HIS INTERPERSONAL RELATIONSHIPS.
        HE APPEARS TO BE AN IDEALISTIC, SOCIALLY PERCEP-
TIVE PERSON WHO IS ESTHETIC AND PERHAPS SOMEWHAT FEMININE IN
HIS INTEREST PATTERNS. HE MAY PURSUE ARTISTIC AND CULTURAL
INTERESTS AND REJECT COMPETITIVE ACTIVITIES.
        THIS PERSON MAY BE HESITANT TO BECOME INVOLVED IN
SOCIAL RELATIONSHIPS. HE IS SENSITIVE, RESERVED AND SOME-
WHAT UNEASY, ESPECIALLY IN NEW AND UNFAMILIAR SITUATIONS. HE
MAY COMPENSATE BY UNUSUAL CONSCIENTIOUSNESS IN HIS WORK AND

Figure 5-6.   This automated, or computer-generated, MMPI report summarizes
Scott's MMPI performance. Much of this material, gleaned by the computer from
the MMPI scores, is strikingly similar to the material written by a clinician after a
single interview with Scott (See Figure 2-1).

inkblots that made up his test was to separate people into Jung's introversive and extroversive personality types.

From this modest beginning the uses of the Rorschach technique have expanded tremendously for both clinicians and researchers. On each of the ten cards is an inkblot design (see Figure 5-7). The subject is shown a card at a time and is asked to tell the examiner everything he or she sees in the card. After going through all the cards once, the examiner and subject turn through them again in order to get additional information for formal scoring purposes. Scoring of each Rorschach response (formally called a *percept*) takes these factors into account: What parts of the card were incorporated in the percept? How much of the card did the subject use in the percept? What element or elements of the visual stimulus did the percept depend upon (color, form, texture, etc.)? What was the content of the percept (human, animal, anatomical, etc.)?

Early in the history of the Rorschach technique, diagnosticians began to use the scores as "signs" of various mental disorders. Piotrowski (1937) identified Rorschach "signs" of organic brain damage, Harrower-Erikson (1945) compiled the "signs" of neurosis, and Beck (1938) described the "signs" of schizophrenia. At about the same time Fosberg (1938) wrote glowingly that the Rorschach was a foolproof device for defining personality.

Since that time of youthful enthusiasm, research on the Rorschach has revealed serious limitations in its usefulness. Psychologists who were once its champions admit that the technique does not have the diagnostic promise they originally thought (Klopfer, 1968, 1973). Instead of using the Rorschach as an all-purpose diagnostic instrument, they now see it as a source of information on personality constructs like ego strength (Glatt, 1972; Holt & Havel, 1960), defensive behavior (Lerner & Shanan, 1972), and character types (Rice & Gaylin, 1973). In part this change in em-

Figure 5-7. Hermann Rorschach, the creator of the Rorschach technique, and an inkblot similar to the ones each of which appears on a Rorschach card. *(Hans Huber Verlag)*

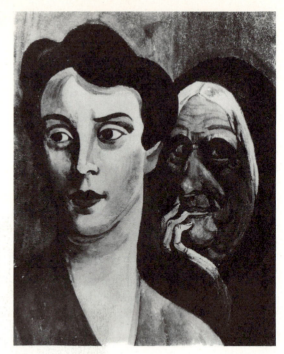

Figure 5-8. Henry Murray, the inventor of the Thematic Apperception Technique (TAT), and a picture like the one found on each TAT card. *(Harvard University News Office)*

phasis reflects a shift from preoccupation with what a patient "has" to what he "does" (Mischel, 1968)—an approach that appears to be more reliable (Goldfried & Kent, 1972). In part it also reflects the lack of "payoff" for efforts to diagnose or to predict behavior directly from Rorschach scores. Most clinicians now believe that Rorschach performance and interpretation are influenced by situational factors rather than just unconscious, unvarying ones (Koscherak & Masling, 1972; Potkay & Ward, 1972).

Seventeen years after Rorschach published *Psychodiagnostik,* Henry Murray's *Explorations in Personality* appeared (1938). That book introduced the Thematic Apperception Technique (TAT) and thereby became a second landmark in the development and popularization of the projective approach to personality.

The TAT contains 31 stimulus cards. Of these, 30 are drawings of various scenes which mostly involve people; 1 card is blank. In the standard presentation the subject is shown 20 cards that have been chosen with his age and sex in mind (see the example shown in Figure 5-8). He is told that the TAT is "a test of imagination" and that he ought to tell as dramatic a story as possible about each card. The story should include what led up to the event in the picture, what is happening now, what the people in the story are thinking and feeling, and what will happen later.

The TAT, like the Rorschach, was originally designed to elicit unconscious fantasy material from patients who were in psychoanalysis. Murray, its originator, stated two important assumptions about behavior on the TAT: (1) The behavior and feelings which the subject describes for the main character in a TAT story represent the subject's own tendencies toward such behavior and feelings. (2) The subject responds to elements in the main character's environment that are most similar to important ones in his own. According to this view, Bill H. would see at least one "problem drinker" in the TAT cards (he did not), as well as at least one person who was having serious marital difficulties (he did).

As with the Rorschach technique, many scoring methods for TAT responses have been suggested in order to convert the test's essentially qualitative (verbal) data to quantitative form. The most widely used is the system proposed by McClelland and his colleagues, which aims to evaluate the subject's *need achievement* motivation (1953). Another TAT scoring system by Zubin and his associates has proved useful for research (1965). So has Murray's own system, which is based on his theory of personality. It scores every TAT story along two dimensions: the subject's *needs* (for food, sex, nurturing, authority, etc.) and the *stresses* he identifies in his environment (say, ill health, poverty, racial bias) which either help him achieve his needs or prevent him from satisfying them.

Though the amount of research which has been done on the reliability and utility of the TAT is second only to that on the Rorschach, "its status as a proven, clinically useful instrument is still in doubt" (Pervin, 1970, p. 54). Part of the doubt stems from the unreliability of the usual method of scoring TAT responses: this involves the qualitative, unsystematic, and largely uncontrolled interpretation of the stories according to psychoanalytic theory. But another aspect of the TAT's low reliability and validity is that it belongs to the group of psychological tests which seek to identify enduring *traits* of character and personality rather than more transitory, situation-specific moods or *states*. Users who like the trait approach (most of whom favor the psychodynamic view of personality) believe that the projective techniques are able to reflect meaningful traits. Critics of this position (many of whom are behaviorists) point to data suggesting that so-called traits have little real value as predictors of behavior. Thus behavioral clinicians tend to avoid projective

tests; instead they prefer to assess behavior as a function of its relevant environmental (situation-specific) determinants.

Future of psychopathologic diagnosis

This chapter has shown that current procedures for diagnosis are generally low in reliability. Furthermore, even the most careful (hence reliable) diagnoses are of limited value in some cases and useless in others.

What is the future of diagnosis in the mental disorders? The answer depends upon which clinician you ask. Pasamanick (1963) and Dreikurs (1963), for example, believe that despite its shortcomings, diagnosis is necessary to a proper understanding of psychopathology. Others (e.g., Kety, 1961) say that it is essential to research on the effectiveness of various treatments. Aside from the practical problems that would result if clinicians had to consider each patient's disorder as new and unique, research on treatment would be virtually impossible if diagnosis and classification were eliminated. On the other hand, it is foolish to continue on and on with the present unsatisfactory system simply because it already exists.

Many solutions to the shortcomings of diagnosis have recently been proposed. Spitzer and Endicott (1969), Nathan (1967, 1969), Lorr (1968), and others believe that the real validity and utility of diagnosis will not be known until diagnostic procedures are made as reliable as they can be. These men and women are therefore concentrating their efforts on reliability. Others, however, are approaching diagnosis through the behavioral model, which emphasizes diagnosis as an aid to development of treatment strategies.

Behavioral approach to diagnosis

Behavioral psychologists have been most active in suggesting diagnostic procedures that are tied directly to treatment planning. One reason is that behavior therapy, in their view, leads to behavior changes which can be measured more precisely than behavior changes following psychoanalytic treatment. Mischel proposes that diagnosis be relabeled *behavior assessment* and redefined as "an attempt to select reasonable treatment objectives" (1968, p. 198). Bill's alcoholism and the circumstances connected with it might be summarized in behavioral terms as "Recurrent uncontrolled drinking when stress is high, money is in adequate supply, and the weather is bad. Treatment, probably most effective during the winter months, might involve desensitization to stress-inducing situations, training in controlled drinking, and development of alternate reinforcing uses for money."

A similar point is made by Tharp and Wetzel in their revolutionary book *Behavior modification in the natural environment* (1969). They argue that current diagnostic procedures must be drastically altered, and that diagnosis and assessment must come before any efforts to change behavior. To Tharp and Wetzel, *accurate description* is the therapist's first task. In their system the diagnostician must:

Assess qualitatively and quantitatively (*a*) the behavioral repertoire of the target; (*b*) the stimulus conditions under which the focal behaviors occur (antecedent events); (*c*) the maintaining stimuli which reinforce the focal behaviors; (*d*) the reinforcement hierarchy of the target; and (*e*) the potentials for mediation in the natural environment. [1969, p. 66]

Here is Tharp and Wetzel's assessment strategy applied to Bill H.'s drinking behavior.

[a] *Target behavior:* Bill H. drinks too much. He drinks every day; he drinks every night. He has continued this maladaptive behavior for more than ten years.

[b] *Antecedent events:* The few times Bill has been sober during the past few years, he has gone back to drinking when he became angry or upset, usually after thinking about the people he has alienated and the chances he has lost in life because of his drinking. At these times he decides that if he takes a drink he won't be so unhappy, because he'll be able to forget.

[c] *Maintaining stimuli:* The powerful stimulus which maintains Bill's drinking behavior once he has begun to drink is the fear of withdrawal symptoms, especially the "horrors"—delirium tremens. To avoid them Bill must continue to drink enough to postpone withdrawal. The stimuli maintaining his return to drink after periods of sobriety are more difficult to specify. They seem to include the superstition that alcohol will help him forget his troubles and be happy again. This belief is a superstition because, in fact, Bill usually becomes more unhappy and more anxious after he has been drinking.

[d] *Reinforcement hierarchy:* Bill's reinforcement hierarchy seems to begin and end with alcohol. Food, clothing, a place to sleep, cleanliness, sex—none of the usual reinforcers seems to hold much allure for Bill once he has begun to drink. Before he begins, though, these things do have some appeal for him. Most attractive to him, perhaps, are the men with whom he shares his skid-row life—the members of his "bottle gang"—for whom he says he would do almost anything.

[e] *Potentials for mediation:* A variety of environmental alterations (group and individual therapy, drugs, A.A.) had failed to alter Bill's drinking behavior. The peculiar role of alcohol as the alcoholic's most potent reinforcer makes this particular behavior change problem an extraordinarily difficult one. Since Bill finds his friendships so reinforcing, it might be that treatment directed toward increasing the relative reinforcement value of *people* and, at the same time, decreasing the reward value of *alcohol* would work for him. Exploratory projects along these lines are described in Chapter 11.

Kanfer and Saslow's diagnostic system, which also stems from the behavioral model, aims to relate diagnostic procedures directly to treatment variables. The system is based on "continuing assessment of the patient's current behaviors and their controlling stimuli" (1965, p. 535). These writers (1969) list the following guidelines for their *behavioral analysis,* which they predict will replace the present-day classification of psychopathology by etiology and symptoms:

1 A detailed description of the particular behavioral excesses or deficits which represent the patient's complaints, and of the behavioral assets which may be available for utilization in a treatment program.

2 A clarification of the problem situation in which the variables are sought that maintain the patient's current problem behaviors. Attention is also given to the consequences of psychiatric intervention on the current adjustment balance of the patient in his social environment.

3 A motivational analysis which attempts to survey the various incentives and aversive conditions representing the dominant motivational factors in the patient.

4 A developmental analysis which suggests consideration of biological, sociological, and behavorial changes in the patient's history which may have relevance for his present complaint and for a treatment program.

5 An analysis of self-control which provides assessment of the patient's capacity for participation in a treatment program and of the conditions which may be necessary to control behaviors with untoward social consequences.

6 An analysis of social relationships which provides the basis for assessing social resources in the patient's environment which have affected his current behavior and may play a role in the therapeutic program.

7 An analysis of the social-cultural-physical environment to assess the degree of congruence between the patient's present milieu, his behavioral repertoire, and the type of therapeutic goals which the therapist can establish. [1969, p. 444]

Toward a dual classification system for the future

Kanfer and Saslow's system, with its emphasis upon the patient's biological and physiological history as well as upon past and present mediating stimuli, is close to our own hopes for a future classification system. We believe that clinicians will evolve a dual classification method that recognizes the fundamental differences between biologically determined and behaviorally determined disorders. Given such a dual approach, we expect that disorders which stem from biochemical, metabolic, or toxic conditions (the organic brain disorders, perhaps the schizophrenias, perhaps the manic-depressive psychoses) would continue to be diagnosed, as they now are, from etiologic factors (e.g., alcohol, cerebral arteriosclerosis, diffuse brain lesion, etc.) This sort of diagnosis "makes sense" for them because they are physical diseases.

But we believe that the behavioral disorders—disorders for which no organic etiology has or will be found—will ultimately be diagnosed by procedures and under assumptions different from those the profession uses today. Instead of being classified almost entirely according to "symptoms," it is possible that the neuroses, for example, may come to be diagnosed as *escape-avoidance disorders*. So conceptualized, these disorders become exercises in treatment design. The focus will be on procedures that enable patients to confront their highest-frequency target behaviors. Rather than avoiding them or escaping from situations which generate anxiety or other maladaptive behavior, patients will gradually evolve methods for spending greater and greater amounts of time in the activities which were once avoided. Similarly, psychopathologists might recast what are now called the personality disorders into *disorders of excess and deficit*. Treatment would concentrate on procedures designed to increase the frequency of a deficient behavior (e.g., assertiveness) and decrease the frequency of an excessive behavior (e.g., suspiciousness).

Summary

The diagnostic system now largely used in the United States, that of the American Psychiatric Association, is heavily influenced by the medical model. It divides the psychopathologic disorders into ten categories: mental retardation, organic brain syndromes, psychoses not related to physical conditions, neuroses, personality disorders and other nonpsychotic mental disorders, psychophysiological disorders, special symptoms, transient situational disturbances, behavior disorders of childhood and adolescence, and nonspecific conditions and maladjustments.

Diagnosis as a process has undoubted strengths in helping the clinician understand and treat psychopathology. But the current diagnostic system also has important weaknesses, particularly its apparent low reliability and unproved validity. Low diagnostic *reliability* means that a diagnostic label given someone today may turn out to be inaccurate next month. Unproved diagnostic *validity* (which is in part a function of low reliability) means that the diagnostic labels now in widespread use give the clinician little help in understanding or treating many mental disorders. For example, an elaborate diagnostic program to analyze Bill H's chronic alcoholism, temporal lobe epilepsy, and other serious behavioral disorders did not produce any real understanding of his difficulties or ideas on how to help him.

Among the elements of the diagnostic process through which Bill H. was taken were a mental status examination, a physical examination, and a detailed personal history. Because these procedures are too dependent upon the subjective impressions and experiences of a single examiner, behavioral scientists have tried for many years to systematize and objectify diagnosis. For the purpose they have developed symptom rating scales—some of which have recently been computer-assisted—and psychological tests. The reliability and validity of some of these instruments have also been questioned. However, the Wechsler Adult Intelligence Scale, the Minnesota Multiphasic Personality Inventory, the Rorschach Inkblot Technique, and the Thematic Apperception Test continue to be used by many psychologists for diagnosis.

Behavioral psychologists have recently proposed that diagnosis be relabeled *behavior assessment* and refocused specifically on identification of reasonable treatment objectives and procedures. Tharp and Wetzel suggest a five-point plan for assessment: analysis of *(a)* a patient's behavioral repertoire, *(b)* the environmental variables which precede his maladaptive behaviors, *(c)* the stimuli in the environment which appear to maintain these target behaviors, *(d)* his reinforcement hierarchy, *(e)* the naturally occurring environmental events whose modification might help modify his maladaptive behavior.

We, the authors, believe that a dual classificatory system for the psychopathologic disorders may ultimately evolve. We expect that those disorders which stem from biochemical, metabolic, or toxic conditions—the organic brain disorders, perhaps the schizophrenias, perhaps the manic depressive psychoses—will continue to be diagnosed as they are now, from proved or presumed etiologic factors within a "traditional" diagnostic system. But we also anticipate that the behavioral disorders—those for which an organic etiology has not and will not be found—will be assessed by procedures and under assumptions which derive from behavioral models. Two such systems of assessment—one proposed by Tharp and Wetzel, the other developed by Kanfer and Saslow—are already being tried out.

CHAPTER SIX

The group of schizophrenias: History, signs, and cues

Lee Harvey Oswald ● Rudolph Hess ● History ● Cues ●
The group of schizophrenias: The "traditional ten" ●
Dimensions of schizophrenia: Alternatives to the traditional
approach ● Assessment of the schizophrenias: Identifying
and evaluating the cues

LEE:
THE GIANT
KILLER

Lee Harvey Oswald was born in Oct 1939 in New Orleans La. the son of a
Insuraen Salesmen whose early death left a far mean streak of indepence
brought on by negleck. entering the US Marine corp at 17 this streak of
independence was strengthed by exotic journeys to Japan the Philipines
and the scores of odd Islands in the Pacific immianly after serving out his
3 years in the USMC he abonded his american life to seek a new life in the
USSR. full of optimism and hope he stood in red square in the fall of
1959 vowing to see his chosen course through, after, however, two years
and alot of growing up I decided to return to the USA. [From Lee Harvey Oswald's autobiography, in *Report of the President's Commission on
the Assassination of President John F. Kennedy,* 1964, pp. 395–397]

Two months before Lee Harvey Oswald was born, his father died of
a heart attack. When Lee arrived the family consisted of his mother
Marguerite, his 5-year old brother Robert, and a half-brother, John,
who was 7. Life was difficult for the Oswalds. By 1941, when Lee
was 2 years old, his mother found the burden of three children so
heavy that she placed the two older boys in an orphanage. Lee was
too young to be sent away, so he was cared for by an aunt and a series
of baby sitters. A year later he joined his brothers in the orphanage.
    When Lee was 4 years old his mother began to date a Texan named
Edwin Ekdahl, who took an interest in the children as well. He married Marguerite and brought the boys to Texas to live with them.
Next fall the older boys were sent to a military boarding school, while
Lee stayed with his mother and stepfather. Years later Lee's older
brother John said that Ekdahl quickly became the father Lee had
never had. Unfortunately his new security did not last; his mother
and Ekdahl were divorced after three years. And once again Marguerite began to feel that the burdens of her life were overwhelming.

*(Flip Schulke from Black
Star)*

145

She was especially worried about money; it had become a lifelong concern, and she encouraged John, the oldest son, to leave school and go to work at the age of 16.

She herself took one job after another. Before Lee was old enough for school, he waited in the car while his mother called on customers for her job of the moment. When he did begin school he usually waked up in an empty house, came home to it and fixed his lunch, and returned after school to be alone again. In part his isolation was the result of his mother's possessiveness, for she discouraged him from playing with other children. In part it was from his own shyness and lack of self-confidence. Yet in spite of his social withdrawal, Lee was able to hold his own in school. His grades were average — below his bright-normal intellectual potential, but acceptable.

However, Lee and his mother moved to New York City in 1952, and he began to have serious academic and social difficulties. At first they lived with his older brother John and his wife, but their visit ended when Lee threatened his sister-in-law with a pocket knife during an argument. Lee and his mother moved into their own apartment, and Lee entered a New York City school that fall. But the other children laughed at him because of his Texas accent and Western clothes, so he stopped going to school. He stayed home and read or watched television, and his mother made only token efforts to send him back. Truancy charges that were finally brought against the boy and his mother led to a psychiatric examination for Lee. The doctor's report said:

This 13 year old well built boy has superior mental resources and functions only slightly below his capacity level in spite of chronic truancy from school which brought him into Youth House. No findings of neurological impairment or psychotic changes could be made. Lee has to be diagnosed as "personality pattern disturbance with schizoid features and passive-aggressive tendencies." Lee has to be seen as an emotionally, quite disturbed youngster who suffers under the impact of really existing emotional isolation and deprivation, lack of affection, absence of family life and rejection by a self-involved and conflicted mother. [President's Commission, 1964, p. 380]

The psychiatrist recommended that Lee be placed on probation and offered psychotherapy. His mother too was urged to seek psychological help.

The social worker who also talked to Lee and his mother at that time reached essentially the same conclusions. She described Lee's mother as a "smartly dressed, gray-haired woman, very self-possessed and alert and superficially affable," but essentially a "defensive, rigid, self-involved person who had real difficulty in accepting and relating to people" and who had "little understanding" of Lee's behavior and of the "protective shell he has drawn around himself" (p. 381).

Lee Oswald in his 1957 high school yearbook. *(UPI)*

By the age of 13 Lee had formed his lifelong pattern of response to a stressful world. He withdrew from unpleasant situations and spent most of his time by himself. He resented authority. He was explosive and impetuous. He had fantasies about his own greatness. Despite these maladaptive patterns of behavior, no one who knew Lee would have predicted that he would someday kill a President. To the contrary, the social worker who knew him best said: "Despite his withdrawal, he gives the impression that he is not so difficult to reach as he appears and patient, prolonged effort in a sustained relationship with one therapist might bring results. There are indications that he has suffered serious personality damage but if he can receive help quickly this might be repaired to some extent" (p. 382). Lee never got that help.

Before the court could take any action to provide care for Lee, he and his mother moved back to New Orleans. There again the other children teased him at school, this time because of his New York accent. His mother, no longer willing or able to control him, left it up to Lee to decide whether or not he went to school. He regularly chose not to. Sixteen years old by this time, still very much alone, he had no close friends of either sex.

Lee left school and went to work after the ninth grade. He began to read Communist Party literature and, according to one of his fellow employees, wanted to kill President Eisenhower because he was exploiting the working people. Yet Lee also felt drawn to the Armed Forces and tried to enlist in the Marines at age 16. He was told to wait until he was 17. In the interim he memorized his brother Robert's *Marine Corps Manual.* Shortly after his seventeenth birthday, Lee Harvey Oswald joined the Marines.

Despite the enforced camaraderie of barracks life, Lee's period in the service did little to change his isolation. His professional performance was generally adequate, but he never rose above the rank of private first class. The President's Commission concluded: "His Marine career was not helped by his attitude that he was a man of great ability and intelligence and that many of his superiors in the Marine Corps were not sufficiently competent to give him orders" (p. 385).

When his unit was sent to Japan, Lee finally found a girl friend. He is said to have become more assertive and self-confident as a result; unfortunately, his new assurance led to a fight with a sergeant whom he felt had a grudge against him. This scrap, for which he spent a month in the guardhouse, was the only serious blemish in Oswald's service record.

Oswald left the Marine Corps three months before his scheduled discharge date because, he said, he needed to take care of his mother. In fact, on discharge he departed almost immediately for the Soviet

Union and applied for citizenship there. But Lee was disappointed at his reception by the Russians, who were not eager to keep him. In fact, they were planning to deport him when he made a suicide attempt. They relented and allowed him to live in Minsk, where he went to work in a factory. But his life was no happier there than it had been in the United States, and he became disillusioned with the Soviet system. In Minsk, however, he did meet and marry a Russian woman, Marina Prusakova.

Just before he met Marina, Lee began negoiating with the United States Embassy to permit his return to the United States. He was thus admitting defeat in his pursuit of a major goal: life in the Soviet Union had brought him no more opportunity or contentment than life in the United States.

Marina says that Oswald was a "changed man" after they returned to America; he seemed more irritable and more isolated. "Our family life began to deteriorate after we arrived in America. Lee was always hot-tempered, and now this trait of character more and more prevented us from living together in harmony. Lee became very irritable, and sometimes some completely trivial thing would drive him into a rage. I myself do not have a particularly quiet disposition, but I had to change my character a great deal in order to maintain a more or less peaceful family life" (p. 395).

By now Oswald had rejected both communism and capitalism, though his feelings about them fluctuated. For example, soon after returning to the United States, he wrote the Soviet Embassy asking for Russian magazines and other literature. He refused to let his wife learn English because he said he hated America. Clearly he was pulled in many directions by emotions he could not reconcile.

The first firm evidence of his potential for violence was his unsuccessful attempt on the life of General Edwin Walker, whom he considered an enemy of the people. Walker, bent over his desk in his Dallas, Texas, study, narrowly escaped death when Oswald's rifle bullet missed his head by inches. Having fired—and not knowing that he had missed—Oswald hid his rifle, boarded a bus, and went home. He thought he had accomplished a deed analogous to the assassination of Hitler. We can only imagine his shock when he learned that he had missed.

The apparent irrationality of this attempt was illustrated by the series of notes he left in his room. If he had succeeded in shooting Walker and had been caught, the notes would doubtless have been found. Actually they are not so irrational in view of Oswald's goal, which seems to have been to ensure a place for himself in history rather than to protect himself.

Marina and Lee brought back their first child, a daughter, when they returned to this country. Oswald found it hard to meet his fam-

(Matt Herron from Black Star)

148

ily responsibilities; he went through a series of different jobs in Fort Worth, Dallas, New Orleans, and other towns. He also became involved in some of the American political activities surrounding the Cuban revolution. Once he even went to Mexico City in an unsuccessful attempt to get permission to enter Cuba.

Oswald's marriage was a difficult one for both parties. Friendships played an important part in Marina's life, but Lee was jealous and tried to control her relationships with other people. His efforts to bully her did not intimidate Marina; she nagged him about many things, including his political views and his sexual failings.

His unsatisfactory marriage may have been a crucial factor in Oswald's decision to assassinate President Kennedy. In the days just before the assassination Lee and Marina had a major quarrel, and she stopped speaking to him. He was finding rejection at every turn; the murder of a great man may have seemed an ideal way to achieve the importance and recognition he desired. A little after noon on November 22, 1963, Lee Harvey Oswald, aiming from a window on the sixth floor of the Texas Book Depository, shot and killed John F. Kennedy.

RUDOLPH HESS: PATRIOT OR PSYCHOTIC?

From a German newspaper, Berlin, May, 1941:

As far as it is possible to tell from papers left behind by Party Member Hess it seemed that he lived in a state of hallucination as a result of which he felt he could bring about an understanding between England and Germany. It is a fact that Hess, according to a report from London, jumped from his aeroplane near the town to which he was trying to go, and was found there injured. The National Socialist [Nazi] Party regrets that this idealist fell as a victim to his hallucinations. This however will have no

(Wide World Photos)

effect on the continuation of the war which has been forced upon Germany. Dr. Karl Haushofer, head of the Geo-political Institute, Willi Messerschmitt, Frau Hess, and others were arrested. [Rees, 1948, pp. 2–3]

From Rudolph Hess:

Next morning, the Duke of Hamilton came to see me after I had requested that. After I told him my name, I explained to him why I had come.
At the end, I told him somehow my feeling of what the future held in store for me and I had had that feeling already in Germany. I told him that I had flown to England to render a service to the peoples that had been involved in the war but had not come to go through a Secret Service third degree. I was regarding myself as an emissary and in that capacity I asked for the protection of the King of England, to whose honour and fairness I appealed. [Rees, 1948, p. 96]

On the night of May 10, 1941, a German pilot parachuted from his Messerschmitt ME110 aircraft and was captured by a farmer, David McLean, in the south of Scotland. The pilot introduced himself as Hauptmann Alfred Horn to McLean, who was amazed to find that he had single-handedly taken such an imposing-looking prisoner. McLean helped the pilot, who had injured himself in bailing out, back to the farmhouse. After Horn was turned over to military officials, he demanded to see the Duke of Hamilton. When the duke appeared at his bedside, Horn revealed himself as Rudolph Hess, head of the Nazi party and the man who was second in command of Nazi Germany. He came, he said, to negotiate peace between England and Germany. He did not wish to see England defeated and more innocent women and children killed. He wanted to draft a peace treaty based upon German terms, though they seemed vague in his mind. The duke notified Winston Churchill, Prime Minister of Great Britain, and they puzzled over their unexpected guest. Was the man actually Hess? If so, what was his real purpose in coming to England?

It turned out that the captured pilot was indeed Rudolph Hess. To understand his bizarre flight it is helpful to know something about his childhood, and about the Germany which he helped to rule.

Hess was born in Alexandria, Egypt, on April 26, 1896. His father owned a family business there which had been established by Rudolph's grandfather. Rudolph, his brother, and two sisters apparently grew up fearing their father, for it is said that they had to be exceptionally obedient whenever he was at home. Playtime was reserved for the hours when he was at work. At the age of 12 Rudolph was sent to a boarding school in Germany. There his records show that he was "a good student and a devoted patriot." Because his father wanted him to become a businessman, he went to a special business school at the age of 15. After that he spent several years as a business apprentice.

In 1916 when Hess was 20 years old, World War I erupted. He joined the German army as a volunteer and served in the infantry. After considerable combat experience, during which he was wounded several times, he was promoted to lieutenant and reassigned for pilot's training. He spent a brief time in flight duty before the armistice was signed. After his discharge Hess went to Munich and became an active member of a newly organized, strongly nationalistic, anti-Semitic group which was a precursor of the Nazi party. He also enrolled at Munich University, where he became a student of Karl Haushofer. This teacher was to have a major influence on the development of Hess's political philosophy.

In 1923 Hess met Adolf Hitler. It is reported that he heard Hitler speaking in a beer cellar in Munich and became an immediate convert to the vision of a renascent German empire. From that time on, Hess devoted himself entirely to Hitler and the National Socialist (Nazi) party. In 1924 he was imprisoned with Hitler and served as his secretary during the time Hitler wrote *Mein Kampf.* Because some of the teachings of Hess's old professor, Haushofer, can be identified in the book, it seems likely that Hess did much of the editing. After his release from prison Hess spent some time in Munich working for Haushofer. Then he became Hitler's secretary and personal adjutant, and in this capacity wrote much of the propaganda which Hitler used during his rise to power. As the National Socialist party grew, Hess's power grew along with it. In fact, he was head of the Nazi party until the day in May 1941 when he climbed into his Messerschmitt and flew to England.

Not much is known about Hess's personal life in Nazi Germany. We get the general picture of a man who complained of many physical ailments and went to all sorts of quack doctors. Often his symptoms appeared to have little physical basis, though some of them may have been induced by tension. He may have acquired his preoccupation with health from his mother, who is said to have experimented with various unorthodox medical treatments. As for other personal details, it is known that Hess refused to allow his wife to take part in his public life. She was rarely seen in public and did not participate in National Socialist Party activities. These facts are too scanty to permit identification of Hess's psychopathology; it was only after he arrived in England that a diagnostic picture emerged.

His reception by the English was hardly what he had expected. Rather than receiving a hero's welcome, he was considered a prisoner of war and put behind barbed wire. Far from going into conference night and day with the King of England, he was guarded around the clock by ordinary British soldiers. Hess responded by developing the belief that he was surrounded by agents who intended to poison him or drive him to suicide. He singled out one or two men on each guard-duty tour and accused them of being the agents who were persecuting him. Though these guards changed from day to day, he was convinced that new agents took their place. Every day he also selected one or two other guards to act as his own agents, "entrusting" them with special messages to be smuggled out of prison. He had no more reason to trust these men than to be suspicious of the others.

Hess reached the point where he was unwilling to eat unless a British officer ate with him from the same platter. He took care to select the slices of meat that were farthest away from him, and he waited until the officer had started eating before he began. In this way he was protecting himself from being poisoned by "agents of international Jewry." He saved samples of his food and medicine to give the representative of the neutral Swiss government who came regularly to see him.

Hess's delusions of persecution also affected his responses to the noises around him. Since his prison was located in a camp which trained military policemen, there were a great many motorcycle sounds, as well as some machine-gun fire and airplane noises. He refused to believe that the sounds were products of military training; he said that they had been devised to upset him.

Early in his imprisonment Hess made a bizarre attempt at suicide. Jumping over a banister and down a flight of stairs, he only managed to break a leg. Afterwards he said that he had tried to kill himself because he preferred death to being driven insane by the powers gathered against him.

The grandiosity which inspired so much of his behavior is illustrated by Hess's plan to "save" Britain and Germany by flying to England to arrange peace. He took on the role of world peacemaker without consulting other members of the Nazi party or even his revered Führer. Yet when he was questioned about his plans for peace, Hess could not explain precisely how peace was to be established.

An excerpt from Hess's autobiography, written while he was a British prisoner, provides a sample of his thinking.

Since there was a great lack of books, I spent a large part of the day in drawing architectural sketches—suddenly my eyes got so bad that I could neither draw nor write nor read. At this time I took my breakfast as my only meal without company, and thus it was the best opportunity to give me poison. For a few days, I merely pretended to eat breakfast and at once my eyes got better. I had hardly started drinking the cocoa again when the visual disturbances reappeared. When it was noticed that I was not eating breakfast any more and that my eyes had recovered, the poison doubtless was put into my other meals. I suspect, though, that it was put in some part of my food which the doctor would be careful not to eat.

152

Soon my eyes deteriorated so badly that I could see only very blurry outlines of near and distant objects. I had to take into account the possibility of becoming blind. My eyes secreted so much liquid that they were completely glued up in the morning; when I told this to the doctor and Major F. their faces took on an expression of demoniac satisfaction. [Rees, 1948, p. 106]

At the end of the war Hess was sent to Nuremberg along with other high-ranking Nazis for the war-crimes trials. He had lost all memory, however, for many events that had taken place in Germany between 1933 and 1945. It was unclear whether his profound memory losses were hysterical amnesia, further indications of his psychosis, or an effort by a trapped man to evade responsibility for his acts. An examining board of psychiatrists from the United States, the Soviet Union, France, and Great Britain interviewed Hess to try to decide whether he was capable of standing trial for his crimes. With one exception they concluded that his amnesia was, at least in part, genuine. However, they also felt that his memory loss would remit once the trial began. The Nuremberg justices reviewed these reports and listened to Hess's testimony that he was quite capable of assisting in his own defense. He claimed that his memory was intact, that he had only pretended to lose it. Yet he continued to show fluctuations in memory during the trial.

Hess in Spandau Prison, 1969. *(Wide World Photos)*

Hess was tried at Nuremberg and found guilty of war crimes, along with Goering, Ribbentrop, Keitel, Rosenberg, Streicher, and von Papen. The sentence for Rudolph Hess—whether he was psychotic or sane, a patriot or a traitor—was life imprisonment in Spandau jail.

Two psychoses that shook the world

Many theories "explain" psychopathology in environmental terms. Family and society—the customs and culture within which one grows up—are often "blamed" for behavior deviations. Chapter 2 is devoted to a review of the theories and facts surrounding the impact of society upon psychopathology. But that chapter does not deal with the issue raised by the case histories of Lee Harvey Oswald and Rudolph Hess: the impact which psychopathology sometimes has upon society.

When Lee Harvey Oswald shot John Fitzgerald Kennedy, he dramatically influenced political events in the United States and no doubt changed the course of American relations with the rest of the world. When Rudolph Hess became Adolf Hitler's secretary, he played a major role in helping Hitler rise to international eminence. In fact, both men altered the course of history. Most schizophrenic persons have little influence on the world, for they lead lives of social isolation. Although they may bring despair into the lives of their families, their serious impact usually extends little further. In this sense Oswald and Hess were atypical schizophrenics. At the same time, they were typical in that their isolation, suspiciousness, delusional thinking, and impulsive behavior were like the symptoms of schizophrenics whose influence does not extend beyond the back ward of a state hospital.

This chapter aims to give you some sense of the complexities involved in the study of schizophrenia. They become obvious just from comparing the case histories of Hess, Oswald, and Daniel Paul Schreber back in Chapter 1. Schreber's schizophrenic label is the most clear-cut of the three because, as he himself wrote in his memoirs, he was "massively hallucinated," "tortured by compulsive acting and obsessive thinking," and at various times "immobile for long periods, impulsive." Rudolph Hess's behavior was more complicated and more obscure. Although paranoid schizophrenia now seems an apt label for him, some people argue that he was simply lying,

others that he should be called neurotic rather than psychotic. But the most complex person from the diagnostic point of view was Oswald, largely because he did not show the blatant thought disorders demonstrated by Schreber and Hess. If Jack Ruby (himself an example of psychopathology) had not assassinated Oswald, we might have obtained the psychological and psychiatric data necessary for an exhaustive and generally agreed-upon diagnosis. Without those data there will always be room for argument. The point here is that diagnosis of schizophrenia is a difficult matter. The traditional categories of schizophrenia may not be adequate for the job that has been assigned to them.

This chapter traces the development by scientists of the concept of schizophrenia. Then it describes the signs and symptomatic behaviors which characterize the group of schizophrenias. In the process it will use details from the cases of Oswald, Hess, and Schreber.

The concept of schizophrenia: History

The history of the concept of schizophrenia (a word that means the splitting of psychic functions) is a relatively recent one. It was not until the last part of the nineteenth century that the group of schizophrenias began to emerge as a distinct entity within the mental disorders.

Kraepelin: Brilliant synthesis, flawed diagnostic system. Emil Kraepelin (1855 to 1926), a German psychiatrist, recognized that groups of seemingly dissimilar patients shared certain distinguishing characteristics. He concluded that there were two major divisions of mental illness: *dementia praecox,* which means progressive insanity and *manic-depressive psychosis,* which consists of extreme mood alterations (Zilboorg, 1941). Within the broad category of dementia praecox Kraepelin included several disorders which had never before been viewed as related: *catatonia, hebephrenia,* and *vesania typica,* a condition we now term paranoid schizophrenia. Eventually, at the urging of Eugen Bleuler, a fellow psychiatrist, Kraepelin added the category of *simple schizophrenia.*

In Kraepelin's opinion all the patients with dementia praecox shared the same grave prognosis: inevitable progressive deterioration to a state of total insanity. Having so defined dementia praecox, he set out to compile an extensive catalog of all the possible behaviors commonly associated with it. Even today his descriptions of schizophrenia are among the most detailed that have been written. Kraepelin did not make much of an attempt to explain the cause or meaning of these behaviors. Simply listing and describing them was his goal.

Credit must be given this man for his brilliance in synthesizing a great deal of previous work in the classification of psychopathology. His writings continue to influence contemporary ideas about diagnosis. Nevertheless, there was a serious flaw in Kraepelin's diagnostic system. His diagnosis of dementia praecox was based upon prognosis—upon the anticipated outcome of the disorder. For this reason a patient could be definitely diagnosed only after he had begun to show progressive mental deterioration. If he recovered rather than deteriorated, he could not be said to have had dementia praecox, even though his initial behaviors may have been those of patients who followed the predicted downward course. Because Kraepelin's system was useful only after the fact, its value was decidedly limited. In physical medicine his diagnostic procedure would be like watching a tumor to see whether a patient dies of cancer.

Bleuler: Not one disease but many. The next major figure in the history of schizophrenia was the Swiss psychiatrist Eugen Bleuler (1857 to 1930). In 1911 Bleuler published a monograph in which he expanded upon Kraepelin's basic ideas as well as adding important new ones of his own. It was he who changed the name of the syndrome from dementia praecox to schizophrenia. The new term eliminated the implication that the disorder was one of progressive deterioration and emphasized the splitting apart of various psychic functions. The name "schizophrenia" suggests that the affect, intellect, and behavior of the schizophrenic are not coordinated, as they are in other people. Rather than the single disease entity which Kraepelin envisioned, Bleuler felt that schizophrenia encompasses a number of disorders. Hence the concept of the *group of schizophrenias.*

Bleuler pointed to two kinds of symptoms in schizophrenia. *Fundamental* symptoms are found to some degree in every schizophrenic patient, while *accessory* symptoms are seen in some but not in others. In addition, accessory symptoms may appear in other forms of psychopathology besides schizophrenia. According to Bleuler, the four fundamental symptoms of schizophrenia, sometimes called the "four A's," are loosening of associations (language difficulties), inappropriate affect (emotion that does not fit the circumstances), ambivalence (conflicting emotions toward the same

Eugen Bleuler. *(The Bettmann Archive)*

object), and autism (excessive preoccupation with fantasy). Examples of accessory symptoms are delusions and hallucinations.

Organic versus psychological explanations. When schizophrenia became recognized as a distinct form of psychopathology, all sorts of theories were formulated to explain its cause. There are now two basic explanations of the etiology of schizophrenia: organic and psychological.

The first organic theory of schizophrenia was Kraepelin's. He hypothesized that dementia praecox was due either to pathology of the brain or to a metabolic disorder. Until the past twenty-five or thirty years most organic theories of schizophrenia had to be accepted on faith, because scientists lacked the biochemical and neurological techniques for testing them. Since World War II, however, these techniques have been developing rapidly. Consequently there has been a trend toward more biochemical and genetic theorizing about the causes of schizophrenia, and some of the theorizing is backed by empirical data (see Chapter 7).

Bleuler, whose work followed Kraepelin's by about fifteen years, was the first person to look for a psychological meaning in the behaviors of schizophrenia. While he thought it was possible that the disorder might have an organic cause, he felt that a patient's specific behaviors had psychological significance. This explanation grew out of the work of Sigmund Freud, whose long period of influence on psychology and psychiatry was just beginning. Since Bleuler's time the Freudian approach to the interpretation of schizophrenic behavior has dominated psychiatric thinking. Only recently have other psychological theories—based upon the patient's social-learning history or on family communication patterns—been put forth as explanations for these behaviors (see Chapter 7).

A theory of etiology generally implies an approach to treatment, and the history of schizophrenia has included many varied attempts at cures. Theorists who believe in a biological cause have looked for an organic

cure. The development of shock therapy with insulin or electricity, the use of psychosurgery (in which portions of the brain are altered or removed), and the prescription of tranquilizing drugs have all grown out of this orientation. On the other hand, theorists who think there is a psychological basis for schizophrenia have turned to such techniques as psychoanalysis, family therapy, and behavior modification in their search for a cure. The merits and demerits of these approaches will be considered in detail in the next chapter.

The following section will describe the specific behaviors which most clearly characterize schizophrenia. These *cues to schizophrenia* are behaviors which can be readily and in most cases reliably observed without recourse to psychological tests or physiological measurement.

Cues to the schizophrenias

Schizophrenic patients show a wide variety of disordered behaviors. Some of these (especially Bleuler's four A's) seem to "belong" to the disorder. Others are better explained as reactions to the stress and turmoil which the schizophrenic often creates in family, work, school, and hospital situations. Ever since Bleuler first suggested in 1911 that looseness of associations, inappropriate affect, autism, and ambivalence were fundamental symptoms of schizophrenia, clinicians have debated his proposition. In particular, they disagree about whether these behaviors characterize every schizophrenic. Research by Nathan (1969) suggests that disordered affect, ambivalence, and autism, although major features of schizophrenia, are not unique to it. Furthermore, associational difficulties have appeared in patients with organic brain disorders as well as among schizophrenics. Rather than discussing schizophrenia in terms of the four A's, this section divides the cues into four kinds of behavior disorders: cognitive, perceptual, affective, and psychomotor.

Cues to the cognitive disorders

The schizophrenic's use of language and his mode of thinking are among the most obvious cues to the seriousness of his psychopathology. While these cognitive disorders take a variety of forms, all are markedly deviant from normal thought patterns. As shown by the letter in Figure 6-1, language loses much of its communication value for the schizophrenic. Paul Meehl (1962) calls this phenomenon *cognitive slippage* instead of using the more traditional term, *loosening of associations,* because his phrase suggests that the deviation may take a very subtle form and still be a sign of cognitive dysfunction.

Regardless of terminology, it is a fact that most schizophrenics show disruptions in the continuity of their thoughts. The pattern of words that they put together may not follow the rules of logic most people use. For example, their associations may be based upon similarities of sounds: the schizophrenic may speak of "house-mouse" or "lead-head." Such combinations based on sound are *clang associations.* Or schizophrenic patients' language may become so disjointed that it is nearly impossible to follow their logic, in which case we say they are talking in *word salad.* In some instances patients make up words, called *neologisms,* to suit themselves. Lehmann describes a patient who coined the word "polamolalittersjittersittersleelita" (1967). With the patient's aid this word was ultimately deciphered: it referred to her feeling that she was suffering from a serious disorder of the nervous system (poliomyelitis), that she felt messy inside (litters), that she was nervous and ill at ease (jittersitters), and that she was both dependent upon and handicapped by her illness (leelita). Note the clang associations (litters-jitter-sitters) within this neologism. Here are other words coined by schizophrenics:

Temperatrist: Patient's ward psychiatrist whom, he said, tempered justice with mercy.
Downworldfucked: This patient said that the world had gotten to be downright fucked up

and so he coined a word to describe such a disorganized world.
MoPoNoLo: This obscure neologism refers to a particularly disorganized patient's family. Raised in a chaotic family situation, the patient felt that neither his mother nor his father (Mo and Po) really loved him (No Lo).
Glogodivisex: Whenever this patient talked about sex, with which she was preoccupied, she had to begin her discussion with some praises to God, lest she be condemned for her evil thoughts. This neologism gradually took the place of her prayers; it means "Glory to God in the Divine for permitting me to talk about sex."
Somatophrenia: This paranoid schizophrenic patient was convinced that his disorder stemmed from somatic causes, probably of biochemical origin.
Pseudotherapy: This patient, for a long time engaged in an unproductive psychotherapeutic relationship, renamed that relationship for what she felt were its real inadequacies.
Vomitory: This schizophrenic woman, quite a religious person, felt sure that her behavior had condemned her to a period of time in purgatory. By associating purging with vomiting, she came up with this word to describe her anticipated residence on her death.

Syllogistic illogic. According to the formal rules of deductive logic, two things are identical if they share identical subjects. For example:

People born in the United States are American citizens.
John Henry was born in the United States.
John Henry is an American citizen.

Contrasting this mode of thinking with schizophrenic thinking, Von Domarus suggested that schizophrenics employ a form of *paralogic* in which things are seen as identical if they share the same adjective. In his words:

Whereas the *logician* accepts only the Mode of Barbara, or one of its modifications, as basis for valid conclusions, the *paralogician* concludes

Dear Mother and Father:

We had a good movie today. It was about the wild west and I thought about you when I watched it. I got wild again like I always do when I think about you two. Too, I remembered how glad I was when you sent me that $2.00 two years ago for my birthday. That was one of the best parties I had here since I came. Dr. J. came and the O.T. volunteer and some of the other patients. I sang offkey which is how I usually sing. Why didn't you get me those voice lessons you promised when I finished first grade choir with an A? I remember things like that, you know.

John Wayne killed three Indians, two bank robbers, and a cattle rustler today. He was wild... wild. Its Spring here now, like it was in the movie. And I have spring in my steps, when I walk outside in the springy turf. But my bed's been giving me trouble again. The mattress and the springs. Too old, I guess. Do you think I'm old enough to get married now or too old? Have you been feeling OK? You don't look old to me though I guess you are. Will I have to stay here when you move to Florida or will I go to Florida to live there? What about when you are incapacitated?

I bought some candy and cigarettes with that money you gave me two years ago. I still have the wrappers. I remember things like that, you know. It was springtime when my birthday came then too.

Well, guess that's all for now. Write soon as its convenient for you. I will find the time in my busy day to read the letters sometime after they arrive.

John

Figure 6-1. This letter shows a young schizophrenic patient's arduous efforts to communicate his love and concern to his parents, about whom he has ambivalent feelings. It illustrates the associational and cognitive difficulties the patient experiences when he tries to set down his thoughts and feelings.

identity from the similar nature of the adjectives. [Italics added. Von Domarus, 1944, p. 111]

Arieti, an American psychiatrist, expanded upon the Von Domarus principle to make it read:

Whereas the *normal person* accepts identity only upon the basis of identical subjects, the *paleologician* accepts identity only upon identical predicates. [Italics added. Arieti, 1955, p. 194]

Note that Arieti substituted "normal person" for "logician" and "paleologician" for "paralogician" in Von Domarus's definition. By the term paleologic Arieti refers to the regressed and primitive thought which he feels characterizes children, schizophrenics, and primitive peoples. Bleuler (1913) provides an illustration of paleologic in the case of the man who thought he was Switzerland because he reasoned:

Switzerland loves freedom.
I love freedom.
I am Switzerland.

The analysis presented by Von Domarus and altered by Arieti has since undergone considerable criticism. Maher, for example, suggests that Arieti's assumptions are more complex than they have to be to explain the behavior in question (1966). While Arieti contends that the schizophrenic is engaging in a form of regressed thinking, Maher argues that the behavior can better be understood as a form of excessive stimulus generalization. After all, he says, normal people do not always follow the rules of formal logic in their thinking. Other researchers have shown that controlling for intelligence and for emotionally provocative stimuli permits schizophrenics to perform like normals on tests of logical reasoning (Gottesman & Chapman, 1960; Williams, 1964). In summary, though the case for excessive stimulus generalization as an important determinant of schizophrenic illogic has not been proved, it seems more tenable now than the Von Domarus principle.

Delusions. The schizophrenic's thinking is sometimes called *autistic* (excessively preoccupied with the self) because he may detach himself from reality and place an excessive value upon his own thoughts. While most people enjoy their fantasies, they are usually able to separate their wishes, fears, and desires from external reality. The schizophrenic cannot always make this discrimination, with the result that some of his behavior may be the result of strong wishes rather than accurate perception of reality. Much of the time, the schizophrenic's autistic thinking is focused upon his delusions. A *delusion* is a false belief which the person will not alter even when he is given facts or commonsense explanations. Most delusions are of persecution, but patients also have delusions that are grandiose (meaning self-important), sexual, reli-

"Now, madam, calm yourself. What makes you think you're getting obscene signals from outer space?" Even though the paranoid schizophrenic may function well in other respects, his or her delusions are likely to cause conflicts with others in the community. *(Drawing by Herbert Goldberg; copyright 1970 by Saturday Review/World, Inc.)*

gious, hypochondriacal, or self-destructive. The overwhelming majority of schizophrenics are delusional. Lucas, Sansbury, and Collins (1962) reported that 71 percent of the 405 schizophrenic patients they studied had delusions and among the remaining 29 percent, more than half were so disturbed that it could not be determined whether or not they were delusional. Rudolph Hess's writings are filled with references to his delusions of persecution. For example:

In November, 1941, I got in touch with the Swiss Envoy in London, and asked him to visit me as the representative of the Protecting Power. I had hardly mailed the letter when, again, huge quantities of brain poison were put in my food to destroy my memory, after I had not been given any of this poison for a long while, or any of the poison which closed my bladder. Again I deceived them into believing I had lost my memory. After I appeared to have lost my memory completely, the Envoy appeared. [Rees, 1948, p. 104]

Sexual delusions are illustrated in this excerpt from the writings of Daniel Paul Schreber:

During that time the signs of a transformation into a woman became so marked on my body, that I could no longer ignore the imminent goal at which the whole development was aiming. In the immediately preceding nights my male sexual organ might actually have been retracted had I not resolutely set my will against it, still following the stirring of my sense of manly honour; so near completion was the miracle. Soul-voluptuousness had become so strong that I myself received the impression of a female body, first on my arms and hands, later on my legs, bosom, buttocks, and other parts of my body. [1955, pp. 147–148]

Lee Harvey Oswald's murder, which directly followed his assassination of John Kennedy, prevented psychologists from discovering whether delusions played a major role in his decision to kill the President. Judging from the delusional themes of persecution and grandiosity which had pervaded his life, it seems likely that he was "driven" to the Texas Book Depository by the belief that he was "saving America," or at least some deserving segment of Americans. The delusions of the schizophrenic occupy much of his time and energy. He must focus his efforts upon proving their truth and upon protecting himself from the fantasied consequences of these misbeliefs.

Cues to the perceptual disorders

Hallucinations. A *hallucination* is the perception of a sensory stimulus which does not in fact exist. The patient may see something which is not there, hear something when no sound has been made, or smell, taste, or touch something for which there is no external stimulation. Schreber, for example, had a variety of tactile hallucinations of a sexual nature.

The most common hallucinations of the schizophrenic are auditory (Goodwin et al., 1971): the patient hears voices talking to him or about him. They may command him to do certain things, or they may call him names and make fun of him. The voices may be those of God, the devil, the patient's mother, or strangers. Schreber reported that "the sun has for years spoken with me in human words" (Schreber, 1955, p. 47). Although visual hallucinations are less common than auditory ones, they are not uncommon among people diagnosed as schizophrenic. The patient may have religious visions, or see frightening or amusing scenes. Schreber wrote: "In early years there sometimes appeared when I was in bed—not sleeping but awake—all sorts of large, queer, almost dragon-like shapes, immediately next to my bed, and almost as big as my bed" (Schreber, 1955, p. 190). Hallucinations of touch, smell, and taste are much less frequent among schizophrenics than either auditory or visual ones.

Hallucinations are not unique to schizophrenia, however. Goodwin and his colleagues observed hallucinations in five patient groups in the diagnostic categories of schizophrenia, manic-depressive psychosis, alcoholism, organic brain syndrome, and hysteria (1971). They found that the modality or form of hallucination (whether it was visual, audi-

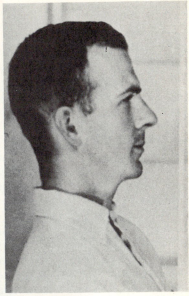

Assassins Sirhan Sirhan and Lee Harvey Oswald, as well as would-be assassin Arthur Bremer, probably suffered from paranoid schizophrenia. Few contemporary psychotics have had as profound an impact on society as these three. *(UPI, Flip Schulke from Black Star, Wide World Photos)*

tory, or so forth) had no diagnostic significance. Auditory hallucinations were the most common form among all diagnostic groups except the organic brain syndrome patients, who had more visual than auditory hallucinations. Similarly, Jansson reported no relationship between the form of hallucination and prognosis (1968).

Impaired body concept and depersonalization. Some schizophrenics report a change in *body image.* As all infants grow, they develop a sense of their own body boundaries. One's body has a certain size and feeling. The distance between head and toes, for example, becomes a known and sensed dimension. But the schizophrenic sometimes experiences profound changes in his or her sense of self. The body feels too big or too small; parts of it become numb or exquisitely sensitive.

Arnhoff and Damianopoulos presented subjects with photographs of bodies, including the subject's own, from which all facial clues had been removed (1964). They found that normal college students were better able than schizophrenics to recognize their own bodies, a result which supports the view that schizophrenics do have less accurate body images than nonschizophrenics.

One consequence of the changes in body image which the schizophrenic undergoes is *depersonalization*—the sense that he is no longer himself. Events that are both external and internal do not seem the same to him as they once did. Some patients actually claim that they are no longer themselves; they conclude that the bodily changes they are experiencing "mean" that they have become Jesus Christ, the Virgin Mary, or the King of England. Schreber felt that he was changing sex.

The experience of depersonalization is not unique to schizophrenics. Neurotic patients sometimes have the same feeling (Chapter 9). And many normal people experience some degree of depersonalization when intoxicated, fatigued, ill, or especially anxious. But when depersonalization occurs in schizophrenics, it is usually more pronounced and intense than in normals or neurotics. In addition, normals can cope better with the changed bodily sensations than schizophrenics can. The normal person does not often resort to such explanations as a change in identity to account for the novel experiences he is having.

Cues to the affective disorders: Failures of emotional response

Schizophrenics are sometimes described as suffering from *anhedonia*—inability to experience pleasure. Another way of saying it is that they show a *blunting* or *flattening of affect.* Affect is a term used to describe emotional state or mood. A person who experiences pleasure and sadness at proper times may be said to have "appropriate affect." Many schizophrenics fail to respond with an appropriate range of emotions to important events. Instead, they may appear withdrawn and indifferent even in situations which should frighten them, or to occasions which should make them happy.

There are, of course, variations between cultures in normal affective response. Lehmann wisely points out that the clinician must be cautious in judging the extent to which an emotional response is or is not appropriate (1967). A Texas cowboy and a New York City sophisticate would be expected to show their feelings in different ways. Likewise, we would expect Anne Frank and Piri Thomas, adolescents from vastly different cultural backgrounds, to differ in their emotional expression.

Along with emotional flatness, some schizophrenics may show *inappropriate emotional responsivity.* They may be indifferent or even take pleasure in a profound loss, such as a death in the family or a terminal illness. Or they may respond with rage to a mild or unintended offense. A patient known to one of the authors always giggled when talking about her impending death from cancer.

Schizophrenics have also been described as *ambivalent* in their emotions. That is, they may experience *simultaneous* love and hate, desire and fear, and similar conflicting emotions toward the same person or idea. Although ambivalence is not unique to schizophrenics—normal people sometimes feel it—it is more intense and incapacitating in schizophrenics than in normals. Lee Harvey Oswald's conflicting feelings about the Soviet Union and the United States and about communism and capitalism led to many inconsistent behaviors on his part. So did Schreber's ambivalence about his sexual feelings.

The more pronounced a patient's lack of appropriate emotional response, the more disturbed he is. The retention of a reasonable degree of affective response is a good prognostic sign (McCabe et al., 1972).

Cues to the psychomotor disorders

When laymen are asked to describe a "crazy" person, they often talk about unusual or bizarre motor behavior. Their stereotyped picture of psychosis is of the excited schizophrenic who giggles, shouts, waves his arms, runs around, and makes faces. Actually, because of the tranquilizing drugs these behaviors are rarely seen today except during acute psychotic episodes.

One dramatic form of motor behavior is the *stupor (catalepsy)* of some schizophrenic patients. They may remain immobile for long periods, apparently unaware of external stimulation. They may also show *waxy flexibility,* when parts of the body that are under voluntary muscle control can be "molded" by other people. For example, a patient's arm will remain suspended in midair once someone has positioned it there. Behaviors this extreme are relatively rare, especially now that modern drug therapy can reduce the intensity of acute psychotic episodes. As a result, someone entering a ward of chronic schizophrenic patients is likely to find many of them sitting quietly in their own chairs engaged in their own reveries.

Schizophrenics do sometimes exhibit repetitive mannerisms such as facial grimaces. Others may show *stereotyped behavior,* in which they pace back and forth all day long on the same spot, or return to the same

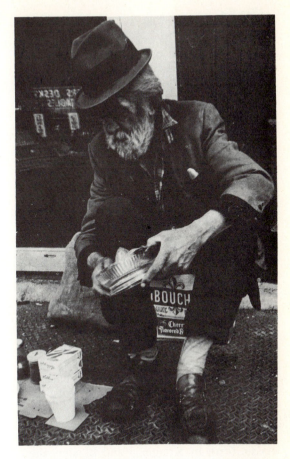

An unconventional life style—such as a "skid row" existence—is often associated with chronic schizophrenia. *(Henry Monroe/DPI)*

place day in and day out to emit the same repetitive behavior.

Schizophrenic patients are often untidy in their appearance and personal hygiene. They have to be urged to wash, change clothes, shave, or apply makeup; even then they do not always comply. They may also neglect conventional social manners, so that they fail to respond to greetings or make "small talk." In evaluating such changes in behavior, the clinician must remember that the boring life in a mental hospital may be a contributing factor. A normal person living in the same tedious, sterile environment might very well begin acting like a patient. He might find little or no incentive to dress up, use good table manners, or feel concerned about social conventions. So it may be true that many of these behavioral deficits are not inherent in schizophrenia but result from the social conditions imposed upon the hospitalized schizophrenic. It is partly for this reason that men like Szasz and Laing so emphatically reject the idea of hospitalization for psychiatric patients.

The group of schizophrenias: The "traditional ten"

The cognitive, perceptual, affective, and psychomotor behaviors just described cut across the various types of schizophrenia. As a result, the categories of what is called the group of schizophrenias must be differentiated by a relative emphasis on certain cues rather than by pointing to any single cue for each category. Because this way of discriminating among otherwise similar patterns of behavior is notoriously difficult, reliable separations between the types of schizophrenic disorders are rarely achieved.

Following the descriptions of simple, hebephrenic, catatonic, and paranoid schizophrenia set forth by Kraepelin and Bleuler, there have been many attempts to further subdivide the group of schizophrenias. The American Psychiatric Association names the following ten categories in DSM II, its current diagnostic manual (APA, 1968).

Simple type. The most striking features of simple schizophrenia are the gradual onset of symptoms that often include loss of ambition, interest, and interpersonal contacts. The simple schizophrenic's disorder usually lacks any dramatic cues. He simply becomes increasingly withdrawn, indifferent, and apathetic. He stays in his room, does not work, avoids contact with people, and shows few emotional responses to anything. Many people with this diagnosis continue to live in a marginal fashion outside the hospital. They may wander around as tramps or hobos

Older women wandering about with all their worldly possessions are a common sight on the streets of many large cities. The isolation and suspiciousness of these unfortunate people are often signs of simple schizophrenia. *(Henry Monroe/DPI)*

or function as isolated members of a tolerant family. When a simple schizophrenic is finally hospitalized, the precipitating event was often a rage response and assaultive attack upon a member of the family (Lehmann, 1967).

Hebephrenic type. The hebephrenic (from the Greek words for "young" and "mind") appears to be the most disorganized of all the patients whose psychoses fall within the group of schizophrenias. His thought is severely disordered and his affective responses are grossly inappropriate. The hebephrenic is noted for his giggling, silliness, and childish behavior. He may experience hallucinations or delusions, but they are usually brief and disorganized.

Catatonic type. There are two subtypes of catatonic schizophrenia: excited and withdrawn. The *excited* catatonic is identified by excessive and sometimes violent motor activity, the *withdrawn* catatonic by stupor, mutism, and negativism. In extreme instances the withdrawn catatonic may also exhibit waxy flexibility. Most withdrawn catatonics, however, are not immobile. They simply show a decreased level of activity, speaking and moving little if at all. They are aware of events that occur around them even though they may not respond. After long periods of inactivity, a catatonic may suddenly become excited and agitated. He will shout, run, and ultimately exhaust himself and those around him from the combination of frantic activity and little or no sleep.

Paranoid type. The behavior of the paranoid schizophrenic is well illustrated by the case histories of Lee Harvey Oswald, Rudolph Hess, and Daniel Paul Schreber. Paranoid schizophrenia, by far the commonest schizophrenic label (Outpatient Psychiatric Clinics, 1963), is most dramatically characterized by delusions and hallucinations. The delusions are usually of a persecutory or grandiose nature. Many paranoids are preoccupied with religion. As a result of their delusions paranoid patients are often suspicious, hostile, and physically and verbally aggressive. Paranoid schizophrenics show the least disruption of intellectual functioning among all the traditional subgroups of schizophrenia (Hamlin and Lorr, 1971). Their delusions are usually systematic and organized—once you accept the basic irrational premise.

Acute type. This phrase is generally applied only to a schizophrenic patient's first psychotic episode. The condition is marked by acute confusion, depression, agitation, and anxiety. It may be resolved in one of two ways. The patient may gradually develop the symptoms of one of the other subtypes of schizophrenia; or else his behavioral deviations may remit. Remission (behavioral improvement) is often but not always followed by a later return to schizophrenic behavior. The term "remission" is used by clinicians who think that a person can recover from schizophrenia. Many other clinicians believe, however, that any person who has once shown schizophrenic behavior is very likely to show it again. They would regard a patient who experiences an initial acute episode followed by a complete recovery as having been incorrectly diagnosed—and as being very lucky. Later in the chapter you will see that some researchers consider the chronic-acute dimension one of the most important for understanding schizophrenia.

Latent type. Latent schizophrenia, also called *borderline* schizophrenia, refers to people who show some schizophrenic behaviors but have never been clearly psychotic. In these cases diagnosis is an especially subtle process; the clinician must be sensitive to the smallest indications of thought disorder. Many clinicians hesitate to use this category, especially in view of the unpleasant consequences a diagnosis of schizophrenia often has for a person (see Chapter 5).

Residual type. The label "residual type" is usually applied to patients who have had a previous schizophrenic episode but are not now psychotic. The residual schizophrenic, like the latent schizophrenic, demonstrates what is left of his psychopathology in mild form. But note once again that many authorities believe a patient is not usually "cured" of schizophrenia, even though he may show only the mild "cognitive slippage" of which Meehl writes, rather than the more blatant "loosening of associations" which is associated with active psychosis.

Schizo-affective type. Schizo-affective schizophrenics exhibit the behavioral excesses of both schizophrenia and affective disorder, a condition which will be discussed in Chapter 8. As a result they are divided into excited and depressed types. The patient may be profoundly depressed and suicidal, or else manic and grandiose. He expresses delusional ideas or other behaviors which clearly reflect thought disorders. The prognosis for improvement in the schizo-affective patient falls between that of the schizophrenic, which is not good, and that of the manic-depressive, which is good (Clark & Mallett, 1963).

Childhood type. Childhood schizophrenia is the category reserved for individuals in whom the behaviors of schizophrenia appear before puberty. Chapter 15 provides a detailed consideration of these syndromes.

Chronic undifferentiated type. Patients who do not show a clear-cut set of behaviors appropriate to any of the other categories of schizophrenia are included in the "wastebasket" category of the chronic undifferentiated type. They show mixtures of disordered thought and affect sufficient to "qualify" them as schizophrenics but inadequate for more precise categorization. The term "chronic" implies a long-standing disorder.

Categories of schizophrenia: How useful are they?

From what you have read in this chapter and Chapter 5, you might conclude that the ten categories of schizophrenia are not as reliable or valid as their incorporation into the "official" diagnostic system would imply. That conclusion, in our view, is correct. To begin with, patients like those described in DSM II, the *Diagnostic and Statistical Manual,* rarely exist; most people seen in clinical practice do not lend themselves to easy categorization. Further, a variety of research suggests that reliable differentiation of the subcategories of schizophrenia is extremely difficult (Hearst et al., 1971; Nathan et al., 1968). Finally, the categorization of schizophrenic patients into the subgroupings given above apparently has little meaning for prognosis. Specific therapies for patients in the various subgroups do not exist. Instead, the major tranquilizers appear to control severe deviations in many schizophrenic patients irrespective of diagnostic subcategory. Though it has often been

said that patients of the paranoid type have a better untreated prognosis than those in other subcategories, even this is essentially unproved (Shakow, 1969).

Dimensions of schizophrenia: Alternatives to the traditional approach

Behavioral scientists have tried and continue to try to reconceptualize schizophrenia along more meaningful dimensions than the traditional diagnostic categories permit. Eysenck has even suggested doing away with the category of schizophrenia altogether (1960c). His idea is to focus instead upon identification and assessment of broad personality dimensions by which all patients would be judged. In Eysenck's proposed system a patient would not be *either* schizophrenic *or* neurotic. Rather, he would fall at a certain point on the continuum of psychosis and at another point on the continuum of neurosis. But the dimensions of schizophrenia which are currently arousing the most interest and study are a little less radical than the ones Eysenck proposes. Research today is emphasizing the process-reactive, chronic-acute, and paranoid-nonparanoid continuums.

Process-reactive dimension

Process schizophrenia is considered a slowly developing disorder in which the symptoms gradually worsen. *Reactive* schizophrenia, in contrast, has a sudden onset and acute symptoms, which seem to arise from a sudden shock or stress in the person's environment. The distinction between process and reactive schizophrenia originated with the differing views about the disorder held by Kraepelin and Bleuler. Kraepelin believed dementia praecox to be a progressive disorder with total mental deterioration as its ultimate end. Bleuler, however, was convinced that some schizophrenics recover, even though the majority of them clearly do not.

Historically, clinicians have tended to agree with Kraepelin. They argue that patients who recover completely from what appears to have been a schizophrenic episode were not really schizophrenic to begin with. The process-reactive dichotomy has developed as one resolution of this circular argument. According to the dichotomy, process and reactive schizophrenics show some behavioral similarities but actually suffer from different disorders. The process schizophrenic has an organic disorder whose course follows Kraepelin's projected deterioration. The reactive schizophrenic is simply responding to a life stress and is potentially curable.

Kantor, Wallner, and Windner listed some apparent differences between process and reactive schizophrenics in a 1953 paper, which is summarized in Table 6-1. But when this scale or similar scales are applied to the life histories of unselected schizophrenics, the patients do not fall into two clear-cut categories. Instead their "schizophrenic history" scores distribute them along a continuum from highly process to highly reactive. Recognizing this, Higgins and Peterson suggest that schizophrenic patients may actually be distributed along a process-reactive *continuum* rather than forming two separate groups of patients with different disorders (1966).

TABLE 6-1. PROCESS—REACTIVE DICHOTOMY IN SCHIZOPHRENIA

Process schizophrenia	Reactive schizophrenia
Birth to the fifth year	
Early psychological trauma	Good psychological history
Physical illness—severe or long	Good physical health
Odd member of family	Normal member of family
Fifth year to adolescence	
Difficulties at school	Well adjusted at school
Family troubles paralleled with sudden changes in patient's behavior	Domestic troubles accompanied by behavior disruptions. Patient "had what it took."
Introverted behavior trends and interests	Extroverted behavior trends and interests
History of breakdown of social, physical, mental functioning	History of adequate social, physical, mental functioning
Pathological siblings	Normal siblings
Overprotective or rejecting mother. "Momism"	Normally protective, accepting mother
Rejecting father	Accepting father
Adolescence to adulthood	
Lack of heterosexuality	Heterosexual behavior
Insidious, gradual onset of psychosis without pertinent stress	Sudden onset of psychosis; stress present and pertinent. Later onset.
Physical aggression	Verbal aggression
Poor response to treatment	Good response to treatment
Lengthy stay in hospital	Short course in hospital
Adulthood	
Massive paranoia	Minor paranoid trends
Little capacity for alcohol	Much capacity for alcohol
No manic-depressive component	Presence of manic-depressive component
Failure under adversity	Success despite adversity
Discrepancy between ability and achievement	Harmony between ability and achievement
Awareness of change in self	No sensation of change
Somatic delusions	Absence of somatic delusions
Clash between culture and environment	Harmony between culture and environment
Loss of decency (nudity, public masturbation, etc.)	Retention of decency

SOURCE: Kantor et al., 1953.

As opposite ends of a continuum, the process and reactive concepts seem to offer a meaningful approach to schizophrenia. One finding that lends support to this dimensional model was a study showing that reactive schizophrenics have a consistently better prognosis (for remission of their psychotic behavior) than process schizophrenics (Higgins, 1964). Another group of studies was designed to look at relationships between male process and reactive schizophrenics and their parents. The data revealed that process schizophrenics more often come from homes with dominant mothers, reactive schizophrenics from homes with dominant fathers (Baxter & Becker, 1962; Garmezy et al., 1961). A similar investigation discovered that censure from fathers has an especially disruptive effect on the behavior of male reactive schizophrenics, while maternal criticism most disrupts the process schizophrenic (Goodman, 1964). In addition, some research has compared the autonomic functioning of male process and reactive schizophrenics with the functioning of normal subjects (Van Zoost & McNulty, 1971). The investigators reported that under stress, the skin resistance and blood pressure levels of normals and reactive schizophrenics were similar. The process schizophrenics had higher skin resistance and lower blood pressure under the same stress. Reactive schizophrenics had the highest heart rate, normal subjects the lowest.

These data, though they do not *prove* the existence of a bimodal distribution, do suggest that the process-reactive dimension is a potentially useful one for studying and understanding schizophrenia. At least it permits meaningful distinctions among schizophrenic patients, whereas the DSM II categories rarely do.

Chronic-acute dimension

Another dimension of schizophrenia which seems to have some prognostic value is the chronic-acute dimension. Many observers have noticed that following an initial acute psychotic episode, schizophrenics (1) may completely recover—to all appearances, anyway; or (2) may become less agitated and much less overtly psychotic, but remain chronically withdrawn, isolated, and confused. On this basis schizophrenic patients can be divided into those who are acutely disturbed and actively struggling with their psychosis (acute) and those who have become apathetic and indifferent to it (chronic).

Acute schizophrenic episodes are often triggered by some upsetting event like a move to a new city, the death of a family member, or a romantic failure. In such situations the patient may be completely overwhelmed by his emotions, to the extent that only psychosis offers a "way out." By contrast, the disordered behavior of the chronic schizophrenic patient develops much more gradually. Often he seems indifferent, sometimes even unaware, that he is in serious trouble.

The acute schizophrenic has a better prognosis than the chronic one. Perhaps the reason is that the acute patient continues to struggle with his deviant behavior, to react to rather than avoid a life crisis, whereas the chronic schizophrenic appears resigned to his disorder, when he recognizes its existence. Although the research in this area is interesting, it is open to serious charges of sampling errors which challenge the value of the conclusions (Strauss, 1973).

Patients do not begin their patienthood as chronic schizophrenics. Instead, at some earlier point in their lives they developed behaviors which led other people to label them as disturbed. In other words, becoming a chronic patient involves a series of steps or "choice points" by society as the people who are around a disturbed individual make decisions about what kind of action to take (Sommer & Witney, 1961).

Paranoid-nonparanoid dimension

Paranoid schizophrenics are almost always less severely impaired in functioning than other schizophrenics (Johannsen et al., 1963; Payne & Hewlett, 1960). It has been suggested that

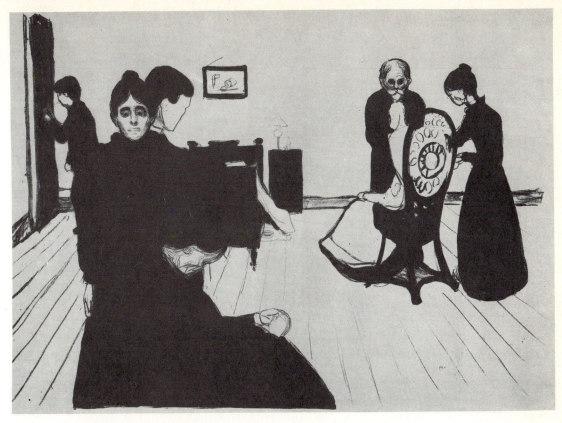

The Death Chamber, by Edvard Munch, suggests the kind of stress that can sometimes trigger an acute schizophrenic episode in a bereaved survivor. *(Collection, Museum of Modern Art, New York)*

paranoid schizophrenics may form a diagnostic category separate from the other kinds of schizophrenia. In any event, many diagnosticians believe that the paranoid-nonparanoid distinction is one of the most important they can make.

Among 17,000 schizophrenics seen at a large number of selected outpatient clinics in 1961, 38 percent were diagnosed as undifferentiated, 36 percent as paranoid, 6 percent as catatonic, 5 percent as simple, and 1 percent as hebephrenic (Outpatient Psychiatric Clinics, 1963). In other words, the paranoid label alone accounted for more than one-third of all these patients. And in a study of the diagnostic decisions made at a large urban hospital, Nathan (1969) found that almost 50 percent of the schizophrenic patients were placed in the paranoid category (see Figure 6-2).

Considerable research supports the legiti-macy of the paranoid-nonparanoid distinction. Shakow found that a group of schizophrenic patients of all subtypes revealed only two distinctly different cognitive patterns (1962, 1963). The first fitted the traditional picture of paranoid schizophrenia (that is, they showed an essentially intact set of cognitive functions), while the other resembled the hebephrenic pattern of severe thought disorder. Heilbrun and Norbert reported that paranoid subjects were more sensitive to maternal censure than nonparanoids were (1971). An interesting result of several studies is that the paranoid-non-paranoid dimension was independent of either the process-reactive (Sanes & Zigler, 1971) or the chronic-acute (Eisenthal et al., 1972) dimensions, despite important similarities among all three.

Clearly, these three dimensions may represent significant bases for a new classification

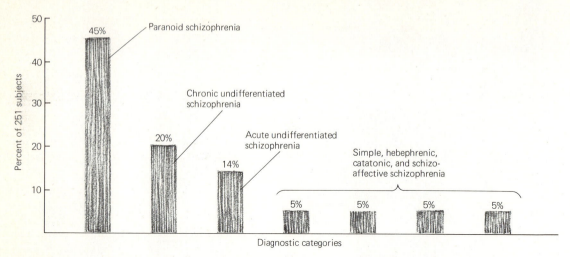

Figure 6-2. Diagnostic subdivisions among 251 schizophrenic patients. *(Nathan et al., 1969)*

system in diagnosing schizophrenia. Such a system could be superior to the present DSM II labels both in reliability (because only two rather than ten distinctions have to be made) and in validity (because these dimensions relate empirically to important prognostic and treatment variables).

Assessment of the schizophrenias: Identifying and evaluating the cues

Efforts to identify the characteristic behaviors of the group of schizophrenias have taken a variety of forms. The search for reliable overt and covert cues has included mental status examinations, psychological tests, behavioral observation techniques, specialized tests of speech and language, and physiological measurements.

Psychological tests as assessment tools

Many tests have been tried out in attempts both to differentiate schizophrenia from the other mental disorders and to discriminate among the subtypes of schizophrenia. Certain objective tests of personality—notably the Minnesota Multiphasic Personality Inventory

(MMPI)—have proved useful as rough screening devices. They provide the clinician with a test profile which can be compared with scores obtained by known schizophrenics as well as by normals. Further, certain items on the MMPI can signal the interviewer that he should probe for the presence of thought disorder. For example, if the patient endorses such items as "Evil spirits possess me at times," or "Peculiar odors come to me at times," these may be signs of serious psychopathology and certainly should be discussed with the patient.

The MMPI has been used successfully to distinguish *groups* of schizophrenic patients from normals, from other psychiatric patients, and from patients with organic brain disorders (Taulbee & Sisson, 1957; Winter & Salcines, 1958; Watson, 1971). However, the ultimate clinical value of this research is questionable, because such group results are rarely valid for individual patients. The Wechsler Adult Intelligence Scale (WAIS) has a similar drawback. Guertin and his colleagues say that it may be possible to distinguish schizophrenics from normals on the WAIS (1962). But they suggest that it is much more difficult to use the scale to separate the schizophrenic from patients in other diagnostic categories—and this is the more common clinical problem.

Thus the diagnostic value of objective personality tests like the MMPI, and intelligence tests like the WAIS, is limited. But the use of projective tests like the Rorschach and TAT for this purpose is even more questionable. The classic study of "schizophrenic" Rorschach responses was undertaken by David Rapaport and his colleagues in 1946. Though it was welcomed then because it identified a set of Rorschach responses unique to schizophrenic patients, Rapaport's study is now considered seriously flawed in design. For example, some of his samples consisted of as few as four subjects. Rapaport also failed to control for such important variables as social class, intelligence, education, age, and sex. Today few clinicians believe that they can point to a particular Rorschach response and call it "schizophrenic," no matter how bizarre or unusual it may be. Recent better-designed studies have not demonstrated the Rorschach's diagnostic value for individual patients, though it does appear to have research value when large groups of cases permit general statements to be made (Goldfried, Stricker, & Weiner, 1971).

One encouraging trend in the use of the Rorschach technique is a movement toward more sophisticated scoring of responses—that is, scoring for less generalized purposes than the aim of overall diagnosis. For example, Quinlan and his coworkers (1972) report a new scoring system which appears sensitive to the presence of thought disorder severe enough to affect patients' responses to the inkblots. The strength of this and other "new" uses of the Rorschach is their approach to it as a standardized, objective sample of behavior and their deemphasis on it as a diagnostic instrument or as a measure of the person's "inner functioning."

Cognitive deficits: Disorders of language and intellectual functioning

Language: Do schizophrenics talk differently?
Language disorder is one sign of the more basic malfunction in schizophrenia called thought disorder. For this reason, behavioral scientists usually regard the pecularities of speech dem-

onstrated by a schizophrenic as reflections of bizarre thinking. The following "schizophrenic writings" are good examples of cognitive dysfunction. The first is from Daniel Paul Schreber:

The purpose of not-finishing-a-sentence is consistent with God's attitude to me throughout: to prevent dissolution in my body which would necessarily result from its attraction. While conditions prevailed which were at least somehow in consonance with the Order of the World, that is before trying-to-rays and trying-to-celestial-bodies were started, . . . a momentary uniform *feeling* was enough to make the freely suspended souls jump down from the sky into my mouth, thus ending their independent existence. [1955, p. 173]

Here are the words of Rudolph Hess:

The heart poison was without any doubt put into my food and the medicines that were recommended to me to take against my abdominal cramps. My broken leg was also massaged with some powder and this powder was also put into my laundry; it dried the skin and caused unbearable itching of the skin and rashes. They gave me vaseline as an antidote which on the other hand contained heart poison. They put chemicals in my supper that would prevent sleep. The sedatives against this lack of sleep contained heart poison. They did not miss any chances of giving it to me. [Rees, 1948, p. 118]

Lee Harvey Oswald wrote in his diary:

I am shocked! ! My dreams!***I have waited for 2 year to be accepted. My fondes dreams are shattered because of a petty offial, *** I decide to end it. Soak rist in cold water to numb the pain, Then slash my leftwrist. Then plaug wrist into bathum of hot water***Somewhere, a violin plays, as I watch my life whirl away. I think to myself "How easy to Die" and "A Sweet Death, (to violins)***. [President's Commission, 1964, p. 392]

Layman and professional alike would agree that these three excerpts show uncommon use of language. Even when they are grammatically correct, as Hess's is, the ideas expressed are very strange. Yet while all three may appear "schizophrenic," notice that each is quite different from the other two. Schreber's writing is more disjointed than Hess's, though both dwell on the theme of persecution. Oswald's statement, the most poetic and the least obviously psychotic of the three, is nonetheless persecuted in tone and disorganized in form. Lorenz has wisely advised social scientists to avoid trying to establish a dictionary of a single "schizophrenic language" (1961). Although schizophrenics do give evidence of psychopathology in their speech and writing, as the examples above show, there is no pattern which can be singled out as *the* schizophrenic language.

Keep this reservation in mind as we turn to the positive evidence concerning language and diagnosis. Research indicates that schizophrenic speech can be reliably identified (Hunt & Arnhoff, 1956) and that experienced clinicians can use it to make valid judgments of the severity of a patient's disorder (Jones, 1959). Many studies have also focused on the formal or grammatical characteristics of schizophrenic language. One finding is that schizophrenics use a smaller vocabulary than nonschizophrenics. Another is that they use more action words and fewer descriptive words than normal subjects (Maher et al., 1966). And when comparisons of formal language usage are made among groups of schizophrenics, process schizophrenics are usually more deviant from normals than reactive schizophrenics are (Maher et al., 1966).

Research on the content of schizophrenic language suggests that the schizophrenics with the most severe thought disorders are apt to be preoccupied with religious, scientific, political, and legal issues—as Schreber, Hess, and Oswald certainly were. Less disturbed schizophrenics are like normal people in that they tend to dwell on issues relevant to their own lives and families (Maher et al., 1966).

Intelligence: Does schizophrenia affect intellectual functioning? Studies of his language give us one guide to the schizophrenic's thought processes. Studies of his intellectual functioning give us another. Is the schizophrenic's ability to function on intellectual tasks impaired? A decline in intellectual

functioning does follow hospitalization for schizophrenia (Kingsley & Struening, 1966). However, the research which demonstrated this decline did not separate the effect of being hospitalized from that of being schizophrenic. The lethargy produced by long-term hospitalization in itself may reduce a person's efficiency on tests where motivation and speed are important factors. Patients who stay in the hospital for some time do not show a continuing decline in intelligence, while those who improve enough to leave it tend to return to their pre-hospital levels of functioning (Payne, 1970). Thus, contrary to Kraepelin's prediction, schizophrenia does not seem to involve progressive deterioration.

Efficient intellectual functioning requires attention, perception, and organization. As the following discussion emphasizes, the schizophrenic who becomes disordered in any of these areas will be impaired in intellectual performance.

Attention and intelligence. The schizophrenic's ability to pay attention to intellectual tasks is apt to be disrupted by factors which do not appear to distract nonschizophrenics. However, when the consequence of not paying attention is physically aversive (like a shock), schizophrenics pay attention about as well as normal subjects (Maher, 1966). In other words, it seems that schizophrenics are capable of normal attention under the proper circumstances. Not surprisingly, reactive and paranoid schizophrenics show better attention skills than process, chronic, and nonparanoid schizophrenics (Payne, 1970).

Perception and intelligence. Some schizophrenics also appear to suffer from deficits in perception. They do not perform as well as normal subjects on tasks like matching and copying patterns or estimating sizes, distances, and weights. These deficiencies, however, appear to be confined to nonparanoid and process schizophrenics (Payne, 1970).

Organization and intelligence. What happens to information once it has been attended to and perceived by the schizophrenic? Researchers have developed two major conceptual models by which thinking processes may be evaluated. These are the *concrete-abstract* continuum (Goldstein, 1944) and the *overinclusive-underinclusive* continuum (Cameron, 1963). The concrete-abstract dimension of concept formation refers to a person's ability to transcend the immediate stimulus properties of a situation and look at it from a broader perspective. For example, interpreting the proverb "Strike while the iron is hot," as "Do your ironing while the iron is heated up," is interpreting it concretely. An abstract interpretation of the same proverb is "Take advantage of an opportunity when it presents itself." Goldstein and many others have concluded that the ability to think abstractly is an important component of intelligence (1944). Note these schizophrenic responses to proverbs:

A stitch in time saves nine.
If you had a tear in your clothing and sewed it up right away, you'd be saving time.
If I would take one stitch ahead of time, I would know nine times better how to do another stitch.
I could do something and it would help everyone else.

People in glass houses shouldn't throw stones.
You shouldn't throw stones at people.
You shouldn't throw stones through windows—that's what I've been trying to avoid doing.

When the cat's away, the mice will play.
There's nobody to watch the kittens—I mean the mice.
If the father is away, things get harmed, too.

Barking dogs seldom bite.
It depends on what they are barking for. When they are loose it is all right, but when they are tied up they get mean and will bite.

[Gregory, 1968, pp. 430-431]

Overinclusion refers to the process of incorporating within a concept objects or ideas which most people would specifically exclude from it. Underinclusion involves omitting objects or ideas from a concept which most people would regard as an integral part of it.

The ability to form concepts, like a person's ability to pay attention and like his competence in perception, varies with different subgroups of schizophrenia. Process schizophrenics tend to be concrete in their interpretations (Johnson, 1966) and to define conceptual boundaries excessively narrowly (Payne, 1970). Reactive schizophrenics are largely overinclusive in their categorizations (Payne et al., 1964).

Taken as a whole, current research on thought disorder seems to underline the importance of the dimensions of schizophrenia. The chronic-acute, process-reactive, and paranoid-nonparanoid dimensions all appear related to the severity of a patient's thought disturbance. In addition, all tend to have more predictive value than the traditional categories of schizophrenia.

Affective and perceptual deficits: Disorders of psychobiological functioning

Many mental health professionals believe that some or all of the disorders which compose the group of schizophrenias are the result of psychobiological malfunction, perhaps hereditary. Others, acknowledging that schizophrenics do show important physiological differences from nonschizophrenics, regard these differences as a result of, rather than the cause of, the psychosis. First, what are some of the differences in physiological functioning between schizophrenics and normals?

Response to stress. On such physiological measures of response to stress as galvanic skin response, heart rate, blood pressure, and respiration, schizophrenics tend to be either "overaroused" or "underaroused" compared with normals. In other words, most schizophrenics appear unable to give suitable emotional responses to stressful stimuli (Epstein, 1967; Fenz & Velner, 1970). See Figure 6-3. This inability to modulate emotional expression during stress relates directly to the overall affective description often given of the schizophrenic: that is, as a person whose emotions are inappropriate. Either they are so "out

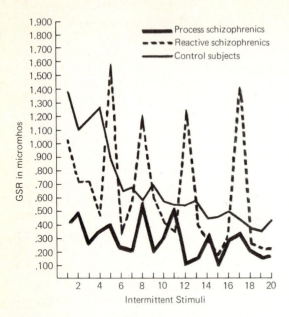

Figure 6-3. Both process and reactive schizophrenic patients show much greater galvanic skin response (GSR) reactivity to intermittent stressful stimuli than do nonschizophrenic control subjects. *(Fenz & Velner, 1970)*

of control" that when they are expressed they are incongruous (the patient laughs when tears are suitable or cries when laughter is called for) or they are so "overcontrolled" that the patient is simply unresponsive ("flat") emotionally to whatever is going on.

Pincus and Hoagland have studied the role of the adrenal cortex in emotional responsivity (1950). They reported that schizophrenic and normal subjects did not show significant differences in hormonal output from the adrenal cortex during resting conditions. Their schizophrenic subjects, however, became markedly "underreactive" during stress conditions. Studies that followed this early project have yielded comparable findings.

In most studies reporting that schizophrenics respond abnormally to stress, paranoid schizophrenics are described as resembling normal subjects more than they do hebephrenic or catatonic schizophrenics (Gruzelier

et al., 1972). This finding is consistent with the many differences described earlier between paranoid and other schizophrenics.

EEG patterns. Many studies have tried to identify differences between the electroencephalograms of schizophrenic patients and normal subjects. As discussed in Chapter 3, various organic brain disorders (including epilepsy and brain tumors) cause abnormal EEGs. Because some researchers consider schizophrenia to be of organic etiology, they have suggested that schizophrenics ought to produce a distinctive EEG pattern. As a group, in fact, schizophrenics show a larger number of abnormal EEGs than normal subjects do (Abenson, 1970). This finding, however, appears to tie in with neurological illness, age, or medication more than with schizophrenia as an organic brain disorder. (Research relating schizophrenia and epilepsy, a form of brain damage, will be reviewed in Chapter 17.)

Sleep abnormalities. Other researchers have proposed that hallucinations—the major perceptual dysfunction of schizophrenics—are a form of dreaming during the waking state. And if so, perhaps schizophrenics dream less when they are asleep than normals do. This hypothesis has had little support from research during the past twenty years. Dement found no difference in amount of dream activity when he compared chronic schizophrenics with normals (1955). Similar negative results were reported more recently by Feinberg and his colleagues (1964) and by other researchers. However, schizophrenics do appear to experience some disruption of stage 4 sleep (deep sleep). Caldwell and Domino found that schizophrenics have significantly less stage 4 sleep than normals (1967). And Koranyi and Lehman reported that sleep deprivation exacerbates the disordered behavior of chronic schizophrenics (1960). However, the extent to which these data relate to either the etiology or the psychopathology of schizophrenia remains to be established.

Summary

Researchers and clinicians have amassed huge quantities of data to describe schizophrenia and to support their theories about this puzzling disorder. The sample of competing arguments and conflicting experiments given here only suggests the chaos of facts available. Still, a few themes and pieces of firm evidence should stand out and stay with you now that you have finished the chapter.

It was not until Kraepelin singled out the behaviors which he labeled dementia praecox (later renamed schizophrenia) that scientists became aware of this distinct category. What were the behaviors that Kraepelin, Bleuler, and the workers who followed them diagnosed as schizophrenic? Bleuler called them the four A's—loosening of associations, inappropriate affect, ambivalence, and autism. Many of the schizophrenic's deviations are cognitive dysfunctions: the schizophrenic shows disturbed logic, peculiar use of language, and preoccupation with his own thoughts. Perceptual disorders, including hallucinations and changes in body image, are also common in schizophrenia. The emotional responses of the person diagnosed as schizophrenic are characterized by "flattening of affect." Schizophrenics may show abnormalities in psychomotor responses: they may be frozen in stupor, they may race about wildly, or they may make repetitive stereotyped movements.

Building on Kraepelin and Bleuler's original diagnostic categories of simple, hebephrenic, catatonic, and paranoid, the American Psychiatric Association now recognizes ten categories of schizophrenia. In addition to the four basic types, these include acute, latent, residual, schizo-affective, childhood, and chronic undifferentiated. Unfortunately, such categories are not reliable or valid enough to be useful. Recognizing the difficulties in the traditional system, many researchers have attempted to find new *dimensions* for the classification of schizophrenia: for example, the process-reactive, chronic-acute, and paranoid-nonparanoid continuums. Research indicates that reactive, acute, and paranoid patients have a better prognosis than patients who fall into the process, chronic, and nonparanoid groups.

Although in group research, the MMPI and the WAIS have successfully differentiated among schizophrenics, normals, and other psychotic categories, they are not accurate enough to make this distinction for single patients. The Rorschach and TAT have even less utility for such a purpose. Psychobiological studies suggest that there may be differences in physiological functioning between schizophrenics and other groups. For example, schizophrenics may have more EEG and sleep pattern abnormalities, although unique patterns to these deviations have not been found.

Lee Harvey Oswald, Rudolph Hess, and Daniel Paul Schreber were all diagnosed as schizophrenic. Certainly the behavior of each man was highly unusual, far exceeding the bounds of what most people would describe as normal. Keep in mind, however, that their reactions and ways of expressing their deviations were almost as different from one another as they were from the majority of people. They are good examples of the diversity encompassed within the category of schizophrenia.

CHAPTER SEVEN
The group of schizophrenias: Etiology and treatment

Rick G. ● Etiology: Biochemical factors ● Genetic factors ● Psychoanalytic theories ● Interpersonal theories ● Drive and arousal theories ● Learning theories ● Treatment: Somatotherapy ● Chemotherapy ● Dynamic therapies ● Milieu therapy ● Behavior modification ● Involuntary hospitalization

FROM A
YOUNG
PSYCHOL-
OGIST'S
CASE NOTES

August 30, 1969

I was assigned the case of Rick G. today; I see him tomorrow. He's going to be a handful. This afternoon I checked his file, which is a folder an inch thick. The bare facts are that he's a white male, aged 26, with a diagnosis of chronic paranoid schizophrenia. Imagine being chronic anything at 26! He's been in the hospital twice before, but this time he was arrested for molesting a 7-year-old girl. Seems he enticed her into the attic when she came around selling Girl Scout cookies. I've never dealt with a child molester; I'm not sure I can get over my feelings enough to be much help to him. Hard

(Jan Lukas from Rapho Guillumette)

177

to understand how anyone could hurt a child, except that when you look at Rick's history you begin to see why. His father has been in and out of state hospitals, his brother was given a medical discharge from the Army for psychiatric reasons, and his mother, the most stable of the four, was arrested for child abuse when Rick was small. She had burned his back with an iron.

September 15

It's a good thing I'm in therapy myself. I'm going to need all the help I can get with my feelings about Rick. Our sessions are interesting and he's providing a lot of material, but much of it is as psychotic as anything I've ever heard or read about. He has experienced stronger sexual feelings and more aggression and anger in his 26 years than most people do in a lifetime. And what is so distressingly psychotic is the way all those impulses come tumbling out with almost no ego control. With me, Rick just says what he is feeling on the most primitive levels. With other people in the past, like that little girl, he does more than just describe his feelings. One of my main goals will have to be strengthening his ego defenses.

October 7

Rick began today's session by saying he had so many things on his mind that he despaired of communicating them to anyone. There was a pause; then he told me that after our last session, he had gone directly to see his mother, for it was during visiting hours. But because he was so upset about the thoughts he was beginning to have about me, he hadn't been able to think about anything else. Later that day he had stopped thinking about me—while he masturbated as he watched one of the secretaries walking to her car. He added— a little obscurely—that he doesn't feel bad if he touches girls who wear tight skirts, because they are sinning against God. Then he said he was afraid that he might have a bad body odor. Then he wondered out loud if his rectum was clean. And then he wondered whether the Virgin Mary's rectum was clean—and how clean mine might be. I amazed myself by sitting quietly and solemnly, every inch the professional woman, while inside I was quaking. How many women my age have heard a man say such things without running for the door?

Despite my personal feelings about Rick's confession, I could still appreciate the sequence of his associations. Unable to acknowledge his anger toward his mother (and maybe his desires for her), he was filled with sexual and aggressive thoughts about me when he was with her. Then he displaced his sexual thoughts onto a girl "bad" enough to deserve them because she wore a tight skirt. All these things must have made him think about himself: "I stink—

I have body odor." The link between his sexual and aggressive thoughts is becoming clearer.

October 28

When I started the session with "What's new?" his instant response was "Not good, not good!" He said that since last week he has been reading his Bible more and more. After he went to bed last night, he felt as if Jesus was in the room with him. He opened his eyes and looked at the picture of Jesus on the wall, and it winked at him. Earlier that night when he was taking a shower, he washed the feet of a black man in the shower because he wanted to do what Jesus had done in the Bible.

November 23

He started today's session by telling me that he had had another homosexual encounter with Dave last night. Afterwards he was afraid he had offended God. Then he said that he had watched me leave the building and had seen my skirt go up when I got into my car. He wanted to know why I left the building with Dr. C. and whether he and I were lovers. He said he felt uncomfortable today. Thought he might smell bad.

The business about odors is clearly tied in with times when he feels he has really offended someone. All the sexual content is getting tough for me to handle. I can see why it is so important for me to be alert to my own feelings. There is no denying that I sometimes have sexual thoughts during the conversations. Sometimes these thoughts have to do with Rick and me. I'm going to have to work on the countertransference elements of our relationship so I can be sure I'm not doing anything to bring out the sexual material. Could be I'm unconsciously acting seductive. But I still think all the sexual talk is just a cover for his anger. I wonder if I'm nearly as afraid of his anger as he is. Then again, I really am afraid sometimes that he might lose control and attack me. Or could it be a wish? I've got to work on that.

December 13

At the start of every session he pokes paper into the keyhole so no one can spy on us.

He said he didn't have much to say today. Then he was silent for a long while. Finally he said he would like to see me in the nude. At the ward party last week he danced with a female patient who "put her private parts on my private parts." A long silence followed this confession. Then, surprisingly, Rick left off his psychosis long enough to talk solemnly and realistically about the understandable feelings of affection he does have for me. The session ended on this,

(Jan Lukas from Rapho Guillumette)

179

the most positive sign of progress yet. Could be we are making some gains against old devil psychosis?

December 15

Two steps back for every step forward. The honesty of the last session scared him. He spent most of today's meeting talking about how much his head ached and his back hurt. A real regression; I guess the intimacy was too much for him to handle. He said he felt uncomfortable around me today because he thought he might smell bad from a homosexual contact last night. Then he said he would like to undress me and put his mouth all over me. I felt certain enough of my sex-equals-anger interpretation to point it out to him. I told him he said those things when he was mad with me. He responded by saying, "My neck has been hurting me since 1958." Then he talked about a woman whom he had met in a movie house and wanted to attack. She had made him mad. I know he didn't realize the implications of this sequence of remarks, but it certainly confirmed my hypothesis. His sexual acting out is based on his anger toward women. His mother is no doubt at the bottom of it.

January 11

Our sessions are focusing more and more on Rick's mother. An amazingly seductive woman: when she wasn't beating him, which she did fairly often, she was inviting him into bed with her. He has made some real strides toward recognizing his anger toward his mother. Now if I can only help him to see how the sex and anger tie together.

April 23

I think he has learned something from our sessions. He is able to recognize his anger, and to see that molesting children was an outlet for the anger. A way to have sex without being forced into contact with a woman. The trouble is that he is still preoccupied with sexual and aggressive thoughts. And he's afraid he will molest children just as before if he's released. He thought Jesus came to see him again last night.

June 11

We have only a couple of weeks of therapy left before I leave the hospital to go back to Denver. I'm not sure how much I've helped Rick. We have a good relationship; he trusts me. He talks freely, but he's just as psychotic as before. Three hours a week for nearly a year—and very little progress. Psychoanalytic treatment of schizophrenia is impossibly long. I honestly don't know what to recommend when I leave. He needs more therapy: years more. I've

(Jan Lukas from Rapho Guillumette)

heard from Dr. C. that they are having some success with schizophrenics on the behavior-modification ward. I wonder if that's the place for Rick? But what can poker chips and candy do for psychosis? Then again, what have I done for him with all my interpretations and theoretical formulations, my warmth and understanding? If only I had more time for Rick. The problem is that no one ever has enough time for people like him. Maybe behavior mod is the way to go. But I'm glad it isn't me who will be treated like a machine, and I hate to think that it's one of my patients. If I just had the time.

On schizophrenia: What will become of Rick?

These excerpts from case notes written by Rick's young therapist raise many issues surrounding the causes and treatment of the schizophrenias. We will focus here on three: Rick's behavior as a sample of what psychologists call schizophrenia, his therapist's thoughts and feelings about her developing relationship with Rick, and the particular therapeutic strategy she chose to employ.

A truism in the mental health professions is that even patients with the same diagnosis can show marked symptomatic differences. Think of Rick and Daniel Paul Schreber, for example. Both had elaborate delusional systems revolving around sexual, aggressive, and religious themes. Both "acted out" their sexual and aggressive fantasies on society to the extent that both were hospitalized. And both showed the cognitive and affective disabilities that are considered characteristic of the schizophrenias. Therefore both received the same diagnostic label: paranoid schizophrenia. But despite these behavioral similarities, Rick and Schreber were not by any means "two peas in a pod." Schreber, product of an aristocratic Prussian family, was urbane, well-educated, and well-mannered, at least when his psychosis did not overpower him. Rick, born into a poor rural American family

split by discord and mental illness, never approached Schreber's social, intellectual, and economic position. And these largely sociocultural differences between the two men were reflected in their psychoses. Schreber's delusions were full of literary and historical references; Rick's were tied to immediate environmental stimuli. Schreber's book about his psychosis was a literate, even elegant, document; we learn of Rick's disorder only because his therapist recalls it. Schreber returned to his family, friends, and social position after his release from the hospital; Rick has never been discharged, in part because no one is willing to take responsibility for him.

The case notes of Rick's young therapist provide insights into a beginner's reactions to severe psychopathology. They also reveal the difficulties which all therapists, even experienced ones, have in dealing with psychotic patients' interpersonal distortions and unrealistic perceptions.

Every new therapist has trouble adjusting to the role of therapist, since it demands wisdom, compassion, unconditional warmth, and empathic understanding from fallible human beings. But for therapists who begin their careers by working with psychotics, it is especially difficult to sort out the interpersonal demands a patient's psychosis places on them from the demands of the therapeutic situation itself. Rick's therapist, a young woman studying for her doctorate in clinical psychology, had to deal with a young man who had committed a variety of serious sexual crimes over which he had had no control. This man consistently and dramatically distorted reality, suffered from profound hallucinatory and delusional impairments, and maintained an unflagging but totally unrealistic sexual interest in her. Rick's therapist was not entirely sure that aspects of her own behavior—her compassion, human warmth, and desire to help a suffering human being—were not contributing to his romantic interest in her. And this young man, one of her earliest clients, was so disturbed that it was highly unlikely that she could have much effect on the severity of his condition. It is not surprising that her feelings were complex as she tried to understand and deal with his psychopathology.

Rick's therapist had been educated in the psychodynamic tradition that predominates at many training centers for mental health professionals. As a result her therapy was aimed at trying to understand Rick's psychodynamics, and then at trying to help him understand them. Her case notes are filled with speculations about how Rick's early experiences with his parents contributed to his current sexual difficulties, how his instinctual urges had overwhelmed his reality-oriented psychic structures, and how his behavior with his therapist seemed to embody transference elements characteristic of most psychoanalytic relationships. All these formulations were focused on one therapeutic goal: helping Rick achieve insight into the causes of his antisocial behavior and his inappropriate transference feelings, in hopes that insight would bring about changes in his behavior.

If this therapist had entered training in 1974 instead of 1969, her approach to Rick might have been very different. Behavioral therapies for serious psychopathology like Rick's have become widely accepted, because they often seem to work more effectively than psychodynamic methods. How would behavior modification have been used with Rick?

Probably a behavioral analysis would have been done first, to define the behaviors that needed changing and to try and discover the relationships between these behaviors and variables in the environment which were maintaining them. In all likelihood, target behaviors for change in Rick's case would have been his inappropriate fantasies regarding sex with children; his inability to control rage and aggression; his delusions revolving around religion, sex, and aggression; and his inability to establish comfortable social relationships.

Rick's therapist referred to behavior modification techniques as treating the patient "like a machine." Actually, behavior therapy does not approach patients mechanistically but rather aims to deal with each maladaptive behavior in whatever way gives the best results. A close relationship with the therapist might be a part of a behavior modification strategy if this reinforcement seemed effective. As for other strategies, inappropriate sexual fantasies might be treated with aversive conditioning. At the same time, the patient might be helped to acquire and practice more appropriate sexual fantasies and activities. Uncontrolled rage and anger would be dealt with by assertive training techniques. Role playing sessions might also give the patient practice in more appropriate rage-control behavior. Specific training in social skills could help him to feel more comfortable in interpersonal relationships. Rick's delusions would be a more difficult problem for therapy, since there are few reports of successful behavioral treatment of delusions. Also, his delusions were so intimately tied to his whole psychosis that they would be difficult to deal with separately. But it could happen that his delusions might become less important to him, and consequently easier to treat, as other elements of his behavior became more manageable. It is also possible that the antipsychotic drugs might eliminate the delusions, leaving other disordered areas of his behavior more responsive to treatment.

Etiology of schizophrenia

Biochemical factors

Schizophrenic behavior often resembles the pathological behavior of persons whose brain chemistry has been disrupted by drugs, poison, trauma, or disease. Does schizophrenia in fact have a biochemical etiology? Perhaps; though investigators have yet to demonstrate it.

Virtually all biochemical theories of schizophrenia derive from the fundamental assumption that a qualitatively or quantitatively abnormal substance in the brain is responsible for the behavior of the schizophrenic. In other words, these theories assume that schizophrenia results either (1) from too much or too little of a usual brain substance, or (2) from the presence of a toxic brain substance. Over the past three decades, different researchers have identified various biochemical agents in the body fluids of schizophrenic patients that seem to be "responsible" for the disorder. But so far, there has been no independent confirmation of the central role of any of these substances in the etiology of schizophrenia (Kety, 1972; Mosher & Gunderson, 1973).

One reason for this lack of confirmation lies in the problem of controls. Researchers cannot control for every variable in schizophrenic patients' environments that might cause deviations in biochemical functioning (deviations which then may or may not have anything to do with schizophrenic behavior). Mann and LaBrosse (1959) and Dastur and his colleagues (1963) cleverly illustrated the research pitfall in the area of controls. It seemed that certain substances present in the urine of a sample of schizophrenic patients but not present in the urine of a "matched" sample of nonschizophrenic patients might be *the* biochemical factors responsible for schizophrenia. But these researchers demonstrated that their schizophrenic subjects drank much more coffee during the day than the nonschizophrenics, and hence excreted more metabolites of coffee in their urine.

Other problems complicate the search for biochemical factors in schizophrenia. One relates to the possibility, currently accepted by many authorities, that what is now called schizophrenia may be a whole collection of abnormal behavior syndromes that have multiple etiologies and multiple symptom patterns (Overall et al., 1972; Harty, 1972). Thus a substance unique to the brains of one sample of schizophrenics—and possibly responsible for their schizophrenia—might not have anything to do with the behavior of another group of schizophrenics of a different subtype.

Another problem is the difficulty of measuring small changes in brain biochemistry by means of changes in other body tissues or in body fluids. Since it is not yet possible to make direct measurements of biochemical changes in the brain tissue of living people, it is necessary to use less reliable indirect measures. Take the case of the investigator who identifies an abnormal substance in the urine of some schizophrenic patients. What can he conclude? He cannot be sure that the substance has any relationship to the behavior of the patients, because he cannot be sure that its metabolic predecessors—the compounds of which this is the waste product—ever exerted an effect on brain function at all.

Norepinephrine. Despite these formidable problems, research continues on biochemical correlates of schizophrenia. One of the first such studies was reported by Osmond and Smythies (1952). They observed that mescaline (a hallucinogen contained in certain cactuses) and norepinephrine (a neurotransmitter) were both derivatives of the same basic chemical (phenylalanine). They hypothesized that some forms of schizophrenia might result from the abnormal metabolism (transformation) of norepinephrine into a substance, like mescaline, capable of producing psychotic-like behavior. Other investigations found that a number of other hallucinatory drugs besides mescaline were also related chemically to normal body metabolites (Wyatt et al., 1971). Hoffer and his co-workers began to give schizophrenic patients niacin in the form of nicotinic acid (a component of the vitamin B complex), both of which were thought to inhibit the metabolism of normal brain metabolites into abnormal psychotogens (1957). Hoffer and his colleagues have continued to report positive results from nicotinic acid therapy (Hoffer, 1966; Hoffer & Osmond, 1968). Unfortunately, most other researchers have been unable to confirm these findings (McGrath et al., 1972; Ban & Lehmann, 1970).

DMPEA. In 1962 Friedhoff and Van Winkle reported the appearance of 3,4-dimethoxy-phenylethylamine (DMPEA) in the urine of patients "with early schizophrenia." Since DMPEA was also a derivative of dopamine (a naturally occurring brain amine) and hence a close chemical relative of mescaline, it was thought that DMPEA might be the abnormal brain metabolite responsible for schizophrenia. Some studies have supported Friedhoff and Van Winkle's original findings (Kuehl et al., 1964; Takesada et al., 1963). Others have reported the successful development of a "pink spot" chemical test for a substance having many of the characteristics of DMPEA in the urine of schizophrenics (Bourdillon et al., 1965). However, most of the studies of DMPEA have failed to confirm the 1962 findings (Charalampous & Tansery, 1967; Jones et al., 1969; Stabenau et al., 1970).

Bufotenine. Bufotenine, a compound which occurs in certain mushrooms, can produce hallucinatory effects and also a schizophrenic-like syndrome when given to humans (Fabine & Hawkins, 1956). The same substance has been found in the urine of schizophrenics, while it has not been found in the urine of nonschizophrenics (Narasimhachari et al., 1970; Rosengarten et al., 1970). Since bufotenine is a derivative of serotonin, a naturally occurring neurotransmitter that affects synaptic transmission, research has aimed to demonstrate that schizophrenia is a consequence of the abnormal metabolism of serotonin into bufotenine. Despite the plausibility of this theory, most of the research supporting it failed to employ a "blind" method for data collection and analysis in order to rule out experimental

bias. Further, many of the studies did not control the diets of the patients. When these controls were utilized, Perry and his colleagues found no evidence of bufotenine in the urine of either schizophrenics or nonschizophrenics (1966).

Adrenochrome. Many other brain amines and their derivatives have been investigated in research on schizophrenia. Some experimenters have reported finding adrenochrome and other abnormal metabolites of epinephrine in the blood of schizophrenics (Hoffer et al., 1954). But more recent research suggests that no qualitative or quantitative differences in the metabolism of epinephrine distinguish schizophrenics from nonschizophrenics (LaBrose et al., 1961). A similar substance, identified by Hoffer and his collaborators, was once thought to be responsible for the appearance of the "mauve spot" on many chromatographs of schizophrenic urine (Hoffer & Osmond, 1963). Other groups of researchers have been able to distinguish schizophrenics from nonschizophrenics by the "mauve spot" chemical test. They have recently concluded, however, that this chemical reaction represents phenothiazine metabolites—products of the drugs routinely given most schizophrenics in hospitals (Ellman et al., 1968; Sohler et al., 1967, 1970).

Taraxein. Another major line of research designed to relate schizophrenia to a biochemical abnormality centers on abnormalities of plasma proteins. These are chemical substances which freely circulate in the blood. Heath and his co-workers found that taraxein, a substance in the blood of schizophrenic patients, caused schizophrenic behaviors when injected into the bloodstream of nonschizophrenic volunteers (1958). When Heath gave taraxein to monkeys, they developed a peculiar electroencephalograph pattern, called "septal spiking," similar to that found in schizophrenics (1966). But a study which was designed to duplicate Heath's work failed to produce psychotic-like behavior in nonschizophrenics who were injected with the blood of schizophrenic patients (Robins, 1957). Likewise, workers who have attempted to replicate Heath's EEG "septal spiking" results have been unsuccessful (Mosher & Feinsilver, 1970).

Heath and his colleagues have proposed an elaborate *autoimmune theory* of schizophrenia (Heath & Krupp, 1967; Heath et al., 1967), based upon the assumption that schizophrenics produce substances called *antibodies* which attack normal substances called *antigens* that are produced in the brain. Though his group has published a great deal of empirical data in support of the theory, other experimenters have failed to confirm the findings (Whittingham et al., 1968; Logan & Deodhar, 1970).

Genetic factors

Research on the genetics of mental illness had begun by the turn of the century, when Emil Kraepelin began to unify many observations of psychotic behavior into the concept of dementia praecox (see Chapter 6). Most of the early genetic research involved efforts to document the widespread belief that madness ran in families. Scientists assumed that several kinds of faulty human genetic material were transmitted from generation to generation as "hereditary traits." Among them were left-handedness, stuttering, hunched backs, hirsuteness (hairyness), and insanity.

About 1911, when Bleuler renamed the disease schizophrenia and said that it was a group of disorders rather than a single entity, Ernst Rüdin established a psychiatric research clinic in Munich that trained virtually all the pioneers of psychiatric genetics. Since then the genetics of mental illness has emerged as a separate discipline that has yielded data important to the entire range of psychological and psychiatric disorders (Shields & Gottesman, 1971).

There are three major techniques for research into the genetics of mental illness: the pedigree method, the family method, and the twin method. Each has special strengths and weaknesses; each emphasizes a somewhat different aspect of a patient's life history and family background.

Pedigree method. In this procedure the distribution of a disorder is traced among the nuclear (close) and collateral (distant) relatives of an "index case"—a patient who has been diagnosed as definitely suffering from that disorder. The pedigree method is designed to show whether a disorder is distributed in strict accordance with the Mendelian laws of inheritance and whether the responsible gene is dominant, recessive, or sex-linked. The method has not proved very useful for study of the genetics of schizophrenia. This failure may indicate that schizophrenia is a collection of separate conditions with different genetic determinants. Karlsson and his colleagues, however, report that their pedigree studies suggest a strong genetic component in schizophrenia (1966). They have concluded that schizophrenia is a function of a dominant gene, but other genetic researchers have failed to confirm their results.

Family method. The family method assumes that even if a mental disorder does not obey the Mendelian laws of inheritance, it is hereditary if it occurs more often in the families of index patients than in the population at large. This questionable assumption ignores the possibility that the increased incidence of a disorder in a family might reflect maladaptive child-rearing patterns and other negative behavioral influences of family membership. Therefore the conclusions of those who have used the family method to "identify" genetic components in schizophrenia are considered suspect by many investigators.

The family method imposes two other obligations on the genetics researcher which he cannot always meet: (1) It requires accurate determination of rates of schizophrenia in the general population for comparison with index-case family rates. Unfortunately, overall prevalence figures are subject to profound sampling error. (2) It requires accurate diagnosis of the relatives of index patients, no matter whether the relatives are dead or alive, easily available or impossible to locate. In many cases researchers must make a guess on the basis of what evidence is at hand. But since diagnosis under the best conditions is not very reliable, diagnosis from indirect methods instead of actual interviews is even less adequate.

The most widely cited study using the family method to explore the genetics of schizophrenia is that of Franz Kallmann (1938). In Berlin he surveyed the families of 1,087 schizophrenic index cases and reported that the closer the genetic relationship between the schizophrenic index case and one of his relatives, the more likely the relative is to be diagnosed schizophrenic. Recent critics of Kallmann's findings, however, say that his data were neither gathered nor analyzed as carefully as they might have been.

Twin method. The twin method is now considered the most effective model for genetic studies of schizophrenia, largely because it controls for the environmental factors that cloud the results of genetic studies employing the pedigree and family methods (Rosenthal, 1967). The twin method depends upon the fact that monozygotic (identical) twins will share genetically determined disorders, since they are genetically identical. By contrast, dizygotic (fraternal) twins may or may not share such disorders.

Because dizygotic twins are presumably raised no differently from monozygotic twins, they provide the experimenter with a control for environmental influences. Differences between monozygotic and dizygotic twins in rates of schizophrenia ought to reflect accurately the genetics of the disorder.

Examination of rates for identical twins *reared apart* is another way to assess genetic influence. This technique permits evaluation of the relative influence of specific environmental determinants (for example, those present in only one home) on the disorder.

One of the most important twin studies of schizophrenia was published by Kallmann in 1946. Twin index cases were singled out from the residents and new admissions to twenty New York State mental hospitals over the nine

years 1937 to 1946. In all, 691 index pairs were located, of whom 174 were monozygotic twins and 517 were dizygotic twins. The study was also designed to reveal rates for schizophrenia among family members of varying genetic *and* familial relationships to the index cases. Therefore it included 2,741 full siblings, 134 half siblings, 74 stepsiblings, 1,191 parents, and 254 marriage partners of the 1,382 twins.

Kallmann found "a rather clear indication that the chance of developing schizophrenia increases in proportion to the degree of consanguinity to a schizophrenic index case" (p. 314). He added, however: "Neither the offspring of two schizophrenic parents nor the monozygotic cotwins of schizophrenic index cases have a morbidity rate of 100 percent as would be expected theoretically in regard to a strictly hereditary trait." This meant to Kallmann that the genetics of schizophrenia can *predispose* a person to the development of the disease, while environment or "strong constitutional defense" determine whether or not the predisposition will lead to schizophrenia. His view has become an increasingly popular one, especially since many physical disorders (for example, migraine headache, gastric ulcers, asthma, and heart disease) have been found to share the same dual etiology.

A recent book by Gottesman and Shields, which summarizes the current status of genetic research on schizophrenia using the twin method, supports Kallmann's fundamental conclusions. It suggests, however, that his data overstate the actual degree of correlation between familial relationship and psychopathology (1973).

Adoption studies. David Rosenthal, a major figure in current genetics research, has developed a new strategy to deal with the major shortcoming of traditional genetics studies: the fact that they do not permit assessment of the separate influences of heredity and environment on psychopathology. Rosenthal investigates child adoptions in order to control for that old bugaboo, unknown environmental effects on incipient psychopathology. Adoption records had been successfully used to study intelligence (Skodak & Skeels, 1949), alcoholism (Roe, 1945), and antisocial behavior (zur Nieden, 1951). But before Rosenthal they had not been applied to genetic studies of schizophrenia, largely because adoption agencies were reluctant to divulge information about biological and adoptive parents and children to outsiders (Rosenthal, 1971b).

Implicit in Rosenthal's research strategy are efforts to resolve two opposed hypotheses: (1) If schizophrenic disorders are inherited, more of these disorders should occur among the *biological* relatives of schizophrenic patients than among the biological relatives of matched nonschizophrenic subjects. (2) But if schizophrenic disorders are learned or modeled from parents whose own behavior is confused, disorganized, erratic, or chaotic, schizophrenic patients should have a greater number of *adoptive* relatives with schizophrenic disorders than matched nonschizophrenic subjects do (p. 193).

The findings of Rosenthal and his large research team strongly support the first of these hypotheses—the one viewing schizophrenia as an inherited disorder. In one study he and his colleagues showed that more of the *biological* parents of thirty-three adopted children who were later diagnosed as schizophrenic were themselves schizophrenic than either the adoptive parents of the schizophrenic children or the biological or adoptive parents of thirty-three matched control children (Kety, Rosenthal, et al., 1968). In another study, they found that a significantly larger number of adopted children of schizophrenic parents were themselves schizophrenic when compared with adopted children whose biological parents had no known history of the disease (Rosenthal et al., 1971). They also found that the biological parents of schizophrenic subjects were "appreciably more disturbed" than the subjects' adoptive parents (Wender et al., 1971).

These and other findings by Rosenthal's group offer strong support for the genetic theory of schizophrenia. But because of the usual design problems associated with genetics

research, it is still impossible to say exactly how large a part inheritance plays in schizophrenia. As a result, few observers assign either no role or the total role to genetics. Most subscribe to what Rosenthal calls the "diathesis-stress model," which assumes that a genetically determined underlying predisposition to development of schizophrenic behavior interacts with environmental determinants (including social learning) to bring the disorder to overt expression (1970). This is essentially the same conclusion Kallmann reached in 1946.

Psychoanalytic theories

Though Sigmund Freud devoted his major efforts to understanding and treating the neuroses, many of the theoretical contributions he made have since been applied to the schizophrenias. Freud rarely dealt directly with the schizophrenias in his writings. His analysis of Schreber's memoirs was actually a discussion of what Freud thought of as paranoia rather than schizophrenia, though most clinicians today would call Schreber's a paranoid schizophrenic psychosis.

Freud's views on etiology. The traditional psychoanalytic (Freudian) view—also called the dynamic view—of the etiology of schizophrenia is that the disorder represents fixation at or regression to the most primitive levels of psychosexual development: those of the oral stage. As a result the schizophrenic fails to develop important personality structures, especially certain defensive ones, which permit adequate response to ordinary environmental stress.

Freud speculated on one of the important consequences of that developmental failure in his paper "Psycho-analytic Notes upon an Autobiographical Account of a Case of Paranoia (Dementia Paranoides)," first published in 1911. This was his classic commentary on Schreber's memoirs. His theory to account for the development of Schreber's paranoid thought processes has influenced psychoanalytic therapists to our own day. Homo-

Freud in his middle years—the period when he wrote his comments on Schreber's *Memoirs. (The Bettmann Archive)*

sexuality was one of Schreber's central preoccupations, and Freud took the position that the paranoid—or as we would call it, paranoid schizophrenic—uses the inadequate, immature defense of projection to counter the unacceptable homosexual wish which is at the root of his condition. From this Freud concluded that the basic homosexual proposition, "I (a man) love him (a man)," is not accepted by the patient, who denies it with the contradictory proposition, "I do not love him; in fact, I hate him." Then, by projection, "I hate him" becomes transformed into the paranoid delusion "He hates me."

Traditional psychoanalytic theory also focuses on the withdrawal and regression characteristic of much schizophrenic behavior. It explains these behaviors as an effort by the patient to recover his ability to function in the world and to reconstruct and put back in order an otherwise confusing environment (Arieti, 1955). The resultant reconstruction is thought to represent the schizophrenic's predominant orientation to the world. Freud described this process in his paper "On Narcissism," published in 1914. He hypothesized that in schizophrenia, libido (psychological energy) is withdrawn from *investment in the world* in favor of *investment in the ego.* The consequence is that patients suffer from "megalomania"—from exclusive preoccupation with their own thoughts and feelings—rather than taking an interest in the world and their place in it.

In a further explanation of his position, Freud wrote in 1923 that neurosis is the result of conflict in which the ego continually struggles to keep the id's largely unacceptable sexual and aggressive impulses from being expressed in overt ways. By contrast, psychosis stems from a direct disturbance in relations between a weakened ego and the environment. The result is that the ego is too weak to modify id impulses, which consequently predominate in the overt behavior of many schizophrenic patients. The following excerpt from Daniel Paul Schreber's memoirs conveys how overwhelmingly he must have been preoccupied by sexual conflict when he was in the midst of a schizophrenic episode:

This process of unmanning consisted in the (external) male genitals (scrotum and penis) being retracted into the body and the internal sexual organs being at the same time transformed into the corresponding female sexual organs, a process which might have been completed in a sleep lasting hundreds of years, because the skeleton (pelvis, etc.) had also to be changed. . . . I have myself twice experienced (for a short time) the miracle of unmanning on my own body . . . for weeks I was kept in bed and my clothes were removed to make me—as I believed—more amenable to voluptous sensations, which could be stimulated in me by the female nerves which had already started to enter my body. [1955, pp. 73–76]

Another excerpt shows the intensity of the suspicious, angry, and aggressive feelings by which Schreber was also clearly absorbed during his period of psychosis:

The talk of the voice has already become mostly an empty babel of ever recurring monotonous phrases in tiresome repetition; on top of this they were rendered grammatically incomplete by the omission of words and even syllables. However, the description of a certain number of phrases used is of interest, because of the sidelight thrown on the souls' whole way of thinking, their idea of human life and of human thinking. Among these phrases are those in which I was called a *"Prince of Hell"*—roughly since the time of my stay in Pierson's Asylum. It was said innumberable times, for instance, that "God's omnipotence has decided that you, the Prince of Hell, are going to be burned alive," "the Prince of Hell is responsible for the loss of rays," "We announce victory over the beaten Prince of Hell." [pp. 139–140]

An empirical assessment of the Freudian view of etiology. A recent attempt to assess the validity of Freudian, or dynamic, views on schizophrenic etiology reveals some of the difficulties associated with making psychoanalytic theory the object of empirical examination. The case histories of forty schizophrenic patients hospitalized for at least three years at Boston State Hospital were examined to test a "psychoanalytic reformulation of psychosis in terms of 'developmental lines'" (Kris, 1972). This "reformulation" does away with the stages of psychosexual development (oral, anal, phallic) and the psychic apparatus (ego, id, superego) to focus instead on schizophrenia as a multifaceted failure in psychological development.

Kris's theory assumes that "progress along the developmental line toward mature object relations" (toward being able to love and be loved, and toward being dependent when dependency is appropriate and independent when independence is suitable) is particularly difficult for psychotic patients. While they are chronologically mature and therefore experience the need to develop these object relations, they are psychologically immature and consequently unable to do so. This part of Kris's theory was given support by his observation that two kinds of environmental

stresses, both having to do with people, were often associated with the first appearance of a patient's psychosis. One was "a new developmental ambition (increased opportunity for sexual activity, leaving home for college) that appears to lead to loss of support, sometimes through conflict with supporting figures." This was observed in seventeen of the forty patients in connection with their first hospitalization. The other environmental stress led to psychosis through "death, departure, or rejection." Most of the rest of the patients in Kris's sample had experienced such a loss before their first admission to the hospital.

Though these observations support Kris's theory and, by extension, the dynamic view of schizophrenic etiology, they were derived from unreliable data collection methods and a subjective approach to data analysis. Researchers who want to apply the standards of science to the behavioral sciences question the reliability of Kris's findings. On the other hand, those who, like Kris, want to test the utility of theories generated in the consulting room on real clinical problems might ask how else they can do it. The answer is one of faith and commitment: the dynamic theorist and the behaviorist continue to develop and employ research strategies that meet their own different standards of acceptability.

Sullivan's etiologic views. Harry Stack Sullivan (1892 to 1949), an American psychoanalyst who "specialized" in schizophrenia, made his most outstanding contributions in the area of treatment. His views on the etiology of schizophrenia, however, were also important in the development of interpersonal and familial theory and research on schizophrenia. While Freud traced the cause of the disorder to a series of traumatic interactions between the individual and the environment during the oral stage, Sullivan said that what goes on between people is as important as what goes on in the psyche. Observing that the child's view of himself is largely constructed from "reflected appraisals" of him by his parents, Sullivan concluded that a mother's anxiety or a father's anger and disapproval, even if un-

Harry Stack Sullivan. *(William Allen White Psychiatric Foundation, Inc.)*

related to the child or his behavior, can implant those behaviors in the child. If the family situation is bad enough, the child may choose to protect his own "sense of self" by eliminating from conscious experience all reflected threats to himself. One of the ways he might accomplish this defensive maneuver is by "parataxic distortion"—distortedly identifying the other real person in the situation with someone else or with a person who exists only in fantasy. Sullivan's *Conceptions of Modern Psychiatry* (1946) contains a thorough and thoughtful presentation of his views on schizophrenia.

Interpersonal theories

Increasing attention has been paid during the past ten years to the study of disturbed communication in the families of schizophrenics. Major figures in this effort include Bateson, Lidz, and Laing, though many others have contributed.

Bateson and the double bind. A crucial aspect of Bateson's theory of schizophrenia is the double bind. The basic double-bind situation has these elements:

1 The subject is involved in an intense interpersonal relationship in which he believes that it is very important to understand exactly what kind of message is being conveyed to him so that he can respond appropriately.
2 But the other person in the relationship gives two conflicting messages at the same time.
3 The subject cannot comment on the conflicting messages in order to find out which message he ought to respond to.

Bateson illustrates the double-bind situation by describing an incident that typifies interactions between schizophrenics and their parents:

A young man who had fairly well recovered from an acute schizophrenic episode was visited in the hospital by his mother. He was glad to see her and impulsively put his arm around her shoulders, whereupon she stiffened. He withdrew his arm and she asked, "Don't you love me any more?" He then blushed, and she said, "Dear, you must not be so easily embarrassed and afraid of your feelings." The patient was able to stay with her only a few minutes more and following her departure he assaulted an aide and was put in the tubs. [Bateson et al., 1956, pp. 258–259]

The patient's dilemma in this situation, like many others he had been in with his mother, was that he could not show his love for her because doing so made her uncomfortable; but if he did not show her that he loved her, he might lose her.

The double-bind concept has been extended to family situations involving mother, father, and child, with the assumption that there are no fundamental differences in pathologic impact between two- and three-person situations (Weakland, 1960). From what we know of his childhood, it seems likely that Lee Harvey Oswald experienced just such a double bind in relations with his mother, Marguerite, and his stepfather, Edwin Ekdahl. Oswald remembered those childhood years as lonely, isolated ones, and indeed, though his mother and stepfather professed love for him, his loving mother placed him in an orphanage; later, his devoted stepfather divorced Marguerite and left them.

The double bind is clearly a component of many, perhaps most, family interaction patterns involving schizophrenic parents and children, but no one has yet proved that it is a central etiologic agent in schizophrenia. One study lent only partial support to the validity of the double-bind theory. Berger hypothesized that schizophrenics would report having heard their mothers give a significantly greater number of commands and comments incorporating double-bind inconsistency than would a group of nonschizophrenic controls (1965). Of course, Berger's study could not be a direct test of the double bind as an etiological factor, since his data represented correlated, not causal, phenomena. In any event, his schizophrenic subjects (males between the ages of 16 and 35) did report more childhood double-bind episodes than his control subjects. However, the difference between schizophrenic patients and those with personality disorder labels was not significant—a finding which suggests that the double bind may not be restricted to schizophrenic families.

Lidz's long-term study of schizophrenic families. Lidz and his colleagues at Yale Medical School (1957a, 1957b) made essentially the same basic assumption as Bateson: that "schizophrenic patients virtually always emerge from homes marked by serious parental strife or eccentricity." But they studied schizophrenics and their families in a broader context and came to different conclusions about the ingredients of the disordered family situations. They observed the families of sixteen schizophrenic patients hospitalized at the Yale Psychiatric Institute. The central method of research was long-term study "in an attempt to recreate the personalities, their interactions, the ways and the atmosphere of the family group." All available family members were interviewed repeatedly (some of them several hundred times) during both therapy and nontherapy sessions. Here is Lidz's summary of some important findings:

The extent and pervasiveness of the family pathology were unexpected. Not a single family was reasonably well integrated. . . . Most of the marriages upon which the families were based were gravely disturbed. The majority were torn by schismatic conflict between the parents that divided the family into two hostile factions, with each spouse seeking to gain the upper hand, defying the wishes of the other, undercutting the worth of the spouse to the children, seeking to win the children to his side and to use them as emotional replacements for the spouse. The remaining families developed a skewed pattern because the serious psychopathology of the dominant parent was passively accepted by the other, leading to aberrant ways of living and of child-rearing. Their acceptance and masking of the serious problems that existed created a strange emotional environment that was perplexing to the child. . . . In each family at least one parent suffered from serious and crippling psychopathology, and in many both were markedly disturbed . . . at least 10 of the 16 families contained a parent who was an ambulatory schizophrenic or clearly paranoid. . . . Still others were chronic alcoholics, severe obsessives, or so extremely passive-dependent that they were virtually children of their spouses rather than another parent. . . . Insecurity and confusion concerning sexual identity, often with fairly obvious homosexual trends, were common, and many of these parents had difficulty in controlling their incestuous impulses, both heterosexual and homosexual. [Lidz & Fleck, 1960, pp. 332–333]

As this summary makes clear, Lidz and his group chose to emphasize general pathology in parents of schizophrenics—their developmental inadequacies, failures as role models, and inability to project love and security—rather than focusing, like Bateson, on the double bind as a prepotent factor in the etiology of schizophrenia.

Lidz's basic findings of disorder and psychopathology in the homes of schizophrenics have been confirmed in many studies by his group and by others (Lidz & Fleck, 1960; Anthony, 1969; Alanen, 1970). But it is difficult to be certain of the causal implication of Lidz's observations. They could support genetic or biochemical theories of schizophrenic etiology just as well as interpersonal ones. After all, if a schizophrenic child's parents are seriously disturbed, the child could have inherited genetic material capable of bringing on disordered behavior through biochemical abnormality.

Laing: Schizophrenia is the way to live in an insane world. One of the most controversial figures in psychiatry is R. D. Laing, the darling of antiestablishment mental health professionals and laymen. A brilliant theorist and an innovative therapist, Laing holds phenomenological views about the etiology of schizophrenia. In other words, he believes that all aspects of the schizophrenic patient's environment contribute to his or her behavior. Thus Laing's position is not strictly an interpersonal one, though he does emphasize the importance of interpersonal relationships.

R. D. Laing. *(Lawrence McKintosh/Newsweek)*

In most of his writings Laing acknowledges that the weight of evidence on schizophrenic etiology supports the genetic-biochemical position. But he claims that the evidence is not strong enough to justify its uncritical acceptance:

That the diagnosed patient is suffering from a pathological process [meaning a mental disorder] is either a fact, an hypothesis, an assumption, or a judgement. To regard it as fact is unequivocally false. To regard it as an hypothesis is legitimate. It is unnecessary either to make the assumption or to pass the judgement. . . . The judgement that the diagnosed patient is behaving in a biologically dysfunctional (hence pathological) way is, I believe, premature, and one that I shall hold in parenthesis. [1964, p. 188]

Laing's own opinion is that schizophrenic behavior, far from being pathological, is a strategy which the person has developed in order to live in what has become an unlivable situation. Viewed in this way, schizophrenic behavior becomes a means of coping with an environment that is itself insane and chaotic.

Laing is persuasive; his logic is often inescapable. He reminds us that schizophrenia is a label some of us pin on others; it is not an illness like tuberculosis or diabetes. More important, it is a social fact, even a political event. Schizophrenia is brought about "by outrageous violence perpetrated by human beings on human beings" (Laing, 1967). Because it is a socially defined concept, the label often defines treatment procedures which tend to reinforce rather than extinguish the behavior of the patient. Laing's equally iconoclastic suggestions for the treatment of schizophrenia are considered later in the chapter.

The "treatment" given Daniel Paul Schreber (a padded cell, "cold packs," even manacles when they were needed) and Rudolph Hess (social isolation, poor food, little exercise) must have reinforced their pathological suspiciousness about the motives of their keepers. Even the more enlightened treatment provided for Rick took place in a sterile hospital setting complete with the traditional patient-doctor hierarchy, enforced celibacy, and the dehumanization of enforced group living.

Naturally, Laing's unorthodox views have attracted as much criticism as praise. They have been dismissed by traditionalists as frivolous at best and destructive at worst, but they have also received thoughtful and objective evaluation. One recent critique, by Siegler and her colleagues, concludes that Laing's theory is a composite of psychoanalytic, "conspiratorial," and "psychedelic" views of personality (1969). It is conspiratorial because one of its major concerns is "the violation of the rights of the person labelled as schizophrenic." Laing's position is similar in this regard to that of Szasz, for like Szasz, he blames the medical model for dehumanizing patients in mental hospitals.

Siegler and her co-workers respond by pointing out that the "medical context" also "permits people called doctors to perform all kinds of unusual actions on people called patients, and this enables them to treat illnesses." But while such an argument is a reasonable justification for medical intervention in cases of physical illness, it is precisely because Laing and Szasz do not believe that psychological disability is equivalent to physical illness that they object to the "medical context." Since we share Laing's opinion of the medical model, we also question Siegler's further statement: "As an individual, Laing is quite free to put forth any view on these matters that he chooses, but as a physician he is not free to put forth the view that the social fiction called medicine is more harmful than helpful." Phrased another way, the same argument is used by politicians to demand support of their policies (like war making) not because the policies are just, but because public objection to them would make it harder to carry them out.

Siegler and her group also challenge Laing's claim that he is treating schizophrenics in a new way; they say that he is really using psychoanalysis. Laing would not agree that his therapy is psychoanalysis, though he might grudgingly acknowledge that psycho-analysis, when it works, does so because of the same therapist skills and experience upon which his own procedures are based.

Siegler terms "psychedelic" the portion of Laing's theory which says that the schizophrenic may experience the same kind of consciousness expanding which is reported by non-schizophrenics who take psychedelic drugs. She argues: "It is heartless to suggest, without the most exact explanation and qualification, to those suffering from tuberculosis, cancer, or schizophrenia that they should look on this as a rare opportunity for self-understanding." However, it does not seem to us "heartless" to stress the positive aspects of what is an overwhelmingly negative situation. Since no definitive treatment for schizophrenia has yet evolved, is it wrong to emphasize the small positives and minimize the profound negatives of this disorder?

On balance we conclude that Siegler and her co-workers, like others in the mental health "establishment," take Laing, Szasz, and others like them too literally, too seriously—and yet not seriously enough. Though history proves that no establishment knows what to do with its gadflys—its Socrateses, Voltaires, Swifts, and Thomas Paines—few, fortunately, have been without them.

Drive and arousal theories

Freud and the psychoanalysts, Kallmann and the geneticists, Kety and the biochemists, and Bateson and the interpersonal theorists all built very different theories of etiology by emphasizing different components of the syndrome of schizophrenia. In the same way, psychologists who observe psychological deficits in the schizophrenic explain the development of the disorder in terms of the particular deficits on which they choose to focus. Because there are almost as many psychological theories of schizophrenia as there are psychological dysfunctions that can be observed in the schizophrenic, we will illustrate this vast area of research with just one example: that of drive or arousal theories of schizophrenia, an especially well-explored research area. Following are descriptions of four such theories, taken in chronological order to illustrate the developmental trends in theory-building.

Pavlov's "neurological" view of schizophrenia. Ivan Pavlov, the Russian physiologist best known for his research on the fundamental laws of classical conditioning, also formulated a theory of schizophrenia (1928, 1941). Basic to Pavlov's theory was his conviction that schizophrenic behavior represents an adaptive response to "overstimulation." Pavlov believed that schizophrenics have "weak nervous systems" which do not react effectively to the ordinary physical, developmental, or social stimuli of life. The mechanism by which schizophrenics respond to excessive stimuli Pavlov termed "transmarginal inhibition," a reflexive, passive, and unconditioned "emergency" response that reduces reactivity to

Ivan Pavlov. *(Tass from Sovfoto)*

stimulation. In performing this "gating" function, however, transmarginal inhibition also disrupts intellectual and emotional functioning.

Pavlov's system has been criticized above all for its complexity. He hypothesized many neurological mechanisms which can either inhibit or disinhibit, depending on an intricate set of interactions among external and internal arousal states, threshold levels, and preexisting states of inhibition and disinhibition. Though this complicated system enabled him to account for many behaviors commonly associated with schizophrenia, it made very difficult the task of "pinning down" the precise mechanisms responsible for a behavior. Another frequent criticism of Pavlov's theory of schizophrenia is its tendency to "neurologize," to posit unproved physiological mechanisms to account for largely psychological or behavioral phenomena. In consequence the theory has been rejected by many behavioral scientists for its faulty physiology, despite its attractiveness on other grounds. Largely for these reasons Pavlov's theory has not generated a great deal of research outside the Soviet Union.

Venables: Schizophrenia is the result of "stimulus overload." Venables has concluded that schizophrenics show an "input dysfunction" (1964). He observed that acute schizophrenics—those in the early stages of the psychosis—exhibit overactive parasympathetic functioning and, as a result, have excessively low resting levels of arousal. He reasons that this "underactivity" makes them susceptible to virtually all internal and external stimuli, and consequently to "stimulus overload" and ultimate disorganization. As an adaptive response, he says, the chronic schizophrenic maintains high levels of arousal and hence reacts little even to strong stimuli. One result is that the acute schizophrenic develops an excessively broad range of attention, while the chronic schizophrenic does just the opposite. This striking behavioral difference may account for the findings, reviewed in Chapter 6, that chronic and acute schizophrenics differ profoundly from each other and from normals in terms of how they perceive and respond to the world about them.

One of the strengths of Venables's theory is the attention it pays to the possibility that the subtypes of schizophrenia—especially acute and chronic—may develop from divergent etiologies. He compels us to look at the defect in regulation of stimulus input which many schizophrenics demonstrate, a defect that may have prognostic and therapeutic significance. Two major weaknesses of his position have also been pointed out. The first stems from its reliance on data gathered for other purposes rather than on data from studies designed specifically to test the theory. The second weakness is that its explanation of schizophrenia focuses on only one of the symptoms—breadth of attention—and ignores all others.

Mednick: Schizophrenia is a state of heightened drive.

One of the most influential recent theories of schizophrenic etiology was formulated by Sarnoff Mednick (1958, 1962). Derived in part from Clark Hull's influential theory of learning (1943), Mednick's hypothesis is that most of the disordered behaviors of schizophrenia are produced by a state of heightened drive. Basic to Hull's theory was the assumption of a strong positive relationship between drive strength (a concept very much like Freud's id impulses) and response strength (a concept that takes into account the organism's prior success in satisfying its drives). Mednick argues that "high-drive" schizophrenics condition more rapidly than nonschizophrenics, whose levels of drive are not as high. Hull's hypothesis was that the strength of a tendency to respond in a particular way is a function both of the response strength and of the intensity of the drive associated with it. The schizophrenic's increased drive level, Mednick says, is related to the development of a variety of responses which come to compete with each other and, as a result, prevent each other from successful execution. Mednick suggests that this process is responsible for the inability of schizophrenics to perform complex tasks: inappropriate

new responses continually develop to compete with appropriate older ones. He uses the same model to explain the formal characteristics of schizophrenic thinking.

The disastrous consequences of competing cognitive stimuli in schizophrenia is evident in the following excerpt from a letter written by one of Bleuler's schizophrenic patients:

> Centraleurope andt centraleuropera No. 3258 Ernest Gisler Troth also the key to Mr. Minister No. Kaiser DDiv. etc. Standdenbank pprr p. 96 or letterpost 3 vvia Imperially andt Royally also Imperially Royally business Titt, Pheinau. Mo work Badd godd 3/8 Herr dr. N.C. 30/7 Bern 27/7 AD 18/7 short 30/7 3/8 Aa 1906 Datum. Tthey pay on presentation of a receipt Frcs 8 thousandd in banknotes also Titt. Bernese Central bank in Berne or BCB frcs. 8000 cash. at 10 per cent. FRCS 8,000 equlaly 800 FRCs time 10 at eleven: Titte. Government chancellory Aaltdorf by reason of damage sustained through Mr. Aalt missionary and hotel-guest, living with Cr. Christaller in Bellevue Andder madtim Poag Francs c 12 half-Octav Trvel-work. [1950, p. 154]

When enough time and effort were spent with this patient to unravel the meaning of the letter, a message that was largely though not completely understandable did emerge:

> We, the Emperor of Central Europe, E. No. 3258 wed to Miss Gisler (whereby the right to be free was given), Possessor and Lord of the bank through which we satisfy our needs by using postal-notes, and owner of the factory in Pheinau, issue the following decree: "You, or the Bernese Central Bank are to pay on demand on the presentation of a note, 8000 francs in cash plus 10 percent. This is to be drawn on the account of the Altdorf government bureau which owes me the sum for damages and injuries caused me both by the government and by hotel-keeper Christaller in Bellevue, Andermatt; each day you are to pay 3 billions and 12 pieces of toilet paper and my freedom." [P. 155]

An additional feature of heightened drive in the schizophrenic is what Mednick calls "the reciprocal augmentation of anxiety and stimulus generalization." By this phrase he means that more and more stimuli, as they are attended to by the overattending schizophrenic, become capable of evoking anxiety. In so doing, they also increase the overall level of drive, which further increases stimulus generalization, overattention to stimuli, and anxiety, in that order. Mednick says that this vicious circle ends in acute schizophrenic disorganization and panic.

Mednick believes that the schizophrenic's high drive level can be a product of heredity, environment, or both. He also suggests that if a person "endowed" with such a predisposition has a life that provides only limited opportunity for high drive excesses, he can avoid developing schizophrenia. Such restricted environments, however, are very rare.

Mednick's theory is important both because it accounts plausibly for many of the major symptoms of schizophrenia and because it has stimulated a great deal of research designed to investigate its hypotheses (Mednick, 1970, 1971). But researchers disagree on the extent to which his fundamental assumptions are supported empirically (Lang & Buss, 1965). In addition, they disagree on the meaning of some of Mednick's constructs (especially "drive," which he sometimes uses to denote Hull's link between a stimulus and a response and sometimes uses as if it were identical with clinical anxiety). Perhaps the most telling drawback of Mednick's theory is its insistence on the etiological significance of the reciprocal relationship between anxiety and stimulus generalization (overattention). The problem with this view, as Lang and Buss point out, is that everyone is anxious at times. So if anxiety always increases stimulus generalization and stimulus generalization always increases anxiety, why doesn't everyone become schizophrenic?

Epstein: Schizophrenia involves a failure to modulate excitation. Derived from a more general theory of anxiety, Epstein's drive-arousal theory of schizophrenia (1967, 1971) makes the following fundamental assumptions:

1 All organisms must defend themselves against excessively high levels of stimulation. They must also be able to respond to relatively low levels of stimulation (say, rustling leaves, sounds from afar) in order to stay alive.
2 Anxiety and arousal are related to each other in different but important ways. Anxiety must be classified as an avoidance motive, while arousal is a nonspecific element of all states of stimulation. In consequence, the organism's defenses against excessive arousal are broader than its defenses against excessive anxiety.
3 A fundamental psychophysiological system to inhibit excessive stimulation must exist. A malfunction of this system is centrally implicated in the development of schizophrenia.
4 As the intensity of stimulation increases, the delicate balance—the "fine tuning"—of the inhibition mechanism may shift over to a more diffuse "all-or-none" process that contains the seeds of an ultimate schizophrenic disorganization.

These premises lead Epstein to the view that schizophrenia consists largely of a fundamental inability to modulate excitation:

To protect himself from being overstimulated, the schizophrenic generally attempts to restrict his subjective and objective world of experience. The only alternative, given an all-or-none defense system, is to be overstimulated (that is, to be bombarded by too many stimuli from the environment.) In either event, he fails to obtain experience in dealing with the repetition of stimulation at appropriate levels of arousal that is necessary for the development of an adequately modulated inhibitory system. [Epstein & Coleman, 1971, p. 39]

Epstein's model is strongest in its capacity to explain virtually all the major "symptoms" of schizophrenia—over- and under-response to the environment, imperfect contact with reality, decreased pleasure in life, inability to control impulses, and attention defects—by reference to the fundamental excitation-control disorder. The fact that the theory is derived from a more fundamental theory of anxiety permits comparison with the non-psychoses, especially the neuroses, in terms of etiology. Its major drawback at the present is its relative newness: so far, Epstein's model is unsupported by empirical data.

Summary. Like other theories of schizophrenic etiology, including those that are primarily physiological and those that are psychological, the drive-arousal theories remain largely unsubstantiated. While they have inspired important empirical studies, none of these have yet established a clear causal relationship between over- or under-arousal and any of the group of schizophrenias.

Learning theories

The drive-arousal theories of schizophrenia are behavioral theories in that they explain development of schizophrenic behavior according to the lawful operation of "observables." But they are not learning theories, because they do not posit learned relationships between present and past behavior. The following learning-theory approaches, including our own, have been formulated very recently in the history of research on schizophrenia.

Bandura's social-learning theory of schizophrenia. Bandura explains the development of many of the most common cues to schizophrenia by referring to basic principles of learning (1968). For example, after viewing Lidz's findings relating disordered family structure to schizophrenia, Bandura concludes that the data "provide ample evidence that delusions, suspiciousness, grandiosity, extreme denial of reality, and other forms of 'schizophrenic' behavior are frequently learned through direct reinforcement and transmitted by parental modeling of unusually deviant behavior patterns" (1968, p. 295). Lidz and his colleagues applied the dynamic model to their observations and decided that the disorganized family took its toll by interfering with the child's normal passage through crucial psychosexual milestones. But as Bandura

Albert Bandura.

points out, the same data can be used to argue that these symptoms were learned directly.

In a similar fashion, Bandura reinterprets the behavior of a schizophrenic patient described earlier by Bateson (1961). The patient had been raised by rigidly moralistic parents who punished virtually all behavior that had positive consequences. Now in adulthood the patient was fearful and anxious even about innocuous actions like taking medicine. Whenever he did complete a sequence of such "forbidden" behavior, he forced himself to undergo a ritual of atonement to cleanse himself of sin:

In the night I awoke under the most dreadful impressions; I heard a voice addressing me, and I was made to imagine that my disobedience to the faith, in taking the medicine overnight, had not only offended the Lord, but had rendered the work of my salvation extremely difficult, by its effect upon my spirits and humors. . . . A spirit came upon me and prepared to guide me in my actions. . . . I was placed in a fatiguing attitude, resting on my feet, my knees drawn up and on my head, and made to swing my body from side to side without ceasing. [Bateson, 1961, p. 28]

Bandura views this patient as

. . . a striking example of how behavior can become completely controlled by fictional contingencies and fantasied consequences powerful enough to override the influence of the reinforcement available from the social environment. . . . It is important to bear in mind that fantasied consequences are no less real, or less aversive, to the people who fear them than those associated with external aversive stimuli. [Bandura, 1968, p. 309]

Ullmann and Krasner's "sociopsychological model" of schizophrenia. Ullmann and Krasner have formulated what is probably the most comprehensive and controversial learning-theory view of schizophrenic etiology (1969). Their "sociopsychological model" explains schizophrenic behavior as the product of "failure of reinforcement for a sequence of behavior." They say that after repeated failure of reinforcement, the schizophrenic learns to stop paying attention to environmental cues. "The crucial behavior, from which other indications of schizophrenia may be deduced, lies in the extinction of attention to social stimuli to which normal people respond" (p. 383). In this way Ullmann and Krasner account for the deficits in attention and thinking that often characterize schizophrenic behavior. Obviously, patients who are attending to internal cues or to uncommon external ones will not respond appropriately when another person praises or criticizes them for actions whose determinants may be hidden from view. The explanation "failure of reinforcement," however, is less useful for interpreting other "schizophrenic" behaviors. For example, Ullmann and Krasner attribute the mood disorders commonly seen in the schizophrenias to a long history of inadequate reinforcement for affective expression (smiling, laughing, crying). But they do not specify the nature and extent of that history or offer empirical data supporting their views.

It is when they must explain delusions and hallucinations that Ullmann and Krasner have the greatest difficulty with their learning model. They say that delusions are dramatic means of eliciting attention and concern from an imperfect environment—that the patient resorts to delusions because he cannot obtain the concern he needs by more conventional methods. This explanation, however, appears plausible only for "overt" delusions that the patient shares with others.

Ullmann and Krasner have devised an even more involved behavioral sequence to explain hallucinations. According to them, hallucinations are "learned" from the mass media, from watching other patients, and from the questions of mental health examiners. This "observational learning" can result in hallucinations if the patient, after shifting attention from the external environment to the internal, has lost the distinction between what is real and what is imagined or thought (McReynolds, 1960). Hallucinations may then become reinforcing in themselves because they fulfill wishes and desires unattainable in the real world.

The strength of Ullmann and Krasner's sociopsychological model is its insistence that schizophrenic behavior is no different from deviant behavior emitted by nonschizophrenics. The model approaches schizophrenia through known mechanisms of learning, so that schizophrenic behaviors do not stand in isolation from mutual interrelationships with the patient's world. In other words, schizophrenia affects the environment and the environment affects schizophrenia.

The sociopsychological model, however, has several serious weaknesses. Ullmann and Krasner must skirt the bounds of probability to explain all schizophrenic behaviors according to the "failure of reinforcement" concept. Their faith in learning theory has led them to soft-pedal the data on the genetics and biochemistry of schizophrenia. And they show a curious willingness to posit a theory unsupported by empirical data, despite their strong insistence on such data in connection with other theories.

Our view. We believe that persons who are labeled "schizophrenic" begin life with an inherited predisposition to development of the disorder, and that this predisposition takes some form of biochemical abnormality ultimately capable of affecting the functioning of the central nervous system. When these people experience the normal stresses of life with which nonpredisposed persons deal adequately (if not always happily), they begin to emit what are called schizophrenic behaviors. In our view, many schizophrenic behaviors are in fact learned, especially those associated with disturbances in attention and affect. But other such behaviors, including delusions, hallucinations, and some of the cognitive dysfunctions, may be the result of a chronic brain disorder associated with the inborn biochemical lesion. Our research and the work of others suggests that these behaviors appear most often in persons who suffer from acute or chronic brain disorder (Nathan et al., 1969a, 1969b, 1969c). A similar hypothesis has been developed by Meehl (1962), although he gives much less attention to the role of learning in the creation of "schizophrenic behavior."

Treatment of schizophrenia

Somatotherapy

Neurosurgery. In the 1930s and 1940s, before the major tranquilizing drugs were synthesized, several neurosurgical procedures were employed as treatment for especially violent and unmanageable chronic schizophrenic patients. Between 1948 and 1955, an average of 1,000 patients a year received a prefrontal leucotomy (Tooth & Newton, 1961). Following the dramatic introduction of the tranquilizing drugs since 1955, neurosurgery (now popularly called psychosurgery) for schizophrenia has become increasingly rare, though it is still occasionally reported (Vaernet & Madsen, 1970; Winter, 1971). While its decline has been due largely to the success of the phenothiazines as tranquilizing agents,

experience also taught that surgery has no value in some of the most common kinds of schizophrenia, while in others it is actually harmful. Beyond the risks attendant upon any major operation involving entry into the brain, neurosurgery often left patients without will and without personality—in short, turned them into the human vegetables sometimes described in the popular press.

Recent years have seen dramatic modifications of surgical techniques—modifications which have both reduced the risks associated with the procedures themselves and increased the precision with which target areas can be functionally separated from the rest of the brain. Research during this time has also been directed toward outcome evaluation. Somewhat unexpectedly, some of it suggests that neurosurgery may be more useful in the management of patients with recurrent affective disorders and intractable pain than with schizophrenics.

Insulin coma therapy. Developed in 1933, insulin coma therapy (ICT) was a relatively common treatment for schizophrenia before the phenothiazines were. It was designed above all to quiet hyperactive, hallucinating patients. ICT involved administration of large quantities of insulin to patients; this caused progressive hypoglycemia (low blood sugar) leading to coma, which lasted fifteen minutes to an hour. Coma was terminated by the infusion of glucose, which ended the hypoglycemia. Insulin coma treatment was characteristically protracted; some patients were given more than a hundred treatments. When it worked, ICT did quiet them down temporarily, but it also had conspicuous disadvantages. The medical risk was considerable (1 in 100 patients died during the course of insulin coma therapy), highly experienced personnel were required for it, and the results were often disappointing. Despite its drawbacks, there are still occasional hospitals where ICT is given for intractable cases of schizophrenia.

Electroconvulsive therapy. Widely used now as a treatment for severe and protracted depression, electroconvulsive therapy (ECT) is not a common therapy for schizophrenia. But when a schizophrenic is extremely excited, depressed, or suicidal, ECT is thought to reduce hyperactivity, alleviate depression, and make him or her more tractable. It is a frequently chosen alternative when the tranquilizing drugs have proved unsuccessful. The details of ECT are given in Chapter 8, which discusses the place of ECT in the treatment of affective psychosis.

Chemotherapy

As the legend goes, chlorpromazine, a drug of proved value for reducing the severity of vomiting during the early months of pregnancy, was given to several hospitalized pregnant French schizophrenics in the late 1940s. Subsequently they showed dramatic reductions in both vomiting and psychotic behavior. Their physicians then undertook controlled research designed to test the antipsychotic "side effects" of the antiemetic drug. The resulting paper by Delay, Deniker, and Harl, "The Therapeutic Use of a Phenothiazine with Selective Central Action," ushered in a new era in the treatment of the functional psychoses (1952).

The major tranquilizers include the large family of phenothiazine drugs and the much smaller group of rauwolfia compounds. The most commonly used phenothiazines are chlorpromazine (Thorazine), fluphenazine (Prolixin), perphenazine (Trilafon), prochlorperazine (Compazine), thioridazine (Mellaril), and trifluperazine (Stelazine). The two rauwolfia compounds in widespread application are deserpidine (Harmonyl) and reserpine (Serpasil). While other drugs, including the "minor tranquilizers," LSD, and some sedatives, are also given to schizophrenic patients, the overwhelming preponderance of drug therapy for them is of the phenothiazine type.

Now we take the powerful effects of the phenothiazines for granted and are not surprised to see "back-ward" patients sitting quietly, watching television, working, sleeping, or talking coherently. But hospital personnel who worked on the back wards of state hospitals before the advent of these drugs still look upon them as little short of miraculous, for they have transformed the screaming, shouting, violent chaos of the predrug back-ward to relative serenity.

Though the incidence of potentially fatal side-effects with phenothiazine therapy is very low, less serious side effects are common. They include muscular rigidity, tremor, loss of associated movements, restlessness, drooling, a "masklike" face, and a shuffling gait. These are also the symptoms of Parkinson's disease, a chronic incapacitating neurological condition for which a promising treatment with a dopamine drug called "L-dopa" has recently been developed. For the side effects of the phenothiazines, specific anti-Parkinson syndrome drugs are given along with the tranquilizer. They usually reduce significantly the severity of the side effects, but if they do not, the phenothiazine can be discontinued for a time or its dosage can be lowered. Other less common side effects are convulsive seizures early in treatment, a skin rash, and blood, liver, and visual problems. These also are treatable, usually by temporary drug withdrawal.

Experimental studies generally bear out the observations of clinicians that the phenothiazines are "magic bullets" (Prien et al., 1973). Such is not often the case with new treatments for serious psychiatric disorders; usually they fizzle out after a brief period of promise. One of the most carefully controlled studies of the phenothiazines (Goldberg, 1967) revealed that 340 newly admitted schizophrenic patients treated with chlorpromazine, fluphenazine, or thioridazine showed significantly greater improvement on both an overall measure of psychosis and on 14 of 21 specific measures of psychotic behavior than did comparable schizophrenic patients given a placebo (a chemically inert substance disguised to look like one of the active drugs). Apathy and motor retardation, common symptoms of schizophrenia, were dramatically reduced by the phenothiazines. Irritability, slowed speech and movement, hebephrenic symptoms, unconcern about

Two views of the "screaming, shouting, violent chaos of the predrug back ward": Hogarth's *In Bedlam* (18th century) and an unknown artist's depiction of a crowded ward of the lunatic asylum on Blackwell's Island, New York (19th century). *(The Metropolitan Museum of Art, Harris Brisbane Dick Fund, 1932; The Bettmann Archive)*

hygiene and grooming, and other signs of indifference to the environment also changed for the better. Further, incoherent speech, hostility, agitation and tension, ideas of persecution, and auditory hallucinations improved markedly. Recent studies have demonstrated that the phenothiazines are more effective in the treatment of schizophrenia than ECT (Kalinowsky, 1967), ICT (Solomon & Patch, 1971), and the other tranquilizers (Denber, 1967). The comparative efficacy of the phenothiazines and psychotherapy is considered later in the chapter.

Note that the phenothiazines do not "cure" schizophrenia; that is, their withdrawal often leads to the full recurrence of the patient's original psychotic symptoms. Maintenance dosages of these drugs, however, enable many schizophrenic patients to leave the hospital and in some cases, to do productive work. Even for patients who remain hospitalized, they have often meant a happier, more interesting life and more hope for eventual release. The phenothiazines are the true "wonder drugs" of our age.

Dynamic therapies

The problem of whether or not to offer psychotherapy to the schizophrenic patient is nicely captured by excerpts from two psychiatric textbooks. The first (Arieti, 1959) was published in America, where the traditions of psychoanalysis have taken deep root; the second (Slater & Roth, 1969) was published in England, where psychoanalysis has for the most part fallen on barren ground.

The methods of treatment for schizophrenic patients may be divided roughly into two categories: physical therapies and psychotherapies. . . . One finds, first of all, marked disagreements as to treatment of choice. My own marked preference, in the average case, is psychotherapy. . . . My "bias" is based on the belief that physical therapies, as far as we know or can infer, produce only a symptomatic improvement, whereas psychotherapy tends to: (1) remove the basic conflicts which led to the disorder, (2) correct the psycho-

pathologic patterns, and (3) permit the regenerative psychological powers of the organism to regain the lost ground. [Arieti, 1959, p. 493]

If the patient is seen by a doctor within two years from the manifestation of the first symptoms, and if the diagnosis of schizophrenia is established, it is nowadays a gross error not to press for his admission to a special unit or hospital where he can receive physical treatment. . . . Prolonged psychotherapy, even in mild cases, can no longer be justified. Psychoanalysis is, indeed, *contraindicated* in any stage or type of schizophrenia; to apply it is, as Freud himself commented to L. Binswanger, a professional error. [Slater & Roth, 1969, p. 325]

Even though ten years separate these strong and conflicting statements, the fundamental issue of the efficacy—and the morality—of psychotherapy for schizophrenics remains unresolved. This is so despite the results of a variety of studies that call into question the ultimate value of psychotherapy in schizophrenia.

Freud concluded early in his career that standard psychoanalytic techniques were not suitable for the treatment of schizophrenia. He felt that the schizophrenic has great difficulty developing close interpersonal relationships, while the establishment of such relationships is central to the therapeutic process of psychoanalysis. Nevertheless, psychoanalytic concepts like regression, transference, and the unconscious have influenced the development of psychotherapeutic techniques specifically oriented toward schizophrenia.

Technique. Psychoanalytic treatment methods for the schizophrenias vary widely, depending in part on whether they are based on the "classical" or "neo-Freudian" model. All, however, emphasize the importance of rapport between patient and therapist. The patient must come to recognize that he is no longer isolated from the world and that he is a worthy person in his own right. And he must understand that neither of these "discoveries" depends upon his becoming something he does not wish to become—in other words, that his therapist's acceptance of him is not contingent upon his being a "good patient." Such acceptance can mean a great deal to a schizophrenic, whose long history of rejection by the world is usually matched only by his long-standing rejection of himself. Sullivan talked of the importance of offering patients an early "relationship of security beyond what they have ever had" (1953). Fromm-Reichman conceived of this early effort at relationship building as "a specific way by which they can trust the world and themselves" (1952).

The therapist is also an important element in many behavioral treatment strategies, but dynamic and behavior therapy differ in the "justifications" each attaches to a close relationship between patient and therapist. The behavior therapist is apt to be pragmatic about the process, sometimes seeing it as the cement required to keep the patient motivated enough to participate in treatment. The psychoanalyst, while acknowledging the usefulness of rapport in motivating the patient, is likely to attach central importance to the relationship between schizophrenic and therapist for another reason: He believes that it offers the patient the sense of basic trust and self-worth which he failed to receive early in life from his parents.

Dynamic therapy with schizophrenics rarely employs "the couch"; most dynamic therapists think that would increase the patient's already substantial difficulty in relating directly to the therapist. Some therapists (such as Arieti) prefer to sit next to the patient, while others (such as Fromm-Reichman) choose to stand, sit, kneel, or lie down with the patient. Numerous short treatment sessions are usually employed, and patients are urged to be punctual (lest they project into the therapy relationship the lack of discipline and order that already characterizes their life).

Dynamic therapy with schizophrenics stresses the supportive—in contrast to intrusive—nature of the relationship between patient and therapist. The therapist asks few questions, so that the patient does not feel under pressure to "give away" parts of himself. If the patient is disorganized, the therapist tries to be alert to the ultimate meaning of his incoherence. If he is unrealistic and deluded, the therapist tries to make it clear that he cannot accept the patient's disordered view of the world even though he understands why the patient sees the world as he does. At the same time, the therapist may attempt to draw the patient away from exclusive preoccupation with the material of his delusions, in order to clarify and bring substance to his unreal view of the world.

Interpretation of a patient's psychotic behavior (for example, explaining to him that his paranoid projections represent unsuccessful efforts to prevent people from coming closer to him) is also a part of psychoanalytic psychotherapy. The degree, nature, and timing of these "insights" depend very much upon how disorganized the patient is.

Evaluation. Dynamic therapy procedures make sense both as practical expressions of psychoanalytic theory and as pragmatic approaches to disturbed patients. Whether they bring about positive therapeutic change is another matter. As the therapist's case notes said at the beginning of this chapter: "I'm not sure how much I've helped Rick. We have a good relationship; he trusts me. He talks freely, but he's just as psychotic as before. Three hours a week for nearly a year—and very little progress. Psychoanalytic treatment of schizophrenia is impossibly long."

Several broadly conceived outcome studies of psychotherapy with psychotic inpatients (most of whom were schizophrenic) failed to prove that psychotherapy was useful. For example, the results of psychotherapy alone were compared with the results of drug therapy alone in a large-scale project by the psychopharmacology research branch of the National Institute of Mental Health (May & Tuma, 1964, 1965). It was found that twenty schizophrenic inpatients who received individual psychotherapy from experienced dynamically trained psychotherapists did not do as well as twenty matched patients given phenothiazines rather than psychotherapy. Outcome measures included the rate of release from the hospital, length of hospital stay, amount of sedation required, change in overall clinical status as judged by experienced psychoanalysts, and final ratings of clinical status. Further, there was no difference in readmission rates between the drug and psychotherapy groups. A later study by the same research group, this time with a population of 228 patients, reported virtually identical findings (May, 1968). Other studies by the group compared psychotherapy alone with psychotherapy and drug therapy together and yielded equivalent conclusions (May, 1968).

For another major study, Grinspoon and his associates (1967, 1968) chose schizophrenic patients who had the best possible pretreatment prognoses: all were young, all had a diagnosis of acute schizophrenia, all were motivated, bright, and in good physical health. They were treated intensively and at length by highly qualified psychoanalysts. Despite these efforts to maximize the likelihood that psychotherapy would be effective, all measures showed that psychotherapy alone failed to produce changes in patients' behavior (Figure 7-1). The same measures reflected marked positive behavioral effects when the same patients were treated with both drugs and psychotherapy. Some critics of this study say: "Although the interpersonal therapies produced no noticeable effects over time, definite conclusions on this point could not be drawn, since suitable controls were not included" (Uhlenhuth et al., 1969). But most commentators have been impressed by the study's design and the value of its findings (May, 1971).

The relative efficiency of drugs and psycho-

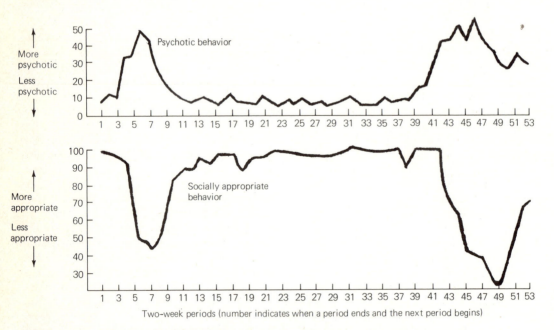

Figure 7-1. This graph shows some of the considerable evidence that, for schizophrenics, psychotherapy is far less effective than drug therapy. When a chronic schizophrenic patient was given a drug (phenothiazine, starting at two-week period 8), his behavior became less psychotic and more socially appropriate. When the drug was withdrawn (at period 41), these behavioral gains disappeared, even though psychotherapy was not discontinued. When the drug was reintroduced (at period 48), the behavioral gains reappeared. *(After Grinspoon et al., 1967)*

therapy for schizophrenia is probably most accurately tested by a research design comparing the outcome following drug treatment alone with the outcome when drugs and psychotherapy are combined. May's research design permitted this comparison. His studies (1968) found no significant differences in outcome between drugs alone and psychotherapy plus drugs, a finding that earlier studies had also reported.

These results lead us to conclude that while psychotherapy apparently does not *interfere* with the effects of drug therapy, it probably does not add to them either. The same data suggest that the major tranquilizers are clearly effective in improving the behavior of schizophrenic patients. They also suggest that psychotherapy is probably not effective for this purpose. As a consequence, we must agree with those who claim that psychotherapy for schizophrenic patients is largely a waste of time, money, and effort.

Milieu therapy and therapeutic communities

Though the roots of the therapeutic-community movement lie in Philippe Pinel's efforts two hundred years ago to humanize mental hospitals, the more recent work in this area was inspired by Maxwell Jones. The founder of the "social rehabilitation unit" at Belmont Hospital near London, Jones first built a community-based therapeutic household in 1947. Its underlying assumption was that since society has made these patients sick, they can be restored to mental health only by living in a wholesome therapeutic society.

A therapeutic community, according to Jones, must convince its members that they are "active participants in the therapy of themselves and other patients and in other aspects of the over-all hospital work—in contrast to their relatively more passive, recipient role in conventional treatment regimes" (1953). Active participation in the community is facilitated by joint involvement of staff and patients in both treatment and administration. Inclusion of patients in these functions was a

revolutionary notion when Jones first proposed it. So too was his suggestion that staff roles might also be in need of alteration. (For example, nurses as well as social workers might visit patient's homes, since nurses might be sensitive to family interactions for which the social workers' training had not prepared them.)

Jones's term "therapeutic community" meant something new, too. It indicated that a therapeutic culture—a treatment ideology—would replace the custodialism which largely characterized prisons and hospitals. Jones felt that these prevailing "antitherapeutic" attitudes and behaviors could be confronted and changed by community meetings bringing together all patients and staff who worked and lived together. He acknowledged the difficulties that community meetings caused those who attended them. For example, the head nurse would be deprived of her valuable "special relationship" with the ward doctor; the ward doctor would have to face patients without the protection of his white coat or prescription pad; and the patient would be forced to abandon the guise of helplessness provided by his psychosis. But Jones also envisioned important compensating benefits from these meetings that would require people to abandon comfortable social roles while relating to each other on new, more equitable grounds.

One sometimes gets the feeling, on rereading Jones from the perspective that the years have brought, that everything he wrote about has now been implemented in the "milieu therapy" programs of our up-to-date state hospitals, prisons, and community mental health centers. In fact, this is not true. Many institutions still foster authoritarian administrations, helpless and irresponsible patients, and nonexistent treatment regimes. Even in institutions which have accepted the promise of the therapeutic community, its evolution continues, as shown by the work of Cumming and Cumming (1962) and Fairweather (1969).

Like his views on the etiology of schizophrenia, R. D. Laing's approach to treatment is iconoclastic. Though his ideas are closer to Jones's than they are to any other more contemporary commentator on schizophrenic treatment, they can be distinguished easily from Jones' much more temperate words:

The following are a few necessarily telegrammatic remarks on therapy. (1) A bare minimum is care and respect for the whole person. In the acute breakdown "he" or "she" is only partially in this world. Although his body is all here, "he" may be all "there." While the patient is *in absentia*, he should be treated with full human dignity. (2) Occasionally another patient, or member of the staff, may have some understanding of the internal drama that is going on. The psychiatrist should realize that nothing in his training as a doctor or psychiatrist gives him any special claim to understand this process. He may, however, be humble and gifted enough to sense when someone else does; and very rarely he may have an understanding of what is involved himself. The patient badly needs guidance, but he is much better not given any advice or "interpretations" made with no genuine authority. (3) Preparation for the person's return to his family and community requires work with his family and other social networks before he leaves hospital, as well as thereafter. Continuity of care is required, without the existing tendency to separate, economically and organizationally, the "cure" of the "illness" from the "care of the person." [Laing, 1967, p. 184]

Laing outlines a novel treatment program for acutely disturbed schizophrenics. It is derived largely from his radical views on the etiology of the schizophrenias and his emphasis on the failure of traditional treatment procedures. He advocates small treatment centers, each housing no more than twenty-four patients, that are neither mental hospitals nor general hospital psychiatric wards. Treatment in these independent facilities consists of life in the therapeutic community—a "tranquil human setting"—where staff and patients alike have experienced important elements of the schizophrenic experience.

While Laing is a little short on the specifics of the treatment program in his therapeutic communities, he implies that it involves a mutual sharing among patients—and between patients and staff—of the experiences they have had during their psychoses. Special efforts are made, apparently, to demonstrate that the insights derived from these experiences will be valuable to the patient as he or she makes more and more concrete plans to reenter society. Intimate group discussions, sharing and openness in all human interactions, humane regard for everyone's essential strength and dignity—all are important elements of Laing's prescription for treatment.

Once a patient has recovered from the acute phases of a "schizophrenic break," he or she goes to work outside the center, though there is no pressure to leave it permanently. Patients who do leave are encouraged to keep in close touch with their friends there and, if the need arises, to return. Flexibility in terms of maximum and minimum lengths of stay is stressed. Laing has established at least one model center of the kind he describes. Located in the heart of London, it has attracted a good deal of attention and controversy in the popular press because of its radical approach.

Controlled studies of therapeutic communities and milieu therapy settings have not been common. One reason is that an "antiscientific" ethic pervades many of them; another is that the treatment effects of a total ward atmosphere are extremely difficult to measure. Rapaport (1960), a social anthropologist, spent more than four years observing Jones's pioneering therapeutic community. His findings, based upon data from 168 patients, are descriptive only, because his study was not controlled. He concluded that the therapeutic community had succeeded; he found a positive relationship between the length of time patients remained in the community and their psychological health on leaving it. That is, the longer they lived there, the more they benefited from it.

Recent studies of therapeutic communities of functionally psychotic patients, of geriatric patients, and of emotionally disturbed children all suggest that this approach to treatment often yields positive results in terms of ward adjustment, release rates, and posthospital performance. What is less certain is the degree to which the enthusiasm, commitment, and extra time put into the projects by hospital administrators and the ward staff are responsible for the results. Is it the staff commitment or the approach itself that works so well? The question is still open.

Behavior modification

Behavior modification comprises a variety of therapeutic techniques now used extensively with schizophrenic and other psychotic patients. The procedures stem almost entirely from the body of operant conditioning research. Central to the work of the behavior modifier is the conviction that *behavior, even maladaptive behavior, is a direct function of its consequences.* Therefore virtually all behavior modification programs seek to change behavior by altering its consequences. These changes in behavioral consequence involve either punishment of unwanted old behavior (to suppress it), reinforcement of wanted new behavior (to increase its frequency), or both.

Lindsley: Schizophrenia is high-frequency psychotic behavior. The pioneering work of Ogden Lindsley at Boston's Metropolitan State Hospital between 1953 and 1965 marked the real beginnings of behavior modification. Most of Lindsley's work centered on exploration of operant responding by psychotics rather than on treatment. But he was one of the first of his generation of laboratory-trained psychologists to "dirty his hands" with real clinical problems. During most of Lindsley's tenure at Metropolitan State Hospital, his basic research paradigm remained as it was first described by Skinner, Lindsley's teacher and first collaborator:

A patient is left alone one hour each day in a small room containing a device similar to a vending machine. The patient may operate the plunger on the machine and this behavior may be rewarded or "reinforced" with candy, cigarettes, or short exposures of interesting pictures.

The rate at which the machine is operated is studied. . . . The rates range from almost zero in the case of catatonics when first exposed to the machine to 10,000 responses per hour in the case of a manic subject. [Skinner, 1954, p. 403]

Lindsley believed that operant methods, at that time completely unproved in the clinical setting, had virtually unlimited clinical potential. His prophetic words were: "The free operant method can be used, with very little modification, to measure the behavior of any animal from a turtle to a normal genius. Since neither instructions nor rapport with the experimenter are demanded, the method is particularly appropriate in analyzing the behavior of non-verbal, lowly motivated, chronic psychotic patients" (1956, pp. 118–119). His research had indicated that psychotic patients differed from nonpatients in several ways. They generally had a lower rate of operant responding and showed extreme resistance to experimental extinction. Further, their operant behavior was sensitive to important concurrent environmental events (routine ward-assignment shifts, changed parole status, insulin therapy). In a subsequent report Lindsley described successful efforts to measure the onset, duration, and offset of what he called "psychotic incidents"—the aberrant behaviors which behaviorists consider to be the defining characteristics of psychosis (1960). He also detailed additional experimental efforts to use operant responding as a sensitive, continuous measure of the therapeutic efficacy of electroshock, insulin coma therapy, drug therapy, and psychotherapy. Lindsley found that patients dramatically altered their usual pattern of operant responding when these therapeutic interventions were made (see Figure 7-2). Thus operant responding might turn out to be an ultimate "barometer" of therapeutic success.

Lindsley's work at Metropolitan State Hospital continued for several years longer, extending into the measurement of psychopharmacologic response (1962), social behavior (1963), the behavior of retarded children (Bar-

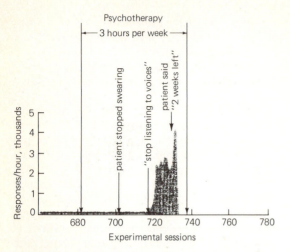

Figure 7-2. An application of conditioning principles to the problem of measuring psychotic behavior. Before he entered psychotherapy, this chronic schizophrenic patient had little time for "normal" behavior (working for cigarettes and candy, as measured by the scale of responses per hour), because he was pacing, hallucinating, and shouting. But after he began psychotherapy (a relationship he valued and therefore a reinforcer), his psychotic behavior decreased enough to permit him to work for cigarette and candy reinforcers. After his psychotherapy ended—shortly after he said "Two weeks left," meaning "I have only two more weeks of therapy left"—his "normal" behavior ceased and he reverted to his early psychotic behaviors. *(Lindsley, 1963)*

rett & Lindsley, 1962), and patient-therapist variables in psychotherapy (Nathan, Schneller, & Lindsley, 1964). Lindsley's major impact on the field of behavior modification, however, was his pioneering research on schizophrenics. Here his contribution was twofold: He demonstrated that schizophrenic patients are subject to the same fundamental laws of conditioning as nonpsychotics and animals. And he had the courage to suggest that the most "humane" approach to schizophrenia is to refuse to permit it to exist unattacked and untreated.

Ayllon: Psychosis can be treated by systematic application of laws of learning. Lindsley's example led Teodoro Ayllon to the first successful application of operant principles in a mental hospital setting (Ayllon & Michael,

1959). Ayllon taught behavioral techniques to the psychiatric nurses and aides working with him at the Weyburn, Sasketchewan, Provincial Hospital. One of these techniques was systematic withdrawal of the nurses' attention from unwanted behavior, and systematic increases in attention paid to wanted behavior. Behaviors treated by withdrawal of attention included psychotic talk and frequent, unnecessary, time-consuming visits to the nurses' station. Lucille, a schizophrenic woman, was successfully treated in this way:

Lucille's frequent visits to the nurses' office interrupted and interfered with their work. She had been doing this for 2 years. During this time, she had been told that she was not expected to spend her time in the nurses' office. Frequently, she was taken by the hand or pushed back bodily into the ward. Because the patient was classified as mentally defective, the nurses had resigned themselves to tolerating her behavior. As one of the nurses put it, "It's difficult to tell her anything because she can't understand—she's too dumb."

The following instructions were given to the nurses: "During this program the patient must not be given reinforcement (attention) for entering the nurse's office. Tally every time she enters the office."

The pretreatment study indicated that she entered the office on an average of 16 times a day. . . . The average frequency was down to two entries per day by the seventh week of extinction, and the program was terminated. [Ayllon & Michael,1959, pp. 326–327]

Though virtually everyone now agrees that inordinate attention to a behavior usually causes it to occur more frequently, it took repeated demonstrations by Ayllon and his colleagues to make the point. Its relevance to the classroom and the home as well as the hospital has since been acknowledged.

A wide range of target behaviors and treatment procedures were explored by Allyon and Michael. For example, assaultive behavior was eliminated by reinforcing behavior incompatible with it (such as lying quietly on the floor or talking to nurses). Patients'

refusal to feed themselves was altered by social reinforcement for self-feeding and punishment for refusing. Hoarding—collecting ward
"junk" and carrying it around beneath clothing—was extinguished by satiation (giving the
patient a flood of whatever junk he prized).

Ayllon and his co-workers continued to
develop individualized operant programs to
alter the behavior of individual patients during
the early 1960s (Ayllon, 1963; Ayllon & Haughton, 1962). Then Ayllon and Azrin set up the
first "token economy" in a psychiatric hospital
ward (1965). The token economy model, in
essence, transfers much of the task of deliver-
ing reinforcement for desired behavior from
the "warder" (the nurse, psychologist, ward

attendant) to the "ward" (the patient). It is
the patient who must assume responsibility
for earning and keeping tokens. They are
"earned" by the emission of appropriate wanted behaviors. They can be used to "purchase"
material reinforcers (food, candy, comfortable
physical surroundings), social reinforcers
(time with a therapist, the attention of a friendly nurse), or both.

Behaviors that Ayllon and Azrin first selected for token reinforcement included ward
duties (serving meals, cleaning floors, sorting
laundry), off-ward hospital tasks (working in
the kitchen, answering telephones, cleaning
laboratory glassware), and reduction of psychotic behavior (mutism, assaultive behavior,

TABLE 7-1. THE TOKEN ECONOMY: REWARDS AVAILABLE FOR TOKENS

	Tokens		Tokens
Privacy (Purchased by the day)		*Devotional opportunities*	
Selection of Room 1	0	Extra religious services on ward	1
Selection of Room 2	4	Extra religious services off ward	10
Selection of Room 3	8		
Selection of Room 4	15	*Recreational opportunities*	
Selection of Room 5	30	Movie on ward	1
Personal chair	1	Opportunity to listen to a live band	1
Choice of eating group	1	Exclusive use of radio	1
Screen (room divider)	1	Television (choice of program)	3
Choice of bedspreads	1		
Coat rack	1	*Commissary items*	
Personal cabinet	2	Consumable items such as candy, milk, cigarettes, coffee, and sandwich	1–5
Leave from the ward		Toilet articles such as tissues, tooth-	
20-minute walk on hospital grounds (with escort)	2	paste, comb, lipstick, and talcum powder	1–10
30-minute grounds pass (3 tokens for each additional 30 minutes)	10	Clothing and accessories such as gloves, headscarf, house slippers,	
Trip to town (with escort)	100	handbag, and skirt	12–400
Social interaction with staff		Reading and writing materials such as stationary, pen, greeting card, news-	
Private audience with chaplain, nurse	5 min free	paper, and magazine	2–5
Private audience with ward staff, ward physician (additional time—1 token per minute)	5 min free	Miscellaneous items such as ashtray, throw rug, potted plant, picture hold- er, and stuffed animal	1–50
Private audience with ward psychologist	20		
Private audience with social worker	100		

SOURCE: Ayllon & Azrin, 1965.

food stealing). Tokens were redeemable for six kinds of reinforcement: *privacy* (a four-bed room was 8 tokens, a two-bed room 15 tokens, a single room 30 tokens); *leave from the ward* (a twenty-minute escorted walk on the grounds was 2 tokens, an escorted trip to town was 100 tokens); *social interaction with staff* (a five-minute private audience with the chaplain was free, while a private audience with the social worker cost 100 tokens); *devotional opportunities* (an extra religious service on the ward was 1 token and off the ward it was 10 tokens); *recreational opportunities* (a movie on the ward was 1 token, a choice of television programs 3 tokens); *commissary items* (candy, milk, cigarettes, etc. were 1 to 5 tokens, toilet articles were 1 to 10, clothing and accessories were 12 to 400). The token price list is shown in Table 7-1.

Despite the relative complexity of the token exchange procedure, the sophisticated system of rewards, and the considerable self-control demanded in return for tokens, most of the chronic schizophrenic patients who took part in Ayllon and Azrin's early studies met the requirements of the token economy. These requirements were varied systematically to permit a behavioral analysis of the reinforcing properties of the token system. During one period tokens were no longer given for popular jobs but only for work that was generally disliked. The patients quickly switched over to the unpopular jobs and performed them adequately. At another stage in the experiments the patients were given their tokens *before* going to work, and the number of hours they spent on the job began to decrease sharply. Only when tokens were again paid after the work was performed did the hours spent at work return to their former levels. And as shown in Figure 7-3, when tokens were no longer given at all for performance of a job (beginning on day 16), the rate of work decreased sharply. It rose again only when reinforcement was resumed on day 31. Thus tangible reinforcement was necessary to maintain the desired behavioral changes in schizophrenics.

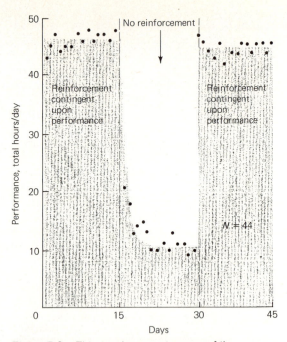

Figure 7-3. This graph presents some of the evidence that principles of conditioning can be used to reduce or even eliminate psychotic behavior. It shows the behavioral changes in a group of schizophrenics who participated in a token economy program. When the patients were given tokens for doing jobs in the hospital, they worked at appropriate levels. When their work was no longer rewarded by tokens (at day 16), it decreased by 80 percent. When they were again reinforced by tokens for working (at day 31), they returned to work with their former zeal. *(Ayllon & Azrin, 1965)*

Atthowe and Krasner: Development of sophisticated token economies. The success of Ayllon and Azrin's experiments inspired rapid expansion of the token economy approach. One of the most innovative and comprehensive "second-generation" token economies was established by Atthowe and Krasner early in 1963 on an 86-bed locked ward at the Palo Alto, California, Veterans Administration Hospital. Their project lasted two years and included sixty patients, most of them chronic schizophrenics who "had, for the most part, obvious and annoying behavioral deficits" (Atthowe & Krasner, 1968). Because of the length of time this token economy was studied, the relatively large number of patients it involved, and its careful research design, the Palo Alto project is regarded as a definitive test of the long-term efficacy of the token economy with chronic schizophrenic patients.

There were some important differences between this project and Ayllon and Azrin's earlier token economy:

Cigarettes, money, passes, watching television, etc., were some of the more obvious reinforcers, but some of the most effective reinforcers were idiosyncratic, such as sitting on the ward or feeding kittens. For some patients, hoarding tokens became highly valued. This latter practice necessitated changing the tokens every thirty days. In addition, the tokens a patient still had left at the end of each month were devalued 25 percent, hence the greater incentive for the patient to spend them quickly. . . . In general, each patient was reinforced immediately after the completion of some "therapeutic" activity, but those patients who attended scheduled activities by themselves were paid their tokens only once a week on a regularly scheduled pay day. Consequently, the more independent and responsible patient had to learn "to punch a time card" and to receive his "pay" at a specified future data. He then had to "budget" his tokens so they covered his wants for the next seven days.

In addition, a small group of twelve patients was in a position of receiving what might be considered as the ultimate in reinforcement. They were allowed to become independent of the token system. These patients carried a "carte blanche" which entitled them to all the privileges within the token economy plus a few added privileges and a greater status. For this special status, the patient had to work 25 hr. per week in special vocational assignments. In order to become a member of the "elite group," patients had to accumulate 120 tokens which entailed a considerable delay in gratification. [p. 38]

Atthowe and Krasner's behavioral analysis of the patients' responses permitted an evaluation of the specific variables which contributed to the power of the token economy method, as well as an assessment of the method itself as a therapeutic tool. At the start of their project, the experimenters established a six-month baseline period during which observers gathered reliable data on the rate at which patients naturally emitted a wide variety of "target" (symptomatic) behaviors. During the three-month "shaping" period which followed, tokens contingent upon specified behavior changes were introduced. Shaping of the behavior of patients who required gradual introduction to the token system was instituted at this time.

At first, the availability of canteen booklets, which served as money in the hospital canteen, was made contingent upon the amount of scheduled activities a patient attended. It soon became clear that almost one-half of the patients were not interested in money or canteen books. They did not know how to use the booklets, and they never bought things for themselves. Consequently, for 6 wk., patients were taken to the canteen and urged or "cajoled" into buying items which seemed to interest them (e.g., coffee, ice cream, pencils, handkerchiefs, etc.). Then all contingencies were temporarily abandoned, and patients were further encouraged to utilize the canteen books. Next, tokens were introduced but on a noncontingent basis. No one was allowed to purchase items in the ward canteen without first presenting tokens. Patients were instructed to pick up tokens from an office directly across the hall from the ward canteen and exchange them for the items they desired. After 2 wk. tokens were made contingent upon performance and the experimental phase of the study began. [p. 39]

Atthowe and Krasner found that introduction of tokens into the ward routine of these sixty chronic schizophrenics significantly increased their involvement in group activities. The patients showed a "widening of interest and a lessening of apathy." There was a marked rise in the number receiving passes to leave the hospital on weekends, drawing weekly cash, and using the ward canteen. Further, infractions of hospital rules decreased dramatically, even though the patients were much more active and hence more likely to come into conflict with hospital or ward regulations. Most important of all, twenty-four patients were discharged from the hospital as significantly improved and eight were transferred to more active wards, whereas there had been only eleven discharges and no transfers during the preceding eleven-month period.

Current trends in behavior modification. The behavior modification–token economy approach to schizophrenia has gone far beyond its modest beginnings. Several trends in the development of these behavioral techniques can be identified.

[1] The token economy paradigm is being extended far beyond the psychiatric hospital ward—to the public school classroom (O'Leary

These girls at the Rebecca Gratz Club—the successor organization to Henderson's Spruce House—can spend their earned allowances in the club's own "boutique." *(Sam Miller)*

et al., 1969; O'Leary & Drabman, 1971), to the exceptional child in the "special" class (Kaufman & O'Leary, 1972; Wolf et al., 1968), and to the institutionalized delinquent (Burchard & Barrera, 1972; Cohen, 1968). Successful application of behavior modification in these settings is described in Chapters 15 and 16.

[2] Token economies and other behavior modification methods have also been introduced into the area of community psychology. There they appear to permit continued effective treatment of chronic schizophrenics (Fairweather et al., 1969; Henderson & Scoles, 1970), autistic children (Herbert & Baer, 1972), retarded children and adults (Sajwaj et al., 1972), and delinquents (Fixsen et al., 1972). The work of Henderson and his colleagues at Spruce House in Philadelphia is notable. Spruce House, "established as an alternative to treatment in a state hospital," employs a token economy which has three goals: to help patients reacquire the "rules" of real work, to help them relate more effectively to persons in a vastly expanded environment, and to help prevent the reappearance of the maladaptive behaviors which led to their original hospitalization. Early outcome data suggest that appropriate work and social behavior are maintained by the token system, which also appears to reduce the frequency of hospital readmission.

[3] On the negative side, some professionals are concerned over the possibility that token economies may reinforce social values which are not especially laudable—values like docility, obedience, and obeisance (O'Leary, 1972; Winett & Winkler, 1972).

[4] Targets for behavior modification are now often focused on specific individual maladaptive behaviors rather than on a patient's overall disorganization. Increased efforts are being reported to alter specific "schizophrenic" behaviors like delusional speech (Liberman et al., 1973), apathy (Weinman et al., 1972), interpersonal isolation (Ravensborg, 1972), and hallucinations (Haynes & Geddy, 1973; Weingaertner, 1971). Early results of this work have been promising, though whether they will eventually justify the inordinate ex-

penditure of time they require has been questioned (Kazdin & Bootzin, 1972).

The future. Behavior modification techniques have yielded extremely encouraging results with schizophrenics. Nevertheless, comparison of the "cost effectiveness" of these procedures with drug treatment, traditional milieu therapy, or both together must be undertaken before anyone can be certain that behavior modification is as effective as enthusiasts claim. Further, long-term outcome studies comparing behavior modification procedures with other therapeutic methods must take place before we can be certain that the behavioral techniques are as useful for keeping schizophrenics and other patients in the community as they seem to be for getting them back there in the first place.

Behavior modifiers have been paying increased attention to behavior modification in the community and by persons in the community. The goals of this effort are to maintain the effective behavioral control over psychotic behavior first achieved in the hospital setting and to exert control over the factors in the community that are associated with development of maladaptive behavior. Atthowe, for example, has recently formulated the concept of *behavior innovation,* meaning a set of procedures by which the community can exert positive behavioral control over both disordered and disordering behavior. Behavior innovation, to Atthowe, is "a continual shaping and fading of all of the relevant behaviors in the complicated rehabilitation chain from its initiation to its stabilization. For many individuals, the rehabilitative process may never end. Shaping, however, cannot be limited to the behavior of patients . . . behavior innovation requires modification in the various social systems (intraindividual, extraindividual) that influence each marginal man" (1973, p. 38).

Atthowe is here asking for nothing less than a radical reshaping of one of the most fundamental functions of society—the process by which it instills modes and morals in its members. Society has failed most, Atthowe believes, with the persons who most need this

Does society have the right to condemn anyone to this kind of existence? *(Jerry Cooke)*

learning—those whom he calls "marginal men." He suggests that society must make the rules by which it wishes its citizens to be guided more explicit and less difficult to learn.

Involuntary hospitalization

An article in a southern California newspaper early in 1973 reported that Jose Martinez, a Mexican-American farm worker, had been a patient in a large central California state hospital for eighteen years—until it was discovered that no one had ever judged him insane. It seems that he had been hospitalized because the 8-year-old daughter of the owner of the farm on which he was working in the summer of 1955 identified him as the man who had "touched her in her private parts" several times. Because no other witness to the crime could be found—and because the child confused Jose Martinez with other farm workers during one police lineup—Martinez was not indicted for child molestation. Instead, a solicitous county welfare worker arranged for his hospitalization so that he would "at least have enough to eat and be kept out of further trouble."

Society often imprisons its social deviants and malcontents. Throughout history two kinds of people have been shut away: those who have committed a crime against society and those who might do so. Criminals largely fall within the first category; "mental" patients within the second. All fifty of the United States have laws which govern commitment of "mental" patients to hospitals for "treatment." There are three common avenues of commitment: (1) voluntary commitment, (2) commitment for observation, (3) involuntary commitment. For obvious reasons involuntary commitment has long been a controversial issue.

In a recent review of criteria for civil commitment, Baynes, a young American attorney, points to a recent increase in efforts to make the four basic commitment criteria more objective and reliable (1971). State laws have long insisted that before he can be committed, a person must fall into one or more of these categories: he must be mentally ill, likely to injure himself or others, in need of immediate care or treatment in a hospital, or lacking in sufficient insight or capacity to make responsible decisions concerning his hospitalization. Baynes points out a variety of problems of definition in the four criteria and reviews recent attempts by the states to reduce such problems.

Baynes also describes an even more recent trend: controversies over patients' "right to treatment," which have arisen in Georgia, Illinois, and Virginia. As he says, if the state cannot furnish the specific treatment that the individual needs, keeping him in a mental institution may be a violation of his constitutional rights under the due process clause.

Though involuntary commitment continues to be a prerogative of every state, that right has begun to be questioned. What seems clear is that involuntary hospitalization cannot be justified as "treatment," but only as society's way of punishing offenders or protecting itself against them.

Summary

So far there is no known cause of schizophrenia, though there is no shortage of theories to account for the range of bizarre behaviors grouped within this category. The theories include biological, psychoanalytic, and learning models of etiology.

Many mental health professionals believe that one or more inborn metabolic disturbances, perhaps transmitted genetically, may be responsible for the schizophrenias. Researchers have tried for years to identify biochemical factors in schizophrenia, because the behavior of many schizophrenics closely resembles the pathological behavior of persons whose brain chemistry has been disrupted by known drugs, poisons, trauma, or disease. Despite the logic of this deduction and the multitude of studies which have attempted to confirm one biological theory or another, the central role of biochemical factors in the etiology of schizophrenia has not been demonstrated. Important control, diagnostic, and methodological problems have prevented generalization of results from one laboratory to another.

Though a biochemical or metabolic abnormality could come about as the result of spontaneous mutation or an undiagnosed illness, it is more likely that such a disorder would be transmitted genetically. The pedigree method, the family method, and the twin method are three forms of experimental design which have attempted to control for environmental circumstances and identify possible genetic factors in the schizophrenias. Results of studies using these procedures strongly suggest that at least some of the schizophrenias are genetically determined.

Psychoanalytic theory traces the roots of schizophrenia to a period of severe environmental trauma during the oral stage of psychosexual development. Supposedly the person then fixates at that primitive level of behavioral development. Unhappiness among psychoanalysts with this conception led to the formation of a series of interpersonal theories of schizophrenia. Chief among them was Bateson's double-bind hypothesis, which is still unproved. It claims that schizophrenia results when a parent's predominant mode of communication with a child involves the delivery of two conflicting messages at the same time. Other interpersonal theories of schizophrenia derive from Lidz's studies of disordered schizophrenic families and from Laing's conclusion that schizophrenia is a strategy adopted to enable a person to live in what has become an unlivable situation.

The drive and arousal theories, formulated by psychologists like Pavlov, Venables, Mednick, and Epstein, state in essence that schizophrenia stems from a person's fundamental inability to modulate the input of stimuli from the environment, resulting in a disorganizing stimulus overload that prevents selection of appropriate responses. The social-learning view, supported by Bandura, Ullmann and Krasner, and others, takes the position that many or most of the symptoms of schizophrenia are learned through direct reinforcement and modeling of deviant response patterns. Like the drive and arousal theories, independent validation of the social-learning model has not been achieved.

Before the phenothiazine drugs were developed in the mid-1950s, neurosurgery, insulin coma therapy (ICT), and electroconvulsive therapy (ECT) were widely employed to treat the symptoms of schizophrenia. Current assessment of these methods suggests that they are not very effective. By contrast, the phenothiazines truly appear to be wonder drugs. In fact, controlled studies comparing treatment using the phenothiazines with treatment using other drugs, alone or in combination with psychotherapy, group therapy, or electroconvulsive therapy, indicate that the phenothiazines are much more effective than any other treatment in reducing the frequency and severity of many of the signs of schizophrenia.

Though their overall efficacy with schizophrenic patients is largely unsupported, psychoanalysis and psychoanalytic therapy continue to be employed. Rick G., this chapter's case study, was treated with a form of psychoanalytic psychotherapy, and the results convinced his young therapist that the therapeutic process would be long, difficult, and not necessarily successful. Recent behavioral approaches to schizophrenia, including behavior therapy and token economies, have shown considerable promise. They appear to enable patients to lead more productive lives both inside and outside the hospital, even though they rarely extinguish the maladaptive behaviors which caused the patients to be hospitalized in the first place.

CHAPTER EIGHT
The affective and paranoid psychoses

Fyodor Dostoevsky ● Clifford Beers ● Historical perspectives ● Affective and paranoid psychoses ● Etiological factors ● Cues to the affective psychoses ● Experimental studies of depression ● Suicide ● Treatment for the affective psychoses

DOSTOEVSKY: NOTES FROM UNDERGROUND

I am a sick man. . . . I am a spiteful man, I am an unattractive man. I believe my liver is diseased. . . .

I have been going on like that for a long time—twenty years. Now I am forty. I used to be in the government service, but am no longer. I was a spiteful official. I was rude and took pleasure in being so. . . . When petitioners used to come for information to the table at which I sat, I used to grind my teeth at them, and felt intense enjoyment when I succeeded in making anybody unhappy. I almost always did succeed. For the most part they were all timid people —of course, they were petitioners. But of the uppish ones there was one officer in particular I could not endure. He simply would not be humble, and clanked his sword in a disgusting way. I carried on a feud with him for eighteen months over that sword. At last I got the better of him. He left off clanking it. That happened in my youth, though.

But do you know, gentlemen, what was the chief point about my spite? Why, the whole point, the real sting of it, lay in the fact that continually, even in the moment of the acutest spleen, I was inwardly conscious with shame that I was not only a spiteful but not even an embittered man, that I was simply scaring sparrows at random and amusing myself by it. . . . It was not only that I could not become spiteful, I did not know how to become anything: neither spiteful nor kind, neither a rascal nor an honest man, neither a hero nor an insect. . . .

I want now to tell you, gentlemen, whether you care to hear it or not, why I could not even become an insect. I tell you solemnly, that I have many times tried to become an insect. But I was not equal even to that. I swear, gentlemen, that to be too conscious is an illness—a real thoroughgoing illness. . . .

Fyodor Dostoevsky. *(New York Public Library Picture Collection)*

"Ha, ha ha! You will be finding enjoyment in toothache next," you cry, with a laugh. "Well? Even in toothache there is enjoyment," I answer. I had toothache for a whole month and I know there is. In that case, of course, people are not spiteful in silence, but moan; but they are not candid moans, they are malignant moans, and the malignancy is the whole point. The enjoyment of the sufferer finds expression in those moans. . . . Come, can a man who attempts to find enjoyment in the very feeling of his own degradation possibly have a spark of respect for himself? . . . In consequence again of those accursed laws of consciousness, anger in me is subject to chemical disintegration. . . . Oh, gentlemen, do you know, perhaps I consider myself an intelligent man only because all my life I have been able neither to begin nor to finish anything. . . .

Oh, if I had done nothing simply from laziness! Heavens, how I should have respected myself then. I should have respected myself because I should at least have been capable of being lazy; there would at least have been one quality, as it were, positive in me, in which I could have believed myself. Question: What is he? Answer: A sluggard; how very pleasant it would have been to hear that of oneself! It would mean that I was positively defined, it would mean that there was something to say about me. "Sluggard"—why, it is a calling and vocation, it is a career. . . .

The long and the short of it is, gentlemen, that it is better to do nothing! Better conscious inertia. And so hurrah for underground! Though I have said that I envy the normal man to the last drop of my bile, yet I should not care to be in his place such as he is now (though I shall not cease envying him). No, no; anyway the underground life is more advantageous. There, at any rate, one can. . . . Oh, but even now I am lying! I am lying because I know myself that it is not underground that is better, but something different, quite different, for which I am thirsting, but which I cannot find! Damn underground! [Fyodor Dostoevsky, 1951, pp. 129–132, 137, 140–141, 153–154]

BEERS: LETTERS FROM NEW HAVEN

I had reached a point where my will had to capitulate to Unreason . . . that unscrupulous usurper. My previous five years as a neurasthenic had led me to believe that I had experienced all the disagreeable sensations an overworked and unstrung nervous system could suffer. But on this day several new and terrifying sensations seized me and rendered me all but helpless. My condition, however, was not apparent even to those who worked with me at the same desk. I remember trying to speak and at times finding myself unable to give utterance to my thoughts. Though I was able to answer questions, that fact hardly diminished my feelings of apprehension, for a single failure in an attempt to speak will stagger any man, no matter what his state of health. I tried to copy certain rec-

(Colorlab)

ords in my day's work, but my hand was too unsteady, and I found it difficult to read the words and figure presented to my tired vision in blurred confusion. . . .

What I had long expected I now became convinced had at last occurred. I believed myself to be a confirmed epileptic. . . . From that time my one thought was to hasten the end, for I felt that I should lose the chance to die should relatives find me in a seizure of the supposed malady. . . . Soon my disordered brain was busy with schemes for death. I distinctly remember one which included a row on Lake Whitney, near New Haven. . . . I also remember searching for some healing drug which I hoped to find about the house. . . . I then thought of severing my jugular vein. . . . During these three or four days I slept scarcely at all. . . . By a process of elimination, all suicidal methods but one had at last been put aside. On that one my mind now centered. . . . The sills of my windows were a little more than thirty feet above the ground. . . . It required no great amount of calculation to determine how slight the chance of surviving a fall from either of these windows. . . . It was now or never for liberation. . . . With the mad desire to dash my brains out on the pavement below, I rushed to that window which was directly over the flag walk. . . . With my fingers I clung for a moment to the sill. Then I let go. [Beers, 1905, pp. 15–19]

Clifford Beers was 30 years old, a graduate of Yale College, and a member of New Haven's "establishment" when he wrote *A Mind that Found Itself* (1905). The book, which catalyzed far-reaching changes in mental patient care in the United States, describes with clarity and beauty the author's own manic-depressive psychosis.

Although Beers remembers that he was given to striking alterations of mood in childhood, he traces the onset of his first severe depression to the time shortly after his graduation from college. This episode seems to have been a depression characterized by auditory hallucinations; a poorly systematized delusional system centered on ideas of persecution; a severely depressed affect accompanied by prominent feelings of guilt, hopelessness, and despair; and pronounced psychomotor agitation, which alternated with periods of depressive stupor. Shortly after these symptoms reached psychotic dimensions, Beers attempted suicide and was hospitalized. He remained in the hospital for two years, emerging from his depression after eighteen months to display significantly elevated mood and psychomotor behavior, a persistent attitude of grandeur, and flight of ideas. This episode lasted five months and was followed by a period of stabilized mood which led to his release from the hospital.

Shortly afterwards Beers told in *The Mind that Found Itself* the story of his experiences at three Connecticut mental hospitals to which he had been confined. The book raised a furor among state government officials, members of mental health commissions, ex-patients, local citizens' groups, and other civic organizations. All were appalled at rediscovering the wretched conditions under which mental hospital patients were forced to live. In 1908 Beers and a group of citizens from all walks of life founded the Connecticut Society for Mental Hygiene. In 1909 the National Society for Mental Hygiene was formed and the national movement was underway. The influence of that movement has waxed and waned with the wars, depressions, racial upheavals, and other competing concerns of American society. But it continues to foster efforts to humanize mental hospitals; to bring enlightened mental hygiene concepts to the schools, ghettos, and ethnic neighborhoods where they have not been popular; to increase the numbers of mental health professionals; and to broaden the socioeconomic base from which these professionals are drawn.

The picture Beers paints of his manic-depressive psychosis is notable for the precision and sensitivity with which he recalls his thoughts and actions during times of irrationality. His chronicle begins with the description given above of his sudden realization that a "nervous condition" he had had for five years had begun to worsen. It continues with the discovery that his attempt at suicide resulted only in a few broken bones and commitment to a private psychiatric hospital. Shortly after being committed, he began to experience the full agony of profound depression.

Certain hallucinations of hearing, of "false voices," added to my torture. Within my range of hearing, but beyond the reach of my understanding, there was a hellish vocal hum. Now and then I would recognize the subdued voice of a former friend, now and then I would hear the voices of some who I believed were not friends. All these referred to me and uttered what I could not clearly distinguish but knew must be imprecations. Ghostly rappings on the walls and ceiling of my room punctuated unintelligible mumblings of invisible persecutors. Those were long nights. [P. 23]

Even worse were his feelings of estrangement from the world which he was convinced had rejected him for his irredeemable sins.

My emotions on leaving New Haven were, I imagine, much the same as those of a condemned and penitent criminal who looks upon the world for the last time. The day was hot, and, as we drove to the railway station, the blinds on most of the houses in the streets through which we passed were seen to be closed. The reason for this was not then apparent to me. I thought I saw an unbroken line of deserted houses, and I imagined that their desertion had been deliberately planned as a sign of displeasure on the part of their former occupants. As citizens of New

Haven I supposed them bitterly ashamed of such a despicable inhabitant as myself. [P. 34]

At last his depression lifted—only to be followed by mania.

I have already described the peculiar sensation which assailed me when, in June, 1900, I lost my reason. At that time my brain felt as though pricked by a million needles at white heat. On this August 30th, 1902, shortly after largely regaining my reason, I had another most distinct sensation in the brain. It started under my brow and gradually spread until the entire surface was affected. The throes of a dying reason had been torture. The sensations felt as my dead reason was reborn were delightful. It seemed as though the refreshing breath of some kind of Goddess of Wisdom were being gently blown against the surface of my brain. It was a sensation not unlike that produced by a methol pencil rubbed ever so gently over a fevered brow. So delicate, so crisp and exhilarating was it that words fail me in my attempt to describe it. Few, if any experiences can be more delightful. If the exaltation produced by some drugs is anything like it, I can easily understand how and why certain pernicious habits enslave those who contract them. For me, this experience was liberation, not enslavement. [P. 81]

But "liberation" to mania, despite its pleasures, was enslavement in fact. It brought, for example, the emptiness of delusions of grandeur:

As for me, the very first night [in another mental hospital] vague and vast humanitarian projects began joyously to shape themselves in my mind. My garden of thoughts seemed filled with flowers which might properly be likened to the quick-growing, night blooming cereus—that Delusion of Grandeur of all flower-plants that thinks itself prodigal enough if it but unmask its beauty to the moon! Few of my bold fancies, however, were of so fugitive and chaste a spendor. . . . My large and varied assortment of delusions of grandeur made everything seem possible. There were few problems I hesitated to attack. . . . Many times a day I would instruct the attendants what to do and what not to do, and tell them what I should do if my requests, suggestions, or orders were not immediately complied with. [Pp. 85, 102]

The consequences of Beers's manic delusions were quixotic:

I know of no better way to convey to the reader my state of mind during these first weeks of elation than to confess—if confession it is—that when I set upon a career of reform I was impelled to do so by motives in part like those which seem to have possessed Don Quixote when he, madman that he was, set forth, as Cervantes says, with the intention "of righting every kind of wrong, and exposing himself to peril and danger, from which in the issue he would obtain eternal renown and fame." . . . What I wish

Don Quixote, after the lithograph by Doré. Cervantes's great tragicomic character showed many signs of being a victim of manic delusions. *(New York Public Library, Print Division)*

to do is to make plain that one abnormally elated may be swayed irresistibly by his best instincts, and that while under the spell of an exultation, idealistic in degree, he may be not only willing, but eager to assume risks and endure hardships which under normal conditions he would assume reluctantly, if at all. [Pp. 85–88]

His "career of reform" sometimes found unusual outlets:

During the latter part of that first week I wrote many letters, so many, indeed, that I soon exhausted a liberal supply of stationery. . . . It was now at my own suggestion that the superintendent gave me large sheets of manila wrapping paper. These I proceeded to cut into strips a foot wide. One such strip, four feet long, would suffice for a mere *billet-doux;* but a real letter usually required several such strips pasted together. More than once letters twenty or thirty feet long were written; and on one occasion the accumulation of two or three days of excessive productivity, when spread upon the floor, reached from one end of the corridor to the other—a distance of about one hundred feet. My output per hour was something like twelve feet with an average of one hundred and fifty words to the foot. Under the pressure of elation one takes pride in doing everything in record time. Despite my speed, however, my letters were not incoherent. They were simply digressive, which was to be expected, as elation befogs one's "goal idea." [P. 89]

When his mania finally subsided, Beers was discharged from the hospital. A portion of the energy and commitment with which he had attacked those strips of paper became translated into zeal for mental hospital reform—with results that were not nearly as quixotic as he had once predicted.

Depression, mania—and creativity

We have chosen to illustrate the affective and paranoid psychoses with descriptions by men who experienced the affective psychoses in their full intensity—the Russian novelist Fyodor Dostoevsky and the American reformer Clifford Beers. Dostoevsky's depression was unremitting. Sometimes psychotic in intensity, it was always painful, often debilitating. Yet Dostoevsky wrote what many believe to have been the nineteenth century's most distinguished prose. His work included *Crime and Punishment* and *The Brothers Karamazov,* both among the world's great novels. Though he described the horrors of his depression through a fictional character in *Notes from Underground,* it seems clear that he was chronicling the physical pain and abject despair that accompanied his own chronic depression.

At the same time one must ask whether Dostoevsky's burden played a role in his incredible productivity. Besides his two greatest novels he wrote two others, *The Idiot* and *The Possessed*, that almost any writer would be proud to claim as his best. And his cluster of short novels, including *Notes from Underground, Uncle's Dream, The Eternal Husband,* and *The Double,* are among the prominent representatives of this form in Western literature. Could Dostoevsky have written even better if he had not been depressed? Or did his depression contribute to his art, forcing him to concentrate on the world of the imagination rather than the material world? One of Dostoevsky's biographers is convinced of the answer:

The distinguishing events of Dostoevsky's life wear an exclusively gloomy hue. The spring which fed him, rendered him great and powerful, and never quite dried up, was suffering. It is hardly exaggerating to call Dostoevsky's burden the heaviest which any man has had set upon his shoulders. Every kind of suffering tormented him; bodily misery, social misery, spiritual misery, everything in excess. [Meier-Graefe, 1928, p. 36]

Beers's psychosis was a manic-depressive reaction, though at the beginning he thought his "nervousness" was "neurasthenia," a label current in his time to describe what we now call anxiety neurosis. That behavioral disorder was troublesome but did not prevent Beers from working. In time, however, his psychopathology became totally disabling. It grew more and more exclusively depressive in character until he experienced psychotic depression in its full intensity: depressive mood, retarded motor behavior and thought, prominent hypochondriacal complaints, and a delusional system centering on feelings of sin, guilt, and the certainty of ultimate and everlasting punishment. But unlike Dostoevsky, whose depression was interminable and unremitting, Beers's depressive psychosis ultimately lifted. It was followed almost immediately by the antithesis of depression, mania: elated affect, rapid thinking and increased motor behavior, and delusions of grandeur.

Either in spite of or because of his psychosis, Beers set to work when he recovered and energized the American mental hygiene movement. Did his psychosis make him a reformer?

Or did it prevent him from being an even more effective one? Like many other questions about the causes and cures of the psychopathologies, these cannot be answered. But what can be concluded by reviewing the productive lives of Dostoevsky and Beers is that psychosis does not always nullify a life.

Historical perspectives on the affective and paranoid psychoses

The paranoid and affective psychoses occupy a central place in the history of mental illness. To begin with, *paranoia* is one of the oldest "state of mind" terms, dating back to the ancient Greeks. The word referred literally to one who was "out of his mind," and for many centuries it simply described insanity. The use of the term to denote conditions as different from each other as delirium, delusions, and schizophrenia continued until Kraepelin restricted it to patients who had chronic, highly systematized, and seemingly incurable delusions but did not show general personality disorganization (1896). It was then that this rare complex of behaviors became identified, as it is today, by the term *paranoid states.*

At the same time that the first edition of Kraepelin's monumental psychiatric textbook appeared, Freud also described paranoia (1896). He pictured it as the result of exclusive reliance upon the defense mechanism of projection. In so doing he reinterpreted as psychologically determined a condition which had previously been considered entirely biological in etiology. Fifteen years later when Freud analyzed Daniel Paul Schreber's memoirs, he carried his view of the workings of projection still further (details of this analysis were given in Chapter 7). Others who have written about paranoia include Adolf Meyer (1948), who focused on the mechanisms by which paranoids attempt to bend objective reality to their delusional thinking; Kretschmer (1925), who identified a constitutional complex with strong paranoid tendencies; and Cameron (1963), who related the adult symptoms of paranoia to failure during childhood to acquire skills in role taking and interpersonal sensitivity.

The manic-depressive reactions were identified very early. Homer, Plutarch, Hippocrates, and Aretaeus all described mania and melancholia, often as accurately as present-day clinicians. They recognized the cyclical nature of the episodes of mania and depression and the relative intactness of thought processes even during times of greatest turmoil. Consequently they were able to differentiate these conditions from what we now term the schizophrenias and the senile (organic) disorders.

Modern views of the manic-depressive psychoses, like those of so many other serious psychopathologies, were heavily influenced by Kraepelin. His ideas in turn were affected by two French psychiatrists, Falret and Bail-

larger, and a German, Kahlbaum, who made a variety of scientific observations confirming the cyclical nature of the disorders. Kraepelin (1896, 1913) integrated their findings, gave the name *manic-depressive insanity* to the syndrome group, and included within the term "the whole domain of periodic and circular insanity, simple mania, the greater part of the morbid states termed melancholia, and also a not inconsiderable number of states termed amentia (confusional or delirious insanity)."

Affective and paranoid psychoses

The affective and paranoid psychoses, like the schizophrenias, are "psychoses not attributed to physical condition." This phrase from DSM II means that they are presently considered *functional psychoses* which do not derive from physical causes.

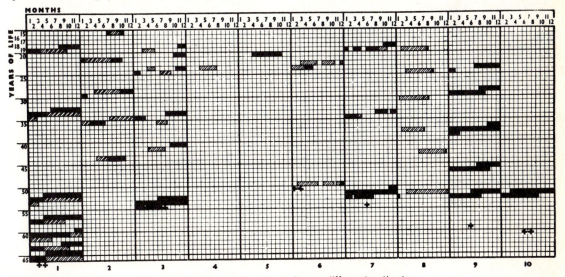

Figure 8-1. The observed courses of affective psychosis in ten different patients. (Key: +, Death from physical causes. ++, Suicide. Black, depression. Shaded, mania.) Note the great variability of the disorder. The first three patients experienced cyclical manic and depressive episodes. The fourth had a single manic episode, the fifth a single depressive episode, the sixth two manic phases each followed by short depressions, the seventh three depressive phases, two of which were followed by short manic episodes. The eighth suffered six prolonged periods of mania, and the ninth five prolonged periods of depression. The tenth was an example of involutional melancholia. Three of the ten patients were suicides. *(Slater & Roth, 1969, p. 216)*

The affective psychoses differ from the other functional psychoses by virtue of the fundamental disorder of mood—either depression or elation—that colors every aspect of the patient's behavior. These extremities of mood are unrelated to environmental circumstances (unlike depressive neurosis, which is almost always a result of unhappy events in the patient's life). As Figure 8-1 shows, the rhythm of moods varies considerably from patient to patient. The following affective psychoses are distinct diagnostic entities:

[1] *Involutional melancholia.* This disorder occurs in both men and women during the involutional period, between the ages of 50 to 60. It is characterized by worry, anxiety, agitation, and severe insomnia. In extreme cases a person may experience profound guilt, the certainty of eventual punishment, and somatic preoccupations, which may include actual somatic delusions.

[2] *Manic-depressive psychosis.* DSM II separates these conditions into three varieties. *(a) Manic-depressive illness, manic type,* is distinguished largely or exclusively by manic episodes during which patients are excessively elated, irritable, and overly talkative. They cannot control the rapid flight of their ideas or slow down their markedly increased activity levels. Though brief periods of depression may occur in the midst of the mania, they are secondary to the fundamental manic condition. *(b) Manic-depressive illness, depressed type,* consists only of episodes of depression. Patients experience severely depressed mood, mental and motor retardation (sometimes progressing to stupor), hypochondria, apprehension, agitation, and perplexity. Hallucinations and delusions, always tied to guilt, frequently accompany severe depression. Dostoevsky and his shadow, the underground man, probably suffered from manic-depressive illness, depressed type. *(c) Manic-depressive illness, circular type,* is an affective psychosis that includes at least one episode each of mania and of psychotic depression. Clifford Beers's manic-depressive psychosis was of the circular variety. As patients age, the frequency of manic and depressive episodes often increases,

with the result that fewer and shorter periods of nonpsychosis may intervene between periods of psychosis.

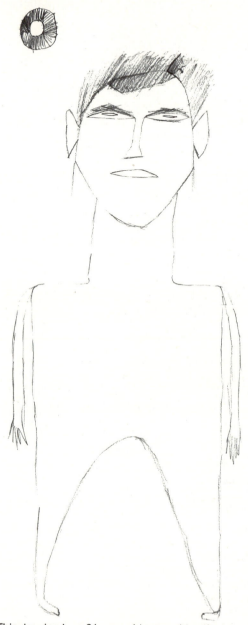

This drawing by a 21-year-old paranoid patient reflects his suspicious, angry approach to the world. Not all "patient art" correlates so well with actual psychopathology.

The *paranoid psychoses* are extremely rare. They are distinguished from the other functional psychoses by a central delusion of either a persecutory or a grandiose nature. Though disorders of mood, activity, and thinking often coexist in paranoid psychosis, they are always colored by the fundamental delusion. Despite this diagnostic cue, many clinicians question the legitimacy of setting off the paranoid psychoses from the affective psychoses or the schizophrenias, with which they share many common features.

A man later given the diagnosis of paranoid psychosis startled New York City during the spring of 1914 when he made an attempt on the life of Mayor John Purroy Mitchel. The shot intended for the mayor hit Frank L. Polk, an aide, injuring him severely. When the assailant, a 71-year-old man named Michael P. Mahoney, was taken to the Tombs prison, he seemed elated and satisfied. "You don't know how relieved I feel!" he exclaimed. Born in the south of Ireland, a blacksmith by occupation, Mahoney had been in the United States for fifty-two years. He was married, had no children, smoked and drank only moderately, and had no history of venereal disease or narcotics addiction.

Mahoney firmly believed that he had been the victim of systematic frame-ups by certain people during most of his life in the United States. Talking to a reporter in calm, reasonable tones, he said, "You may be one of them and it won't do me any good to tell you." He finally admitted that it was the Masonic order which was against him, and since Mayor Mitchel was a member of the order, he must have been a part of the conspiracy. Mahoney believed that the Masons would stop at nothing to get opponents out of their way and to protect their brethren. He himself had repeatedly tried to find a job, traveling from one state to another looking for work, but the Masons always interfered to spoil his chances. Mayor Mitchel, Mahoney felt, had clearly used influence to prevent him from obtaining employment in New York City.

Etiological factors in affective and paranoid psychoses

Genetic factors

Genetics and the manic-depressive pyschoses. Many mental health workers now believe that hereditary and constitutional factors play important roles in the etiology of the manic-depressive psychoses. Early support for this hypothesis came from the work of Kretschmer (1925), who concluded that 81 of 85 schizophrenic patients had what he labeled "leptosomatic physique," while 58 of 62 manic-depressives had a so-called "pyknic" one. But of the many subsequent studies designed to explore the relationship between physique and psychopathology, only a few have confirmed Kretschmer's findings (Rees, 1960). Further, close examination of the studies which did support Kretschmer (Wittman et al., 1948; Anastasi & Foley, 1949) suggests that their positive findings may well have resulted from intervening relationships involving the subjects' ages and nutritional status. We therefore conclude that Kretschmer's early formulations were not valid.

Several investigators, among them Kallmann (1952) and Slater (1953), believed that some persons are carriers of a specific predisposition or vulnerability to manic-depressive psychosis. Kallmann reached this conclusion after surveying 461 manic-depressive patients and their families. He computed the following expectancy rates for manic-depressive psychosis among blood relatives of the patients:

.4% in general population
16.7% in half siblings
23.0% in full siblings
23.5% in parents
26.3% in fraternal (dizygotic)
100.0% in identical (monozygotic) twins

Slater, who also employed the twin method, found an incidence of manic-depressive psychosis that was significantly higher among identical twins (1953), though his findings did not reach Kallmann's 100 percent concordance level. More recent research in the same area has tended to confirm these early results (Stenstedt, 1959; Hopkinson, 1964).

In a modification of the family method, a study of the Hutterites (a small, inbred, "fundamentalist" sect living in Canada and the northern plains states of the United States) showed that they have roughly four times the usual rate of manic-depressive psychosis (Eaton & Weil, 1955). On the surface these data appear to support the hereditary view of manic-depressive psychosis. But since the Hutterites' community is a rigid, formalized one which permits little spontaneous expression of emotion, it may be that their life style, rather than genetics, plays the major role in their predisposition to affective psychosis.

Other studies that seem to relate the affective psychoses to genetic determinants are marred by unsatisfactory design features. Among these are diagnostic unreliability (Was the patient manic-depressive, schizophrenic, or something else?), bias in selection of twins (Were they truly representative of all available twins?), and inaccurate assessment of twinship (Were the twins who were identified as monozygotic really dizygotic, and vice versa?).

Beck, a major figure in research on the affective psychoses, concludes: "Excessive frequency of a particular psychiatric disorder among relatives of a patient does not in itself prove that the disorder is hereditary. Genetic transmission is only one inference from the findings; noxious environmental influences with particular family groups could also account for the findings. The available research data does not establish conclusively whether affective disorders are genetic, environmental, both or neither" (1967, p. 132).

Genetics and the paranoid psychoses. Genetics do not play a major role in the etiology of the paranoid psychoses. One of the very few investigations of this matter observed that of 400 patients included in a survey of patients hospitalized with paranoid reactions, only 8 had forebears in whom distinct paranoid trends could be identified (Tyhurst, 1957). No biochemical or neurophysiological lesions could

be found in any of the 400. As a result of these and similar findings, the most common etiological view of the paranoid disorders continues to derive from Freud's conviction that they develop when homosexual trends can no longer be repressed. A corollary is that the person who develops a paranoid reaction is basically homosexual and that his homosexuality derives from fear of castration experienced first during the oedipal period. One problem with this formulation is that Schreber, whose memoirs enabled Freud to develop the theory, would today unquestionably be diagnosed as schizophrenic rather than paranoid. Another is that clinical evidence and clinical research during the last forty-five years have failed to relate incidence of paranoia and homosexuality (Cameron, 1967). For these reasons we conclude that Freud's etiologic equation is not a valid one for the paranoid disorders. But it is also important to add that no other view of the etiology of the paranoid psychoses has yet gained wide acceptance.

Because of the rarity of the condition and the considerable debate about its use as a legitimate diagnosis, there will be no additional discussion of paranoid psychosis in the present chapter. The reader is referred to the accounts of paranoid schizophrenia in Chapter 6 and the paranoid personality in Chapter 13 for related information.

Metabolic studies of the affective psychoses

A tremendous increase in the amount of research on physiological and biochemical aspects of affective disorder has taken place during the past decade. One of the major efforts of the work is to identify metabolic differences between the manic and depressive phases of manic-depressive psychosis. This line of inquiry was started by Cameron, who compared the two phases with respect to basal metabolic rate, blood pressure, blood glucose level, gastrointestinal activity, parotid gland secretion, and gastric acid activity (1942). He reported that apparent differences between the manic and depressive states were due more to the activity-level differences between them than to fundamental biochemical differences. Specifically, Cameron observed that "tense or agitated persons . . . may show more in common in their biological function with elated and excitable persons than they do with other depressive syndromes. This is not compatible with the hypothesis that elation and depression are fundamentally opposed metabolic processes" (p. 192).

Mineral metabolism and the affective psychoses. Others have systematically studied changes in metabolism associated with changes in mental status during periods of prolonged affective turmoil. Klein and Nunn described a 67-year-old patient who had alternated between manic and depressive cycles every week for fourteen years (1945). As regularly as clockwork, five days of depression were followed by two days of mania. The only positive metabolic findings were retention of water and salt during depression and their release during mania. These findings, however, were probably related to the patient's drinking more water during mania. Crammer, in 1959, reported on two chronic psychotic patients who also showed gains and losses in body weight associated with water retention during periods of mania and depression.

Several investigators have recently analyzed metabolic function during periods of depression. Gibbons found that on recovery from serious depressive episodes, most of a group of twenty-four patients showed a decrease in levels of "exchangeable" sodium (1963). Russell identified a similar trend (1960). In a study which has had considerable impact on recent research, Flach found that depressed patients who received electroconvulsive or antidepressant drug therapy excreted significantly less calcium after than before treatment (1964). This finding suggests a relationship between clinical improvement and calcium levels in the blood. Coppen (1967) and Shaw (1966) have also related disturbances in the distribution of sodium and potassium in the body to the onset of depression and mania.

To summarize: Water and mineral metabolism are likely to be disturbed during depression. However, the predictability of this effect and its relationship to the etiology of depression remain uncertain.

Steroid metabolism and the affective psychoses. A good deal of evidence suggests that changes in steroid metabolism are predictive of the phases of depression, though similar changes have also been observed in other forms of psychopathology (specifically schizophrenia). In comprehensive reviews of work in the area, Michael and Gibbons (1963) and Rubin and Mandell (1966) concluded that normals who experience a change in emotion or are confronted with stressful situations often show an associated rise in blood levels of cortisol, a steroid hormone produced by the adrenal glands. They also found that dramatic increases in these and other blood steroids have been observed in clinically anxious and depressed patients and in acute schizophrenic patients in great turmoil. Further, they noted that clinical improvement in most patients was associated with decreases in levels of circulating 17-hydroxycorticoid.

For example, a study of urinary steroid excretion in five neurotically depressed patients and five manic-depressive, depressed patients reported that excretion of 17-ketogenic steroids was significantly related in both groups to depressive episodes (Kurland, 1964). In a variation on the same theme, other researchers found that three depressed patients who successfully committed suicide showed very high 17-hydroxycorticoid levels just before their suicides (Bunney & Fawcett, 1965).

In summary, these data suggest strongly that increased steroid output is associated with depression. Specifically, they indicate that as depression increases, steroid output increases. Further, steroid-level decreases seem to relate to improvement in or recovery from depression. Unfortunately, since steroid output also occurs during acute schizophrenic episodes and at other stressful times (Sachar, 1967), the specific relationships between mania and depression and steroid metabolism are not known. Research on this problem is underway.

Mendels has reported on relationships between levels of sex hormones in the blood and concomitant mood change (1969). His study was prompted by the facts that depression is more common in women, that the involutional period (a time of significant change in hormone levels) is associated with an increase in periods of depression, and that oral contraceptives (compounded from sex hormones) sometimes precipitate depressions.

Biogenic amine metabolism and the affective psychoses. The biogenic amines are a group of chemicals found in the brain that play vital but as yet undefined roles in central nervous system functioning (Brodie & Costa, 1962). They have been implicated in the etiology of schizophrenia; research on that aspect is discussed in Chapter 7.

Two groups of brain amines, the catecholamines (epinephrine, norepinephrine, and dopamine) and the indole amines (serotonin and histamine), seem to affect mood. This conclusion is based on the following clinical and experimental observations:

1 Many drugs used in the treatment of depression (Tofranil, Elavil, Nardil, Marplan) increase the level of available amines (especially norepinephrine) in the brain (Hillarp et al., 1966: Scheckel & Boff, 1964).
2 The same drugs which increase brain amine levels in humans also produce "over-activity" and alertness in experimental animals (Ganrot et al., 1962).
3 Other drugs (reserpine, for example) which lower existing levels of amines in the brain produce sedation and inactivity ("depression") in experimental animals (Costa et al., 1962).
4 Many of the drugs that deplete brain amines also cause depression in humans (Cole & Davis, 1967).

Schildkraut summarizes this body of research as follows: "Some, if not all, depressions are associated with an absolute or relative deficiency of catecholamines, particularly norepinephrine. . . . Elation conversely may be associated with an excess of such amines" (1965). Some researchers believe that other brain amines, for example serotonin, are involved in the etiology of depression (Glassman, 1969). Few investigators now fail to acknowledge that at least some of the brain amines seem to play an important role in the etiology of serious depression.

Psychodynamic and psychological theories of etiology

Classical view of depression. Karl Abraham, one of Freud's early followers, is most closely identified with the "classical" psychoanalytic view of depression. In 1911 Abraham compared the depressions (neurotic and psychotic) with normal grief. He concluded that depression and grief both stem from loss, but that while the normal mourner is preoccupied with his loss of a friend or relative, the depressed person is overwhelmed by the feelings of guilt that surround his loss. Abraham believed that the depressed person turns against himself the unconscious hostility he felt toward the lost person. Later, in *Mourning and Melancholia* (1917), Freud said that whereas in mourning the "object" is a person lost because of death, in depression the "object" is often not a person. Instead, the depressed patient suffers the internal loss of an object that had been "incorporated" in the psyche by the process of identification.

Neo-Freudian views of depression. Sandor Rado, a "neo-Freudian," concluded that persons predisposed to depression have very strong narcissistic needs (needs for personal satisfaction), in part because they did not develop a secure sense of self-worth during the crucial first years of life (1928). When they suffer a loss, they react with anger that ultimately turns inward as the ego (which incorporated the "introjected," now lost, love object) is "punished" by the superego.

Melanie Klein, another neo-Freudian personality theorist, believed that the roots of depression lie in the nature of the mother-child relationship during the first year of the child's life (1934). When this relationship is unsatisfactory, the infant reacts to frustration and to the absence of gratification with rage and with fantasies of sadistic "acting out" on the environment. In the face of these strong, frightening wishes, the child grows up feeling helpless, sad, guilty, and filled with regret over his life circumstances. He also lives in fear of annihilation because of his anger at his mother. According to Klein, mothers who do not recognize the existence of this complex of circumstances and who fail to provide their children with noncontingent love may be permitting the children to develop a potential for serious depression.

Contemporary views on the psychodynamics of depression. Contemporary dynamic theorists have also amplified on the basic psychoanalytic theme of object loss as the prime etiologic factor in depression (Bibring, 1953; Jacobson, 1954; Hammerman, 1962). Zetzel, a leading spokesman for this position, refers to depression and anxiety as "developmental challenges" which the person must meet and master in order to cope with the stresses of normal adult life. Failing to meet these challenges may lead to symptom formation, erection of rigid defenses, or perhaps chronic depression (1966).

Beck's experimental psychodynamics. Like most research on psychoanalytic theory, validation of the dynamic view of depression derives primarily from case studies (Cohen et al., 1954; Spielberger et al., 1963). One notable exception is the experimental work on depression by Beck and his colleagues. As Beck states their central premise: "In undertaking a study of the psychodynamic factors of depression, I felt that it would be necessary to satisfy two prerequisites. First, it should be possible to isolate a particular psychodynamic constellation or construct that has a meaningful relationship to depression but not to other syndromes. Second, it should be possible to develop methods for

identifying the referents of this construct in the clinical material" (1967, p. 169).

Some researchers might feel that Beck is laboring the obvious here, but the obvious and the unambiguous are not the usual characteristics of experimental studies of psychodynamics. It is for this reason that we view Beck's work as a model for investigators who aim to validate psychodynamic theories in a scientifically acceptable manner.

Beck's ambitious research project started shortly after he noted that five soldiers who had accidently killed a comrade had become psychotically depressed and suicidal (Beck & Valin, 1953). All five wanted to be punished for their deeds; all but one had attempted suicide. Putting these observations together with psychoanalytic views of depression, Beck concluded that a central feature of depression is the need to suffer.

Three stages of Beck's research program designed to validate this view of depression have now been carried out. The first was a series of projects to evaluate the reliability and utility of methods for separating depressed patients into the traditional diagnostic groupings (Beck et al., 1962; Ward et al., 1962). The second aimed to develop a reliable inventory for measuring depression (Beck et al., 1961). The third, which was the program's principal goal, undertook to test the idea that "depressed patients are characterized by a number of distinctive patterns that lead to suffering disproportionate or inappropriate to the reality situation." In this stage Beck and his colleagues began to explore "ideational material" (dreams, responses to structured projective tests, and free associations) and the use of controlled experimental stress situations as ways to validate their hypotheses.

A pilot study of the dream content of 12 depressed and nondepressed subjects had revealed that the depressed patients dreamed significantly more "masochistic" dreams than the control subjects (Beck & Hurvich, 1959). As a large-scale follow-up, Beck and Ward analyzed the dreams of 287 patients drawn at random from the out- and inpatient departments of two large Philadelphia general

The Sleep of Dreams Produces Monsters by Goya suggests the frightening dreams depressed patients often have. *(The Metropolitan Museum of Art, Gift of M. Knoedler and Co., 1918)*

felt that this finding lent support to his psychoanalytic view of depression.

Studies of depressed patients in experimental stress situations by the same researchers also supported Beck's original hypotheses. For example, when severely depressed patients were told that their performance on a word-completion test had been inferior (which was not necessarily true), they reported a greater drop in mood level than mildly depressed patients who were given the same information (Loeb, Beck et al., 1964). Conversely, when severely depressed patients were told that their performance had been superior, they showed a greater rise in mood level than mildly depressed patients.

Beck's research has been reviewed here not because it has led to more effective treatment for depression or because it permits earlier or more accurate detection of incipient depression. Its contribution is its successful blending of hypothesis and scientific method in the quest for validation of theory. His studies have been criticized on specific points: for example, the absence of normal control groups for comparison, the lack of validation for dream interpretation methods, the questionable relevance of "masochism" to "guilt over object loss." But his work also represents some of the best current research on experimental psychodynamics.

Behavioral views on depression

Behavioral approaches to depression are very recent, so that experimental work on the learning mechanisms which may be involved has just begun. The studies which have been reported (e.g., Lewinsohn & Libet, 1971; Lewinsohn & Shaffer, 1971) mostly support the behavioral theories of depression summarized below.

Lazarus views depression as the result of inadequate or insufficient reinforcers (1968). Redefined in operant terms, this means that depressed patients probably have a weakened behavioral repertoire. In other words, they are on an extinction schedule—their behavior is never followed by reinforcing consequences.

hospitals (1961). Of this group, 25 percent were neurotically depressed and 10 percent were psychotically depressed. As predicted, significantly more dreams of severely depressed patients were "masochistic" than dreams of nondepressed patients ($p < .01$). A corollary study examined relationships between early childhood bereavement and later depressive psychopathology in the same patients (Beck et al., 1963). Among the variety of diagnostic labels in the group, significantly more severely depressed patients had suffered the loss of mother, father, or both during childhood than moderately depressed and nondepressed patients. Beck

They experience loss and deprivation: loss of security or salary, status or influence, love or popularity. This statement seems to be simply a redefinition of the psychoanalytic theory of depression in learning terms, for "extinction trial" and "object loss" appear to be parallel concepts. But such a behavioral redefinition does successfully "operationalize" abstract concepts to make them accessible to empirical inquiry.

Another behavioral view of the etiology of depression has been advanced by Costello (1972). Acknowledging the crucial etiologic importance of Lazarus's "loss of reinforcers" theory, Costello suggests the existence of another etiologic factor: "general loss of reinforcer effectiveness." He explains the loss of effectiveness in two ways: (1) biochemical or neurophysiological events occurring "in the head," and (2) disruption or interruption of the usual chain of reinforcing events. In essence, Costello believes that the concept "loss of reinforcers" by itself cannot explain the depressed person's withdrawal of interest from reinforcers which he or she had previously valued.

Lazarus's answer to this argument is instructive. He says: "To describe [depression] as a 'general loss of reinforcer effectiveness' neither explains the phenomenon, nor does it generate a logical treatment modality. . . . It is never-theless encouraging that many behavior therapists no longer hypothesize that depression is merely a consequence of 'protective inhibition when anxiety is very prolonged and intense'" (1972, p. 248). With this statement Lazarus puts the focus back on the utility of etiologic hypotheses for treatment planning, a distinctly behavioral strategy. As noted in Chapter 5, Kanfer and Saslow make a persuasive case for diagnostic procedures aimed at treatment.

Cues to the affective psychoses

Behavioral cues to depression and mania

Though most of us think first of depressed affect—of sadness, melancholy, despondency, and despair—when we think of depression as a psychopathologic entity, clinicians look for other behavioral cues when they evaluate the seriousness of a depression. Among these are insomnia, early-morning awakening, diffuse anxiety, poor appetite, loss of energy, and lessened motor activity. Very serious psychotic depressive conditions often include delusions of persecution (centering on sin, guilt, and the certainty of punishment), somatic delusions (in which part of the body is believed

TABLE 8-1. CUES TO PSYCHOTIC DEPRESSION, NEUROTIC DEPRESSION, AND THE SCHIZOPHRENIAS

Cues	Psychotic depressed patients ($N = 40$)	Neurotic depressed patients ($N = 161$)	Schizophrenic patients ($N = 251$)
Psychomotor retardation	65%	21%	18%
Hallucinations	20%	–	50%
Retarded thinking	40%	3%	17%
Delusions of sin, etc.	35%	1%	8%
Hypochondria	30%	6%	8%
Depression	95%	100%	23%
Anxiety	50%	50%	36%

SOURCE: Summarized from Nathan et al., 1969.

to be nonfunctional or absent), auditory hallucinations of a persecutory nature, and disorders of thinking. Dostoevsky alludes to many of these in writing about the underground man.

Table 8-1 shows the cues to depression found by Nathan and his co-workers among various patient groups (1969). They discovered that psychotically depressed patients were set off from either neurotically depressed or schizophrenic patients by the symptoms of psychomotor retardation, retarded thinking, delusions of sin and self-accusation, and hypochondria. Depressed affect differentiated the psychotically and neurotically depressed groups from the schizophrenic group. Anxiety did not discriminate among the three groups.

The manic phase of manic-depressive psychosis offers fewer useful diagnostic cues. As you would guess, they include elation and euphoria, markedly increased psychomotor activity, and a dramatic acceleration in the flow of thoughts. All these were prominent in Clifford Beers's description of his own manic behavior given at the beginning of the chapter. Data from Nathan's system analysis support this impression: 91 percent of his sample of manic patients had significantly increased their psychomotor behavior as compared with 29 percent of his sample of schizophrenic patients and 26 percent of his neurotic patients (Nathan et al., 1969). Similarly, 55 percent of Nathan's manic patients demonstrated flight of ideas (a rapid, often uncontrollable succession of thoughts) as compared with 21 percent of the schizophrenics and no neurotics. And 91 percent were pathologically elated as compared with 6 percent of the schizophrenics and no neurotics.

There have also been attempts to distinguish among depressed patients by factors other than intensity and severity of disordered mood, thinking, and motor behavior. The variable most often chosen in this regard is the degree to which the patient's depression is based upon environmental circumstances that appear to justify it. People whose depressions seem to be reactions to recent loss—the death of a close friend or relative, a major financial setback, a geographic displacement—are considered "reactive" or "exogenous" depressives. They are often less seriously depressed than patients whose depressions do not seem to arise from a recent loss. The latter are "process" or "endogenous" depressives; they are often psychotic.

The usefulness of the exogenous-endogenous distinction has been debated for years, in part because some nonpsychotic depressives have suffered no apparent recent loss while some psychotic depressives have. Recent work by Martorano and Nathan supported the validity of this dichotomy (1972). From a factor analysis of symptom data on 924 psychiatric patients whose psychopathologic behavior was rated by a new diagnostic checklist, the authors identified one cluster of cues to both neurotic and psychotic depression (severe anxiety and depression, pronounced psychomotor agitation), one cluster that was restricted only to psychotic depressives (disordered behavior unrelated to recent loss), and one that was restricted only to neurotic depressives (behavior clearly related to recent loss). Other evidence for the validity of the endogenous-exogenous dichotomy is equivocal (Garside, 1971; Klerman, 1971; Malmquist, 1970).

Assessment of depression by tests and rating scales

A variety of rating scales and self-report instruments designed to quantify depression has been developed over the years (Costello & Comrey, 1967; Humphrey, 1967; Lubin et al., 1967; Zung, 1965). Several items from one such scale are given in Table 8-2. The value of these instruments in diagnosis continues to be debated, largely because some clinicians feel that interviewers can identify the symptomatic behaviors related to depression better than psychometric measures can. The instruments have been of unquestioned value, however, as indexes of response to antidepressant medication (Rose et al., 1965) and as survey instruments reflecting the prevalence of mild and moderate depression in nonpsy-

TABLE 8-2. SELECTED ITEMS FROM THE WITTENBORN PSYCHIATRIC RATING SCALES TO MEASURE DEPRESSION

Item	Score
Face shows at least ordinary expressive variability in response to others.	0
Facial expression slow to change in response to others, i.e., shows more or less constant mood.	1
Facial expression does not change appreciably.	2
Face flaccid and without discernible change.	3
Participates in most available activities and routines.	0
Avoids certain activities and is reluctant to participate in them.	1
Participates in one or two activities only.	2
Will not participate in activities.	3
No evidence of social withdrawal.	0
Does not appear to seek out the company of other people.	1
Avoids many people.	2
Attempts to avoid almost all people.	3
Reveals interest in others and emotional resonance during interview.	0
Expresses feelings only about self during interview.	1
Expresses concern about self, but only with shallow display of feeling.	2
Does not participate in interview or participates with no evidence of affective involvement.	3

NOTE: Interviewer checks one item in each group. The higher the point total, the more depressed the patient.
SOURCE: Wittenborn, 1965.

chiatric medical patients (Schwab et al., 1967). Other more general diagnostic instruments (e.g., the MMPI, the IMPS, and the WPRS, as discussed in Chapter 5) have yielded factors related directly to the depressions. For the most part these include the cues to psychotic depression, because the normative samples of patients used to develop the measures were psychotic. Though projective tests have also been tried out for diagnosing and quantifying depression, the results have been disappointing (Wittenborn, 1965).

Mania is rarely diagnosed by psychometric testing. One reason is the difficulty of convincing a manic patient to sit down long enough to take a test. Another is that test data are not really needed to detect mania.

Biophysiological measurement of depression

One of the most interesting recent developments in efforts to distinguish among the depressive syndromes and between them and other mental disorders has been the use of biophysiological measurement techniques. For many years clinicians have believed that a beneficial response to electroconvulsive therapy is strong indication that a patient is primarily depressed (Mendels and Hawkins, 1967). Now there are more precise biophysiological assay methods for depression, most of which have evolved from empirical investigation of biophysiological differences between depressed and nondepressed persons.

Some investigators claim that depressed patients' "resting" EEGs (electroencephalographic recordings taken during periods of relaxation) are often abnormal in one way or another (Denber, 1958), but experimental evidence has not identified consistent abnormalties (Mendels, 1970). However, several investigators have shown that *interruption* of the resting EEG pattern causes EEG changes which do differentiate between depressed and nondepressed subjects (Paulson & Gottlieb, 1961; Snyder, 1969). Interruption by auditory or visual stimulation (for instance, by a tone or a bright light) causes greater *alpha wave suppression* (suppression of a regular EEG rhythm of 8 to 13 cycles per second) in depressed than in nondepressed persons. Other investigators claim that the *recovery period* which follows initial alpha suppression is longer in depressives than in nondepressives. (Shagass & Schwartz, 1962).

These results must be regarded with caution both because they are based on small numbers of subjects and because they come from studies that failed to control for variables (like age and diagnostic grouping) which might themselves relate to alpha suppression. Despite their tenative nature, however, they are important because they support the hypothesis that depressed patients are often in a state of unstable neurophysiological hyperexcitabilty (Whybrow & Mendels, 1969). The significance of alpha patterning in an entirely different context—treatment for some of the psychosomatic disorders—is discussed in Chapter 14.

Since sleep disturbances, such as early-morning awakening and insomnia, are frequent complaints of depressed patients, depression research has also investigated EEG activity during sleep. The Dement-Kleitman EEG recording system (1957) is most often used for this purpose. It divides sleep into four separate stages according to frequency (speed) and amplitude (size) of EEG waves, changes in muscle tension, and changes in eye movements during sleep. *Stage 1 sleep*—light sleep—is characterized by low-amplitude, high-frequency EEG waves. It is during stage 1 sleep that most dreaming occurs. This conclusion is based upon data from many studies which have correlated *rapid eye movement* (REM) of a particular kind (periodic bursts of horizontal, "jerky" eye movements) with "fast" EEG activity and an absence of muscular tension (Jacobs et al., 1971; Karacan et al., 1970). *Stage 2 sleep,* the stage at which most of the night is spent by most people, is marked by EEG *sleep spindles*—short periods of exceptionally fast EEG activity. *Stage 3* and *stage 4 sleep*—slow-wave sleep—are dominated by very slow, high-amplitude EEG activity.

Mendels and Hawkins (1970) examined the EEG sleep patterns of nondepressed control subjects and depressed patients newly admitted to a hospital. They found significant differences between the two groups in total sleep time, actual sleep time (composed of sleep time minus time spent lying awake or drowsing), stage 1 (REM) sleep, and stage 4 sleep. After substantial clinical improvement in thirteen of the depressed patients, the quality of their sleep also improved, though they still remained awake longer than the nonde-

pressed control subjects. Data from more recent studies confirm Mendels and Hawkins's conclusions that EEG activity and dreaming behavior during sleep reflect severity of depression (Detre & Jarecki, 1971).

The electromyograph (EMG), a measure of muscle tension, has also been used to quantify depression. Some investigators have observed that depressed patients maintain significantly higher resting levels of muscular tension than schizophrenic patients (Whatmore & Ellis, 1959, 1962) and nondepressed controls (Goldstein, 1965). Other researchers have failed to confirm these findings (Rimon et al., 1966), perhaps because of crucial differences in patient groups or perhaps because of the method used to analyze muscular tension.

Experimental studies of depression

The animal model: "Depression" in infant monkeys, "learned helplessness" in dogs

Virtually all studies employing animals as subjects in experimental studies of depression have examined the effects of early maternal separation on later development of "depression." This behavior in animals is similar in important ways to the behavior of human depressives. One of the earliest of the studies was Kaufmann and Rosenbloom's 1957 demonstration that infant monkeys separated from their mothers withdrew from age mates, "looked sad," ate badly, and otherwise seemed lethargic and isolated. In a study by Seay and his colleagues four baby monkeys were separated for three weeks from their mothers (1962). Their initial response, "violent and prolonged protest," was followed shortly by "despair and depression." A more recent study by the same group identified certain similarities between adolescent depression in humans and monkeys (McKinney et al., 1972). These researchers have also observed that the range of behaviors available to monkeys for reacting "emotionally" to maternal loss is clearly narrower than that available to human beings (Harlow et al., 1972).

Another promising research program, by Seligman and his colleagues at the University of Pennsylvania, investigated the behavior of dogs who received a series of inescapable shocks early in their lives. Seligman found that afterwards, the dogs could not learn to escape shock even when it was possible for them to do so (1969; 1972). He labeled this phenomenon "learned helplessness." Seligman also reported that animals which were first trained with escapable shock—and then were subjected to the inescapable shock situation—could reacquire the escape behavior later. He regards the pretraining in escapable shock as a kind of *inoculation* against development of learned helplessness. Seligman draws interesting parallels between these behaviors in the animal laboratory and human depressive reactions. He even suggests that humans be given training which will prepare them to react with energy and conviction instead of helplessness in the face of catastrophe and failure.

The human model: How are moods labeled?

The most extensive investigations of experimentally induced affect in human beings were undertaken by Schachter and his colleagues (Schachter, 1964; Schachter & Singer, 1962; Schachter & Wheeler, 1962). Though their work was not focused on depression, it provides relevant insights into the process by which affects are labeled.

All the subjects were normal males and females. In the first study in the series, they received an injection of the drug adrenalin, which raised their arousal and energy levels. However, they were not told the name of the drug or what effects it would have on them. Next, some of them were placed in an experimental situation designed to be frustrating (they were confronted with a set of insoluble tasks) while others were placed in a setting supposed to generate pleasant feelings. Afterwards Schachter asked all subjects to label the moods which the unknown drug had gen-

erated in them. He found that those who had been placed in the frustrating setting experienced the drug-induced arousal as *anger,* and those who had been in the pleasant setting experienced it as *elation.*

In another study in the series, subjects were given accurate information on what bodily sensations to expect when they received the injection of adrenalin. (They were told that it would make them more energetic, nervous, and restless.) Under these circumstances they did not feel angry even when they were placed in the frustrating setting, or elated when put into the pleasant one.

Schachter concluded that when people experience a state of physiological arousal for which they have no explanation, they will label it with the affect that best "fits" the environmental circumstances. But when they believe that a state of arousal has a physiological explanation, they will not label it further.

Schachter's findings have led other psychologists to speculate about affective states besides elation and anger. Kagan felt justified in extending Schachter's conclusions to *all* forms of affects: "The primary component of an affect is a perceived change in the intensity and quality of the mosaic of internal stimulation from muscles and viscera. . . . Specific affects are linked to differing intensities. . . . The [affect] label chosen depends on (1) the direction of the change [the subject] notices in arousal, (2) the content of the images and thoughts he is having when the change in arousal is perceived, and (3) the immediate contextual situation" (1968, p. 14).

Generalizing from Schachter's findings, we suggest that depression might be a dual function of *lowered arousal* and *unhappy circumstances.* We wonder, in this context, whether the behavioral differences between neurotic and psychotic depression might stem less from differences in state of arousal than from differences in environmental precipitants (given the apparent legitimacy of the exogenous-endogenous distinction). Since researchers have not yet employed drugs that *lower* arousal in order to investigate affective states, no empirical data can be cited.

Sometimes suicide appears to be the only way out for the lonely, depressed person.
(Charles Gatewood)

Suicide

Published figures on suicide indicate that in any recent year, about one American citizen out of ten thousand (0.01%) committed suicide (*Vital Statistics of the U.S.*, 1973). There is evidence that this figure significantly understates the real suicide rate, because many seemingly accidental deaths, especially those from drug overdose, alcoholism, and automobile accidents probably represent concealed suicide (Stengel, 1962).

In contrast to these "unselected" figures are others which indicate that approximately 5 percent of all manic-depressive patients ultimately commit suicide (Lundquist, 1945; Rennie, 1942). Researchers who have compared rates of suicide among a variety of psychiatric patients conclude that the suicide rate for depressed patients is between twenty-five-

and thirty-five-times the unselected national rate. The depressed-patient rate is also substantially higher than that for groups of patients suffering from other mental disorders (Pokorny, 1964; Temoche et al., 1964). Women attempt suicide more frequently than men, but they succeed less often (Kraines, 1957). Men and women also seem to differ in their choice of suicide method: men prefer firearms, while women prefer poison and drug overdoses (Beck, 1967).

Suicide predictors—individual demographic, behavioral, and social variables associated with suicide—have recently begun to attract attention (Krauss & Tesser, 1971; Resnick & Kendra, 1973). The cliché is that the person who talks about suicide will not attempt it, but empirical data say otherwise (Rudestam, 1971; Stengel, 1962). In fact, one of the predictors of suicide is the person's communication of a suicidal intent (Robins et al., 1959), though the best predictor is a previous suicide attempt (Motto, 1965). Though it has been recognized for some time that women are more prone than men to attempt suicide, specialists have only recently begun to attend to two other large segments of our society who choose suicide more frequently than the average: young adult blacks and adolescents of both races.

Seiden begins his provocative review of the subject with wry humor: "It is often assumed, particularly by black persons, that suicide represents a white solution to white problems. As Dick Gregory once cracked, 'you can't kill yourself by jumping out of the basement' .... And Redd Foxx scoffed, 'Only three Negroes have jumped off the Golden Gate Bridge, and two of them were pushed'" (1970, p. 24). Nevertheless, Seiden cites figures to show that young adult blacks actually do commit suicide more often than their white counterparts. He adds: "The suicide rate among young urban blacks would leap far higher if we included in it a significant number of deaths that are, technically speaking, homicides, but that seem essentially to be suicides in which the victim arranges or demands to be killed. Some militant black revolutionaries may be suicidally motivated, and their activity may serve them as a subculturally acceptable alternative to the so-called 'inadvertent' overdose" (p. 24). One has only to recall Malcolm X's memories of his early and middle adolescence or remember James Baldwin's observation, "To be a Negro in this country and to be relatively conscious is to be in a rage almost all of the time," to acknowledge the apparent reasonableness of Seiden's conclusions—though without much more empirical data, they must be viewed as speculation.

As an example, Seiden describes a "hidden" suicide:

Malcolm Jayson was a 25-year old black youth worker whose job involved him in frequent, almost daily contact with policemen. Jayson and four others had driven to the San Francisco Hall of Justice to arrange bail for a young man booked on a misdemeanor charge. Two of their party went to get a bail bondsman; two others remained in the car. Jayson walked across the street to a bar known to be favored by off-duty policemen.

Jayson ordered a drink, drank it and ordered another. He then declared he wouldn't pay because the drinks were watered or weak. He complained loudly, waved his arms, had words with the bartender, and was thrown out. He then walked to the car, got a loaded pistol, and walked back to the bar. The glass doors of the bar were being shut by a customer Jayson presumably knew was an off-duty policeman. Jayson smashed the glass door with his gun and pointed his weapon

"I didn't realize Akerman, Burbee & Smith had women in key jobs." *(Drawing by Whitney Darrow, Jr.; © 1970 The New Yorker Magazine, Inc.)*

at the policeman-cum-customer. Another off-duty policeman shot Jayson through the heart. [P. 24]

Recent work has also explored the subject of suicide during childhood and adolescence. This attention is overdue: suicide now ranks fourth as a cause of death among adolescents. In certain large urban general hospitals (New York's Bellevue, Brooklyn's Kings County, Los Angeles's USC Medical Center) between 10 and 18 percent of the children admitted are there because of a suicide attempt (NIMH, 1970). It has been estimated that there are more than 60,000 attempted suicides a year among persons under the age of 20 in the United States (Peck & Schrut, 1971).

Teicher (1970) and Jacobs (1971) have recently reported on a large-scale study of adolescent suicide. Begun in 1964, the project compared the life situations of fifty adolescents who had attempted suicide with those of fifty controls (young persons who were matched for age, race, sex, and family income). All the subjects were southern California residents between 14 and 18 years of age. At least one parent of each suicidal adolescent, usually the mother, was included in the study. Girls composed 75 percent of the sample group; blacks, whites, Mexican-Americans, Protestants, Catholics, and Jews were represented.

Following a structured interview with each adolescent suicide attempter, his or her matched control and the parent, the subject's "life history chart" was constructed. It chronicled such events as residential moves, school changes, the onset of various behavioral problems, parental separation, divorce, remarriage, and deaths in the family. It focused on the sequence of events leading up to the crisis or crises which preceded the suicide attempt.

Suicide attempters (SAs) and controls (Cs) differed in several important ways. Though 72 percent of the SAs and 53 percent of the Cs came from homes broken by divorce, 58 percent of the parents of SAs and only 25 percent of the parents of Cs had remarried. Further, when C parents remarried they did so early in the child's life and stayed married;

SA parents remarried later or remarried several times (Jacobs & Teicher, 1967). Just 38 percent of the SAs said that their childhoods were happy, while 94 percent of the Cs did. Much of the unhappiness of the SAs came from their sense of isolation, from the feeling that they had no one to turn to in time of trouble. This suicide note, written the night before a 17-year-old attempted suicide for the second time, is poignant testimony to the isolation from family and friends that many of Teicher's subjects experienced.

Dear Father, I am addressing you these few lines to let you know that I am fine and everybody else is and I hope you are the same. Daddy, I understand that I let you down and I let Mother down in the same way when I did that little old thing (first suicide attempt) that Wednesday night. Daddy, I am sorry if I really upset you, but Daddy after I got back I realized how sad and bad you felt when I came back home. . . . Daddy I tried as hard as I could to make it cheerful, but it does get sad. Daddy I am up by myself. I've been up all night trying to write you something to cheer you up, because I could see your heart breaking when you first asked Sam's wife if they would have room and that Sunday Dad, it was hard but I fought the tears that burned my eyes as we drove off and Daddy part of my sickness when I had taken an overdose I did just want to sleep my self away because I missed you Dad. . . . But when I left I felt like I had killed something inside of you and I knew you hated to see me go, and I hated to go, but Daddy, well, I kind of missed Mother after I had seen her. I miss you. [Teicher & Jacobs, 1966, p. 1254]

Treatment for the affective psychoses

Electroconvulsive therapy and depression

Despite the continuing controversy over electroconvulsive therapy (ECT), it is still the "treatment of choice" for psychotic depression. ECT has undergone many changes since it was first introduced by the Italian psychiatrists Cerletti and Bini in 1933. Most of the changes have been initiated to make ECT safer, less frightening, and less likely to cause unwanted aftereffects. As a consequence, current procedures for administering ECT result in few of the fractures and almost none of the fatalities which were formerly associated with it. Also, patients no longer have to be borne kicking and screaming into the ECT room, because the terror formerly associated with it has been reduced significantly by pretreatment medication. And changes in ECT technique have reduced (but not eliminated) the posttreatment amnesia that so often diminished the overall effectiveness of the method.

In standard ECT technique, patients are given a short-acting intravenous barbiturate to induce unconsciousness, usually before they are removed to the treatment room. A muscle relaxant, most often succinylcholine, is then administered to decrease the likelihood that the shock-induced convulsion will cause bone fracture. With the patient lying prone on a table in the treatment room, electrodes are applied to both temples. From 70 to 130 volts of alternating current are passed between the electrodes for 0.1 to 0.5 seconds. It has been estimated that between 200 and 1,600 milliamperes of current go through the brain during this brief period (Detre & Jarecki, 1971).

The immediate consequence of ECT is a convulsive seizure. If an insufficient amount of current has been used, the patient may experience an unwanted *petit mal* seizure. If enough has been administered, it causes an immediate *grand mal* convulsion, the *tonic phase* of which begins at the moment of stimulation. This phase, during which virtually all voluntary muscles contract, generally lasts about ten seconds. The *clonic phase,* which follows instantly and usually lasts 30 to 40 seconds, is characterized by a rapid series of alternating contractions and relaxations of the voluntary muscles. After the convulsive movements have stopped, the patient remains unconscious for a few minutes. Afterwards he or she may be in a confused, "clouded" state for as long as an hour.

Though dramatic clinical improvement of severe depression may take place after a single ECT treatment, two to ten are usually given in order to "clear a depression." Variability in the spacing of treatments is common; one to five a week may be used. More than five usually aggravate memory and confusion problems, while one or less sometimes fail to have the cumulative effect necessary for quick remission of symptoms.

Recent studies have shown ECT to be effective with 40 to 100 percent of seriously depressed patients (Mendels, 1967). But these encouraging figures must be viewed in the light of the high natural remission rates which characterize the depressions. Complete untreated recovery from an episode of depression occurs 70 to 95 percent of the time (Beck, 1967). Younger patients are at the high end of this estimate. The average length of an untreated depression that requires hospitalization is 6.3 months; when it does not involve hospitalization it is less that 3 months. Both sets of figures are low compared with the other functional psychoses (especially schizophrenia) and with the chronic organic psychoses (which often do not remit at all).

However, between 47 and 79 percent of depressed patients have a recurrence of depression. There is some evidence that the naturally remitting depressions recur less frequently than those treated with ECT (Hordern, 1965). Authorities agree that the neurotic depressions do not respond to ECT (Cole, 1964; Hordern, 1965). Schizophrenia, as discussed earlier, responds to ECT only when depression is a major component of a schizophrenic's behavior.

ECT is one of those "organic" treatments that social psychologists claim are given significantly more often to blacks and other patients with low socioeconomic status. But despite the complicated sociopolitical determinants of its use, this organic therapy does alleviate depression. Actually, private psychiatric hospitals frequently administer ECT for schizophrenia—a procedure which the evidence suggests is the real malpractice.

Antidepressive drugs

Two groups of drugs, the tricyclic compounds and the monoamine oxidase (MAO) inhibitors, have been favored during the past fifteen years for treating psychotic depression. Imipramine (Tofranil) is the most thoroughly studied and widely used of the tricyclic compounds. As Table 8-3 suggests, it may be the most effective antidepressant available, compared with placebos, other antidepressive drugs, and even ECT (Klerman & Cole, 1965; Friedman et al., 1966). It is clearly better than either no treatment or psychotherapy for psychotic depression (Hollister, 1972), but researchers still disagree over whether or not it is as effective as ECT for the most serious depressions (Detre & Jarecki, 1971).

The MAO inhibitors are used to treat depression less frequently than the tricyclic compounds, largely because they can have serious side effects (including headache, hyper-tension, and blood disorders). The one comparative review of studies contrasting the two groups of drugs reported that imipramine was superior to the MAO inhibitors in four studies, equal in six, and inferior in none (Davis, 1965).

One of the major advances in drug therapy for the psychoses during the past ten years has been the recent widespread use of lithium carbonate for mania. Introduced by Cade in 1949, lithium now plays a major role in both the treatment of mania and its prevention. When taken in maintenance doses every day, lithium appears to lessen the severity and frequency of recurring manic episodes (Hullen et al., 1972; Prien et al., 1973).

Dynamic therapy and manic-depressive psychosis

As with schizophrenia, there is controversy over the use of psychoanalytic psychotherapy and classical psychoanalysis for manic-de-

TABLE 8-3. COMPARATIVE EVALUATION OF DIFFERENT ORGANIC THERAPY USED TO TREAT DEPRESSION

Antidepressant drugs	Number of studies in which drug is:	
	More effective than placebo	Equal to or less effective than placebo
Imipramine (Tofranil)	22	8
Amitriptyline (Elavil)	8	1
Iproniazid (Marsilid)	3	2
Phenelzine (Nardil)	4	3
Tranylcypromine (Parnate)	2	1
Amphetamine (Benzedrine)	0	3
Chlorpromazine (Thorazine)	2	0

Antidepressant drugs and ECT	Number of studies in which treatment is:		
	More effective than imipramine	Equal to imipramine	Less effective than imipramine
Electroconvulsive shock therapy	3	4	0
Amitriptyline (Elavil)	2	5	0
Phenelzine (Nardil)	0	5	2
Tranylcypromine (Parnate)	0	3	0
Chlorpromazine (Thorazine)	0	3	0

SOURCE: Adapted from Davis, Klerman, and Schildkraut, 1968.

pressive psychosis (Cohen, 1967). For involutional melancholia, however, most authorities agree that psychotherapy is much less effective than either drugs or ECT (Ford, 1967).

Few studies have compared the efficiency of drugs alone and psychotherapy alone for the treatment of the affective psychoses. This research gap is almost certainly a function of medical ethics, which prohibit the researcher from withholding proved therapeutic methods like the tricyclic drugs from patients who need them. The handful of studies which have attempted the comparison suggest that drugs and psychotherapy together may be more effective than either alone (Lesse, 1966; Ostow, 1966). The sparsity of research, however, makes conclusions very tentative.

Virtually everyone who writes about psychotherapy with depressed patients speaks of the importance of establishing a therapeutic relationship; yet it is extremely difficult for patients to relate easily to others during depression. They may consider themselves unworthy of a therapist's concern, interest, and commitment. As a result they may suspect the motives of a dogged therapist, seeing him as an agent of retribution if they are psychotic, or as a misguided do-gooder if they are not. Establishing a relationship with a manic patient is usually even more difficult, since his hyperactivity and distractibility render him inaccessible to interpersonal relationships. As a result, advocates of psychotherapy for manic or depressed patients suggest that the therapist try to form a "supportive" relationship during the patient's periods of active psychosis and follow up with more intensive, insight-oriented psychotherapy afterwards.

The form of the therapy is dictated largely by the theoretical views of the therapist and the special circumstances of the patient. Often it aims to identify the environmental elements which seem to be related to the onset of depressive or manic episodes. Those who favor supportive psychotherapy for a manic-depressive patient stress the importance of reassurance (telling him that the condition is self-limiting and that he will surely improve) and the opportunity for ventilation and catharsis (unburdening). Those who believe in insight-oriented psychotherapy emphasize the necessity for a thorough survey of the patient's life history to obtain data on the stage of psychosexual development at which the disorder has its roots.

Many dynamically oriented psychotherapists believe in active intervention by the therapist. Beck (1967), a psychoanalyst, suggests that the therapist provide active guidance toward and help with environmental change. He also proposes that the therapist try to neutralize the "automatic thoughts" of self-depreciation that often accompany serious depression, and attempt to modify the patient's mood by induced fantasy (that is, by encouraging the patient to think pleasant, hopeful thoughts). These are therapeutic strategies more commonly associated with behavior therapy than with psychoanalytic psychotherapy.

Behavior therapy for severe depression

Depression, especially serious depression, has not so far been a principal target of treatment by behavior therapists. Increasing numbers of such case reports, however, are appearing in the behavior therapy journals (Seitz, 1970). For the most part, they deal with behavioral treatment of neurotic depression rather than of depressive psychosis.

Earlier, this chapter described Lazarus's view of depression as "a consequence of inadequate or insufficient reinforcement." His 1968 paper, "Learning Theory and Depression," proposes a variety of treatment procedures designed to confront loss of reinforcement directly.

Lazarus used three behavioral techniques with patients for whom "reactive depression," as he defines it, was the primary complaint. The first, "time projection with positive reinforcement," grew out of the common observation that time heals many depressions simply by giving patients the opportunity to acquire new reinforcers to take the place of those which have been lost. The technique involved projecting the person into a future time that is full of increased activity and enjoyment of old and new occupations. He said to one patient:

"It is almost 3:15 p.m. on Wednesday, April 14, 1965. [This was the date of the actual consultation.] Apart from sleeping, eating, etc., how could you have occupied these 24 hours? You could have gone horseriding for a change, or taken your guitar out of mothballs. . . . Let's push time forward another 24 hours. You are now 48 hours ahead in time. Enough time has elapsed to have started a painting and done some sculpting. You may even have enjoyed a ride in the country and attended a concert. Think about these activities; picture them in your mind; let them bring a good feeling of pleasant associations, of good times." [P. 87]

Though some might consider this a simple-minded approach to a serious disorder, Lazarus claims that it has worked: "Although depressed patients are usually deaf to advice and guidance, the cognitive effects of this procedure are similar to the old 'pull-yourself-together-sufficiently-to-do-something-creative-and-then-you-will-feel-better' doctrine."

Second, Lazarus prescribes "affective expression" for depressed patients. He assumes that while they rarely respond to affective stimuli, what stimuli do break through their depression have at least a temporary positive effect. He recommends that the therapist try to arouse anger, amusement, affection, sexual excitement, or anxiety, all in an effort to break the depressive cycle. Third, Lazarus suggests using "behavioral deprivation and re-training" to achieve the same ends. He means that patients should be subjected to a prolonged period of inactivity, even including

"Thank you, Doctor. You do wonders for my fits of depression." This therapist's approach is very close to the technique Lazarus calls "affective expression." (Starke © PUNCH 1969)

sensory deprivation. Afterwards almost any stimulation will be positively reinforcing. If patients are then exposed to a graduated series of tasks which reintroduce them to the stresses of everyday life, he says that their depression may well lift. It should be emphasized, however, that these techniques are speculative and untested. Even though Lazarus has used them in his own clinical work with patients, they empirically remain unproved (Lazarus, 1971, 1973).

Of several recent papers on the behavioral treatment of depression, only one reports on a psychotic depression (Todd, 1972). The remainder describe treatment of less severe neurotic depressions and acute grief reactions. The techniques chosen included reinforcement reinstatement, contingency management and task completion (Burgess, 1969), interpersonal feedback (Lewinsohn & Shaw, 1969), assertive training and self-reinforcement (Todd, 1972), self-reinforcement (Jackson, 1972; Robinson & Lewinsohn, 1973), and desensitization (Wanderer, 1972).

Todd employed an interesting behavioral treatment procedure to alter the disordered behavior of a 49-year-old woman who was psychotically depressed (1972). She had three times attempted suicide, had undergone unsuccessful psychotherapy for three and a half years, had been hospitalized once, and had tried a variety of antidepressant drugs. Mrs. M. had clearly reached the end of her rope by the time she sought help from a behavior therapist.

Following a detailed behavioral analysis of her problems, a behavior therapy program involving multiple techniques was developed for her treatment. Systematic desensitization was decided upon for her many "phobias"; conditioned relaxation responses for certain of her psychosomatic complaints; behavior rehearsal, assertive training and reinforcement by therapist during a series of increasingly more demanding tasks to reinstate social behaviors. Finally, marital counseling based on operant principles was planned to deal with conflicts with her husband. [Pp. 91–92]

None of these techniques directly treated the patient's self-punitive behavior, which in Todd's opinion was at the root of the total depressive syndrome. To attack it, he first asked Mrs. M. to describe herself in single words or phases. As predicted, all her initial responses were self-condemnatory. After prolonged prompting, support, and social reinforcement, she produced six positive statements about herself. These statements were then printed in large letters on sheets of notepaper and on a card which fitted into a cigarette pack. Todd explained to Mrs. M. that the frequency of a desired behavior (in this case, thinking positive thoughts about herself) could be increased by coupling it with an existing behavior that already had a high probability of occurrence (smoking). He told her to read one or two of the positive statements about herself whenever she lit a cigarette. Within a week her depression lifted. At the same time she thought of another seven positive things to say about herself. At the end of the second week she "felt better than she had in years" and was able to increase the list to twenty-one. On termination of therapy shortly thereafter, Mrs. M. had become active in social and political causes and reported no significant depression. A three-year follow-up indicated that her improvement had continued.

While it is possible that Mrs. M.'s depression lifted as a function of spontaneous remission, an undocumented change in life circumstances, or the effects of other unspecified behavioral interventions, it is also possible that Todd's behavioral interventions brought about the change. In the future, procedures such as these must be subjected to careful and repeated investigation in order to isolate whatever active ingredient or ingredients are responsible for their effectiveness.

Summary

The affective psychoses, recognized by the ancient Greeks as among man's most common and troublesome afflictions, differ from the other functional psychoses by virtue of the fundamental disorder of mood—either depression or elation—that colors every aspect of the patient's behavior. They are now divided into two diagnostic categories: (1) involutional melancholia, a disorder occurring between the ages of 50 and 60 and characterized by severe worry, anxiety, agitation, and insomnia; (2) manic-depressive psychosis, a complex disorder which may consist of periods of manic behavior separated by periods of normality, periods of severe depression and relative normality, or alternating periods of mania, depression, and normality. Clifford Beers was the victim of the circular type with alternating mania and depression, while Dostoevsky and his fictional character, the underground man, suffered almost perpetually from severe depression.

The paranoid psychoses are rare conditions distinguished from the other functional psychoses by the presence of a delusion, either persecutory or grandiose, that is usually the only sign of the disorder. Because many professionals question the legitimacy of this diagnosis (compared with paranoid schizophrenia, for example), it is rarely applied in clinical practice.

A number of mental health workers now believe that genetic factors play important roles in the etiology of the manic-depressive psychoses, a conclusion stemming in large part from the twin and family research of Slater and Kallmann. Beck, criticizing this work, points to crucial design problems that mar its results. A tremendous upsurge of research on physiological and biochemical factors in manic-depressive psychosis has also taken place during the past decade. Much of it centers on efforts to identify metabolic differences between the manic and depressive phases. The three metabolic processes which seem to be implicated are those involving mineral, steroid, and biogenic amine metabolism.

The classical psychoanalytic view of depression was formulated by Karl Abraham, one of Freud's earliest followers. He believed that while depression and grief both stem from loss, it is only the depressed person who is overwhelmed by feelings of guilt and unconscious hostility that surround the loss. Later, Freud added that the loss can be an internal one that does not involve death or physical removal of another person. Successive generations of psychoanalysts have amplified and modified these early theoretical statements so that there are now several dynamic explanations of depression (for example, those of Rado, Klein, Bibring, and Zetzel). Behavioral views of depression, articulated much more recently, see it as the result either of a loss of reinforcers or a loss of reinforcer effectiveness. The few behavioral studies undertaken to validate this position have largely supported it.

Although both mania and depression are fairly obvious behavioral deviations, psychological tests, rating scales, and more recently and impressively, biophysiological measures have proved of some value in the early detection of these disorders. It may be that interruption of resting EEG patterns by direct stimulation provides a characteristic depressive pattern. Sleep disturbances reflected by the EEG may also yield meaningful diagnostic patterns among depressed patients.

Both psychoanalytic psychotherapy and behavior therapy are used with seriously depressed patients, but the most effective single treatment for this condition appears to be somatic. Thus despite the controversy that continues to surround electroconvulsive therapy, ECT still appears to be the "treatment of choice" for psychotically depressed patients who have not responded to antidepressive medication. A variety of controlled studies of ECT attest to its utility in this regard. During the past 15 years two groups of antidepressive drugs, the tricyclic compounds and the monoamine oxidase inhibitors, have also been employed with success.

CHAPTER NINE
The neuroses: History & cues

Bertha P. ● Davey B. ● Historical perspectives ● Cues
● Categories of neuroses ● Assessment of neuroses ●
Experimental studies of neurosis

BERTHA P.:
THE TALKING
CURE

When Bertha P. was 21, her father fell ill and she became his devoted nurse. She worked so hard that her family was not surprised when her own health began to fail. She finally reached the point where she could not take care of him; she was weak and anemic, had no appetite, and needed constant rest. She developed a severe cough and went to the family doctor, Josef Breuer, who was a prominent physician in Vienna in the 1880s. He diagnosed the cough as *tussis nervosa* (nervous cough) but could do nothing for it. During the winter following the onset of her father's illness, Bertha took to her own bed and stayed there until spring. She complained of headaches, visual disturbances, paralysis of the neck, and loss of movement and feeling in her limbs.

Before her illness Bertha had been an attractive, intelligent young woman, compassionate, and unselfish, and generally pleasing. She had never been in love, however, and was unusually naïve about sex. In Dr. Breuer's opinion her upper-middle-class Jewish family was extremely puritanical. They had shut themselves into a home-life that was monotonous and restrictive, and Bertha had told him that she escaped from the tedium into fantasies which had gradually become a constant preoccupation.

As he studied her illness Breuer came to realize that Bertha had two different states of consciousness at different times. In one state she was sad and anxious but normal in behavior; in the second, she acted like a naughty, disobedient, spoiled child. At the height of her illness Bertha experienced few intervals of normality. In the afternoons she usually fell into a drowsy state that lasted until after sundown. Then she would awaken from her semiconsciousness and repeat the phrase "tormenting, tormenting" over and over except for one two-week period when she was unable to speak at all. After observing these behaviors and listening to her disjointed comments, Breuer concluded that there was something she did not want to talk about.

When her father finally died, Bertha became violently agitated

"Bertha P." (Bertha Pappen-heim) in 1888. *(Courtesy of Congregation Solel and Dr. Dora Edinger)*

and irrational, then fell into a stupor which lasted two days. Afterwards her symptoms subsided, only to be replaced by new ones. Her field of vision grew so restricted that she could no longer recognize most people. Breuer himself was the only person to whom she responded consistently, and she began to refuse to eat unless he fed her. She started speaking only English, although German was her native tongue. Her drowsy autohypnotic states continued.

About ten days after her father's death Dr. Breuer had to leave Vienna for a few days, and without him Bertha deteriorated dramatically. She ate nothing, became extraordinarily anxious and agitated, and developed frightening visual hallucinations of deaths'-heads and skeletons.

Breuer discovered that the best way to communicate with Bertha was to put her into a hypnotic trance. He also found that when she talked about her hallucinations after he had hypnotized her, she awakened in a relatively calm and cheerful mood. Despite this encouraging trend, Bertha's overall condition continued to grow worse. That summer she had such strong suicidal impulses that it became necessary to institutionalize her. Breuer went to see her in the hospital every two or three days in the evenings and listened to her talk about the hallucinations she had developed since his last visit. Bertha referred to their sessions as the "talking cure," because they were followed by periods of greater calm for her. Then her symptoms would gradually reintensify until Dr. Breuer's next visit.

Bertha gradually improved. Her appetite increased; she was able to move more freely; she became more responsive to people. But whenever Breuer stayed away for more than a few days, she grew much worse. When he returned he would have to see her every day for several days in order to relieve the buildup of symptoms which had occurred. This convinced Breuer that "talking out" her fear and anxiety helped reduce their intensity.

In the fall Bertha went home to Vienna to live with her family in a new house. Breuer hoped that she would continue her gradual improvement, but instead she developed strange new symptoms. She began to experience each day as though it were the same day in the previous year. Christmas of 1881 seemed to her to be Christmas of 1880. She was also convinced that she was back in the old house; she would even bump into walls where there had been doors in the old structure. She continued literally to "live in the past" until late spring, when this symptom remitted.

Bertha also began to refuse all liquids and had to eat fruit in enormous quantities to avoid serious dehydration. This unusual symptom led to a major breakthrough in her treatment, for one day in a hypnotic trance she told Breuer that her English governess had allowed a puppy to drink from a glass. Bertha had found it disgusting. After

Bertha Pappenheim in her later years. *(Courtesy of Congregation Solel and Dr. Dora Edinger)*

giving vent to these feelings, Bertha asked the astonished Breuer for a glass of water and drank it with gusto. He decided that if he could trace a symptom back to the circumstances in which it had first occurred, his patient would be permanently freed of the symptom. The method worked, and Bertha's recovery was rapid.

In Breuer's opinion, the etiology of Bertha's symptoms could be traced to the time when she was nursing her father. The doctor based this conclusion on many of her memories, particularly on a story she had told him of sitting by her father's bed asleep, her arm over the back of her chair. In a state that was half-asleep and half-awake, she had seen a black snake coming out of the wall to attack her father in bed. When she tried to beat off the snake she discovered that her arm was paralyzed. It was her right arm, the one which had been resting over the back of the chair and had grown numb from lack of circulation. When the snake vanished, Bertha tried to pray but in her anxiety could only recall some English children's verses. The next day she was out in the yard and bent down over some bushes. She saw a branch which reminded her of the snake she had dreamed about, and suddenly her right arm became paralyzed. When Breuer traced Bertha's later symptoms to this and other memories of her childhood, they vanished. The "talking cure" seemed miraculous.

Breuer later reported that Bertha remained normal from the time of her cure onwards. But a younger colleague of Breuer's, Dr. Sigmund Freud, disputed his recollection. Freud contended that Bertha suffered some relapses, though on the whole she was much improved. Both men agreed that Bertha P. went on to a successful social work career, that she devoted much of her energy to feminist causes and the protection of children, and that she never married.

DAVEY B.: LEARNING TO SAY HELLO

Davey B. was born in a small town 50 miles west of Tulsa, Oklahoma. His father was the town policeman; his mother, fifteen years younger than her husband, was a housewife who had never wanted any other occupation. Davey had an older sister, Joanne, who was 7 when he was born.

Mrs. B. remembered her pregnancy with Davey as a difficult one, for the morning sickness that often accompanies the early weeks of pregnancy did not go away until she was well into her sixth month. By the time the nausea cleared up, her ankles had become so swollen that the doctor made her stay off her feet most of the time. Her ninth month of pregnancy was in July, and she was hot and miserable until the day Davey was born.

All Davey's baby pictures show him smiling or laughing. He was an active, friendly baby who seemed to enjoy having people around him. Later he told his therapist that it must have been because he was too young to understand what his parents were saying to him.

When his mother first took him to kindergarten, however, Davey cried and cried; it was weeks before his teacher could persuade him to stop crying and play with the toys. Even then he played alone and broke into tears if another child approached him. When he woke up in the morning, he often claimed to be sick so that his mother would let him stay at home. He was much happier there, sitting in a big rocking chair and slowly turning the pages of a book. His mother used to say that he looked as if he were reading long before he actually learned how, because he had memorized his favorite bedtime stories. He knew them so well that he would correct his mother whenever she made a mistake. In the first grade when he did learn to read, he enjoyed it and quickly became one of the best readers in the class. Arithmetic did not come so easily, and he often cried over the multiplication tables.

Davey frequently had nightmares. He was afraid to go to sleep lest he die before morning, and he would wake up in the middle of the night crying for his mother. His nighttime fears were so intense that he would not sleep without a night-light until he was 12 years old.

Davey describes his father as a frightening man who sometimes hit him without provocation. He teased Davey because the boy was small and bad at sports, and the first and last time that he took his son on a hunting trip, he was disgusted when Davey cried over a dead deer. On the other hand, Mrs. B. had plenty of time for her boy. She enjoyed having him around the house and encouraged him to stay at home rather than play with other boys. She would not allow him to have a bike until he was 13 years old, and then it was only at her husband's insistence that she consented to what she con- sidered a dangerous toy. In her fear for Davey's life and health she protected him from many of the normal bumps and falls that most children have. She taught him to think of the world as a dangerous place.

His parents first became concerned about Davey when he entered junior high school and his grades showed a sharp decline to the C level. Davey, the boy who loved books, stopped reading them and for several years read only comic books—stacks at a time.

Davey remembers high school mainly in terms of the misery he felt. Excluded from the school's regular social groups, he had friends only among social outcasts like himself. Since his mother didn't approve of the friends, she wouldn't allow him to bring them home.

Davey was not well coordinated and did poorly in physical edu- cation. The worst part of it for him was undressing and showering in the locker room, for he was slow to mature and physically inferior to his classmates. Whenever he set out for the gym his heart pounded, his hands grew sweaty, and his stomach churned.

In high school one girl in his class seemed to like him, but he never mustered the courage to ask her for a date. Sometimes when he masturbated, he imagined that he was with her or with his young, attractive drama teacher, but fantasies like this only made him more miserable. He wondered why he couldn't meet girls and sometimes thought that he might be homosexual.

At home Davey's relations with his parents deteriorated to sullen hostility. He rejected their attempts to approach him even while he accused them of not caring about him. He blamed his mother for being too protective and his father for ignoring him.

Although his high school grades were not very good, he was finally admitted to the state college, where an uncle of his taught. But the summer after he graduated from high school Davey nearly decided not to go to college. He was afraid of having to live away from home, afraid he would not do well in college, afraid that it would be nothing more than the misery of high school all over again. His sister Joanne, by now married and living in a nearby town, managed to persuade him to start classes. But once they were underway his fears were confirmed; though he did fairly well in classwork, he was lonelier than he had ever been before in a very lonely life.

He spent a lot of time walking the campus at night, his head down, hands in his pockets, deeply absorbed in his unhappiness. He found himself thinking about suicide; it seemed to him that he was a worthless person who didn't deserve to live. Feelings of deep anxiety would strike him, sometimes at random, sometimes in particular situations: riding in a bus or car, talking in class, walking toward the student center, standing in the quadrangle between classes. Because his anxiety in these circumstances was predictable, he spent most of his time alone in his room.

In short, Davey had reached the point where he planned each day largely to avoid fearful experiences. His life had become a series of maneuvers to reduce or avoid anxiety-provoking situations. Since there were so many of them, his involvement with the world became ever more limited. Davey had had similar feelings in high school, but they had been milder and briefer. At last in desperation, frightened that he might finally be driven to kill himself, he went to the college counseling center.

After talking to Davey, a counselor decided that their immediate goal should be to help him become comfortable enough to return to class. Once that was done they could begin to deal with his upsetting social and interpersonal problems. For the first few sessions they simply talked about the things which were troubling him in his family life and his life on campus. They tried to define his fears

(M. E. Warren/Photo Researchers, Inc.)

253

more precisely so that they would know exactly what circumstances made him anxious.

When this difficult task was finally accomplished, the therapist used the technique of systematic desensitization in an effort to eliminate his most disabling fears. The method worked well; it helped reduce his panic in cars and buses as well as his anxiety in social situations. Then, in the safety of the therapy room, Davey practiced the kinds of things a boy says to girls. Once he had rehearsed these behaviors, he began gradually trying them out in the real world. The transition was planned: The first week he simply had to smile at a strange girl; the next week he had to smile and say "hello." Ultimately he was able to approach a girl in his class, talk to her, and ask her for a date. Both he and his therapist were enormously pleased the first time a girl accepted his invitation.

Davey and his therapist talked often about his relationship with his parents and concluded that he was not able to be assertive enough with them. He was intimidated by his father's temper and manipulated by his mother's possessiveness. Once Davey began to recognize how unfounded these attitudes were for a young man of his age, he began to rehearse with the therapist some better ways of responding to his parents.

It was nearly a year before he and his therapist felt satisfied that he was ready to terminate therapy. At that time he was dating fairly often, he had made several good male friends, and he was earning a B average as a history major. He was not transformed by therapy; he remained a quiet boy who had occasional moments of anxiety. But he felt much better about himself, and better prepared to grow on his own.

Three years after his therapy ended, Davey made an appointment with the therapist and brought in his fiancée. They had wanted to stop by and thank the therapist for all she had done for him. On the side, Davey told the therapist that he had had some initial problems adjusting to sex with his girl friend but that they had diminished with experience. He was planning to start graduate school in the fall. The fiancée, an attractive first-year law student, told the therapist that she and Davey were very happy.

Fears from living

The case of Bertha Pappenheim, best known by the pseudonym Anna O., is a famous one in psychoanalytic history. Her treatment was first discussed in the book *Studies in Hysteria,* jointly written by Josef Breuer and Sigmund Freud and published in 1895. Though she had been Breuer's patient a dozen years before, it was only at Freud's urging that her story was

Josef Breuer. *(The Bettmann Archive)*

told. One of the reasons for Breuer's reluctance to report on this interesting case was that late in her treatment, he realized that Bertha had become very much attached to him (Jones, 1963). In fact, she underwent false pregnancy (pseudocyesis) when the treatment was terminated.

Breuer was shaken by this, especially since he feared that he had not acted professionally in allowing her to become so emotionally attached to him. Freud, however, reassured him that such an attachment (he called it *transference*) was a normal, even inevitable, part of psychological treatment. Freud recounted his own experiences with patients who had become similarly attached to him. Thus persuaded, Breuer added the case of Anna O. to the collection of case reports and theoretical articles in their book. The birth of psychoanalysis is usually dated from its publication.

The disordered behavior that Bertha P. showed in such incredible profusion was

diagnosed as hysterical by Breuer, but such a diagnosis in the 1880s had a very different meaning from what it would imply today. Furthermore, Ellenberger (1972) suggests that Bertha was not really a "classic case of hysteria" even then. By current standards most of her pathology, especially her hallucinations and disordered thinking, seems more schizophrenic than hysterical, although some of her difficulties—her loss of vision, loss of movement, changed states of consciousness, unpredictable panic, and extreme dependence on her therapist—can be found in "modern" hysterical neurotics. Her case is presented here mainly because of its historical importance, for it was the first extensive report of distinctly psychological therapy for a psychological disorder.

Davey B. was born some seventy-five years after Breuer treated Bertha P. Among other things, his case report illustrates the ways in which therapy for neurotic disorders has changed during that period. Davey's problems were primarily those of phobic neurosis, so his therapist treated him with a variety of behavior therapy techniques, including systematic desensitization, assertion training, and behavior rehearsal. His fears improved rapidly under this regime.

Davey's personal and social problems are not unique among people of his age. Many late adolescents remember their childhoods as Davey remembered his. Many harbor angry, resentful feelings toward their parents. Many conclude that life is not worth living and think of suicide. We believe it is important that this book's readers realize how widespread such feelings are—and how responsive they can be to time or to active therapeutic intervention.

Taken together, Bertha's and Davey's neuroses are grossly dissimilar. What unites them is the pervasive anxiety which both people experienced. Anxiety is the symptom that has caused the very different behavior disorders now termed "neurosis" to be put into the same category. The legitimacy of this shot-gun marriage of very different conditions will be discussed below.

Historical perspectives

Psychotic behavior—hallucinations, delusions, bizarre behaviors, strange, idiosyncratic speech and thought—is difficult for anyone to ignore. It is easy to understand why even primitive peoples were impressed by it and created myths to account for it. But the behavior of people we call neurotic is more subtly disordered. The neurotic's discomfort is often evident only to those who know him well; to others he may not appear to be especially troubled. Consequently the neuroses did not receive the attention in ancient times that the psychoses were given. While there are occasional references to neuroses in writings from the distant past, they are infrequent and sketchy. Najab ud din Unhammad, an Arab physician of the ninth century, described a disorder he called *janoon* which closely resembled what we now call depressive neurosis. He also wrote of *murrae souda,* a state similar to today's obsessive-compulsive neurosis (Zilboorg & Henry, 1941). The neuroses remained largely neglected, however, until the eighteenth century.

The one exception is hysteria (now called hysterical neurosis), which has been described in detail for several thousand years. Its dramatic symptoms, which include paralysis, loss of bodily sensation, total memory loss, and strange physical disabilities, were catalogued by the early Greeks. Hippocrates concluded that it was an illness of women caused by the wanderings of the uterus about the body. His prescription for it was marriage (a chauvinistic treatment strategy).

The history of hysteria, and ultimately of the other neuroses, is closely linked to the history of hypnosis. Anton Mesmer, a Parisian adventurer, played a major but controversial role in bringing hypnosis to the attention of scientists in the eighteenth century. Claiming that he had discovered "animal magnetism," Mesmer induced hypnotic trances in many affluent Parisians with a treatment machine he called the *baquet.* In 1784 the French Academy of Science appointed a distinguished committee including Benjamin Franklin, Lavoisier, and Guillotin (inventor of the machine that bears his name) to investigate the phenomenon of animal magnetism. The committee concluded that the effects of hypnotic treatment resulted from the imagination rather than from any change in body fluids, and decided that hypnosis was potentially harmful.

Following this condemnation of "mesmerism," few reputable scientists ventured into the area. Those who did (Elliotson and Braid, both English physicians, and Liebeault, a French physician) earned the disapproval of

L'hypnotiseur (1813)—a satirical French comment on animal magnetism." *(New York Public Library Picture Collection)*

A Clinical Lecture by Charcot at the Saltpetriere by A. Brouillet. *(Culver Pictures, Inc.)*

their colleagues. Nonetheless, by the 1880s hypnosis was again being used fairly widely in Europe for the relief of physical discomfort. The question of how and why it worked had not been answered, but two major theories about it were soon offered. Jean Martin Charcot, whose followers came to be known as the Salpetriere school of hypnosis, produced the first. Hippolyte Bernheim, head of a rival group referred to as the Nancy school, quickly advanced the second. Contention between these two groups was a major focus of interest in the scientific community.

Charcot, a well-known neurologist, contended that hypnotic phenomena, like hysteria, resulted from changes in the nervous system. He believed that both hysteria and susceptibility to hypnosis were the result of nervous system degeneration and that both were therefore reflections of abnormality. Bernheim argued instead that hypnosis and hysteria were both products of the imagination—that they were not physical disorders.

One significant consequence of the Charcot-Bernheim controversy was the attention it drew to the group of disorders (which included hysteria) that shortly came to be called the neuroses. Another important result was Bernheim's recognition that the neuroses stemmed from psychological rather than physical causes. (Charcot finally acknowledged that Bernheim was right.)

Sigmund Freud was one of the few Austrian physicians of his time to accept that daring French theory. His innovative mind led Freud from his early studies of the testes of the eel to the subject of neurology, and from there to the neuroses. He studied with both Bernheim and Charcot during his formative years and then returned to Vienna to specialize in the private practice of psychiatry. Soon he found himself working primarily with female hysterics. It was during this time that Freud learned of Josef Breuer's treatment of Bertha Pappenheim. After some unsuccessful efforts to use hypnosis himself, Freud began to develop his own treatment methods. Out of them came his theory of personality (see Chapter 4) and the psychoanalytic method for the treatment of the neuroses (Chapter 10).

The evolution of Freud's views on theory and technique, the history of the psychoanalytic movement itself, and the current status of the dynamic approach to the neuroses are also described in Chapters 4 and 10.

Another historical thread in the story of neurosis is the one which leads ultimately to behaviorism and the behavioral approaches to neurosis. The seventeenth- and eighteenth-century philosophers Locke, Hartley, and Bentham were probably behaviorism's most influential ancestors. Prominent nineteenth- and twentieth-century figures like Darwin, Dewey, Sechenov, and Bekhterev also made major contributions to the developing behavioral movement in psychology, though not specifically in the area of neurosis. The greatest impact on early behaviorism was made by Ivan Pavlov, who gave substance to the entire movement through his classical conditioning model (Chapter 4) and who also influenced behavioral conceptions of neurosis.

Working largely with dogs, Pavlov found that "experimental neuroses" could be demonstrated in a variety of ways, all involving a "breakdown" in conditioning. This would happen when an animal could no longer meet task requirements he had learned to meet during initial conditioning. Pavlov noticed that different dogs responded differently to his efforts to induce experimental neurosis, and he began to classify the animals according to their reactivity to stressors. He developed a four-part theory of "personality" types to account for their differences in vulnerability to experimental neurosis. He had the idea that the breakdowns he observed in his dogs were simplified versions of neurotic breakdowns in men. Accordingly he attempted to categorize human neuroses as he had done animal neuroses, but this effort has met with little acceptance by others. To summarize, Pavlov is important in the history of neurosis for two contributions: his classical conditioning studies, which established a paradigm that others such as Wolpe have used to explain the etiology of the neuroses, and his experimental-neurosis work, which set the stage for later studies, like those by Masserman, that have had a considerable impact on theories of etiology.

John B. Watson, an American psychologist of the same general period as Pavlov and Freud, also played a major role in the history of behaviorism (Chapter 4) and of behavioral approaches to the neuroses. In his classic experiment with phobia, Watson conditioned

Freud and his fiancée Martha Bernays, about the time that Breuer treated "Bertha P." *(Culver Pictures, Inc.)*

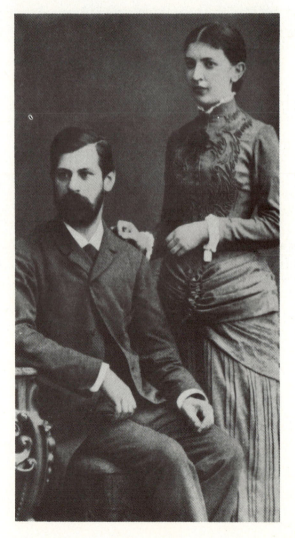

John B. Watson. *(Culver Pictures, Inc.)*

a variety of fear responses to a white rat in a child who, before conditioning, had shown only interest and pleasure in the animal (Watson & Rayner, 1920). This demonstration convinced Watson and others who followed him that naturally acquired human neuroses might have been learned in much the same manner. Jones's later demonstration that phobic behavior could also be unlearned by means of conditioning fostered the development of behavioral approaches to treatment of the neuroses (1924).

Freud and his disciples, and Pavlov, Watson, and their students, laid the groundwork for a debate about the etiology and treatment of the neuroses that is still continuing. Simply stated, the question is this: Does neurotic behavior reflect underlying personality conflict, or is it a set of learned maladaptive responses? The details of that conflict are given in Chapter 10, which compares and contrasts behavioral and psychoanalytic views on the etiology and treatment of the neurotic disorders.

Cues to the neuroses

Neurotic behavior does not involve a break with reality. That is, the neurotic person recognizes the internal nature of his discomfort and does not distort reality to explain it, as does the psychotic. Further, no matter how disturbed, depressed, or anxious he may be, the neurotic retains the ability to recognize that his functioning is impaired. By definition, *the symptomatic behavior of the neurotic is the same behavior exhibited by the normal person under grossly stressful conditions.*

Ever since Freud brought together the neurotic disorders under the psychoanalytic umbrella, the hallmark of the neuroses—the concept which has justified their inclusion under a single heading—has been anxiety. DSM II, the *Diagnostic and Statistical Manual of Mental Disorders,* says: "Anxiety is the chief characteristic of the neuroses. It may be felt and expressed directly, or it may be controlled unconsciously and automatically by conversion, displacement and various other psychological mechanisms. Generally, these mechanisms produce symptoms experienced as subjective distress from which the patient desires relief" (APA, 1968, p. 39).

This description presents two major diagnostic problems. The first is that agreement on what constitutes conversion, displacement, and "various other psychological mechanisms" has been notoriously low (Goldfried et al., 1971). The second is that anxiety is a symptomatic behavior common to virtually all psychopathology. For that reason it is not useful for differentiating between any of the diagnostic categories, including the neuroses. Nathan points out that in a large sample of patients, diagnosticians described as "anxious" the following proportions of each category: 45 percent of patients who had a diagnosis of affective psychosis, 36 percent of the schizophrenics, 43 percent of those in the personality disorder category, 38 percent of those with acute brain disorder, and 54 percent of the neurotics (1969). The neurotic disorders are, therefore, among the most difficult on which clinicians try to reach diagnostic consensus.

Categories of neuroses

DSM II divides the neuroses into eight categories: anxiety, hysterical, phobic, obsessive-compulsive, depressive, neurasthenic, depersonalization, and hypochondriacal neuroses. Figure 9-1 gives an approximation of the number of patients in each.

Anxiety neurosis. The most common of all neuroses, anxiety neurosis is the label assigned 30 to 40 percent of all neurotics (Coleman, 1972). It is characterized by the presence of *free-floating* anxiety, which refers to the inability of the anxiety neurotic to identify the source or sources of his anxiety. Wolpe believes that this is because the source of the fear is so subtle or diffuse that the patient has not learned to identify it (1969). Psychoanalytic theorists hold that the source is unknown because of repression.

In any event, the anxiety neurotic lives in a state of chronic, low-level anxiety which is

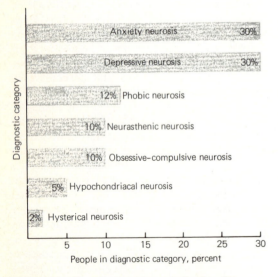

Figure 9-1. These percentages indicating the frequency of seven categories of neurosis are rough estimates, because there are wide variations in diagnostic practices. Depersonalization, another category of neurosis listed by the APA's *Diagnostic and Statistical Manual,* is such a recent label that few figures are available on its use.

periodically interrupted by acute episodes of panic. He will say of himself, "I usually feel tense," or "I keep feeling that something bad is going to happen to me, but I don't know what," or "I'm just nervous all the time." He may also describe such somatic sensations as headaches, dizziness, nausea, and difficulty in breathing, all associated with the tension that he constantly suffers.

The anxiety neurotic may also describe his psychological state as one of worry, concern, dread, or a sense of impending disaster. He is afraid without knowing what he fears. He may feel that he is "losing his mind." His mood is probably depressed, and he is probably irritable. During an interview he may show a variety of motor deviations: his hands may shake, or he may shift restlessly in his chair, shuffle his feet, wipe his sweaty hands. He is likely to talk a great deal, but with frequent disfluencies such as "Ah" or "Umm" (Pope et al., 1970). If he is acutely anxious he may be unable to keep from pacing and trembling.

No anxiety neurotic shows all these behaviors. Hamilton (1959) and Buss (1962) did factor-analytic studies of the behaviors exhibited by anxiety neurotics and found that the patients formed two distinct groups. One group showed largely physiological indexes of anxiety (sweating, heart palpitations, etc.). The second group demonstrated disorders in the cognitive and motor spheres (worry, restlessness, muscular tension). These two studies support Eysenck's contention that there are two kinds of anxiety reactions, one which derives from physiological overreactivity and is expressed by somatic reactions, and another which stems from conditioned anxiety and is characterized by cognitive and motor reactions (1961).

Panic states lasting from a few minutes to an hour or more may strike anxiety-neurotic patients at unpredictable times. During these episodes, called *anxiety* or *panic attacks,* patients become extraordinarily fearful, anxious, and disorganized. Sometimes they become convinced that their feelings mean they are going to die.

The anxiety neurotic is likely to be viewed

by the people around him as frightened, tense, timid, exceptionally sensitive to the opinions of others, and lacking in self-esteem. Despite these traits, he may set unrealistically high goals which he exhausts himself trying to achieve.

Hysterical neurosis. The hysterical neuroses are the descendants of Freud's hysteria. Like hysteria, they are characterized by symptoms which seem to be physical in origin but have no underlying organic basis. The hysterical neuroses are subdivided into the conversion type and the dissociative type.

• CONVERSION TYPE. The term *conversion hysteria* comes from the psychoanalytic explanation of this disorder: that it represents a "conversion" of repressed sexual energy into physical "equivalents." These equivalents usually involve one or more of the senses or some portion of the voluntary nervous system. Thus the patient may be blind, deaf, mute, paralyzed, or anesthetic (unable to feel sensation) in a portion of his body. Or he may suffer "writer's cramp," convulsive movements, tunnel vision (vision through only a narrow channel of sight), frequent and intense headaches, coughing, nausea, or vomiting. Or, as with Bertha P., the patient may experience a pseudopregnancy. This brief list suggests how dramatic and incapacitating the effects of conversion hysteria can be. The hysteric is often said to receive *secondary gain* from his condition in that it exempts him from certain demands which might normally be made upon him. For example, Bertha P. could no longer care for her father after she became ill; further, her bizarre and frightening behavior brought her concern, care, compassion —and Dr. Breuer.

The diagnosis of conversion reaction is sometimes relatively simple. One excellent diagnostic cue is that the hysterical behaviors may disappear following hypnotic suggestion. Another is that the naïve hysteric may manifest physical disabilities which fail to make anatomical sense. For example, he may complain that his hand is paralyzed, even though a paralysis from the wrist down without any involvement of the arm does not accord with the neuroanatomy of the hand and arm. Similarly, in a hysterical condition called *astasia abasia,* the patient will be able to move his lower extremities while he is sitting or lying down but not while he is standing.

At other times, however, conversion hysteria is most difficult to recognize. A person who complains of vague intestinal pain which is difficult to isolate may be a hysteric, suffering from a psychosomatic disorder, or the victim of an organic disorder without psychological determinants.

According to clinical tradition, many hysterics lack serious concern about their disability. This characteristic, called *la belle indifférence,* is regarded by some clinicians as instant evidence of hysteria. The person who wakes up one morning to find himself paralyzed from the waist down and then rolls over and goes back to sleep is most likely to be labeled hysterical.

But like many other bits of "clinical lore," this one has not been strongly supported by empirical data. Several studies have shown that excessive unconcern is observed in only about one-third of all hysterics (Stephens & Kamp, 1962; Zigler et al., 1960). Further, more than one-third of all hysterics are at least moderately depressed about their bodily dysfunctions.

Another item of clinical lore concerning conversion hysteria is that it has become increasingly rare in recent years, largely because people nowadays are more sophisticated psychologically and know that the dramatic symptoms of conversion reaction are signs of neurosis. But a study by Stephens and Kamp (1962) revealed that the national incidence of hysteria in the periods 1913 to 1919 and 1945 to 1960 remained steady at the 2 percent level, a conclusion which Woodruff and his colleagues drew more recently in 1971.

It has also been widely believed that women are more prone to develop hysteria than men. In fact, hysteria was once viewed as a result of uterine dysfunction. Yet in wartime, many conversion reactions are observed in combat soldiers (Mucha & Reinhardt, 1970). In part the more frequent diagnosis of women as hysterics may be a function of expectation: the clinician who does not expect to find a male hysteric is not likely to see one. Nevertheless, Woodruff and his co-workers interpret their research to indicate that there is a higher incidence of hysteria among women (1971). Another study by the same research group reports that blacks and women have more multiple conversion symptoms than do whites or men (Guze et al., 1971). Taken together, these studies suggest that while women may more often be diagnosed as hysterics, the condition is not unique to them.

•DISSOCIATIVE TYPE. In the *dissociative states* of hysterical neurosis, the patient reports a change in his state of consciousness or in his identity. The dissociative states, which are described below, are a relatively rare form of neurosis.

Amnesia refers to a partial or total loss of recall of past experiences. It is often caused by organic brain disorders, in which case there is usually a lack of selectivity in the content of lost memory. In amnesia of hysterical origin, on the other hand, the patient tends to forget anxiety-laden material. The person suffering from neurotic amnesia may be unable to remember his own name or address or to recognize members of his family, even though he can still speak, read, and use other skills he has learned. He may appear troubled only when he must recall facts about himself.

A *fugue state* is an even more intense disorder of memory than simple amnesia. A person may leave his home to wander about for long periods of time. Days, weeks, or years later, he suddenly finds himself in a strange place, not knowing how he got there or what he has done during the "lost" interval. Occasionally there have been reports of individuals who established whole new lives and then suddenly regained the memory of their past existence.

Multiple personalities are extremely rare. Their dramatic nature always catches public attention, but through time there have been fewer than a hundred recorded cases. It is an error to equate multiple personality with schizophrenia. Multiple personality is not a "split personality"; it is a form of dissociative state in which the patient has two or more distinct personalities. He or she may change back and forth between them for periods ranging from minutes to days. One personality is not usually aware of the other, though in rare cases a state of co-consciousness has been reported. The most famous contemporary case of multiple personality was recorded by Thigpen and Cleckley in their book *The Three Faces of Eve* (1957).

Morton Prince wrote the classic description of a multiple personality in *Dissociation of a Personality:*

Miss Christine L. Beauchamp . . . a person in whom several personalities have become developed; that is to say, she may change her personality from time to time, often from hour to hour, and with each change her character becomes transformed and her memories altered. In addition to the real, original or normal self, the self that was born and which she was intended by nature to be, she may be any one of three different persons. I say three different, because, although making use of the same body, each, nevertheless, has a distinctly different character; a difference manifested by different trains of thought, by different views, beliefs, ideals, and temperament, and by different acquisitions, tastes, habits, experiences, and memories. Each varies in these respects from the other two, and from the original Miss Beauchamp. . . . And so it happens that Miss Beauchamp, if I may use the name to designate several distinct people, at one moment says and does and plans and arranges something to which a short time before she most strongly objected, indulges tastes which a moment before would have been abhorrent to her ideals, and undoes or destroys what she had just laboriously planned and arranged. [1925, pp. 1–2]

Somnambulism or sleepwalking, the most common of the dissociative reactions, occurs in 5 percent of all children. Typically the sleepwalker falls asleep normally, but gets up later and carries out what appear to be

Acrophobia can be terrifying to those who suffer from it—as this photograph is meant to suggest. *(Alfred Gescheidt)*

purposeful acts (Taves, 1969). Afterwards he goes back to bed and has no memory of his somnambulistic behavior when he awakens. Kales and his colleagues report that sleep-walking occurs during sleep periods devoid of dreams so that, contrary to general belief, the condition does not appear to be an acting out of a dream (1966).

Phobic Neurosis. The person who suffers from phobic neurosis is subject to periods of intense fear of objects or situations which he usually recognizes are not objectively harmful or dangerous. His experience of anxiety is similar to that of the anxiety neurotic, except that the phobic neurotic can point to the source of his fear. So long as he is able to avoid that phobic object he does not become uncomfortable. Phobic neurotics constitute

8 to 12 percent of all neurotics seeking treatment (Eiduson, 1968). More women than men and more younger people than older are diagnosed as phobic. Here are some fairly common phobias:

Acrophobia—Fear of high places
Agoraphobia—Fear of open places
Claustrophobia—Fear of closed places
Nyctophobia—Fear of darkness
Ochlophobia—Fear of crowds

While there is an esoteric Greek name for nearly every fear known to man, most phobias are usually described in plain English. Thus one is more likely to be "afraid of thunderstorms" than "astraphobic." The most prevalent phobia among adults is fear of open spaces (agoraphobia). This fear occurs in approximately 50 percent of all phobic patients, the majority of whom are female. Such patients tend to be passive, anxious, shy, and dependent (Marks, 1970).

Minor fears are common to everyone. Snakes, insects, high places, or closed places may cause discomfort in many people. What makes a fear neurotic is its incapacitating nature; the neurotic person will go a long way to avoid having to face a feared situation. And if he tries to force himself to confront the feared object, he may become so anxious and disorganized that he can no longer function effectively.

Some phobias are only mildly disruptive in that they can be avoided without seriously interfering with the phobic person's life. The person who is afraid to fly can usually arrange some other method of transportation, while the person who fears snakes can usually manage to live in a snake-free environment. In some cases, however, a phobia can prevent a person from living a normal life. The patient who is afraid to be alone, afraid of crowds, afraid of open spaces, or afraid to speak in public has to plan his life with great care. He may even find himself seriously incapacitated. Davey B. eventually reached the point where he could not attend classes or meet people socially; his life was severely disrupted. The same was true of Jay Meredith, whose sexual and social disabilities are detailed in Chapter 12.

The phobic often has the additional prob- lems of mild depression, depersonalization, and mild obsessive and compulsive behavior (Marks, 1970). Frazier and Carr point out that phobias can also occur in other psychopathology, including hysterical neurosis, depression, obsessive-compulsive neurosis, and paranoia (1967). They suggest, in fact, that it may not even be appropriate to regard phobic behavior as a separate diagnostic category. At the present time, however, the *Diagnostic and Statistical Manual of Mental Disorders* retains this diagnostic label.

Obsessive-compulsive neurosis. The obsessive-compulsive neurosis is characterized by insistent unwanted thoughts, urges, or activities. *Obsessions* are unavoidable preoccupations with thoughts or ideas; *compulsions* are behaviors which the individual is impelled to perform. Although some professionals feel that these two conditions should be diagnosed separately, most believe that they occur together often enough to justify their being considered two facets of the same disorder. Estimates of the frequency of obsessive-compulsive neurosis vary from 4 to 20 percent of all neurotics (Coleman, 1964; Goodwin et al., 1969). It usually begins early in life: over two-thirds of all obsessive-compulsive patients

The obsessive-compulsive, faced with a decision, may simply avoid conflict altogether. *(Drawing by Frascino; © 1971 The New Yorker Magazine, Inc.)*

"A hamburger, please."   "Rare, medium, or well done?"   "Never mind."

in one study had developed the disorder by the age of 25 (Nemiah, 1967).

•OBSESSIONS. Buss divides obsessive behavior into two subcategories: obsessive doubts and obsessive thoughts (1966). The *obsessive doubter* is the individual in a constant state of indecision. Even the choice between two desirable options becomes a source of severe discomfort. He spends all his time forming plans to act, but he rarely does any acting. He worries about making a choice up to the time when he can no longer prolong the decision, and then he may act in a foolish, impulsive manner. Not only does the obsessive doubter worry about the future; he also broods about the past. His life is a continual process of worry about decisions past, present, and future.

Obsessive thoughts usually involve repeated fantasies about prohibited activities. The person may have sexual or aggressive fantasies whose content is unacceptable and hence very much out of character. Such thoughts are called "ego-alien." Typical obsessive thoughts include standing up in church and shouting obscenities, raping or being raped, pushing one's mother down the stairs, or stabbing one's child with a butcher knife—though not all obsessive thoughts are so aversive. Sometimes, in fact, the person is simply obsessed with an idea or an old tune which refuses to leave his mind. We have all been haunted by a phrase, a television jingle, or a popular song. For the obsessive neurotic this is a more pervasive and persistent experience that actually interferes with his concentration on work or attention in social interaction.

•COMPULSIONS. The patient suffering from compulsions must emit certain stereotyped behaviors again and again. Even though he may recognize their irrational or nonfunctional nature, he cannot stop. If he tries, he becomes increasingly anxious until he must finally "give in" to his compulsion. Compulsive behavior can vary from minor acts like lining up shoes in a precise manner each night or avoiding all the cracks in the sidewalk to complex rituals in which occupations like bathing or dressing may take several hours. If the obsessive feels that he has performed his ritual in an unsatisfactory manner, or if he is interrupted in the middle of it, he may have to repeat the whole compulsive sequence. The two most common forms of compulsion are repetition and symmetry. In a *repetition* compulsion, the neurotic must repeat the ritual over and over again. In a *symmetry* compulsion, the neurotic feels "driven" to ensure that his or her actions balance each other out.

All of us engage in minor compulsive patterns in our daily routine. We wake up, brush our teeth, wash our face, get dressed, and prepare breakfast in a set way. But when we are faced with the necessity to alter that routine temporarily or permanently, we do not become anxious or disorganized. The true compulsive cannot permit such variations.

Depressive neurosis. Neurotic depression, most clinicians believe, is triggered by genuine loss or failure in the patient's life. A death, divorce, or other painful separation, the failure to get a promotion, be given a job, or be admitted to a college or university—all have the potential to precipitate neurotic depression. It differs from normal depression in the unusual degree of sadness involved and in its persistence past the time when an improvement in mood would normally be expected. It differs from psychotic depression in that it is less intense and long-lasting and does not include such psychotic behaviors as hallucinations and delusions. While a neurotic depression may last for months, it ultimately remits. But psychotic depressions may continue for years without letup. Fyodor Dostoevsky may well have been seriously depressed for much of his adult life; the same may have been true of Abraham Lincoln.

Neurotic depression is a common neurosis; 20 to 30 percent of all neurotics fall into the category (Coleman, 1972). Nathan reported that 75 percent of his sample of 215 neurotic patients were diagnosed as depressive neurotic (1969). The fact that these patients came from a predominantly poor area of urban

Boston may account for the high rate of depression.

The neurotic depressive can be thought of as a person in prolonged mourning. That is, even though the interval of appropriate grief over a loss has passed for most people, he remains dejected and downhearted, reports a reduced sense of self-worth, and shows little interest in making plans for the future. He may complain of having trouble concentrating. All of life seems a great effort; getting up in the morning requires more strength than he feels he has. He may also find it hard to get to sleep, and once he does, he may sleep fitfully. On the other hand, he may sleep almost constantly. In either case he wakes up feeling as tired as he was when he went to bed. It has been reported that depressives show a relative lack of stage 4 sleep compared with normal control subjects (Hawkin & Mendels, 1966), though the meaning of this finding remains unclear. Since in some cases the neurotic depressive may be suicidal, it is one of the few forms of neurosis that may warrant hospitalization.

Neurasthenic neurosis. The neurasthenic neurotic is chronically fatigued, weak, and exhausted. Unlike the hysterical neurotic, his disabilities are not dramatic, and he fails to derive secondary gain from them. He is simply in a state of perpetual fatigue, or sometimes of physical pain. The neurasthenic patient often experiences a mild depression which tends to be more enduring but less intense than the depression suffered by the depressive neurotic. Neurasthenia is observed in about 10 percent of neurotics (Coleman, 1972). It is familiarly known as the "neurosis of the frustrated housewife."

Depersonalization neurosis. This neurotic disorder is marked by a sense of unreality and a feeling of estrangement from oneself (depersonalization) or one's surroundings (derealization). It is both the most recently recognized and the least explored of the neurotic disorders listed in DSM II.

As Weckowicz (1970) and others have emphasized, depersonalization is peculiarly difficult to define clearly, because the term refers to highly private events—the individual's own thoughts—which are impossible for an observer to share. The clinician is entirely dependent upon the patient's self-reports, yet the patient finds his sensations difficult to convey and talks in metaphors as he tries to describe them.

Acker identified five characteristics of depersonalization among the subjects he studied: (1) a feeling of change, (2) a feeling of unreality, (3) an unpleasant quality to these feelings, (4) loss of affective response, (5) a nondelusional quality to the experience (1954). The last point refers to the ability of the normal or neurotic subject to recognize that what he is experiencing is simply a feeling and not a fact. He knows that his body remains real, that it is only the external world that appears unreal. In contrast, the psychotic who experiences depersonalization may not retain this degree of "reality testing"; he may conclude that his body has actually become someone else's (see Chapter 6).

Depersonalization is a common experience (Roberts, 1960). A study of 57 normal British students found that 23 had felt it. In another survey of 112 normal American students, between one-third and one-half reported having had it (Dixon, 1963). Furthermore, the descriptions students give of their depersonalization experiences resemble those given by patients (Myers & Grant, 1971). The frequency of depersonalization among both normal and psychiatric populations has led Sedman to speculate that about 40 percent of any population may possess a built-in mechanism which leads to the experience under the proper circumstances. Clinically, depersonalization is reported most often by younger patients who are anxious, introverted, and depressed (Sedman, 1970).

The term "depersonalization neurosis," however, should be reserved for people with whom depersonalization is a primary complaint serious enough to disrupt their functioning. Reliable diagnosis of the syndrome remains difficult.

Hypochondriacal neurosis. In this neurotic disorder the person is preoccupied with his body and his health. Although he is not delusional, the hypochondriac finds it difficult to believe that he is not seriously ill. But unlike the hysterical neurotic, he does not suffer from an actual loss of physical function. The syndrome occurs in approximately 5 percent of all neurotic patients (Coleman, 1972). Pilowsky suggests that three basic factors are found in hypochondriasis: (1) bodily concern, (2) disease phobia, (3) inability to accept reassurance about health (1967).

The hypochondriac keeps up with the latest events in the medical world; he knows all of the symptoms of cancer, tuberculosis, and brain tumor, as well as those of leprosy, schistosomiasis, and Courvoisier's gallbladder. And he is constantly anticipating the appearance of the symptoms in his own body. A mild headache leads him to conclude that he has a brain tumor; a cough is interpreted as lung cancer. His preoccupation with bodily functions causes the hypochondriac to attend to minor body changes which other people ignore.

Though this kind of neurotic is often certain that he is fatally ill, he does not appear as anxious about it as might be expected from a patient with a terminal illness. Hypochondriacs are prime targets for quack physicians who encourage them to believe that their complaints have physical bases. On the other hand, the reassurance of a reputable physician rarely does the hypochondriac any good, whereas he can be the bane of the doctor's existence.

Diagnosis of hypochondriacal neurosis is complicated by several factors. First, the symptoms of hypochondriasis are not confined to this syndrome. Many neurotics and psychotics have unfounded worries about their health; so do normal people from time to time. Second, hypochondriasis is especially difficult to distinguish from neurasthenic neurosis, since the two disorders share many common features. Theoretically there is a qualitative difference in the emphasis which patients in the two groups place on their complaints, but in practice this difference is difficult to detect. Consequently, some diagnosticians believe that neurasthenia and hypochondriasis would better be viewed as one syndrome rather than two.

Categories of neurosis: How useful are they?

Now that you have read the descriptions of the eight "official" categories of neurosis, you can begin to weigh the assets and liabilities of the DSM II system. Examination of this material strongly suggests that many of the separate diagnostic categories are more alike than different. Two psychopathologic cues—anxiety and depression—are important components of virtually every neurotic disorder, including the two major neurotic syndromes, anxiety neurosis and depressive neurosis. Claghorn argues that these two syndromes should be merged into one "anxiety-depressive syndrome" to reflect the frequent simultaneous occurrence of anxiety and depression (1970). Nathan and his colleagues observed that depression and anxiety characterized sizable numbers of patients in all categories of neurosis identified in their sample population (1969). These studies and many others suggest that depression and anxiety by themselves have little differential diagnostic value. A few recent treatment-outcome surveys offer data that dispute this conclusion; for example, one study of anxious and depressed patients found that patients who were more depressed than anxious had a better prognosis than those who were more anxious than depressed (Schapira et al., 1972). Despite this differentiation between the two groups, it seems best to follow the advice of Derogatis and his co-workers, who suggest that the complex issue of the interaction of anxiety and depression requires much more study before it can be set down as a diagnostic formula (1972).

Essentially the same generalization can be made about the other behavioral cues to the neuroses. Concern about physical health and complaints of fatigue are found among patients with all diagnoses, as well as among normal people. Depersonalization is a frequent complaint by normals, psychotics, and neurotics. And for that matter, no psychiatric disorder is free from conversion behaviors (Guze et al., 1971). In sum, the mere presence or absence of any of the so-called neurotic cues is not sufficient to allow definitive diagnosis of either neurosis or any of the subtypes of neurosis. While the current official diagnostic categories have merit in areas such as the organic disorders, they reveal serious flaws when it comes to classifying the neuroses.

Assessment of neurosis: Identifying and evaluating the cues

Psychological tests as assessment tools

Many studies have explored the utility of the subscales of the Minnesota Multiphasic Personality Inventory (MMPI) as a reliable way to discriminate between neurotic patients and other diagnostic groups. For example, Goldberg (1965), Gough (1963), Guthrie (1963), Meehl (1963), and Schmidt (1963) all have reported success in differentiating groups of neurotic patients from groups of schizophrenics, psychotically depressed patients, and manic-depressives, as well as from patients with personality, conduct, and psychosomatic disorders. The MMPI has also been used to make reliable discriminations between patients with anxiety neurosis and those with hysterical neurosis labels (Hovey, 1963), and between patients with hysterical conversion reactions and those with early multiple sclerosis (Dodge and Kolstoe, 1971).

But while the MMPI is useful for identifying group differences in patterns of neurotic psychopathology, authorities caution that it is *not* useful for diagnosis in actual clinical settings because of the great variability and overlap in neurotic patients' disordered behavior (Modlin, 1963; Williams et al., 1972). It has been demonstrated that groups of neurotic, psychotic, and character-disorder patients in a private hospital population could not be reliably separated on the basis of MMPI performance (Blum, 1970).

It was long believed that intelligence test patterns could discriminate among the neurotic subtypes—that, for example, obsessive-compulsive and anxiety neurotics had higher verbal than performance facility, while hysterics achieved higher performance scores than verbal scores (Rapaport, 1945; Schafer, 1948). However, this belief has not been supported by recent research (Matarazzo, 1972). Again contrary to widespread early conviction, distinctive "neurotic" patterns on the standard intelligence tests have failed to discriminate neurotics from other psychiatric patients (Rosecrans & Schaeffer, 1969).

Attempts to use the Rorschach or Thematic Apperception Test (TAT) to discriminate neurotics from other patient groups have generally come to nothing. Although several researchers have claimed that they identified neurotic "signs" on the Rorschach, none of their findings have survived efforts to "cross-validate" them with different clinical populations (Goldfried et al., 1971). The TAT has also failed to make more than a minimal discrimination between neurotic and other psychiatric or normal groups (Ritter & Eron, 1952). Further, TAT studies which do report identification of differences between these groups neglect to detail procedures for achieving practical clinical utility from the test (Foulds, 1953). Murstein concludes that diagnostic differentiation using the TAT is generally unsatisfactory (1965).

Psychophysiological techniques as assessment tools

Psychophysiological assessment of neurosis has centered on measures and techniques which reflect anxiety level. It has been shown that increased heart rate distinguishes neurotic patients from normal control subjects (Glickstein et al., 1957). Anxiety neurotics have higher systolic blood pressure than either schizophrenics or normals (Milliken, 1964). Neurotic patients also show greater GSR responsivity than normal subjects under stress conditions (Lader, 1967).

In a related research area, experimenters have reported that anxious subjects exhibit greater GSR conditioning than normal subjects (Howe, 1958). Other physiological measures, including muscular activity (Malmo, 1966), stomach activity (Mahl & Karpe, 1953), and pupillary reactivity (McCawley et al., 1966), likewise differentiate neurotics from normals.

It seems correct to conclude that psychophysiological assessment of neurotic behavior, which provides more "direct" measurements of neurotic anxiety, has proved much more successful than assessment by psychological tests.

Experimental studies of neurosis

Two central elements of the neurotic disorders, anxiety and conflict, have been given intensive scrutiny by experimental psychopathologists. Most of their work has involved two simultaneous efforts: to develop objective and reliable measures of anxiety and conflict, and to induce in human and animal laboratory subjects analogues of real-life anxiety and conflict.

Anxiety and fear as measurement problems

In the vocabulary of the psychopathologist, *fear* is a realistic response to a dangerous situation, while *anxiety*, the hallmark of neurosis, is an unrealistic response to a situation with little if any real danger. Because the subjective sensations involved in fear and anxiety are similar, differentiation of the two by objective methods is very difficult. For example, Davey B. sweated profusely, felt sick to his stomach, and reported a great deal of tension whenever he had to ride a bus or go to class; Anne Frank described many of the same reactions whenever the Dutch police or the Gestapo came near her family's hiding place. Davey's response was anxiety, because his apprehensions about riding buses or being near people had no foundation in reality;

During acute anxiety attacks the anxiety neurotic is overwhelmed with panic—a condition suggested by *The Shriek,* a lithograph by Edvard Munch. *(Collection, the Musuem of Modern Art, New York.)*

Anne's was fear, because the dangers associated with discovery were very real.

While it is not difficult to label Anne Frank's autonomic responses "fear" and Davey B.'s "anxiety," that task is rarely easy in the clinical setting, where the determinants of the behaviors are not so obvious. Partly for this reason, researchers have attempted to measure anxiety in controlled settings first, with an eye to later clinical application.

Measurement of anxiety

Several basic strategies have been used to select subjects for research on anxiety. One involves screening by experienced clinicians to determine which persons are anxious. A second employs paper-and-pencil tests to identify "high-anxious" and "low-anxious" people in a pool of otherwise normal subjects. A third technique involves placing randomly selected subjects in a situation deliberately designed to elicit anxiety. The second and third methods are not mutually exclusive; some studies preselect high- and low-anxious subjects and then subject them to situations which the experimenter believes will elicit anxiety. The obvious ethical problems associated with research of this kind have not so far been resolved.

The variety of methods that have been devised to measure anxiety includes self-report questionnaires, physiological measures, and behavioral measures. These methods of assessment do not always agree with one another, partly because the measurement techniques are subject to error. Also, researchers and research subjects differ among themselves and with each other in their definitions of anxiety. Thus a person who shows physiological changes which a researcher would label as indicative of anxiety may not describe himself as anxious at all.

Physiological measures of anxiety. As already discussed, most of the psychophysiological techniques for assessing neurosis do so by measuring anxiety level. These procedures, which include indexes of heart rate, vascular response, galvanic skin response, palmar sweat, muscular activity, and pupillary reactivity, may also be used singly or in various combinations to measure anxiety as such (Wing, 1964). The measures can discriminate between high- and low-anxious subjects when both groups are placed in a stressful situation (Malmo, 1957). However, they do not reliably differentiate between high- and low-anxious subjects under nonstressful conditions (Martin & Sroufe, 1970).

Some researchers have investigated biochemical measures of anxiety, which include assessment of adrenocortical hormones, adrenal gland extracts, and substances which are indirect reflections of these two factors (Pitts and McClure, 1967). They report an increased output of adrenocortical hormones among high-anxious as compared with low-anxious subjects (Martin & Sroufe, 1970).

Behavioral measures of anxiety. Behavioral measures of anxiety depend upon systematic observation of such functions as motor disturbances (Buss et al., 1955), speech (Kasl & Mahl, 1965), perceptual-motor coordination (Ryan & Lakie, 1965), perception (Goldstone, 1955), memory (Basowitz et al., 1955), speech (Pope et al., 1970), simple learning (Taylor & Spence, 1966), and complex learning (Katahn & Lyda, 1966).

In general, data from most of these studies suggest that when the task is a simple one and the response a dominant one, anxiety improves performance. For example, high-anxious subjects show faster conditioning and slower extinction than low-anxious subjects in a simple eye-blink task (Taylor, 1951). Conversely, when the task is a difficult one and the correct response a nondominant one, anxiety hampers performance. In a complicated maze-tracing assignment, for example, low-anxious subjects were superior to high-anxious ones (Farber & Spence, 1953).

Self-report measures of anxiety. The most widespread self-report measures of anxiety are the Taylor Manifest Anxiety Scale (TMAS; Taylor, 1953), the "Pt" and Welsh anxiety subscales of the MMPI (Welsh, 1952), and the "Neuroticism" scale of the Maudsley Personality Inventory (Eysenck, 1959). These scales correlate highly with one another (Eriksen & Davids, 1955).

The TMAS consists of 90 true-false items, of which 50 are designed to measure anxiety and the rest are simply filler. The anxiety items were selected on the basis of agreement among clinicians that they reflect important dimensions of anxiety. Although created for research, the TMAS has also been used with some success for clinical purposes. Examples of TMAS items include the following:

1 I am often sick to my stomach.
2 I do not tire quickly.
3 I work under a great deal of tension.

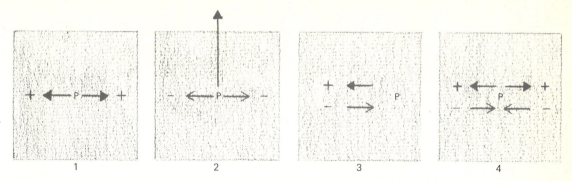

Figure 9-2. The four basic patterns of conflict. **(1)** Approach-approach conflict. The person *P* is attracted at the same time by two incompatible goals. He or she may, for example, want to marry yet want to remain in close proximity to parents. **(2)** Avoidance-avoidance conflict. The person is threatened by two strongly aversive stimuli. The ghetto child who hates school but fears the truant officer is caught in just such a conflict situation. **(3)** Approach-avoidance conflict. The person is drawn to a positive goal which also contains negative elements. A man may enjoy his work and want to excel in it, yet be conscious that the extra time which he devotes to his career is time which he could be spending with his wife and children. In this case the positive goal of his career has the disadvantage that it takes time away from his family. **(4)** Double approach-avoidance conflict. The person is torn between two goals, each of which contains positive and negative elements. The black who can remain within the ghetto and lead a secure life might also think about venturing into the white world, with its material advantages but increased psychological stresses.

These paper-and-pencil measures of anxiety do not correlate as highly with physiological or behavioral measures of anxiety as they do with one another. Maher, summarizing research that attempts to relate TMAS scores to physiological measures of anxiety, says: "The correlations with physiological measures are significant when the latter are measures of physiological changes in stress situations but not significant when they are measures of physiological functioning in resting or non-stressful circumstances" (1966, p. 179). Martin and Sroufe believe that the self-report measures are better indicators of general maladjustment than of anxiety in stressful situations (1970).

Conflict: Which way to turn?

Whenever a person must choose between two or more equally attractive or equally unattractive options, he is in a *conflict* situation. The normal person resolves conflict situations by weighing the pros and cons of each alternative and then choosing one of them. But the neurotic finds himself incapacitated by conflicts that the normal person settles quickly. As he tries ineffectually to cope with the decisions he must make, the neurotic suffers from high tension, hesitation, and fatigue.

One of the conflict situations that Davey B. found difficult to resolve was the conflict between going to college (having to grow up) and staying at home in safe, familiar surroundings (remaining dependent). Unable to make this decision, Davey spent an entire summer in conflict. Tense, unhappy, and unsure what to do in the fall, he finally let his sister make the decision: he followed her advice to go to college.

Models of conflict. Work by Kurt Lewin (1935) and Neal Miller (1959) has led behavioral scientists to outline the four basic patterns of conflict shown in Figure 9-2.

• APPROACH-APPROACH CONFLICT. Approach-approach, the simplest form of conflict, requires the person to choose between two equally attractive alternatives. The approach-approach conflict is unstable because it is likely to be quickly and fairly easily resolved. For example, the high school senior who is accepted by two equally good colleges feels little pain when he or she has to make a choice.

• AVOIDANCE-AVOIDANCE CONFLICT. Avoidance-avoidance conflict is not nearly as pleasant as approach-approach, since it offers two equally unattractive options. Common solutions are to find some sort of compromise, devise a new option, or "leave the field" altogether. (Suicide is the ultimate act of leaving the field.) But some people simply remain, endlessly vacillating within the avoidance-avoidance situation. As soon as they begin to move toward one choice, it becomes more strongly aversive and they move away from it, thus shuttling back and forth between the "frying pan and the fire." Dostoevsky's underground man describes an avoidance-avoidance conflict when he talks of his inability to decide whether it is better to be unknown, unobserved, and unattended to as he is, or to be evil, hated, and despised.

• APPROACH-AVOIDANCE CONFLICT. In an approach-avoidance conflict the same goal or object has both attractive and repellent characteristics. This form of conflict is even more painful than the avoidance-avoidance situation. At one point in her illness, Bertha P. would not drink liquids; drinking had become repulsive to her after she saw her governess let a dog drink from a glass. Thus, even though she craved a glass of water for relief from her thirst, she remained unable to drink.

"Just row away! That's *your* answer to everything!" One way out of a conflict is to withdraw from it. *(Drawing by Claude; © 1970 The New Yorker Magazine, Inc.)*

•DOUBLE APPROACH-AVOIDANCE CONFLICT. Most human conflicts are more complex than any of the three models described above. It is the double approach-avoidance conflict that is the model most appropriate to our daily lives. In this common conflict situation two or more goals are involved, each of which has both attractive and repulsive features. In the conflict that college represented for Davey B., it is possible to identify a double approach-avoidance situation: Davey's two choices—going to college or staying at home— each had two aspects. An attractive part of going to school was the chance to be on his own. But going away also involved the risk of loneliness. Staying at home would allow him to remain in a familiar situation; but staying at home would also mean the usual daylong conflict with his parents. Many other approach-avoidance factors can be identified in Davey's conflict.

The neurotic paradox

One of the questions raised most frequently about neurotic behavior is why the neurotic continues his self-defeating behavior even though he usually recognizes that it is irrational and maladaptive. Why doesn't he withdraw from his neurotic conflicts? If he realizes that it is not reasonable to be afraid of cats or to wash his hands incessantly or to be anxious all the time, why doesn't he just stop? Neurotic behavior persists despite social punishment, personal misery, and the weight of logic. Dollard and Miller refer to the seemingly illogical persistence of neurotic behavior in the face of its aversive effects as "stupid" (1950). As Chapter 10 will show, they recognize that the stupidity arises out of particularly unfortunate life experiences.

Mowrer and Ullman label this so-called stupidity the "neurotic paradox" (1945). They believe that the crucial factor in sustaining neurotic behavior is the unavoidable delay in delivery of the negative consequences. That is, behavior followed immediately by reinforcement and only later by punishment will be maintained even if the delayed punishment is severe and the immediate reinforcement inconsequential. Immediate reward can be vastly more potent than remote punishment. A child who steals a cookie in the morning and is spanked by his father that night will continue to steal many more cookies than the youngster whose hand is slapped as he pulls the cookie out of the jar. It often happens that neurotic behavior serves the immediate function of reducing anxiety. A later punishment—social disapproval, lowered self-esteem, or a sterile existence—may have little effect when set against the potency of the immediate reduction of anxiety. Davey B.'s refusal to enter social situations served the immediate function of reducing his anxiety about coping with social demands. The resultant lack of friends, depression, and boredom were delayed but ineffective consequences of his neurotic behavior.

The behavior of the neurotic does not remain paradoxical when the details of his learning history become known. Its seemingly paradoxical nature arises only from ignorance of the sequence of its development. Neurotic behaviors, like all human behaviors, are lawful. The next chapter will have more to say about them.

Summary

Systematic attempts to describe the neuroses began in the late 1800s when Freud, building on the work of Charcot and Bernheim, suggested that the symptoms of hysteria were psychological rather than organic in etiology. His review of the case of Bertha Pappenheim provided support and documentation for this psychoanalytic view.

A short time later John Watson, by demonstrating the learned nature of a phobia, provided a model for early behavioral views of the etiology of neurosis. These two views, psychoanalytic and behavioral, have long been in conflict about a basic issue: Does neurotic behavior reflect underlying personality conflict, or is it a set of learned maladaptive responses?

What behaviors does the clinician respond to when he applies a label of neurosis? First, the neurotic—no matter how upset he may be—does not fail to recognize that his behavior is impaired. Second, the primary characteristic of the neuroses, the feature which binds the various categories together, is anxiety (though anxiety is not unique to the neuroses).

The American Psychiatric Association recognizes eight categories of neurosis. As listed in DSM-II they are anxiety, hysterical (subdivided into conversion and dissociative types), phobic, obsessive-compulsive, depressive, neurasthenic, depersonalization, and hypochondriacal neurosis. Unfortunately, upon close examination these categories appear more alike than different.

Considerable research has been devoted to differentiating the neuroses from the other forms of psychopathology. The MMPI permits the researcher to distinguish *groups* of neurotics from other diagnostic groups, but the test loses much of its utility in individual diagnostic decisions. The WAIS, the Rorschach, and the TAT have failed to show more than minimal ability to separate neurotics—in groups or individually—from other patients. It has been demonstrated, however, that neurotic patients have some physiological responses which are different from those of either normal or schizophrenic subjects.

Since anxiety has been named repeatedly as the hallmark of neurosis, considerable energy has been devoted to attempts to measure it. As in the case of psychological testing, the differentiation of degrees of anxiety between groups of patients has proved easier than measuring it in single subjects. As well as being anxious, the neurotic person is often in a state of conflict. Davey B., for example, could not choose between staying home and going to college. Conflict situations are generally described in terms of approach and avoidance.

One of the critical questions raised about neurosis is why the neurotic continues to engage in his "stupid," self-defeating behavior. Usually he recognizes the foolishness of what he does, so why doesn't he stop? This persistence of neurotic behavior in spite of logic and common sense has been called the neurotic paradox. In terms of the laws of learning, the neurotic keeps on with his maladaptive behavior because it is followed immediately by reinforcement and only later by punishment.

CHAPTER TEN

The neuroses: Etiology and treatment

Will M. ● Truda S. ● Etiology ● Treatment ●
Psychotherapy, behavior therapy, or drugs: The great
controversy

**WILL M.:
ONE MAN'S
PRIVATE
CHAOS IN
NEWARK**

By the time of the Newark riots in 1967, Will M. was so sunk in his own trouble that he hardly noticed them. A black civil servant, he "had it made" economically and socially to an extent that few other black residents of Newark could hope for. But the greyness that had begun to color his world—the sameness he saw in his job, his home, and his family—all gave him the feeling that life is something to be endured, not enjoyed.

Will was born in 1915 outside a small "black belt" town in south-western Alabama. The eldest of nine children, he spent the first four years of his life on the tenant farm where his mother and father (Mae and Will, Senior) raised cotton. But when things got bad shortly after World War I, in part because of a succession of drought years, the family moved up North. First they went to Cleveland to live with one of Mr. M.'s brothers, then to Newark to live with Mrs. M.'s favorite cousin, who had left Alabama before Will was born.

Will took the move away from Alabama harder than the two younger M. children because he missed his grandparents. Though he never admitted it to his mother and father, he felt much closer to his grandparents, especially his grandmother, than to his parents. Down South his parents had to spend exhausting hours in the fields, especially when the weather was warm and the cotton needed tending, while his grandparents took care of the children. And because Will was the first grandchild, he had always been the favorite.

Will's parents were family-centered people, and in Newark it was hard for them to leave the children with a local girl while they worked in nearby factories. But living was expensive in Newark, partly because the M. family was continuing to grow, so both parents had to work even longer hours than they had "down home."

On Sundays and holidays the family's life centered on the African Methodist Episcopal Church, a substitute for the small Pentacostal

(Dorothea Lange from Magnum)

275

church in Alabama where the parents had been active. As a result, Will's home was pervaded by a fundamentalist approach to the Bible and a strict code of morality that was applied to all thought and behavior. On Sundays the family went to church in the morning, returned home for afternoon meditation, then went back to church for gospel singing, revelation, and faith healing. In the same dedicated spirit, weekdays were for school. The M.'s believed that education was the path to social and economic mobility, security, and respect, middle-class goals that they wanted their children to achieve. Only on Saturdays did Will and the other M. children have any time to themselves. Even then, somehow, they felt a little guilty when they played in the park or on the street or went downtown with friends. It seemed as if they should be doing homework, earning money, or helping the people in the neighborhood who were less fortunate than the M.'s. Will took a job as soon as he could, working in the kosher meatmarket down the street. Mr. Kassell, the proprietor, acknowledged that Will was as bright, ambitious, polite, and hardworking as any of his own children, an oft-repeated remark which Will and his family took as a compliment.

Like most of his brothers and sisters, Will did well in grammar school and even better in high school, where he devoted himself to his studies and not to the "idle socializing" that his parents said was the work of the devil. At that time Newark's schools were widely regarded as the best in the state and among the best in the country—a far cry from most urban schools today. When he graduated from Central High School, it was hard for Will to accept the fact that he could not go to college. But it was 1933, the height of the Depression, and the M.'s had no money. Any last hope that Will might be able to afford college was lost when his father had a stroke and died in 1935.

Will is one of those rare men who married the first (and only) girl he ever kissed. He and Jolynn, a girl from as fundamentalist a family as his own, met (at a church social) when both were high school seniors. After their marriage, which took place in the church where they had met, Will and Jolynn moved down the street from his mother and lived there until early 1942, when Will was drafted.

Because of his prewar job in the mail room of a large Newark life insurance company—about the only white-collar job a black could get then—Will was sent to clerk-typist school at Fort Dix. He was older (27) than most of the draftees and had bad eyesight, so he was assigned to spend the duration of the war at an army hospital in Pennyslvania. He worked as an admitting clerk, then as payroll NCO, then as NCO-in-charge of the whole enlisted company servicing the hospital administrative structure. After the war his excellent service record qualified him for a good job in the admitting office of a Veterans Administration hospital near Newark, the same hospital in which Webster R., a distant cousin, was to spend many months twenty-five years later. (The story of Webster R., a Vietnam veteran whose brain was severely damaged by shrapnel, is told in Chapter 17.)

As a civil servant Will was able, responsible, and hardworking, not surprising in view of the respect for these virtues that he learned during his youth. For a black without a college degree, he rose rapidly; by 1965 he was supervisor of medical records at a VA regional office near his home and earned good pay as a GS-9. He and his wife had two children—both of whom were healthy, hardworking, and seemingly happy—a small home in Newark's central ward, and a harmonious marriage. If Will did not possess Newark's most sparkling personality—if he did not smile easily or laugh readily—he was a loving father and husband, a good friend, and a person who seemed largely satisfied with a satisfactory lot in life.

Then Will's mother died, and gradually he began to change. He himself didn't notice it until Jolynn, not a person given to nagging, said with some heat that he had become irritable around the house, picking on the children, criticizing her housekeeping, finding fault with the neighbors. Not only was it out of character for Jolynn to complain, but the behavior she complained about was out of character for Will. Though he had always been a quiet, reserved man, he and his family had enjoyed unusually close relationships characterized by mutual respect and affection. Jolynn's criticism worried Will a great deal, especially because he himself began to notice anger rising suddenly when he did not expect it. He did increasingly feel, however, that it was justified anger. It seemed to him that everyone took him for granted, that he only existed to bring home the paycheck, not to be praised or supported or given some tangible sign of love.

Will began to notice that his work was becoming a burden to be carried, an eight-hour daily episode to be lived through. Before, it had given him satisfaction to know that the records under his charge were up to date, in excellent order, and instantly available. He had been proud that the seven people under him liked him, respected him, and looked to him for leadership. Now he began to doubt the adequacy of his leadership and the quality of his section's work. Previously he had taken pleasure in the fact that his was the best job held by a noncollege graduate in the regional office. Now he compared himself unfavorably with others who had better jobs and earned more money.

There were obvious behavioral changes too. His appetite, never particularly robust, fell off, and he lost a lot of weight. He had always been able to get a good night's sleep, but now it was hard for him to drop off, and often he came awake an hour or two before he had to get up in the morning. Will and Jolynn's sexual relationship, always one of the best aspects of their excellent marriage, deteriorated because he rarely wanted to make love any more. Jolynn became convinced that Will had lost interest in her, that she was too old to have any sex appeal, and his sexual rejection made her snappy with him in other situations.

It was not until about a year and a half after his mother's death that Will began to experience the depressed mood which his therapist later felt was basic to the other changes in his behavior. To him these feelings of depression were the worst of all the strange things that were happening to him. He had never been one to toot his own horn, but he had always lived with the quiet conviction that he was as bright, as hardworking, and as successful as the next man. Now it seemed to him that he was not only not as good as the next man, but much worse. As father, husband, employee, lover, citizen, or black man, he perceived his own limitations in strong, insistent terms.

Things came to a head when Will M.—husband, father, valued employee, church deacon, upright citizen—attempted suicide one night by carbon monoxide poisoning. Found unconscious by his son shortly before it would have been too late, Will was first treated medically, then as an inpatient on the psychiatric ward of the nearby VA hospital. Now receiving antidepressive medicine and outpatient counseling from a VA social worker, as well as lots of support from an understanding wife and children, Will M. seems to be safely through the worst period of his life.

(G. D. Hackett)

TRUDA S.: BRINGING ORDER TO CHAOS IN TEREZIN

Born in 1929, the first child of well-to-do parents, Truda Steiner lived until she was 13 in Brno, Czechoslovakia, a middle-sized city southeast of Prague. Remembering those years now with fondness and nostalgia, Truda speaks of the warmth and closeness of her family and the emphasis her parents placed upon secular and religious learning, even for girls. She recalls with pleasure the delight she and the other Jewish children in Brno took in the return of spring to the fields surrounding the Brno ghetto after the long, harsh Czechoslovakian winter. About the only flaw she remembers in those early years was her parents' efforts to get her to use the toilet on their schedule rather than her own. Like most other well-educated, "modern" Brno Jewish parents, they felt it was important to toilet-train their children early and efficiently. Truda did not agree, and before and after her second birthday she and her mother went through six months or so that were traumatic for both of them.

Starting around her eleventh birthday, Truda can remember low-flying airplanes with black swastikas on their wings, hard-faced German soldiers in grey uniforms, German tanks in the streets. Suddenly there was not enough to eat, and there was the frightening awareness that her parents were no longer certain of their ability to raise their children in serenity and security.

Things grew even worse for a patriotic family who had thought that the German occupation of Czechoslovakia was quite bad enough. Truda's father lost his position in a leading Brno law firm; the family had to move from their comfortable apartment to a cramped one elsewhere; Truda's uncle was arrested and imprisoned. These changes came because the Steiners were unlucky enough to be Jews in a Europe occupied by Hitler's Third Reich. For the same reason Truda had to stop her education; the Jewish secondary school she attended was closed by the Nazis.

Truda remembers that her brother Jiri and some of his friends got into a fight with a group of Hitler Youth, near the cathedral in Brno. Because they were young, naïve, and filled with love of country, Jiri and his friends fought valiantly and won. As a result the Steiner family was visited late the following night by a young Gestapo captain and his aide, who informed them that such a thing was never to happen again, that Jews were to accept whatever they were given, that Hitler Youth had rights which others did not.

Transports for Terezin began to leave Brno in early 1942. The Steiners received their transport notice in March; friends, relatives, and non-Jewish neighbors came to say goodbye and to be given the family's belongings, for the Steiners knew they could take nothing with them. Truda had to present her dressing table, a gift on her twelfth birthday, to a rosy-cheeked classmate "who promised to keep

(G. D. Hackett)

279

it for me until we returned to Brno." Her canopy bed went to a neighbor down the street; her lithograph of the Joseph II fortress was taken by her father's tailor, the only Gentile tailor in Brno.

The trip to Terezin was in stages, first to a town no more than 20 miles from Brno, where the Steiners and sixty other families lived for a week in a school building that had been cleared out for them. Then they boarded a train for the three-day trip to Terezin, which was punctuated by long stops, continuous head counts, little food, less water, and always the German soldiers and the hatred in their eyes. It was Truda's first train trip, though she had often dreamed of traveling firstclass to Prague or Vienna.

Despite the stresses to which she had been exposed under the German occupation, it was only after the Steiners arrived at Terezin that Truda began to show the unusual patterns of behavior that have dominated her life ever since. In many ways the move to Terezin was harder on her than the rest of the family, though objectively she lost the least. Her psychological suffering, however, was intense. In Terezin families had to live apart, husbands separate from wives, boys and girls separate from parents and from each other. While families could occasionally meet together, the time and frequency of such reunions was rigidly controlled. But it was not so much the separation from her family, or even the constant fear of a forced movement to another more terrible concentration camp, that tormented Truda; what she could not bear was the material, psychological, and social disorder of Terezin. Raised in a totally predictable middle-class household, she had entered adolescence protected by cleanliness, order, and serenity. Now that everything around her was chaotic, disorganized, and unpredictable, her life seemed intolerable, and her behavior began to change gradually but profoundly.

In Brno she had liked having her room clean and neat, her furniture placed just so, her dresses and skirts hung straight and in an order she had worked out. Now in Terezin Truda developed a passion for order. Her sleeping mat had to be fastidiously made up and arranged, her few worn, soiled clothes hung just so, her one extra pair of shoes exactly aligned with the foot of her mat. Some of the people who lived around her began to feel that her behavior was exceeding the normal when Truda, who was one of the most enthusiastic members of an amateur dance group, began to excuse herself from rehearsals, then from the weekly performances at the Terezinstadt library. Her rituals of orderliness were simply taking most of her time; she had none left for dancing.

Now, in what others called a "stupid" reaction to the dirt and filth which were constants in Terezin life, she developed a passion for preventing her clothes and body from getting dirty. Though water was often in short supply, Truda took every opportunity to wash her hands and face. When water was relatively plentiful she would make as many as forty trips a day to the washbasin, and her hands and face grew red and chapped. And because clothes got dirty so easily in Terezin, Truda spent a great part of her day washing and then pressing her few dresses.

Trying to avoid coming into contact with dirt in the first place was most difficult of all, since the thousands of people who came to live in the camp's overcrowded quarters brought with them disease, filth, and insect parasites that swarmed everywhere. Truda's solution was to circumscribe her life space. She stopped going out of her house altogether, even when the spring sun warmed up the usual Terezin chill. At one point she would not leave her own small living area for fear that it would become disordered and dirtied in her absence. Her father arranged for someone to take her food once a day. When he could he also sent her Czech novels by Hasek and Polacek (himself a Terezin resident), Czech plays by Capek and Stech, Czech poems by Dyk and Neruda—all offering nourishment for Truda's soul that was as important as the pitifully little food she ate.

And so Truda remained for almost a year—confined by invisible but nonetheless inviolable psychological bonds to the simple order of straw mat, clean hands, and unsullied dresses. Yet all around her, Terezin bustled with life, learning, and sometimes laughter. Then, a few months before the Steiner family was transported from Terezin to Auschwitz (where her parents, a sister, and a brother died in the gas chambers), Truda began to venture out of her web of security. She had made friends with a girl, Eva, who was becoming frustrated at Truda's unwillingness to accompany her to school, to concerts and plays, and on visits to the boys' and parents' areas.

As her affection for Eva grew, Truda did for her what she could not earlier do for her parents: she left the safety of her ordered room and the security of her rituals for the disordered stimulation of Terezin. From small beginnings she began to spend more and more time away from her house, and go longer and longer periods without having to wash her hands, face, and clothes. She tolerated the company of people who might be carriers of dirt or disease or disorder. Toward the end of her stay in Terezin, in what was a great personal triumph for Eva, Truda appeared onstage in the chorus of the children's opera *Brundibar* in a performance watched by both her parents.

Shortly afterwards, Truda and her family reentered the familiar transport vans, this time for Auschwitz. Truda survived and is now a married woman in her middle forties living in Prague. She remembers her years in Terezin with the curious detachment that the passage of time and the intensity of the trauma she suffered during

An inmate's drawing of a makeshift theatre in the Terezin prison camp—perhaps the one where Truda Steiner sang in *Brundibar*. (Council of Jewish Communities, 1965)

the war have given many people. Even now she is a person who finds it difficult to "relax and enjoy life." Her house is spotless, she herself is always spic and span, and she orders her life and those of her husband and two children with a firm hand. Today, however, she can withstand the considerable psychological pain that results when things are not "quite right"—which for her means not in order. Truda is married to another former prisoner in Terezin—one of the few remaining Jewish physicians in all Czechoslovakia. Truda often wonders why she broke down precisely as she did under the stresses of Terezin, instead of showing the psychotic behavior, depression, or overwhelming anxiety that many of the other inmates did. Her husband, who is an internist, not a psychiatrist, does not know either.

Is neurotic behavior really stupid?

As the last chapter pointed out, one of the central questions about neurotic behavior concerns its paradoxical qualities. Specifically, why is it maintained? Obviously it is maladaptive and unpleasant, and there is no readily apparent reason why the neurotic keeps on with behavior that is so "stupid," as Dollard and Miller have called it (1950).

Think about the neurotic behavior of Truda Steiner and Will M.; was it stupid? Perhaps not completely. While Truda's compulsions did prevent her from entering into the rich and busy life of Terezin, they also lessened for her the daily ration of humiliation, anxiety, and degradation that everyone else had to put up with. Further, her behavior probably increased the amount of attention she received from her father, who sent her food and books and worried about her condition. Perhaps most important, her compulsions permitted her to be legitimately special and out of the ordinary—self-perceptions which may have contributed to her success in staying alive at Auschwitz.

Making sense out of Will M.'s neurotic depression is more difficult, because it really did seem a stupid response to a life that appeared to be a happy one. Though Will was not an outstanding success by the standards of white society, he did have a secure job with some status for which he had worked very hard. He also had a loyal wife, two healthy, bright children, and a future he could look forward to. Yet Will became more and more unhappy, more and more depressed. Was his behavior only stupid, or did it serve a function?

The traditional psychoanalytic view would be that Will's behavior was prolonged mourning for his mother: a reasonable hypothesis, since his behavior changes began soon after she died. Furthermore, psychoanalytic theory would trace his neurosis back to its antecedents—perhaps to his childhood mourning when he had to leave his grandparents. Despite the apparent congruence between dynamic theory and fact in this instance, one must ask how many nondepressed persons could point to comparable losses without comparable symptomatic behavior. One must also ask whether this theoretical statement makes sense out of Will's behavior. In our view, it does not.

On the other hand, if Will's behavior is viewed as an effort (though not a calculated one) to elicit a whole set of new responses to him from his environment, it makes somewhat more sense. His depression brought him sympathy, compassion, and understanding from persons in his environment (wife, children, friends) who had previously treated him with affection but with relatively little understanding. Will himself said to one of the psychologists at the VA regional office where he worked, "Getting depressed brought out all kinds of concern from people who had never really acknowledged that I was a person with real feelings." Though it is not a complete explanation of Will M.'s neurotic depression, this *functional analysis* of his behavior does effectively remove the "stupid" label.

How well do Will M.'s neurotic depression and Truda Steiner's obsessive-compulsive neurosis fit the DSM II descriptions? The answer reveals something of the process by which textbook definitions of psychopathology are converted to diagnostic labels that describe real behavior.

Will's increasing irritability, self-doubts, loss of self-esteem, deepening depression, disturbed sexual activity and sleep habits, loss of appetite, distractibility, and finally, suicidal behavior all point to depression as the diagnosis. And the facts that these behaviors took shape soon after the death of the patient's mother, and occurred "out of the blue" in a person whose adjustment to life had been excellent, indicate that the depression was neurotic (though in a "textbook" case, the precipitating circumstances would have been more obvious).

The other diagnoses which are usually considered in cases of depression—involutional melancholia, manic-depressive psychosis, and schizo-affective schizophrenia—do not apply to Will. Manic-depressive psychosis and schizo-affective schizophrenia are psychotic reactions involving loss of reality testing, loss of contact with reality, and actual distortion of environmental events. Though Will was certainly making his life much worse than it really was, he did not apply the irrational logic of the psychotic to it. As for involutional melancholia, it is true that Will's depression occurred during what is commonly considered the involutional period (between 50 and 60 years of age). But two facts oppose this diagnostic decision. First, the roots of his overly severe judgment of his own competence can be clearly seen in his rigid, moralistic upbringing, his parents' high standards of conduct and achievement, and his consequent high expectations for himself. In other words, Will's difficulties with self-esteem can be traced to his background. Second, Will's depression was debilitating but did not totally disable him, whereas involutional melancholia is usually a completely disruptive disorder with prominent psychotic behavioral elements.

Truda Steiner's obsessive-compulsive neurosis, like Will M's neurotic depression, was not a textbook case. In large part this was because of the special circumstances which provoked its appearance. If Truda had gone through adolescence at home in Brno uninterrupted by war, her compulsions might simply have been expressed as a need for excessive cleanliness and order. Her relationships with other people almost certainly would not have suffered as they did in Terezin, because her compulsive behavior would not have been so all-encompassing. In Terezin, however, there was no other way for Truda to order her life than to withdraw as completely as possible from the chaos of the concentration camp. What is observed in Truda's behavior is not only the compulsions which label her disorder, though they were present in good quantity. What is also seen is Truda's life reduced to its basics, to a monastic existence that was the only way in which she could manage her extreme anxiety.

By now the theme of this book—the diverse ways by which society influences psychopathology—ought to be taking on meaning and substance for you. Certainly the life circumstances surrounding Truda and Will's behavior had important effects on their psychopathology. During more ordinary times, Truda's compulsions might have taken a more benign form than they did under the severe physical, emotional, and environmental stresses of Terezin. And though Truda's psychopathology protected her from some of the most trying aspects of Terezin, it also took a toll that showed itself later when she was free as continuing nervousness, apprehension, and inability to enjoy life.

As for Will M.'s psychopathology, one important social influence was the fundamentalist religious tradition in which he grew up. Emphasizing as it did the pervasiveness of individual sin and moral responsibility, it must have played a major role later in Will's harsh condemnation of his own competence. Speculating about the impact of his race on his psychopathology is riskier. But it is possible to argue that if he had been a white man with the same intelligence, drive, and social skills, his level of achievement would have been a good deal higher and he might not have been so scornful of it. Further, if Will's mother had not been forced to work when he was young, his feelings about her death might not have caused the emotional turmoil he experienced. That is, one popular theory of depression treats it as a response to the loss of a loved one about whom the person feels considerable ambivalence. While Will acknowledged his love and respect for his mother, these feelings were combined with some anger that she had been away so much during his early years. In fact, in the rare moments when he permitted himself to speculate, Will wondered how his life would have turned out if he had been a white child in a white family in which only the father had to work.

Etiology of the neuroses

As with the schizophrenias, a proved etiology or set of etiologies to explain the neuroses has not been established. Instead there is a great variety of theories to suit every scientific taste. Some, like "classical" psychoanalytic theory and the other dynamic theories, have been in existence since the turn of the century, when the neuroses were set off as disorders distinct from the dementias and the organic conditions. Others, like the interpersonal theories of the "neo-Freudian" psychologists, evolved from psychoanalysis during the 1930s and 1940s. Still others, namely the existential

Freud around the time he put forth his theory of neurotic etiology. *(Culver Pictures, Inc.)*

and behavioral theories of etiology, are very recent but very important additions that have generated a great outpouring of research and therapeutic experimentation.

Classical psychoanalytic theories

Since most of Freud's clinical work was with neurotic patients, he built psychoanalytic theory largely on the psychic mechanisms he observed in them. As a result, *the psychoanalytic theory of neurosis is psychoanalytic theory's most important etiologic statement.* The successive refinements and alterations which this statement underwent through Freud's life mirror changes in Freud's thinking that affected the whole structure of psychoanalytic theory.

Freud's earliest theory of the etiology of the neuroses arose after he began using the "cathartic" method with hysterics. He encouraged patients to relate in sometimes painful detail the specifics of early encounters with parents, siblings, and other people who were important to them. Freud believed that this "unburdening" would directly alleviate his patients' discomfort. After a time he noticed that many of the female hysterics he treated by this technique "remembered" a sexual seduction at an early age, usually by their fathers.

As a result, Freud concluded that all hysterical neuroses are brought on by unconscious memories of early seductions. This was a change from his earlier opinion that anxiety neurosis and neurasthenia (a common neurotic syndrome that includes fatigue, listlessness, headache, irritability, and digestive disturbances) were associated with disturbances in the biochemistry of sexuality. Specifically, he had believed that anxiety neurosis was induced by sexual stimulation which failed to culminate in orgasm and that neurasthenia was caused by excessive masturbation.

Later, however, Freud changed his mind a third time, because he was unable to validate the existence of so many early seductions. He decided that most of the sexual seductions his patients remembered were fantasy rather than fact. Discarding his early-seduction hypothesis, he undertook the formulation of a consistent etiology for all the neuroses.

Freud's "classical" psychoanalytic model explains the development of a neurosis as a sequence with four elements:

1 The patient experiences inner conflict between drives and fears (that is, between id and superego functions—see Chapter 4). The conflict prevents "drive discharge" (overt or disguised expression of desires, impulses, or wishes). For example, Freud said that Little Hans, whose case was analyzed in Chapter 4, suffered from conflict between his sexual feelings for his mother and his love for and fear of his father.
2 Sexual drives are usually involved in these conflicts. (Hans's drives were sexual as well as aggressive.)
3 The conflict cannot be "worked through" to resolution by the logical, rational in-

fluence of the ego. In consequence, energy from the unacceptable drives which have been repressed from consciousness begins to plague the individual in the form of anxiety or other neurotic behaviors. According to Freud, Hans failed to resolve the conflict caused by his unacceptable love for his mother. Proof of this came only indirectly: Freud assumed that if Hans had worked through his conflict, he would not have been so ambivalent about his father or his wish to "coax with" (caress) his mother, and would not have shown such insatiable curiosity about sexual functioning. Most important, Freud believed that if Hans had not been in neurotic conflict, he would not have been phobic.

4 Repression does not eliminate powerful drives. It simply forces them "underground," where they seek expression through neurotic symptoms. Thus Hans's phobias were "conscious equivalents" of the unacceptable sexual and aggressive feelings he had for his mother and father.

Empirical efforts to validate some of the key elements of psychoanalytic theory began shortly after Freud set forth the bulk of it. They reached their peak during the 1930s and 1940s, in part because the Rorschach and TAT projective techniques were coming into widespread use. Experimental psychodynamics research continues still, though no longer with such vigor. This decline in enthusiasm reflects the disappointing results of earlier efforts to validate its structures and mechanisms (Eysenck, 1972; Goldfried & Kent, 1972; Maher, 1966). Current research includes studies designed to relate the timing and nature of early experiences to later psychopathology (Kokonis, 1972; Sarnoff, 1971), to identify relationships among levels of psychosexual development and defense mechanisms (Renik, 1971; Rosenwald, 1972), to illuminate relationships among behavior and its psychic mediators, the ego, id, and superego (Cooperman & Child, 1971; Lancaster, 1970), and to trace the many behavioral pathways of the drives (Fancher & Strahan, 1971).

Dynamic researchers have also made some impressive efforts to relate psychoanalytic theory and practice to contemporary problems. An example was the 1969 conference on the contribution of psychoanalysis to community psychology, held at Adelphi University. The records of that conference suggest that psychoanalytic constructs may be directly relevant to such current concerns as drug addiction, alcoholism, community-action projects, and urban crime (Milman & Goldman, 1971).

Other psychoanalytic theories

C. G. Jung, the first of Freud's followers to set forth a separate theory of neurosis, traced the development of neurosis to the "neurotic problems" of the patient's mother and father. Among these problems, Jung said, were disguised or unacknowledged parental discord, the influence of the parents' repressed instinctual needs and desires, and the impact of their anxieties (1915). Jung rejected what he saw as Freud's inordinate emphasis upon sexuality as the all-pervasive etiological factor in the development of neurosis. In another deviation from classical Freudian theory, Jung said that neurotics sometimes repress acceptable as well as unacceptable personality components.

In therapy with neurotics Jung therefore tried to help them develop and expand their strengths as well as adjust to their weaknesses. If he had been treating Will M. for his depression Jung might have encouraged him to become more assertive with his family and friends, more competitive on the job, and more energetic in his pursuit of pleasure for himself. "Repression" of these behavioral potentials may have been adaptive for Will in that they "smoothed his way" interpersonally. But it may also have contributed to Will's negative view of himself and his own capabilities —a factor with undoubted etiologic significance for the development of his depression.

Alfred Adler, another of Freud's early followers, traced the neuroses to feelings of

C. G. Jung. *(The Bettmann Archive)*

inferiority that he believed all children experience in relation to their bigger, stronger, wiser parents. These early feelings, Adler wrote, cause adult neurotics to experience severe inferiority feelings—"inferiority complexes"—which derive specifically from "organ inferiority" during childhood (1917). Organ inferiority refers to the presumed inadequacy that little boys feel, for example, when they observe their father's penis and despair of ever having one that size. In reaction to these omnipresent feelings of inferiority, Adler continued, the neurotic overcompensates by striving endlessly to prove to himself and others that he is not really inferior.

Adler later came to regard the inferiority complex as a reaction not simply to the physical inferiority of the child's sexual organs but also to his total smallness and helplessness in relation to adults. As a consequence, over-

Alfred Adler. *(The Bettmann Archive)*

Erich Fromm.

compensation of many kinds is considered neurotic by Adlerians. They now include the "masculine protest" and the "will to power" in this category. The gay liberation and womans' liberation movements are regarded by Adlerians as responses to feelings of inferiority.

Interpersonal theories

Personality theorists have also explained the development of neurosis from the vantage point of cultural and interpersonal influences. Though these authorities accept the intrapsychic (psychoanalytic) model, they assume that environmental as well as personal factors are involved. Their approach appears to some people more relevant to contemporary concerns than the older, exclusively psychoanalytic models of psychopathology.

One of the first of the "neo-Freudian" interpersonal psychologists, Karen Horney, published a thoughtful cultural redefinition of neurosis in 1937. She added a cogent criticism of Freud's libido (sexual) theories in 1939.

In both publications Horney stressed the etiological importance of the patient's present-day life situation, although she acknowledged that persons with whom a patient had come into contact during maturation had exerted a powerful influence on the development of his behavior, including neurotic behavior. But Horney believed that later attitudes toward authority are not, for example, identical with the individual's feelings about his mother at the age of 3. Though such early feelings form the base on which attitudes toward authority develop later, they are added to and changed during the process of growing up by subsequent experiences with parents and other authority figures. The final transference picture is an end result of all such experiences.

Another important figure in the gradual "culturalization" of psychoanalytic concepts of neurosis was Erich Fromm, whose *Escape from Freedom* (1941) remains required reading for many liberal arts students. Fromm's thesis in the book was that modern men and women become neurotic because they are not equipped to handle the freedom of opportunity, choice, and association which modern culture gives them. Fromm believed that as people come to realize how separate they are from each other in modern society, they come to feel more and more isolated, more and more alone. As a result they begin to want to return to their earlier state of solidarity with one another. Unfortunately, they no longer have such an option. While they have gained freedom from the institutions of society, they have not acquired the complementary freedom to develop as separate yet intact persons. As a consequence they may evolve irrational, counterproductive methods to rejoin the group. Among these are sado-masochism, destructiveness, or automaton conformity.

To Fromm, Nazism was a composite of all these neurotic methods for effecting the "escape from freedom." There are echoes of Fromm's thesis in some of Rudolph Hess's behavior (Chapter 4), though most of it stems more clearly from psychosis. Truda Steiner's retreat from the realities of Terezin also can be seen as a flight from freedom—from the anxieties that uncertainty, disorder, and lack of structure fostered in her.

Existential theories

Existential or phenomenological approaches to neurosis—and especially to anxiety—conceptualize people not as collections of static, unchanging behavioral or intrapsychic elements, but as organisms that are continually changing. Man is always either being or becoming; he never just *is*. And existential theorists (May, Minkowski, Straus, and Binswanger) believe that a person can be understood only in terms of what he is becoming—what he is moving toward—rather than in terms of what he is at any given moment.

In the existential viewpoint it is important to recognize that man is the only animal who knows that there will be a time when he is not, when he will be a nonbeing. Recognition of his future makes man's present existence meaningful; it also creates the "existential anxiety" which sets man off from lower organisms. But too intense an awareness of the imminence of nonbeing—the certainty of death—precipitates anxiety intense enough to prevent a satisfactory relationship with the world. Neurosis to the existentialist, then, is an awareness of future nonbeing that is too intense to permit present "being" and "becoming."

Behavioral theories

John Dollard and Neal Miller's *Personality and Psychotherapy* (1950) was the first coherent attempt to apply the principles of learning theory to the etiology and treatment of abnormal behavior. Though their work benefited considerably from the learning theory and earlier research of Clark Hull (1943), Dollard and Miller's book set off on its own in an important new applied direction. This new direction, however, departed only slightly from dynamic approaches to psychopathology. In essence, Dollard and Miller's model of psychopathology took psychoanalytic concepts and translated them into behavioral terms.

John Dollard.

An excerpt from *Personality and Psychotherapy* illustrates the important bridge that the book built between psychoanalysis and behaviorism:

In a phobia acquired under traumatic conditions of combat the relevant events are recent and well-known. . . . Such cases provide one of the simplest and most convincing illustrations of the learning of a symptom. The essential points are illustrated by the case of a pilot who was interviewed by one of the authors. This officer had not shown any abnormal fear of airplanes before being sent on a particularly difficult mission to bomb distant and well-defended oil refineries. His squadron was under heavy attack on the way to the target. . . . As they came in above the rooftops, bombs and oil tanks were exploding. The pilot's plane was tossed violently about and damaged while nearby planes disappeared in a wall of fire. Since this pilot's damaged plane could not regain altitude, he had to fly back alone at reduced speed and was subject to repeated violent fighter attack which killed several crew members and repeatedly threatened to destroy them all. When they finally reached the Mediterranean, they were low on gas and had to ditch the airplane in the open sea. The survivors drifted on a life raft and eventually were rescued. Many times during this mission the pilot was exposed to intensely fear-provoking stimuli such as violent explosions and the sight of other planes going down and comrades being killed. It is known that intense fear-provoking stimuli of this kind act to reinforce fear as a response to other cues present at the same time. . . . Because he had already learned to avoid objects that he feared, he had a strong tendency to look away and walk away from airplanes. Whenever he did this, he removed the cues eliciting the fear and hence felt much less frightened. A reduction in any strong drive such as fear serves to reinforce the immediately preceding responses. . . . To summarize, under traumatic conditions of combat the intense drive of fear was learned as a response to the airplane and everything connected with it. The fear generalized from the cues of this airplane to the similar cues of other airplanes. This intense fear motivated responses of avoiding airplanes, and whenever any one of these responses was successful, it was reinforced by a reduction in the strength of the fear. . . . In phobias the responses of avoidance and their reinforcement by a reduction in the strength of a fear is almost always quite clear. The origin of the drive of fear may be obvious or obscure; it often traces back to childhood conflicts about sex and aggression. [Pp. 157–158, 161]

This explanation combines behavioral themes, occasional Hullian assumptions, and scraps of psychoanalytic theory. Behavioral themes include the assumption that phobic behavior can be learned, that specific fears can generalize to related stimuli, and that avoidance responses can be explained by direct reference to the original phobic stimuli. Hull's theory is apparent in the references to the "strength of fear" and the formal mechanisms responsible for this "habit strength." The psychoanalytic tradition probably caused the "origins of the drive of fear" to be discussed in relation to sexual and aggressive impulses experienced during childhood. Although

J. Wolpe.

present-day behavioral views of the etiology of the neurosis differ considerably from Dollard and Miller's, their contribution was substantial. The revolutionary aspect of their approach was its insistence that the neuroses could be explained by known laws of learning rather than solely by intrapsychic mechanisms whose existence can only be deduced because of the existence of a neurosis.

The immediate effect of *Personality and Psychotherapy* was to stimulate heated discussion of its radical premises. A more important delayed reaction was an effort to develop a "purer" theory of psychopathology that would be independent of psychoanalytic influence. One of the earliest theorists engaged in this effort was Hans Eysenck of the Institute of Psychiatry in London, who took the position that neurosis can be defined according to two objective behavioral dimensions: neuroticism-nonneuroticism and extroversion-introversion (1957). He claimed that both these dimensions of neurosis have strong underlying genetic components (1961). He described neuroticism as "an inherited autonomic overreactivity," concluding from his own research and that of others (Franks, 1960) that introversion is characterized "by strong conditionability." Hence, he concluded, the focal neurotic symptom of anxiety appears most often in "dysthymics"—neurotic introverts.

Despite the elegance of his research and the volume, brilliance, and wit of his writings, Eysenck has had little direct influence on current behavioral conceptions of the etiology of the neuroses. One reason is that his commitment to his own theories has prevented him from being objective about those of others. By contrast, Wolpe's views on the etiology and treatment of the phobias, the anxiety reactions, and the obsessions have had a profound impact on other theorists. Yet Wolpe has been thoroughly criticized for performing what many (Bandura, 1969; Eysenck, 1972; Wilson, 1973; Wilson & Davison, 1971), but not all (Reid, 1973), researchers consider to be unwarranted extrapolation from the animal laboratory to the consulting room.

Neal E. Miller.

Wolpe's view, in essence, is that human neuroses are parallel to "experimental neurosis" (see Chapter 9) in animals in three important respects: (1) acquisition by learning, (2) primary stimulus generalization, and (3) elimination by unlearning. Following his demonstration of these variables in the "experimental neuroses" of cats (1952, 1958), Wolpe conducted a series of studies on his patients and concluded that human neuroses follow the same laws of learning and unlearning (1969). Regarding acquisition, he said: "It was invariably found that neurotic reactions whose origin could be dated to . . . either a particular occasion of great distress or else the repeated arousal of anxiety in a recurrent situation . . . had come to be evocable by stimuli similar to those that were to the forefront in the precipitating situation" (1969, p. 9). Regarding the generalization of human neurotic reactions, he said: "As in the animal neuroses, their intensity is determined by the degree of similarity of the evoking stimulus to a zenithal stimulus that is often identical with the original conditioned stimulus" (p. 9). He believes that experimental extinction is the necessary treatment for these conditions; the specific technique to be used is systematic desensitization, which "is effective in all neuroses and not only in unitary phobias" (p. 13).

A number of recent studies have raised serious questions about Wolpe's belief that phobic behavior in humans is a conditioned autonomic response. For example, Rappaport (1972) and Leitenberg and his co-workers (1971) report that their phobic subjects showed reduction in phobic avoidance behavior without consistent changes in physiological responses. Leitenberg also reports no consistent pattern of heart rate and avoidance behavior. Some of the subjects in these studies experienced an increase in heart rate as avoidance decreased; others showed a decrease in heart rate under the same conditions; others registered no change in heart rate. Several subjects showed a decrease in heart rate only after phobic avoidance behavior had decreased.

An alternative explanation of the reduction of avoidance behavior suggests that it is the person's *cognitive state* which determines the interpretation he gives to physiological responses. The specifics of this view, put forth by Schachter (1964) on the basis of extensive research, were applied to depression in Chapter 8. Research derived from Schachter's hypothesis would predict that subjects who were told that they were showing physiological signs of reduced anxiety would display a reduction in avoidance behavior. Valins and Ray investigated the hypothesis and found data to support it (1967). Unfortunately, several later attempts to replicate the Valins and Ray study failed to confirm its findings (Rosen et al., 1972; Sushinsky & Bootzin, 1970). Thus, a satisfactory explanation of the alteration in avoidance behavior and changes in physiological responses which accompany anxiety has yet to be provided.

Wolpe's views on the etiology of neurotic behavior have also been attacked on other grounds. Dynamic theorists criticize the simplicity of his unitary explanation for a complex, multifaceted phenomenon (Freeman, 1968), his unwillingness to attend to cogni-

tive, interpersonal, and unconscious determinants of behavior (Birk, 1970), and his essentially ahistorical view of human behavior (Breger & McGaugh, 1965). Behaviorists, while they acknowledge Wolpe's central role in the development of rational alternatives to psychoanalytic treatment, condemn what they say is his confused intermingling of classical and operant learning paradigms (Davison, 1968; Davison & Wilson, 1973). Behaviorists also criticize Wolpe because in speaking of human neurotic reactions, he clings to the outmoded medical model of maladaptive behavior as symptomatic of underlying pathology rather than as an inappropriate learned response to the environment (Ullman & Krasner, 1969).

As a preface to stating his own opinion, Bandura cogently summarizes the current status of the etiology of neurosis:

Psychotherapists of different theoretical affiliations tend to find evidence for their own preferred psychodynamic agents rather than those cited by other schools. Thus, Freudians are likely to unearth Oedipus complexes and castration anxieties, Adlerians discover inferiority feelings and compensatory power strivings, Rogerians find compelling evidence for inappropriate self-concepts, and existentialists are likely to diagnose existential crises and anxieties. . . . Skinnerians, predictably, will discern defective conditions of reinforcement as important determinants of deviant behavior. In the latter explanatory scheme, however, the suspected controlling conditions are amenable to systematic variation; consequently, the functional relationships between reinforcement contingencies and behavior are readily verifiable. [1969, p. 9]

Bandura himself believes that "when the actual social-learning history of maladaptive behavior is known, principles of learning appear to provide a completely adequate interpretation of psychopathological phenomena, and psychodynamic explanations in terms of symptom-underlying disorder become superfluous" (p. 10). So far as Bandura is concerned, the potential complexity of any given neurotic patient's relevant social-learning history is much greater than that of the restricted models proposed by Wolpe or the Skinnerians. That is, social-learning variables can include modeling, classical learning mechanisms, and operant learning mechanisms; all can play a role in the development of a person's neurotic behavior. Further, Bandura believes that "response feedback processes" (self-reinforcement) and "internal symbolic central mediational processes" (hypotheses about the principles governing the occurrence of rewards and punishments) are also involved in the acquisition of neurotic behavior.

Because he is convinced that all these learning mechanisms have a share in neurosis, Bandura does not accept the idea that the neuroses ought to be subject to any single unifying concept (such as anxiety, conditioned avoidance, or underlying sexual disorder). Instead, he believes that they are maladaptive behaviors which may or may not have common antecedents and may or may not respond to a single treatment regimen. He says that even the degree to which they are labeled as maladaptive, sick, or troublesome is determined by a variety of subjectively arrived-at criteria, including "the aversiveness of the behavior, the social attributes of the deviator, the normative standards of persons making the judgements, the social context in which the behavior is performed, and a host of other factors" (p. 62).

Bandura's position, which represents the etiologic thinking of many research-oriented behavioral psychologists, has some shortcomings. For instance, is one justified in positing an etiology only among variables one can currently measure? Is all behavioral deviation truly culture-specific? But Bandura's theory does have the ultimate virtue of stressing the importance of empirical data in an area where they have been in very short supply.

Constitutional, genetic, and biophysiological factors in neurosis

Research into constitutional, genetic, and biophysiological factors in the etiology of neurotic behavior is sparse in comparison with similar work on the psychoses, but it has a surprisingly long history. In a pioneering twin study reported more than thirty-five years ago by Newman and his colleagues, interviews and psychological tests given to 19 pairs of identical twins raised apart showed that they were strikingly similar in "temperament" even though their environments had been different (1937). A recent survey by Shields analyzed 44 pairs of separated monozygotic twins and 44 pairs of monozygotic twins reared together and yielded essentially the same findings (1962). Shields reported that both groups of twins resembled each other in "normal" behavior (mannerisms, voice quality, esthetic and sexual preferences) and "neurotic" behavior (anxiety, personal inflexibility, "moodiness," hostility).

The evidence provided by both these studies that some of the behavioral components of neurosis are mediated by constitutional factors is supported by data from a few investigations which reveal higher concordance rates for neurosis among monozygotic than among dizygotic twins. Only one of these studies (Shields, 1962) reports such findings across the entire range of the neuroses; others (such as Gottesman, 1962, 1963) claim that only some of the neuroses are inheritable: "It would appear that neuroses with hypochondriacal and hysterical elements have no or low genetic component, while those with elements of anxiety, depression, obsession and schizoid withdrawal have a substantial genetic component" (Gottesman, 1962, p. 226).

Malmo's biophysiological theory of neurosis proposed that anxiety, which is central to almost every neurotic disorder, is associated with the state of overarousal (1957). Many neurotic patients, according to Malmo, exist in a state of chronic arousal that has gradually eroded their normal ability to inhibit arousal. One result is that they have a lower threshold of arousal and therefore respond with anxiety to a wider variety of stimuli than less anxious persons. This theory, a by-product of research on the general adaptation syndrome (Selye, 1957), also bears some relationship to the drive-arousal theories of schizophrenia reviewed in Chapter 7. The attraction of a model which uses a single concept like "over-arousal" to explain both neurosis and psychosis is that it enables investigators to view these very different disorders along one continuum. The problem with the model, however, is that no one has been able to explain on either a conceptual or a biophysiological basis when and how neurosis stops and psychosis starts.

A more recent effort to relate neurotic behavior to biophysiological mechanisms centers on the role of lactate in the body. Lactate is a normal product of cell metabolism that accumulates in small but measurable amounts in the body before it is further broken down by metabolic processes. Pitts reports that administration of additional amounts of lactate to anxious-prone (neurotic) persons generally induces a severe anxiety attack within a few minutes (1969). While Pitts's nonpatient controls also reported some increase in anxiety, this increase was much less than that reported by his neurotic subjects. Concluding from his research that lactate probably induces anxiety in virtually everyone, Pitts also assumes that some persons are more responsive to its anxiety-producing effects than others. In particular, he hypothesizes that anxiety neurotics are people whose higher levels of adrenalin secretion already subject them to higher than normal amounts of lactate. Thus additional lactate only adds more anxiety. In a later review of the possible biochemical factors involved in the etiology of anxiety neurosis, Pitts names other substances besides lactate which may be of potential etiological significance in anxiety neurosis. He also suggests that anxiety attacks might be prevented by the introduction of agents which block the accumulation of metabolic substances capable of producing anxiety.

Treatment of the neuroses

Classical psychoanalysis

Even after more than fifty years a mystique surrounds the psychoanalytic movement. An excellent description of the "special" feeling that suffused the movement from its beginnings is given by Ellenberger in his fascinating history of psychoanalysis:

Almost from the beginning Freud made psychoanalysis a movement, with its own organization and publishing house, its strict rules of membership, and its official doctrine, namely the psychoanalytic theory. The similarity between the psychoanalytic and the Greco-Roman philosophical schools was reinforced after the imposition of an initiation in the form of the training analysis. Not only does the training analysis demand a heavy financial sacrifice, but also a surrender of privacy and of the whole self. By this means a follower is integrated into the Society more indissolubly than ever was a Pythagorian, Stoic, or Epicurean in his own organization. [1970, p. 550]

As Chapter 9 described, the classical psychoanalytic method gradually evolved from Freud's early efforts to treat hysterical patients by hypnosis (Breuer & Freud, 1905), a technique Freud first learned from Charcot in Paris. Hypnosis often made it easier for his patients to remember events in their past that appeared to bear a relationship to their behavior. The method also had its failings, however. Some patients could not be hypnotized; some who could still did not remember the past; some who were given therapeutic posthypnotic suggestions failed to experience symptom relief. As a consequence, Freud developed the free-association method, a technique that remains central to psychoanalytic treatment. Between the years 1910 and 1915, he published nine papers on psychoanalytic technique which form the basis for the classical psychoanalytic method (Freud, 1959b–1959j).

Goals of psychoanalysis. The ultimate aim of psychoanalysis is resolution of the "infantile neurosis"—the basic psychopathologic core

Freud's famous couch in his consulting room, Vienna. *(Edmund Engelman)*

that is presumed to be at the root of the adult's neurotic behavior. A more immediate aim is to make the unconscious conscious, in order to permit the previously forgotten or forbidden instinctual impulses that "cause" neurotic "symptoms" to well up and be dealt with. One can also say that psychoanalysis aims to strengthen the ego so that it can mediate among the conflicting demands of the id, the superego, and the external world without having to resort to ineffective defensive maneuvers.

In jargon-free terms, psychoanalysis aims to help the individual deal with the world as a function of his realistic place in it and its realistic impact on him, rather than on the basis of his own particular, biased view of the world gained from his own past history. Seen in this way, the goals of psychoanalysis are virtually identical with those of most other "psychological" therapies (including its otherwise antithetical competitor, behavior therapy).

Selection of patients for psychoanalysis. Most psychoanalysts agree on the following selection criteria for patients.

[1] The patient must be in adequate contact with reality, show intact cognitive (thinking) and affective (feeling) functions, and have a history of adequate functioning in the past. In short, the patient's ego functions, though under attack from the id and the superego, must be adequate both to deal with the stresses of psychoanalysis and to serve as a base for the development of more effective personality functioning. This criterion eliminates schizophrenic patients, others in the midst of acute turmoil, and patients whose psychological problems derive from organic brain disorders that impair thinking. As one prominent psychoanalyst said, "Actually, one has to be a relatively healthy neurotic in order to be psychoanalyzed without modifications and deviations" (Greenson, 1959).

[2] The patient must also be motivated for

treatment—he must want to get better—or else he will drop out when the psychoanalytic process becomes unpleasant for him. One measure of motivation, presumably, is his willingness to pay the high fees that psychoanalysts charge most patients. This particular measure of motivation has long been a bone of contention between psychoanalysts and those who favor methods that are available to larger segments of the population (Mintz, 1971). The ability-to-pay criterion effectively restricts psychoanalysis to people of upper socioeconomic status who can afford the typical psychoanalysts's weekly charges of $200 or so. While clinics have been established which offer psychoanalysis for reduced fees, the economics of highly-trained professionals seeing small numbers of patients keeps psychoanalysis a very precious commodity. An alternative treatment is psychoanalytically oriented psychotherapy, which requires a less intensive patient-therapist relationship, and is available to more patients.

[3] The patient must be able to do the "psychological work" that is necessary during psychoanalysis. He must be verbally facile, intellectually competent, able to grasp the notion of psychological causality, and willing to tolerate the analyst's insistence on making connections between current behavior and events in the past. In practice, this criterion generally rules out members of most minority groups, most poor people, and people of foreign parentage who are not fluent in the psychoanalyst's language. Halleck, a social psychiatrist who takes an irreverent view of psychoanalysis, says:

Psychiatrists who are well-educated and have been raised in middle- or upper-class environments will obviously have some difficulty communicating with a relatively uneducated client. This probably accounts for much of their reluctance to treat the poor person with therapies that require verbal interaction and expansion of awareness. Many psychiatrists seem to have a subtle kind of prejudice toward lower-class persons, which increases the probability that they will treat such patients with nonverbal techniques. [1971, p. 111]

Psychoanalysis is expensive because of the frequency with which patient and therapist meet. Most psychoanalysts consider four hour-long sessions per week to be the minimum for effective therapy. The psychoanalyst must come to know a patient intimately, because the patient must have the opportunity to react to the psychoanalyst on a wide variety of occasions and under a broad range of emotional states (in order for "transference" to develop). Also, the patient will place psychoanalytic treatment in proper perspective—that is, first and foremost—only if he must make it part of his daily regimen. For this reason some psychoanalysts believe that once-a-week psychoanalytic psychotherapy, even though it is based on the theoretical assumptions of classical psychoanalysis, cannot achieve the goals of the classical method. They claim that treatment once a week does not permit development of the kind of relationship which patient and therapist must share for successful therapeutic change.

Free association: The basic rule. Free association remains the basic rule—the major analytic technique—of psychoanalysis. It requires the patient to renounce, to the extent that he possibly can, all usual efforts to "censor" his thoughts and words. He is asked to verbalize all thoughts, feelings, and wishes without worrying about their logic, order, social acceptability, or significance.

One reason why many psychoanalysts still use the couch is that they believe the patient who does not have to face the therapist can bring out uncensored material more easily. Parenthetically, the couch also takes the pressure off therapists, who would otherwise undergo many hours of patients' scrutiny every day. Another important justification for the couch is that it fosters development of the "transference neurosis." That is, it keeps the patient-therapist interaction to a minimum so that the patient can more readily project onto the analyst the desires, wishes, and thoughts he experiences toward parents, siblings, and other important persons in his life.

Dream interpretation. No single element of psychoanalytic technique has been so criticized and so praised as the interpretation of dreams. When Freud published *The Interpretation of Dreams* in 1900, he made one of his most original and controversial contributions to analytic psychology. In this book he detailed the uses to which the dreamer puts dreams, the mechanisms by which dreams are "disguised," and the procedures by which the analyst tries to ferret out their meaning.

Freud explained dreams as symbolic representations of unconscious conflicts reawakened by the day's activities. Their function was to protect the sleep of the dreamer by permitting him to "work through" concerns, anxieties, and desires that would otherwise awaken him. Because much of this material was unacceptable to the patient's standards of morality (it was too sexual or too aggressive), various dream mechanisms to disguise the true meanings of the dreams had to be employed. This was called the *dream work*. The analyst's job in interpreting a dream was to uncover its real meaning while protecting the patient from coming into too rapid or too direct confrontation with the unwanted and disguised material.

This vastly condensed presentation of an extraordinarily complex matter must be accompanied by an example of dream interpretation that is equally abbreviated. The example was given by Freud:

A dream consisting of two short pictures: The dreamer's uncle was smoking a cigarette, although it was Saturday—A woman was fondling and caressing the dreamer as though he were her child.

With reference to the first picture, the dreamer (a Jew) remarked that his uncle was a very pious man who never had done, and never would do, anything so sinful as smoking on the Sabbath. The only association to the woman in the second picture was that of the dreamer's mother. These two pictures or thoughts must obviously be related to one another; but in what way? Since he expressly denied that his uncle would in reality perform the action of the dream, the insertion of the conditional "if" will at once suggest itself. "If my uncle, that deeply religious man, were to smoke a cigarette on the Sabbath, then I myself might be allowed to let my mother fondle me." Clearly, that is as much as to say that being fondled by the mother was something as strictly forbidden as smoking on the Sabbath is to the pious Jews. You will remember my telling you that in the dream-work all relations among the dream-thoughts disappear; the thoughts are broken up into their raw material, and our task in interpreting is to reinsert these connections which have been omitted. [Freud, 1953, p. 195]

Other phenomena of psychoanalytic treatment. Among the great number and variety of events that take place during psychoanalysis, some are central to the treatment process. One which appears very early in the psychoanalytic relationship is *resistance,* defined as both conscious and unconscious efforts by the patient to defeat the aims of the therapy. Among the resistances psychoanalysts identify in their patients are lateness and forgetting of appointments, inability to free-associate, intensification of symptoms, and removal of the therapy hour from "real life." Resistances are overcome, according to psychoanalytic theory, by interpreting their unconscious determinants so that therapy can proceed. The following excerpt from a psychoanalytic session shows how a patient's unwillingness to return to normal functioning is expressed as resistance to progress in therapy.

A patient with a phobic reaction extended to subway travel made a trip to my office by subway for the first time since treatment had started. She entered the room sullenly and remarked fretfully that she was furious with me. Her anger had started when she discovered that she had no great anxiety riding on the train. A fragment of the session follows:

Patient: I am so angry and resentful toward you. (pause)
Therapist: I wonder why.
Patient: I feel you are gloating over my taking a subway. I feel mother is gloating too. I resent her too. I felt she was pushing me, trying to force me to break away from her. She gloats if I do something that makes me independent. I feel that when I go ahead you gloat too.

Therapist: It sounds as if you are angry about being able to travel on the subway.

Patient: Mother seems to be anxious to give up her responsibility for me. I resent that. But I also don't like the idea of my being so close to mother, too.

Therapist: I see, as if you want to continue being dependent and yet resenting it.

Patient: When I get sick at night, I ask her to make me some tea; and then I resent her patrician attitude when she does this.

Therapist: But what about your feeling about me?

Patient: It's like giving in to you. But yesterday I felt liberated by the idea that I'm in the middle of a conflict and that coming here offers me hope. I realize that my neurosis is threatened by my getting well. (laughs)

Therapist: What part of your neurosis do you want to hold onto?

Patient: (laughs) None. But I have a feeling that I don't want to be normal, that in giving in to you, I'll be like anybody else. Also that you'll expect more things of me. And (laughs) that if I get too well you'll kick me out. [Wolberg, 1954, pp. 468–469]

"After all these years, you still feel guilt? You should be ashamed of yourself." Psychoanalysts are supposed to keep their personal feelings out of the therapy situation. When they do not, they are betraying what is called "countertransference." (Drawing by Handelsman; © 1972 The New Yorker Magazine, Inc.)

The patient's resistance to getting better is obvious even to her. Getting better means losing the "secondary gains" from her disability. Above all, it means losing her relationship with the therapist, whose professional concern for her has come to stand for the love and nurturing from her mother about which she is in so much conflict.

One of the most common sources of resistance is the *transference* phenomenon. At the same time, transference is thought to provide much of the patient's motivation to try and change. Transference refers to the feelings the patient experiences toward the analyst—feelings which are in the large part products of his interactions with important persons in his past. The main source of these feelings is almost always the patient's parents. Because psychoanalytic technique deemphasizes the therapist's verbal activity and physical presence so that he can function as a "blank screen," the patient's feelings about the therapist are often little-disguised feelings about parents.

The great value of transference in the psychoanalytic process is that it can provide, for patient and therapist alike, the clearest view of the determinants of the patient's neurotic behavior. Those who accept the idea that psychoanalysis aims to uncover the roots of the "infantile neurosis" in order to "cure" the adult neurosis believe that the transference relationship offers an excellent vehicle for doing it. By interpreting all the neurotic displaced, inappropriate, and irrational reactions of the patient to him, the therapist can help the patient identify a significant portion of his current maladaptive behavioral repertoire. Since transference in this sense can be useful even for behavior therapists, some of them have begun to pay increasing attention to the nature of their relationship with their patients.

Here is a typical illustration of transference in the context of a classical psychoanalytic relationship:

An unmarried male laboratory technician of thirty underwent psychoanalysis for the relief of his lifelong loneliness and general dissatisfaction with himself and what he was getting out of existence. Early in the process he described his father's reserve and aloofness. Later, however, he made similar observations about one of his teachers and then about his employer. Ultimately, of course, it was the analyst who seemed reserved, cold and aloof. A little later, however, he recalled certain earlier experiences with a girl cousin whose warmth was a sharp contrast to the chill formalities in his own home. He felt guilty, however, because of certain of his responses to her advances and feared particularly what his father's reaction might be. Something similar was repeated with a young woman he met in college. The analyst was not surprised, accordingly, when some months later the patient dreamed of the analyst in the form of a seductress, which evoked reproach that the analyst was expecting too much of him and encouraging him in forbidden directions. Next, it developed that there had been in his childhood a particularly stern aunt whose judgements were feared by all the relatives and, indeed, by the entire neighborhood. She evidently represented to him, then, what law and order, the police court and purgatory came to represent to him later. This began to appear in the transference when the analyst, who had previously been accused both of coldness and of seductiveness, became a stern figure of retribution from whom the patient expected punishment and dismissal. . . . In all of these aspects of transference one sees the irrational roles in which the analyst is cast, the ways in which the earlier models are used. [Menninger, 1958, p. 82]

This patient's subsequent successful therapy consisted of efforts to make him aware of the distortions he characteristically introduced into his relationships with important people in his life. These distortions were largely functions of the power and longevity of his early experiences with a reserved, aloof, cold father and a stern, demanding aunt.

Interpretation, one of the major ways in which transference phenomena are translated into therapeutic gain, is "a statement, phrased in one of various ways, which the therapist makes in reference to something the patient has said or done. The therapeutic intent of the statement is to confront the patient with something in himself which he has warded off and of which he is partially or totally unaware" (Colby, 1951, p. 82).

Among the targets for interpretation are the defenses the patient uses to protect himself against his own impulses or the environment (the therapist might say, "Its hard for you to trust anyone, isn't it?"), the impulses against which the patient is defending (the therapist: "Thinking about your father makes you remember the anger you felt at his lack of interest in you"), transference feelings (the therapist: "I wonder whether the feelings you say you have about me relate to similar feelings you had for your mother when you and she went on that cross-country trip"), and dreams.

Though psychoanalysts on television and in the movies alter a patient's behavior by making a single unerring interpretation, real-life analysts say that a great deal of time and effort are required to bring about real-life therapeutic change. Repeated interpretation of the transference relationship, resistances, and irrational behavior outside the therapy hours is required before the patient "buys" a connection, whatever its importance or validity.

Psychoanalytically oriented psychotherapy

Though classical psychoanalysis still has great prestige among many middle- and upper-class urban Americans, it is not the treatment that most Americans choose, regardless of their socioeconomic status. Psychoanalytically oriented psychotherapy, a more direct, less intensive, and less expensive process, is the treatment more often adopted by patients for whom dynamic therapy is judged appropriate. This method, essentially a modification of classical psychoanalysis, aims for less than the total personality reorganization which is the goal of classical psychoanalysis. It focuses instead on helping the individual come to terms with the realities of his environment: ego functions are clarified, defenses are strengthened, if necessary, and the reality of current environmental situations is clarified.

Therapy, often only once or twice a week, is devoted less to exploration of forgotten early experiences and current unconscious determinants of behavior, and more to everyday reality. The therapist is much more active: consequently free association is deemphasized. Dream interpretation, another "royal road to the unconscious" in classical psychoanalysis, is also employed less often. Transference is no longer a prime vehicle for a cure. Though attention is paid to the patient's distortions of his relationship with the therapist, it is not the major focus of therapy that it is in classical psychoanalysis.

The following case report illustrates a number of the important components of short-term dynamic therapy. As you read, notice its differences from the examples of classical psychoanalysis given above.

A physician, a German refugee 45 years old, came for psychotherapy because of an intense depression resulting from extreme irritation with his son. He was seen for a single consultation with excellent results. . . . The patient had had no serious neurotic difficulties before. He had been in this country for ten months, and his wife and only child, a nine-year-old boy, had only recently joined him. His chief complaint was that he felt extremely irritated by his son, that he could not concentrate on his work in the boy's presence, that he was annoyed by his demanding attitude and his constant need for attention. He was now so discouraged over his inability to adjust himself to the child that he had become exceedingly depressed and decided to consult a psychiatrist. . . . In the course of the discussion, the patient's attention was distracted from his complaints about his son with a few questions about the way he had lived before his family joined him. He then talked freely about the circumstances of his immigration and about his first attempts to reconstruct his life in the new environment. Although he had had a hard time in the beginning, he had been fairly successful in getting established in his profession. . . . As he talked it became clear to him that his son and wife had joined him "too soon," that they had come before he was ready to offer them the security they needed. With considerable emotion—at first hesi-

tantly, then with conviction—he said he realized that life would be easier now if his son and wife were not with him. He saw that the demands of his son were really not exaggerated but seemed so because he himself felt insecure—not only within himself but also in his economic adjustment. He felt guilty and responsible, and even saw some justification for his son's behavior, since his own difficulties in the new environment did not allow him to be the ideal father his standards demanded. As he talked the whole situation over, he gained more and more insight into these feelings (which were not far under the surface) and with this insight he experienced marked relief. . . . But insight alone was not enough. It was necessary also to help this patient make some practical arrangement whereby he could adjust his way of working to the American style of life—chiefly through having an office outside the home. This made it possible for him to divide his energies; he could be a hardworking doctor part of the time, and an attentive father and husband the rest of the time. [Alexander & French, 1946, pp. 155–156]

Though the results of psychoanalytically oriented psychotherapy are rarely achieved so quickly and with so little apparent effort by patient or therapist, the methods of single- and multiple-session therapy are comparable. The focus is on a pressing environmental problem; the therapist actively interprets, suggests, exhorts, and directs; there is little emphasis upon fantasy, dreams, or other unconscious material. While the therapy described in the example was doubtless expedited by a willing, motivated, and intelligent patient whose problem was amenable to quick solution, those who write about psychoanalytically oriented psychotherapy often report such rapid "symptomatic" improvements.

Controlled research on the outcome of classical psychoanalysis is uncommon; the usual research report is the written analysis of a successful case, examined in the effort to validate one or another of the basic tenets of psychoanalytic theory. Controlled research involving psychoanalytically oriented psychotherapy occurs more frequently. The so-called A-B therapist variable, for example, has been an important recent research direction (Berzines et al., 1972; Razin, 1971). The A-B distinction, first proposed by Whitehorn and Betz (1960; Betz, 1963), grew out of the common observation that therapist personality variables can play an important role in treatment outcome. Chartier describes A-type therapists "as possessing a problem-solving approach, including genuineness, respect, sympathetic independence, perceptive attunement to the patient's inner experience, and expectation of responsible self-determination." He pictures B-type therapists as "mechanical, passively permissive or authoritatively instructive, concerned with symptom reduction rather than the use of assets, and solicitous of deference and conformity" (1971, p. 23). The importance of the A-B distinction, if it can be validated, is potentially great; it could have a major impact on professional training, therapist and patient selection and matching, and psychotherapy processes and outcomes.

Other psychoanalytic approaches

For the most part, other psychoanalytic approaches to treatment are variations on the classical (Freudian) psychoanalytic theme. Most psychoanalysis which is carried out today is not of these varieties, but they are described briefly here in order to show that divergent theory can lead to convergent therapy.

Adlerian psychoanalysis. The meaning of the therapeutic relationship is the focus of differences between classical psychoanalysis and Adlerian psychoanalysis (also called *individual psychoanalysis*). Specifically, the Adlerian therapist acknowledges the importance of the transference relationship but interprets it in terms of power and status rather than tying it to sexual (oedipal) themes. As a result the Adlerian therapist is most sensitive to patients' irrational efforts to "control" treatment by complaining of terrible psychic pain, by developing more and more disabling symptoms, or by introducing into therapy the threat of suicide for which the therapist would be responsible.

The therapist must "head off" these maladaptive defensive behaviors by making real efforts to conduct therapy on the basis of genuine cooperation and mutual trust, as an exercise in problem solving. If he must, he assumes a nurturing role with the patient. In this way he avoids the "duel for power" that would doom therapy to failure. Implicit in Adlerian psychoanalysis is use of the therapeutic relationship as a model for the patient's social improvement outside the therapy situation. That is, when the patient begins to relate to the therapist as a mature, self-confident person does, presumably he is also showing this behavior outside the consulting room.

Jungian psychoanalysis. The ultimate goal of Jungian psychoanalysis is self-realization—arriving at the kind of personal balance represented by the Mandala, a traditional oriental symbol. In Jungian psychology the

Mandala stands for reunification of the personality. The Jungian therapist stresses dream interpretation as the best way to discover the relative strengths and weaknesses of the male and female elements that he is convinced reside within every human psyche. The fundamental aim of his therapeutic efforts is to bring these conflicting forces into equilibrium. In so doing he deemphasizes the relationship between patient and therapist, the cornerstone of many other psychological therapies. Though non-Jungian therapists do not accept this specific aspect of Jungian therapy, they acknowledge the value of Jung's respect for the inherent dignity of human beings and his corresponding insistence that therapeutic gain must be based on the healthiest components of a patient's personality.

Perhaps the weakest part of Jungian theory and therapy lies in its assumption that every person has an accumulated store of racial wisdom passed from generation to generation by genetic transmission. This hypothetical system remains unproved and some critics believe that it strengthens tendencies toward preoccupation with fantasy life in those patients whose hold on reality is tenuous to begin with. Therefore some observers conclude that it is unwise to use Jungian therapy with psychotic patients.

Interpersonal psychoanalysis: The methods of Horney and Fromm. The interpersonal psychoanalysts, among them Horney and Fromm, also evolved distinct therapeutic strategies to accompany their neo-Freudian theories of behavior. In Horney's case, theory emerged from therapy rather than the other way around. She said in 1939, "My desire to make a critical reevaluation of psychoanalytic theories had its origin in dissatisfaction with therapeutic results."

Horney stressed the supreme importance of understanding the patient's current life situation—at home, at work, and in the context of his hopes for the future. This therapeutic emphasis on the present rather than the past resembles Adler's approach, though Horney's insistence on a broad understanding of the patient is less limiting than Adler's view that the "will to power" is at the root of all "neurotic" difficulties (Kelman, 1971). But Horney's emphasis upon the present has been criticized because patients may fail to recognize that their present behavior is the sum of past experiences. As a result, her opponents

argue, patients may feel guilty that they have developed so many "bad habits" for no apparent reason.

Horney has also been criticized for expecting all patients to become hostile toward the therapist when they realize that he is the enemy of their defenses. As Thompson summarizes Horney's position: "In the presence of the threat of losing his neurotic pseudo-security, the patient becomes more anxious and hostile, and a struggle for power ensues" (1950, p. 203).

It has been said that classical psychoanalysis aims to enable patients to adjust to an imperfect society. In our view, this is a valid picture of one of the ultimate goals of any behavior-change process. Erich Fromm's "humanistic psychoanalysis" sets an alternative and equally admirable goal: to permit patients to realize their own distinctive human potentialities and abilities irrespective of the society in which they live. Fromm, who developed many of his theories during the tumultuous years before the beginning of World War II, felt that successful therapy changes behavior from "culture-bound" to "culture-free" actions—to behaviors which express the person's full range of abilities and interests. Though the bulk of Fromm's writings dealt with social ethics and cultural responsibility, they also had an impact on conceptions of therapy. His emphasis upon respect for the patient, his focus upon the patient's healthiest core elements, and his concern with therapists' natural but irrational tendencies to become authoritarian with patients (just as patients themselves accept authoritarianism as an "escape from freedom")—all these have influenced the evolution of psychoanalytic theory and technique.

Rogers: Client-centered therapy

Carl Rogers's client-centered therapy developed from a theory of therapy rather than a theory of personality. His approach is epitomized by fourteen principles which he not only carries out in therapy but has himself chosen to live by:

1 In my relationships with persons I have found that it does not help, in the long run, to act as though I were something that I am not.

2 I find I am more effective when I can listen acceptantly to myself, and can be myself.

3 I have found it of enormous value when I can permit myself to understand another person.

4 I have found it enriching to open channels whereby others can communicate their feelings, their private perceptual worlds, to me.

5 I have found it highly rewarding when I can accept another person.

6 The more open I am to the realities in me and in the other person, the less do I find myself wishing to rush to "fix things."

7 I can trust my experience.

8 Evaluation by others is not a guide for me . . . only one person can know whether what I am doing is honest, thorough, open, and sound, or false and defensive and unsound, and I am that person.

9 Experience is, for me, the highest authority. . . . It is to experience that I must return again and again, to discover a closer approximation to truth as it is in the process of becoming in me.

10 I enjoy the discovering of order in experience.

11 The facts are friendly . . . painful reorganizations are what is known as learning. . . .

12 What is most personal and unique in each one of us is probably the very element which would, if it were shared or expressed, speak most deeply to others.

13 I have come to feel that the more fully the individual is understood and accepted, the more he tends to drop the false fronts with which he has been meeting life, and the more he tends to move in a direction which is forward.

14 Life, at its best, is a flowing, changing process in which nothing is fixed. [1961, pp. 16–27]

Though they are a poetic and very personal expression, these fourteen tenets also represent the essence of Rogers's pragmatic philosophy of treatment. Its assumptions can be condensed in more commonplace terms: (1) Progress in therapy is almost always associated with therapeutic relationships in which the client comes to have affection and respect for his counselor. By the same token, the counselor who has similar feelings for his client, who cares for him but is not demanding or possessive, is more apt to succeed than the counselor who sets himself at a distance from his client. (2) The client's progress in therapy involves moving away from situational problems dealt with in an intellectual fashion and moving towards an emotional, "experiencing" way of relating to the counselor. (3) During successful therapy the client also becomes aware of new perceptions about himself—perceptions that are often less defensive and less condemning than before. (4) Successful counselors convey genuine, empathetic, nonpossessive warmth when they learn to respect and value their clients regardless of the clients' human failures and inadequacies.

The value of these tenets has been confirmed by a good deal of empirical research which centers on defining the therapist variables that best predict success in the counseling situation. (Rogers et al., 1967; Truax & Carkhuff, 1967). With some exceptions (Gar-

Carl R. Rogers

field & Bergin, 1971), the research strongly suggests that the therapist must have empathy (real concern for the client's suffering), warmth, and genuineness for a successful therapeutic outcome. Furthermore, even professionals who question the methods and goals of client-centered therapy praise the insistence of Rogers and his colleagues on the necessity for continuing assessment of the results of therapy.

Some mental health professionals call client-centered therapy unidimensional, meaning that the therapist simply mirrors the client's feelings by a succession of sympathetic "um-hms." The following excerpt from one of Roger's own cases suggests that this view of his therapy is not an accurate one. The excerpt also shows that client-centered therapists must respond to transference phenomena, which to them as well as to dynamic therapists are an important component of the patient-therapist relationship.

It would appear to be correct to say that *strong* attitudes of a transference nature occur in a relatively small minority of cases, but that such attitudes occur in *some* degree in the majority of cases. . . . If we take one of the minority of cases in which definite transference attitudes are experienced and discussed by the client, we may see something of what occurs. [This is the] beginning of a fifth interview with a young married woman, Mrs. Dar. In the previous interviews she had brought out material about which she felt quite guilty.

Client: Well, I have had a very curious dream. I almost hated to think about coming back again, after the dream. Uh . . .
Therapist: You say you almost thought about not coming back again after the dream?
Client: M-hm. (Laughs.)
Therapist: It was almost too much for you.
Client: Yeah. Well, uh, last Friday night I dreamt that, uh, I went to New York to see you, and you were *terribly* busy, and were running in and out of offices, and you had so much to do, and finally I looked at you pleadingly and you said to me, "I'm sorry. I haven't got any more time for you. Your story is much too sordid. I—I just can't be bothered." And you kept running in and out of

rooms, and I kept sort of following you around. I didn't, uh, know what to do, and I felt very **help-less**, and at the same time I felt very **much** ashamed, and shocked by the fact that you **said** what you did.
Therapist: M-hm.
Client: And it's—it's stayed with me ever **since** then.
Therapist: That had a good deal of reality.
Client: Yes.
Therapist: You sort of felt that somehow I **was** judging your situation to be pretty, pretty bad.
Client: That's right. That you were—I was up for trial, and you were the judge, and— (Pause.)
Therapist: The verdict was guilty.
Client: (Laughs.) I think that's it. (Laughs.) That's it all right. I didn't see how I could come back into the situation. I mean the circumstances, you already judged me, and therefore I didn't really see how I could possibly talk any more.
Therapist: M-hm.
Client: Except about other things. And uh, it hasn't left me. I've been thinking about it a great deal.
Therapist: You almost felt that you *were* being judged.
Client: Well, why should I feel that? Uh—well, of course I probably transferred my own thoughts into your mind, and therefore I, uh, there was no doubt about it. It just couldn't be changed. It was *the* verdict. I suppose in my own way I was judging myself.
Therapist: M-hm. You feel that perhaps *you* were the judge, really. [1951, pp. 199–202]

Only a few centers provide training in client-centered therapy, while many offer advanced training in several varieties of psychoanalysis. Nevertheless, client-centered therapy continues to be widely employed, especially in college counseling centers.

Group and family therapy

Therapeutic relationships involving more than just a patient and a therapist are called *group therapy* when they bring together persons who are unrelated to one another and *family therapy* when the persons are members of a

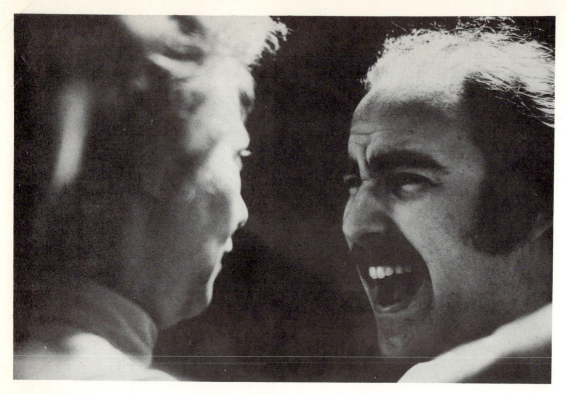

In encounter-group meetings—a type of group therapy—feelings can run high as members release or reexperience suppressed emotions. *(Hella Hammid from Rapho Guillumette)*

family. One reason for the great popularity of the group therapy movement is the undoubted efficiency associated with having one therapist see several patients at a time. In addition, however, group therapy brings important new advantages to the therapy process. It gives a patient the opportunity to ask for and receive feedback on his behavior from a wide range of people. It fosters feelings of support and comradery, because the members of the group share intimate details of their personal lives with each other. And it enables patients to observe the adaptive and maladaptive behavior of others in close proximity and to model those behaviors when it seems appropriate.

Many group and family therapists come from psychoanalytic backgrounds, though behavior therapy groups and client-centered counseling groups also have a large place in the movement. A group therapist's theoretical background, of course, determines much of his

therapeutic behavior. Psychoanalytic group therapy is apt to focus on unconscious determinants of each person's group behavior. Group behavior therapy often employs group desensitization and role playing to confront behavior problems that group members share. Rogerian group therapy is concerned with enabling each group member to feel competent, accepted, and adequate in his own right.

Family therapy has inspired a variety of new therapeutic techniques. One of the leaders in this movement, Norman Paul, has developed a method which involves recording a family's therapy sessions and then replaying them during a subsequent session. As the following excerpt suggests, these playbacks can foster therapeutic growth for all concerned:

Burt S. was a 30 year old single schizophrenic male who had been incapacitated for eleven years with delusions of grandeur and persecution, bizarre behavior, and repeated vituperative explosions, primarily directed at Mr. S., his father. He was the younger of two children, having a sister four years his senior, who was married and had three adopted children. Burt had an insidious lifelong history of being withdrawn, avoiding social contacts, and being unable to compete comfortably with his peers. . . . Both Mr. and Mrs. S. were living. Mr. S. was a successful, forceful, hard-driving educator; Mrs. S., a cool, remote, detached housewife. Mr. S. had great aspirations for his son who had been well endowed intellectually. A singular problem for the patient over the years had been his inability to decide what he wanted for himself in light of Mr. S.'s over-zealous need to condition Burt to meet his expectations. . . . His clinical condition had improved minimally by late fall, 1963. At that time, his most recent psychotherapist, who had seen Burt in intensive psychotherapy for the preceding two years, referred him and his family for conjoint family therapy. . . . During the 27th meeting, I played back the beginning twenty-five minutes of the eleventh meeting. . . . The following is excerpted from the final six minutes of the twenty-five minutes segment played back:

Mr. S. (Father): We don't talk at home. There's nothing. We have no conversations at all. If we come in, he goes out. If he comes in, we have to get out of the way, and it isn't a question of "GET OUT OF MY WAY." Yesterday, we got up early; we did some chores around the house, cleaned up the house, had breakfast; 12 o'clock we went out on the road. We had lunch in a Johnson's; from there we went to Jane and Stanley's house [sister and brother-in-law] and intentionally stayed there to 5 or 6 o'clock . . . came home. Came home: Burt [Patient] is locked in his door—in the den, not in his bedroom. Now, Burt gets out and I'm in the hall. I walk into the kitchen and Burt pounds his way out of the kitchen "GET OUT OF MY WAY." Now, incidentally, that's the first words we've had now in 24 hours. It is *impossible* to live under those conditions.

Therapist: Well, that's not true.

Mr. S.: Well, look we just can't keep on. Day in and day out and day in and day out.

Therapist: You lived under those conditions for a long period of time.

Mr. S. plans for a brief vacation with his wife; he is concerned about where to leave Burt. He considers having Burt stay with Mr. S.'s sister and brother-in-law in the country.

Mr. S. (with annoyance): Well, he's going to, he'll have an automobile. He could ride back and forth or go anywhere he wants. He could have our car. He wouldn't be isolated. He'd be able to do more there than he could do at our home. He'd have a picnic with the automobile.

Stanley (Brother-in-law): How would you manage without a car?

Mr. S.: Well, for a few days, until I could straighten out, I could do very nicely without a car and then go away . . .

Therapist: Burt, how would you feel about their going away? For anywhere from a week to ten days?

Burt (Patient): When I see it, I'll believe it.

Therapist: You don't think think they can make it.

Burt: I've never been offered the car or anything else. When I see it, I'll believe it.

Mr. S. continues to plan for Burt.

Mr. S. (defensively): Well, I like to have Burt have hot meals. I'd like to have him sleep with Jim and Alice in their home, the same as sleeping with you (to Stanley). I wouldn't want him to just spend . . . whether it's one week or two weeks or three weeks all alone in that big house. For 24 hours a day, every single day, day in and day out.

Stanley: But he's really alone in it now. From what you just described . . .

Mr. S.: He may be alone in there, but still we're sleeping there every single night. And mother does get up and make his breakfast and does have his hot meals at night. They're all made for him. Every meal is made for him. . . .

During the playback, Stanley held his head in his hands; both parents and Burt listened intently while periodically looking at the tape recorder. After fifteen minutes of playback, Mr. S. darted his eyes from side to side, appearing distressed. Playback had to be discontinued after twenty-five minutes because Burt began to argue loudly with the father heard during playback, looking intently at the tape recorder. The following are the responses to playback:

Therapist: Because you're interrupting, I wonder what you people thought about hearing this. Do you remember it?

Mr. S.: I remember it almost verbatim.

Therapist: How does it sound to you?

Mr. S.: A little distressing.

Therapist: In what sense?

Mr. S.: Well, that it brings back bad memories.

Therapist: Do you know that you operate in the way you hear yourself on the tape? Do you know the impact you make?

Mr. S. (soberly): I do now.

Therapist: Did you before you heard this? What kind of impact does this sound have to you?

Mr. S.: A very rioting and disturbing and antagonistic.

Burt: Rumpelstiltskin, stomping as the Savoy, that's what I call it . . .

Mr. S.: I can see where it, it, it actually challenges a person to, to argue, to fight back . . .

Therapist (to Mrs. S.): How did this sound to you: Was it that distressing to you?

Mrs. S. (Mother): Yes.

Mr. S.: Why?

Mrs. S.: Yes, actually this isn't how, how I see my husband.

Therapist: You mean, you were unaware that he sounded this way too?

Mrs. S.: That's right.

Therapist (to Stanley): How did it sound to you?

Stanley: Oh, I don't know. I guess each takes their own part. Each takes their own part. I certainly felt antagonistic at that meeting. I found . . . I felt antagonistic toward both Burt and my father-in-law in terms of both—the way I felt at that time, their inabilities to see right, both of them to see anything . . .

Mrs. S.: How does it sound to you, Dr. Paul?

Therapist: Just the way it sounds to you. Yes.

Mr. S.: Did you find that all along?

Therapist: Oh yes. You see, the question I have . . . the reason I played it back to you people that way; you have your own images as to how to relate to one another and the question in my mind is are you aware of what the others hear? Because this is crucial to know this. You can come here and sound off, and Burt doesn't believe that this has very much of an impact on you, but he doesn't know what you understand of yourselves,

or what you don't; and the thing that's most amazing to me is not that you, Mr. S., didn't know, but that your wife didn't know.

Mr. S.: She could very well over such a long, long period of time become forgiving, tolerant, and used to a thing.

Therapist: And pretend.

Mr. S.: And pretend.

Therapist: Well, you see, when you hear this, you have an idea of what Burt's been up against.

Mr. S.: It's very irritating.

Burt: Well, isn't it a little bit better to make a person's life worth living and not give them any money than to drive them insane and give them money to live on and keep reminding them about anything? [1966, pp. 178–182]

Behavior therapy

Behavior therapy, which is still in its early adolescence, means different things to different people. Consider the definition given by Wolpe, whose "systematic desensitization," one of the earliest behavior therapy procedures, is still one of the most widely used. Wolpe says that behavior therapy is limited to "the use of experimentally established principles of learning for the purpose of changing unadaptive behavior. Unadaptive habits are weakened and eliminated; adaptive habits are initiated and strengthened" (1969). Lazarus, originator of "broad-spectrum behavior therapy," defines the term more broadly. To him behavior therapy involves "all the usual psychotherapeutic techniques, such as support, guidance, insight, catharsis, interpretation, environmental manipulation, etc., but in addition . . . the behavior therapist applies objective techniques which are designed to inhibit specific neurotic patterns" (1971). To authorities like Bandura and Ullmann and Krasner, who view behavior in its social-learning context, behavior therapists must study the relevant social-learning histories of their patients in order to plan operant strategies for behavioral treatment.

These differences in definition partly reflect professional "power politics," but they also have real consequences. Specifically,

"Hey, everybody! It's exactly three years ago today that I stopped smoking! How about that?" Psychoanalysts believe that behavior therapy often results in "symptom substitution," by which symptoms eliminated through behavior therapy reappear in different forms. *(Drawing by Ross; © 1973 The New Yorker Magazine, Inc.)*

Wolpe's view of behavior therapy prohibits use of certain procedures that might in fact be effective, while Lazarus's broader definition legitimizes techniques that might not actually contribute to therapeutic gains. Leonard Krasner, an early figure in the field, sees the dilemma this way: "It is especially crucial to determine the scope and limitation of the field of behavior therapy since too comprehensive a view (e.g., equating it with all of psychology) renders it meaningless, and too narrow a view (e.g., equating it with a specific technique) will render it useless" (1971, p. 484).

A provocative article by psychologist Perry London restates the controversy:

The early growth of behavior therapy as a professional specialty was largely polemical and political, not theoretical, and most of its scientific hoopla evolved to serve the polemical needs of the people who made it up. . . . The study of learning for behavior therapists, in fact, was always more for the purpose of metaphor, paradigm, and analogy than for strict guidance about how to operate or about what it all means. [1972, p. 914]

From this basic premise London concludes that what is most important is to know which techniques work and which do not—that it is unprofitable to deliberate about the theoretical underpinnings of a therapy method or the reasons for its effectiveness.

We believe that some of the dramatic distinctions which have been drawn between behavior therapy and psychoanalysis are real and some are not. Behavior therapy and psychoanalysis are alike in that they both ultimately aim for behavior change, enhanced personal effectiveness, and an increase in the satisfaction that the patient derives from life. Neither is associated with physical manipulations or the use of drugs. Both require extensive training and experience.

But psychoanalysis and behavior therapy differ in their fundamental view of how mental disorders come about: the psychoanalyst attributes them to early traumatic experiences which result in deep-seated psychological malfunctioning, while behavior therapists regard them either as learned maladaptive behaviors or as behaviors of unknown etiology. The two approaches also differ in their short-term therapeutic aims: the psychoanalyst sets himself to uncover repressed memories of early trauma in order to "cut out" the diseased core of unconscious conflicts that is causing the symptoms; the behavior therapist tries to modify or eliminate unwanted maladaptive behaviors. As for the methods employed to bring about these aims, the therapist in psychoanalysis is relatively inactive; he relies primarily on natural development of transference, resistance, and insight, though he helps them along with occasional interpretations. In contrast, the behavior therapist is more active and the relationship between patient and therapist is more collaborative. In behavior therapy it is common for patient and therapist together to identify and then employ a range of behavioral methods to confront specific unwanted behaviors—though it is the therapist's job to be the expert consultant in these efforts.

Systematic desensitization. Systematic desensitization and its associated procedures were the first behavioral methods to be used in treating neurotic behavior. Though others before Wolpe attempted to substitute preferred incompatible behaviors for unwanted "neurotic" ones (Jones, 1931; Holmes, 1936; Terhune, 1949), it was his "reciprocal inhibition therapy" that generated the outpouring of clinical research and application that have established systematic desensitization as a useful treatment for many of the neurotic behaviors.

Wolpe's basic premise was that human neuroses are "persistent unadaptive learned habits of reaction" whose "unlearning can be procured only through processes which involve this primitive level." He concluded that "elimination of anxiety response habits is usually accomplished by the inhibition of anxiety by a competing response. . . . If a response inhibitory of anxiety can be made to occur in the presence of anxiety-evoking stimuli it will weaken the bond between these stimuli and the anxiety" (1969, p. 15). The systematic desensitization procedures which will be described here were used successfully in one of

the clinical examples you will read in Chapter 12 ("Jay Meredith's Secret").

The stimulus most often used to "countercondition" anxiety is deep muscle relaxation. In preparation for it, the early sessions of therapy include regular periods of relaxation training. The most common technique for teaching deep muscle relaxation is Jacobson's "progressive relaxation" method (1938). It focuses on successive selected muscle groups, requiring their alternate contraction and relaxation in order to teach the patient to discriminate between gradations in tension level. The first of these exercises teaches relaxation of muscle groups in the hands and arms. Initial instructions include the following:

"Now I want you to get as comfortable as you can in your chair. If you feel more relaxed with your eyes closed, then close them. Now, try to concentrate your mind's eye on the most relaxing, pleasant thing you can think of. Perhaps it's sitting somewhere that's quiet, reading a book, occasionally looking out the window at some trees in the distance. Now, while you're relaxing, thinking of that pleasant, comfortable scene, I'd like you to tighten your left fist just as tight as you can . . . and hold the fist . . . and now relax . . . Let the relaxation spread from your fingers through your hand . . . and up your arm . . . Study the relaxation . . . And now clench that left hand again and hold the fist . . . tighter and tighter . . . and now relax again and feel the release of tension spread through your arm . . . Now I want you to do the same thing, only with your right fist. Clench your right fist as tight as you can and hold it . . . Study the tension . . . and relax . . . Feel the tension dissolve and feel the relaxation spread through your fingers and your hand, your lower arm." [Jacobson, 1938, p. 74]

Successive relaxation exercises focus upon face and shoulders, trunk and abdomen, thighs, legs, and feet. Jay Meredith, whose case history is given in Chapter 12, began to learn deep muscle relaxation during his fourth therapy session. He continued the exercises through the eighth therapy session and practiced them daily at home.

Training in assertive behavior is often an

integral part of the systematic desensitization procedure. It is a useful technique in its own right and is employed with patients for whom desensitization is not appropriate. But it often happens that patients undergoing desensitization can also benefit from assertive training. One reason for this is that assertive behavior—self-expression, self-control, and self-assertion in interpersonal situations—inhibits interpersonal anxiety by reciprocal inhibition much as deep muscle relaxation does.

Assertive training can take several forms. Jay Meredith was given training in assertiveness toward both his father and girls because he felt that he could not be properly forthright with either. He role-played a variety of assertive responses with his therapist before he was given the assignment to use a certain number and kind of assertive responses toward specific people in his environment. When these responses were not met with counter-hostility, ridicule, or rejection, they reinforced further assertive efforts on Jay's part. Recent reports on the use of assertive training to treat compulsive behavior (Tanner, 1971), homosexual pedophilia, or attraction to children (Edwards, 1972), and interpersonal anxiety in group settings (Rathus, 1972) supplement earlier findings that it is effective with more traditional neurotic behaviors (Lazarus, 1971; Wolpe, 1969; Yates, 1970).

As relaxation and assertive training proceed during the early stages of systematic desensitization therapy, therapist and patient together develop anxiety or fear hierarchies for use in the coming desensitization. These hierarchies list the situations that trigger the anxiety or fear for which the patient first sought therapy. The items on each list are arranged in the order of their capacity to elicit fear or anxiety.

Many kinds of hierarchies are described in recent reports. For example, a hierarchy associated with anxiety about childbirth: "Typical themes were the obstetrical examination, leaving home for the maternity hospital, receiving injections, feeling uterine contractions, being in the labor ward, and experiencing the phases of childbirth" (Kondas & Scetnicka, 1972,

p. 52). A hierarchy of fears about flying: "A desensitization hierarchy of 56 items, based on the temporal sequence involved in planning, anticipating, and executing a commercial flight, was constructed. The items ranged from deciding to make a flight, getting tickets, making preparation, and going to the airport, to various aspects of taking off, flying, and landing" (Bernstein & Beaty, 1971, p. 260). And a hierarchy of themes in a hand-washing compulsion: "Picking up objects from the floor without touching floor, picking up objects from the floor with touching floor, emptying dirty ash tray, picking up dirty clothes, touching husband's genitals, cleaning commode, vacuum cleaning, having dirty hands" (Rackensperger & Feinberg, 1972, p. 124).

The desensitization procedure itself is straightforward. After the patient, using his new relaxation skills, informs the therapist that he has relaxed completely, the therapist asks him to imagine a neutral or "control" scene (say, lying on a beach on a warm summer day). This scene serves as a non-anxiety-provoking image to which the patient can return as desensitization proceeds. The therapist then starts desensitization by describing in detail the scene lowest in the patient's hierarchy—the item that causes him least anxiety or fear. If the patient, now fully relaxed, can imagine that scene in detail without experiencing anxiety, the therapist moves up the hierarchy by one scene. When the patient does come to a scene in the hierarchy which arouses his anxiety, the therapist asks him to return either to the control scene or to a scene lower on the hierarchy.

Desensitization continues until the patient can imagine the entire hierarchy without experiencing the anxiety or fear that it previously elicited. According to Wolpe (1969), desensitization of most anxiety- or fear-provoking stimuli takes fewer than fifteen therapy sessions.

Behavior therapists point with pride to the relative accessibility of their techniques to experimental investigation. Much of this research is focused on outcome measurement—comparisons of the rates of success among

Group desensitization for severe dog phobias. *(The New York Times)*

various therapies (it will be reviewed later in the chapter along with research on the efficacy of the dynamic therapies). But the desensitization process also lends itself to empirical study of the various components of therapy, in part because it contains elements which can be readily separated and therefore easily varied. Recent studies have explored therapist and client variables that influence therapeutic outcome (Borkovec, 1972; Lang, 1970; Lomont & Brock, 1971a), relationships between the duration of scenes in a hierarchy, their timing and ordering, and the outcome (McNamara & MacDonough, 1972; Paul, 1969a & 1969b) and the extent to which relaxation training plays a central role in the desensitization process itself (Garlington & Cotler, 1968; Hyman & Gale, 1973; Sue, 1972). Results of these and other studies must be regarded as tentative because they have not yet been replicated. But in general they suggest that the rather rigid format for desensitization advocated by Wolpe and his colleagues for many years may in fact be unnecessary to the overall success of the method.

Implosion therapy and flooding. Implosion therapy is a dramatic variant of the Wolpean desensitization paradigm. As described by its originators, Stampfl and Levis, it involves exposing patients to the top (most arousing) scenes in their fear and anxiety hierarchies so that they will experience these emotions at full intensity (1967, 1968). Stampfl and Levis's research and that of others (Boudewyns & Wilson, 1972; Fazio, 1970, 1972) suggest that the method is useful with phobic and anxious patients who can withstand its rigors.

Flooding, a kind of implosion therapy, has similar goals. It differs from implosion therapy in that it involves exposing the patient to actual fear- or anxiety-evoking situations. Following is a dramatic instance of the successful use of flooding. The patient was—

. . . a 41-year-old Protestant (woman) with a 13-year-history of severe obsessive compulsive neurosis. She first sought psychiatric help after the birth of her second child. There was a marked exacerbation of symptoms soon after the terminal illness of her father who died of cancer.

... She experienced difficulty in handling objects she believed to have been in physical contact with her father shortly before his death. ... Later this generalized to a pervasive cancer phobia in which a multitude of objects in her home came to be seen as disease carriers. Chief among these were raw meat, particularly pork. ... By the time of her referral for behavior therapy in May 1968 she had become almost totally incapacitated. She was unable to make routine decisions, could not prepare meals, expressed anxiety about her children's welfare and complained about numerous obsessive preoccupations. ... Flooding took the form of bringing her into a small, almost windowless room, in which there was a table and two chairs. A large piece of raw pork as well as some minced pork meat lay on the table covered by a cloth. In presence of the therapist the patient was asked to remove the cloth. This she did gingerly, then averted her face and quickly began to sob. At the therapist's request she then returned to the table, touched the raw carcass and made meat balls from the minced pork. Because she did this with outstretched arms, taking care not to have the meat touch more than her fingers, the therapist picked up a meat ball and threw it to her. She caught the meat ball and complied with the request to throw it back and forth to the therapist. At this point she remarked "I know you hope that one of these will disintegrate and spatter all over me." This did, in fact, happen at which time she was brought a dish of rather dirty water in which to wash her hands. She continued to do this for about 15 min. after which one brief implosion session was carried out in the same room. ... Following this experience the patient was urged not to change her dress for a week and no further treatment was given for a few days. During that time, she reported and soon after demonstrated she could handle meat but the obsessive thoughts remained. They were subsequently dealt with by further flooding, thought-stoppage, assertive training and desensitization *in vivo*. ... She was discharged early in January, 1969. ... When last heard of, 18 months after termination of treatment, she was still managing the household. ... She reported some residual preoccupation with her former fears but these did not seem to prevent her from functioning as a mother, wife, and housekeeper. [Baum & Poser, 1971, pp. 251–252]

Though implosion therapy and flooding appear to possess proved utility, a variety of studies suggest that they are not applicable to all phobic reactions. For example, Jay Meredith in Chapter 12 tried to "cure" his subway and bus travel phobia by spending long Saturdays riding on buses and subways. He was overwhelmed by anxiety and panic during many of these rides and ultimately had to stop his self-administered flooding, because his fears and anxieties seemed to be getting worse rather than better.

Positive reinforcement and extinction. Though most clinical applications of positive reinforcement and extinction have been with schizophrenic and other psychotic patients (Chapter 7), or with children in classrooms, at home, and in institutions (Chapter 15), efforts have also been made to use operant reinforcement and extinction to alter neurotic behaviors. Assertive training occurs within the operant paradigm. That is, patients are first taught this additional behavioral option through reinforcement by the therapist; then they are reinforced for assertive behavior by social approval from persons in their environment; finally, assertive responses are maintained by the patients' own "self-reinforcement" system.

One of the most innovative continuing research and development programs involving operant treatment strategies for neurotic problems is that of Leitenberg, Agras, and Barlow. An early study by this group used positive reinforcement to treat two female adolescents suffering from anorexia nervosa. (This is an exotic psychiatric syndrome characterized by severe and rapid weight loss. It is caused by a voluntary reduction in eating, uncontrollable vomiting, or both). When praise from a therapist was made contingent upon eating a gradually increasing amount, the patients' food intake increased dramatically and remained at adequate levels during a prolonged follow-up (Leitenberg et al., 1968a).

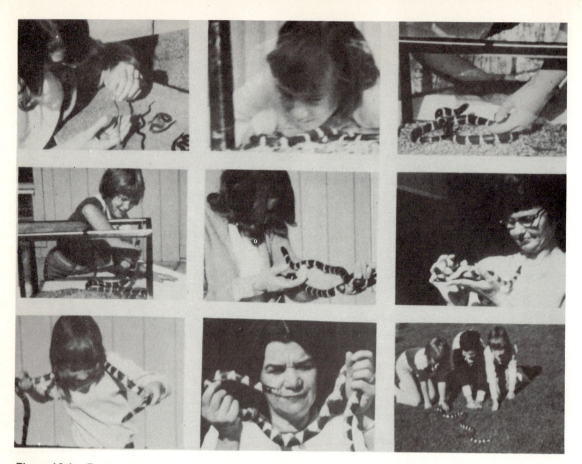

Figure 10-1. Frames from a movie shown to the "symbolic modeling" group of subjects during an experiment for snake phobia. The relative effectiveness of this and two other types of behavioral therapy are presented in Figure 10-2. *(Bandura et al., 1969)*

Other studies by the same group have employed positive reinforcement and extinction procedures with a variety of "chronic neurotic patients." For example, patients were reinforced by a therapist's praise for increasing progress along a one-mile "course" from the medical center to a downtown area. Following the introduction of this social reinforcement, the distance that patients would walk increased. When the reinforcement was withdrawn, their therapeutic progress stopped, and reappeared only when praise was resumed (Agras et al., 1968). In another study, praise given a severely claustrophobic woman for increasing the periods of time she spent in a small room had a profoundly positive effect on her phobia (Leitenberg et al., 1968b).

Leitenberg summarizes the strategy behind his entire line of research as follows: "When expectations of success are combined with repeated practice in the feared situation together with praise and feedback, all the ingredients for an effective treatment of phobia are present" (1972). This therapy strategy, called *reinforced practice,* continues to be explored (Callahan & Leitenberg, 1970; Leitenberg et al., 1971), though its current development centers on treatment of *nonclinical* fears—fears that are not disabling (for example, fear of heights, animals, thunder, darkness, and lightning).

Modeling. During the 1960s Bandura's ambitious research program focused upon the roles of modeling, imitation, vicarious learning, and vicarious reinforcement in normal learning. At the end of the decade he undertook to develop a procedure for use with "adolescents and adults who suffered from snake phobias that, in most cases, unnecessarily restricted their activities and adversely affected their psychological functioning in various ways" (1969, pp. 182–183; Bandura et al., 1968). Some of the subjects could not accept jobs that required them to risk the possibility of coming in contact with snakes; others refused to garden or to hike for the same reason.

Four matched groups were made up from the sample of subjects. The first, the "symbolic modeling" group, saw a movie in which children, adolescents, and adults engaged in increasing interaction with a large king snake (see Figure 10-1). The subjects were also taught relaxation exercises to be used during the film, and they could regulate the speed at which the film was projected. Armed with these desensitization skills, the "symbolic modeling" group watched the film again and again until the members were able to view it from beginning to end without experiencing anxiety.

A second group of subjects was labeled the "live modeling with participation" group. Its members first watched a live model touch, hold, fondle, and stroke a king snake with gradually increasing fearlessness. Then the subjects themselves were led by the model to perform the same behavior, although much more gradually and slowly. This process, called "contact desensitization," continued until they reported no anxiety with a wide range of snake-touching behavior.

Subjects assigned to the third, or "desensitization," group received Wolpe's standard desensitization treatment until they no longer experienced anxiety even while imagining very intimate and prolonged contact with a snake. Subjects in the fourth (control) group completed the full battery of behavioral and attitudinal assessment instruments given all subjects before and after treatment. They did not receive therapy for their snake phobias.

Figure 10-2 shows that while the control subjects experienced essentially no change in the severity of their phobic avoidance be-

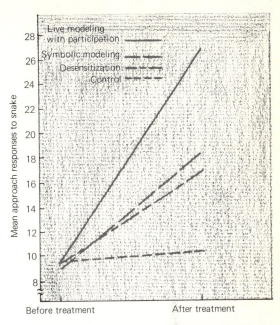

Figure 10-2. Results of the experiment in snake-phobia therapy. The groups of patients who were treated by "symbolic modeling" and by desensitization improved after treatment: they were more willing than before to approach snakes. The greatest improvement of all in snake-approach behavior was in the subjects who were treated by live modeling with participation. Control subjects, who received no treatment, showed no significant change. (Bandura et al., 1969)

havior, members of the symbolic modeling and desensitization groups showed substantial improvement. It was the subjects who received live modeling with participation, however, who improved dramatically: the number of approaches they made to snakes more than doubled during treatment. A follow-up one month later showed that these therapeutic gains were maintaining themselves. More important, some of the subjects in all three treatment groups (but not in the control group) had begun to alter preexisting behavior patterns by putting themselves in places where they might come in contact with snakes.

Since publication of these findings, clinicians have begun to try out modeling for treatment of neurotic behaviors (Kazdin, 1973; Rappaport et al., 1973.) For example, one study applied modeling and guided participation in an attempt to modify a 6-year-old boy's extreme social withdrawal (Ross et al., 1971). His entry into public school had been delayed because of his unwillingness to interact with other children. The boy was normal in intelligence and normal in psychological development except for his withdrawal behavior.

The patient was seen three times a week for seven weeks. During the first four individual therapy sessions, the boy was trained to imitate a variety of behaviors modeled by the experimenter. He was given "tangible and social rewards" for imitative responses. At the end of the fourth session, he showed a strong attachment to the experimenter and readily imitated him. Following this first phase of treatment, the patient watched the experimenter, or model, begin a graduated series of social interactions with other children at the school which the boy would attend. Other verbal techniques designed to teach him to apply "cognitive rehearsal" and desensitization to his fears of social involvement were also introduced. In addition, the model and patient role-played potential child-child interactions. Then the experimenter began to initiate actual social interaction with other children, gradually bringing the patient into these situations. Treatment was concluded after seventeen sessions. Assessment measures revealed that "treatment was effective in increasing subject's social interactions to approximate those of the socially competent baseline control children. . . . Treatment was also effective in reducing the frequency of subject's avoidance behavior." A follow-up after two months indicated that the patient had maintained his gains in social competence.

Another study compared the differential effectiveness of flooding and modeling with ten chronic obsessive-compulsive patients (Rachman et al., 1971). The experimenters concluded that both techniques produced significant clinical improvement. Since none of the ten patients in the study had been able to function normally before treatment, these positive findings supported Rachman's earlier

view (1968) that flooding is now a proved treatment method.

Rachman has also said: "The fact that flooding and modeling methods proved to be equally successful in the treatment of chronic obsessional patients . . . suggests the possibility that all three fear-reducing techniques— modeling, desensitization and flooding—are variations on a single theme. A fairly obvious candidate for consideration in this connection is the phenomenon of extinction. . . . Another possibility, closely related, is that the underlying process in all three procedures is one of habituation to sensitized or sensitizing stimulation" (1972, pp. 391–392). Others will doubtless argue that it is simplistic to posit a common mechanism underlying three important behavior therapy procedures. Still, the idea that such a mechanism might exist is intriguing.

Self-control. Another focus of behavior therapy research is self-control procedures— methods for self-management, self-reinforcement, and self-regulation—as ways to handle anxiety, depression, fears, and other neurotic behaviors. Kanfer (1970a, 1970b; Kanfer & Karoly, 1972) and Bandura (1971) have done important basic research in this area. In a recent critical review of such research, Mahoney (1972) divides what he calls the self-management area into three subareas:

1 *Self-reinforcement.* "Any self-management (SM) enterprise designed to increase the probability of some target behavior either by the self-presentation of positive consequences or by the removal of negative consequences."

2 *Self-punishment.* "Any SM enterprise designed to decrease the probability of a target behavior via the self-presentation of negative consequences or the removal of positive consequences."

3 *Auxiliary techniques.* "SM procedures which emphasize stimulus variables and incompatible response."

Positive self-reinforcement has been employed successfully to treat "social anxiety" (by a gradual increase in self-exposure to social situations for which self-reinforcement was given; Rehm & Marston, 1968) and obsessional thoughts of worthlessness (by increasing the frequency of interfering positive self-references; Mahoney, 1971). Positive self-reinforcement was also used to treat problem behaviors in classrooms (Glynn, 1970) and study problems (Lovitt & Curtiss, 1969). No studies of negative self-reinforcement or positive self-punishment have yet been reported, though negative self-punishment (berating or condemning oneself after behaving badly) is a frequent human behavior pattern.

Broad-spectrum behavior therapy. Broad-spectrum behavior therapy is the term applied to the cluster of therapeutic techniques that Lazarus and others use to deal with a wide range of behavior disorders, including neurotic ones. As described in his recent book *Behavior Therapy and Beyond* (1971), these techniques include conventional behavior therapy procedures like systematic desensitization, behavior rehearsal, modeling, assertive training, and aversive conditioning. However, broad-spectrum therapy also utilizes pragmatically derived methods less closely connected to the learning-theory base from which the behavioral methods are derived. While Lazarus has been severely criticized (Edwards, 1972, Wolpe, 1969) for deviating from Wolpe's reciprocal inhibition model, Lazarus and others have argued persuasively against such a restrictive view of behavior therapy. Who is right? The question can be answered only by more research that compares the results of "conventional" and broad-spectrum behavior therapy in matched groups of subjects.

One of the techniques in Lazarus's broad-spectrum therapy (which he has recently renamed *multimodal therapy*) is the "blow-up" method. Here he describes its use:

I had a 22-year-old male patient with several debilitating obsessive-compulsive reactions. One of his most distressing habits was a tendency to keep checking the men's room at a theatre or

Arnold A. Lazarus.

movie for a possible outbreak of fire. Typically, at intermission, or before taking his seat in the movie, he would visit the men's room, smoke a cigarette, and then go inside the theatre. Soon he would feel a mounting panic. He would ask himself, "I wonder whether I accidentally started a fire in the men's room?" He would leave his seat and rush back to the men's room and carefully check. . . . This was repeated about 15 to 20 times during the average movie. . . . I then gave him the following instructions: "When the urge to check comes over you, do not leave your seat. Instead, I want you to imagine that a fire has indeed broken out. First, picture the toilet paper and then the toilet seats catching fire and spreading to the doors, then going along the floor, so that eventually the entire men's room is ablaze . . . soon the entire movie house . . . is a roaring inferno. This blaze is like no other. It cannot be stopped . . . imagine the entire neighborhood on fire . . . the entire city is devoured . . . One city after another is demolished . . . until the entire country is ablaze. The flames even spread across the oceans until the entire world is on fire. Eventually the whole universe is one raging inferno." . . . The patient practiced this sequence when he next attended a movie and reported that after an initial acute feeling of panic, he became calm, somewhat amused, and "realized how ridiculous it was to keep checking." [1971, pp. 230–231]

Lazarus's broad-spectrum treatment for the neurotic and sexual disorders is similar in many ways to another approach, Ellis's rational-emotive therapy. Ellis says that his therapy has three successive goals: (1) to help the patient identify the irrational beliefs and assumptions which determine his inappropriate emotional reactions to the world, (2) to enable him to challenge those beliefs and assumptions, and (3) to encourage him to modify his philosophy of life in order to regain rational control over his emotions (1962, 1971). The procedures and techniques that Ellis uses to bring about these therapeutic goals are like many of Lazarus's, a fact both acknowledge. In some cases his contributions predate Lazarus's, in others they postdate him.

Drug therapy

When tranquilizing drugs are given to neurotic patients, they are most often prescribed to relieve severe or chronic anxiety, insomnia, agitation, or depression. Drugs used for these purposes are almost always selected from the group of minor tranquilizers, among which are benactyzine (Suavitil), chlordiazepoxide (Librium), diazepam (Valium), meprobamate (Miltown, Equanil), and oxazepam (Serax). The most widely used and most effective of these drugs are Librium and Valium. The minor tranquilizers differ from the major tranquilizers in several important ways: they have fewer and less serious side effects, they are less amenable to addiction, they attack nonpsychotic rather than psychotic symptoms, and their therapeutic effects are more often due to "placebo reactions" than are those of the major tranquilizing drugs.

Controversy continues among mental health professionals on the proper use of these drugs. Some dynamic therapists, for example, feel that the anxiety which the drugs are designed to alleviate is an important component of the treatment setting, since it motivates patients to continue psychotherapy even when it becomes painful. Some mental health professionals accuse some psychiatrists of dispensing minor tranquilizers to avoid undertaking psychotherapy with patients who cannot afford it. In this regard it is worth remembering that disproportionate numbers of low-SES patients are apparently given "organic" therapy, which includes tranquilizers, rather than psychotherapy.

Psychotherapy, behavior therapy, or drugs: The great controversy

One of the most hotly debated issues in the mental health area concerns the relative effectiveness of the various treatment approaches to the neurotic behaviors. The neuroses are omnipresent in most Western societies. Their alleviation would represent an extraordinary step forward—perhaps equal in importance to the successful treatment of poliomyelitis or syphilis.

Both psychoanalysis and behavior therapy trace their roots to initial successes with specific neuroses. Yet there is no proved best treatment for these conditions, unlike the schizophrenias, for which the major tranquilizers are clearly helpful. Though some psychiatrists employ behavior therapy and many psychologists use psychoanalysis and psychoanalytically oriented psychotherapy, behavior therapy is seen as largely the province of psychologists, while psychoanalysis is most closely identified with psychiatry. As a result the struggle for therapeutic primacy is also a battle for professional power.

Our review of this issue will include (1) an evaluation of research which has studied the efficacy of psychoanalysis or psychoanalytically oriented psychotherapy alone, (2) an assessment of studies directly comparing the differential efficacy of psychoanalysis, psychotherapy, and drug therapy, and (3) an evaluation of findings comparing psychotherapy and systematic desensitization. For discussions which go beyond our brief summary the reader must turn to some of the books on the subject (Bergin & Garfield, 1971; Bergin & Strupp, 1972; DiLoreto, 1971).

Eysenck's 1952 review of the effects of psychotherapy. More than twenty years after its publication, Eysenck's 1952 review of the effects of psychotherapy remains the starting point for discussions of the effectiveness of psychotherapy with neurotic patients. For analysis he chose twenty-four studies which met the research criteria that he felt were necessary for objective and valid evaluative purposes. Practically all the patients in the studies he selected had been given one or another of the "neurosis" labels. After reviewing the data, he concluded that psychotherapy does not help in the treatment of neurosis:

Patients treated by means of psychoanalysis improve to the extent of 44 per cent; patients treated eclectically improve to the extent of 64 per cent; patient treated only custodially or by general practitioners improve to the extent of 72 per cent. . . . There thus appears to be an inverse correlation between recovery and psychotherapy; the more psychotherapy, the smaller the recovery rate. . . . In general, certain conclusions are possible from these data. They fail to prove that psychotherapy, Freudian or otherwise, facilitates the recovery of neurotic patients. They show that roughly two-thirds of a group of neurotic patients will recover or improve to a marked extent within about two years of the onset of their illness whether they are treated by means of psychotherapy or not. [1952, pp. 324]

Despite the flood of criticism which followed this report (Luborsky, 1954; Rosenzweig, 1954), and despite the masses of data that have accumulated since, Eysenck has held to his position (1961, 1966, 1967). He stated it even more strongly in 1966 than in 1952:

The writer must admit to being somewhat surprised at the uniformly negative results issuing from all this work. In advancing his rather challenging conclusion in the 1952 report, the main motive was one of stimulating better and more worthwhile research in this important but somewhat neglected field. . . . Such a belief does not seem to be tenable any longer in this easy optimistic form, and it rather seems that psychologists and psychiatrists will have to acknowledge the fact that current psychotherapeutic procedures have not lived up to the hopes which greeted their emergence fifty years ago. [P. 40]

Bergin's response to Eysenck. Criticism of Eysenck has concentrated on his lack of objectivity, the ambiguity with which he reported the substance of studies of which he was critical, and an apparent lack of comparability between patients who received psychoanalytic therapy and those who were given eclectic therapy (Kiesler, 1966; Luborsky et al., 1971; Strupp, 1964). One of the most telling of critiques comes from Bergin, a behaviorist and hence presumably a sympathizer with Eysenck's viewpoint. After reanalyzing the original data on which Eysenck based his conclusions, Bergin wrote:

Despite the limitations of the studies published prior to 1952, the results up to that time must be considered encouraging . . . the longer and more intensive the treatment, the better the results. The eclectic therapy studies frequently involved very brief and superficial treatment. [They] yielded the poorest results. [1971, pp. 227]

From his own review of forty-eight recent studies of therapy outcome, Bergin concluded:

In general, it may be stated at the outset that the picture here is similar to that already presented in regard to studies appearing prior to 1952. While the methodological sophistication and precision of studies have improved markedly, the evidence continues to yield the general conclusion that psychotherapy, on the average, has modestly positive effects . . . most of these studies are quite gross in character. They are tests, for the most part, of whether therapy has any effect at all, but they usually do not examine whether specific methods have specific consequences, nor do they examine the notion that only a small proportion of therapists and patients may be accounting for the positive effects when they do occur on averaged data. [p. 262]

Drugs *versus* psychotherapy. Fewer studies have been made during the past twenty years on the comparative efficacy of drugs and psychotherapy for the treatment of the neuroses. In perhaps the most thorough (Koegler & Brill, 1967), 299 neurotic outpatients were assigned at random to one of six groups receiving the following treatments: prochlorperazine (a major tranquilizer), meprobamate (a minor tranquilizer), phenobarbital, placebo, psychotherapy, and no treatment (the control group). Therapist ratings of the outcomes revealed two nonsignificant trends: patients in the meprobamate and psychotherapy groups improved the most; those in the phenobarbital and prochlorperazine groups changed the least. Patient ratings of outcomes were quite different: they judged meprobamate to be significantly more effective than any other treatment.

Drugs *and* psychotherapy. In a study of neurotic outpatients who were given psychotherapy and drugs or psychotherapy and a placebo, Rickels and his co-workers found that the combination of psychotherapy and meprobamate (Equanil) was most effective as judged by patients and therapists (1966). Studies of mixed groups of outpatients with a preponderance of neurotic diagnoses yield comparable results. Thus Lorr and his colleagues (1962), studying 150 outpatients of whom 82 percent were neurotic, found that chlordiazepoxide (Librium) had a positive effect on overall severity of illness in the context of a short-term therapy situation.

Reviewing these and other findings, May concludes that so far as drugs and psychotherapy for neurotic patients are concerned, "the main trend of opinion is that although drugs may perhaps be helpful as an adjunct in certain situations, it is generally preferable to use psychotherapy alone to help the patient to identify and to solve his problems" (1971, p. 499). The opposite conclusion was reached

by Unlenhuth and his colleagues, also following an extensive review of the research (1969). They claimed that while drugs and psychotherapy are of no greater benefit to patients than drugs alone, the combination is consistently superior to psychotherapy alone.

Our own view differs from both May's and Unlenhuth's; we are not convinced that either the "traditional" psychotherapeutic methods or the minor tranquilizing drugs have been effective for the neuroses. Therefore we are dubious that a combination of two apparently weak therapeutic agents would function better than either alone. Instead, we anticipate further growth in innovative therapeutic strategies—specifically in the behavioral techniques—and trust that they too will receive careful and objective evaluation. Paul's comprehensive and thoughtful review of the efficacy of desensitization therapy is an excellent beginning in this regard. He wrote:

While 55 of these papers were uncontrolled case reports or group studies without sufficient methodological controls to establish independent cause-effect relationships, 20 of the reports were controlled experiments, and 10 of the controlled experiments included designs which could potentially rule out intraclass confounding of therapist characteristics and treatment techniques. The findings were overwhelmingly positive, and for the first time in the history of psychological treatments, a specific therapeutic package [systematic desensitization] reliably produced measurable benefits for clients across a broad range of distressing problems in which anxiety was of fundamental importance. "Relapse" and "symptom substitution" were notably lacking. [1969a, pp. 158–159]

Other reviews of the efficacy of systematic desensitization conclude, as did Paul, that the method is clearly superior both to no treatment controls and to dynamic psychotherapy (Eysenck, 1971, 1973; Marks & Gelder, 1968; Krasner, 1971). The authors of these review articles, however, are committed behavioral psychologists; further, most of the studies they reviewed had evaluated the success of systematic desensitization for behavior problems like speech anxiety (as against "clinical problems" like diffuse anxiety, depression, or obsessions).

Because the other behavioral methods that are promising so far as the neuroses are concerned (positive reinforcement and extinction, aversive conditioning, modeling, and self-control) have been developed only recently, objective reviews of their efficacy have not yet appeared. Thus, while early reports on these methods are promising, their utility in comparison with psychotherapy or drugs has not been established.

Summary

The psychoanalytic theory of neurosis, Freud's most important etiologic statement, has gone through successive refinements since his work in the late nineteenth century. Basing his initial conclusions upon a limited sample of female neurotic patients, Freud ultimately produced what has become the "classical" psychoanalytic view of neurotic etiology. It claims that the neuroses result from inner conflict between drives (largely sexual) and fears—between id and superego functions. Central to development of the conflict, according to Freud, is the oedipal situation, which forces all children to deal with conflicting feelings aroused by love for the opposite-sex parent and fears of retribution for this love from the same-sex parent. The conflict, suitably disguised and repressed, was thought by Freud to account for adult neurosis. Though empirical validation of the theory has not been convincing, Freud's model continues to influence psychoanalytic approaches to the neuroses.

Other psychoanalytic theorists, among them Jung and Adler, were unwilling to accept the central role that Freud gave to sexual factors in the etiology of neurosis. They formed alternative theories emphasizing the importance on nonsexual dynamic factors in the development of neurosis. The interpersonal theorists Horney and Fromm, writing somewhat later, stressed the influence of relationship variables on the initiation and maintenance of neurotic behavior. Existential theorists like May and Binswanger, on the other hand, explained neurosis as a direct function of man's unique recognition of his future nonbeing—his death.

The first distinctly behavioral theory of neurosis was articulated by Dollard and Miller in 1950. Though it was explicitly designed to bridge the gap between psychoanalytic and learning conceptions of psychopathology, Dollard and Miller's position was clearly that many important neurotic behaviors are learned. More recently, behaviorists like Eysenck, Wolpe, and Bandura, among others, have formulated explicit learning-based models of neurosis derived to a greater or lesser extent from laboratory studies of animal analogues to human neurosis.

The goals of psychoanalysis, which is preferred by many mental health professionals for the treatment of neurosis, can be stated as follows: Psychoanalysis aims to help the individual deal with the world as a function of his realistic place in it and its realistic impact on him rather than on the basis of his own biased view of the world attained from his own particular set of experiences. Despite its position as the most-favored treatment for neurosis, psychoanalysis is not for everyone. Patients who do best in dynamic treatment are in good contact with reality, are intact emotionally and intellectually, are bright, well motivated, and verbally facile, and are wealthy enough to afford an expensive and time-consuming form of treatment.

Among the most important techniques employed in the psychoanalytic treatment of the neuroses are free association, dream analysis, and interpretation. Among the invariable phenomena with which the therapist must deal during psychoanalysis are resistances and transference. For people who do not have the time and money for psychoanalysis, psychoanalytic psychotherapy, a shorter and less intensive treatment that focuses more on current than on historical issues, may be appropriate. Another therapy that concentrates on the "here and now" is client-centered therapy, developed by psychologist Carl Rogers. One of its major contributions has been the productive research it has fostered, some of which suggests that empathy, warmth, and genuineness are necessary for therapists of all theoretical persuasions in order to achieve successful therapeutic outcomes.

Wolpe's reciprocal inhibition therapy, first set forth in 1954, stimulated much of the outpouring of clinical research and application that has established systematic desensitization as a popular treatment for many of the neurotic disorders. A central element of the therapy involves training the neurotic patient in a behavior which will compete and, it is hoped, inhibit the anxiety which often accompanies neurotic behavior. The competing behavior most often chosen for this purpose is deep muscle relaxation which, together with assertive behavior, has successfully displaced anxiety in the response hierarchies of many neurotic patients. Implosion therapy and flooding, positive reinforcement and extinction, modeling, training in self-control, and broad-spectrum behavior therapy have also been employed by behaviorally trained clinicians to deal with neurotic behavior.

CHAPTER ELEVEN
Alcoholism and drug dependence

Ralph Lyon ● Piri Thomas ● Who is an alcoholic? ●
Etiology, cues, assessment, treatment ● Who is a drug
addict? Etiology, cues, assessment, treatment

SALLY LYON
VISITS THE
ALE-HOUSE

When Sally Lester gave her hand in marriage to Ralph Lyon, she
was a delicate, timid girl of 18, who had passed the springtime of life
happily beneath her father's roof. To her, care, anxiety, and trouble
were yet strangers. The first few years of her married life passed
happily, for Ralph was one of the kindest of husbands, and suffered
his wife to lean upon him so steadily that the native strength of her
own character remained undeveloped.

Ralph Lyon was an industrious mechanic, who always had steady
work and good wages. Still, he did not seem to get ahead as some
others did, notwithstanding that Sally was a frugal wife and did all
her own work, instead of putting him to the expense of help in the

An 1884 view of Demon Rum:
"The first result of the introduction of the bottle. Laziness and craving for more
liquor, to relieve the feeling
of despondency produced by
indulgence in drunkenness."
(New York Public Library)

family. Of course, this being the case, it was evident that there was a leak somewhere, but where it was neither Ralph nor his wife could tell. . . .

"I am sure it isn't your fault—at least I don't think it is," reflected Ralph, "but something is wrong somewhere. I don't spend anything at all, except for a glass or two every day, and a little tobacco; and this, of course, couldn't make the difference."

Sally said nothing. A few glasses a day and tobacco, she knew, must cost something, though, like her husband, she did not believe it would make the difference between security and their own precarious situation. But let us, gentle reader, see how it really is. Perhaps we can find the leak that wasted the substance of Ralph Lyon. He never drank less than three glasses a day, sometimes four; and his tobacco cost, for smoking and chewing, just twelve and a half cents a week. Now, how much could all this amount to? Why, to just sixty-five dollars a year, provided but three glasses a day were taken, and nothing was spent in treating a friend. But the limit was not always observed, and the consequence was that, take the year through, at least eighty dollars were spent in drinking, smoking, and chewing. Understanding this, the thing is very plain. In four years, eighty dollars saved in each year would give the handsome sum of three hundred twenty dollars. Mrs. Lyon came to this very realization. It was, in fact, Ralph's drinking and smoking that were keeping them on the ragged edge.

At length, Sally ventured to hint at the truth. But Ralph met it with—"Pooh! nonsense! Don't tell me that a glass of liquor, now and then, and a bit of tobacco, are going to make all that difference. It isn't reasonable. Besides, I work very hard, and I ought to have a little comfort with it. When I'm tired, a glass warms me up and makes me bright again; and I am sure I couldn't do without my pipe."

The condition of Ralph Lyon and his family grew worse and worse. From not being able to save anything, he gradually began to fall in debt. Poor Mrs. Lyon felt very miserable at the aspect of things; more especially since, in addition to the money squandered at the ale-house by her husband, he often came home intoxicated. The grief to her was more severe, from the fact that she loved Ralph tenderly, notwithstanding his errors.

One day she was alarmed by a message from Ralph that he had been arrested while at his work, for debt, by his landlord, who was going to throw him in jail. She asked a kind neighbor to take care of her children for her, and then, putting on her bonnet, she almost flew to the magistrate's office. There was Ralph, with an officer by his side ready to remove him to prison.

"You shan't take my husband to jail," she said, wildly, when she saw the real aspect of things, clinging fast hold of Ralph. "Nobody shall take him to jail."

"I am sorry, my good woman," said the magistrate, "to do so, but it can't be helped. The twenty dollar debt must be paid, or your husband will have to go to jail. I have no discretion in the matter. Can you find means to pay the debt? If not, perhaps you had better go and see your landlord; you may prevail on him to wait a little longer for his money, and not send your husband to jail."

Mrs. Lyon let go the arm of her husband, and, darting from the office, ran at full speed to the house of their landlord.

"Oh, sir!" she exclaimed, "you cannot, you will not send my husband to jail."

"I both can and will," was the gruff reply. "A man who drinks up his earnings as he does, and then, when quarter-day comes, can't pay his rent, deserves to go to jail."

It was vain, she saw, to strive with the hard-hearted man, whose face was like iron. Instead, she hastened home. On entering her house, she went to her drawers, and took therefrom a silk dress, but little worn, a mother's present when she was married; a good shawl, that she had bought from her own earnings when a happy maiden; a few articles of jewelry, that had not been worn for years, most of them presents from Ralph before they had stood at the bridal altar, and sundry other things, that could best be dispensed with. These she took to a pawnbroker's, and obtained an advance of fifteen dollars. She had two dollars in the house, which made seventeen; the balance of the required sum she borrowed from two or three of her neighbors, and then hurried off to obtain her husband's release.

For a time, the rigid proceedings of the landlord proved a useful lesson to Ralph Lyon. But then, instead of getting better, things grew worse, year after year. At last even the few dollars Mrs. Lyon had received every week from her husband's earnings ceased to come into her hands. The wretched man worked little over half his time, and drank up all that he made.

Matters at last reached a climax. Poor Mrs. Lyon had not been able to get any work to do herself for a week, and all supplies of food, except a little meal, were exhausted. She was truly at her wit's end. Wrapping each of her two little children around with a piece of an old shawl, and after putting on her bonnet, she took them by the hands and left the house. It was a chilly night in winter. The wind swept coldly along the streets, piercing through the thin garments of the desperate mother, who was leading forth her tender little ones on some strange, unnatural errand. At length she stopped before the window of an ale-house, within which she saw her husband sitting comfortably by a table, a glass by his side, and a pipe in his mouth.

Mrs. Lyon remained without only a few moments; then taking hold of the door she walked firmly in, and without appearing to notice her husband, went up to the bar and called for three glasses of brandy. Mr. Lyon jumped from his chair and stood before his wife, just as she had taken her seat at the table, saying in an undertone, as he did so—

"For Heaven's sake, Sally! What brings you here?"

"It is very lonesome at home, Ralph," she replied, in a calm but sad voice. "Our wood is all gone, and it is cold there. I am your wife, and there is no company for me like yours. I will go anywhere to be with you. I am willing to come even here. God hath joined us together as one, and nothing should divide us."

Sipping the burning liquid that had been brought to their table, and smacking her lips, Sally looked into her husband's face and smiled. "It warms to the very heart, Ralph!" she said. "I feel better already." Then turning to the children, whose glasses remained untouched before them, she said to the astonished little ones.

"Drink, my children! It is very good."

"Woman! Are you mad? My children shall not touch it."

"Why not?" said his wife, "If it is good for you, it is good for your wife and children. It will put these dear ones to sleep and they will forget that they are cold and hungry. To you it is fire and food and bed and clothing—all these we need, and you will surely not withhold them from us."

The drunken husband was confounded. He knew not what to do or say. The words of his wife smote him to the heart; for she uttered a stunning rebuke that could not be gainsaid.

"Sally," he said, after a pause, in an altered and very earnest tone, "I am going home, and I intend staying there. Won't you go with me, and try to make it as comfortable as it used to be. Here, once and forever, I solemnly pledge myself before God never again to drink the poison that has made me more than half a brute, and beggared my poor family. Come, Sally"

"The Lord in Heaven be praised!" Sally said, solemnly, "for it is His work. Yes, come! Our last days may yet be our best days."

The hopeful declaration of Mrs. Lyon proved indeed true. There was soon light, and fire, and food again in that cheerless dwelling; and the last days of Ralph and his family have proved to be their best days, for he has never since tasted the bitter cup. [Arthur, 1850, pp. 184–195]

PIRI THOMAS VISITS DOGIE

"Look," I said bad-like, "I've used this stuff before, But some wise motherfucker don't seem to know that I did and maybe like punks gotta be shown." Looking dead at Alfredo, I inhaled, first through one nostril, then through the other. Then, turning quickly away, I went into the cold street. Almost immediately I felt a burning sensation in my nose, like a sneeze coming. I pulled out my handkerchief and had barely enough time to put it to my nose when the blood came pouring out. *Man, I thought, this cap has blown out the insides of my nose.* But, in a few seconds the bleeding stopped just as it had started. Now the night lights seemed to get duller and duller, my awareness of things grew delayed. But the music was clearer and I felt no pain, nothing at all. I seemed sort of detached. I felt a little sick in my belly, but the good-o feeling was even better. I saw Trina coming to meet me, and I crossed the street and walked toward her, walking real light, real dreamy and slow, so she would have to meet me more than halfway. Sometimes I'd make her walk all the way to me, but tonight I felt good.

"Hi, Marine Tiger," I greeted her. She was a beautiful girl—dark, curly hair, large black eyes, red mouth, and a real down figure. Tonight she had a new dress. *Man*, I thought, *she's action come alive.* But when she asked me how she looked, I merely grunted, "*Buena, nena.*"

"She told me she felt good to be by my side. *Man, I love you, Trina, I feel good.* I felt my face. It was like touching someone else. A little voice bugged me: *You're on your way, baby, you're walking into junkies' alley.* "Aw, the hell with you," I half blurted out and turned the corner, my arms tightly around Trina.

Heroin does a lot for one—and it's all bad. It becomes your whole life once you allow it to sink its white teeth in your blood stream. I never figured on getting hooked all the way. I was only gonna play it for a Pepsi-Cola kick. Only was gonna use it like every seven days, that is until the day I woke up and dug that I was using it seven times a day instead. I had jumped from a careful snorter, content to take my kicks of sniffing through my nose, to a not-so-careful skin-popper, and now was a full-grown careless mainliner.

At first it was like all right, because I had some bread going for me, but them few hundred bucks melted real fast and all I had was a growing habit. I still had some clothes and a wrist watch but they went the same way the money went. I got a job for a while, but forty bucks or so weren't enough and the more I used, the more I needed.

"Yet there is something about dogie—heroin—it's a superduper tranquilizer. All your troubles become a bunch of blurred memories when you're in a nod of your own special dimension. And it was only when my messed-up system became a screaming want for the

Mainlining, like snorting (inhaling), is an effective route to oblivion by heroin. *(Eugene Anthony from Black Star)*

next fix did I really know just how short an escape from reality it really brought. The shivering, nose-running, crawling damp, ice-cold skin it produced were just the next worst step of—like my guts were gonna blow up and muscles in my body becoming so tight I could almost hear them snapping. [Thomas, 1967, pp. 110–111, 200–201]

Dealing with society's stepchildren

DSM II, the APA's *Diagnostic and Statistical Manual* (1968), brings together a variety of different behavior disorders under the heading, "Personality Disorders and Certain Other Nonpsychotic Mental Disorders." Two of these syndromes, alcoholism and drug dependence, are discussed here; two others, the sexual deviations and the personality disorders, are considered in Chapters 12 and 13. These disorders share several common features. First, they are not characterized by psychotic or neurotic psychopathology (delusional and hallucinatory behavior, severe anxiety and depression, etc.). Second, they are probably not of organic origin. Third, they tend more often than not to be lifelong patterns of adjustment to the environment. Fourth, people who are given these labels sometimes come into direct conflict with society owing to the antisocial nature of many of their actions.

Because we, the authors, think that society bears some responsibility for their antisocial acts, we believe that people with personality disorder, alcoholic, drug addict, or sexual disorder labels are at least partly *failures of society*. Some of these failures of society have failed to learn the fundamental rules by which society feels it must operate; they grew up in subcultures which had not accepted the rules. Malcolm X and Piri Thomas fit into this group. Others emit such behaviors in an effort to cope with an intolerable environment. Many ghetto blacks say they use heroin to escape the bleakness of life without hope. Others rebel against society for what they consider its hypocrisies—

for permitting some of its citizens, for example, to profit from legal alcohol and cigarettes while it condemns those who use marijuana or choose the homosexual way of life. This group of rebels, which includes the middle-class "speed freaks" and "acidheads," is perhaps the largest and least understood of all those we call failures of society.

We have chosen to illustrate alcoholism and drug addiction with excerpts that contrast the behavioral effects of the drugs, the consequences of their prolonged use, and the standards by which their addicts were judged 100 years ago and now. The first portrays Sally Lyon's sad plight as seen through the eyes of a mid-nineteenth-century temperance worker. Her story describes the unhappy consequences of having an alcoholic husband—consequences that are the same today as they were in 1850. Sally's tale also conveys a sense of the harsh moral judgment made about alcoholism a century ago. It may be significant that Dostoevsky's father was an alcoholic, since the impact of having a father whom society considered morally reprehensible must have been great.

Though its effect on the alcoholic and everyone around him is still profound, alcoholism is viewed more objectively today. It is seen as a social, psychological, and perhaps physical problem rather than as a clear sign of moral degradation. (Even so, the issue of "will power," a holdover from the old moral concerns, sometimes still intrudes into discussions of alcoholism.) Current treatment focuses on attempts to alter patients' social and environmental circumstances rather than their morality or their will power. The case notes on Bill H. at the beginning of Chapter 5 epitomize current "enlightened" approaches to alcoholism. Though Bill's case was described in Chapter 5 because it illustrates contemporary problems in diagnosis, it also illuminates several important features of chronic alcoholism whose discussion properly belongs here:

1 The alcoholic is rarely only overindulgent. When he comes to the hospital for treatment, he usually has a variety of physical illnesses, some of which may stem directly from his alcoholism (for example, an enlarged, malfunctioning liver), some of which probably have nothing to do with it (for instance, Bill's tests showed that he might have temporal lobe epilepsy), and some of which may or may not be related to it (hallucinations or delusions).

2 Alcoholism is rarely the only diagnosis that the clinician is called upon to make in the patient who drinks to excess. Clinical signs of schizophrenia, epilepsy, psychopathy, and hysteria can be recognized at various points in Bill's chronicle.

3 The alcoholic patient's alcoholism is never his problem alone. Bill's alcoholism affected many people, including his family, his friends, and workers in a variety of public agencies. In this regard, alcoholism and the drug dependencies differ dramatically from other physical illnesses, whose effects are often confined to a single person's pain and suffering.

4 The alcoholic's motivation for treatment is rarely high. It must be increased before a reasonable hope for successful treatment can be entertained. In Bill's case most of the hospital staff considered him "just another old crock," and it was partly for this reason that he was lost to treatment.

5 The fact that Bill was admitted to a psychiatry service in the first place is unusual. Any person who has worked in a large urban hospital knows how unwelcome alcoholics are on the hospital's emergency floor, and how unwilling hospital personnel are to admit them to medical or psychiatric wards unless they are experiencing delirium tremens or are seriously ill from other physical illnesses. The tragedy of Bill's case was not that he was admitted to the hospital but that once he was there, no one could help him.

Most cases of alcoholism have even less drama than Bill's. The moderately depressed, moderately anxious, middle-class housewife who begins to forget things, scold her husband and children, lose interest in sex, and worry about the drinks she "must" have before social gatherings; the successful, hard-driving, ambitious middle-management executive who admits to "one or two" double martinis at lunch to see him through the pressure-filled day; the physician who has always been conscientious about his work and professional responsibilities but begins to slip a little, especially first thing in the morning—all are people who may be on the way to alcoholism, more quietly and more discreetly but no less surely than Bill H.

But given the gross errors of judgment—the hospital staff's insensitive mistakes of approach—that resulted in Bill H.'s decision to pass up continued treatment for his alcoholism, a genuine effort was made to understand his problem and help him with it. In other words, Bill H. was not simply condemned by all those who saw him as a weak-willed reprobate who deserved everything bad he had received at the hands of society.

By contrast, Piri Thomas introduces the issue of morality again and again into his discussion of his drug addiction. Though it is possible to read between the lines and conclude that he also sees his antisocial behavior as a response to social injustice—to job discrimination and unequal opportunities in life—he evaluates his actions in fundamentally moral terms. As this chapter will show, some scientists share with Thomas the inability to take an objective view of the socially destructive behaviors associated with alcoholism and drug addiction.

Alcoholism

Historical perspectives

Alcohol and alcoholics have been part of man's history ever since he learned that fermented grain or fruit yields an intoxicating substance with pleasant effects on mood and conviviality.

Noah might have been mankind's first recorded inebriate. The Old Testament says: "And Noah the husbandman began, and planted a vineyard. And he drank of the wine, and was drunken; and he was uncovered within his tent" (Genesis 9:20, 21). The authors of the Book of Proverbs emphatically condemned social drinking: "Look not upon the wine when it is red, when it sparkleth in the cup, when it goeth down smoothly; at the last it biteth like a serpent and stingeth like an adder" (Proverbs 23:31, 32).

The use of alcohol has waxed and waned through the ages. It waxed under the Greeks and Romans and waned in the lands controlled by Islam during the dark ages. In more recent times, it waxed during the lusty hedonism of the Elizabethan era and waned as efficiency and productivity became bywords during the industrial revolution. At the beginning of the industrial era, ardent tracts condemning the effects of alcohol appeared, and groups were formed in England and the United States to take up the cause of temperance. The calculatedly heartrending story of Ralph Lyon's redemption is the product of one of these groups. The most prominent of them in the United States was Carrie Nation's Women's Christian Temperance Union (WCTU). The WCTU was influential in bringing about Prohibition, the "experiment noble in purpose," as President Hoover called it, which began in 1920 and ended in 1932.

The end of Prohibition marked the beginning of a more scientific approach to alcoholism, brought on in large part by recognition of the dismal failure of the Prohibition laws to change public morality. A variety of alcoholism research projects began, encouraged by the newly founded Yale Center of Alcohol Studies and its *Quarterly Journal of Studies on Alcohol*. The advent of the "vitamin age" led to the discovery that many diseases which had been considered alcoholic in origin were actually products of malnutrition and vitamin deficiency (see Chapter 17). Alcoholics Anonymous was also formed shortly after the end of Prohibition. Society's more objective approach to alcoholism has even recently resulted in legislation defining alcoholism as a medical disease instead of a criminal offense (though whether this new attempt to legislate public opinion will be more successful than the one which led to Prohibition remains to be seen).

THE

SONS OF TEMPERANCE

OFFERING:

FOR

1850.

"—— Health consists with Temperance alone,
And Peace, O virtue! Peace is all thine own."
POPE.

EDITED BY
T. S. ARTHUR.

NEW YORK:
PUBLISHED BY NAFIS & CORNISH.

Who is an alcoholic?

There is no single definition of alcoholism. Nevertheless, several behavioral criteria taken together help mental health professionals make judgments about the severity of a drinking problem: (1) The person reports a loss of control of his drinking behavior. (2) He needs a drink to get going in the morning, to keep going during the day, or to prepare himself for stressful events—he has become psychologically dependent upon alcohol. (3) He has lost jobs or alienated his family or friends because of his drinking. (4) He has experienced blackouts, increasing tolerance for alcohol, or both. (5) He reports withdrawal symptoms when he stops drinking; he is physically dependent upon alcohol.

In this set of criteria the term *psychological dependence* describes a strong, sometimes overwhelming need for a drug. *Physical dependence* refers to need for a drug that is accompanied by painful symptoms of physiological withdrawal (for example, restlessness, nausea, vomiting) when the drug is no longer taken. After a fixed dose of a drug has been ingested at regular and frequent intervals, certain of its effects progressively decrease in intensity. This phenomenon is drug *tolerance*. It necessitates taking larger and larger doses to produce the desired effect. *Blackouts* are characteristic short-term memory deficits that appear after a person has been a heavy drug user for a long period of time. These terms describe effects that are common to all drugs, not just to alcohol.

Varieties of alcoholism

The two most common formal systems for categorizing problem drinkers and alcoholics are those offered by Jellinek (1960) and DSM II, *The Diagnostic and Statistical Manual* (1968). Jellinek classes the varieties of alcoholism as follows: (1) *Alpha alcoholism* represents reliance upon alcohol to relieve bodily or emotional pain but does not lead to loss of control. The major damage is to interpersonal

Most "skid rowers" are gamma alcoholics. *(Joel Gordon)*

relationships. This alcoholic is often termed the "problem drinker." (2) *Beta alcoholism* describes the kind of alcoholism that is associated with physical complaints such as gastritis or cirrhosis of the liver but that does not involve either physical or psychological dependence upon alcohol. (3) *Gamma alcoholism* refers to patients who have acquired increased tissue tolerance to alcohol, experience withdrawal symptoms when they stop drinking, have become psychologically dependent upon alcohol, and have lost control of their drinking. Most skid row alcoholics are of this type. (4) *Delta alcoholism* differs from gamma alcoholism in one way: Delta alcoholics cannot abstain from drinking, while gamma alcoholics, though they have lost control of their drinking, are nonetheless capable of periods of sobriety. The Frenchman who loves his wine and drinks a bottle or so at every meal might be a Delta alcoholic without knowing it, since he never tries to stop.

DSM II categorizes the physical and psychological effects of alcohol abuse in three separate places. The brain damage that is caused by heavy, prolonged drinking is grouped with the other *organic psychoses* (see Chapter 17). Simple drunkenness that does not involve psychotic-like behavior is listed separately as a *nonpsychosis of physical origin.* The largest group of alcohol-related problems are included within the broad *personality disorder* category. In this category the "alcoholism" label includes four subgroups: episodic excessive drinking, habitual excessive drinking, alcohol addiction, and "other" alcoholism. Though it is a more objective and hence more verifiable system than Jellinek's, DSM II's scheme is essentially a static one and may not fit the actual behavior of alcoholics as well as Jellinek's system does. As will become clear from the empirical data on the drinking behavior of alcoholics, their pattern of alcoholism often changes as time and circumstances change.

Some of the limitations of both the Jellinek and DSM II systems become obvious when we try to fit them to the lives of Malcolm Little and Ralph Lyon. Little's drinking was likely to be very, very heavy on one occasion and almost nonexistent on another. Neither system adequately describes this unusual pattern, which presumably developed both to relieve some of the stresses associated with his competitive, hostile urban environment and to meet or exceed the consumption standards of his peers. Such a complex of determinants of drinking behavior is probably as powerful as any purely physiological ones. So far as the story of Ralph Lyon is concerned, it is difficult to pigeonhole the behavior portrayed in that fictionalized moral tale, largely because of the amazing rapidity and ease with which Ralph made the decision to stop drinking. The term "loss of control" characterized his drinking for many years, and the ability to regain control so suddenly and completely is inconsistent with this concept.

On the other hand, Bill H.'s alcoholism fits nicely into Jellinek's gamma alcoholism category—though that category, like the DSM II pigeonholes, fails to suggest a treatment approach which Bill would have accepted. This is the major limitation of both systems: most of their diagnostic categories have little real value beyond the mere ritual of classification itself. Affixing diagnostic labels does not help prevent others from making the same mistakes in their drinking behavior, nor does it point the way to effective treatment.

Etiologies of alcoholism

No definitive etiology of alcoholism has been established, although biophysiological, sociological, psychoanalytic, and behavioral theories have been proposed.

Biophysiological theories. One of the first and most persistent of the biophysiological theories of alcoholism hypothesized that alcoholics and nonalcoholics differ in the rate at which they metabolize alcohol. If it could be demonstrated, this difference would have profound etiologic significance. However, a number of recent studies have reported that the rate of ethanol metabolism between groups of alcoholics and nonalcoholics does not differ (Mendelson, 1968). Efforts to detect differences between alcoholics and nonalcoholics in cellular adaptation to ethanol, or in adrenal medullary and adrenergic mechanisms (which influence tolerance phenomena), have also failed. These mechanisms clearly depend upon alcohol consumption and nutritional variables rather than on innate or acquired differences in bodily function between alcoholics and nonalcoholics (Mendelson, 1970).

Although no physical bases for alcoholism have yet been found, research into biophysiological determinants continues. Lately this effort has focused on the possible role of genetic factors in alcoholism. Support for a genetic view comes from human twin studies (Kaij, 1960), which indicated that monozygotic twins have a higher concordance rate for alcoholism (more often share the disorder) than dizygotic twins, and from animal research that produced strains of inbred mice which prefer alcohol (Rodgers & McClearn, 1962).

Sociological theories. Many investigators have demonstrated the profound impact that cultural patterns of drinking have on rates of alcoholism. First-generation Italian-Americans and Jewish-Americans, both from cultures in which drinking takes place in a family or religious context, drink frequently but have low rates of alcoholism (Cahalan et al., 1969; Lolli et al., 1958). The Irish, who drink in pubs, have lower consumption rates but higher alcoholism rates than the other cultural groups. As all these groups become acculturated within the American "melting pot," their rates of alcoholism become more similar. Recent data indicate that second- and third-generation American Jews have a significantly higher rate of alcoholism than first-generation Jews; the reverse is true of Irish-Americans (Secretary of HEW, 1971).

Though cultural influences can predispose a person to alcoholism, social variables play a major role in translating that predisposition to actual addiction. They can also operate to keep the alcoholic drinking. Peer pressure, for example, has a powerful influence in the development of deviant drinking patterns among adolescents (Jessor et al., 1972; Braucht et al., 1973).

Psychoanalytic theories. Psychoanalysts explain alcoholism in several ways. Some see the alcoholic as fundamentally suicidal in his efforts to destroy a "bad, depriving mother" with whom he has identified. Others claim that he is "defending" himself against an underlying depression by drinking to oblivion. Still others say that the alcoholic drinks in defense against overwhelming anxiety (deVito et al., 1970). Critics of the psychoanalytic approach to alcoholism point out that there are no empirical data to support these hypotheses and that psychoanalysis does not help most alcoholics who seek treatment (Franks, 1970).

Behavioral theories. The behavioral view of alcoholism etiology has not yet been well articulated. Most behavioral approaches are variations on the basic theme that drinking is a learned means of reducing conditioned anxiety. They differ as to which learning mechanisms are responsible for the anxiety.

Implicit in the hypothesis that alcohol is a tension reducer is the assumption that it eases anxiety for alcoholics. However, a recent study comparing alcoholics and matched non-alcoholics on a variety of behavioral dimensions found that this assumption is not completely valid (Nathan & O'Brien, 1971). The investigators reported that following an initial twelve- to twenty-four-hour period of drinking during which levels of anxiety do decrease, alcohol actually *increases* levels of anxiety and depression in alcoholics. Other researchers who obtained the same results concluded that the presence of alcohol may act as a discriminative stimulus with both positive and negative properties for the alcoholic (Okulitch & Marlatt, 1972).

While these findings do not invalidate the behavioral view of the etiology of alcoholism, they do paint a picture of alcoholism that is more complex than the simple "anxiety reduction" model. They explain the alcoholic's decision to initiate new episodes of drinking by assuming that he remembers only the immediate effects of liquor in alleviating his anxiety and depression and not its end result of increasing them. This phenomenon reflects the influence of "blackout," a deficit in short-term memory function associated with chronic alcoholism and brought on by high blood-alcohol levels (Lisman, 1973; Nathan et al., 1972).

Cues to alcoholism

Efforts to identify behavioral cues to alcoholism have not been successful. Nathan's systems analysis failed to identify psychopathological symptoms that differentiate alcoholics from other psychiatric patients. Sober alcoholics with no physical or neurological complaints displayed virtually no symptoms at all. Sober alcoholics with physical or neurological complaints showed symptoms of "organicity" indistinguishable from those of other "organic" conditions with psychological concomitants. And intoxicated alcoholics manifested symptoms that were not significantly different from those of patients intoxicated with other drugs (Nathan, 1969).

Assessment of alcoholism

For every study reporting that the alcoholic is an "oral character," "dependent," "masochistic," or a "masked depressive" on the basis of projective test results or depth interviewing, another three fail to find such distinguishing characteristics (Tremper, 1972; Zucker & Van Horn, 1972). Objective tests, however, have identified what seem to be reliable behavioral differences between alcoholics and nonalcoholics. For example, scale 4 of the MMPI, the "psychopathic deviant" subscale, differentiates alcoholics from nonalcoholics (MacAndrew, 1965) and is sensitive to treatment changes in hospitalized alcoholics (Rohan et al., 1969; Rohan, 1972). Other MMPI scales—those measuring levels of depression and anxiety—also appear to be sensitive to individual differences in the severity and intensity of alcoholism among a range of drinkers (Overall & Patrick, 1972; Whitelock et al., 1971).

Examination of the items from scale 4 which differentiate drinkers from nondrinkers shows that the scale's sensitivity to alcoholic behavior is largely a result of three items: those which ask whether the subject has ever used alcohol to excess, has ever been in trouble with the law, or feels that he has not lived the right kind of life. Consequently one must consider whether it might not be simpler to ask suspected alcoholics these three questions and skip the rest.

Experimental psychopathology

The animal model. Until recently a major stumbling block in using animals as models for human alcoholism was that alcohol was not a demonstrated reinforcer for laboratory animals (Mello, 1973). This behavioral difference between humans and "lower" animals meant that many of the most important causes and effects of human drinking—those having to do with psychological factors—were not open to exploration through animals. Woods and his co-workers, however, have now developed an animal model of alcoholism which seems to include the reinforcement component important to the human model (1971). In this promising research advance Woods has been able to "shape" monkeys into emitting operant responses reinforced by ethanol.

The human model. Through the years the "social psychology of psychological research" has exercised a powerful influence on the scope and nature of alcoholism research. The influence was felt in two ways: (1) It delayed controlled research into the behavior of drinking alcoholics until society's opposition to giving alcohol to alcoholics was outweighed by its interest in the benefits of such research. (2) It led researchers to concentrate on the behavior of skid row alcoholics, because their low social status and lack of political power rendered them "expendable" as research subjects.

Studies involving the acute (short-term) administration of alcohol to alcoholics and nonalcoholics were begun before chronic (long-term) studies were undertaken. The acute studies focused mainly on the effects of measured doses of alcohol on physiological, metabolic, and behavioral functioning of alcoholics as compared with nonalcoholics.

Docter and his co-workers found that acute ingestion of alcohol by alcoholics leads to increases in heart rate, rapid eye movements (REMs) during sleep, and EEG alpha activity (1966). These investigators were intrigued to find that maximum increases in EEG activity were induced by very light alcohol dosages, and that performance on a task demanding continuous attention to an auditory signal did not worsen after the alcoholics had begun to drink. Talland and other researchers have also showed that even relatively large amounts

GETTING DRUNK DOESN'T MAKE YOU... TALL ...

RICH... STRONG... HANDSOME...

SMART ... WITTY... SOPHISTICATED...

OR SEXY... ...JUST DRUNK

IN FACT IT DOESN'T DO A
THING FOR YOU – EXCEPT
GET YOU DRUNK.

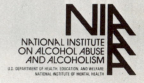

NATIONAL INSTITUTE
ON ALCOHOL ABUSE
AND ALCOHOLISM

U.S. DEPARTMENT OF HEALTH, EDUCATION, AND WELFARE
NATIONAL INSTITUTE OF MENTAL HEALTH

FOR INFORMATION OR FOR HELP, WRITE: NATIONAL CLEARINGHOUSE FOR ALCOHOL INFORMATION, BOX 2345, ROCKVILLE, MARYLAND 20852

D GPO : 1972 O—319-206

of alcohol do not interfere with some perceptual and motor performances by alcoholics (1964). Some investigators (reviewed by Mello, 1972) have actually observed an *increase* in the ability to perform these and other tasks when alcoholics are drinking at moderate levels. Others, however, have found the opposite (Talland, 1966).

One drawback to acute drinking studies is that they do not portray the customary drinking behavior of chronic alcoholics. Mendelson and Mello were the first investigators to study prolonged drinking by alcoholics in a controlled laboratory setting. Their early studies (1964) were done in a hospital ward at Boston City Hospital, an appropriate research site since according to Efron and Keller's recent figures (1970), Boston has the second-highest per capita incidence of alcoholism in the United States. (San Francisco has the highest.) Among the most important findings of Mendelson and Mello's first set of studies were the following:

1 Tolerance (behavioral adaptation to alcohol) was exhibited by most of the alcoholics. It was reflected by a gradual increase in adequacy of performance on a number of tests of thinking and of coordination as drinking continued.

2 A change in cardiac function associated with both alcohol ingestion and alcohol withdrawal was identified.

3 "Craving" for alcohol, a phenomenon thought to doom the recovered alcoholic who takes as much as a single drink after a period of sobriety, was not observed even when subjects were given a drink after a period of sobriety. In fact, craving failed to appear until large quantities of alcohol had been consumed over a period of many days.

4 Observation of relationships between alcohol ingestion, spontaneous cessation of drinking, and onset of alcoholic gastritis (irritation of the stomach lining intense enough to cause vomiting) suggested that susceptibility to serious stomach upset in the face of prolonged drinking might be one of the major determinants of the drinking patterns of many alcoholics.

Since the first set of laboratory studies, Mendelson and Mello's work has been supplemented by that of Nathan and his colleagues in independent research designed to illuminate the physiological and psychological effects of prolonged drinking by alcoholics. Both groups of researchers have demonstrated that certain behaviors associated with prolonged drinking appear to be relatively unaffected by

"My parents taught me to fear God and respect my fellow-man. I was president of my class at college and was voted most likely to succeed. After graduation, I joined the staff of a large corporation and devoted all my energy to my work. I neither drank nor smoked nor let pleasure deflect me from my objective. As the years passed, my devotion was rewarded with increasing responsibilities until finally I was elected Chairman of the Board. I was given an honorary degree by Columbia, and the President of the United States bestowed on me the Medal of Merit for services in my country's behalf. At the height of my career, I was invited to pose for an advertisement featuring men of outstanding accomplishment. I accepted this honor. The photographer posed me before his camera and placed in my hand a glass of liquid. Out of curiosity, I took a sip—and then another sip—and another . . ." *(Drawing by Cobean; Copr., 1948, The New Yorker Magazine, Inc.)*

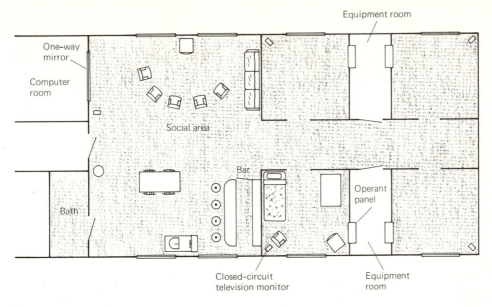

One-way mirror

Computer room

Social area

Equipment room

Bath

Bar

Operant panel

Equipment room

Closed-circuit television monitor

Figure 11-1. A hospital research ward where the behavior of alcoholics was studied. The four small patient rooms are individual bedrooms, each equipped with a closed-circuit TV monitor and devices ("operant panels") which registered the subjects' responses. The larger "social area" has a television set, a dining table, and a fully equipped bar. The layout is useful in studying patterns of socializing that are connected with alcohol consumption. One of Nathan and O'Brien's findings from a study using this ward was that alcoholics are social isolates before, during, and after drinking. *(Modified from Nathan & O'Brien, 1971)*

psychological or social factors. These behaviors include a characteristic and often dramatic increase in levels of depression and anxiety that often occurs shortly after drinking begins, and an equally common cycle of "spree" and "maintenance" phases within a single prolonged drinking episode (Mello, 1972; Nathan et al., 1971).

In a study at Boston City Hospital comparing the social, affective, and drinking behavior of skid row alcoholics and skid row nonalcoholics, Nathan and O'Brien brought the two groups of subjects at different times to the research ward diagrammed in Figure 11-1 (1971). Four alcoholics and four nonalcoholics took part in these identical thirty-three-day experiments. Major results were as follows:

1 Though both alcoholics and nonalcoholics reached the same high blood-alcohol levels early in drinking, the alcoholics remained at these levels longer and returned to them more frequently. Hence they drank almost twice as much as the nonalcoholics.

2 Alcoholics began drinking with a 6- to 8-day "spree," followed by a longer "maintenance" drinking period (a period when levels of intoxication are lower and more stable); nonalcoholics were only "maintenance" drinkers.

3 Unlike the nonalcoholics, the alcoholics were social isolates before, during, and after drinking.

4 Once drinking began, the alcoholics became significantly more depressed and less active and demonstrated significantly more psy-

chopathology (anxiety, manic behavior, depression, paranoia, and the neurotic behaviors of phobia and compulsions) than nonalcoholics.

The results of the study, like those from other studies by Mello, Mendelson, and Nathan, suggest that, contrary to widespread belief, the alcoholic may not be an "all-or-none" drinker and may not drink to reduce high levels of depression and anxiety. They also suggest that the uncontrolled drinking behavior of the alcoholic rather than a set of presumed personality quirks may be his distinguishing characteristic. This hypothesis suggests that the behavioral (as against the dynamic) approach to therapy may be most appropriate for alcoholism.

Treatment of alcoholism

Detoxification and drugs. "Detoxification" is the term that describes the process by which patients intoxicated by alcohol (or any other drug) are withdrawn from it. More detoxification of alcoholics takes place in city jail

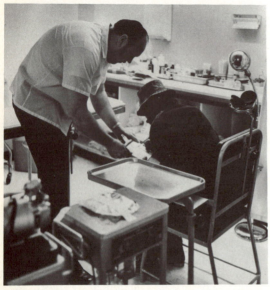

Drying out in Manhattan: An alcoholic gets help at a hospital-based detoxification project in New York City. *(The New York Times/William E. Saure)*

lockups than in any other institutional setting. The danger of detoxification in a nonmedical setting is the possibility of serious, perhaps fatal, withdrawal symptoms. Civil authorities have become worried enough about lockup withdrawals to speak out publicly in favor of more adequate detoxification facilities. In such facilities alcoholics who wish or need to terminate a drinking episode can be helped to reduce blood-alcohol levels without also precipitating serious consequences of withdrawal. Where blood-alcohol levels are very high to begin with, the alcoholic can be given alcohol in gradually decreasing amounts to lessen the chance of severe withdrawal effects. Tranquilizers like Librium and Valium may also be used.

Withdrawal from alcohol is a very serious matter—more serious than most people realize. After a prolonged period of heavy consumption, withdrawal is more dangerous to life and limb than withdrawal from heroin. The untreated mortality (death) rate for alcoholics who have delirium tremens, a relatively common withdrawal symptom, is 10 to 15 percent. Furthermore, significant numbers of alcoholics die or are permanently disabled by complications arising from the severe vomiting, dehydration, and malnutrition that can accompany alcoholic withdrawal.

Although no drug exists which by itself prevents uncontrolled drinking, there have been two drugs which for a while were thought to be "magic bullets" for alcoholism. Flagyl, a drug used to treat fungi in the vagina, recently attracted attention following the observation that women alcoholics who were taking the drug sharply reduced their alcohol intake. Flagyl quickly gained a host of supporters who testified to its therapeutic efficacy with alcoholism. But careful, controlled clinical trials on large numbers of alcoholics finally disproved these claims (Penick et al., 1969).

Antabuse interferes with the metabolism of alcohol so dramatically that its presence in the bloodstream in even trace amounts when alcohol is drunk causes dramatic, prolonged, and extremely unpleasant effects. They include sudden nausea, vomiting, dramatically increased heartbeat and respiration, and "cold sweats." Though at first many clinicians considered it a panacea for alcoholism, Antabuse must now be viewed more realistically. When taken as directed—on awakening in the morning, before the "impulse to drink" strikes—it is an effective deterrent to drinking for two or three days. On the other hand, when the "mood to drink" does strike, Antabuse can be easily avoided and the alcoholic can resume drinking in a few days. A recent study by Lubetkin and his co-workers found that less than 1 percent of all patients receiving maintenance doses of Antabuse under optimal conditions in the hospital after detoxification continued to take it after their release (1971). The authors of this study concluded that for Antabuse to work, patients must be well motivated, in which case it does serve the useful function of protecting the recovered alcoholic from occasional "reversion impulses."

Alcoholics Anonymous. The history of Alcoholics Anonymous—A.A. to its worldwide coterie of members and friends—is usually dated from a weekend in May 1935. At that time Bill W. (not to be confused with Bill H., whose case we have already discussed) and Dr. Robert S., both alcoholics, met to discuss the formation of a treatment milieu free from the medical and moral domination that characterized therapy for alcoholism. In the second edition of his book *Alcoholics Anonymous* (1955), Bill wrote: "In addition to . . . casual get-togethers, it became customary to set apart one night a week for a meeting to be attended by anyone or everyone interested. . . . Aside from fellowship and sociability, the prime object was to provide a time and place where new people might bring their problems" (Bill W., 1955, p. 159).

The latest edition of A.A.'s *World Directory* (1973) provides a glimpse of the phenomenal growth of the organization during the first 39 years of its existence. From the initial two-man group, there are now over 16,000 autonomous A.A. groups holding over 20,000 weekly meetings throughout the United States, the Canal Zone, the Bahamas, the Virgin Islands,

> ## THE TWELVE SUGGESTED STEPS OF A.A.
>
> *1—We admitted we were powerless over alcohol—that our lives had become unmanageable.*
>
> *2—Came to believe that a Power greater than ourselves could restore us to sanity.*
>
> *3—Made a decision to turn our will and our lives over to the care of God as we understood Him.*
>
> *4—Made a searching and fearless moral inventory of ourselves.*
>
> *5—Admitted to God, to ourselves and to another human being the exact nature of our wrongs.*
>
> *6—Were entirely ready to have God remove all these defects of character.*
>
> *7—Humbly asked Him to remove our shortcomings.*
>
> *8—Made a list of all persons we had harmed, and became willing to make amends to them all.*
>
> *9—Made direct amends to such people wherever possible, except when to do so would injure them or others.*
>
> *10—Continued to take personal inventory and when we were wrong promptly admitted it.*
>
> *11—Sought through prayer and meditation to improve our conscious contact with God as we understood Him, praying only for knowledge of His will for us and the power to carry that out.*
>
> *12—Having had a spiritual awakening as the result of these steps, we tried to carry this message to alcoholics and to practice these principles in all our affairs.*

Figure 11-2. The "twelve steps" of Alcoholics Anonymous, from an A.A. pamphlet. The pamphlet also says: "The only requirement for A.A. membership is a desire to stop drinking."

and Puerto Rico. Though firm figures are not available, it is likely that there are well over 211,000 active A.A. members in the United States. The *World Directory* also lists over

2,000 A.A. groups in Canada and close to 4,800 other groups scattered through the rest of the world.

On referral to the A.A. "fellowship" by a friend, a relative, a clergyman, a professional, or the police, the prospective member is immediately introduced to the "twelve steps," which are listed in Figure 11-2. They form a set of rules for living not unlike the sets of moral tenets used by many religious groups. Two other fundamentals of the A.A. philosophy are that the alcoholic must recognize that he can never drink again and must concern himself only with abstaining for "one day at a time" rather than with the long-term problem of his alcoholism.

On making his first contact with A.A., the prospective member is usually provided with a sponsor, a recovered alcoholic who assumes responsibility for helping the new member deal with the personal crises that accompany the decision to stop drinking. The sponsor accompanies his "prospect" to A.A. meetings, where the new member begins to learn A.A.'s ideology, rules for living, and expectations. It is an impressive experience for people who are "down on their luck" and without hope to listen to a well-dressed man or woman tell of the depths from which he or she has emerged, with A.A.'s help, never to return to the bottle again.

Though objective data on the therapeutic efficacy of A.A. are difficult to come by, most professionals familiar with the movement believe that it represents the most effective current treatment for alcoholism. For this reason, it is striking that A.A.'s "cure" rate seems to be just 30 to 35 percent (Ditman, 1967), a rate that would be condemned as grossly inadequate for any other major social problem.

Dynamic therapies. Although Freud referred only occasionally to alcoholism, dynamically based individual and group treatment probably remains the predominant therapy for alcoholics by mental health professionals. Yet Freud himself was dubious about the utility of psychoanalysis for "character neuroses,"

among which alcoholism usually is classed. The results of a recent careful review of forty-nine papers published between 1952 and 1963 reporting on studies of psychotherapy with alcoholics draws the unhappy conclusion that the authors were "unable to form a conclusive opinion as to the value of psychotherapeutic methods in the treatment of alcoholism" (Hill & Blane, 1967).

Other researchers have claimed success with alcoholics through psychoanalytically oriented psychotherapy (Silber, 1970), psychoanalysis (Shentaub & Mijolla, 1968), and dynamically oriented group therapy (Smith, 1969). Unfortunately, these reports are unaccompanied by empirical research data, forcing us to conclude that the utility of psychotherapy for alcoholics remains to be established.

Behavior therapy. In the dramatic upsurge of interest in behavior modification that has taken place during the last decade, alcoholism has been a "target" disorder. Franks observes that over time, behavioral treatment of the alcoholic has fallen into three distinct phases (1970). The first, the direct application of classical conditioning techniques to alcoholism, generally involved efforts to pair the sight, taste, or smell of alcohol with an aversive agent in order to establish a conditioned avoidance response to alcohol. In an early study cited by Franks, fifteen alcoholic patients were subjected to the following conditioning procedure (Sanderson, et al., 1963). Each was given a bottle containing his favorite beverage and told to hold it, look at it, smell it, and then put it to his lips and taste it. After five such "familiarization" trials, the paralytic drug succinylcholine was injected intravenously. The patient was then handed the bottle again, at which point the effects of the drug made their dramatic entry. The patient became totally paralyzed, unable to move or breathe. After a few such conditioning trials, the majority of patients "developed a conditioned aversion to alcohol in any form" so that its sight, taste, and smell brought back the feelings of fear and paralysis they had experienced during the pairing of alcohol and succinyl-choline. Despite the experimenters' conclusion that their method resulted in "favorable recovery rates," similar studies with more extensive follow-ups have not been so enthusiastic (Holzinger et al., 1967; Farrar et al., 1968).

The use of succinylcholine presented moral and medical problems as well as problems of therapeutic effectiveness. So behaviorists working with alcoholics began to evaluate the utility of other aversive agents, such as electric shock and unpleasant covert stimuli (that is, stimuli in the patient's own thoughts). According to Franks, the second phase of the behavioral approach to alcoholism began when the aversive techniques, which punished the preference for alcohol, were combined with other procedures which reinforced the avoidance of alcohol.

The classic application of electrical aversion conditioning combined with operant reinforcement of alcohol avoidance was undertaken by MacCulloch and his colleagues (1966). They modeled it after their use of similar procedures, described in the next chapter, to treat homosexuality (Feldman & MacCulloch, 1965). Alcoholics were shown "photographs of beer and spirits, the sight of an actual bottle of alcohol (stoppered), the sight of an open bottle of alcohol, and alcohol in a glass." A tape repeating an invitation to have a drink of the patient's favorite beverage was also played. Slides of orange squash—a soft drink—were used as "relief stimuli."

The actual conditioning procedure was as follows: Patients were shown one of the alcohol-related stimuli. If they pushed a switch to remove the stimulus within eight seconds of its onset, they avoided an electric shock. In so doing, they also illuminated the non-alcohol-related stimulus, the soft drink—which presumably signaled aversion relief to them. In essence, these investigators were attempting to use painful shock the way Sanderson and his colleagues used succinylcholine: to develop a conditioned reflex linking the sight and smell of alcohol to the aversive stimulus (pain) precipitated by the shock.

Obviously this was a more sophisticated use

of the aversive paradigm than the succinylcholine project, aiming as it did to instill both conditioned aversion to alcohol and conditioned aversion relief to non-alcohol-related stimuli. But MacCulloch, and his group obtained only limited results with it, in part because its effects remain active only for limited periods of time. More recent projects have added follow-up "booster" sessions of electrical aversion conditioning, which have "significantly increased time to relapse" (Vogler et al., 1970).

The treatment of alcoholism by covert sensitization, or inducing aversive stimuli in the patient's own thoughts, was developed by Cautela. He suggests asking alcoholics to imagine a covert sensitization scene like this: "You are walking into a bar. You decide to have a glass of beer. You are now walking toward the bar. As you are approaching the bar you have a funny feeling in the pit of your stomach. Your stomach feels all queasy and nauseous. Some liquid comes up your throat and it is very sour. You try to swallow it back down, but as you do this, food particles start coming up your throat to your mouth. You are now reaching the bar and you order a beer. As the bartender is pouring the beer, vomit comes to your mouth." A graphic, detailed description of the mechanics and sensations of vomiting then ensues, followed by, "As you run out of the barroom, you start to feel better and better. When you get out into the clean, fresh air you feel wonderful. You go home and clean yourself up" (Cautela, 1970, p. 87). Thus, covert sensitization and MacCulloch's aversion relief procedures both aim to couple alcohol with unpleasant associations *and* its absence with pleasant associations.

The third phase of behavioral therapy for the alcoholic, Franks says, is a multidimensional approach. One exciting trend in this developing cluster of techniques involves the possibility of retraining alcoholics to become social, controlled drinkers, even though the effort contradicts one of A.A.'s fundamental tenets. In the first such study, made by Lovibond and Caddy (1970), alcoholics were given a short period of training in estimating their

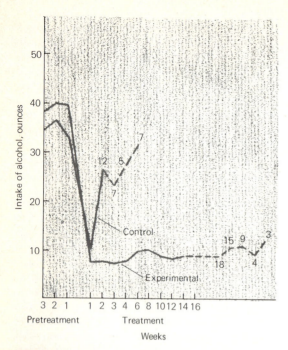

Figure 11-3. Can alcoholics be retrained as social drinkers? In this experiment they were punished with electric shock when their blood-alcohol levels rose above a certain amount. The control group was given random shocks. The experimental group's posttreatment alcohol intake was significantly lower than that of the control group. *(Slightly modified from Lovibond & Caddy, 1970)*

own blood-alcohol levels (largely on the basis of subjective feelings of intoxication). Then they were given beverage alcohol, according to a predetermined schedule, to generate desired (moderate) blood-alcohol levels. When they drank at blood-alcohol levels above a specified cutoff point, they received strong electric shock on a variable schedule. A control group of alcoholics was given random shocks instead of shocks contingent upon blood-alcohol levels. As seen in Figure 11-3, the posttreatment alcohol intake of the experimental group was significantly lower than that of the control group. Although these results are intriguing, a much more extensive follow-up period is required to explore their long-term effectiveness.

In another study of controlled drinking, thirteen hospitalized male alcoholics were treated during a series of experimental drinking sessions (Mills et al., 1971). Subjects could avoid painful electric shock by drinking "like a typical social drinker" (by drinking mixed drinks in small sips and in small amounts), but they received shock whenever they behaved "like alcoholics." Four of the subjects adopted the required social-drinking behavior from the first day: they never ordered more than three mixed drinks and consumed each of them in very small sips. The remaining nine subjects acquired these social-drinking behaviors over twelve to fourteen sessions. In a subsequent twelve-month follow-up of these subjects, Schaefer found that seven out of nine experimental subjects who could be located (but only two out of eight control subjects) were either abstinent or drinking in socially acceptable ways (1972). He concluded that "drinking in a socially acceptable manner should be trainable as long as relevant behavioral parameters for such behavior are known."

An additional report by the same group evaluated "individualized behavior therapy" that employed whatever was needed in the way of assertive training, aversive conditioning, and training in social behaviors (Sobell & Sobell, 1973). Follow-up indicated that the seventy subjects in the long study seemed to have maintained sobriety or controlled drinking more successfully than patients in studies which did not "individualize" treatment procedures.

The behavioral approach to alcoholism treatment, though it is new and unproved, appears to hold considerable promise for the future. As additional behavior-change procedures are developed, however, their utility and applicability will continue to be assessed.

Drug dependence

Historical perspectives

People have used opium and its derivatives— morphine, heroin, and codeine—throughout recorded history. Europeans cultivated the poppy, from which the natural opiates are derived, for at least 4,000 years; opium ("the plant of joy," according to the ancient Sumerians) is mentioned in the early writings of the Babylonians, Egyptians, Greeks, and Romans. In some cultures these drugs were used as part of a religious ritual, in others simply for pleasure, in still others to dull severe pain or lighten the burdens of psychological depression. Today they are taken for all these purposes, sometimes legally, often illegally. Together with their synthetic equivalents—which include Demeral and methadone—these drugs are the narcotics. Narcotics which are legal in the United States must be purchased only on prescription; neither opium nor heroin is legal.

The flowering tops and leaves of the hemp plant were used before 500 B.C., when they played a part in religious rites in India. The drugs produced from hemp have been important ever since as marijuana and as hashish, a concentrated substance that is several times more powerful than marijuana.

The use of leaves from the coca tree for ritual purposes was reported as early as the twelfth century. At that time, it is written, the Incas of South America chewed them in order to achieve greater communion with the gods. We now call the active substance of coca leaves cocaine.

While alcohol, the opiates, cocaine, marijuana, and hashish, gifts from a bountiful mother nature, have been known and used for thousands of years, the nonnarcotic, non-alcohol drugs of dependence are much more recent. The barbiturates came into wide use to relieve anxiety and to induce sleep only in the early twentieth century. As late as 1938, there was considerable doubt as to whether they caused physical dependence. As for the amphetamines, their stimulant properties were not discovered until around 1915. While some of the psychedelic drugs (such as mescaline and psilocybin) are also natural products that have been used for many years in religious rituals, their synthetic equivalents, including LSD, have become widespread only during the last ten years as the result of their "discovery" and popularization by Timothy Leary and Robert Alpert.

What are the drug dependencies?

Though DSM II lists ten separate items under the heading "drug dependence," not all of them are significant in contemporary society. The dependencies that are important today include those which are related to opium, sedatives, cocaine, *Cannabis sativa,* the psychostimulants, and the hallucinogens.

Opium, opium alkaloids, and their derivatives; synthetic opiates. Dependencies on these drugs are both physical and psychological. Opium is a substance derived from the sap of the poppy-seed capsule *(Papaver somniferum);* synthetic opiates are manufactured compounds with morphine-like properties. The major drugs of abuse from the poppy seed are opium, morphine, codeine, and heroin. Within the synthetic opiates, the primary abused drugs include meperdine (Demerol) and methadone. Opium, once common in parts of Asia and other areas as both a medicine and an intoxicant, is now in relatively little demand, because some of its derivatives are stronger and more predictable in their effects. Of these morphine and codeine are widely and legally used as powerful pain-killers. Significant numbers of narcotics addicts in the United States were first "hooked" when they were given the drugs for the relief of pain.

Heroin ("horse," or "H") is the drug preferred by American narcotics addicts (Ball & Chambers, 1970), even though there are no apparent differences in the subjective and objective effects of morphine and heroin (Martin & Fraser, 1961). Heroin is sold "on the street" as a white powder that is usually "cut" with milk sugar or another inert sub-

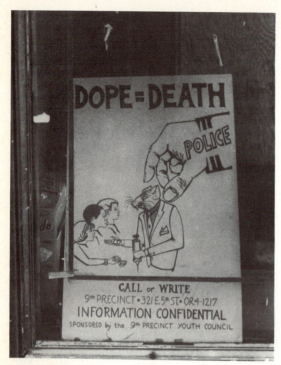

(Dan McCoy from Black Star)

stance. The heroin now bought by American addicts is less than one-tenth as pure as the heroin that was peddled before World War II (Wilner & Kassebaum, 1969).

Heroin dependence often begins by sniffing or, less commonly, by injection under the skin ("popping"). Once the person develops physical dependence, a process that rarely requires more than a few experiences with the drug, he usually shifts to "mainlining"—intravenous injection—because its effects are both more rapid and more predictable. At this point, tolerance forces the addict to feed his addiction with more and more of the drug to achieve the same effect. Ultimately the "high" disappears, no matter how much heroin the addict is taking. Either he must go through withdrawal, to lower his tolerance so that he can reexperience heroin's effects, or he will die of an overdose—a common event in the addict community.

The characteristic syndrome of narcotics

intoxication includes some sedation, decreased "drive," and a profound sense of inner pleasure and well-being (the "rush"). Shortly after the addict has taken heroin, his reaction may include drowsiness (the "nod"), flushing, constriction of the pupils, decreased rate and depth of breathing, decreased blood pressure and temperature, and a slowed pulse (Solomon & Patch, 1972). Many of these effects were reported more graphically by Piri Thomas.

The effects, if any, of the "hard drugs" on sexual behavior and sexual experience have been the subject of a great deal of speculation "on the street." Little reliable data have been available until very recently, when De Leon and Wexler summarized the results of their survey of the sexual behavior of thirty-one male drug-free heroin addicts who were residents of a halfway house in New York City (1973). Their report indicates that during addiction periods, most subjects reported decreased frequencies of intercourse, masturbation, and nocturnal emissions. Further, the frequency of orgasms dropped, ratings of desire and the quality of orgasm were lower, and the latency to ejaculation was increased. During the postaddiction period, sexual desire and performance appeared to recover almost completely.

Abstinence from heroin for just a few hours leads to a variety of painful withdrawal symptoms. These include, first, restlessness, anxiety, and craving for the drug; next, yawning, crying, a running nose, perspiration, and insomnia; then dilation of the pupils, gooseflesh, loss of appetite, hot and cold flashes, involuntary fine-motor-muscle contractions, and both muscle and joint pain; finally, profound insomnia, elevated temperature, increased rate and depth of breathing, increased pulse and blood pressure, marked restlessness, nausea, vomiting, diarrhea, weight loss, and occasionally, spontaneous, unenjoyable orgasm. The unpleasantness of these symptoms explains the willingness of the heroin addict to commit crime for the money that will prevent withdrawal. As we pointed out before, though, most mental health professionals agree that the process of withdrawal from alcohol is more painful, more prolonged, and more dangerous than withdrawal from heroin.

Dependence on sedatives. "Downers" of both the barbiturate and nonbarbiturate variety create profound physical and psychological dependence. On a worldwide basis the social, financial, and medical impact of barbiturate addiction has been estimated as second only to that of alcoholism (Solomon & Patch, 1972). The most important barbiturates in this context include pentobarbital, secobarbital, and amobarbital. Major nonbarbiturate drugs frequently abused include glutethimide (Doriden), meprobamate (Miltown and Equanil), and chlordiazepoxide (Librium).

Addiction to the barbiturates is both more serious and more widespread than addiction to nonbarbiturate sedatives. Barbiturate addiction sometimes begins as a nightly capsule at bedtime to help the tense businessman or harried housewife get to sleep. It also starts when a friendly neighborhood pusher convinces an unwary purchaser that "yellow jackets" are cheaper, safer, and as much fun as heroin.

The effects of a moderate dose of barbiturates include feelings of relaxation and euphoria, accompanied a little later by nystagmus (fine lateral movements of the eyes that signify brain dysfunction on either an acute or a chronic basis), speech and balance difficulties, and impaired mental alertness. At high dosages slowed breathing, shock, coma, and death can occur. As with alcohol and the opiates, continued use of the sedatives, especially the barbiturates, leads to increased tolerance. Recent studies have revealed, for example, that barbiturate addicts are able to consume a dose more than ten times strong enough to kill a nonaddict (Freedman & Kaplan, 1967).

Abrupt discontinuation of the barbiturates by a physically dependent person inevitably leads to one of the most potentially fatal of all withdrawal syndromes. It involves, in this order, muscular weakness, restlessness, and tremulousness; anxiety and insomnia; elevated body temperature, generalized convulsions, and psychosis. If convulsions occur, they usually do so on the second or third day of withdrawal; psychotic behavior, if it appears, does so on the fourth to seventh days.

Dependence on cocaine. Addiction to "coke" is unusual in this country because of the relative unavailability of the drug on the street and the fearsome hallucinations it can evoke in some people. Malcolm Little, however, was a devotee of cocaine early in his hustler days. As he describes its appeal: "Cocaine produces, for those who sniff its powdery white crystals, an illusion of supreme well-being, and a soaring overconfidence in both physical and mental ability. You think you could whip the heavyweight champion, and that you are smarter than everybody. There was also that feeling of timelessness. And there were intervals of ability to recall and review things that had happened years back with an astonishing clarity" (Malcolm X, 1966, p. 134). While cocaine probably does not induce physical dependence, it can cause a high degree of psychological dependence.

Not many people know that Sigmund Freud, founder of the psychoanalytic movement, was the first person systematically to explore the effects of cocaine on human physical and psychological functioning. During the 1880s when Freud was still training to be a neurologist, he reported that cocaine seemed to have striking pain-relieving and depression- and tension-reducing properties. Some of his observations in this regard were made on himself after he had taken small doses of the drug. Because no one else had thought that the leaves of the coca tree might have particular therapeutic effects, Freud was for a time the world's expert on cocaine. He relinquished this position because of his growing interests in psychological phenomena. Freud did not realize until later that cocaine can also produce profound psychological dependence—that it was not a "wonder drug"—which is surprising in view of the care he usually took to look at all sides of new issues.

Dependence on Cannabis sativa. The flowering tops and leaves of the hemp plant produce a resin containing THC (tetrahydrocannabinol), the active component of both marijuana ("pot," or "grass") and hashish ("hash"). Both are usually smoked in cigarettes ("reefers," "joints") or pipes. There is no evidence that physical dependence accompanies prolonged marijuana or hashish smoking, although psychological dependence may develop. A decreased or "reverse" tolerance is thought by some to characterize regular use of these drugs—that is, their continued ingestion seems to reduce the amount needed to produce the usual effect. Despite these largely anecdotal observations, recent controlled studies of the behavioral pharmacology of marijuana suggest that tolerance does in fact ultimately accompany its prolonged ingestion (*WHO Chronicle* 26, 1972; *2nd Report to Congress,* 1972).

Because marijuana and hashish do not cause physical dependence, abrupt cessation of chronic or heavy marijuana or hashish smoking does not cause physiological withdrawal symptoms. But since prolonged use of these drugs may lead to psychological dependence, withdrawal is sometimes associated with the appearance of anxiety, depression, agitation, insomnia, and decreased interest in sex.

Dependence on psychostimulants. The psychostimulants include amphetamine (Benzedrine), dextroamphetamine (Dexedrine) and methamphetamine (Methedrine). Their continued use leads to psychological dependence and tolerance, but probably not to physical dependence. The tolerance that accompanies psychological dependence on the amphetamines develops rapidly and dramatically. The daily dose of the drug may be raised to several hundred times the initial level as the addict seeks to achieve the powerful subjective effects that he used to experience. The amphetamines were formerly widely prescribed by physicians as mood elevators in depression and as appetite suppressants for weight reduction. But the legal consumption of the amphetamines has dropped as the medical profession has come to recognize their limited therapeutic utility. The United States Food and Drug Administration, aware of the manufacturers' unwillingness to reduce supplies of the amphetamines, has also begun to take steps to this end.

When a person first takes one of the amphetamines, he has a characteristic "high" accompanied by euphoria, enhanced self-confidence, vastly increased physical energy and alertness, and unbounded optimism. These positive feelings are followed by a mild "down" when the effects of the acute dose wear off. Chronic users of the amphetamines ("speed freaks") experience much more pronounced "downs" (sometimes called "crashes"), with lethargy, emotional "dulling," and severe psychological depression lasting for long periods. Overdoses of the amphetamines, which are common when the user is a chronic abuser who has begun to take increasingly large amounts, may precipitate psychotic episodes characterized by frightening auditory and visual hallucinations, paranoid delusions, or both.

Here is a description of one pattern of amphetamine use by residents of Haight-Ashbury in San Francisco. It shows how the drug quickly assumes first place in the life of the amphetamine addict.

Methamphetamine interrupts sleep patterns and suppresses appetite. The individual may go on a "speed binge" lasting three or four days in which he "shoots up" from one to ten times a day, always going for the peak experience. He does not eat or sleep during this time. He is in a continuous state of hyperexcitement until, for one of various reasons, he decides to terminate this "speed binge." This may occur for several reasons—exhaustion and fatigue, abnormal psychological circumstances that are frightening to him, or inability to obtain the drug.

For whatever reason, the "speed binge" is terminated and we then see the reaction phase of the speed cycle. The reaction phase to the "speed binge" is classically the exhaustion syndrome. The individual often lapses into a deep sleep for periods of from 24 to 48 hours, depending on the duration of the "speed binge"; and upon awakening he may eat ravenously.

Unfortunately many of the amphetamine users do not return to a baseline level of personality function. They have a prolonged subacute phase in which profound depression dominates. Very often the "speed freak" shoots methamphetamine again to treat his depression and another cycle begins. [Smith et al., 1969, p. 153]

The amphetamines, unlike the barbiturates, do not create physical dependence and therefore do not precipitate physiological withdrawal symptoms that are potentially fatal. Nevertheless, they are said to cause more medical problems than any other drugs of abuse except alcohol and heroin (Hawks, 1971; Ladewig & Battegay, 1971). These problems include severe and protracted psychological depressions which sometimes require hospitalization, cardiac decompensation, and psychosis, all of which accompany prolonged ingestion.

Dependence on the hallucinogens. Addiction to LSD (lysergic acid diethylamide), morning glory seeds, mescaline, peyote, and psilocybin is of the psychological variety only, though tolerance to LSD has been reported (Pahnke, 1971). While Leary, Alpert, and their colleagues began their experiment with the "natural" hallucinogens, most current "acid heads" confine their drug taking to LSD, a synthetic drug which is cheaper, more easily procured, and somewhat more reliable in its effects than mescaline, peyote, or psilocybin.

The following description of an LSD experience by a former associate of Timothy Leary and Richard Alpert provides a firsthand account of the intensity and disarray of an acute LSD psychosis:

The physical world I could see had begun slowly to come apart. No cubic inch of space had to do with any other. Everything in my field of vision turned into bright jelly. There was no time and place, nothing but a flow. I got up and waded through the room, making my way unsteadily. Around me the music, the fire, and the candle dripping, the lights of nearby buildings, all combined and flowed. Yet I could see Ralph and Arthur watching me, and I saw my own situation with terrible clarity. I had gone too far out and couldn't get back! I called to Ralph, remembering what Arthur had said in the beginning: ". . . if you get hung up, always move toward your partner." I did, crying: "Help me. I want to get back!"

The jelly before my eyes separated. The universe cracked into bright globules and separated; then I was in little pieces, about not to exist anymore, and being borne away on something like a jet stream, and this was the stream Arthur had mentioned, streaming unconsciousness that one was supposed not to fight. Ralph caught my hand and said: "Go with it!" But I said: "Get me out. I want to go home. Where is she?" They were like people trying to help me in my envelope of flowing air, not being able to do anything but sympathize. But we could see each other with amazing clarity all this time. They were making notes on me! Arthur had a chart. [Harrington, 1963, p. 82]

Though LSD, like the amphetamines, does not produce physiological withdrawal symptoms, it probably does cause emotional difficulties, and perhaps physical ones, during and after prolonged use. It has been reported that LSD can impair intellectual processes, precipitate chronic psychosis, or both following acute or chronic ingestion (Taylor, 1971). But a psychotic reaction, if it occurs at all, does so only in persons who are already on shaky psychological ground. Some researchers have also claimed that chronic use of LSD causes chromosomal changes, but this finding has been widely questioned (McGlothlin et al., 1970) and should be considered an open question for the time being.

Chronic use of LSD probably exerts its most profound effect by cutting the person off from his social environment. Like the heavy marijuana user, the acid head who begins to look to his drug as the prime source of his intellectual, emotional, and social stimulation may drop out while he turns on, with dramatic effects on his school or job performance and his interpersonal effectiveness.

Etiologies of drug dependence

No definitive etiology of the drug dependencies has been established.

Biophysiological theories. The pharmacology and physiology of physical dependence and tolerance are being constantly explored, but so far no one has developed an adequate etiological theory of drug dependence based on biophysiological factors. This is so for largely the same reasons that alcoholism has not been identified as primarily a biophysiological entity: no differences have been found in rate of metabolism, route of metabolism (how the drugs are broken down in the body), site of metabolism (where metabolism occurs), or susceptibility to the effects of drugs between persons who become addicts and those who do not. The history of medicine suggests that such differences are crucial to the ultimate discovery of biophysiological (organic) etiologic factors.

An important step forward in the search for biophysiological factors in drug addiction appears to have been taken recently by Snyder and Pert (1973). These investigators report that they have identified the sites of action in the brains of heroin and other opiate addicts. They also note that the drugs appear to become chemically bound to specific kinds of brain cells in specific areas. Unlike the addictive drugs, the nonnarcotic drugs fail to bind at these sites.

Snyder and Pert also report that the opiates become concentrated in receptor areas located in the *corpus striatum* area of the forebrain—an area with an especially high concentration of the neurotransmitter acetylcholine. In fact, the receptors that bind the opium seem to be closely linked with the availability of acetylcholine in other portions of the brain too.

Psychoanalytic theories. Dynamic theories of drug addiction are like dynamic theories of alcohol addiction: they describe the addict as a person whose addiction represents a return to the oral stage of psychosexual development. As a result, dependency needs are paramount, but the individual is frustrated by his inability to derive satisfaction of these needs. Since he cannot satisfy his "oral dependency needs," in more appropriate ways, the addict uses drugs and alcohol to do so.

This brief summary vastly oversimplifies the complex psychoanalytic formulation of drug addiction. Nonetheless, its validity has just begun to be investigated empirically (by Gilbert & Lombardi, 1967; by Sutker, 1971), so its value as an explanatory device is still unproved.

Behavioral theories. Abraham Wikler, a psychiatrist who has used the behavioral model to explore alcoholism and drug addiction, was probably the first to offer a behavioral theory of drug addiction. He views drug addiction as a product of instrumental (operant) learning (1965). He assumes that each injection or ingestion of a drug reinforces drug-seeking behavior by providing immediate, powerful positive reinforcement. Hustling for drugs becomes a secondary reinforcer be-

Many people believe that alcoholism and drug addiction stem from virtually identical causes. *(Heath © PUNCH 1972)*

cause of its relation to the primary reinforcement furnished by injection and the resultant "drive reduction." Wikler explains the extremely high rate of return to drug addiction by detoxified addicts as "due simply to incomplete extinction of reinforced drug-seeking behavior."

The role of modeling, another learning mechanism, in the development of patterns of drug use is beginning to be explored. A recent study of 8,865 Canadian high school students found a positive correlation between the parents' use of tranquilizing drugs, alcohol, and tobacco (as reported by the students) and the students' use of hallucinogenic drugs (Smart & Fejer, 1972). This relationship was strongest when both students and parents took psychostimulant and sedative drugs. The researchers conclude that many adolescents do model their drug use after that of their parents. They believe that the use of drugs by these adolescents can be reduced only when the parents cut down too.

Sociological theories. There are few other psychopathological disorders where the influence of sociocultural factors is as striking as in the drug dependencies. Sociocultural variables play two key roles in drug addiction: They differentiate drug users from nonusers and they determine the kind of drug a user selects.

By now everyone knows that heroin addiction is endemic to the ghetto. Unlike so many other items of "common knowledge," this one seems to be true. The now-classic Chein study, which evaluated the social and economic characteristics of fifteen high-drug-use areas of New York City, found significant relationships between juvenile delinquency and drug (largely heroin) addiction, between delinquency and poverty, between poverty and drug addiction, and between the proportion of blacks in an area and the rate of drug use there (1964). In twelve of the fourteen areas studied, blacks and Puerto Ricans made up more than 70 percent of the population. But Chein also observed that while "the highest-drug-rate areas are all high-delinquency areas, delinquency is not [caused by drugs], except in the sense that the varieties of delinquency tend to change to those most functional for drug use; the total amount of delinquency is independent of the drug use" (pp. 64–65).

Thus these data do not justify the conclusions, drawn by some authorities, that drug addiction "causes" juvenile delinquency, that blacks are more commonly drug addicts because they are black, and that poverty and drug use are invariably linked. Significant correlations like those reported by Chein are deceptive because they imply causality (cause and effect) without in any way proving it. Two facts are clear, however, from such studies: (1) Heroin is a poor, usually a black, man's drug, at least in the United States. (2) Its use is intimately associated with high crime rates (Bender, 1963; Murray, 1967).

By contrast, other drugs of abuse, especially marijuana and LSD, are not largely the property of blacks living in the ghettos of large American cities. The Shafer Commission on marijuana, appointed by President Nixon, summarizes the demographic characteristics of marijuana users as follows:

On the basis of the Commission-sponsored National Survey, we have concluded that contemporary marihuana use is pervasive, involving all segments of the U.S. population. The Survey estimated that about 24 million Americans over the age of 11 years (15% of the adults 18 and over, and 14% of the 12–17 year olds) have used marihuana at least once. . . . Marihuana use does not appear to vary significantly by race. With respect to the religious affiliation of the users, Jews and Catholics appear to be slightly overrepresented as compared to Protestants. . . . Usage is highest in cities, towns and suburbs but not uncommon in rural areas. . . . Use is found in all socioeconomic groups and occupations, though slightly more predominant among persons with above-average incomes. . . . At the same time, the incidence of use seems to vary according to education attainment. Among all adults now in school, 5% of those with an eighth grade education or less have used the drug, contrasted with 11% of those who completed some high school, 14%

(Charles Gatewood)

of those who graduated from high school, 25% of those who completed some college and 21% of those who graduated from college. [National Commission, 1972, pp. 38–39]

Studying the group of moderate to heavy users of marijuana (defined as those who smoked it from eleven times a month to several times a day), the Shafer Commission found that their mean age was 23, that they were superior in intelligence, that they had completed an average of 2½ years of college, and that they came from all socioeconomic groups (though *daily users* came more often from low-SES broken homes).

Comparable demographic data on LSD users have also been gathered (Braucht et al., 1973; Kuehn, 1970). Like marijuana, LSD now seems a drug most commonly used by college students. Again as with marijuana, heavy users of LSD appear to be significantly more maladjusted—more "hung up"—than either occasional users of the drug or those who do not use it (Smart & Jones, 1970), though the precise nature of the relationship between frequency of LSD use and psycho-

logical impairment has not been determined. That is, no one yet knows whether heavy LSD use precipitates psychological difficulties, or whether only people who are already impaired psychologically are willing to become abusers of LSD. Surprisingly, despite the "bad trips" and "flashbacks" that LSD is capable of providing both habitual abusers and "one-shot" experimenters, the incidence of overt psychosis directly linked to the drug appears to be very low (Clark & Done, 1972).

Habitual abusers of the amphetamines and barbiturates are more often disturbed emotionally than heavy users of LSD and marijuana. In themselves these drugs are extremely serious hazards to psychological well-being, and their abuse is so patently dangerous that a person must be foolish, desperate, or both to use them (Louria, 1969). A recent study of heavy amphetamine users reveals that they were significantly more intelligent and had completed significantly more years of education than the average heroin addict (Fischman, 1968), though the fact that they were predominantly white means that important relationships between race, performance on IQ tests, and opportunity for higher education were not controlled.

What is the exact nature of the relationships among sociocultural variables and the etiology of drug abuse? We do not know. While many research reports claim that a poor black urban dweller is more likely to become a heroin addict than a white resident of the suburbs, it is also a fact that most poor urban blacks are addicted to nothing "harder" than the fervent wish to escape from the ghetto. On the other hand, while it makes sense to conclude that heroin addicts use the drug to escape the frustrations of the ghetto (and that "acid heads" take LSD to flee the monotony of college life), it is difficult to marshall empirical data to justify those positions. We can talk about the importance of sociocultural variables in the etiology of the drug dependencies without being able to point out causal relationships between drugs and demography.

In fact, it seems wisest to conclude that no single etiologic factor leading to the drug dependencies will ever be identified. As the authors of the *Interim Report* on the non-medical use of drugs in Canada put it: "There is no single or simple explanation available— nor is one likely to be found. Motives vary widely between users and groups of users. The motivation of the individual user may vary through time. Motivation is also a function of the real and expected effects of the various drugs" (1971, p. 28). This does not mean, of course, that a predominant causal factor for a particular *group* of drug abusers (say, ghetto-dwelling heroin addicts) might not be identified. It means that a heroin addict in Harlem and one in New Rochelle might have developed their addictions for very different reasons.

Cues to drug dependence

Like alcoholism, drug dependence cannot be reliably distinguished from the other personality disorders by any other behavioral cue than the fact of drug abuse itself (Chynoweth, 1969; Whitlock, 1970). That is, drug abusers, unless they are physically ill, in the midst of a drug-related psychotic episode, or undergoing withdrawal, cannot be distinguished from other persons who are experiencing severe emotional turmoil. It is equally difficult to identify potential drug addicts or differentiate addicts from nonaddicts on the basis of psychological measures. Some researchers have developed an MMPI drug-addict profile showing scores substantially above normal on the "psychopathic deviant" subscale, along with scores somewhat above normal on the "mania," "schizophrenia," and "depression" subscales (Berzins et al., 1971; Greaves, 1971). But essentially the same pattern of MMPI responses occurs in populations of nonaddicts with histories of other kinds of antisocial behavior (Davis & Sines, 1971; Persons & Marks, 1971).

Because the same problems have arisen from efforts to use other standard tests to identify drug addicts, the Addiction Research Center (ARC) at the Lexington, Kentucky, Federal Narcotics Center designed the ARC Inventory specifically to facilitate personality research

with drug addicts (Haertzen, 1965). The inventory consists of 550 items taken from the MMPI and other objective behavior checklists. Studies of narcotics addicts made with the inventory suggest that it may be better able than the MMPI to discriminate among addicts, "psychopaths," and alcoholics (Haertzen & Hooks, 1969).

Experimental psychopathology

The animal model. The behavioral pharmacology of the "drugs of abuse" has been thoroughly explored in animal studies. Those reviewed by Wikler in 1967 had produced a number of sophisticated results. For example, they made possible the controlled assessment of the relative "potency" of various drugs within a drug family (they found that codeine is one-twelfth as potent, Dilaudid is five times more potent, and heroin is two to three times more potent than morphine). They led to discovery of the sites and modes of action of a class of drugs (e.g., the opiates seem to exert a combination of depressant and excitant actions at all levels of the central nervous system, with the sites and modes of action progressively more difficult to localize the higher they are in the CNS). The studies Wikler covered also explored mechanisms of tolerance and physical dependence (one finding was that definite evidence of tolerance in the dog can be elicited during one eight-hour intravenous infusion of a moderate dose of morphine; at the end of that time, withdrawal phenomena will be precipitated by a single injection of a morphine antagonist).

The relevance of these and similar studies to human addiction is clear in some instances, remote in others. Unfortunately, the development of drug dependence in man depends as much upon sociocultural and behavioral factors as on the pharmacological activity of the drugs, and animals offer little help in exploring these factors. But no matter what the shortcomings of animal research, controlled investigation of the effects of new drugs which have potential or unknown danger for man can only be attempted with animals. The modes and sites of action of many drugs are similar in the higher animals and man, and animal studies of this kind have been very helpful.

The human model. Many of the same ethical and moral issues that prevented researchers from studying alcoholism in the human laboratory setting also discouraged human research with drugs in the laboratory. Now a few controlled studies of the effects of the drugs of abuse have begun to appear (Carlin et al., 1972). It is interesting that one of the groups of researchers now studying drugs in the laboratory is led by Jack Mendelson, the man who first gave alcohol to alcoholics in controlled laboratory studies ten years ago.

There have been several studies which, though uncontrolled, provide valuable observations on the psychological, physiological, and psychopathological effects of the drugs of abuse. Chein's monumental survey of drug addiction was the first and in many ways remains the most thorough investigation of this kind (1964). Valliant's paper, "The Natural History of Narcotic Drug Addiction" provides another perspective, one gained by examining the multiple social factors that influence addicts' behavior during their addictions (1970). Valliant studied two very different groups of narcotics addicts: every addict from Kentucky who was admitted to the Lexington Federal Narcotics Center between 1936 and 1959 (266 in all), and a random sample of 100 addicts from New York City who were first admitted to the same hospital in 1952. The Kentucky group was middle-aged, 80 percent male, and of old American (Caucasian) stock. Most of the members of this group had originally become addicted during treatment with legally prescribed drugs. Their socioeconomic status was "equal or superior to that of the state as a whole." By contrast, the New York group was young (mostly between the ages of 22 and 25), only 20 percent Caucasian, and largely composed of addicts who had become addicted "on the street." Most of the subjects in the New York group were high school dropouts from welfare families.

Despite these striking differences between the two samples, their histories of addiction appear to have been surprisingly similar. So far as etiological factors were concerned, more members of both groups had lost a parent or parents before the age of 6 than comparable groups of nonaddicts, more had higher delinquency rates from nonnarcotic causes, and more had lower preaddiction employment rates. There were also remarkable similarities in the course of their addictions. Eleven years after hospital treatment, 65 percent of the living members of the Kentucky group were free of drugs—but 50 percent of the original sample were dead, and many of those still alive were misusing alcohol. Twelve years after treatment, 57 percent of the living members of the New York group were no longer addicted—but many of the persons in the original sample had died, despite their relative youth, while many more were abusing alcohol. Only 21 percent of the members of this group had worked for three or more years during the twelve-year follow-up period. Over 90 percent of the members of both groups had returned to drugs as soon as they left Lexington. Valliant summarizes the fate of the others as follows: "Roughly 50 percent of addicts who achieve abstinence for a year will subsequently relapse. . . . As the years pass, however, the likelihood of abstinence for a given sample at one point in time goes up" (p. 491).

Valliant's unhappy conclusion was that addicts rarely become abstinent voluntarily. He also found, unexpectedly, that the widely held view that addicts "mature out" of addiction or die is not supported by fact. In his Kentucky sample, the people who abstained from drugs did so because narcotics gradually became unavailable to them (that is, both legal and illegal sources "dried up"); in the New York group, those who became abstinent did so because their continued use of drugs led to arrest and subsequent involuntary abstinence.

A recent study of heroin addicts in Washington, D.C., provides startling statistics on the drug epidemic that is now sweeping our urban centers (DuPont, 1971). According to the study, best estimates are that there are about 17,000 heroin addicts in the nation's capital. Two-thirds are under 26 years of age, and 91 percent are black. In one large section of center-city Washington, it is estimated that 20 percent of boys 15 to 19 years old and 38 percent of young men 20 to 24 years old are heroin addicts.

Treatment of drug dependencies

Detoxification and chemotherapy. As with alcoholism, the first step in the treatment of the drug dependencies is detoxification—withdrawal from physical and psychological dependence on the drug. Detoxification from the physically addicting drugs (opiates and barbiturates) is best carried out in a drug-controlled setting where medical care is available. The patient is first stabilized for a day or two on a dosage of the drug just sufficient to prevent the appearance of withdrawal symptoms. Withdrawal can then be accomplished over five to ten days, depending on the initial level of addiction, by successively reducing the dosage. Detoxification by the "cold turkey" route (complete, immediate drug cessation), while unpleasant, is the method preferred by some addicts, for whom it is a painful experience but not usually a serious medical problem. Abrupt withdrawal from the barbiturates, however, is a different story: "cold turkey" detoxification can be fatal.

For addicts whose drug dependency resulted from efforts to tranquilize themselves for anxiety or depression, tranquilizers are sometimes helpful in preventing a return to addiction. Heroin addicts are rarely saved from a return to the drug this way, but detoxified barbiturate and amphetamine addicts, as well as abusers of LSD and marijuana, sometimes derive enough relief from tranquilizers to head off a return to dependence.

Methadone (Dolophine), a synthetic compound with heroin- and morphine-like pain-relieving activity but without their capacity to produce euphoria, holds promise for the treatment of heroin addicts. Though its chemical structure is not like that of heroin, methadone inhibits heroin withdrawal symptoms when it is substituted for the drug. When the "transfer of dependence" from heroin to methadone has taken place (for methadone is physically addicting too), methadone either can be withdrawn gradually, with fewer and less painful withdrawal symptoms than heroin, or can be given the patient on a more or less permanent basis, much the way insulin is given to diabetics. Methadone maintenance is now the treatment of choice for many hard-core narcotics addicts because it can interrupt the "treadmill of despair" described by Malcolm Little and Piri Thomas (Dole et al., 1968). Of more relevance to pragmatic city officials who must decide whether or not to fund methadone treatment centers is the dramatic role these centers played in reducing urban crime (DuPont & Katon, 1971) and the other costs to society (Cushman, 1971, 1973) for which hard-core criminal addicts are responsible.

A certain percentage of heroin addicts refuse to enter methadone programs and, as a result, continue the life of crime which heroin addiction necessitates. The psychologist Thomas Stachnik, who recently served as director of the Michigan Governor's Office of Drug Abuse, has proposed that these addicts be furnished with legal heroin at the same clinics which now dispense methadone to other addicts (1972). Stachnick bases his radical proposal on the belief that existing legal sanctions against hard-drug use have failed to stem the tide of heroin addiction. He concludes that the availability of heroin through clinics would reduce crime; decrease the hepatitis, septicemia, tetanus, and phlebitis commonly associated with illicit heroin injection; diminish the likelihood of accidental heroin overdoses; and "most important, for the first time [establish] some contact between a benign 'establishment' and the heroin subculture" (p. 642). Though startling and even heretical, Stachnik's imaginative proposal deserves further study.

Synanon. Synanon (a manufactured word that means, roughly, a group of anonymous members) was founded in 1958 by a member of Al-

A Synanon meeting. *(Robert Foothorap)*

coholics Anonymous who had experimented extensively with hard drugs (Endore, 1968). Though it was modeled directly on A.A., Synanon has become sharply different in style, orientation, and therapeutic techniques.

On joining Synanon the addict is expected to renounce his former way of life, including all his addicted friends. Typically he enters a house owned and run by the group, in which he is given a job appropriate to his skills and sense of personal responsibility. Continual group pressure from ex-addicts who have "come up through the ranks" forces him to reexamine his beliefs about life and to strive for the ultimate goal, "staying clean." Group pressure is exerted most directly during the "synanon," a kind of group therapy usually held three times a week. The synanon focuses specifically on the self-deceptions that addicts devise to justify their continued use of drugs. The group leader, because of his own history, is "tuned in" to attempts to evade individual responsibility for drug use. He may use ridicule, sarcasm, or direct confrontation to strip

away the various rationalizations advanced by the members of his group.

Partly because the philosophy of Synanon stresses total involvement in the program, impartial data on its success rates are rare. For the same reason there is no objective information on the number of Synanon houses and Synanon members. It seems clear, however, that Synanon reaches a relatively small percentage of addicts, just as Alcoholics Anonymous reaches only a small percentage of alcoholics. Only one study, published in 1963, has detailed the background characteristics and response to treatment of Synanon residents. In it Volkmann and Cressey reported that fewer than half of a group of fifty-two early Synanon members had completed high school, 81 percent had had "unstable work records," and the thirty-eight males in the group had averaged 5.5 previous institutional confinements before entry into the program. Following up their study, the researchers found that 8 percent of the original group had returned to the community and were free from drugs, 44 percent had remained in the Synanon residence, and 48 percent had left and were "unaccounted for." Presumably, most of that 48 percent had returned to drugs.

Comparably current data have not been published, so it is difficult to assess the overall effectiveness of the Synanon program. One can only conclude that Synanon seems to have promise for the successful residential treatment of drug addicts.

Dynamic therapies. Though there is some evidence that Freud himself abused cocaine during his twenties when he was studying its analgesic properties, his interest in understanding and treating the drug addictions appears to have been no more substantial than his interest in alcoholism. Some addicts continue to undergo dynamically oriented psychotherapy, but most data suggest that these treatment techniques by themselves are not especially effective (Freedman, 1968; Neuman & Tamerin, 1971).

Behavior therapy. The use of behavior therapy to treat drug addiction has only just begun. One of the earliest reports described the treatment of a 21-year-old college senior who was "taking morphine two or three times a week" but had not become fully addicted (Lesser, 1967). Treatment techniques included training in relaxation (both to overcome tension and as a substitute for drug-induced relaxation), training in self-assertion (as a means of overcoming the need for drugs and to help the patient say no to the pusher), and aversive conditioning with electric shock to the behaviors associated with actual administration of the drug. Follow-ups 7 and 10 months after the 4½ month treatment revealed that the patient had not returned to drugs and was apparently leading a productive life.

Behavior therapists have more recently employed aversive conditioning by itself (Liberman, 1968; Thomson & Rathod, 1968) and in conjunction with other behavioral techniques, including desensitization and assertive training (O'Brien et al., 1972). Preliminary results have been strongly positive; significant proportions of the addicts treated have achieved abstinence quickly and maintained it through follow-up periods. Nevertheless, much more extensive follow-ups on the behavioral techniques are necessary before their effectiveness can be considered proved.

One of the most exciting new applications of the behavioral approach to drug addiction involves contingency contracting, a method previously used most often with families suffering from discord. The first published report on the use of contingency contracts with a drug addict describes the treatment of a female graduate student at a Midwestern university who had become addicted to amphetamines originally prescribed for a physical disability (Boudin, 1972). A contingency contract, lasting for three months and signed by both patient and therapist, required the patient to keep the therapist continuously informed of her whereabouts, to call him three times a day to report on her activities, to call him "out of phase" whenever she became involved in situations exposing her to possible drug use,

and to give up all drugs. The therapist arranged his schedule so that the patient would know where he was at all times.

A joint bank account, in the names of both patient and therapist, was established in the amount of $500 (all the money the patient had). They agreed that in the event of any actual or suspected drug use by the patient, the therapist would make out a fifty-dollar check and send it to the Ku Klux Klan. Since the patient was black, this was thought to be an effective contingency.

Though the therapy had its trials, the patient did remain drug-free, with only one slip, over the three-month contract period. Follow-up later revealed that she had remained abstinent and was making satisfactory progress toward her Ph.D.

Contingency contracting as an adjunct to or central component of the behavioral treatment of drug addiction is in its very early stages of development, though its use in other problem areas is well established.

Legislation. While few informed persons disagree with efforts to strengthen existing laws against the illegal possession or sale of the hard drugs, it is becoming increasingly clear that the influx of these drugs from outside the United States must also be stemmed. Eliminating the importation of drugs is easier said than done, given the political realities of our time. For example, a report prepared by the CIA and the State and Defense Departments for the President's cabinet in 1971 stated: "The corruption, collusion and indifference at some places in some governments, particularly Thailand and South Vietnam . . . precludes more effective suppression of traffic in narcotics" (*New York Times,* July 30, 1972).

It is enlightening to review briefly the reaction of society and government to suggestions that penalties for the possession and use of marijuana be made much less severe. These suggestions stem largely from the recognition that marijuana is probably less dangerous to the health and well-being of society than alcohol or tobacco (Clark et al., 1970; Clark, 1972). The President's National Commission on Marihuana and Drug Abuse made the following recommendation, based upon their review of all available information on marijuana—its possible health hazards, its current and projected use in society, and the pragmatic consideration of the degree to which its use could actually be controlled: "We recommend to the public and its policy-makers a social control policy seeking to discourage marihuana use, while concentrating primarily on the prevention of heavy and very heavy use" (1972, p. 168). The commission suggested the following changes in federal law:

1 Possession of marijuana for personal use should no longer be an offense (it is currently a misdemeanor, punishable by up to one year in jail and a $1,000 fine for first offense), but marijuana possessed in public would remain contraband subject to summary seizure and forfeiture.
2 Casual distribution of small amounts of marijuana for no remuneration, or insignificant remuneration but not involving profit, should no longer be an offense. (It is currently punishable by imprisonment for up to five years for the first offense and by up to ten years for the second.)

No change in the penalties for cultivation, importation and exportation, or sale or distribution for profit was proposed by the commission. All are felonies punishable by imprisonment for up to five years for a first offense and by up to ten years for a second; penalties are doubled for sale to a minor.

Following completion of the commission's report, President Nixon put out a strongly worded rejection of its findings and recommendations. By contrast, many authorities on the uses and abuses of marijuana praised the commission's dispassionate conclusions, although some (for example, Grinspoon, 1972) felt that it had not gone far enough.

Today the possession, use, and distribution of any amount of marijuana is still illegal. No one knows what legalization of the drug would do to the incidence of adverse reactions to it. But it is clear that a critical, objective decision on the legalization of marijuana awaits a time when politics, passion, and pedantry are no longer so interwoven into the fabric of national decision making.

Summary

Though not everyone agrees, many people believe that it is possible to specify the behavioral criteria which signal the onset of alcoholism. These criteria usually include "loss of control" of drinking; psychological and physiological dependence upon alcohol; loss of jobs, family, or friends because of drinking; and the experience of "blackouts," increasing tolerance, or both.

The two most important systems for categorizing problem drinkers and alcoholics are Jellinek's, which divides them into four groups according to the severity and duration of the problem, and the APA *Diagnostic and Statistical Manual's*, which categorizes alcoholics who have suffered brain damage under one general heading and the largest group of persons with alcohol-related problems under another. The category of alcohol-related problems has subheadings: episodic excessive drinking, habitual excessive drinking, alcohol addiction, and "other" alcoholism. Although few professionals are satisfied with either classification system, efforts to categorize alcoholic behavior by other means (by psychological tests, for example) have also proved unsuccessful. One promising new approach to assessment involves observation of alcoholics drinking within controlled laboratory environments where their behavior can be studied while elements of the environment are varied.

Alcoholism treatment has been largely ineffective, an observation with which Bill H. would certainly agree. Drugs (both tranquilizers and Antabuse), Alcoholics Anonymous, psychotherapy, behavior therapy—none have yet demonstrated efficacy with more than a small percentage of the alcoholic patients in this country. New therapeutic approaches to the disorder continue to be developed. Among the most promising are behavioral efforts to take alcoholics for whom abstinence has never worked and retrain them to become controlled drinkers.

Among the various kinds of drug dependence recognized in DSM II are dependence on opium, opium derivatives, and synthetic opiates (opium, morphine, codeine, heroin, Demerol, and methadone); dependence on sedatives (pentobarbital, secobarbital, amobarbital, Doriden, Miltown, Equanil, and Librium); dependence on cocaine; dependence on marijuana or hashish; dependence on psychostimulants (Benzedrine, Dexedrine, and Methedrine); and dependence on the hallucinogens (LSD, mescaline, peyote, and psilocybin).

Although no biophysiological explanation for drug addiction has been widely accepted until now, investigators have recently reported that they have identified the sites of action of heroin and other opiates in the brains of addicts. They have also discovered some of the modes of action of these drugs in their "binding sites" in the brain.

Both psychoanalytic and behavioral theories of drug dependence have been advanced, but there are few empirical data to support them. It is known that drug addiction is strongly influenced by socio-cultural and demographic variables. Specifically, heroin is a poor, usually black, person's drug, and its use is intimately associated with high crime rates. Marijuana and LSD, on the other hand, are used mostly by middle-class college-educated young adults.

Data from a long-term study of two contrasting groups of narcotics addicts confirm a conclusion reached by most clinicians who work with addicts: they rarely become abstinent voluntarily. No current treatment method, including drug therapy, psychotherapy, and behavior therapy, has achieved significant success with these patients, though some behavioral techniques that are being developed seem encouraging. One of the most promising approaches to drug addiction, Synanon, a therapeutic community model based in part on the Alcoholics Anonymous program, reaches only a small proportion of addicts but apparently does well with many of these.

More informed legislation dealing with drug addiction is badly needed. Among the enlightened recommendations of the National Commission on Marihuana and Drug Abuse was the suggestion that possession of small amounts of marijuana be made legal. Though the conclusions of this commission have not been acted upon by federal authorities, they appear to be forerunners of more realistic attitudes in the future toward use of the so-called soft drugs.

CHAPTER TWELVE

The sexual disorders

Jay Meredith ● Steve Habillier ● Sexual deviations ●
Sexual dysfunctions ● Etiology ● What is "normal?" ●
Prostitution ● Pornography ● Treatment

JAY
MEREDITH'S
SECRET
PROBLEM

Jay Meredith was working and living in New York City—doing neither very happily—when he decided to go to a behavior therapist. He was vaguely depressed, lethargic, dissatisfied with himself, and unsure where he wanted to go in life. After graduating from an Eastern state university he had taken a job with a large industrial firm in the city. Because he became very anxious when he had to ride in crowded trains, buses, and subways, he had rented a "bachelor pad" near work, two blocks from Greenwich Village. But the lifestyle that most young bachelors would have envied was giving him no satisfaction.

Jay was the elder of two sons of a stable, middle-class suburban couple. Although he and his parents had differed through the years over many issues, including drugs, sex, religion, and politics, they did feel love and concern for each other. He recalled a reasonably happy childhood and adolescence and four good years at college. He noted, in passing at first, that his sex life in college had been a good deal less active than his fraternity brothers had imagined. In fact, though most of them had considered him a "real stud," Jay had never actually been able to complete intercourse because he could never maintain an erection whenever intromission became imminent. This problem had begun to dominate his sex life after college; in the therapist's view, it was probably the real reason for his decision to seek psychological help.

Jay's sexual problem was impotence—inability to complete the sex act. He lost his erection whenever sexual intercourse became a real possibility. He could achieve and maintain an erection easily during masturbation or the early stages of petting, but he lost it when sexual contact became intimate and began to involve mutual digital-genital touching—especially if his sexual partner began to give evidence of wanting to have intercourse. Jay had begun to limit himself to girls with whom there was no chance for the development of a sexual liaison. As a result his anxiety about his sexual inadequacy

had decreased, but so had his self-esteem, while his sexual frustration had grown.

Because Jay's sexual problem was one that often responds well to behavior therapy, he and his therapist agreed to center on that problem rather than on his feelings of interpersonal discomfort, depression, and personal dissatisfaction. The therapist was convinced that successful treatment of his impotence would probably result in significant improvements in other areas of his life.

During the early sessions, which took place once a week, Jay and his therapist made a "behavioral analysis" of his complaints. This process is central to effective behavior therapy. It focuses on the relationships between environmental or psychological events (which in Jay's case consisted of any "petting" session that showed promise of "getting out of hand") and the "target" behavior to be altered (the loss of an erection). Therapist and patient also constructed an "anxiety hierarchy" around the events leading up to the problem situation.

While they worked on these two tasks—behavioral assessment and hierarchy building—they began the process of assertive training. The technique is designed to provide patients who are deficient in assertive behavior with the skills necessary to advance their own ideas in social situations where they might otherwise remain silent. Jay lacked assertive behavior in two crucial situations. He was unable to respond effectively to his father's criticisms of his somewhat hippy life-style, long hair, predilection for "soft" drug taking, and unwillingness to share his life with his family. Jay was also unable to be direct with girls, so that they sometimes took his silence for disinterest in them and his unwillingness to disagree with them for tacit acceptance of their ideas. Despite his passivity in these situations, he reported that he "boiled inside" whenever his father attacked his values, because he believed that values like his father's were responsible for much of the chaos in the world. Similarly, though he wanted girls to like him, he was uncomfortable because he could not easily tell a girl where she stood with him.

Given these deficits in Jay's behavioral repertoire, the therapist felt that an increased ability to be assertive would have a pronounced positive influence on his view of himself and his social competence. Furthermore, Jay could not experience interpersonal anxiety or fear at the same time that he was being assertive since these two feeling states are incompatible.

Assertive training began with homework exercises for Jay—assignments to report on his assertive behaviors from the preceding week. Behavior rehearsal helped Jay practice a variety of assertive behaviors toward his father and important girls in his life in the security of the therapy relationship (with his therapist playing all the other roles). At first Jay found it difficult to get into the imagined scenes, but gradually he began to experience the same feelings of frustration and anger in them that he had felt in the real situations. The therapist's variety of roles included that of "anger modulator," since one of the most important goals of assertive training is to teach the distinction between assertive behavior and hostility.

During the fourth week of therapy Jay began relaxation exercises in which he focused on the prevailing tension levels in successive voluntary muscle groups of his body. After several sessions he could identify the relative activity of these muscle groups and modulate it to produce feelings of relaxation. He practiced the exercises at home once or twice a day for ten or fifteen minutes each, and week by week he became better able to relax quickly and effectively.

Systematic desensitization was begun in the sixth therapy session. Jay was instructed first to induce a state of deep muscle relaxation. Then the therapist began a detailed description of the earliest scene from the hierarchy that he and Jay had constructed. Jay imagined himself in the scene, and when he could hold it in mind for several seconds without experiencing the anxiety associated with it in real life, the therapist moved up the hierarchy to a scene which both patient and therapist had considered a little more anxiety-provoking. Usually Jay imagined five or six scenes during a session, though the number dropped when the scenes began to precipitate anxiety. Any scene that made him anxious was terminated, and relaxation exercises were reintroduced briefly until he calmed down. Then the therapist would describe a scene farther down the hierarchy or a "neutral" scene completely outside the hierarchy.

When Jay was about halfway through the hierarchy, he began to report more and more examples of successful assertive behavior. He was surprised and gratified that this behavior had not caused his father to reject him for being impertinent. Instead, his father had begun to talk more rationally about their differences, as though he recognized the futility of trying to make his son over in his own image. Jay also found that some of the girls with whom he had begun to be more assertive seemed to be looking at him in a new light. He said, "Somehow, I get the impression that they don't think I'm the same old wishy-washy Jay but someone who has ideas of his own."

At about the same time, Jay and his therapist agreed to start direct desensitization of his subway and bus phobia. To begin with, he rode the subway a few stops on Sunday mornings when it was uncrowded. Then, with the help of his relaxation exercises, he began gradually to increase the length of the rides and to ride at times when there were more passengers. By the end of the ninth week of therapy, he could ride crowded subways and buses with relative ease.

Jay and the therapist had agreed that he should tell his girl friend that his doctor had forbidden him to attempt intercourse. This effectively removed a great deal of the anxiety he usually experienced during the preliminaries to sexual intercourse, because it eliminated the possibility that he would have to try and then fail again. The "fear of failure" syndrome that had attached itself to Jay's sexual performance was broken.

Simply by virtue of this change Jay reported that the anxiety he usually associated with petting, kissing, and mutual manual manipulation of genitals was largely gone, making his involvement in these activities more heartfelt and hence more reinforcing. His girl friend also recognized a profound change in his sexual interest in her. The change heightened her enjoyment of their lovemaking and became another source of increased satisfaction for Jay.

The rate and quality of Jay's sexual activity grew gradually, at a pace agreed upon by therapist and patient. It was governed largely by the gradual dispersal of Jay's anxiety. When he felt that he could attempt intercourse without the anxiety that had been associated with it, Jay was instructed to attempt only partial intromission and to withdraw relatively quickly once it had been achieved. Successful partial intromission was then followed by less and less rapid withdrawal until prolonged intromission could be accomplished without anxiety.

After twelve sessions Jay reported that he had had totally satisfactory sexual intercourse several times during the preceding week, much to his own and his girl friend's satisfaction. In a follow-up session three months later, Jay said that he had consolidated his social and sexual gains. A year later Jay had changed girl friends but had retained his sexual capabilities. He was happier than he had ever been, though he still griped about life in the "canyons of Manhattan."

Steve has several posters of himself as "Diana." They hang on the walls of his home. His favorite shows him in a blonde wig and tight sweater, smiling out over the family-room bar. Although he changes occasionally to a black wig, a blouse, skirt, and heels are his basic costume. Perhaps it is his size that makes two-piece outfits look best: he is 6 feet tall and weighs more than 200 pounds. When Steve is not dressed as Diana, he is sales manager for a large company,

the father of three children, a master sergeant in the Marine Corps Reserves, and a devoted football fan. But in any clothes, Steve is a warm, kind person, with a sense of humor, a tendency to be introspective about himself, and the gift of sympathy toward others.

One night at a regular meeting of fellow "cross-dressers" and their mates, Steve (attending as Diana) was reminded of the early death of a close friend at whose funeral he had been a pall bearer. The emotion he expressed at the memory and the love he showed for his friend were both deeply felt. At other times that evening, when the group spoke of other forms of social defiance than its own—of promiscuity, drugs, alcohol, and homosexuality—Steve radiated understanding and the unwillingness to judge people harshly. In the same way, to Steve friendship is a constant; it does not depend upon whim or mood, as it does with some others in the group.

Steve's wife Mary is a pretty woman in her middle thirties. When she attends the meetings she is apt to drink too much and say too much in a loud, rather defensive way. Perhaps insecure as a "straight" person in that setting, and disquieted at seeing her husband dressed "in public," she clearly finds these functions difficult. Yet in private, Mary often speaks of her love for Steve and the importance of keeping her marriage going, of transvestism and how much better it is than adultery, of how, since Steve's problem has been out in the open, most of the troubles that made them unhappy early in their marriage have disappeared.

One of their difficulties had been that Steve had tried to keep his secret life to himself. But after several years of marriage, the pressures involved in lying about his evening absences from home, explaining why there were cosmetics in his closet, and justifying his American Express charges for local motels became too great. One night the truth came out, and for several months Steve and Mary's marriage hung in the balance. Mary first decided to leave Steve. Then she decided to stay but to move out of the bedroom they shared. Finally, recognizing that Steve was actually the same person he had been before, Mary resolved to build a new relationship with him that included her startling new knowledge.

"Better with him than without him," says Mary now. "I always thought he was special anyway—something not quite right. He's a soldier and a man, a husband and a father, but he's an alien too." Steve interjected, "We've even tried sleeping together 'dressed' but that doesn't work . . . and anyway, I don't have to 'dress' to enjoy our bed; once I found the group and Mary knew the truth things have gotten much better. Now, even if I don't dress one week, I don't get uptight. I know the group is there and that makes life easier. I don't have to lie to Mary. The kids will never know. We

are very careful. Besides, Mary always gets beautiful presents. Transvestites love to shop for their wives!"

Steve also speaks of the erotic feelings he experiences when he dresses up as Diana. He describes the evolution of a nonspecific sensuality that does not demand immediate and complete sexual gratification, like male-female sex demands: "Its enjoyable all over. I can even have this experience when I look at fashion magazines or try out an eye make-up or a foundation cream." Steve anticipates a trying time in the future when "Diana" will have to be much more careful—when the children are older and around more at night, when dressing at home will not be so easy. "I might have to pack Diana into my suitcase and dress only at a meeting. But I know after the kids grow up she'll be at home again. You know, even though it's clearly a deviation and you could call me a sexual deviant—even though it's made for trouble in my life—if you gave me a pill to stop dressing, I don't think I'd take it." [Feinbloom, 1972, pp. 30–33]

Sexual disorders are for keeping secret

These two case histories are very different not only in the two different sexual disorders they present but in the reactions of the two people to their disorders and their motivation for change. One of the interesting features of Jay Meredith's case is that he was sucessfully treated by behavior therapy. This is not yet the "treatment of choice" for primary impotence, although it is amassing an impressive record of success. The therapist's decision to focus on Jay's impotence was made only after behavioral analysis had indicated that the impotence was not associated with other serious behavioral deficits. If it had been, Jay's therapist could not have anticipated that successful treatment of the impotence would "generalize" to areas of functioning at some distance from sexuality.

Jay's very strong desire for a change in his pattern of sexual functioning contrasts with Steve's ready acceptance of the status quo regarding his transvestism. Perhaps a major reason for this difference is that Jay's impo-

tence caused him nothing but anxiety and distress, whereas Steve seems to have derived an uncomplicated pleasure from cross-dressing. Steve often said that he was as satisfied with his sexual adjustment and sexual behavior inside and outside of his marriage as he observed most "straight" men and women to be. This is an important point; we often assume that people whose sexual behavior is different from the norm are sick and unhappy. Since neither of these terms seems to describe Steve, apparently it is possible to lead a productive, useful life under such circumstances.

Sexual disorders in history

Current Western views on sexuality are heavily influenced by the Judeo-Christian tradition, which maintains that procreation is the only legitimate aim of sexual behavior. The tradition explicitly condemns all forms of sexual activity, ranging from homosexuality to masturbation, which are not directly oriented toward this goal. The Mosaic laws were specific: "And if a man lie with mankind, as with womankind, both of them have committed abomination: they shall surely be put to death; their blood shall be upon them. . . . And if a man lie with a beast, he shall surely be put to death; their blood shall be upon them" (Leviticus 20:13, 15). While they were single-minded in their condemnation of all forms of sexual deviation, the Old Testament writers were also contemptuous of men who could not perform the male sexual role, and were offended by women who failed to meet their sexual obligations. In the middle ages the church punished heresy with death, and the inquisition often raised the issue of homosexuality in connection with its victims' heresies. The charges were based on an interpretation of the sins of Sodom and Gomorrah that is still current.

The ancient Greeks apparently felt very differently from their Hebrew contemporaries about homosexuality. It is widely believed that Greek society reinforced personal homosexuality by institutionalizing it through religion. In fact, this is probably not true. While a Greek citizen was expected to assume responsibility as mentor and guide to a boy, and while a strong emotional relationship often developed between them as a result, overt sexual acts between student and teacher (the Greek for it was *stuprum:* vile behavior) were forbidden on penalty of death by the code of Lycurgus (825 B.C.). Female homosexuality, similarly idealized and essentially asexual, was also part of ancient Greek culture, though little is known of it beyond the poems of Sappho of Lesbos. (Sappho's birthplace and sexual behavior have been memorialized in the term "Lesbian" and the name of the gay activist group "Daughters of Sappho.")

Transsexuality was a major theme of Greek myths, presumably reflecting its presence in everyday Greek life. The Tiresias fable is probably the best known. It tells of Tiresias, a soothsayer from Thebes, who came upon two snakes having intercourse. When he killed the female, he became a woman. When he said that the sexual pleasure he received as a woman during intercourse was ten times what

he had experienced as a man, he was changed back into a male. Hermaphroditos, portrayed in late Greek art as an effeminate youth, was one of a number of bisexual or androgynous Grecian deities. *The Witches' Hammer,* the infamous medieval tract written to justify the murder of the insane, contains an eyewitness account of a girl changing into a boy at the command of the devil. (Presumably this was to justify the claim that heresy and sodomy had the same diabolic origin.)

Homosexuality, transsexualism, and the other sexual deviations and dysfunctions have continued to appear in the literature of many peoples, doubtless attesting to their presence in the life of the societies. In cultures such as the Chinese and the medieval Arabic, the mores did not condemn these behaviors as strongly as the Judeo-Christian ethic does, and they were a recognized part of the society. In all likelihood, however, they probably occurred no more often than they do in our own culture.

In the Christian world, homosexuality continued to be regarded as a grievous sin until two major events. The first was the publication of the Napoleonic Code at the beginning of the nineteenth century. This legal milestone abolished all penalties for homosexual acts occurring between adults in private and without violence. The second was the appearance at the end of the nineteenth century of the works of Krafft-Ebbing and Kraepelin, who viewed the "sexual perversions" as forms of "degeneracy" caused by a "hereditary taint" rather than as tangible signs of moral weakness and sinfulness.

Though civil libertarians now condemn Freud for his "old-fashioned," parochial thinking about the sexual deviations, his views on sexuality were at the time distinctly progressive. He rejected both the "hereditary taint" position of the Kraepelinians and the Victorians' view that all sexual deviation was morally reprehensible. Freud took the position that the sexual deviations resulted from an imperfect interaction between the child's developing personality structure and his family environment (1905). While this statement

(Charles Gatewood)

I was a heterosexual all the way up to a certain point and then all of a sudden here I am a queer. But it doesn't happen that way. You are a person and you go through puberty and at some stage you develop sexuality. You become attracted to something sexually, whether it be a fence post, a man or a woman, or a cat or something. . . . Psychiatric oppression is one of the most vicious forms of oppression that the homosexual can experience. He is told that he is an invalid human being. The most valid things about himself, the most giving and the most loving, are the very things that he is told are bad, evil, and horrible. It is no wonder that the homosexual stumbles into the psychiatrist's office. They are taught early to despise themselves and the psychiatrist tells them to despise themselves again. This is the traditional psychoanalytic perspective." [Holmes, 1971, pp. 131–132]

Despite the prevalence of this "old-fashioned" view of homosexuality, the growing influence and effectiveness of the gay liberation movement demonstrate that it is successfully bringing the psychological and legal plight of the homosexual to public attention. Many state legislatures and Congress itself have begun to consider bills to protect the employment status of homosexuals and to legitimize homosexual marriages.

Sexual deviations

The *Diagnostic Manual,* or DSM II (1968), lists but does not describe eleven sexual deviations within a diagnostic category for "individuals whose sexual interests are directed primarily toward objects other than people of the opposite sex, toward sexual acts not usually associated with coitus, or toward coitus performed under bizarre circumstances." The category of sexual deviations in turn is an integral part of the more general "personality disorder" grouping. This chapter uses the term *deviations* to refer to the eleven sexual disorders, reserving the term *sexual dysfunction* for other sexual disorders which involve a reduction in or loss of sexual capacity. Thus sexual dysfunctions include

did place homosexuals in the ranks of the psychopathological, it removed the moral and biological stigmata that they had previously carried.

Many mental health professionals have come to believe that homosexuality and the other sexual deviations may be learned behaviors rather than symptoms of underlying psychopathology. But other professionals, the general public, and some homosexuals themselves still view these behaviors in the traditional light. The consequences of the traditional position can be destructive, as the following excerpt suggests:

"I don't consider [homosexuality] a sickness. I am a homosexual. I have never been anything else. The girl in the back of the room was trying to get to the point of, 'When did I change?' Like frigidity in women and premature ejaculation and impotence in men.

Homosexuality

Homosexuality, the first of the sexual deviations listed in the DSM II, occurs among both sexes, although male homosexuality has been given more attention by more people. The true incidence and prevalence of homosexuality in the United States is unknown, presumably because of the stigma which historically has been attached to it. The anthropologists Ford and Beach say that homosexuality may not be the universal cultural phenomenon which many scientists (including Freud) have assumed (1951). They found that homosexual behavior was either "totally absent, rare or carried out only in secrecy" in 29 of 76 societies which they surveyed.

Homosexuality takes as many forms as heterosexuality. Some persons become homosexual only by necessity (that is, while in institutional settings), others are happily bisexual, while others remain exclusively homosexual their entire lives. Some homosexual relationships have a stability and permanence that rivals heterosexual marriage. Others last only an evening; they begin at a "gay bar," steam bath, or public toilet and are consummated in those places or in a hotel room. Some homosexuals are always the active sexual partner, others characteristically prefer the passive sexual role, while others like variety. Some homosexuals remain hidden, as "closet queens"; others, especially now that the stigma of homosexuality appears to be waning, are more open about their sexual preferences.

Some homosexuals are totally committed to and satisfied with their way of life. They are as unwilling to become heterosexual as any satisfied heterosexual would be to become homosexual. Other homosexuals, though they strongly prefer homosexuality, are unhappy with the "hassles" that crop up in their relations with the "straight" world. Finally, some homosexuals are unhappy with both the sexual components and the life-style of homosexuality. Accordingly, one cannot conclude that "all" homosexuals are either happy or unhappy with their way of life, just as one must beware of generalizing about any other "universal" human condition.

Though some homosexuals are doubtless victims of serious psychopathology, others give no evidence of underlying psychological disorder. Mental health professionals of the psychoanalytic persuasion believe that homosexuality always signals deep psychological disorder. However, a classic study of that issue by the UCLA psychologist Evelyn Hooker strongly refutes the "disease concept" of homosexuality (1958). Hooker matched 10 male homosexuals, none of whom were in treatment and all of whom were judged to be reasonably well adjusted, with 30 heterosexual, males. All took a complete battery of psychological tests and gave detailed information on their life histories. Several experienced clinical psychologists analyzed the data and concluded that there were no differences between the groups in terms of clinical symptoms of mental illness.

A recent study of 127 male and 84 female homosexuals (Thompson et al., 1971) yielded essentially the same results: groups of white, well-educated homosexual volunteers, matched for sex, age, and education with heterosexual control subjects, did not differ from the controls in defensiveness, personal adjustment, self-confidence, or self-evaluating. (These characteristics were measured on self-report rating scales.) Actually, male homosexuals were somewhat less defensive and female homosexuals were somewhat more self-confident than their controls.

While some male homosexuals are effeminate in their gestures, posture, or speech, others are masculine in appearance (Solomon & Patch, 1971). A homosexual's physical appearance rarely bears a relationship to the kind of sexual activity he prefers. Similarly, while female homosexuals may be masculine ("butch") or feminine ("femme") in appearance, these characteristics do not appear to be related to their preferred homosexual behavior.

Fetishism

Fetishism, usually a male sexual deviation, is defined as sexual arousal and gratification from inanimate objects (hats, undergarments, etc.) or from nonsexual parts of the body (say, hair or feet). The fetishist may buy or steal the inanimate fetish object in order to masturbate while wearing or fondling it. The fetishist who focuses on a body part fondles or fantasizes about it during masturbation. Or some fetishists need only to look at the fetish object or touch it very briefly in order to experience orgasm.

Some social critics have suggested that the inordinate interest American males display in the female breast is of such intensity as to render it a fetish object. Certainly other cultures regard the human breast with a good deal more equanimity than our own (Ford & Beach, 1951).

No adequate figures exist on the prevalence of fetishism in the United States. But most experts conclude that while fetishistic behavior is a common element of the sexual repertoires of both sexually normal and sexually deviant persons, it is uncommon as a preponderant form of sexual expression (Berest, 1971; Stekel, 1971).

Pedophilia

This rare sexual deviation, confined largely to males, consists of a sexual relationship between an adult and a child. The child may be of the same or the opposite sex. The pedophile presents a social problem that neither homosexuality nor fetishism do, because the pedophile may physically damage his sexual object in his pursuit of sexual satisfaction. Equally important, the pedophile can cause profound psychological damage to a child, especially insofar as pedophilic molestation or rape can seriously disrupt a child's own developing sexuality.

Transvestism

Males and females who derive sexual gratification from wearing the clothes and adopting the role of the opposite sex are transvestites. Kinsey's data suggest that several times as many men cross-dress as women do. His studies also indicate that only some transvestites are homosexual, supporting the newly emerging view that transvestism is not a variety of homosexuality but a separate sexual deviation. Steve Habillier, though a transvestite, was not a homosexual. While he derived pleasure from cross-dressing, he also experienced sexual arousal and ultimate orgasm during sexual intercourse with his wife.

Some transvestites are more properly termed *transsexuals*. These are individuals who have irreversibly accepted a gender identification opposite to that of their natural biological identity. Nontranssexual transvestites do not wish to change gender and do not consider themselves as belonging to the opposite sex. The transsexual, however, wants so much to deny and change his or her biological sex that this wish often becomes an all-consuming preoccupation in life. Surgical and hormonal means do exist by which transsexuals can achieve the anatomical appearance and some of the sexual functions of the opposite sex.

Green and Money's classic text on the subject of transvestism and transsexuality, *Transsexualism and Sex Reassignment* (1969), contains the lucid and revealing portrait of a person who showed elements of both behavior patterns:

A thirty-two-year-old farm laborer with transvestic and transsexual feelings since the age of fourteen sought admission [to a psychiatric hospital] when his wife threatened to leave him. Aged ten to twelve, he would dress in his mother's old clothes for family games which they called "backyard concerts." Two years later he felt different from other boys and often wished he were a girl. Aged seventeen, he began cross-dressing completely with a feeling of comfort but not direct sexual excitement. Three years later a girl who was a friend of his sister gave him a doll as a "present for a joke." This pleased him and he kept the doll in his bed.

(Charles Gatewood)

Aged twenty-two, he married his friend at his mother's suggestion. During courtship and the first year of marriage his transvestism diminished. Sexual intercourse took place regularly at first, but gradually diminished. The cross-dressing feelings returned, and for some years produced sexual arousal. Aged twenty-five, cross-dressing occurred every night, and his transsexual feelings became stronger with desires for pregnancy and for taking over the household tasks. This caused repeated quarrels with his wife. . . . He became depressed, took an overdose of his wife's contraceptive pills, and was admitted to another hospital before entering The Maudsley Hospital in London. When first seen, the patient said "my body cries out to be a woman." [Pp. 406–407]

Transsexuality is no longer an esoteric sexual deviation whose sole significance lies in its instructional value for students of psychology or its shock value in circus sideshows. It is a human problem of considerable dimension. In 1972, for example, the front pages of New Jersey newspapers carried the story that a male junior high school teacher, Paul Grossman, had undergone a successful "change-of-sex" operation and was then fired because "her sex change would be confusing to her pupils, who were themselves just approaching the time of puberty." As Paula Grossman, she brought suit against the New Jersey school board which had dismissed her. That suit is still pending. Appearing before a sympathetic college student audience, Grossman recently observed that "Not one case has ever been cured, or even significantly helped by psychiatrists. The only known cure is a medical sex change operation" (*Rutgers Daily Targum,* March 5, 1973).

Voyeurism

Strictly defined, voyeurism is a sexual deviation characterized by inability to attain sexual satisfaction except by looking at nude people or watching a couple engaged in sexual inter-

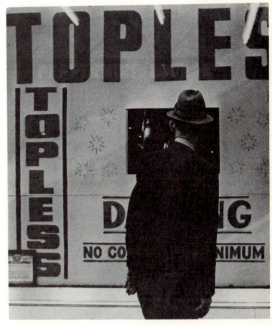

(Charles Gatewood)

course. In truth, there is more than a little of the voyeur in most men and many women. For example, many people derive sexual pleasure from pornographic movies, "suggestive" books, and *Playboy* and other sexually oriented magazines. It is only when the pleasure from looking and reading exceeds the pleasure from participating that the mental health professional becomes concerned about a person's voyeurism. Clinical voyeurism is extremely rare nowadays, perhaps because legal means of satisfying the desire have proliferated. That is, it is now legal to do what the nineteenth-century voyeur was executed for doing.

Sadism and masochism

Sadism and masochism are opposite sides of a single coin. Sadism refers to sexual gratification from pain inflicted upon one's sexual object; masochism is sexual gratification that depends upon the experience of pain oneself. Krafft-Ebing coined the word "sadism" after the Marquis Alphonse Francois de Sade, eighteenth-century French novelist and revolutionary, whose confessions even now are devoured for the delicious detail with which they portray a full range of sadistic sexual encounters. The word "masochism" derives from the novels of Leopold von Sacher-Masoch, a nineteenth-century Austrian writer whose stories often centered on the feverishly promiscuous activity of sadomasochistic heroes.

Sadomasochistic fantasies occasionally excite many normal American males and females, and sadomasochistic behavior is a component of the sexual relationship shared by some normal married couples in our culture. The syndromes in themselves, however, do not figure largely in our sexual way of life. It is rare for a person to go to a mental health professional because he or she is sadistic or masochistic.

Exhibitionism

A relatively common sexual deviation first described in 1877, exhibitionism is a syndrome whereby a male obtains sexual gratification by exposing his genitals, usually to women or small children (Freedman & Kaplan, 1967). Virtually all little boys and many little girls exhibit their genitals freely and happily in the context of exploratory sexual games, but such behavior continued to adulthood presents a problem for society. Though the exhibitionist is not often the same man who physically molests little children, society deals harshly both with those who molest and with those who exhibit themselves. Mental health professionals disagree over the amount of psychological damage the exhibitionist can cause children (Schonfelder, 1970). In our view, a single experience of this sort is not sufficient to cause permanent psychological damage to an otherwise healthy child.

Incest

Incest is considered a sexual deviation in all modern Western societies. Though most of the cultures surveyed by Ford and Beach in 1951 maintained incest taboos of varying intensity, there have been those in which incest, at least among some members of the society, was explicitly encouraged. This was true in the royal families of ancient Greece and England, because incest guaranteed an uncomplicated royal lineage.

Since incest is illegal in our society, marriage between a parent and a child or between siblings cannot take place. Incest as a clinical problem does occur, however, usually as a sexual relationship between a parent and a child. It is not exceedingly uncommon, for example, for a family doctor to be told by a patient that her husband has seduced their daughter, or (though this is rarer) that a brother and sister's exploratory sexual play has progressed to intercourse. Where such occurrences are isolated events, they may not involve psychopathology. But where they are continuing relationships—substitutes for more appropriate or more mature relationships—they may well be signs of serious mental disorder.

Bestiality

Gratification from sexual contact with animals is called bestiality. Kinsey reports that this behavior is the least common form of human sexuality (1948). It is most often found among farm workers whose access to women is restricted, but even within this group of males, it is a rare deviation.

Sexual dysfunctions

DSM II includes the sexual dysfunctions within the group of psychophysiologic disorders, which are disabilities characterized by physical symptoms that are of presumed psychological etiology. Most of the psychophysiologic disorders are discussed in Chapter 14. The sexual dysfunctions are treated here, however, both because they and the sexual deviations often coexist in a single individual and because the two kinds of sexual disorders share many etiologic theories and treatment techniques.

Impotence

Impotence is defined as an inability on the part of the male to obtain or maintain an erection suitable for sexual intercourse. It is a common sexual dysfunction that is also extremely anxiety-provoking. When it occurs in early adulthood, impotence is often accompanied by concern about the mechanics and meaning of sexual intercourse. Jay Meredith, for example, told his therapist that he thought his impotence problems were connected with concerns about sexuality—about its proper role in life and about the legitimacy of moral tenets surrounding it—which he had had ever since childhood. When impotence occurs later in life, often after a prolonged period of sexual adequacy, it may be caused by boredom with a stereotyped sex life or may reflect marital discord that centers on matters which are not strictly sexual.

The form that impotence took in Jay Meredith's case—normal ability to obtain and maintain an erection until a certain point in the sexual sequence was reached—is relatively common. Less common is total inability to obtain an erection, either with a specific person or with all persons of the opposite sex.

The impact of his impotence on the male's sexual partner is sometimes major, but its effects on him—especially in terms of his view of his own sexual adequacy and masculinity—are usually more profound. For that reason, planning for the treatment of impotence must involve some consideration of the "meaning" of the behavior to the patient.

Before psychological treatment for impotence begins, other possible explanations for the condition should be considered. Any physical disease which brings on general malaise and weakness (for example, tuberculosis, diabetes, malnutrition) has the distinct potential for diminishing sexual potency. Aging is another factor. Virtually no men in Kinsey's sample (1948) were impotent at the age of 35, while 77 percent of his sample of 80-year-olds was impotent. (It may surprise and encourage some readers to learn that 23 percent of a sample of 80-year-olds was *not* impotent.) Finally, neurological disease, diseases of the genitals themselves (such as venereal disease), and drug abuse (especially of the sedative, tranquilizer, and opiate variety) can all cause short- or long-term impotence.

Premature ejaculation

Premature ejaculation is a frequent sexual dysfunction among males, certainly among young men. The term describes a sexual behavior whereby the male attains orgasm and ejaculation before he wishes to, often immediately after and sometimes even before intromission. Premature ejaculation is most common among young men whose sexual appetite is greater than their opportunity for heterosexual satisfaction. Beyond the sense of frustration and inadequacy that premature ejaculation gives the male, it also creates problems for his sexual partner, who is often left frustrated and angry that her partner has satisfied himself at her expense.

Frigidity

Frigidity, the female equivalent of male impotence, can be as disruptive to a woman's self-concept as impotence is to a man's. The word describes a range of sexual dysfunctions in women which range in seriousness from mild diminution of pleasure in sexual relations and less frequent orgasm during intercourse, to complete lack of responsivity toward sexual stimulation and total absence of orgasm during intercourse. Frigidity of any severity can be lifelong or can develop at any period in life.

As with male impotence, frigidity (primary orgasmic dysfunction, as the syndrome is increasingly termed) may derive from underlying organic disorder. This etiology must be ruled out before the disorder can be considered psychological.

Dyspareunia and vaginismus are varieties of female sexual dysfunction characterized, in the first instance, by painful or difficult sexual intercourse and, in the second, by painful, involuntary spasms of the vaginal muscles. These conditions occur much less frequently than simple frigidity. They are often associated with serious psychological problems which make effective treatment difficult.

Etiology of the sexual disorders

Genetic factors in homosexuality

Kallmann reported concordance rates for homosexuality of less than 50 percent among forty-five pairs of fraternal twins and 100 percent among forty pairs of identical twins (1952). At face value, these data suggest very strongly that homosexuality depends at least in part upon genetic factors. However, no other investigator has been able to replicate Kallmann's findings. Further, Kallmann's research has been criticized because it failed to control for the amount of environmental experience the twin pairs shared. That is, perhaps identical twins share more environmental experiences than fraternal twins.

Other investigators have used newly developed techniques for comparing the genetic material of matched heterosexual and homosexual males. These researchers failed to identify chromosomal differences between the two groups (Pare, 1956; Pritchard, 1962). Pare, a leading experimenter in the area, concludes from his work that "gross abnormalities of the sex chromosomes are not necessarily important in the etiology of homosexuality" (1965).

Hormonal factors in homosexuality and transsexualism

If homosexuality does not arise directly from genetic factors, what about the possibility that an acquired hormonal imbalance might be responsible? After reviewing current literature on this possibility, Perloff, an authority on hormones and homosexuality, concludes:

It must be clear by now that, despite intense and widespread interest in the possible influence of hormones on sexual behavior, this type of research has proven to be extremely frustrating and disappointing, particularly as, after the discovery of the role of gonads as producers of hormones and specifically after the isolation, purification, and synthesis of the steroid hormones, biologists believed that a simple explanation of sexual behavior was at last available. [1965, p. 47]

More recent data call Perloff's pessimistic summary into question. For example, Kolodny and his colleagues classified thirty 18-to 24-year-old homosexuals according to degree of sexual deviation and then compared them with a matched group of heterosexual males along a variety of physical and physiological dimensions (1971). The homosexual subjects' physical examinations and buccal smears (a test of chromosomal material) were within normal limits. But their average level of plasma testosterone (a male hormone) was significantly below that of the control group. Further, there was a significant relationship between plasma testosterone level and sperm count: the average homosexual subject was producing less testosterone and less active sperm than the average heterosexual male.

Other recent reports that have confirmed Kolodny's findings (e.g., Evans, 1972) support the conclusion that homosexual males may differ from heterosexual males in hormone level. While these differences do not prove that hormone deficiency plays a central role in the etiology of homosexuality, they do suggest the possibility that it does. In turn, genetic factors of an unknown kind might cause these hormonal differences, perhaps through a chromosomal abnormality that has not yet been identified. Evidence for these speculations, however, has not yet been found.

Biophysiological data on the etiology of transsexualism are even more contradictory than those for male homosexuality. Some researchers have reported that there is no evidence of abnormality in plasma and urinary steroids, hormone levels, or physical characteristics among male or female transsexuals (Migeon et al., 1969; Walinder, 1969). Yet Benjamin (1966) found that 40 percent of a sample of transsexual men were underdeveloped sexually, while Blumer (1969) discovered "good evidence for an occasional close relationship between sexual aberrations (for instance. transvestism) and paroxysmal temporal lobe disorders" (a specific variety of abnormal brain functioning). However, Blumer also reported that none of his sample of fifteen transsexuals gave an abnormal EEG reading. On balance, the available evidence for a biophysiological view of transsexualism appears somewhat weaker than the evidence for a biophysiological view of male homosexuality.

Aging and illness in the etiology of sexual dysfunctions

In contrast to the sexual deviations, the sexual dysfunctions often result from physical illness or increasing age. Male impotence may be a direct result of debilitating disease, advancing age, or diseases specific to the sexual organs. Frigidity, dyspareunia, or vaginismus may stem from similar causes or from a physical malformation of the female genitals that requires surgical correction. Thus unlike homosexuality or transsexualism, physical causes account for many cases of male and female impotence and must be ruled out before a psychological etiology can be assumed.

Psychoanalytic views on homosexuality and other sexual deviations

The classical psychoanalytic view of the etiology of homosexuality and the other sexual deviations has been well articulated. Three interlocking tenets of Freud's theory come together in this psychoanalytic position. The first is the assumption that heterosexual behavior terminating in sexual intercourse and orgasm is normal and healthy, while homosexual behavior or heterosexual behavior that does not culminate in sexual intercourse is unnatural and perverted. While this Freudian tenet is dissonant with modern views on the sexual deviations, it makes more sense in the context of the times in which it was formulated. Freud's willingness to discuss matters of sex and morals and his attempts to treat the sexual deviations were both revolutionary, despite the conventionality of his judgments about what constitutes normal and abnormal sexuality.

The second part of Freud's position on the sexual deviations was his assumption (which he shared with many colleagues) that every human being possesses crucial elements from the behavioral repertoire of the opposite sex. The special twist Freud applied to this widespread belief was that a (male or female) person's male component was "active," while his or her female component was "passive." Using faulty logic uncontaminated by empirical data, he concluded that it was perverse—a sign of underlying pathology—for men to be passive and women to be active.

The third part of Freud's theory of homosexual etiology derives from the general libido theory. As discussed in Chapter 4, that theory traces the development of personality through the stages of psychosexual development. During each of the stages libido (psychosexual energy) is "invested" in a different organ. Freud believed that homosexuality and the other "perversions" represented a person's fixation at or regression to a stage of psycho-sexual development less "mature" than the genital stage. The kind of perversion the patient showed depended upon the stage to which he had regressed.

Modern dynamic theorists have diverged in important ways from Freud's original position on homosexuality. In part this reflects the natural process by which an innovator's students alter his original contributions. But these changes also reflect a dramatic transformation in our society's views on homosexuality that came before rather than after changes in the views of mental health "opinion makers."

Theoretical statements by the psychoanalysts Karen Horney, Harry Stack Sullivan, and Sandor Rado show some of the ways in which modern views have departed from Freud. Horney's position stresses the cultural determinants of homosexuality as they interact with personality (1939). That is, Horney sees homosexuality as the response on the part of some individuals to the most pathological elements of our culture: exploitiveness, competitiveness, and authoritarianism. Her approach is strikingly like those which have come after it in its emphasis upon the importance of culture and personality in understanding psychopathology. Similarly, Sullivan's theory of psychopathology firmly places homosexuality in the interpersonal sphere, viewing it as a consequence of the imperfect resolution of the adolescent's major interpersonal needs (1953).

Rado's more complicated adaptational theory of homosexuality focuses on the inevitability of the oedipal situation and explains homosexuality as an adaptation to the overwhelming fear of attack for engaging in heterosexual activity (1956). Bieber's elaboration of Rado's theory makes this position clear:

Pathological sexual behavior is directed toward preserving sexual gratification while attempting to cope with the threat of anticipated injury by engaging in a series of adaptive maneuvers usually referred to as defenses. The defenses may circumvent the threat or combine the threat with a defense and include both in the sexual act itself, or they may deal with the threat in a variety of other ways. In homosexuality, threat is avoided by substituting a homosexual object for a heterosexual object, which is perceived as threatening. [Bieber, 1967, p. 961]

Current psychoanalytic views on homosexuality—for example, those of the psychoanalyst Charles Socarides (1970)—are less insistent on giving the oedipal situation the central role in etiology. Instead, homosexuality is seen as a consequence of crucial traumatic events occurring much earlier in the child's life than the oedipal period. In a study that provided empirical support for this point of view, Bieber and his colleagues found that traumatic family experiences early in life (for example, experiences with an abusive father or an overprotective mother) correlated strongly with homosexuality in a comparative study of 106 male homosexuals and

Karen Horney. (Karen Horney Clinic)

100 heterosexual males in psychoanalytic treatment (1962). While research of this kind raises questions about the adequacy of experimental control, bias on the part of researchers who are also therapists, and imperfect techniques for establishing the validity of the data collected, the study does lend some support to the "modern" psychoanalytic position on homosexuality.

Behavioral theories

The first behavioral theory of sexual deviation was set forth by McGuire and his colleagues (1965). It evolved from detailed examination of the case histories of forty-five sexually deviant patients. In essence, McGuire's group concluded that the thoughts, fantasies, and experiences which first become associated with masturbation during early adolescence can later come to be the specific sexual cues to which the adult responds. Thus if the early stimuli are of a predominantly homosexual nature, the adult may develop as a homosexual.

McGuire put his theory in the context of the classical conditioning paradigm: "Any stimulus which regularly precedes ejaculation by the correct time interval should become more and more sexually exciting. The stimulus may be circumstantial (for example, the particular time or place in which masturbation or intercourse is commonly practiced) or it may be deliberate (for example, any sexual situation or a fantasy of it, be it normal intercourse or wearing female apparel)" (McGuire et al., 1965, p. 186). Modest laboratory support for McGuire's hypothesis was found by Evans (1968), while clinical confirmation of the theory has also been reported (Davison, 1968; Marquis, 1970).

If McGuire's theory applies to Steve Habillier's transvestism, it means that Steve must have associated women's clothing, perhaps his mother's or a sister's, with the pleasure he experienced as an early adolescent during masturbation. Certainly Steve may have had such a set of experiences at that time of his youth, since he lived in a crowded home where he was surrounded by sisters.

Bandura's social-learning approach to psychopathology (1969) incorporates three social-learning mechanisms that are relevant to the development of deviant sexual behavior. The first is represented by parents who "model" sexually deviant behavior patterns in overt or subtle ways. Bandura cites the study by Giffin and his co-workers which traced the development of a 17-year-old boy's exhibitionism to his mother's seductive behavior with him while he was growing up (1954). She would shower with him, have prolonged discussions of sex with him, let him know that she enjoyed the sight of his naked body, especially his "beautiful masculine endowment" —his penis. There seemed little doubt of the central role she played in the development of his deviance.

The second learning mechanism that Bandura stresses is the association of sexually deviant responses with positively reinforcing events when the responses first appear. Specifically, he concludes that if these behaviors are associated with expressions of affection, close physical intimacy, and other reinforcing consequences by parents or friends, they are more likely to remain in the person's sexual repertoire. Stoller, who studied the mothers and wives of thirty-two transvestites, provided strong supporting data for this view (1967). He found that sexual deviance had been strongly rewarded by the wives and mothers, in that whenever many of the men had dressed in feminine clothes, they had been explicitly aided and implicitly rewarded by being taught how to dress, how to apply cosmetics, and how to emit "feminine" behavior.

Third, Bandura makes the point that sexually deviant behavior can become strongly self-reinforcing. Once it acquires stress-reducing capabilities, it is independent of aversive external feedback. He says: "First, sexual activities can produce sufficiently intense pleasurable experiences to contravene feelings of apprehension or frustration. Secondly, performance of sexual behavior also changes the stimulus situation by temporarily directing the person's attention away from stress-producing events" (1969, p. 514).

However, many of the case histories Bandura cites to support his social learning view of sexual disorder could also be used by dynamic theorists to justify their own theoretical position. They would doubtless claim, for example, that the 17-year-old boy's mother in Giffen's study and the mothers of the thirty-two transvestites in Stoller's had simply reactivated traumatic early memories in their boys, causing regression to immature levels of sexual functioning. Nevertheless, there are some laboratory experiments that provide more specific support for the behavioral point of view. These replicate hypothesized mechanisms of social learning initially derived from case history data. For example, Rachman (1967; Rachman & Hodgson, 1968) showed that initially neutral stimuli (say, boots) can be invested with sexually arousing properties by repeated association with primary sexual stimuli (say, pictures of nudes). Like McGuire's theory, this view of sexual deviation derives from the classical conditioning model of etiology. Thus Rachman and Hodgson demonstrated in the laboratory an important etiological mechanism in fetishism that previously had only been presumed to exist. Unfortunately, no other studies of the experimental psychopathology of sexual deviation have been published.

Sociocultural factors

Reports by Gagnon (1965) and Gagnon and Simon (1969; 1973) add a valuable cultural perspective to the social-learning view of the sexual disorders. Central to Gagnon's approach is the thesis that "a prerequisite in any discussion of the sexuality of children is some description of the sexual value system of the adult members of the community" (1965, p. 213). Gagnon and Simon emphasize the pervasive influence of a culture's behavioral norms on the development of patterns of sex-linked behavior in its young people. These writers observe, for example, that demand for aggressiveness in boys and submissiveness in girls has a profound influence on overt sexual behavior, even though aggressiveness and submissiveness do not directly relate to sexuality. In other words, the different roles that a society instills in men and women affect sexual behavior even though the behavior demanded by the roles does not directly relate to sexual behavior.

While Gagnon offers no empirical data to support his theory, it is interesting and plausible. For example, contrast it with the social-learning point of view: it seems clear that learning specific sexual behaviors according to Bandura's modeling paradigm (for example, acquiring homosexual behavior by modeling a mother who then reinforces those behaviors in her child) is no more important to the development of adult sexual behavior than modeling social behaviors that have relevance to sexual behavior (for instance, acquiring a general attitude of submissiveness by modeling a submissive father—and then demonstrating one's submissiveness in sexual situations).

What is "normal" sexual behavior?

Just as people can identify abnormal behavior more easily than they can characterize normality, so they can describe deviant sexual behavior more easily than normal sexuality. As you study the sexual disorders, however, you should know at least the general outlines of research findings on normal sexual behavior.

The Kinsey reports

Before Alfred Kinsey's epochal books *Sexual Behavior in the Human Male* (1948) and *Sexual Behavior in the Human Female* (1953), empirical data on normal human sexuality did not exist. For that reason conservative "traditional" views on sexuality predominated, and most scientists agreed that normal sexual behavior probably conformed largely to the teachings of organized religion and the psychoanalytic movement. As a result, many of Kinsey's findings, especially those having to do with masturbation and pre- and extramarital intercourse, were considered "beyond the pale." Kinsey himself was even accused

Alfred Kinsey. *(The Bettmann Archive)*

of inflating his data in a quest for personal publicity.

In retrospect, few of Kinsey's findings now shock or surprise us. Likewise we now accept the studies of Masters and Johnson (1966) detailing the physiology of the sex act with equanimity, though when they first appeared they too created a sensation. Both Kinsey and Masters and Johnson consider normal sexual behavior to be a *statistical construct,* just as Eysenck approaches normal human behavior through the statistical model (Chapter 1). In other words, normal sexual behavior to these researchers comprises the full and diverse range of physiological and interpersonal sexual events that are shared by most well-adjusted adults. Their objective position enables Masters and Johnson and Kinsey to avoid moral judgments in assessing normality as it relates to sexuality.

Among Kinsey's notable findings were the following:

[1] *Male premarital petting:* 88 percent of his 1948 sample of males had engaged in some sort of petting. Petting to orgasm was most common among college-educated, urban groups with high socioeconomic status. These are the groups which tend to delay marriage the longest.

[2] *Female premarital petting:* 40 percent of Kinsey's 1953 sample had had heterosexual petting experience by the age of 15. Between 69 and 95 percent of the sample had had such experiences by the age of 18. In the sample of "petters," 10 percent had confined themselves to one petting partner before marriage, 32 percent had petted with two to five males before marriage, 23 percent had petted with six to ten partners, and 35 percent had petted with more than ten different partners before marriage. Petting in females, as in males, was positively related to educational level, socioeconomic status, and urban residence.

[3] *Male premarital intercourse:* Most males (80+ percent) had experienced intercourse before marriage. Surprisingly, 22 percent of the sample had attempted intercourse before puberty. Rates of premarital intercourse and educational level were negatively related: Among college males 67 percent had had intercourse before marriage. Comparable figures for high school and grade school graduates were, respectively, 84 percent and 98 percent.

[4] *Female premarital intercourse:* While two-thirds of the married females in Kinsey's sample had experienced orgasm prior to marriage, only 17 percent of this group had done so as the result of premarital intercourse. Nonetheless, nearly 50 percent of the females in Kinsey's total sample had experienced coitus prior to marriage, much of it during the year immediately preceding their marriages (presumably with husbands-to-be). Relationships between educational level and rates of premarital intercourse in this sample were the reverse of those in Kinsey's sample of males: Only 30 percent of the grade school females had had premarital intercourse, while more than 60 percent of the college girls in the sample had done so.

[5] *Extramarital intercourse:* By the age of 40, 26 percent of married women and 50 percent of married men in Kinsey's sample had experienced extramarital intercourse. Of the married females in his sample who had had extramarital sex, 41 percent of them had confined these experiences to a single partner, 40 percent to two to five partners, and 19 percent to six or more.

[6] *Masturbation:* Over 90 percent of the males and 70 percent of the females in Kinsey's sample had masturbated at some time in their lives. Frequency of masturbation during adolescence was, on the average, two to three times a week for boys and two to three times a month for girls. After adolescence, masturbation frequency decreased in men and in-

creased in women, so that by middle age women masturbated more frequently than men. Frequency of masturbation varied directly with education: Single college-level men in the 20 to 30 age range masturbated significantly more frequently than single men of the same age who had not attended college.

[7] *Homosexuality:* Kinsey estimated that approximately 4 percent of Caucasian males in the United States were exclusively homosexual. Further, 37 percent of his sample of white males had experienced at least one homosexual relationship during their lives. Many of these were brief experiences during the early teen years. Corresponding figures for female homosexuality were about one-third those for males.

Publication of Kinsey's books was followed rapidly by heated criticism of his findings on scientific grounds (Hyman & Barmack, 1954; Terman, 1948) as well as on moral and religious ones (e.g., Wallin, 1949). Though some reviewers praised Kinsey's research extravagantly (Sewell, 1955), most combined praise for the overall goals of the project with strong methodological objections. In our view, the significance of the Kinsey reports lay as much in the impact they had on public views about sexuality, especially on the necessity for people to face facts they may have previously chosen to ignore, as on the specifics of Kinsey's data.

From the perspective that the years give us, it seems clear that Kinsey and his colleagues were dedicated men who gathered and reported data that were both important and accurate. Some of their findings (for example, those on masturbation) probably remain largely accurate today. Other Kinsey data, however, are probably on the low side now. The "sexual enlightenment" of our era has almost certainly raised the figures for such behaviors as premarital petting and intercourse. Recent research confirms this conclusion (Reiss, 1967; Wagner et al., 1973).

The psychologist Keith Davis, discussing the results of a study comparing contemporary attitudes toward premarital sex with the attitudes that Kinsey reported in the 1950s, concluded in a recent interview:

"All that nudity must be for middle-agers who missed out on the sexual revolution." Standards of sexual conduct have changed over the last 20 years; looking and leering have, for many, given way to experimenting and trying. *(Drawing by R. Martin; Copyright 1969 by Saturday Review/World, Inc.)*

Students consider sexual intercourse before marriage much more acceptable than before. But it is strongly tied to affection, caring for the partner, which is a continuation of core traditional values. And the women feel this more strongly than men. In the 30's and 40's the criterion was that you had to be married or engaged. Now the criterion is that you have to care for each other. [Paige, 1973, p. 1]

Masters and Johnson's
Human Sexual Response

Even though Kinsey's books had prepared the way, the publication of Masters and Johnson's *Human Sexual Response* (1966) was greeted by almost as much public and professional uproar. And despite major differences in content and intent, Kinsey's 1948 report and Masters and Johnson's 1966 book generated surprisingly similar kinds of criticism, ranging from charges that the authors were seeking publicity, to moral objections, to attacks on methodological grounds.

Human Sexual Response reports on a twelve-year study of the sequential pattern of muscular, glandular, and vascular changes that accompany sexual response in men and women. Drawing on self-report measures and on the observation and measurement of the laboratory performance of 382 women and 312 men who actively participated in the study, Masters and Johnson captured much of the complex interaction of physiology and psychology that constitutes normal adult sexuality. In so doing, they also succeeded in debunking several of our culture's most important and longest-lived sexual myths.

Masters and Johnson describe four distinct stages in the normal sexual sequence. The first, the *excitement stage,* is signaled in men by penile erection which occurs within a few seconds of adequate erotic stimulation. Initial physiological response to sexual stimuli by women usually takes place with thirty seconds of stimulation. It includes vaginal lubrication, breast enlargement, and nipple erection. The excitement stage can last from a few minutes to several hours for both sexes.

The *plateau stage* involves a continued development of the physical changes initiated during the excitement stage. These alterations in body functioning are maintained for varying lengths of time depending upon both the nature of the original erotic stimulus and the state of sexual deprivation of the two sexual partners. By the end of this stage, a "sexual flush" covers the woman's breasts, chest, and neck.

The *orgastic stage* of the sexual sequence, its climactic event, occurs suddenly and lasts only a few seconds. Male orgasm is characterized by ejaculation of semen, followed by a rapid reduction of tension and by detumescence. Variation in the duration and intensity of orgasm among women is much greater than among men. One reason may be that many more distinct anatomic and physiologic changes occur during female orgasm. In this regard, Masters and Johnson report one of their most controversial findings—that the female orgasm centers on the clitoris and depends primarily on clitoral stimulation. This conclusion, based upon convincing empirical evidence, flies in the face of psychoanalytic theory that posits the existence of separate "clitoral" and "vaginal" orgasms, the first of which is more "immature" than the second because it is not so directly related to sexual intercourse.

Immediately after orgasm comes the *resolution stage,* when the physical changes described in the excitement stage are reexperienced in reverse order. If the woman has not achieved orgasm, the resolution changes occur very slowly, sometimes requiring up to three hours. In men a recovery period of variable length is necessary before further sexual stimulation will initiate another sexual sequence. Some women, however, can become reexcited almost immediately after orgasm.

Masters and Johnson's choice of experimental subjects has been questioned. For example, some were prostitutes, while others were sexually inexperienced unmarried women, and some critics have claimed that such "special" subjects limited the generalizability of the data. Most experts in the field, however, praise Masters and Johnson's book and value their findings.

"Normal" sexuality: A contemporary view

Prevailing opinion among mental health professionals, educated laymen, and sex counselors is that whatever sexual practices a couple finds satisfying and pleasurable ought to be viewed as "normal" and "healthy" for them. While heterosexual lovemaking usually does include sexual intercourse, intercourse can be accomplished in many different positions and can be preceded and accompanied by a very wide range of associated sexual behaviors (such as fellatio, cunnilingus, mutual masturbation, flagellation). What this means is that any particular sex act cannot be regarded as a "perversion" without also considering the circumstances in which it occurs, the individuals who engage in it, and the modes, morals, and sexual standards of the society in which they live. While undoubtedly "permissive,"

this view of human sexuality is also probably "healthier" than more rigid views that bear little relation to the infinite variety of human sexual behavior.

Prostitution: Profession or perversion?

Despite its status as "the world's oldest profession," prostitution remains one of those paradoxical human activities that is both omnipresent in most human societies and the object of profound misunderstanding, repression, moral outrage, and hypocrisy. For this reason, there is very little objective information on the role and influence of prostitution in American society, on those who have chosen to become prostitutes, and on those who use the services of prostitutes. One of the few things known for sure about prostitution—defined as the giving of sexual favors promiscuously, anonymously, and without affection, for a fee—is that it exists in most modern

(Jan Lukas from Rapho Guillumette)

societies and has existed for as long as recorded history. Authorities are also fairly certain that while prostitution usually refers to the purchase by males of female sexual favors, markets for male sexual favors by females and for homosexual favors by both sexes exist as well. Finally, most observers of the sexual scene are convinced that professional prostitutes are decreasing in number in many places as the modern climate of moral permissiveness encourages amateurs to provide for little or no money what professionals used to sell.

Authorities are less sure about what effect prostitution has on those who work as prostitutes, how they enter the profession, and what factors go into the decision to employ the services of a prostitute. One of the researchers who has studied the effect of prostitution on prostitutes most carefully is Harold Greenwald (1970). This psychologist writes sympathetically and thoughtfully about the life-style of call girls, a distinct subgroup within prostitution. Many of them live in large convention cities, rent expensive apartments in fashionable neighborhoods, and earn their living (often totaling more than $30,000 a year) by spending the night with middle-aged convention delegates for $100 or more. Greenwald writes that status is a preoccupation with many of these young women—at least in relation to the ordinary streetwalker or "house girl." Call girls, he says, are anxious to distinguish themselves from other prostitutes and are often more scornful of the streetwalkers than the most puritanical reformer.

Despite the clear picture he gives of the kind of person who enters the life of the "elegant prostitute," Greenwald deals only briefly with the reasons why she enters it. Other investigators have studied this matter in more detail. The sociologists Jackman, O'Toole, and Geis interviewed fifteen prostitutes (most of whom were streetwalkers) about the determinants which led them to choose that life (1964). They concluded that the self-images of the prostitutes they had interviewed differed from those of otherwise comparable women in three important ways: (1) Because they are isolated

from the mainstream of society, the prostitutes defined as acceptable some patterns of behavior (such as prostitution) that are condemned by most people. (2) Despite their rejection of many social values, the prostitutes were very much aware of them. As a result they tried to rationalize their violation of traditional moral standards: for example, by pointing to environmental circumstances in justification of their unorthodox way of life. (3) Their rationalizations for violating social taboos were usually accompanied by a reciprocal exaggeration of other values, especially those having to do with financial success. In some cases they emphasized the point that they had to support someone else, such as an aged parent or a child of their own.

Many of Jackman's prostitutes also linked their choice of occupation to a disordered, cold, or rejecting early family situation. Though not a general phenomenon, it seemed that a chaotic childhood, insensitive or hostile parents, or both played a role in the decision by many of these women to enter the world's oldest profession. Sexual deviation or dysfunction may also have a part in this decision-making process. Greenwald, for example, reported that fifteen of the twenty-six call girls he studied had had homosexual relationships. Others writing before and after Greenwald have also observed a relationship between homosexuality and prostitution (Caprio, 1954; Ellis, 1915; Ward & Kassebaum, 1965). According to this view, hostility to men, culminating in the decision to profit from male sexual desire, leads naturally to homosexuality—in their eyes a purer, more ideal form of sexual expression. Ward and Kassebaum quote a homosexual prostitute as saying:

Most prostitutes become homosexual, that goes along with their life, you can't even see the man as a human, you think all men are looking for a profit—then you meet bisexual girls who are hustling. . . . Feelings of hostility against males develop, and the need for something more satisfactory comes, and this is the homosexual relationship. I had one affair like this and it took me a long time to get over it. [1965, p. 129]

In other words, homosexuality develops in women who were heterosexual before they adopted the life of the prostitute. Whether their initial heterosexuality was genuine and whether their "reactive" homosexuality continues after they are no longer prostitutes are questions which have not been answered.

Other mental health workers have pointed out that many prostitutes are sexually frigid (Glover, 1953). But as with the circumstances surrounding prostitutes' homosexuality, it is unknown whether frigidity plays a causal role in the choice of prostitution as a career or whether frigidity is brought on by prostitution as a way of life.

Generalizations about why men frequent prostitutes are even more difficult. Some of the "normal" reasons for doing so include a desire for sexual variety or such factors as advancing age or physical handicaps that make it difficult to succeed with women in more socially acceptable ways. More or less "abnormal" reasons for frequenting prostitutes include unwillingness to accept the obligation for monogamy in Western marriage, inability to attract women because of social ineptitude, or psychological problems that prevent the development of longer-term relationships with women. Thus while some men who are attracted to prostitutes are doubtless disturbed psychologically, it is also likely that many men who achieve sexual release in this way do so for nonpathological reasons.

Pornography: Are dirty movies a risk that society can afford?

Like politics and religion, pornography is a matter about which even people of good will rarely agree. In the first place, what is it? Consider the following five definitions:

> The term "pornography" has no real meaning in the legal sense, or even in the psychological sense.
>
> Pornography is a kind of romance, but no more socially or psychically pernicious than the romance of passion that dominates the lives of Emma Bovary or Heathcliff.

(Charles Gatewood)

> Pornography is like a squalid, unnecessary little country which owes its independence to a vagary of history.
>
> Because it is not taught at university, pornography is unknown to most historians of literature, and for the same reason to most judges—even to those who officiate at obscenity trials.
>
> In short, pornography is sinful. [Barber, 1972, pp. 77–78]

For now, a working definition might be that pornography consists of writings, pictures, movies, or other material whose sole aim is to arouse its audience sexually.

In the second place, does pornography represent a threat to the social order? Public controversy over pornography has largely centered on the effects of an increasingly permissive cultural climate in the Western countries. This climate is characterized by willingness to permit "hard-core" X-rated movies and equally licentious paperback books to be marketed openly and more or less indiscriminately. But do they have a bad influence on the mental health and morals of those who consume them? People who view society's increasing permissiveness as a mark of decline in public morality often believe that pornography plays a crucial role in sexual crimes and other illicit sexual activity. Those who look on pornography more benignly as just a "sign of the times" think that it plays no role at all in crime or corruption.

People who want to prohibit the use or sale of pornography base their arguments on the following assumptions: (1) Pornography "dehumanizes" sexual relations between men and women by portraying what should be a spiritual and psychological act as simply the coupling of two passionate animals. (2) Pornography is a sin because, contrary to Biblical prohibition, it describes sexual activity that is not directed toward procreation. (3) Pornography fosters the belief that everyone is capable of superhuman sexual performances; when people move from pornography to real life, they are bound to be disappointed in their own modest sexual abilities. (4) Pornography unleashes passions which man, a sexual animal, cannot control. Overwhelmed by these primitive sexual impulses, some men will be driven to commit crimes of passion.

Early in 1968 Congress established an advisory commission to "study the causal relationship of such materials to antisocial behavior and to recommend advisable, appropriate, effective, and constitutional means to deal effectively with such traffic in obscenity and pornography" (*Commission on Pornography Report,* 1970).

The commission's central finding was that pornography by itself has *not* caused an increase in the frequency of sex crimes or antisocial behavior in the United States. On the contrary, it was suggested that pornographic materials might actually reduce the incidence of sex crimes by serving as a "safety valve" for sexual expression. Specifically, the commission concluded:

1. The production and distribution of pornographic movies and books has increased enormously during the past decade and is now close to a two-billion-dollar-a-year business.

2. "If a case is to be made against pornography in 1970, it will have to be made on grounds other than demonstrated effects of a damaging personal or social nature. Empirical research designed to clarify the question has found no reliable evidence to date that exposure to explicit sexual materials plays a significant role in the causation of delinquent or criminal sexual behavior among youth or adults" (p. 139).

The commission's study depended upon several different research strategies, of which the three central elements were: (1) Survey studies in which normal adults and young people were asked about their experiences with pornographic materials and their attitudes toward sexual behavior. One of the largest of these studies involved a national survey based on long face-to-face interviews with a random sample of 2,486 adults and over 700 teenagers 15 to 20 years old. (2) Direct comparisons of experiences with and attitudes toward pornography between normal adults and teenagers and convicted sex criminals. Findings from one of these studies are reviewed below. (3) Experimental studies using two or more matched groups of normal subjects, one of whom received controlled exposure to erotic materials. Follow-up or outcome measures provided an index of the extent to which controlled exposure to sexual materials caused a change in sexual attitudes or behavior.

One of the most thorough studies reviewed by the commission directly compares the uses to which sex offenders and normal adults put pornographic materials. It was published by sociologist Harold Kant and psychologist Michael Goldstein (1970). They compared 60 newly admitted patients to a state hospital in California, all of whom had been charged with or convicted of rape or child molestation, with 133 normal adult males from the Los Angeles area. Their major finding was that both the rapists and the child molesters had actually seen *less* pornography of all kinds than the normals had. Specifically, the rapists had seen significantly fewer "representations of fully nude women, of normal intercourse, of mouth-genital contact or of sadomasochistic activity," while the child molesters had seen less pornography of almost every kind than the normal group had. When questioned about the uses to which they had put the pornography they had seen, the rapists and child molesters admitted to more masturbatory activity than the normal group during and after exposure to these materials, but not to any increase in the rate of deviant or criminal sexual activity. Finally, the study revealed that significantly more rapists and child molesters had grown up in families with repressive attitudes toward sexuality, a result parallel to the finding that alcoholics come more often than nonalcoholics from families which prohibit alcohol.

Turning from its review of these and other findings attesting to the relative innocuousness of pornographic materials, the *Commission on Pornography Report* states the commission's opinion that a large part of the "pornography problem" in this country results from our unwillingness or inability to talk frankly about sexual matters. Accordingly the commission recommended that a sex-education program be launched on a national basis, to be supplemented by open forums and other informational campaigns designed to confront the problem of pornography directly.

Moving to legislative recommendations, the commission proposed what has turned out to be its most controversial recommendation: that federal, state, and local laws prohibiting the sale, exhibition, or distribution of sexual materials to consenting adults be repealed. In a less controversial recommendation, the commission advocated prohibition of the sale or distribution of pornography to minors, of public display of sexually explicit pictorial materials, and of the mailing of unsolicited advertisements of a sexual nature.

As could have been predicted, the commission's conclusions and recommendations were applauded by civil liberty groups and condemned by church groups and other organizations convinced of the decline in American morals. Further, the Administration went on record as opposing the commission's recommendations for liberalized laws on obscenity. This position may have led to the recent Supreme Court decision which moved away from its liberal interpretations in the past to one permitting local governments to censor pornography in accordance with local tastes and sensibilities. Whether the Court's decision marks the end of the national controversy on pornography remains to be seen.

Assessment of the sexual disorders

Students of the sexual disorders are increasingly coming to agree that a sexually deviant person cannot be identified simply by his appearance or behavior (Braaten & Darling, 1965; Thompson et al., 1971). That is, reliable behavioral cues to the sexual deviations, other than the deviation itself, have not been discovered.

Though the Minnesota Multiphasic Personality Inventory (MMPI) contains a scale designed to be sensitive to homosexuality (the Mf or "masculinity-femininity scale"), most (but not all) studies testing the validity of the Mf scale for the purpose of identifying homosexuals have demonstrated its uncertain sensitivity in this regard (Carson, 1969; Manosevitz, 1971). One reason for the inability of the Mf scale to differentiate between homosexuals and heterosexuals is that it reflects a person's level of education and socioeconomic status (Zucker & Manosevitz, 1966). In other words, these two variables—which are independent of sexual identity—play an important part in determining where a subject falls on the Mf scale. Persons who are well-educated and high in socioeconomic status may well be interested in art, music, and other cultural activities. They will endorse the many "cultural items on the Mf scale—just as the developers of the MMPI expected homosexuals to do. By contrast, the few items on the Mf scale which do enable differentiation of homosexuals and nonhomosexuals (for example, "I have engaged in unusual sexual practices") are lost among the items which do not discriminate.

The projective tests, especially the TAT and the Rorschach test, have also been used for purposes of diagnosis (say, to answer the question "Is he a homosexual?") and personality research (for example, to find out by what personality variables, if any, homosexuals differ from heterosexuals). There is a great deal of conflict among psychologists as to whether these instruments can do either job (James, 1970; Piotrowski, 1965).

A recent study by Chapman and Chapman (1969), part of an ambitious research program begun earlier (1967a, 1967b), illuminated some of the key determinants of the Rorschach test's insensitivity to homosexuality. Central to the study's design were two facts that had been established by other investigators: (1) Of the seven most common "homosexual signs" on the Rorschach, two appear to be empirically valid, while the other five have not been validated despite a number of efforts to do so (Hooker, 1958; Wheeler, 1949), (2) The valid and invalid Rorschach signs have dramatically different "face validities." The two kinds of responses to Rorschach stimuli which are valid (that is, those which distinguish reliably between groups of homosexual and heterosexual males) are "a human or animal—contorted, monstrous, or threatening" on a certain Rorschach card and "a human or humanized animal" on another. Neither valid sign has much "face validity," in that neither by itself suggests its valid relationship to homosexuality. By contrast, all five invalid signs do have pronounced "face validity." They include the following responses to any of the Rorschach cards: human or animal anal content, feminine clothing, humans with sex confused, humans with sex uncertain, and male or female genitalia.

When thirty-two experienced clinical psychologists were asked by the Chapmans to list the kinds of Rorschach content they associated with men who have homosexual problems, their five most frequent responses were the five invalid diagnostic signs! They almost *never* selected the two Rorschach signs that are valid. These data have since been replicated and extended by Golding and Rorer (1972).

There are a few procedures for the behavioral assessment of homosexuality, however, that have recently begun to yield promising results. Freund (1963, 1971), for example, has developed a technique for measuring changes in penile volume while subjects observe slides of male and female nudes. Each slide is exposed for seven seconds; genital volume is measured immediately before and during the exposure and then seven seconds afterwards. In a validity study of this assessment procedure, the test successfully differentiated among normal heterosexual males, heterosexual and homosexual pedophiles, homosexuals with a special attraction for adolescents, and homosexuals who prefer adults (Freund, 1967).

The penile-volume assessment technique has been criticized as both cumbersome and in itself contributory to sexual arousal (Bancroft et al., 1966). Other researchers have explored the GSR (Hain & Linton, 1969), cardiovascular changes (Wenger et al., 1968), and changes in pupil dilation (Lawless & Wake, 1969) as behavioral measures of sexual interest. But none of these methods has yet achieved the diagnostic differentiation that the penile-volume technique seems to permit, despite its drawbacks.

Few assessment efforts specifically directed to sexual disorders other than homosexuality have been reported. While projective tests have been used in an effort to identify transsexuals (Randell, 1971; Stoller & Newman, 1971) and sex offenders (Jensen et al., 1971), the results have not encouraged widespread use of projective techniques for these purposes. Marks and Gelder did record changes in the magnitude of penile erections to visual stimuli associated with fetishism and transvestism in five sexually deviant subjects before, during, and after aversive conditioning for their disorders (1967). This measurement procedure reflected changes in sexual preference as the therapy proceeded, suggesting that the penile-volume technique may well have diagnostic utility through the range of sexual deviations.

Experimental psychopathology of sexual disorders

The animal model

Few studies have employed animals to explore issues relevant to sexual disorder in humans. Those that have done so have looked at sexuality from one or the other sides of a single coin: they have examined sexual adequacy as a function of early social deprivation or of early social overstimulation (overcrowding).

The bulk of the "early social deprivation–later sexual disorder" experimentation has been done by Harlow and his colleagues at the University of Wisconsin, with rhesus monkeys as experimental subjects. In these studies infant monkeys are usually reared with their mothers for certain periods of time, then separated from them for specific periods, then reunited. Predictably, the infant monkeys become extremely agitated immediately after their mothers are taken away. If separation is continued beyond two or three days, they begin to show marked reductions in the frequency of behavior of all kinds, an effect Harlow terms "behavior depression." Upon reunion with the mother, an infant's behavior gradually returns to baseline levels in some behavioral areas. But depending upon the total length of the separation and the age of the infant during it, the monkey's later adult behaviors, including those identified as sexual, may remain at variance with behaviors emitted by monkeys who were not subjected to early maternal separation (Seay et al., 1962; Seay & Harlow, 1965; Suomi, 1973).

In a study focused specifically on several early social deprivation variables as potential factors in later sexual disability, Suomi, Harlow, and Domek separated four rhesus monkeys (two males and two females) from their mothers at birth and raised them together until they were three months old (1970). A twelve-week separation cycle was then initiated, during which each monkey was physically separated from his peers for four days and then returned to the "group cage" for three days. At the end of this separation sequence, all monkeys (by then six months old) were returned to the group cage, where they lived together for a period of six weeks. Next a second separation cycle, identical to the first and lasting eight weeks, was programmed. It was followed by four more weeks of group living.

One of the ten categories of behavior to which observers were instructed to attend was termed "sex and play," defined as "any sexual advance or posturing directed toward another S and/or any type of socially-directed play activity (including rough-and-tumble, approach-withdraw, and noncontact-type play)." This category was frequently observed following the first separation series. Although "sex and play" virtually always increases in duration and frequency as baby monkeys mature, it was not observed in the behavior of the four subjects in this study. As a result, the experimenters concluded that social deprivation had altered the subjects' usual patterns of sexual approach. The researchers also assumed that the early behavioral deficit would affect the adequacy of later sexual behavior.

Missakian recently investigated the extent to which an intensive social group experience during adulthood can alter atypical sexual patterns developed earlier by rhesus monkeys reared under social deprivation conditions (1972). In other words, Missakian created a behavior-modification program designed to permit "deviant" monkeys to model appropriate sexual behavior shown by "normal" monkeys. Subjects of this "therapy" program were three adult male rhesus monkeys who had been raised in social isolation and showed prominent deficits in social and sexual behavior. They were given three to six months' experience in social settings with monkeys who had no deficits in social or sexual behavior. This experience modified the social and sexual behavior of two of the three deviant monkeys, who increased their rates of social grooming and mounting (copulatory) behavior and decreased their rates of physical aggression against others, all of which were changes in the "normal" direction. Missakian's study supports the view that social and sexual behavior in animals is strongly influenced by learning and modeling variables, which have an effect both early and later in life. This view is essentially identical to the behavioral view of human sexual behavior.

Virtually all other programmatic research employing the animal model to study the experimental psychopathology of sexual disorders has used rats and mice. Its major concerns have also been with the effects of early social deprivation and early social stimulation (overcrowding) on later sexual behavior. In both conditions significant effects have been demonstrated. Rats raised alone or with other rat pups (but without their mothers) do not exhibit normal copulation and ejaculation behavior at 200 days of age while those raised with mothers alone or with mothers and other pups do show this behavior (Gruendel & Arnold, 1969). Gerbils raised in overcrowded conditions fail to develop reproductive organs of normal weight significantly more frequently than gerbils raised in uncrowded situations (Dunn, 1971).

The human model

For many years anthropologists have considered primitive societies to be "fair game" for naturalistic studies of human sexual behavior (Ford & Beach, 1951; Mead, 1935). Comparable studies of our own sexual behavior have only recently begun to appear, no doubt encouraged by recent changes in public willingness to subject sexual practices to open scrutiny. While Kinsey's books probably helped these changes along, other less "scientific" surveys have begun to appear in both scientific and general publications (Bartell, 1970; Roebuck & Spray, 1967; Hoffman, 1969).

So far, however, the only research program designed to study disordered (rather than normal) human sexuality in a controlled laboratory setting was Rachman's (1967, 1968). His studies demonstrated that initially neutral stimuli can be invested with sexually arousing properties through conditioning. While Masters and Johnson's *Human Sexual Response* reported additional laboratory-derived data, their research was not designed to test any specific hypothesis, and they made no effort to apply appropriate controls to permit generalization of results from individuals to groups.

The need for controlled laboratory studies of human sexual disorder seems far to outweigh moral objections to them. It is probable that such studies will soon begin to proliferate as scientists "catch up" with the changed views of sexuality which are emerging in society as a whole.

Treatment of the sexual deviations

Drugs, hormones, and surgery

Some supporters of the biophysiological view of homosexuality have energetically "treated" homosexuality with appropriate sex hormones (androgen for male homosexuals and estrogen for female homosexuals). These treatment efforts, however, have not been very successful (Bieber, 1967).

On the other hand, the treatment of transsexualism by a combined regimen of hormone treatment, surgery, and counseling now appears to offer great promise (Green & Money, 1969). Before selecting patients for the "change-of-sex" operation that is at the center of this regimen, Green, Money, and their co-workers at Johns Hopkins require a thorough psychological, psychiatric, hormonal, and physical status evaluation. Patients who emerge successfully from the evaluation process receive endocrine and surgical treatment in varying proportions, depending upon many factors.

For example, Green and Money's hormonal

From man to woman: Jan Morris, a well-known British Journalist who had been James Morris, changed sex over an eight-year period by means of lengthy hormonal treatment and, finally, surgery. Here she is shown in 1974, after her transition. *(Henry Grossman—PEOPLE)*

treatment for males consists almost entirely of estrogenic preparations in doses large enough to bring about "hormonal castration"— inactivation (and size reduction) of the male's own sex glands—and feminization. Feminization of males with the estrogens results in growth of breasts to the size normally found in a girl in her late teens. Long-continued estrogen therapy may also change the distribution of subcutaneous fat to the feminine mode and cause a reduction in muscular strength. Despite massive and prolonged hormone therapy, the beard and other masculine hairiness usually remain unchanged, as does voice pitch.

Treatment of females with male hormones involves massive doses of a testosterone preparation. In such cases menstruation is suppressed, facial hair grows, and the voice deepens. Skeletal muscles occasionally develop more fully. Only rarely does continued administration of androgens cause regression of women's breasts. As a result plastic surgery is almost always necessary to remove them.

The aim of surgery for transsexualism is alteration of the tissues and organs which do not respond to endocrine treatment. In males this means castration, surgical removal of the penis, and surgical formation of a "vaginal cavity"—all surprisingly easy for surgeons experienced in the techniques involved. In women surgical sex change means removal of the breasts, womb, and Fallopian tubes. A penis is then surgically constructed—an extremely difficult and prolonged procedure which produces an organ serving little if any sexual function.

Because this radical approach to transsexualism is new, adequate follow-up studies of patients treated at Johns Hopkins have not been reported. But the intermediate-term follow-ups (at one- and two-year intervals) are most encouraging (Money, 1971).

Dynamic therapies

Since dynamic therapists believe that homosexuality always signals serious underlying psychological disorder, they argue that treatment must center on efforts to return the patient to exclusive heterosexual functioning. Even so, psychoanalytic theory and practice have undergone many changes since Freud stated this theoretical position. Despite the value judgment that psychoanalysis makes, many modern dynamicists are neither as harsh in their evaluation of homosexuality nor as certain that they are right as their words might suggest.

Many of these clinicians, for example, have adopted the psychoanalyst Sandor Rado's views, which emphasize the anxiety- and conflict-producing factors of family, society, and accidental circumstances in attempting to explain homosexual behavior. This "modern" dynamic approach stresses the importance of concentrating on the homosexual's "basic" problems with competition, dependency, and power rather than on his homosexuality in itself.

There have been numerous efforts to assess the effectiveness of the dynamic approach to homosexuality and the other sexual deviations. Though many of these studies have concluded that dynamic treatment designed to alter long-term patterns of homosexual behavior is largely ineffective, psychoanalytic treatment with more modest goals (for example, therapy to help the homosexual adjust more effectively to life as a homosexual) appears to yield more positive results (Bieber, 1969; Faulk, 1971; Mayerson & Lief, 1965; Zechnick, 1971). As a result, many dynamic therapists support the basic validity of Freud's views on the efficacy of psychoanalysis for homosexuals, summarized most clearly in a letter he wrote in 1935 to an American woman concerned about her homosexual son:

By asking me if I can help, you mean, I suppose, if I can abolish homosexuality and make normal heterosexuality take its place. The answer is, in a general way, we cannot promise to achieve it. In a certain number of cases we succeed in developing the blighted germs of heterosexual tendencies which are present in every homosexual, in the majority of cases it is no more possible. It is a question of the quality and age of the individual. The result of treatment cannot be predicted. What analysis can do for your son runs in a different line. If he is unhappy, neurotic, torn by conflicts, inhibited in his social life, analysis may bring him harmony, peace of mind, full efficiency, whether he remains a homosexual or gets changed. [Freud, quoted by Jones, 1957, p. 195]

Behavior therapy

The increasing application of behavior therapy to the sexual disorders has provided widespread hostility from dynamic therapists and homosexual groups, based on some fact and some misinformation. According to one homosexual college student, most behavior therapy for homosexuals goes as follows:

"I would be put in a chair and they would show me pictures of nude men until I was sexually aroused, if I were sexually aroused by pictures, which I probably wouldn't be, and then they would give me a shock. Then they would show me pictures of nude women, and they wouldn't give me a shock. Then they would do it again, and I would soon be petrified of having a relationship with a man, I would also not have any sexual attraction for a woman at all, so I would go home and mutter, talk to the cat, and drink coffee, and maybe masturbate. I would probably be so messed up by that time that I wouldn't do it." [Holmes, 1971, p. 131]

Bieber, a psychoanalyst whose research on homosexuality is highly regarded by dynamic theorists, expresses an understandably negative (if biased) view of behavior therapy for homosexuality: "Although good results have been reported by some investigators, this type of treatment seems to add injury to preexisting injury. It has given little promise of lasting results and at best is ineffective" (1967, p. 973). As in most controversies among people of good will, there is probably some truth and some error in what these critics of the behavioral approach to the sexual disorders have to say.

Some behavior therapists attempt to treat homosexuality by reducing the anxiety that often accompanies it (e.g., DiScipio, 1972; LoPiccolo, 1971). Their efforts have centered on the use of systematic desensitization and relaxation training to enable homosexuals to respond without anxiety to overt and covert responses to their behavior that were previously capable of eliciting anxiety. The main efforts of behavior therapists, however, have been directed toward altering the primary homosexual orientation through the use of aversion therapy. Aversion therapy for homosexuals dates back to 1935, when Max successfully employed electric shock to alter a male homosexual's deviant behavior. Surprisingly, aversive conditioning of deviant sexuality was not reported again until 1956, when Raymond used apomorphine, a drug that induces nausea and vomiting, to treat a fetishist. Despite these encouraging findings, subsequent use of the aversive paradigm alone to change sexual orientation has had only modest success. Freund, for example, treated forty-seven homosexuals with apomorphine and reported that fewer than 25 percent of them subsequently altered their deviant patterns of sexual behavior (1960). This is an unimpressive rate of treatment success roughly comparable to that reported for psychoanalysis (Bieber et al., 1962).

Working to improve on Freund's results, Thorpe and his colleagues developed a behavioral technique for the treatment of homosexuality that they called aversion-relief therapy (1964). This procedure combined aversive conditioning (to extinguish unwanted homosexual responses) with reinforcement techniques (to "build in" desired heterosexual responses). All five of the patients treated with aversion-relief therapy altered their usual sexual behavior, though the absence of any long-term follow-up detracts from the findings.

Feldman and MacCulloch describe a procedure based on the aversion-relief principle that provides much more relevant and immediate presentation of both positive reinforcement and punishment (1965, 1967, 1971). Their method, termed anticipatory avoidance learning, is based on techniques developed from laboratory studies of avoidance conditioning. Slides of male and female figures judged capable of stimulating sexual arousal are shown to a patient seated in front of a screen. He is told before treatment begins that when a "homosexual" slide appears, an electric shock will be given within eight seconds unless he switches off the slide. Removing the slide before the shock occurs brings on a "heterosexual" slide, which is supposed to become associated with reinforcing feelings of relief.

Once a patient begins consistently to avoid shock by turning off the "homosexual" slides, the original shock-avoidance contingency is changed. Regular avoidance of the homosexual slide now brings on one of three different consequences: (1) *reinforced,* in which (as before) the learned avoidance response succeeds immediately, (2) *delayed,* in which the avoidance response does not work at once, though it finally does before the eight-second interval has elapsed, (3) *nonreinforced,* in which the avoidance response does not work and the patient receives a brief painful shock, at the termination of which the "homosexual" slide finally disappears. The nonreinforced consequence was included to ensure that all patients received electric shock in association with the homosexual stimulus at least occasionally. All three behavioral consequences are presented equally, in random order.

A total of forty-three homosexual patients were treated by MacCulloch and Feldman's method of anticipatory avoidance learning. All were volunteers who wished to change their deviant pattern of sexual behavior. Following completion of treatment, the behavior of all patients was monitored at systematic intervals during the year. When appropriate, "booster" treatment sessions were provided for the patients who needed them. At the end of the year it was found that the technique had been successful with nearly 60 percent of the forty-three patients. Success in each instance was defined as (1) cessation of homosexual behavior, (2) the use of no more than occasional or mild homosexual fantasy, and (3) the development of strong heterosexual fantasy and overt heterosexual behavior.

Critics inside and outside the behavior therapy camp have criticized the Feldman and MacCulloch method for design shortcomings (MacDonough, 1972; Rachman & Teasdale, 1969), terminological inaccuracy (Lovibond, 1970; Wilson, 1972), and insensitivity to ethical issues. Nevertheless, anticipatory avoidance conditioning does appear to offer real promise for the successful treatment of homosexuality. On the whole, recent reports on the method have been encouraging (Bancroft, 1971; Birk et al., 1971; Callahan & Leitenberg, 1973).

Lately some workers have tried to directly train heterosexual behavior patterns without first attempting to extinguish homosexual arousal. Davison, for example, has described the successful treatment of a male homosexual by gradually teaching him to become aroused by previously neutral stimuli (magazine nudes) in the context of a carefully directed sequence of masturbation (1968). Other clinicians (among them Lazarus, 1971) prescribe the "broad-spectrum behavior therapy" approach to the sexual deviations. Such an approach combines a variety of different behavioral techniques including modeling, behavioral rehearsal, assertive training, and practice homework assignments. This method is very similar to procedures outlined in Masters and Johnson's second book, *Human Sexual Inadequacy* (1970).

Treatment of sexual dysfunctions

There is also an extensive literature on the behavioral approach to the sexual dysfunctions, disorders with which dynamic therapy methods have been largely ineffective. The most common male dysfunctions—impotence and premature ejaculation—have both been treated successfully by a combination of systematic desensitization (to reduce the anxiety associated with sexual arousal, sexual intercourse, or both) and assertive training (as a means of helping the male feel a greater sense of control in relationships with women). Among reports of the successful use of these techniques with male sexual dysfunction are those by Wolpe (1958), Kraft and Al-Issa (1968), and Friedman and Lipsedge (1971).

Graded actual sexual experiences are an important part of treatment of the sexual dysfunctions by systematic desensitization and relaxation training. A man who cannot complete the sexual act because he cannot maintain an adequate erection during the preliminaries to intercourse sometimes finds it possible to do so when he and his wife are instructed to share sexual intimacy only to a certain point in the sexual sequence. Then as he gains confidence from successful practice, the "stopping point" in the sexual sequence may be moved farther along until

sexual intercourse is achieved. Lazarus (1971) describes such techniques in detail and claims considerable success with them, and their comparability to the Masters and Johnson approach is striking. Jay Meredith employed these methods with excellent success.

In 1966 Brady drew a useful distinction between two kinds of frigidity. The first is characterized by pleasureless, anxiety-filled sexual intercourse without orgasm, while the second is associated with actual pain during intercourse. Lazarus (1963) and Brady (1966), who were among the first behavior therapists to treat these conditions with systematic desensitization, claimed success rates of over 50 percent with conditions that had prevailed for many years. Their success rates have recently been questioned, however, because of the simplicity of the outcome criteria and the lack of long-term follow-ups.

A recent case report by Brady, the clinician most closely associated with the development of behavioral treatment methods for frigidity, portrays some of the elements of this treatment approach:

This 22-year-old patient had always been uncomfortable in petting situations although she did experience sexual arousal fairly easily. Her first coitus was with her present husband, five months before their marriage. Although she experienced some sexual excitement and pleasure she did not reach an orgasm. Three months later she became pregnant and the couple, who had been planning to marry in another year, decided to do so without delay. Shortly after their marriage, when the patient was three months pregnant, sexual arousal during intercourse began to be replaced by feelings of disgust and repulsion. She optimistically assumed that this problem would improve after the birth of the child. However, the problem only worsened to the point that almost any sexual advance by her husband failed to induce sexual arousal but provoked feelings of repugnance instead. Finally, 13 months after the onset of the sexual difficulty, the couple sought professional help from a gynecologist who referred the patient to the present writer. A hierarchy of sexual situations was constructed with the aid of the patient. The list of nine items to be imaged began with "your husband is kissing you on the lips" and ended with "ventral-ventral intercourse." After 7 desensitization sessions with Brevital (a drug that enhances relaxation efforts) the patient was no longer experiencing disagreeable feelings during sexual activity and some positive feelings had returned. After an additional five treatments she was experiencing more sexual arousal and satisfaction than ever previously and looked forward to coitus. However, she was yet to achieve an orgasm when treatment was unfortunately terminated due to her husband obtaining a position in California. Follow-up on this patient revealed that further improvement occurred without additional treatment and coitus was regularly accompanied by orgasm after another four months. She has maintained this improvement as of the last inquiry some two years after treatment was terminated. [1971, p. 79]

Masters and Johnson's behavioral approach to sexual dysfunctions

In 1959, five years after they began the investigations into normal sexual functioning that culminated in *Human Sexual Response,* Masters and Johnson established a clinic for the treatment of human sexual dysfunction on the grounds of the Washington University School of Medicine. The work done at that clinic, "founded on a combination of 15 years of laboratory experimentation and 11 years of clinical trial and error," resulted in publication of Masters and Johnson's *Human Sexual Inadequacy* (1970). The book details the results of a total treatment program for both male and female sexual dysfunctions, a program which appears so promising that it is now the preferred treatment for these conditions.

Masters and Johnson have developed procedures for dealing with the full array of sexual dysfunctions—including premature ejaculation, impotence, and "ejaculatory incompetence" in men, and orgasmic dysfunction, vaginismus, and dyspareunia in women. The preliminaries to treatment for any of these

disorders are the same in all cases. They derive from Masters and Johnson's basic premise that both marital partners bear some responsibility for either partner's sexual inadequacy.

The first visit for couples who have been accepted for the two-week, $2,500 course of treatment, now located at the Reproductive Biology Research Foundation Clinic in St. Louis, is a brief interview lasting ten to fifteen minutes, during which the couple is welcomed by their cotherapists and given a brief outline of what to expect during therapy. They are told that all sessions will be recorded, that history taking will occupy both partners for the first two days, and that a third day will be allotted to medical history taking, physical examinations, laboratory evaluation, and a "roundtable session." Husband and wife are requested to refrain from asking questions about each other's responses to the history-taking routine until after the roundtable. They are also asked to refrain from any overt sexual activity until they are directed otherwise.

The roundtable session brings together wife, husband, and both cotherapists so that the cotherapists can "tie together" their basic knowledge of human sexual function and dysfunction with what they have learned about the couple's individual and joint personal, social, and sexual histories. Treatment following the roundtable (during days 3, 4, and 5) centers on instruction and practice in *sensate focus.* This process involves learning to touch and explore one another's bodies with the aim of taking pleasure in touch rather than always proceeding immediately to sexual contact. As Masters and Johnson say, "Introduction by either partner of the pressures of sexual performance by goal-orientation to end-point release (ejaculation, orgasm) is verbally discouraged" (1970, pp. 71–73).

During the two or three days of sensate-focus training, regular meetings with the cotherapists are held to discuss the couple's apprehensions, feelings of guilt, and inability to understand either the sense of the procedure or the overall goals of the therapy. Such

Virginia E. Johnson and William H. Masters.
(UPI photo)

feelings and misunderstandings are common at this phase.

Next, therapeutic procedures specific to the specific sexual dysfunction which brought the couple to the foundation are begun. *Premature ejaculation,* for example, is treated by teaching both partners ways to reduce the sensory stimulation the penis receives during intercourse and to use the "squeeze technique." This is a manual procedure which, if properly employed, causes the male immediately to lose his urge to ejaculate. The squeeze technique involves strong pressure on the top and bottom surfaces of the penis immediately below the *glans penis* (the head of the penis).

Masters and Johnson distinguish between *primary impotence,* which they define as failure ever to achieve or maintain an erection sufficient for intercourse, and *secondary impotence,* defined as a failure in sexual performance after at least one and sometimes many successful sexual experiences. Of the men consulting the foundation for problems of impotence, fewer than 15 percent suffer from primary impotence.

Masters and Johnson's treatment plan for male impotence has three major goals: (1) removal of fears surrounding sexual performance—fears generated by a past history of sexual failure; (2) reorientation of his pattern of sexual behavior to make the male a more active sexual participant, rather than the passive spectator he has become; (3) removal of the woman's fears concerning her husband's sexual performance. A necessary prerequisite for the treatment of impotence is immediate restoration and subsequent strengthening of communication between marriage partners. It is important that each learn to tolerate his or her partner's concerns and fears about sexuality. And each must feel comfortable about telling his or her partner how things are going and how things could be improved sexually during and after therapy.

The couple is also told not to attempt sexual intercourse during the first few days following the roundtable. Instead, emphasis upon sensate-focus training and upon the "opportunity to think and to feel sexually without orientation to performance" may enable the male, perhaps for the first time in many months, to achieve and maintain an erection for as long as he wishes. As a result he and his mate will be free to enjoy the luxury of sensuality without fear of performance deficit. After "erection control" has been achieved, Masters and Johnson prescribe a variety of graduated exercises involving greater and greater penetration. Ultimately they culminate in intromission but, it is hoped, remain free from the time demands inherent in the old, unsuccessful patterns of sexual behavior. A very similar sequence of therapeutic events took place during Jay Meredith's successful treatment for primary impotence.

Of 32 cases of primary impotence treated at the foundation during its early years, thirteen (41 percent) failed to respond to treatment. Such a failure rate is not surprising, given the average length of time these men had had the condition. By contrast, of 213 cases of secondary impotence, 157 (74 percent) responded to treatment, certainly an encouraging rate of response.

Fundamental to treatment for *orgasmic dysfunction, vaginismus,* and *dyspareunia* is recognition by the woman that these conditions are strongly influenced by her feelings about her own body, the legitimacy of sexual pleasure, and the function of sex in marriage. If she has learned to view sex as distasteful, morally reprehensible, or legitimate only as a means of reproduction, these beliefs will certainly affect her sexual relationship with her husband even if she rejects them as irrational.

Sensate-focus training is directed toward giving the woman experience in feeling and enjoying a variety of new physical sensations with her husband that do not have to end in sexual intercourse. As a consequence, sometimes for the first time in her married life, physical closeness and touching can be prolonged, without any time demand for intromission: "The cotherapists must make it quite clear to the husband that orgasmic release is not the focus of this sexual interaction. Manipulation of breast, pelvis, and other body areas varying from the lightest touch to an increase in pressure only at partner direction, should provide the wife with the opportunity to express her sexual responsivity freely, but without any concept of demand for an endpoint (orgasmic) goal" (Masters and Johnson, 1970, p. 304).

Graduated instruction and practice in a variety of new coital positions, all designed to provide the wife with maximum pleasure, are introduced as sensate-focus training becomes more and more effective. Of 342 females labeled as suffering from orgasmic dysfunction and treated at the foundation, only 66 (19 percent) failed to benefit immediately from these therapeutic procedures.

In conclusion, it is important to acknowledge the encouraging success that Masters and Johnson's approach to human sexual inadequacy has had. At the same time, now that man's unfettered ingenuity is free to operate within the sphere of the sexual disorders, it is probably fair to anticipate continued development of other techniques and procedures to the same end.

Summary

Popular views of the sexual disorders, even "enlightened" ones, are still heavily infused with the moral indignation that Biblical injunctions against sexual behavior for anything other than procreation have fostered through the ages. The sexual deviations have traditionally been the most stigmatized of all the sexual disorders.

Eleven sexual deviations are included in DSM II. They include homosexuality (by far the most common), fetishism, pedophilia, transvestism, voyeurism, sadism and masochism, exhibitionism, incest, and bestiality. The sexual dysfunctions, defined as a reduction in or loss of sexual capacity, include impotence and premature ejaculation (problems experienced by males) and frigidity (the female equivalent of male impotence).

Because homosexuality is conspicuous among the sexual deviations both because of its frequency and because of its impact on society, most of the work done in this area has concentrated on the homosexual. Though genetic factors responsible for homosexuality have not been identified, recent data suggest that homosexuals and heterosexuals may differ in plasma testosterone levels. This is a difference with obvious etiologic significance that could be mediated by genetic factors.

Psychoanalytic views on homosexuality have come under increasing attack during the past few years, largely because they conclude that homosexuality is evidence of serious underlying psychological disorder. This theory was developed by Freud, who believed that homosexuality and the other "perversions" are the result of fixation at or regression to immature levels of sexual development. By contrast, behaviorally oriented clinicians consider the sexual deviations, including homosexuality, to be learned maladaptive behaviors. Bandura, for example, has named three mechanisms by which he believes homosexuality can be learned: (1) modeling of deviant sexual behavior shown first by parents or siblings, (2) positive reinforcement by others of deviant sexual behaviors when they first appear in the individual, (3) self-reinforcement of these behaviors by the person once they acquire stress-reducing capabilities. Other theorists believe that sociocultural factors, especially sex roles learned during childhood, play important etiologic roles in homosexuality.

Although it is easier to recognize deviant sexual behavior than to define normal sexuality, it is important to do both. Kinsey's and Masters and Johnson's normative sexual data are valuable because they show how very common such behaviors as masturbation, premarital sex, homosexuality, and variants of heterosexual behavior are among normal people. By contrast, though prostitution and pornography have long been accepted as more or less inevitable (if not totally palatable) forms of sexual expression, they are also destructive in important ways to some of those who come in closest contact with them.

Unlike treatment methods for other so-called personality disorders like alcoholism and drug dependence, recent developments in therapeutic strategy for the sexual disorders have begun to yield promising results. A regimen combining counseling, hormone treatment, and surgery appears to hold great promise for the treatment of transsexualism. And though behavior therapy has received a bad name among homosexuals for the inaccurate but widespread belief that all behavior therapists treat homosexuality with aversive electric shock, newly developed behavioral techniques, some of which do involve aversion conditioning, have been very encouraging. They are used, of course, only with homosexuals who are unhappy about their sexual orientation and seek treatment to change it. Extensive application of Masters and Johnson's behaviorally oriented treatment for the sexual dysfunctions seems to have yielded a good deal of independent evidence confirming its utility with problems of secondary impotence and frigidity.

CHAPTER THIRTEEN

The personality disorders

Charles Manson ● On innocence and guilt ● Historical perspectives ● Cues ● Etiology ● Treatment

CHARLES
MANSON:
"I HAVE
NO GUILT"

In August 1969 five bodies were discovered inside an expensive home in the hilly woods that surround Hollywood, California. All five, including the pregnant movie star Sharon Tate, had been brutally murdered and horribly mutilated. Their killers left one message behind—the word "pig" written in blood on the front door of the house. Their search for the killers finally led the police many months later to a 35-year-old man, Charles Milles Manson, and a group of young people who composed his "family."

Charles Manson was born November 11, 1934, the son of a teen-age prostitute. Allegedly his father was an Army officer. Shortly after Charles's birth his mother married another man, William Manson, to give her child a name. Manson left his wife soon after the marriage, and Charles grew up knowing neither his namesake nor his father.

When the boy was 5 years old his mother was arrested for robbery, and Charles was sent to live with an aunt and uncle in West Virginia while his mother served her jail term. He remembered his aunt as a very strict woman, his uncle as a kind, compassionate man who took him hunting and fishing in an effort to be the father Charles had never had. Unfortunately the uncle developed tuberculosis when Charles was 13, and his mother, now out of jail, fetched him home to Indianapolis.

Mrs. Manson was not a good mother for Charles; she drank a great deal and often left him alone all night. At times, remorseful over her neglect, she would give him money and make promises to reform, promises she never kept. In part because she knew that she was a poor mother and in part because she wanted to be free of responsibility, Mrs. Manson tried to place Charles in a foster home. This effort failed, and she sent him to a Catholic boarding school in Terre Haute, Indiana. He stayed there only a short time because his mother could not afford the tuition. He was 14 when he returned to Indianapolis, and he moved out of his mother's home and rented a room of his own.

Sometimes Charles supported himself with odd jobs, for example,

NEW YORK, SUNDAY, AUGUST 10, 1969

Actress Is Among 5 Slain At Home in Beverly Hills

Sharon Tate, 2d Woman and 3 Men Victims— Suspect Is Seized

By STEVEN V. ROBERTS
Special to The New York Times

LOS ANGELES, Aug. 9—Five persons, including the actress Sharon Tate, were found this morning brutally murdered in a home in a secluded area of Beverly Hills.

The home, perched on a wooded hillside overlooking the city of Los Angeles, was being rented by Miss Tate and her husband, Roman Polanski, the movie director, who was in London at the time writing a script for a new movie.

The other victims were identified as Jay Sebring, a men's hair stylist well known in Hollywood social circles; Voyteck Frykowski, a Polish film director said to be a close friend of Mr. Polanski; Mr. Frykowski's girl friend, Abigail Folger, a member of the Folger coffee family, and a fifth man who remained unidentified.

The police arrested William Garretson, a 19-year-old caretaker, and charged him with suspected murder. Mr. Garretson was asleep in a small cottage near the main house of the property when the police arrived this morning.

The Los Angeles coroner, Thomas Noguchi, told a news conference that there was no evidence that a party had taken place or that narcotics had been used. He said that no murder weapon had been found. He also said that there was no

Continued on Page 60, Column 1

Sharon Tate

Associated Press

(The New York Times; Associated Press)

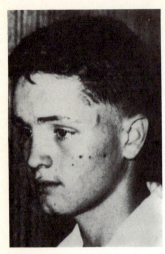

Charles Manson at 14. *(UPI photo)*

as a Western Union messenger; sometimes he did so by petty theft. Not long after this career of juvenile crime had begun, however, Charles's mother turned him in to the authorities. Sent to the Indianapolis Juvenile Center, Charles met a Catholic priest who was impressed by the boy's courage in adversity, desire to make a new start, and eagerness to listen to advice. The priest arranged for him to be sent to Boys' Town near Omaha, Nebraska, instead of to the state reformatory. "Even then, the youth displayed one of his marked adult traits, a charismatic personality. 'He was a beautiful kid for his age, a warm and friendly boy; he won everybody over,' the priest remembered" (Roberts, 1970, p. 30).

Despite the promise of a better, more hopeful life in Boys' Town, Charles ran away after three days. Soon he was arrested for robbing a grocery store and sent to a reformatory, from which he escaped without much delay. Escaping from such places, in fact, became a source of pride. In all, he escaped from eighteen state schools, reformatories, and other juvenile institutions during the next four years. Then he was arrested in Utah on a federal car-theft warrant, and for that more serious crime he was sent to the maximum-security National Training School for Boys in Washington, D.C.

Released from the National Training School in 1954 at the age of 20, Manson returned to West Virginia and not long afterwards married a local girl, Rosalie Willis. Though she became pregnant only a few months after their marriage, Charles was back in jail in Los Angeles for car theft by the time the baby was born. While Charles was serving his time, his wife and baby came West to be near him. In an uncharacteristic display of maternal concern his mother also moved to Los Angeles to help take care of her grandchild. But by 1958 when Charles, now 24, was released from prison (with considerable time off for good behavior), his wife had divorced him and his mother had returned home. Charles continued his solitary life of crime as before—with results as before. He was arrested, though not imprisoned, several times for car theft and pimping, then was arraigned in 1960 on a federal charge of forging government checks. This offense resulted in a ten-year sentence in the McNeil Island Penitentiary in Washington state.

In prison Manson acquired some knowledge of philosophy and scientology (a controversial philosophy focusing on the development of human potential). He learned to sing and play the guitar, and he composed several songs. Above all, this term in prison made him a harder, more careful, more determined man, a man resolved never again to be forced to repay debts to a society he felt he owed nothing. Armed with this new philosophy, Charles Manson was released from prison—totally unrepentent—in 1967 at the age of 33.

The hippie movement was enjoying its fleeting moments of glory that year. Nowhere was its promise more spellbinding than in San Francisco's Haight-Ashbury section, where the residents, many of whom cherished a naïve belief in love, peace, and man's humanity to man, were unfortunately easy targets for those who exploit the vulnerable. Manson was such an exploiter. An attractive and charismatic presence, he soon gathered an adoring coterie of young girls. He had enormous physical energy, magnetic charm, and sensual good looks. One observer said of him in those years: "You either hated Charlie or had a strong attraction to him. He cut right to it; he cut through the pitter-patter. It was sex and the women knew it; there was no foreplay involved" (Roberts, 1970, p. 30).

In short, Manson was a man who had learned to perfection the art and science of exploitation. Schooled in state and federal "reformation" facilities that are well equipped to teach the subject, Manson had discovered that charm, threats, sexuality, and brutality could be combined to draw vulnerable young people to him. Girls who had never felt loved or beautiful, boys who had never had a sense of personal strength or of belonging: both were attracted. They then became the willing bait he used to attract still more followers.

The arrival of opportunists and exploiters like Manson, of motorcycle gangs, of hard-drug users and pushers, and of a variety of other criminals and antisocial types led to the rapid decline of Haight-Ashbury. By 1968, in fact, it was no longer the sanctuary of peace, humanity, and contemplation it had once briefly been. Like much of the world that surrounded it, Haight-Ashbury had become a place of violence and exploitation, of hatred and confrontation. Around that time Manson and a group of his followers packed themselves into a converted bus and left for southern California. Along the way the "Manson family" met and spent time with a variety of people, including Gary Hinman, a musician whom they were later accused of murdering. The family ultimately settled down at an old, decaying ranch north of the San Fernando Valley. The aging owner, blind, weak, and terrified of Manson, was so grateful for the housecleaning given his place by the girls in the family that he allowed them to remain on his land. The family stayed for about a year, leaving only after several abortive raids by local police, who said they had come looking for stolen cars.

Charles Manson has been "credited" with the remarkable ability first to recognize and then to exploit the vulnerabilities of virtually all those who fell under the spell of his charm and presence. That he could also adapt himself to many roles in response to the needs and expectations of those around him clearly fostered this process. Alternately cruel and kind, brutal and gentle, father and brother, he became what each person wanted him to be—without ever really being what anyone believed him to be.

Manson in custody. *(UPI photo)*

397

It remains unclear just why Charles Manson and his family chose the Tate home in Hollywood as the place for their ritual acts of murder. One probable reason was that the previous owner of Sharon Tate's house, a Hollywood record producer, had aroused Manson's anger when he was unable to arrange a recording contract for Manson. Another may well have been Manson's inability to understand why the "beautiful people" who surrounded Sharon Tate had achieved fame and fortune while he, no less accomplished, charming, and ambitious, was a failure.

One might also ask why the young people who made up Manson's family joined him in that act of unspeakable barbarism. To this question too a definitive answer is not possible. Young, lonely, unsure of their places in the world from which they had sought refuge with Manson, perhaps the family members found such a sense of belonging with Manson that they would do his bidding without question. While loneliness and the need for love seem insufficient motives for brutal murder, history is filled with examples of man's inhumanity to man for reasons that continue to escape us. Does anyone really know what led the Nazis and the Germans whom they ruled to kill on such a monumental scale? Does anyone know what causes drug pushers, who are well informed about the life of horror that follows addiction, to sell drugs to children?

In short, behavioral scientists can talk with understanding and compassion of unfulfilled needs and deprived environments that lead to drug addiction, murder, and genocide. But the horror and inhumanity of those crimes — as well as their ultimate senselessness — remains largely beyond our knowing.

On innocence and guilt

Charles Manson acted upon society in an unbelievable variety of antisocial ways. At one time or another he robbed, deceived, assaulted, exploited, seduced — and murdered. But despite the extraordinary range of antisocial acts for which he had been responsible, perhaps his most surprising characteristic was that at no time did he show guilt or remorse about anything he had done. During his trial for the Tate murders, he said, "I've considered innocence and guilt and I know the difference between them and I have no guilt" (*New York Times,* Dec. 25, 1969). A man who could be charming and captivating, brutal and ruthless, Manson could not be guilty, at least in his own eyes. What kind of human being feels no remorse over murder? Why would a person keep committing crimes despite repeated punishment? How can a man charm so many people and yet never relate with genuine feeling to anyone?

These are difficult questions, largely because they tap moral and ethical issues as well as psychological and psychiatric ones. Mental health professionals have had to sidestep them —since in fact there are no answers—to look instead for answers to more specialized questions. Among them is the question of diagnosis: What label should be applied to behavior that falls so far beyond the pale of normal experience? But even the diagnostic question has not been resolved in Manson's case. He has been categorized as paranoid schizophrenic, manic-depressive, obsessive-compulsive, anxiety reaction, hysterical conversion reaction, and psychopathic personality. A "real" diagnosis of Charles Manson's behavior, like that of Lee Harvey Oswald's behavior (described in Chapter 6), will remain an issue for prolonged debate.

We believe, however, that Charles Manson's behavior is most appropriately put into the psychopathic personality group, one of the numerous subcategories of psychopathology that appears under the heading "personality disorder." While most of the other categories of personality disorder are far less dramatic and certainly less destructive than the psychopathic personality, men like Charles Manson whose "character disorders" are very severe have always exerted an influence on society far out of proportion to their numbers. For that reason, our examination of the personality disorders will put special emphasis upon the psychopathic personality.

Historical perspectives

If a man have a stubborn and rebellious son, that will not hearken to the voice of his father, or the voice of his mother and though they chasten him, will not hearken upon them; then shall his father and mother lay hold on him, and bring him out onto the elders of his city. [Deuteronomy 21: 18-22]

With these words the Old Testament identifies a group of people who have continued to present problems for the rest of society— the psychopathic personalities (Rotenberg & Diamond, 1972). Surprisingly, even though the writers of the Old Testament recognized the existence of persons who refuse to fulfill the expectations of society, it was many centuries before this behavior pattern came to be regarded as a form of psychopathology rather than of sin.

In fact, recognition of the personality disorders as a distinct form of psychopathology occurred very recently. Even the psychiatric texts of the 1930s and 1940s did not discuss such syndromes as the explosive, inadequate, or asthenic personalities. They did, however, devote considerable space to the psychopathic or sociopathic personality, which came to the attention of students of psychopathology more than 150 years ago.

Philippe Pinel, the French psychiatrist best known because he freed psychiatric patients from their shackles 175 years ago, called psychopathy *manie sans delire* ("mania without insanity"). Somewhat later J. C. Prichard, a British psychiatrist who renamed the disorder *moral insanity,* made the following comment about these patients:

There is likewise a form of mental derangement in which the intellectual faculties appear to have sustained little or no injury, while the disorder is manifested principally or alone, in the state of feelings, temper or habits. In cases of this nature, the moral and active principles of the mind are strongly perverted or depraved; the power of self-government is lost or greatly impaired and the individual is found to be incapable, not of talking or reasoning on any subject proposed to him, but of conducting himself with decency and propriety in the business of his life. [1835, p. 15]

Emil Kraepelin provided an extensive discussion of the psychopathic personality in his *Textbook of Psychiatry* (1913). He broke down the general category into seven subgroups: the excitable, the unstable, the impulsive, the eccentric, "liars and swindlers," the antisocial, and the quarrelsome. Kraepelin believed that the disorder was hereditary (as he believed many other mental disorders were) but he provided no data to support this view.

Karpman treated a number of psychopaths

by psychoanalytic psychotherapy (1946). He concluded that the majority, whom he called *secondary psychopaths,* were actually neurotic or psychotic. But he categorized a small group which was unresponsive to therapy as *primary psychopaths.* This system of labeling has remained popular to our time.

In spite of such occasional references to psychopathy, Hervey Cleckley commented in his classic text *The Mask of Sanity* (1950) that he was "impressed and sometimes appalled by what seemed to be the refusal of psychiatry to concern itself with the psychopath" (1950, p. 525). Since then a good deal more systematic research into the nature of psychopathy has taken place. Now it is the subtler forms of personality disorder, such as cyclothymic personality, explosive personality, asthenic personality, and passive-aggressive personality, which remain relatively neglected. Virtually the only systematic research currently underway with such patients is Thorne's (1970, 1973).

Cues to the personality disorders

Personality disorders are deeply ingrained habits or patterns of behavior which can be recognized at a relatively early age. To say that a person has a long-standing habitual way of dealing with the world is not, of course, to say that he is exhibiting psychopathological behavior. All of us develop customary, comfortable patterns of handling ourselves within our environments. But in the individual diagnosed as having a personality disorder, these patterns show a rigidity which makes them counteradaptive. He carries the same mode of behavior with him into all circumstances and is unable to adapt himself to the demands of external events. This rigidity often leads him to behave in a self-defeating fashion.

From even the brief summary of Charles Manson's early behavior at the beginning of the chapter, it is clear that his psychopathy was not a recent addition to his behavioral repertoire. Indeed, it had characterized his approach to life from his first years. The same case materials also indicate that his psycho-

pathic behavior was pronounced enough even in his youth to prevent him from adapting very well to life's inevitable ups and downs. Later, his permanently fixed suspiciousness, hostility to conventional society, and inability to form permanent relationships dictated the arrangement of his life-style. The nomadic, antisocial existence he created for himself and his family led finally to the August 1969 murders at Sharon Tate's home in Hollywood.

Typically, the person labeled as a personality disorder is not bothered by his behavior, even though it may disturb or concern those around him. He usually regards it as a "natural" part of his self that cannot or should not be tampered with. Psychoanalytic theory makes the distinction between *ego-alien* and *ego-syntonic* behaviors. The focal behaviors of the neurotic are *ego-alien*—he does not feel comfortable with them and does not regard them as an integral part of himself. But the behaviors of the individual with a personality disorder are more often *ego-syntonic*—that is, because they are consistent with the individual's perception of himself, they do not cause him great discomfort. For this reason most people with personality disorders do not view themselves as disturbed. They are more likely to be brought to the attention of professionals by other people than they are to seek help for themselves.

It was mainly this cue that led us to label Charles Manson's behavior as psychopathic. Far from being remorseful or guilty about any of the greater or lesser crimes of which he had been accused during his life, he was clearly convinced that everything he had done was justified—because he was born out of wedlock, because he had been passed from relative to relative during his early years, because he had had to live on his own as a teenager, because he had become neither rich nor famous despite his energy, charm, and hard work. Difficult as it is to accept the elaborate web of rationalizations that he used to "explain away" his antisocial behavior, those rationalizations satisfied him: Charles Manson felt no guilt.

The personality disorder category is the most vaguely defined of all the separate forms of psychopathology. The heterogeneous range of behaviors under this umbrella label complicates the proper use of the diagnosis. The line between the neuroses and the personality disorders is particularly obscure. Nathan and his co-workers, for example, report their inability to identify a consistent behavioral pattern to distinguish personality disorder patients from psychoneurotic patients (1968). Specifically, their research raised serious questions about "the nature and extent of the inability of these [usual] procedures to enable diagnostic differentiation between psychoneuroses and the personality disorders" (p. 715). The reader of this chapter ought to be particularly critical in evaluating the meaningfulness of the personality disorder category.

Paranoid personality

The individual with this diagnostic label is likely to be extremely sensitive to other people's behavior, and he tends to interpret it in a suspicious light. He sees a glance, a smile, or a frown and puts a highly personal construction on it. Note that suspiciousness in itself is not a sign of personality disorder; there are times when suspicion is justified. But for the paranoid personality, suspicion has become a way of life. He blames others for his shortcomings and failures and usually has few friends as a result. The paranoid personality differs from the paranoid schizophrenic in that he is not psychotic: he does not experience hallucinations or delusions, and he has a much better capacity to "test reality" than the paranoid schizophrenic.

Truda Steiner, whose obsessive-compulsive neurosis in Terezin was described in Chapter 10, received a letter a few years ago from the girl who had been her friend there. It was Eva, now herself a middle-aged woman, who had helped Truda moderate her compulsive fears of dirt and disorder. But now Eva was having psychological difficulties of her own, apparently also caused by her concentration camp experiences. Parts of her letter, translated and reproduced here, illustrate aspects of the paranoid personality. They also suggest

"Harry, you must stop going 'Zap' to people who don't happen to see eye to eye with you." The paranoid individual often misjudges others' intentions toward him. *(Drawing by O'Brien; © 1969 The New Yorker Magazine, Inc.)*

that traumatic events in a person's life can precipitate a behavioral disorder, sometimes long after the experience itself.

Dear Truda:

I'm not certain whether you will remember me after all the years that have passed. You and I lived in the same children's barracks in Terezin the fall and winter of 1942. And I think it was partly because of my urging that you performed in *Brundibar* late in the fall. I felt so proud of you then! You must wonder what's become of me. Well, after the war (I was sent "to the East" early in 1944 with my parents), I met and married my husband back in Zatec, my hometown. His aunt, who lives in Prague, sells you groceries and that's how I knew you had survived and where you lived.

I'm writing you now, though, to tell you about some odd things that have been happening to me off and on for the past ten years or so and to see if you have had similar things happen to you. Often I find myself becoming extremely suspicious about another person's motives or feelings about me without any very good reason. I may become convinced that the greengrocer is shortchanging me because I'm a Jew or that the streetcar conductor misses my stop for the same reason. Even a smile is enough for me to conclude that a man wants me for you know what. And with every German I meet, I feel that he's thinking, "Well, that's one Jew we didn't get rid of."

Now I *know* that these thoughts are stupid and that *all* these people really aren't out to get me— but sometimes I wonder. And because of these things, I don't go out as much as I should and I don't have the friends I should. Why I wrote you is to ask whether you have feelings like this, because if you do, I'll feel a little better about my suspicions. Please answer this letter.

Yours,

Eva Veresova (née Hajkova)

Cyclothymic personality

People with a cyclothymic personality are characterized by pronounced alterations in mood. They have recurring phases of elation and depression. During their cheerful phases they are a pleasure to be with: outgoing, warm, friendly, and enthusiastic about new tasks. Unfortunately, these periods of elation and energy alternate with episodes of depression, futility, and pessimism. Their vacillations in mood can rarely be related to external events. Although the cyclothymic personality pattern may signal an impending manic-depressive psychosis, cyclothymic personalities usually live out their lives without experiencing psychosis.

All of us have ups and downs of mood that may not be tied to events in our environments, but cyclothymic behavior is distinctly different from normal mood alteration. Consider, for example, the following excerpt from an interview with a student at the women's college of a Northeastern university:

"Though I've always considered myself a pretty nervous person, things have gotten even worse during the past year or so. Where before I was just moody, at least I could come out of it when I had to. Now, though, I might wake up one morn-

ing to discover that I can't sit still, that my mind's racing a mile a minute, that I have all sorts of schemes for improving student government or easing out the college administration or something like that; and when things are that way—and they sometimes last for days at a time—of course I can't do much work or even sit still long enough to attend lectures. . . . The other side of the coin is worse. That's when I get really depressed, sometimes over such little things, that I lose most of my energy and I just spend a lot of time in my room sleeping or reading novels. Sometimes I also have trouble sleeping when I'm depressed— and it's times like that that I can't stand having people around me. I guess I'm the kind of person you have to call more than just moody."

Schizoid personality

People who are given this label tend to be withdrawn and seclusive. They avoid close interpersonal relationships and make their emotional investments more often in ideas than in people. They have an exceptionally difficult time expressing aggressive feelings, even under provocation. Their need to protect themselves from closeness to other people makes them appear cold and aloof. They also tend to think autistically—although they do not lose their capacity to test reality, and their autistic thoughts remain within the realm of daydreaming. The schizoid personality differs from the schizophrenic by his or her continuing ability to maintain contact with the environment.

Barry was an extremely bright and sensitive boy who excelled academically in a selective private preparatory school. He was admitted to an Ivy League college and continued to do good work. At the same time, he was not one to enter into the social life of the college or even of his dormitory. When his classmates gathered at a local college hangout on Friday nights to drink beer and flirt with the waitresses, Barry usually spent the evening in the library or in his room listening to Beethoven, his favorite composer "because he gets to the soul of things." He did not pay much attention to girls, though he did have a brief relationship with the sister of one of his freshman roommates. It ended when Barry found out that she wanted a friendship based on more than shared intellectual interests. During college Barry made what he considered some good friends, though many of them were the sort of people who "used" him: they would ask him to do their homework, or they would borrow money or stick him with the check when they ate out together.

On graduating with high honors from college, Barry went on to a prestigious law school and did very well. He was offered a variety of lucrative positions as a junior associate in respected law firms—the usual sort of position for graduates of his excellent law school. But Barry chose to accept a position as junior law librarian in the library of a law school in his own hometown. Today, twenty years after his graduation, he still has this job. He never married, and he leads a solitary life taking care of his aged, senile mother in the home he has lived in all his life. In contrast to the terrible crimes of a psychopath like Charles Manson, Barry's schizoid personality seems commendably innocuous. Certainly he is mildly useful, gentle, kind—and wasted.

Explosive personality

The explosive personality pattern is described as one in which episodes of rage or physical or verbal aggression occur unpredictably. For long periods such a person shows good control; then comes an episode of violent anger. He or she is usually repentant and remorseful once the outburst has passed. In summary, these individuals are excitable, aggressive, and exquisitely irritable in response to pressure from the environment.

Obsessive-compulsive personality

People who are classified as obsessive-compulsive personalities seem to be driven by the need to attain perfection and orderliness in everything they do. They find it difficult to cope with ambiguity in their lives and may insist, once they have selected a path of action, that they must carry it through. They may also be inhibited in their expression of feelings, meticulous in their behavior, excessively diligent and duty-bound in their execution of responsibilities, and unable to relax.

As Brody and Sata point out, a certain degree of compulsiveness may be adaptive in Western society (1967). We value people who remain loyal to their goals and who work beyond the call of duty. Also, an individual with an obsessive-compulsive personality who is in an occupation requiring considerable attention to detail and concentration on a repetitive task may find his behavior adaptive in that situation. Even so, there will be times when his lack of flexibility hampers his capacity to function effectively. In dealing with other people the obsessive-compulsive personality may attempt to impose his standards of perfection upon them. His high standards may also make it difficult for him to find people whom he regards as adequate.

Distinguishing between the obsessive-compulsive personality and the obsessive-compulsive neurotic is not always easy. The most valid difference is probably the degree to which the obsessive or compulsive behavior in question interferes with daily living. For while the patient with a personality disorder may behave oddly, his behavior does not keep him from carrying out his everyday obligations. The obsessions or compulsions of the neurotic patient, on the other hand, often do prevent him from living a normal life. To see this difference clearly, compare the case of Truda Steiner, the helpless neurotic described in Chapter 10, and the following account of Professor Edwards, an able man who performed his obligations all too thoroughly.

The union representing the faculty at the medical school of a Western university was recently asked to consider the problem of Edwards, a tenured professor. His perfectionism, passion for order, and excessively high standards had caused him to come into such conflict with other members of the department of biochemistry and the university's administration that he was in some danger of being dismissed. The union was brought into the situation at Edwards's request, because he believed that his tenure protected him from discharge except for reasons of incompetence or moral turpitude.

Professor Edwards had enraged his colleagues by attempting to use his position as department chairman to make elaborate changes in the curriculum which no one else in the department wanted. He had always been known for the persistence with which he put forth his own ideas—which ranged from complex schemes for reorganizing higher education in the United States to ambitious but unworkable proposals for formalizing hiring policies within the university. But in this instance, he had even threatened to block future promotions for his junior colleagues if they did not support his changes in the curriculum.

To the medical students, Professor Edwards was well known as a lecturer who went into extraordinary detail on minor points, "usually missing the forest for the trees," as one student publication put it. To his colleagues, he was a perfectionist who drove himself in preparing manuscripts for publication. He demanded twice as many subjects, three times as many statistical tests, and extraordinary controls before he would write up an experiment. Even then he could not let the manuscript go until he had put it through innumerable revisions. When it came time to type the final version, he would not allow the typist to make a single erasure for fear that the editor would think him hasty in his scientific work.

Edwards would dwell on almost any subject interminably. Consequently his colleagues took every opportunity to avoid talking to him, although the essence of what he had to say was usually sound. It is interesting that despite the order which Professor Edwards introduced into so many areas of his life, his office at the university was crammed with papers, books, and lectures heaped everywhere—on chairs, tables, the desk, and the floor. He explained this paradox by pointing out that he was interested in ordered, logical thinking, not in unimportant external order.

Hysterical personality

The hysterical personality exhibits a pattern of behavior marked by excitability, self-centeredness, rapidly shifting but shallow (not genuine) affect, and overreactivity. These people may strive to be the focus of attention through dramatic, often striking behavior. Some of them are coy and sexually seductive, but unresponsive when called upon to react with genuine emotion or sexuality.

Kate, a senior at a large Eastern state university, went to the psychological clinic of her school complaining that she was dissatisfied with her aimlessness and inefficiency and with her sparse social life. Later she confessed that her real problem—one that had plagued her since her early teens—was that while she wanted very much to meet men, whenever she did she began to think ahead to the possibility of a sexual relationship. That worry quickly translated itself into nausea and, on occasion, actual vomiting. As a result Kate found herself having to lead a solitary life almost totally devoid of any kind of social involvement.

At the same time, for reasons which Kate could not identify, men were very attracted to her. She often received one or two requests a day for dates from men who sat in classes with her, saw her in the student union, or shared rides with her on the campus bus. Because she could not understand why men were so attracted by her inattention and indifference, Kate agreed to let the therapist observe her behavior in campus settings. During the next days her therapist sat in Kate's classrooms, rode the bus with her, and observed her in the student union, the library, and around the quadrangle.

This period of observation was enlightening. It showed that Kate's behavior, which she saw as demure, aloof, and retiring, was in fact seductive, forward, and provocative. Eyes downcast, forehead wrinkled, she would drop a pencil or a spoon, confess that she could not open a door for herself, or make a self-condemnatory statement, all of which guaranteed that the men who were near her would come to the aid of a pretty girl. In other words,

Kate had learned how to attract attention in almost any situation, despite her seeming desire to be left alone. When confronted with this paradox, Kate was amazed, and unable to understand how the behavior that she had felt would isolate her from men drew their rapt and devoted attention instead. In their subsequent sessions Kate and the therapist focused on this paradox. They also explored the use to which she put the nausea and vomiting as both excuses for interpersonal avoidance and unrecognized tactics for gaining attention. So far, therapy has enabled her to increase the range of her social relationships with men, though this increase has in turn aggravated her anxiety about sex.

Asthenic personality

Individuals with this diagnosis lack energy, interest in life, enthusiasm, and an ability to enjoy themselves. Much of life appears to be a burden which they carry with considerable effort. They also tend to be overly reactive to any sort of physical or emotional stress. Their passivity makes it unlikely that they will bother other people enough, or have enough initiative themselves, to come to professional attention.

Passive-aggressive personality

People with this disorder are marked by both passivity and aggressiveness and hostility. The aggressive aspect of their behavior may be expressed in a passive mode, as "disguised hostility." For example, the passive-aggressive person may impede the work of others by being obstructive, slow with his own work, or stubborn. Because he cannot express his aggression directly, he structures his life in such a way that he can say, wide-eyed and innocent, "I didn't do a thing. I was just standing there." Using these tactics, he is sometimes found out, much to his chagrin and genuine surprise.

The extent to which the passive-aggressive personality relies upon active or passive forms of expression determines which of the following three subcategories he will be assigned

to: (1) passive-dependent, (2) passive-aggressive, or (3) aggressive. In a seven- to fifteen-year follow-up of 100 passive-aggressive patients, Small and his colleagues found that their behavior remained amazingly stable over time (1970).

The overall diagnostic problems associated with the personality disorders have prevented the accumulation of objective data on the relative frequencies of the subgroups within this category. But it seems probable that a large number—perhaps the largest number—of people falling within the personality disorders best fit the passive-aggressive subgroup. Many of us have friends or acquaintances who couple every positive statement about someone with "but then again" or similar qualifying phrases that amount to "damning with faint praise." It is likely, in fact, that every reader knows several persons whose significant feelings of hostility are only thinly veiled by a veneer of passivity and acquiescence. This veil may fall away in the presence of alcohol or stress (as when a colleague or friend has too much to drink and tells you off at a party). On the other hand, because all of us sometimes wish to express anger or hostility in a veiled way, the line between normal controlled anger

"Why not admit it—you despise me." The passive-aggressive individual often avoids direct expression of his hostility. (Myers © PUNCH 1972)

and the passive-aggressive personality is a difficult one to draw.

Inadequate personality

The inadequate personality deals with social, interpersonal, physical, and emotional demands in a weak and ineffectual fashion. Although he is usually physically healthy and at least average in intelligence, he appears to lack the resourcefulness, stamina, judgment, and stability to enable him to cope with life's demands. Often he does not seem to share the goals of the achievement-oriented society which surrounds him. He gets by in life by assuming roles and responsibilities that make minimal demands upon him.

Charlie Brown of the "Peanuts" gang is a whimsical version of the inadequate personality. He seems to have at least average physical coordination, social skills, and intelligence, but he does not play baseball well, he is an ineffective leader of people, and he does less well at school than he should. He is a dreamer for whom the competitive hurly-burly of American childhood is confusing and troublesome. As a comic-strip character Charlie Brown is a playful exaggeration of the inadequacies that we all feel: he has so many of them that he becomes the archetype of the inadequate personality.

Psychopathic personality

The one personality disorder to receive attention from researchers and clinicians alike is the psychopathic personality. A variety of terms have been used for this disorder, including "moral mania" and "sociopathic personality." DSM II labels it "antisocial personality."

A related term in DSM II, "dyssocial personality," refers to people who engage in antisocial behavior in response to the expectations of their subculture or subgroup. They may be respected and admired within that subculture and may have strong loyalties to its members. The criminal behavior of Malcolm Little should be viewed in this light, as should the antisocial behavior of members of organized-crime groups. Such dyssocial personalities are not the subject of this discussion.

The psychopathic individual is an unsocialized person who comes into conflict with society because he refuses to conform to established rules of conduct. He lacks any sense of loyalty to group, friend, or value system; he is selfish, self-centered, impulsive, and unable to learn from his experiences. He cannot tolerate frustration or cope with demands to delay reinforcement. He wants what he wants when he wants it. Many notorious crimes have been committed by people who could have been diagnosed as psychopaths, though not every psychopath is a mass murderer like Charles Manson or a swindler on a grand scale like the successful con men you may have read about. Most psychopaths lead amoral lives on a much more limited scale. They confine the spreading of misery to the small group of people who come in contact with them.

Hugh Johnson, however, operated on the peaks of big-league swindling. This middle-aged man was recently arrested in a large Northeastern city on the complaint of three elderly sisters, who had given him $3,000 to invest for them in a "sure-fire" Florida land deal. His photograph was sent around the country by the FBI and drew inquiries from law enforcement agencies in thirty-seven states. When everything was sorted out, complaints from twenty-seven states seemed to be justified by circumstantial evidence linking him to sixty-four crimes.

Johnson was confronted with the mass of evidence which had been gathered against him—evidence proving that he had forged stocks, bonds, money orders, and checks; that he had worked an astounding variety of confidence games; that he had impersonated a number of doctors, lawyers, and other professional men; and that he had committed many other types of sophisticated crimes. At this he readily admitted his guilt and supplied additional details about most of the charges. When he was asked why he had defrauded so many people out of so much money and property, he replied with some heat that he never took more from a person than the person could afford to lose, and further, that he was only reducing the likelihood that other more dangerous criminals would use force to achieve the same ends. Unfortunately for Johnson, the judge before whom he was tried did not regard this explanation as mitigating circumstance.

Cleckley has identified sixteen factors as important components of psychopathic behavior. As you read his list, keep Charles Manson in mind.

The psychopathic personality

1 Superficial charm and good intelligence
2 Absence of delusions and other signs of irrational thinking
3 Absence of "nervousness" or psychoneurotic manifestations
4 Unreliability
5 Untruthfulness and insincerity
6 Lack of remorse or shame
7 Inadequately motivated antisocial behavior
8 Poor judgment, and failure to learn by experience
9 Pathologic egocentricity and incapacity for love
10 General poverty in major affective reactions
11 Specific loss of insight
12 Unresponsiveness in general interpersonal relations
13 Fantastic and uninviting behavior with drink and sometimes without
14 Suicidal impulses, rarely carried out
15 Sex life impersonal, trivial, and poorly integrated
16 Failure to follow any life plan
[Cleckley, 1964, pp. 362–363]

The psychopath may verbalize the appropriate emotion for a specific situation, but he does not feel it; or he may use all the proper phrases to apologize for something he has done, but they will be obviously hollow. Cleckley coined the term *semantic dementia* to describe the gap between the verbalizations and the affect of the psychopathic personality. Charles Manson's charm, which was persuasive

enough to win him a devoted band of exploited disciples, is a good illustration of this kind of behavior.

In a study investigating the degree of agreement among clinicians on the behaviors which characterize the psychopathic personality, Gray and Hutchison asked nearly a thousand Canadian psychiatrists to list the features they felt were most important in the diagnosis of psychopathy (1964). Of the 677 who responded to the questionnaire, 89 percent felt that the concept of psychopathic personality was a meaningful one. The respondents identified ten behaviors (very similar to those listed by Cleckley) as being most important in the diagnosis of psychopathy. In their view the psychopath has these characteristics:

1 Does not profit from experience
2 Lacks a sense of responsibility
3 Unable to form meaningful relationships
4 Lacks control over impulses
5 Lacks moral sense
6 Chronically or recurrently antisocial
7 Punishment does not alter behavior
8 Emotionally immature
9 Unable to experience guilt
10 Self-centered
[Gray & Hutchison, 1964]

Data on the incidence of the antisocial personality indicate that the diagnosis is applied to men more often than women in a ratio of roughly five to ten males for each female (Robins, 1967).

Assessment of the psychopathic personality

Researchers and clinicians dealing with psychopathic personalities have sought reliable diagnostic cues to differentiate their patients from other groups. But their success, like that of workers attempting to isolate diagnostic cues for neurosis or schizophrenia, has been limited.

Self-report measures such as the MMPI have been given to psychopathic subjects in an effort to define a distinctive psychopathic pattern. It has been found that groups of psychopaths do tend to obtain higher scores on the "psychopathic deviate" and "hypomania" scales of the MMPI than normal subjects, patients in other diagnostic groups, and nonpsychopathic criminals (Hare, 1970). Fould and his colleagues, using selected items from the MMPI, found that psychopaths admitted to more "acting-out hostility" and criticism of others than did neurotics or normals (1960). Other investigators have also claimed that the MMPI can differentiate psychopaths from a wide variety of patient groups (Benton, 1963; Guthrie, 1963; Meehl, 1963; Schmidt, 1963). But the fact that these are group distinctions implies that the MMPI is probably less successful as an individual diagnostic measure (Modlin, 1963).

Comparison of the anxiety levels of psychopathic criminals with those of neurotic criminals on various paper-and-pencil tests of anxiety suggests that psychopathic criminals are less anxious than neurotic criminals (Lykken, 1955). This parallels Cleckley's findings. But while the test differences are significant on a group basis, they are not large enough by themselves to permit a definitive diagnosis of psychopathy.

Research on the intellectual functioning of psychopaths provides support for the notion that they have normal or better than normal intellectual ability (Hare, 1970). Attempts to identify patterns of IQ subtest performance unique to the psychopathic personality have not been successful (Craddick, 1961; Fisher, 1961; Guertin et al., 1956; Manne et al., 1962).

Projective tests have also been used to study the antisocial personality. Kingsley gave the Rorschach test to psychopathic and nonpsychopathic residents of Army disciplinary barracks (1956). He reported that psychopathic soldiers appeared to be more impulsive, immature, emotionally shallow, self-centered, and aggressive on the Rorschach than nonpsychopathic soldiers. Knopf, however, could not differentiate psychopaths from neurotics or schizophrenics on the Rorschach (1965). According to one TAT study, psychopaths express their sexual feelings more openly but have fewer feelings of guilt and less need for

recognition than nonpsychopathic subjects (Silver, 1963).

Thus the few psychometric studies of the psychopathic personality that have been done generally agree that such people are intelligent, impulsive, and immature, as well as aggressive and deficient in anxiety.

Etiology of the psychopathic personality

Physiological functioning

The many researchers who have looked for physiological explanations of psychopathy have usually concentrated on either cortical activity or autonomic functioning. Their definitions of psychopathy and their techniques for its identification varied enormously from one study to the next, however, so that comparisons across studies cannot always be made validly.

Cortical activity: EEG studies. A variety of studies has used the electroencephalogram (EEG) to study the electrical activity of the brains of antisocial persons. But in evaluating studies which report EEG abnormalities, one should remember that between 10 and 15 percent of normal people also show abnormal EEGs (Solomon, 1967).

Hughes has reviewed the large body of research on a form of brain-wave activity called the *positive spike phenomenon* (1965). Positive spikes arise in the temporal lobe and have a frequency of 6 to 8 and 14 to 16 cycles per second (cps). While they are very rare in the general population, they have been identified in 20 to 40 percent of persons with severe behavior disorders. Further, patients who show positive spiking on the EEG often have documented histories of impulsive, extremely aggressive behavior (Schwade & Geiger, 1965). In such instances, a minor irritation may trigger a violent and destructive episode resulting in property damage, injury, or death. Although not all individuals with positive spike records are psychopaths, Kurland, Yeager, and

Arthur believe that as many as 40 to 45 percent of highly aggressive psychopaths may yield this kind of record (1964). In a recent study, however, Greenberg challenged the relationship between positive spiking and aggressive behavior; he did not find it in a large number of subjects (1970).

In an early review of research on brain activity in psychopaths, Ellingson reported that in thirteen of fourteen studies, 31 to 58 percent of the subjects showed some form of EEG abnormality (1954). In many the abnormality took the form of *slow-wave activity.* Slow-wave or theta-wave activity is most characteristic of young children. Consequently, its appearance in the EEG record of an adult is thought to mark that record as an *immature* one.

Studies which have been made since Ellingson's review have tended to confirm the earlier findings. Arthurs and Cahoon, for example, observed that 55 percent of their 87 psychopathic subjects had EEG records that were "borderline" or clearly abnormal (1963). Another study reports that among a group of 82 psychopaths, the behavior of 32 percent improved as they reached the age of 30 (Robins, 1966). These observations are consistent with the increasingly accepted belief that one "outgrows" psychopathy as his cortical functioning "matures."

Autonomic functioning: Learning studies. It has also been suggested that psychopaths fail to experience anxiety and to learn from their mistakes because their autonomic nervous systems are somehow defective. Eysenck, for one, believes that the psychopath is an extrovert whose nervous system is defective in some fashion so that certain kinds of behaviors condition slowly and extinguish rapidly (1964).

Research exploring the ability of psychopaths to learn has revealed some consistent trends. First, under conditions of positive reinforcement, they apparently learn as well as other subjects (Bernard & Eisenman, 1967; Painting, 1961). That is, they are not deficient in the ability to learn. Nevertheless, they do not learn conditioned avoidance responses

easily (Hare, 1965a; Hetherington & Klinger, 1964; Johns & Quay, 1962; Lykken, 1955; Quay & Hunt, 1965). And they do not show the same anticipatory fear responses given by other subjects when told that they are about to receive a strong electric shock (Hare, 1965b; Lippert & Senter, 1966). This means that behavior which most of us learn out of fear— "bitter experience"—may not be so readily acquired by antisocial persons. Psychopaths may not become anxious about the possible outcome of their behavior because fear has not been conditioned in them.

The learning history of Charles Manson is a case in point. Despite the multiple "second chances" that society gave him, Manson, "the man who felt no guilt," was never able to learn from his experiences that crime and violence do not pay off as well as honest endeavor.

Various explanations have been offered for the psychopath's "failure to condition." Schachter and Latane believe that psychopaths fail to learn fear because of their consistently high levels of autonomic arousal (1964). They say: "An emotion can be considered a function of a state of physiological arousal and cognitions appropriate to that state of arousal. Given specific cognitive conditions, an individual will react emotionally or describe his feelings as emotions only to the extent that he experiences a state of physiological arousal" (p. 222). In other words, the psychopath never learns to attach certain cognitive states (for example, "I should not steal because I will be arrested") with certain physical arousal states (the physiological concomitants of anxiety) because his normal bodily state is already one of high arousal. Even inconsequential stimuli, Schachter and Latane report, trigger large autonomic responses in the psychopath. As a result, he cannot learn to differentiate autonomically a range of environmental cues. They hypothesize that it takes a very special circumstance, like the added arousal provided by an injection of adrenalin, to make the psychopath aware of a variation in his bodily state and thus to make him amenable to avoidance learning.

But more recent research has seriously

challenged the validity of Schachter and Latane's observations. In particular, Hare failed
to find this extreme responsivity in psychopaths (1968, 1970, 1972; Hare & Quinn, 1971).
Hare suggests that rather than being overaroused, psychopaths inhibit sensory input in
order "to 'tune out' or at least greatly attenuate
stimulation that is disturbing. The result
would be that threats of punishment and cues
warning of unpleasant consequences for misbehavior would not have the same emotional
impact that they would have for other individuals" (1970, p. 69).

Hereditary factors

Most studies investigating hereditary factors
in psychopathy have been poorly designed.
The two most frequently cited investigations
of psychopathy in twins (Lange, 1930; Rosanoff et al., 1941) have both been roundly criticized for their failure to establish or maintain
reliable diagnostic criteria. Thus there is real
doubt about the reliability of the diagnoses of
psychopathy upon which they depended.

One study of the EEG records of psychopaths and their biological or foster parents did
report an excess of abnormal EEGs, particularly slow-wave activity, in psychopaths and
their biological parents (Knott et al., 1953).
No such relationship was found between the
psychopaths and their foster parents. This
study raises the possibility of a hereditary
factor in cortical functioning, but the fact that
Knott's control group of foster parents was
very small diminishes the ultimate importance
of the findings.

Recent chromosomal studies of criminals
have raised the possibility that a specific genetic defect—the XYY mosaic form—might
be involved in the etiology of psychopathy.
While this defect occurs only in 13 out of
10,000 births, several studies report a significantly higher percentage of XYY males among
men convicted of violent crimes (Hunter,
1968; Nielson, 1968; Telfer et al., 1968). Also,
Nielsen reports that the larger the size of a
subject's Y chromosome, the greater the probability that he will commit a violent crime

(1971). However, researchers have recently
been urging their colleagues to interpret the
meaning of the XYY genotype with caution.
Kessley and Moos insist that the environmental
influences upon a person with an XYY genotype must be carefully considered (1970). In
a recent review of the literature in this area,
Owen states that so far, research does not
allow any firm conclusions about the influence
of the XYY genotype upon phenotypic criminal behavior (1972).

Family theories of psychopathy. Many psychopathic personalities, like Charles Manson,
have undergone early parental loss. Greer
reports that 60 percent of the 79 psychopaths
he studied had experienced a parental loss,
as against 28 percent of 387 neurotic subjects
and 27 percent of normal subjects (1964).
Furthermore, Greer's psychopaths suffered
their losses at an earlier average age than the
control subjects. It has also been reported
that psychopaths are more likely to have been
separated from their fathers rather than their
mothers (Oltman & Friedman, 1967).

McCord and McCord point to emotional
deprivation and parental rejection as crucial
factors in the development of psychopathy
(1964). Bandura and Walters report that
relationships between father and son were
especially poor in a sample of aggressive
adolescent boys (1959). They suggest that
serious delinquency may reflect not only a
failure to internalize parental standards, but
also feelings of anger and opposition toward
the parents. Parents of aggressive children
tend to use physical punishment as their predominant training mode, thereby providing the
child with a model of aggression (Bandura
et al., 1963; Bandura & Walters, 1959, 1963a).
Note that this research cannot be applied
directly to the psychopathic personality: not
all aggressive youngsters are diagnosed as
psychopaths, just as not all psychopaths had
aggressive parents who used physical punishment.

An important study by Robins followed the
development over thirty years of more than
500 people who were first referred to a child

psychiatric clinic (1966). She found that adult psychopaths came from homes in which the father had been psychopathic, alcoholic, or both, and in which the family had been broken by separation or divorce. Paternal behavior appeared more important in the development of psychopathy than maternal behavior did. Robins wrote:

If one wishes to choose the most likely candidates for a later diagnosis of sociopathic personality from among children appearing in a child guidance clinic, the best choice appears to be the boy referred for theft or aggression who has shown a diversity of antisocial behavior in many episodes, at least one of which could be grounds for a Juvenile Court appearance, and whose antisocial behavior involves him with strangers and organizations as well as with teachers and parents. With these characteristics, more than half of the boys appearing at the clinic were later diagnosed sociopathic personality. Such boys had a history of truancy, theft, staying out late, and refusing to obey parents. They lied gratuitously, and showed little guilt over their behavior. They were generally irresponsible about being where they were supposed to be or taking care of money. They were interested in sexual activities and had experimented with homosexual relationships. [P. 157]

Thorne believes that the sociopathic life-style is adopted by an initially healthy person who becomes conditioned to rely upon unhealthy mechanisms to satisfy his needs (1959). According to this view, an attractive child (like young Charles Manson) may learn to charm other people into granting him the things he wants. Or a bright child may learn to use his intelligence to avoid work. Both children may then grow up without ever learning to assume responsibility for themselves, always having been able to "con" their way out of problem situations. The demands of adulthood lead these persons to intensify their already established maladaptive life-styles.

While family theories of psychopathy are appealing because they account for much of the behavior of the psychopath in a common-sense way, they have not been confirmed by independent, objective inquiry. And the fact that many normal adults suffered similar family losses or deprivations when they were children prevents any easy acceptance of this point of view.

Treatment of the personality disorders

The prognosis for treatment of personality disorder patients is not good, largely because the person who is not disturbed by his behavior is not likely to want to change it. Many people with personality disorders never even come to professional attention. They do not experience enough discomfort to need help, and they do not cause enough trouble to come to the attention of the authorities. The failure of therapy for the personality disorders is most obvious in the case of sociopaths. Their lack of anxiety, lack of emotional responsiveness, and lack of long-term goals are major obstacles to successful treatment. Cleckley, commenting on his own and others' failure to help psychopathic patients, said that after seeing them treated by a variety of therapies, he remains discouraged about all attempts to alter the behavior of the psychopath (1964). McCord and McCord also wrote that most of the studies they reviewed failed to demonstrate meaningful changes after many different kinds of therapy.

Dynamic therapy

The same kinds of traditional psychotherapy —psychoanalysis, group therapy, client-centered therapy, and similar techniques—that have traditionally been applied to the neuroses (Chapter 10) have also been used with personality disorder patients. But as you might expect, most "talking therapy" has not been effective with them. It has been suggested that group therapy may be best for these patients, since regular and intensive verbal interaction with a group might motivate them to pay attention to the group's "feedback" about their maladaptive social behavior. While it is appealing in principle, this approach in fact has not proved any more effective than a one-to-one relationship with a therapist (Hare, 1970).

Perhaps the treatment of psychopaths by completely restructuring their lives within a therapeutic community offers more hope for rehabilitation. Patients are placed in a residential treatment setting where every activity is structured as an aspect of their treatment. One study compared a highly structured, authoritarian environment that provided firm discipline and limited psychotherapy with another environment where the residents were self-governing and had considerable group psychotherapy (Craft et al., 1964). It was discovered that patients from the more authoritarian community had fewer convictions for crimes a year after discharge than those from the permissive one. Similar results have been found in other carefully structured therapeutic communities.

Behavior therapy

There has been relatively little research on behavioral means of modifying sociopathic behavior. Behavioral techniques have been applied to delinquents and adult prisoners, however, and obviously some of the people in those groups must have been sociopaths and other cases of personality disorders.

Experimenter-subject psychotherapy is an innovative approach to the treatment of delinquent behavior in which the delinquent subject is paid to serve as an "employee" in research (Slack, 1960). As such he also becomes engaged in a therapeutic contact. Two of Slack's students, Ralph and Robert Schwitzgebel, have extended his work and provided more data regarding its effectiveness. In the book *Streetcorner Research* (1964), Ralph Schwitzgebel provided an extensive discussion of these projects. Follow-up data a year or two later on the delinquents who took part in the research revealed an encouragingly low rate of arrests among them.

Working with institutionalized delinquents, Tyler and Brown compared the effectiveness of contingent "time-out," verbal reprimand,

This young man was one of Schwitzgebel's experimental subjects. The small black case, resting on the pinball machine by the subject's right hand, contained telemetry equipment that enabled Schwitzgebel to keep track of his whereabouts 24 hours a day. *(The New York Times)*

and a combination of these two upon unwanted behaviors (1967). Time-outs (periods of enforced isolation) were effective behavior-change procedures, while verbal reprimand alone had no effect on behavior.

In a 1968 study at the National Training School for Boys (the institution where Charles Manson once served time), a complex token-economy environment was created for forty-one adolescent delinquents. The emphasis was upon reinforcement for appropriate behavior rather than punishment for "bad" behavior. According to the detailed reports which have been published, it was very successful in changing social and attitudinal variables as well as in modifying more objectively measured school-related behaviors (Cohen et al., 1968).

In summary, some behavioral techniques for the treatment of psychopathy seem extremely promising. Research on these methods, however, is still in its early stages.

Summary

Personality disorders are deeply ingrained patterns of behavior whose persistence and rigidity have made them counteradaptive. The individual with a personality disorder shows little flexibility in his approach to life. He cannot adapt himself to the demands of external events, with the result that, like Charles Manson, he behaves in self-defeating ways. Yet the failures and the troubles that he brings on himself may not worry him, because the behavior which others consider maladaptive is often consistent with his perception of himself.

Included in this heterogeneous, diagnostically unreliable group of conditions are the paranoid, cyclothymic, schizoid, explosive, obsessive-compulsive, hysterical, asthenic, passive-aggressive, inadequate, and psychopathic personalities. Most diagnosticians call Charles Manson a psychopathic personality, which is the personality disorder label most often used and most intensively studied.

There have been many efforts to identify biophysiological, psychological, and sociocultural determinants of psychopathy. Investigators have variously claimed that psychopaths show abnormal EEGs, possess defective autonomic nervous systems, have inherited a tendency to psychopathy, or have lost one of their parents early in life. None of these theories has been substantially confirmed.

The prognosis for treatment of personality disorder patients is poor, largely because few of them are sufficiently disturbed by their disturbing behavior to want to change it. Neither dynamic nor behavior therapy can claim much success with the personality disorders. However, one promising variant of behavior modification, Slack and Schwitzgebel's experimenter-subject psychotherapy, did achieve good results by paying juvenile delinquents to be "consultants" to a research project which was really designed as a therapeutic milieu.

CHAPTER FOURTEEN

The psychophysiologic disorders

The M. Family ● Body and mind ● Nine organ systems ● Etiology ● Cues ● Experimental psychopathology ● Treatment

THE M. FAMILY:
THE PAIN OF
ONE BECOMES
THE PAIN OF
ALL

All day Mrs. M. had been in bed with a pounding headache that left her writhing, crying, moaning. Several times she had had to stumble to the bathroom to retch and vomit, though the relief it gave was short-lived. Her misery was so bad at times that she prayed to God for respite and found herself thinking of death as a blessed deliverance. When her 7-year-old son Richie came home from school, he found her sitting on the edge of her bed holding her tear-stained face in her hands. Despite her pain, she opened her eyes for a minute and smiled weakly at him. Then she turned back to her suffering. Though Richie wanted to show her the picture he had drawn at school, he knew that he must not disturb her when she was sick. He tiptoed from the room and walked slowly downstairs.

Richie had seen his mother's agony before, and he knew that the best thing to do was to leave her alone with it. So he took his dog Pooch and went outside to sit on the front steps, where he could watch a colony of ants nearby climbing in and out of their anthill. He felt very bad. He wasn't sure why, but he sometimes wondered whether it was God's way of saying that the headaches were really his fault. That morning, for instance, he had spilled half a bottle of milk on the floor by accident. His mother had looked upset, but then the school bus came and Richie had left in a hurry. He wondered if he had hurt his mother by dropping the milk; he would have to be more careful from now on. The ants climbed in and out of their hill, and Richie sat and thought about God and wondered why people had to get sick, especially kind, precious people like his mother.

That night she didn't come down for dinner. Before he and his father ate the TV dinners his father had defrosted, Richie heard the loud but muffled voices of his parents in the bedroom above. Then his father came downstairs and threw their dinner in the oven with irritation. Usually Richie and he talked a lot—about school

(Al Forsyth/DPI)

415

and baseball and when to go fishing and things like that. Mrs. M. would sometimes laugh at the two of them and call them her chatterboxes. But that was when she wasn't sick; when she was they hardly talked at all.

His father was often irritable and impatient when his mother had a headache. One time after Richie had got up early one morning and come downstairs to watch television, his father ran into the room, jerked him off the floor, and slapped him, yelling "I told you to turn that God-damned television off! You're making your mother sick with the noise." Richie ran into his room and closed the door. He huddled in the corner, sobbing into Pooch's fur for a long time until his father came in and said he was sorry. His father explained how helpless he sometimes felt about his mother's pain—but that was hard for a 7-year-old to understand. A kiss and a hamburger helped some, but Richie still remembered his father's words about making his mother sick.

Despite Mrs. M.'s headaches and their effects on her husband and son, they are in many ways a happy family. Mr. and Mrs. M. married young and struggled hard until he opened a gas station on the interstate highway near their home. After the station was established, the M.'s became comfortable financially, although he still works longer and harder than either he or his wife would like. Richie, born several years after their marriage, was a healthy baby with a big smile and a good disposition who brought his parents intense pleasure.

The family's stability and happiness is very different from everything Mrs. M. knew as a child, for she was a timid little girl who played alone and never stuck up for herself. Illness seems to have dogged her footsteps; she was allergic and had more than her share of colds. Then in early adolescence she began to suffer from severe headaches three or four times a month. The pain was so intense that she could tolerate it only by taking heavy doses of pain-killers and sleeping pills. At such times she might sleep for two or three days, getting up only to take more medicine. The headaches were pounding, blinding migraines that left her dizzy, unable to focus her eyes, nauseated, and incontinent.

In her junior and senior years of high school, the headaches became less frequent and Mrs. M. began to lead a more active social life. She met her husband early in her senior year and they were married the day after graduation. For several years afterward the headaches diminished, so that she could go for three or four weeks without distress. As she got older, however, the frequency increased again, until now they come about once a week.

After a neurological examination (which included skull x-rays and an EEG) failed to show any evidence of brain abnormality, Mrs.

(Al Forsyth/DPI)

M.'s doctor advised her to seek counseling. He felt that emotional problems might be playing an important role in her attacks of migraine. Unfortunately, the M.'s live in a small town which does not have adequate facilities for such "nonessential" professional services. The nearest psychotherapist is 75 miles away, she does not drive, and she has simply not been able to follow her doctor's advice about further treatment.

She often worries about whether the headaches mean that she is really crazy. Her husband, while he is usually sympathetic about her pain, blows up sometimes and tells her it is all her imagination. He even suggests that she is using the headaches as an excuse to avoid having sex with him. Although the pounding pain in her head hardly seems like imagination to her, Mrs. M. has never enjoyed sex with her husband very much, and she admits to herself that there are times when the headaches provide an easy excuse. She also knows that Richie becomes very upset by her headaches. It bothers her a great deal—especially when he cries out in his sleep, "I'm sorry, Momma. I didn't mean to do it." At times like these Mrs. M. realizes that her agony has truly become the pain of her entire family.

Body and mind: Psyche, soma, and the psychophysiologic disorders

The psychophysiologic disorders, which are also referred to as the psychosomatic disorders, are physical illnesses which have either psychological origins or a prominent psychological component. Among them are stomach ulcers, some kinds of high blood pressure, hives, and migraine headaches. Of course, all these conditions can also be exclusively physical in etiology.

It was only after a thorough physical examination had failed to indicate an underlying physical cause for Mrs. M.'s headaches that the doctor suggested she see a counselor. Because she never went for a psychological examination, it is difficult to say what psychological factors may have influenced the headaches. Nevertheless, there are hints in her case history which suggest sources of distress that could relate to her physical disorder.

We know, for example, that as a child Mrs.

M. was unable to stand up for her rights. A timid person, she never learned to express her own needs and demand the respect she was due. It is possible that her family paid more attention to her during her frequent bouts of illness than they did at other times. Even as an adult Mrs. M. avoids arguments rather than confront problems: Though she is reluctant to have intercourse, she is afraid to discuss the problem with her husband. She admits to herself that there are times when the headaches are a convenient excuse to avoid unpleasant situations. Yet Mrs. M. is not lying about her headaches; they are authentic and agonizing. Nevertheless, environmental factors do play an important role in determining when and where she will have the pain.

This chapter examines the paradox of the psychophysiologic disorders—functional as well as disabling. It explores the unique ways in which body and mind may be reflected in physical illness.

Historical perspectives

The history of psychosomatic medicine parallels the history of the mind-body problem in psychology and philosophy. Theories about the relationship between the mind and the body have ranged from those of Hippocrates and Descartes (who viewed mind and body as separate entities and concluded simply that the mind influences the body or the body influences the mind, or that both happen together) to theories which assign the primacy to either the mind *or* the body.

The prevailing approach to the mind-body question is that events of the mind should be viewed as a function of the context in which they are perceived. Thus physiologists attend to certain structural and functional elements of the mind (cells and biochemical processes), psychologists to others (theories of learning and purposive behavior), and philosophers to still others (for example, epistomological issues). A review of this very complex issue is available in Boring (1950).

Psychophysiologic disorders: Nine organ systems

The *Diagnostic and Statistical Manual* (1968) groups together nine psychophysiologic disorders, each of which involves a separate organ system. This group of disorders "is characterized by physical symptoms that are caused by emotional factors and involve a single organ system, usually under autonomic nervous system innervation" (p. 46). Differentiation of the psychophysiologic disorders from conditions that are similar (organic disorders or conversion reactions) is often difficult. Many cues have been suggested for making these distinctions, but few authorities agree on the cues.

Psychophysiologic skin disorders. These conditions include eczema, acne, psoriasis, rashes and hives (which may also occur as allergic reactions), alopecia (sudden loss of hair), Raynaud's disease (vascular spasm of the superficial blood vessels), and hyperhydrosis (overactive sweat glands). They should not be confused with normal skin reactions to emotional stimuli like blushing, pallor, cutis anserina ("goose flesh"), and sweating.

Psychophysiologic musculoskeletal disorders. This category covers physical symptoms like backache, muscle cramps, muscle pain, and tension headache. In addition, rheumatoid arthritis and torticollis (a rare repetitive spasm of the neck muscles) may be psychosomatic, though the data are inconclusive. The most common normal musculoskeletal response to stress is the increase in muscular tension which most of us experience during times of emotional arousal.

Psychophysiologic respiratory disorders. Conditions include bronchial asthma, the hyperventilation syndromes (overbreathing—meaning deep breathing with the mouth open—or shallow, rapid breathing), vasomotor rhinitis (allergic reactions which involve swelling of the nasal mucous membrane, nasal fluid discharge, itching, and sneezing), bronchitis, laryngitis, and chronic hiccoughs. Normal respiratory reactions to stress include sighing, gasping, laughing, and crying.

Psychophysiologic cardiovascular disorders. This category brings together such diverse physical disorders as coronary heart disease (including heart attack, cardiac embolism, and thromboses), functional cardiac dysrhythmias (disturbances of rate and regularity of heartbeat), hypertension (high blood pressure), angina (episodes of intense pain in the chest wall associated with lack of oxygen to the heart muscle), and migraine headaches. There are also many normal cardiovascular reactions to emotional stimuli. They include changes in heart rate, amplitude, and regularity, dilation and constriction of blood vessels, and changes in blood pressure. Some experimental data even suggest that changes in blood-corpuscle content and in the chemical composition of the blood can accompany environmental stress (Lachman, 1972).

Among the most intriguing observations on the psychosomatics of cardiovascular disease were made by Ernest Harburg, a social psychologist at the University of Michigan. Studying racial differences in blood pressure, Harburg recently reported that while middle-class whites and blacks in Detroit do not differ in average blood pressure, lower-class blacks living in "high-stress" ghetto areas have significantly higher blood-pressure levels (Fried, 1973). His data suggest that social and environmental factors play a direct role in cardiovascular malfunctioning.

Psychophysiologic gastrointestinal disorders. Peptic or duodenal ulcer, chronic gastritis, colitis, chronic constipation or diarrhea, hyperacidity, chronic heartburn, and "irritable colon" can be psychosomatic in origin. When most of these conditions occur infrequently or in a mild form, they are normal consequences of the interplay of emotion and digestive processes.

Psychophysiologic genitourinary disorders. These disorders are separated into three groups: (1) disorders of sexual function, (2) disorders of reproductive function, (3) disorders of urinary function. The disorders of sexual function, including impotence, premature ejaculation, frigidity, and vaginismus, were reviewed in Chapter 12. Disorders of reproductive function for the most part involve menstrual difficulties of psychogenic origin, including psychogenic amenorrhea (decrease in or cessation of menses) and psychogenic menorrhagia (excessively heavy or protracted flow during menstruation). Disorders of reproductive function also include spontaneous abortion (miscarriage) without clear organic causes. The inability to urinate in certain situations (say, in public toilets), frequent or involuntary urination, and enuresis (bed-wetting) are considered disorders that may be psychogenic in origin. Of course, any of the genitourinary disorders can be normal reactions to stress.

Other psychophysiologic disorders. The psychophysiologic endocrine disorders, disorders of sensory organs, and hemic and lymphatic disorders are included in DSM II to "round out" coverage of the human body's organ systems. However, evidence of psychosomatic disease in these three organ systems is not well established. There are some sketchy indications, but no proof, that the course of certain endocrine disorders—including hyperthyroidism, goiter, diabetes, and Addison's disease (adrenocortical insufficiency)—is influenced by psychological factors. Some equally scanty data suggest that a few of the sensory disorders, mainly angiospastic retinopathy (spasms of retinal blood vessels), glaucoma, and Ménière's disease (a disease of the inner ear) are psychosomatic in origin. The view that disorders of the blood or lymph systems have psychogenic etiology is supported by even less evidence than that available for the endocrine and sensory systems.

Etiology of the psychophysiologic disorders

Theories of the etiology of the psychosomatic disorders do not break down easily into dynamic, biophysiological, and behavioral ones. Most current hypotheses are dynamic *and* somatic or, in one instance, behavioral *and* somatic.

Dynamic-somatic theories

The question of "symptom choice"—why one patient develops hypertension and another colitis—is central to all theories about the etiology of the psychophysiologic disorders. Within the dynamic-somatic system, the three dominant theoretical models that confront this question are the specificity model, the nonspecific model, and the individual response specificity model.

Specificity model. The assumption here is

that specific psychopathological events occurring during childhood produce specific psychophysiologic disorders. Franz Alexander, a prominent psychoanalytic theorist, was the leading spokesman for the specificity model. According to Alexander, the psychophysiologic disorders arise when repressed infantile conflicts are resurrected by current environmental circumstances (1935, 1948, 1962). These conflicts are experienced as anxiety, with the result that the patient "regresses" to an immature mode of psychosexual functioning. His or her regression is accompanied by specific physiological concomitants.

The specificity in this model derives from Alexander's view that the stage to which a patient regresses—presumably the same stage during which the original traumatic conflict or conflicts occurred—determines the specific psychosomatic disorder the patient experiences. For example, Alexander and his colleagues "explained" stomach ulcers as follows:

The central dynamic feature in duodenal peptic ulcer is the frustration of dependent desires originally oral in character. The craving to be fed appears later as a wish to be loved, to be given support, money, and advice. This fixation on early dependent situations of infancy comes in conflict with the adult ego and results in hurt pride, since the infantile craving for help is contrary to the standards of the adult, to his wish for independence and self-assertion. Because of this conflict, the oral craving must be repressed. . . . The most common defense against both oral dependent and oral acquisitive impulses is overcompensation. The latently dependent or acquisitive person overtly appears as an independent, hard-working individual who likes responsibility and taking care of others. . . . To be loved, to be helped is associated from the beginning of life with the wish to be fed. When this help-seeking attitude is denied its normal expression in a give-and-take relationship with others, a psychological regression takes place to the original form of a wish to ingest food. This regressive desire seems to be specifically correlated with increased gastric secretion. . . . The crucial psychological finding in all ulcer patients is the frustration (external or internal) of passive, dependent, and love-demanding desires that cannot be gratified in normal relationships. [1968, pp. 15–16]

Dunbar (1954) and Grace, Wolf, and Wolff (1951) have also written in support of the specificity model. Despite the theory's attractiveness to many professionals, it has received only partial support from empirical research. Mirsky found that high rates of gastric secretion correlated positively with "dependency problems" among soldiers (1958). Engel and his co-workers concluded from clinical observation that adults with bowel diseases were often the products of "pathological mother-child relationships" (Wenger et al., 1961). Although other clinical studies have provided additional support for the specificity model (Hokanson & Burgess, 1962; Poussaint, 1963), few of them utilized the experimental control necessary to ensure reliable observations and valid conclusions.

Further, clinical and experimental data that are incompatible with the specificity hypothesis have also been gathered. A number of researchers have reported, for example, that patients with a wide variety of psychophysiologic disorders have many different psychological problems and correspondingly divergent psychiatric diagnoses (Kreitman et al., 1966; Wittkower & Lipowski, 1966). Others have observed that the specific nature of a person's psychological problems rarely predicts his psychophysiologic status, and vice versa (Mordkoff & Parsons, 1967). Finally, it has been demonstrated that animals exposed to a nonspecific stress will often develop a specific psychophysiologic disorder—increased gastric secretion—which is a precursor to gastric ulcers (Porter et al., 1958).

Nonspecific model. This model is not as widely accepted as the specificity model. It claims that the psychosomatic disorders are caused not by specific psychological or psychodynamic factors, but by psychological factors in general. Mahl, the principal proponent of the nonspecific model, based his position on the following empirical findings:

(1) virtually every stressor is capable of producing a state of chronic anxiety, if the stressor is strong enough and the subject vulnerable enough (Claridge, 1973), (2) the physiological correlates of anxiety are identical, regardless of its etiology.

Critics of the nonspecific model point to its diffuseness, its limited utility, and its dubious assumption that the physiological concomitants of stress are always the same. Psychoanalytic critics also attack its failure to acknowledge what they believe to be the crucial importance of specific early trauma on the later development of psychosomatic disorders. Although the nonspecific model of etiology does not occupy a prominent position among theories of the psychophysiologic disorders, it has had an important impact on the development of the behavioral-somatic view of these disorders.

Individual response specificity model. A widely used model, this theory differs from both the specificity and nonspecific approaches (Lacey & Lacey, 1962; Malmo, 1967). It does not assume relationships between specific psychodynamic patterns and specific psychosomatic disorders, and it does not posit generalized affective arousal (for example, diffuse anxiety) as a response to early or later stressors. Instead, it maintains that each individual reacts with characteristic and consistent physiological responses to a wide variety of emotional stressors. In other words, it assumes individual response specificity but stimulus generality. Because this model does not posit an invariant relationship between events occurring early in life and later psychosomatic disorders, it is compatible with a wide range of theoretical orientations. The individual response specificity model has become the theory of choice for many pragmatic researchers because it conforms most closely to recent empirical findings (e.g., Claridge, 1973).

Behavioral-somatic theories

Lachman has developed a model of psychosomatic disorder based upon learning theory and research (1963, 1972). His premise, that "with few exceptions psychosomatic disorders are learned," leads naturally to the view that these disorders result from prolonged exposure to stressful situations. Such exposure causes what Lachman calls "implicit reactions," meaning physiological events like alterations in heart rate, blood pressure, muscle tension, and gastric secretion rates.

Lachman names five possible learning mechanisms that could lead to the psychophysiologic disorders:

1 *Stimulus-substitution learning:* Neutral stimuli can acquire the capacity to elicit implicit affective and physiological reactions by association with stimuli which have those properties. For example, the infant Albert learned a fear response to the sight of Watson's white rat (1920).
2 *Emotional redintegration:* A single element in a stimulus-response chain that includes physiological components can itself elicit the implicit reaction. A person who has experienced the physiological sensations of fear during an automobile accident might afterwards begin to experience them on seeing a certain kind of auto, hearing a loud horn, etc.
3 *Stimulus generalization:* Over time, an implicit reaction that was initially associated with a specific environmental stimulus can be elicited by similar stimuli. Watson's little Albert quickly generalized his learned fear of white rats to other furry white objects.
4 *Symbolic stimuli:* Symbolic stimuli (that is, language) may also become capable of eliciting implicit reactions to environmental stimuli identified by or associated with those symbols. The word "Dallas" still arouses in many people the physiological responses they experienced on hearing of the assassination of President Kennedy.
5 *Ideation:* A person can sometimes experi-

ence implicit responses by thinking about the situations which typically elicit them. Thus a claustrophobic person, by imagining himself shut up in a closet, can elicit the visceral fear response he actually experiences in enclosed spaces.

Lachman makes two other assumptions in presenting his behavioral view of the psychosomatic disorders. The first is that particular autonomic responses can be learned on the basis of differential reinforcement. It may seem surprising that someone can develop a psychosomatic disorder because it is rewarded, but it makes sense. The child whose asthma keeps him home from school and the husband whose ulcers make his wife more sympathetic to his personal inadequacies both benefit from their disabilities. Whether these benefits are strong enough to have played a role in the development of the disorders remains to be tested empirically.

Second, Lachman assumes the existence of a "vicious circle" that both maintains and at times intensifies a psychosomatic disorder. For example, the asthmatic who worries continuously about his asthma probably makes his attacks worse when they do occur.

Lachman's theory, although it "makes sense" from the behavioral perspective, remains unvalidated. It has not yet generated the research necessary to justify its acceptance as anything more than an interesting alternative to the better-established dynamic-somatic theories.

Cues to the psychophysiologic disorders

There seems to be no characteristic pattern of maladaptive psychological behavior predictive of or associated with any of the psychophysiologic disorders. That is, patients with these disorders are not more depressed, anxious, obsessive, or compulsive than patients with other troublesome psychological or physical problems (Hinkle, 1957). As a result, one of the most difficult tasks confronting the clini-

cian in a general hospital setting is distinguishing among patients with organic illnesses, conversion neuroses, and psychophysiologic disorders.

The importance of making this distinction lies in the different treatment provided for patients in the three groups. Organic disorders are treated entirely by physical methods, conversion neuroses by psychological techniques, and the psychosomatic disorders by a combination of the two. Table 14-1 illustrates Lachman's effort to increase the precision of the diagnostic process. While they are unproved, the diagnostic criteria he lists do accord with the clinical consensus and for this reason deserve further evaluation.

Assessment of the psychophysiologic disorders

Many studies have explored the utility of traditional psychological tests for discriminating between patients with functional psychiatric disorders and patients with psychosomatic disorders. The majority of studies claiming success in this context have "proved" Alexander's specificity hypothesis. The Rorschach test has enabled various investigators to differentiate control subjects from asthmatics (Barendregt, 1961), from ulcer patients (Osborne & Sanders, 1950; Weiss & Masling, 1970), from patients with hypertension (Thomas, 1961), and from patients with neurodermatitis (Levy, 1952), though other investigators have had no success in using the Rorschach to distinguish between control groups and groups with psychosomatic illnesses (e.g., Miles et al., 1954). The TAT has identified adult ulcer and ulcerative-colitis patients (Poser & Lee, 1963), children with ulcerative colitis (Arthur, 1963), and hypertensive adults (Weiner et al., 1962), while the MMPI has been employed with diabetics (Slawson et al., 1963). But critics of this entire body of research find fault with the control subjects used in many of the studies. Specifically, the patients in many of the control groups were neither physically nor psychologically disordered, making their compara-

TABLE 14-1. DISTINCTIONS BETWEEN ORGANIC ILLNESS, COVERSION REACTION, AND PSYCHOSOMATIC DISORDER*

	Organic illness	Conversion reaction	Psychosomatic disorder
Determinants			
General	Physiogenic	Psychogenic	Psychogenic
Specific	Microorganisms, laceration, concussion, contusion	Difficult situation Earlier familiarity with symptoms	Stimuli provoking physiological changes (i.e., emotional reactions)
Structures involved	Any part of organism	Typically sensory or motor systems	Typically structures involved in or closely associated with autonomic nervous system innervations
Tissue pathology	Present	Absent	Present
Effect of suggestion	Pathology unchanged	Symptoms can be modified	Pathology unchanged (usually)
Effect of motivation on symptoms	Usually none obvious	Important; plays a determining or selective role	Usually none obvious
Reactions	Physical incapacity	Selective functional incapacity	Physical incapacity
Physical treatment	May have positive effect	Typically no effect	May have positive effect
Patient's typical attitude	Concern	Belle indifferénce	Concern
Consistency and anatomical feasibility of symptoms	Anatomically consistent and dependent on nature of the damage	May not correspond to feasible anatomical patterns (e.g., glove anesthesia, shoe paralysis)	Anatomically consistent and dependent on nature of the damage

*Terms such as "usually," "typically," or "generally" should qualify each statement, since there are occasional exceptions to almost every one.
SOURCE: Lachman, 1972.

bility to the psychosomatic patients very questionable.

Perhaps the most productive use of traditional psychological assessment instruments in the psychophysiologic disorders has been the continuing research program of Fisher and Cleveland. Evolving a set of Rorschach and other test criteria to reflect a person's concepts about his own body, these researchers identified two contrasting groups early in their studies. The people in one group view their bodies as impenetrable and well protected by a definite boundary; the people in the other feel that they do not have adequate body protection and hence are vulnerable to attack from without.

In the process of validating their theory, Fisher and Cleveland found that patients with external and internal cancers (1956), neurotic and schizophrenic patients (1958), and rheumatoid-arthritic and ulcer patients (Cleveland & Fisher, 1960; Fisher & Cleveland, 1960) all differed in their "body barrier" scores. For example, schizophrenics felt extremely vulnerable to attack from outside their bodies. Neurotics have a more definite sense of the body as being relatively impenetrable and felt better able to protect themselves from intrusions. Although others have failed to confirm these findings (e.g., Eigenbrode & Shipman, 1960), we believe that the work of Cleveland and Fisher is the most convincing of the projective-test research that has been done on the psychophysiologic disorders.

Experimental psychopathology of the psychophysiologic disorders

The animal model

The psychophysiologic disorders lend themselves to animal research, because relationships between environmental variables and resulting organic lesions can readily be demonstrated. It is not necessary in such experiments to demonstrate "feelings" in animal subjects, as many other areas of research require.

The experiment most often cited to illustrate the research strategy for investigating psychophysiologic disorders in animals is that by Brady and his colleagues (1958). Their study of the "executive monkey" employed rhesus monkeys that were divided into pairs, strapped into separate chairs, and subjected to brief electric shocks every twenty seconds. Each shock could be delayed for twenty seconds if the experimental animal of every pair pressed a lever. The yoked control animal of the pair also had a lever in front of him, but it had no effect on the shock. Each pair of animals re-

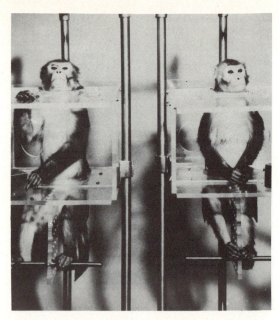

Brady's monkey subjects. The "executive monkey," at left, was responsible for delaying the delivery of electric shocks to both monkeys. The yoked control monkey, at right, could do nothing to alter the timing of the shocks. *(U.S. Army Photograph)*

ceived six-hour conditioning sessions alternating with six-hour "off periods" twenty-four hours a day, seven days a week. A red light signaled to the monkeys when they were in a conditioning phase of the study.

Within a few hours after the study began, the experimental animal in each pair developed a stable pattern of responding to avoid shock. As a result neither animal in the pair received more than an occasional shock. Unexpectedly, though, the experimental monkeys began to die one by one. Cause of death was always the same: "In all instances, gross and microscopic analysis revealed the presence of extensive gastrointestinal lesions with ulceration as a prominent feature of the pathological picture in the experimental animals (Brady et al., 1958, p. 72). None of the yoked control animals who were killed and then examined at the same time showed any sign of comparable pathology.

Other animal studies have investigated the

determinants of ulcers (Sawrey et al., 1956), asthma (Turnbull, 1962), arthritis (Selye, 1956), and cancer (Kazansky, 1955). Brady's reports, however, stand as classics in the area (1958; Brady et al., 1958). His studies confirmed the common view that ulcers are psychosomatic—that psychological factors (such as the stress of decision making) can cause physical pathology. They also disproved the prevailing opinion that psychodynamic factors are responsible for the development of these disorders. No psychoanalyst, despite his commitment to the dynamic model, would acknowledge that monkeys experience the same psychosexual traumata (the dynamic etiologic agents) as humans. Finally, the Brady studies introduced a research paradigm —the operant conditioning model—that has since proved to be productive in the broader exploration of psychopathology.

The human model

Two central lines of research with humans have direct relevance to the psychosomatic disorders. The first involves the experimental production of short-lived benign psychophysiologic disorders in humans. For the most part this research has demonstrated the relevance to the human condition of the more extensive animal literature in the same area. It has also strongly suggested that a number of unexpected disorders (e.g., cancer, heart disease) are influenced at least in part by emotional or psychological factors (Erickson et al., 1961; Ikemi & Nakagawa, 1965; Phillip, 1970).

The second major line of research to be reviewed here is a very new one. It involves exploration of *biofeedback* as a means of controlling or altering disordered body functions (DiCara, 1970; Miller, 1961, 1964). Biofeedback describes a variety of processes by which information on bodily functions—including heart rate, respiration, and the electrical activity of the brain—is "fed back" to the individual to enable him to alter these functions.

The specific research programs to be reviewed here were both *basic,* in that they endeavored to explore the general laws which

govern autonomic functioning, and *applied,* since they also generated techniques useful for altering disordered bodily functioning. Of the two important research projects we will discuss, the first explored biofeedback techniques for altering cardiovascular functioning, and the second explored biofeedback of alpha-wave EEG patterns.

Biofeedback of cardiovascular functioning. The work of Shapiro, Tursky, Schwartz, and their colleagues centers on development of operant conditioning techniques to control cardiovascular functioning. It grew out of earlier work which showed that humans can learn to increase or decrease their systolic blood pressure (the pressure at which blood is forced from the heart) without corresponding changes in heart rate, and that they can learn to increase or decrease their heart rate without corresponding changes in blood pressure (Shapiro et al., 1969, 1970a, 1970b). In one of their latest studies this group conditioned two autonomic responses—heart rate *and* blood pressure—at the same time (Schwartz et al., 1971). Ten male subjects, each with normal blood pressure and heart rate, were divided into two groups. Five received feedback (a brief light and a tone) when their heart rate and blood pressure increased simultaneously; the other five received the same feedback when their heart rate and blood pressure decreased simultaneously. Whenever a subject generated twelve consecutive correct heart rate–blood pressure combinations, he was reinforced with slides (landscapes and attractive nude females) and a cash bonus.

As Figure 14-1 shows, the subjects achieved significant control of both blood pressure and heart rate in a single conditioning session. Further, their ability to maintain control improved with time and training, so that by the final group of conditioning trials (trial 8), they attained consistent control. These dramatic results were important because they provided both impetus and a technology for further exploration of the determinants of autonomic integration and differentiation. They also offer promise of practical, immediate clinical goals.

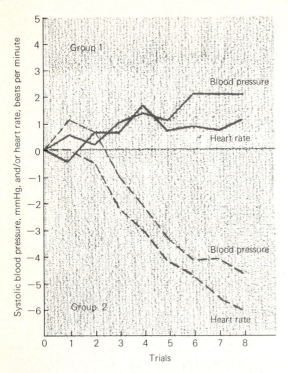

Figure 14-1. Evidence that operant conditioning can be used to control cardiovascular functioning. When two groups of subjects received a combination of biofeedback (to let them know how they were doing) and reinforcement for successful performance, they were able to simultaneously increase their heart rate and blood pressure (group 1) or simultaneously decrease them (group 2). *(Schwartz et al., 1971)*

Another study by the same research group was directed toward such a clinical goal. In it the experimenters successfully used the same operant conditioning feedback system (a light and a tone) to lower systolic blood pressure in seven patients with essential hypertension—high blood pressure of unknown etiology (Benson et al., 1971). Patients were studied on consecutive weekdays. Five to sixteen control sessions (during which blood pressure was recorded but no feedback was given) were programmed to begin the study.

During the subsequent conditioning sessions, a 100-millisecond (100 milliseconds = 1/10 second) flash of light and a *simultaneous* 100-millisecond tone of moderate intensity signaled to the patient that his systolic blood pressure was decreasing. Patients were told that the tone and light were desirable and that they should try to make them appear. Scenic slides and money were given following every twenty tone-light combinations. Conditioning continued until no further reduction of blood pressure occurred during five consecutive conditioning sessions. The researchers found that differences between control and conditioned blood pressures were significant beyond the .02 level: thus the likelihood that these differences occurred as a function of chance was only 2 in 100 (.02). Such findings strongly suggest that median systolic blood pressure can be reduced below baseline levels following a period of operant conditioning.

Though it was largely an exploratory study, these results are most encouraging. A technique for reducing high blood pressure, without the necessity for surgical or pharmacological intervention, would be a significant advance in therapeutics. Beyond that, the findings provide additional justification for efforts to apply biofeedback methods and technology to an increased range of psychophysiologic disorders.

A recent review of the expanding literature on self-control of cardiac functioning focused on this important point (Blanchard & Young, 1973). It acknowledged that the fact of the self-control of four cardiac functions has been demonstrated convincingly, but it asked whether the modest magnitudes of the control achieved by the patients might be statistically but not clinically significant. This is an open question which deserves considerable empirical study.

Biofeedback of alpha activity. The possibility of conditioning central nervous system functions for therapeutic purposes has also intrigued many researchers. Recent reports that humans can be trained to control the electrical activity of the brain, as reflected by the EEG (Kamiya, 1962, 1969; Mulholland, 1964; Nowlis and Kamiya, 1970), have encouraged investigators to seek potential clinical applications. Epileptic patients for whom abnormal EEG spiking signals a seizure have been conditioned to suppress these spikes (Miller, 1969). And patients with mood disturbances have been trained to control their alpha-wave activity as a means of altering unwanted mood states (Kamiya, 1968).

Alpha rhythm is electrical activity of the brain of a specific sort (8 to 13 cycles per second at an amplitude averaging $30\mu V$). It occurs most frequently in humans during periods of "relaxed wakefulness" (Lindsley, 1960). One of the most important characteristics of alpha is that it disappears when attention to external stimuli is first required, only to return after a few repetitions of such stimuli (Berger, 1929). Though a variety of brain centers responsible for the production of alpha activity have been proposed through the years, experts now generally agree that the thalamus is involved in the process (Andersen & Andersson, 1968). The consistency of most people's alpha-wave activity is great enough to suggest a constitutional basis for subject differences in alpha patterns (Walter, 1959). However, efforts to relate these individual-specific patterns to personality patterns have not succeeded (Ellingson, 1956; Fenton & Scotton, 1967).

Many variables affect alpha frequency, including direct visual stimulation, attention to visual stimuli, and oculomotor activity. Attention-arousal factors also exert an influence on alpha in that moderate levels of arousal precipitate maximum alpha activity. "If the subject is too aroused, alpha activity will be diminished, and conversely, if the subject becomes too drowsy, alpha will be diminished" (Lynch & Paskewitz, 1972, p. 203). Relationships between alpha and the setting in which alpha conditioning is undertaken have also been identified. Lynch and Paskewitz say that among these factors are "the feedback situation itself, the attention which it demands of the subject, the eventual boredom of the task, and the feeling he has about being evaluated by the experimenter."

One of the major incentives for studying alpha patterning comes from reports that Zen and Yoga practitioners experience high levels of alpha activity continuously during periods of meditation (Bagchi & Wenger, 1959; Kasamatsu & Hirai, 1966). Another stems from the heightened pleasure, relaxation, and interesting dissociative phenomena that subjects in alpha feedback situations report (Brown, 1970; Hart, 1967). Mankind has searched for centuries for the means of achieving serenity "on command." So far no drug, trance state, or unusual environment has been able to produce such a state. Abraham Maslow, the late president of the American Psychological Association, wrote shortly before he died:

What is seminal and exciting about this research [on alpha patterning] is that Kamiya discovered quite fortuitously that bringing the alpha waves to a particular level could produce in the subject a state of serenity, meditativeness, even happiness . . . it is already possible to teach people how to feel happy and serene. The revolutionary consequences not only for human betterment, but also for biological and psychological theory, are multitudinous and obvious. [1969, p. 728]

Despite the enthusiasm for alpha activity shown by Maslow and other sober and serious behavioral scientists, there are also researchers as thoughtful and respected as Neal Miller who have expressed skepticism concerning alpha as mankind's ultimate salvation (Miller, 1973). It is probably wise to withhold final judgment on alpha as either a "cure" for the psychophysiological disorders or as mankind's source of eternal peace and serenity until more objective data, free from the bias of enthusiasm, are in.

Treatment of psychophysiologic disorders

A psychophysiologic disorder must be treated on two fronts at once: with somatic therapy for the physical disorder, and with therapy directed toward the psychological cause or causes of the disorder. For example, an ulcer patient should receive medical treatment in the form of diet and drugs to hasten healing, or failing that, surgery to remove the ulcer.

In either case drugs, psychotherapy, or behavior therapy might also be employed in an effort to reduce the stress and resultant anxiety presumably associated with development of the ulcer.

Psychotherapy

Both "supportive" and "insight-oriented" psychotherapy have been provided for patients with psychophysiologic disorders. Supportive therapy, by offering encouragement, protection, and approval, is supposed to relieve the anxiety that accompanies physical illness. This approach to therapy is of special value during times of acute turmoil. It is considered only palliative, however, in that its soothing effects are short-lived; they usually last only as long as the patient-therapist relationship continues (Kaplan, 1967).

According to psychoanalytic therapists, more permanent relief from anxiety—hence from the psychophysiologic disorders with which it is associated—can result from a course of "insight therapy." Central to dynamic treatment of the psychosomatic disorders is the belief that the anxiety which causes them can be conquered only by transforming the personality itself. To work such a change the therapist must give the patient insight into his unconscious fears, conflicts, and desires. Once he has brought himself to face and deal with these anxiety-provoking elements of the unconscious, it is believed that his physical condition will improve.

Dynamic theorists acknowledge that psychoanalysis and psychoanalytic psychotherapy with psychosomatic patients are especially difficult. Somatic symptoms, despite the pain and suffering they cause, effectively "legitimize" anxiety by giving patients something tangible to be anxious about. Patients with physical symptoms are consequently less motivated to seek alleviation of their anxiety than patients for whom anxiety is a primary source of discomfort (Kleeman, 1971). Also, people with psychophysiologic disorders often receive a great deal of sympathy, which again "compensates" them for their very real pain and suffering. As a result, the clinician who undertakes psychotherapy with a psychosomatic patient must be prepared for a long, arduous struggle to help him choose confrontation with his psychological problems rather than a life of physical illness. The few recent reviews of psychotherapy with psychosomatic patients indicate that the traditional psychotherapies do not work very well with such patients (Solomon & Patch, 1971).

Behavior therapy

Behavior therapy has also been used to treat the psychophysiologic disorders, especially the sexual dysfunctions (Chapter 12 described this work). Behavior therapists have designed treatments for dermatitis (Walton, 1960a), myopia (Giddings & Lanyon, 1971), vertigo (Fowler et al., 1971), migraine headache (Lutker, 1971), and excessive urination (Yates & Poole, 1972). Most of their work, however, has concentrated on asthma (Cooper 1964; Walton, 1960b) and anorexia nervosa, which is pathological loss of appetite (Blinder et al., 1970; Leitenberg et al., 1968; Scrignar, 1971).

In a well-controlled study of behavior therapy with asthmatics, Moore treated twelve patients who had been unresponsive to drugs (1965). He used three behavioral methods: relaxation and reciprocal inhibition, relaxation with the suggestion of improvement, and relaxation alone. Reciprocal inhibition (that is, systematic desensitization, which was described in Chapter 10) was provided in order to reduce the anxiety that patients felt in the presence of stimuli associated with onset of asthmatic attacks. Each of the twelve patients in the study received two of the three treatments in random sequence over a period of two months. Results were assessed as changes in the frequency of asthmatic attacks. Figure 14-2 shows that all three behavioral treatment methods reduced the frequency of the patients' attacks. But only the effects of the relaxation-reciprocal inhibition method lasted; improvement brought about by the other two methods began to wear off in weeks 7 and 8.

A recent paper by Neisworth and Moore

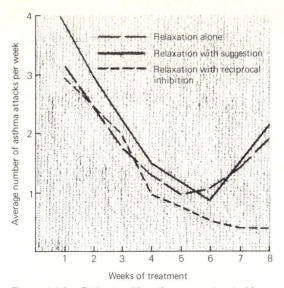

Figure 14-2. Patients with asthma were treated by three different behavioral techniques: relaxation alone, relaxation with suggestion by the therapist that they would improve, and relaxation with reciprocal inhibition (to reduce their sensitivity to stimuli which they associated with the onset of asthma attacks). All three methods helped cut down the number of asthma attacks the subjects had, but only the effects of relaxation with reciprocal inhibition were long-lasting. The improvement produced by the other two methods began to wear off in the seventh and eighth weeks. *(Moore, 1965)*

reported another behavioral approach to asthma (1972). The patient, a 7-year-old boy, had been seen by many medical specialists since the age of 2 for asthmatic attacks. Medication and diet had not reduced their severity. Because all else had failed, the patient was brought to a behavior therapist. The therapist observed almost immediately that the behavior of the child's mother during his attacks might well be supporting and aggravating his asthma. Specifically, the therapist hypothesized, "first, that asthmatic responding was being maintained or amplified by the presentation of verbal and tactile attention (as well as medicine) during or immediately after a seizure, and second, that behavior incompatible with coughing, wheezing, and generally "being sick" was not being reinforced" (p. 96).

Following a baseline period of observation, two systematic treatment strategies were devised. First, both parents agreed to avoid giving attention and medicine during bedtime asthmatic attacks; instead, the child was to be put to bed affectionately but firmly. Second, the child was to be told that he could have lunch money instead of having to take lunch to school if he coughed less often on a given night than the night before. (Lunch money was thought to be a powerful reinforcer for the patient.) The positive effects of these two simple behavioral interventions were dramatic. (See Figure 14-3.) Duration of each asthmatic attack fell from approximately seventy minutes to less than ten minutes a night during the first and second periods of conditioning. Reversal of contingencies—a return to the baseline conditions—caused some increase in the duration of the attacks. At a follow-up period eleven months later, after the child's parents had continued to ignore bedtime asthmatic attacks and to reward their absence, it was found that the duration of his asthmatic responding had decreased still further to one to two minutes of coughing a night.

Anorexia nervosa, or pathological loss of appetite, is not classified officially as a neurosis, a personality disorder, or a psychophysiologic disorder but as a "special symptom." It has been successfully treated, however, by behavioral techniques like those used for the psychophysiologic disorders. One of the classic descriptions of behavior therapy with an anorexic patient was published by Bachrach and two colleagues (1965). A 37-year-old woman had been admitted to the University of Virginia Hospital following the loss of 71 pounds over nineteen years. The authors described her in the following words:

. . . a creature so . . . shrunken about her skeleton as to give the appearance of a poorly preserved mummy suddenly struck with the breath of life. Her pasty white skin was mottled a purple hue over her feet and stretched like so much heavy spider webbing about the bony prominences of her face. . . . Cavernous ulcers opened up over the right buttocks, pubis, and back of the skull while

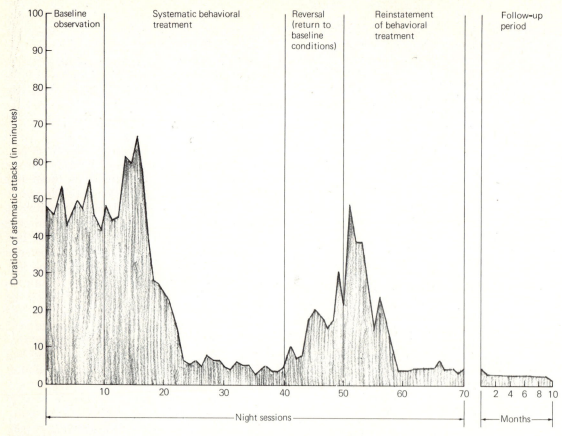

Figure 14-3. Systematic behavioral treatment sharply reduced the duration of asthma attacks suffered by a 7-year-old boy. *(Slightly modified from Neisworth & Moore, 1972)*

smaller ulcers stood out over the knees, elbows and ankles. Delicate silky threads of hair hung lifelessly from her skull. Broken, gray teeth peered out between thin, white lips through which there weakly issued forth a high pitched distant voice, remarkable for its lack of pressing concern and alarm, which to the passing observer might have seemed a bit incongruous. [P. 153]

Therapy focused on efforts to increase eating behavior—the crucial behavioral deficit in this case—by systematic manipulation of the consequences of eating.

While she was an inpatient, she was transferred from her attractively furnished hospital room on the medical ward to a barren room on the psychiatric ward. Then one of the three authors of the report began to sit with her during each of the three daily meals. When she emitted behaviors appropriate to eating (lifting a fork to her mouth, chewing food, swallowing, etc.), she was reinforced with conversation about subjects in which she was interested. She was also reinforced (with a radio, television set, or phonograph, brought in by a nurse) for small increases in overall amount of food consumed. After her weight rose from 47 to 63 pounds under these contingencies, she was no longer reinforced simply for eating; she actually had to gain weight to earn reinforcements.

On her release from the hospital, the pa-

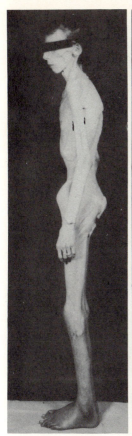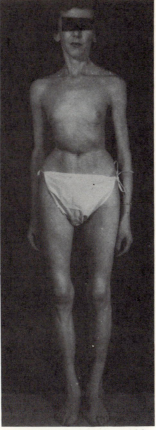

Behavior therapy administered by Bachrach and his colleagues increased the eating behavior of this emaciated anorexic woman to such a degree that she regained considerable weight (right). *(Bachrach et al., 1965)*

also become much more active in community activities.

Another distinguished report on the successful use of behavior therapy to treat anorexia nervosa was published by Lang (1965). The patient was a 23-year-old registered nurse who came to a university psychological clinic after having lost 20 pounds in six months for not eating and for vomiting. A number of different behavioral techniques were used to treat her. She was given training in deep muscle relaxation and was instructed to practice the exercises at home for fifteen to twenty minutes a day. Following this training, relaxation was used with systematic desensitization in order to "countercondition" specific anxiety responses. The situations to which she characteristically responded with anxiety had to do with travel, with criticism by important people in her life, and with being the center of attention in social or educational settings. These stimuli to anxiety were arranged in three anxiety hierarchies to which she was deconditioned during systematic desensitization that lasted for seventy sessions and extended over eleven months.

Results came quickly. Gains in her ability to imagine formerly anxiety-arousing hierarchy scenes without anxiety were paralleled by her increased ability to function in those situations outside the treatment setting. Her reduced anxiety generalized to mealtime situations, so that a "nervous stomach" and the fear of vomiting no longer prevented her from eating. As Lang summarized the course of treatment:

During the eleven months of therapy, N. made considerable progress. Her distress over travel was eliminated. She had purchased a car, drove freely around the city, and had successfully made a long vacation trip with friends. She gained back most of the weight that she had lost and only rarely had problems in eating. N. no longer had difficulty with school and was considering the pursuit of an advanced degree. Her improved command of social relationships proved to be an occupational asset. [1965, p. 221]

Despite the wide range of psychophysio-

tient's family became intimately involved in the reinforcement of her eating. Following a set of explicit instructions designed to make eating pressureless, pleasant, and reinforcing in itself, her family began to "wean" her from the hospital's material reinforcers to social reinforcers: praise from her family and friends for her weight gain, for her growing attractiveness, and for her increased energy. Her weight rose to 88 pounds approximately fifteen months after her release from the hospital. An eighteen-month follow-up showed that she had not only maintained her weight gain but logic disorders that have been successfully treated by behavioral procedures, no single disorder (with the possible exception of the sexual dysfunctions) has been the target of enough work to make possible an overall assessment of these procedures. Further, even with the disorders which have been the focus of the behavioral effort (sexual dysfunctions, asthma, and anorexia nervosa), so many different behavioral techniques have been employed that assessment of their differential effectiveness is not yet possible. Consequently, as we have done so often before in this book, we must conclude that behavior therapy has generated exciting, wide-ranging and often successful treatment efforts whose long-range value and specific "active" mechanisms remain to be determined. Even so, studies of behavior therapy have provided hard data on both the intensity and severity of the psychophysiologic disorders, as well as data on their alleviation by therapeutic invention.

Summary

The psychophysiologic disorders—also called the psychosomatic illnesses—are physical ailments either of proved psychological origin or with a prominent psychological component. Among the illnesses within this diagnostic grouping are stomach ulcers, some kinds of high blood pressure, hives, and migraine headaches. It was Mrs. M.'s migraines that caused her family to live in constant fear of precipitating or exacerbating her pain.

The psychophysiologic disorders include psychophysiologic skin, musculoskeletal, respiratory, cardiovascular, gastrointestinal, and genitourinary disorders. Many relatively common physical ailments are in this group; it sometimes surprises those who look carefully at the list to find so many "real" physical illnesses which would not seem to have an important psychological component.

Most current etiologic theories of the psychosomatic disorders are both psychological and somatic, whereas either psychological *or* somatic etiologic factors are posited for most of the other disorders considered in this book. Alexander's specificity model hypothesizes that specific psychopathological events occurring during childhood produce specific psychophysiologic disorders. Mahl's nonspecific model of psychophysiologic disorders assumes that they are related causally to psychological factors in general, not to specific psychological or psychodynamic factors. Malmo's individual response specificity model says that each individual reacts with characteristic and consistent physiological responses to a wide variety of emotional stressors. Lachman's behavioral-somatic theory begins with the assumption that most psychosomatic disorders result from prolonged exposure to stressful situations, which elicits implicit physiological reactions that can be damaging.

One of the most exciting current research efforts concerns the effects of biofeedback of psychophysiological functioning on psychosomatic disorders. Shapiro and his colleagues demonstrated that biofeedback of heart rate and blood pressure enabled normal subjects to decrease the two functions simultaneously. The same investigators reported that systolic blood pressure in patients with essential hypertension could be lowered in much the same way, a finding of enormous potential importance. Recent reviews of the rapidly expanding literature on the self-control of cardiac function, however, suggest that the actual long-term therapeutic benefits remain to be demonstrated.

Treatment of the psychophysiologic disorders should proceed on two fronts at once: somatic treatment for the physical disorder, and psychological treatment for its psychological components. A number of psychoanalysts have evolved therapeutic methods for dealing with these disorders; unfortunately, empirical data on the value of psychoanalysis for such patients has not been convincing. Behavior therapy has been used with some documented success on disorders such as dermatitis, myopia, vertigo, migraine headache, excessive urination, asthma, and anorexia nervosa.

CHAPTER FIFTEEN
Psychopathology during childhood

Matt, Calvin, and Leroy ● Roger G. ● Defining deviations in children ● Official categories ● An alternative view ● Prognosis ● Treatment

MATT, CALVIN,
AND LEROY:
CHILDREN
OF HOPE

Mrs. R. first brought Matt, Calvin, and Leroy, three of her eight children, to the psychological clinic of an Eastern university to have them evaluated intellectually. All three boys were in special classes for slow learners, but Mrs. R. was convinced that they had greater intellectual potential than many of the other children in those classes.

Mrs. R., a 36-year-old black woman, has lived in Newark for many years. She has considerable charm and talked easily and comfortably to the psychologist who interviewed her. Two years ago, she said, her husband and oldest son had been killed instantly in an automobile accident. Mrs. R. appeared to have resolved much of her grief about the deaths; she said that her remaining children had also made their own adjustments. The interviewer, a graduate student in clinical psychology at the university, was impressed by the dignity and sense of calm with which Mrs. R. discussed the deaths.

Mrs. R. described her marriage as a satisfactory one. She had left high school in her senior year to get married because she was pregnant. She and her husband, Arthur, had lived for several years in the small town near Birmingham, Alabama, in which both had been born. After the textile factory where Mr. R. worked had to close because of competition from imports, the R. family moved to Newark because they had heard that jobs were easier to get. But once he was there, the best work Mr. R. could find was menial labor that did not pay very well. Nonetheless, Mrs. R. noted with obvious pride that despite his small paycheck, "We never asked for welfare until Arthur left us."

Mrs. R. is now dating a bachelor who is good to her and the children. She cares enough for him to marry him, and she is convinced that the children need a father. But he does not make enough money to support both the R. family and his own aging mother; and if they married, Mrs. R. would lose a large part of the welfare benefits which

(Ken Heyman)

435

support her family. The R.'s live in a three-bedroom "project" apartment which is cramped for a family of nine. Their financial condition, however, is considerably better than it was before Mr. R's death because of the welfare payments.

A protective mother, Mrs. R. keeps close track of her children. She calls home once or twice while she is out shopping at the local supermarket, even though it is less than ten minutes away. She is extremely concerned about the ghetto environment, mainly because she fears that the children will be enticed by the illegal but tempting activities they see all around. She is also upset by the schools; she feels that the principals and teachers care more about union organizing activities than about her children's education. A regular and vocal member of the PTA, she often says at the meetings that the long strikes which Newark's teachers have imposed on the community have been sinful and self-serving. On the other hand, she respects education and feels that a teacher deserves a decent week's pay.

Matt is the 7-year-old baby of the family. His parents were not happy when they learned that Mrs. R. was pregnant; they felt that they could not afford a ninth child. But Mrs. R. takes pains to point out that Matt became a full and welcome member of the family the day he was born. His birth was full-term and normal. He walked at an average age and was readily toilet-trained. However, he did and still does have difficulty speaking clearly, a characteristic he shares with a number of his brothers and sisters. Partly for this reason, partly for others, Matt had to repeat kindergarten twice. In first grade he was put into a special class for "neurologically impaired" children, largely because his IQ score on a short form of the Stanford-Binet test was 85—in the "dull normal" range of intelligence.

Matt, his father's pet, was especially upset by Mr. R.'s death. Afterwards he refused to leave his mother for more than a few minutes; he said he was afraid to let her out of his sight for fear she might die too. He would pretend to be sick so that he could stay home from school and be with her. Matt and his mother share this fear of being apart: Matt is afraid of losing his mother to catastrophic injury or terminal illness, and Mrs. R. is fearful of losing Matt to the violence of the streets. Consequently she walks him to and from school, an arrangement which pleases both mother and child.

Calvin R. and Leroy R. are 14-year-old twins who were born prematurely. Calvin, born several hours before Leroy, has always been the healthier of the two boys. Though Calvin and Leroy both walked at about the normal time, Calvin was toilet-trained easily and quickly learned to speak well, while Leroy wet the bed until he was 9 and began to stutter shortly after he stopped sucking his thumb. Despite these striking differences between them, both Calvin and Leroy were

(Ken Heyman)

436

held back for a year before entering school because of "general immaturity." And in the sixth grade both were placed in special classes for the "educable retarded," after psychological tests had confirmed the counselor's impression that both boys were mildly retarded (their IQ scores were in the low seventies). As it happened, their shift of classes took place right after their father's death. Calvin soon became a serious behavior problem at school and was twice suspended for "insubordination and lack of respect." Leroy, who is dependent upon Calvin, becomes very upset when his brother misbehaves in school. As a result he too has been getting into trouble with his teacher and his classmates.

At the present time both Mrs. R. and the child-study team at the school that Matt, Calvin, and Leroy attend have begun to consider alternatives to their present classroom placements. No one believes that these placements have worked out, but no one is very sure what else should be done.

ROGER G: THE BABY WHO WAS TOO GOOD

Roger G. is 7 years old. No one has ever seen him respond to any kind of social contact in the seven years of his life. He has never spoken a word to anyone, not even to his parents. Roger doesn't look up when someone calls his name, when his mother comes into the room, or when his father tries to toss him a ball. He does seem to enjoy playing with the top of an old pressure cooker that he hauled out of the kitchen cabinet several years ago. Roger carries the top around with him, spinning it and watching it fall with apparent delight. There is also the toy car that his grandparents gave him a while ago; he likes to turn it on its back and spin the wheels around and around. He plays with these two toys for hours, and if he is interrupted he kicks and screams and bites until he is allowed to return to his car and his top.

It is difficult for anyone to understand how parents like Mr. and Mrs. G. could have had a child like Roger. They are both warm and friendly people who seem to be ideal parents. Mr. G., now in his late thirties, is a successful insurance salesman who enjoys the challenge of selling and has a genuine liking for other people. He is an even-tempered, good-natured man. He went to college but dropped out after his sophomore year; although his grades were good enough, he was restless in school and wanted to be "doing something." After two years in the Army he was discharged as a corporal and returned to Minneapolis, where he had grown up.

(Joel Gordon)

437

Mrs. G., who is several years younger than her husband, had known him slightly in high school. When he returned from the Army he began to date her regularly, and they soon married and settled down in Minneapolis. Mrs. G. is a warm, gentle person who had always wanted to be a wife and mother. She worked in her husband's office for several years while he struggled to get his insurance business underway, and then to their delight, she discovered that she was pregnant.

Roger was a much-wanted and much-loved little boy. Both sets of grandparents filled his room with stuffed teddy bears, trucks, and cowboy suits. He was a good baby, rarely cried, and seemed most content when he was left by himself. He never reached to be picked up, and he never cuddled up when he was held. He was bottle-fed and easily weaned to a cup. He sat up and walked early, but he failed to show any speech development. As Roger grew beyond the normal age of speech, his parents gradually came to realize that although he was a handsome, well-coordinated, very "good" child, there was something very wrong with him. Not only did he not speak, but he seemed to be in a world of his own.

When Roger was 3 years old the G.'s told the pediatrician about their worries, adding that Roger was probably only hard of hearing or something. The doctor, who was more concerned about the behavior the G.'s described than they imagined, gave Roger a complete physical examination and found him to be in fine physical health. Then he sent the boy to a child neurologist, who found no signs of neurological pathology in Roger. The neurologist did feel, however, that there was the possibility of a serious psychological or psychiatric disorder, and he referred the G.'s to the mental health center at the university near their home in Minneapolis. There the child psychologists and psychiatrists who saw Roger were all in reluctant agreement about the severity of Roger's problem and the nature of his diagnosis. He was, they concluded, an autistic child.

Parents, children, and the world they share

The R. children and Roger G. come from very different social, cultural, and economic worlds. Nonetheless, Roger—the only child of upper-middle-class Midwestern parents—and the R.'s —products of a fatherless ghetto family of eight children in Newark—are alike in important ways. Above all, they are alike because all of them are troubled. All have worried the people who love them and take care of them, so much so that all were eventually brought to professionals for evaluation.

The R. children are examples of the complex diagnostic and therapeutic tasks facing the clinician who works with a socioeconomically diversified clientele. Their case histories show elements of mental retardation, neurological impairment, emotional disturbance, and cultural deprivation. The professional who attempts to assess their problems needs to know, among other things, a lot about the cultural specificity of family interaction patterns, biochemical factors in autism, behavioral theories of childhood psychopathology, and the genetics of mental disorders. Even then his knowledge would not ensure a reliable or valid diagnosis; each of the three R. children might be given a variety of labels ranging from school phobia to retardation to minimal brain damage to cultural deprivation to psychological normality.

Though none of these labels is especially helpful so far as "remediation" or therapy is concerned, recent research does suggest that there is hope for the R. children. Many of the classroom management projects recently undertaken by behavioral psychologists, for example, seem to hold real promise of helping pupils like the R. children "learn to learn." Several of these programs are described here.

Roger G.'s diagnosis, unfortunately for his parents, is unequivocal. So is his prognosis for limited positive behavioral change. Only the etiology of Roger's autism remains unknown, and in all likelihood, effective treatment for autism awaits a definitive answer to the question of etiology. As this chapter will show, that answer does not yet exist.

Historical perspectives: The changing face of childhood

No written discussions of psychological disorders in children appeared before the nineteenth century. And it was not until the twentieth century that students of human behavior, suddenly recognizing that children are something other than miniature adults, fully acknowledged the existence of emotional problems in children. Now contemporary Western society is accused of being too child-centered, too indulgent toward its young people. Regardless of the merits of this argument, it is true that children have come to be seen *and* heard as never before. To appreciate the magnitude of the change in attitudes toward children, it is useful to review the status of children in other societies and earlier times. The interested reader will find a more complete discussion in Louise Despert's book *The Emotionally Disturbed Child—Then and Now* (1965).

Sparta. In ancient Greece the Spartans evaluated newborn infants in terms of their ability to survive and serve the state. Those who were judged inadequate were exposed to the elements to die. There was no discussion of the inherent value of the infant's life and no interest in his mother's emotional state. Children who were allowed to live began a rugged life at the age of 7. Boys were separated from their families and sent to live in barracks where they were given limited food, went barefoot summer and winter, and slept without coverings on straw mats. The emphasis was on physical toughness, not psychological development. Self-expression was subordinated to building the kind of bodies and endurance which could defend a military state. Girls were kept at home but educated much like boys, except that their bodies were being strengthened for the rigors of childbirth, not battle. There was little time in this society for the luxury of concern about a child's emotional security.

Rome. The early Roman family was strongly patriarchal. The father, the most powerful figure, had the right of life and death over his newborn children. He could welcome the infant into the family, sell it into slavery, or simply banish it from the household. In reality he often consulted the rest of the family, especially the child's mother, about these decisions. But banishment or slavery, while uncommon, were the father's privilege. Roman schools carried on the tyrannical rule of the father; there was little room in them for individual differences and little attention to the needs of children as they grew emotionally and intellectually.

The Romans were somewhat more liberal than the Spartans in that they allowed children to remain with their mothers during childhood and did not impose the harsh physical regime of the Spartans. Actually, the strong Roman family structure deteriorated rapidly in the later Roman empire, and there was corresponding increase in child indulgence. Some people have suggested that this was one of the causes of the fall of Rome.

The middle ages. The church in the middle ages was preoccupied with the concept of original sin in children. Christian philosophy was that the infant is selfish, self-centered, and sinful; he appears innocent only because he is physically incapable of hurting others. The sin with which every child is endowed is Adam's, and all must carry its mark from birth. In the writings of St. Augustine, however, one begins to find some recognition of the fact that children are real people with real feelings, even though Augustine too believed that their nature is essentially sinful.

During this time children were regarded as less than human by their physical caretakers as well as by their spiritual ones. They were often neglected, and were rarely consulted about their own fate; it was common, for example, to send a child to a monastery at age 4 to enter training as a monk. Sometimes children had to forage for their own food and clothing, and as a result, they died in great numbers from disease and exposure. Children were also targets of the inquisition, so that many of them were burned as heretics and witches.

Into the twentieth century. The idea that children are worth something less than a man's cattle but something more than his fowl was accepted for many centuries. When the industrial revolution came, children were the logical victims: the wretched lives of the children who worked in factories are difficult to imagine. The poet William Blake (1757 to 1827) was put to labor in a silk mill at the age of 7. Among other poignant memories, he described his horror at waking up one morning to realize that he was late for work. Running all the way, falling repeatedly on the ice, he felt

Child abuse for profit: Coal mining in England around 1840. *(New York Public Library)*

terror and a great guilt that he was ungrateful for the chance to earn bread for his family. Ironically, a few years later he might have been spared his suffering, for a factory owner proudly told the House of Lords in 1817 that he did not employ children under 10 in his business.

Today we do not need to look farther than the inner city to find children who still lack life's basic physical and emotional comforts. Compared with the abuses of the past, however, most children in Western society lead lives of greater ease. Also, the twentieth century has brought us some understanding of the child's emotional life.

The increasing sympathy with the child's needs and the child's viewpoint has had predictable effects on ideas about children's mental health. In 1896 Dr. Lightner Witmer founded the first psychological clinic in the United States. His clients included children and adolescents as well as adults, and in 1906 when he began to publish a journal, *The Psychological Clinic,* it included articles about childhood psychopathology. In 1909 the Juvenile Psychopathic Institute was established in Chicago by the psychiatrist William Healy. These pioneering efforts by Witmer and Healy were the start of a major movement throughout the country in creating child-guidance clinics. The translation of the work of Anna Freud in the late 1920s and the publication of Melanie Klein's work in 1932 brought a sophisticated psychoanalytic view of child psychopathology to the United States. In 1935 Leo Kanner's textbook on child psychiatry was published and earned him the title of the father of American child psychiatry.

It is easy to condemn the child abuse of earlier eras, but before passing such a judgment we should consider the rigor of life in those times. Sensitivity to psychological adjustment can come only after people's basic physical needs are reasonably well met. While a society need not be industrialized to allow its members time for emotional growth, a bountiful environment is probably necessary for this growth. To a person preoccupied with an empty belly or an attacking enemy, worries about shyness, fears, or basic insecurity are an undreamed-of luxury. It has taken the unparalleled standard of living that most of us now enjoy to allow society the indulgence of psychological sensitivity.

Child health care today. The report of the Joint Commission on Mental Health of Children (1970) measures American society by the Western world's new standards of child care and finds it wanting:

We are the richest of all large nations, yet we have fallen shamefully behind other industrial countries in our programs for children and families. Other nations far less well endowed than ours with resources of all kinds have developed comprehensive programs to insure the health and well-being of their people, from birth to old age. These countries recognize and act upon what we, as a nation, have failed to comprehend: that life truly begins at conception, that the developmental potential of the individual's total life is critically and pervasively affected by the care his mother receives before he is born and the services that are available to him and his family during the first few years of his life and thereafter. Because of the very demanding and complex nature of our society, each individual needs a wide range of services throughout the life cycle—educational, physical and mental health, and social welfare. The provision of these needed services is most crucial at the very beginning of life. [P. 138]

Child health care facilities in the United States are in fact poor. We rank thirteenth among the Western nations in infant mortality, with a death rate of 24.7 per 1,000 live births. And once an American child is born, he or she can anticipate receiving health services that are less adequate than those of many other nations less affluent than ours. For the child reared in poverty this fact is more significant than for the affluent child. Consider these statements from the report of the joint commission:

1 Although a number of factors other than psychological ones play into the incidence of school failure, early school dropout, unemployment, juvenile delinquency, drug addiction, family

Harlem and other inner-city ghettos aren't the only places with dilapidated schools; this one is in rural Alabama. *(Bob Fitch from Black Star)*

breakdown, and illegitimacy, the far higher rates of these problems for poor people indicate, among other things, the corrosive impact of poverty on the mental health of children and youth in low-income families.

2 Poor and nonwhite children show high rates of physical disabilities—tuberculosis, chronic diseases, blindness, etc. In many instances, institutionalization for these disorders could have been prevented by early diagnosis and treatment.

3 Disadvantaged children, particularly those from minority groups, show high rates of cumulative educational retardation. It is estimated, for example, that 85 percent of the eighth-grade students in Harlem are "functional illiterates." Typically, such youngsters know only dilapidated, understaffed, and ill-equipped schools. [pp. 183–184]

Defining behavioral deviations in children

It is more difficult to identify behavioral deviations in children than in adults, mainly because the child is in a state of change and development. His behavior is not as stable as that of his elders. Also, he cannot describe his feelings as clearly. And in the process of defining their own identities, children "try on" myriad roles that change from year to year, often from moment to moment. As a result, in evaluating a child's psychological status one must discriminate the transient behavior problem or the concern of the moment from more enduring pathological stigmata.

Who seeks help for a child —and when?

If it is normal for a child to show transient adjustment problems, when does a child's behavior become abnormal? How do parents decide whether a child should be seen for professional evaluation or simply allowed to outgrow his problems with family guidance? Frequently these decisions are not made on the basis of objective data or rational deliberation. Some parents may seek professional guidance for minor behavior deviations; others may wishfully ignore behaviors that should be taken as signs of a seriously troubled child. Naturally, parents with more money tend to bring their children for treatment sooner and for less serious problems than poorer parents do (Harris, 1974). Lower-income black children may be referred to clinics only when their behavior is seriously disruptive to the community or school. For example, when mothers' descriptions of twenty black children who had been brought to a clinic were compared with those of twenty black children serving as a normal control group, the two samples were found to differ on only three items: disobedience, fighting, and poor schoolwork (Shechtman, 1971). A study of white clinic and control children found many more behaviors to distinguish the two groups (Shechtman, 1970a). These data suggest the extent to which social and cultural factors may influence clinic referrals.

Since a child rarely refers himself for psychological treatment, it is parents, teachers, family doctors, and clergymen who determine whether he will be seen for psychological evaluation and treatment. In pragmatic terms, it seems that what bothers adults about a child is what they come to label as abnormal. It is interesting that when the parents of children seen at a clinic were asked to describe their child's self-concept, they tended to underestimate the child's appraisal of his own worth. By contrast, the parents of normal children overestimated their child's self-esteem. In fact, children seen at the clinic had slightly but significantly lower self-esteem scores than normal children (Piers, 1972). This finding suggests that parental attitude may be a more important factor than child behavior in bringing a child to a clinic.

Kessler (1966) suggests the following guidelines for parents in making the decision to seek professional help for a child:

1 *Age discrepancy:* The child acts inappropriately for his age.
2 *Frequency of the troublesome behavior:* The behavior occurs often, even under very mild stress.
3 *Number of troublesome behaviors:* The greater the number of problem behaviors, the more disabled the child probably is.
4 *Degree of social disadvantage:* Parents should be more concerned about difficulties that place their child at an obvious social or educational disadvantage.
5 *The child's inner suffering:* The child who is unhappy about himself can often benefit from professional help.
6 *Intractability of behavior:* A behavior which persists in spite of efforts to modify it should probably receive professional attention.

Official categories of child psychopathology

The diagnostic categories employed for the description of adult psychopathology have serious limitations in their applicability to children, largely because deviant, maladaptive, or unusual behavior in children does not have the same meaning as it does in adults. A severe problem of adulthood may be a transient difficulty of childhood. Also, a given behavior does not have the same meaning among children of different socioeconomic groups. And the greater fluidity of children's behaviors makes it difficult to fit them into adult diagnostic patterns. As a consequence the diagnosis of childhood psychopathology is even less satisfactory than diagnoses of adult psychopathology.

DSM II labels

The American Psychiatric Association's system for categorizing children's deviant behaviors is given in the *Diagnostic and Statistical Manual* (1968). Under the heading "behavior disorders of childhood and adolescence" the system employs six major categories and one catchall label, "other reaction of childhood." The APA system also allows for the diagnosis of transient situational disturbances and childhood schizophrenia.

DSM II categories of child psychopathology

BEHAVIOR DISORDERS OF CHILDHOOD
AND ADOLESCENCE

Hyperkinetic reaction of childhood
Withdrawing reaction of childhood
Overanxious reaction of childhood
Runaway reaction of childhood
Unsocialized aggressive reaction of childhood
Group delinquent reaction of childhood
Other reaction of childhood

TRANSIENT SITUATIONAL DISTURBANCES
Adjustment reaction of infancy
Adjustment reaction of childhood
Adjustment reaction of adolescence

PSYCHOSES
Schizophrenia, childhood type

As Bemporad and his colleagues point out, the DSM II system encompasses a confusing mixture of labels based upon temporary behavioral deviation, more prolonged but still temporary rebellion against authority figures, and largely permanent psychopathology of psychotic proportions (1970). Jackson has also criticized the system for its failure to define terms and its inadequacy in covering the problems of children (1970).

GAP classification system

In 1966 the committee on child psychiatry of the Group for the Advancement of Psychiatry (GAP) proposed a new classification system designed to overcome some of the limitations of the DSM II categories. The categories of the GAP system are given below. In addition, there is a twenty-page set of cues for differentiating the categories.

GAP categories of child psychopathology

HEALTHY RESPONSES
a Developmental crisis
b Situational crisis
c Other responses

REACTIVE DISORDERS

DEVELOPMENTAL DEVIATIONS
a Deviations in maturational patterns
b Deviations in specific dimensions of development
   1 Motor
   2 Sensory
   3 Speech
   4 Cognitive functions
   5 Social development
   6 Psychosexual
   7 Affective
   8 Integrative

PSYCHONEUROTIC DISORDERS
a Anxiety type
b Phobic type
c Conversion type
d Dissociative type
e Obsessive-compulsive type
f Depressive type
g Other psychoneurotic disorder

PERSONALITY DISORDERS
a Compulsive personality
b Hysterical
c Anxious
d Overly dependent
e Oppositional
f Overly inhibited
g Overly independent
h Isolated
i Mistrustful
j Tension-discharge disorders
   1 Impulse-ridden personality
   2 Neurotic personality disorder
k Sociosyntonic personality disorder
l Sexual deviation
m Other personality disorder

PSYCHOTIC DISORDERS
a Psychoses of infancy and early childhood
   1 Early infantile autism
   2 Interactional psychotic disorder

3 Other psychoses of infancy and early childhood

b Psychoses of later childhood
1 Schizophreniform psychotic disorder
2 Other psychosis of later childhood

c Psychoses of adolescence
1 Acute confusional state
2 Schizophrenic disorder, adult type
3 Other psychosis of adolescence

PSYCHOPHYSIOLOGIC DISORDERS

a Skin
b Musculoskeletal
c Respiratory
d Cardiovascular
e Hemic and lymphatic
f Gastrointestinal
g Genitourinary
h Endocrine
i Of nervous system
j Of organs of special sense
k Other psychophysiologic disorders

BRAIN SYNDROMES

a Acute
b Chronic

MENTAL RETARDATION

OTHER DISORDERS

[GAP, 1966, pp. 217–219]

One feature of the GAP system is the "healthy responses" category, the first item in the list. It is for children who are showing a healthy response to stress and for those whose parents have brought them to a clinic when the problem is not serious. The list's length and the detail into which it goes are designed to furnish specific guidance where DSM II is vague. But the GAP system has been criticized by some clinicians for being so very complex that it cannot be reliably applied in the usual clinical setting.

A difficulty that the APA and GAP classification systems share is their failure to adhere to one consistent classification principle. Zigler and Phillips, for example, insist that a diagnostic system should be based entirely upon "meaningful and observable behaviors" (1961). By contrast, these two systems base diagnoses upon behavior (e.g., "runaway reaction," APA), age ("developmental deviation," GAP; "adjustment reaction of infancy," APA), severity ("psychotic disorder," GAP), and etiology ("brain syndrome," GAP).

How do the clinicians who must use these diagnostic systems in their daily work feel about them? Bemporad and his co-workers, reporting on twelve months of experience with the GAP system, found that the percentages of children falling within each major diagnostic category were as shown in Figure 15-1. They pointed out a major deficiency in the GAP system: its failure to include a diagnostic category labeled "minimal brain damage." They praised the GAP list for including the category of "healthy responses," since almost 9 percent of their clinic's children were without serious difficulty and received that happy diagnosis. These are often children whose parents were excessively worried about them.

Most clinics apparently respond to the shortcomings of current diagnostic systems either by applying no diagnosis or by using a label so general that it is meaningless. Rosen and his co-workers reported that 32 percent of the child clients of 1,200 psychiatric clinics were not diagnosed, while another 30 percent were labeled simply "adjustment reaction" (1964). Dreger and his colleagues found that 40 percent of the children seen at seventeen clinics in Florida had been given the same insubstantial label. They wrote: "Looked at realistically, what this means is that after the elaborate diagnostic procedures used in most clinics are completed, the child is placed in a category, which says exactly what we knew about him in the first place, that he has a problem" (p. 1).

Thus an adequate system for child diagnosis has yet to be devised. In this chapter we present a system based upon our own behavioral biases. We have divided the problem behaviors of childhood into two categories: those for which the learning theorist has been able to provide a satisfactory theory of etiology, and those for which there is as yet no adequate learning-based model.

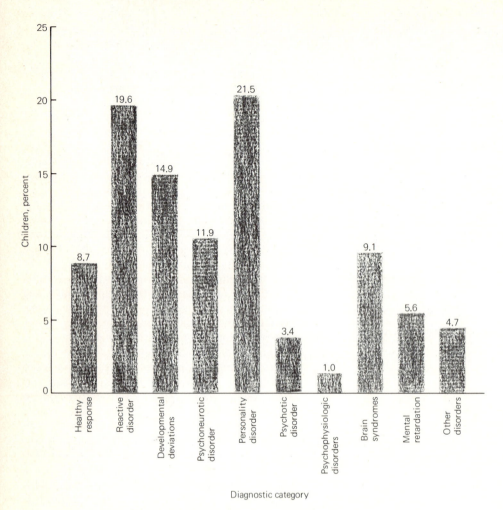

Figure 15-1. Use of GAP diagnostic categories in one clinic for twelve months. In all, 310 children were diagnosed. *(Bemporad et al., 1970)*

Child psychopathology: An alternative view

Deviant behaviors of known etiology

Healthy responses. Children in this category, which also exists in the GAP system, have come to professional attention even though their behavioral problems are integral to the developmental process. Such children are seen in a clinic or by a professional privately only if their parents are unusually concerned about minor behavioral anomalies. These are likely to be the same parents who call the pediatrician whenever a child has a temperature half a degree above normal or has coughed twice. The young thumb-sucker, bed-wetter or "shrinking violet" might well be placed in this diagnostic category, pending the advent of more years, more experience with the world, and more confidence in himself and his parents.

Some of the children Mrs. R. did *not* bring with her to the clinic—for example, 15-year-old Alice—would have fitted into the "healthy responses" category. After their father died, Alice mourned for several months. But she was able after a time to resume her schoolwork and social activities without the major decline in functioning that afflicted Calvin and Leroy.

Enuresis. The diagnosis of enuresis (bed-wetting) can only be made in relation to the child's age and stage of physical development. Infants are expected to wet; adolescents are not. The age at which bed-wetting ceases to be only annoying and becomes both annoying and worrisome can be identified only within the behavioral context.

There is a widespread lack of consensus on what constitutes nocturnal continence. Is a 4-year-old who wets the bed once a week enuretic? How about an adolescent who wets once a month? Yates points out that social-class bias evidently enters into parental reports of wetting (1970). Lower-class parents are likely to be more tolerant of wetting than affluent parents. One study reported that 20 percent of 5-year-old children wet their beds often enough for their mothers to report it in a survey (Jones, 1960). The prevalence of enuresis declines steadily throughout childhood, with almost no nocturnal wetting reported after the age of 10.

All sorts of theories to explain enuresis have been proposed. Psychoanalytic theorists, predictably, regard it as a symptom of underlying psychological conflict. They believe that symptomatic treatment of enuresis (treating the symptom without resolving the underlying conflict) is futile or dangerous or both. Behaviorally oriented psychologists, on the other hand, focus their treatment planning upon the complex behavioral sequence required to learn nocturnal bladder control.

The first behavioral treatment approach to enuresis was developed by Mowrer and Mowrer (1938). The enuretic child is put to sleep in an ordinary bed made with ordinary blankets and sheets beneath which is a special pad connected to a bell. As soon as a drop of urine touches the pad, an electric circuit is completed, ringing a bell which wakes the child. After being repeatedly waked by the bell, the child is increasingly aware of the sensations of bladder tension which precede actual urination and becomes increasingly able to control it. (A commercial version of this device is shown in Chapter 1.) Many studies have demonstrated the efficacy of this technique (DeLeon & Mandell, 1966; Lovibond, 1964; Werry & Cohrssen, 1965). In a thorough follow-up study of twenty-one children treated for enuresis with the Mowrer technique, DeLeon and Sacks found that 81 percent had remained dry four years later (1972). The other 19 percent showed a reduction in the severity of their wetting compared with the pretreatment level.

The experienced behavior therapist also recognizes that for some children, more than a mechanical device may be necessary to treat enuresis successfully. For example, the child who is receiving social rewards for his wetting behavior in the form of increased attention from his parents will not respond to behavioral treatment until their role in the disorder is pointed out and they stop rewarding the unwanted behavior.

Neurotic behaviors. In many respects the deviant behaviors called the "childhood neuroses" resemble the neurotic disorders of adulthood. But these behaviors are less clearly defined in children, and are often associated with developmental hurdles which, once overcome, mean the end of the disorder. For example, the transient phobias of the preschool child have a different, less pathological meaning than the irrational fears of the adult which they may resemble (Miller et al., 1972a). And the early school-age child may demonstrate certain compulsive behaviors which are a usual accompaniment of this developmental stage. The schoolchild who recites "Step on a crack, you'll break your mother's back," and carefully avoids all the cracks in the sidewalk—or carefully steps on all of them—is acting in an age-appropriate fashion. An adult who says the same verse and takes the same care would

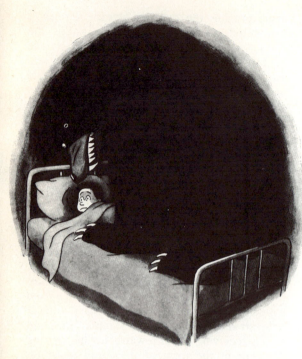

"Now, go to sleep. There's nothing to be afraid of."
A child's fears often seem irrational and trivial to
adults, but they are fully as anxiety-provoking to him
as adult fears are to adults. *(Drawing by O'Brian;*
© 1964 The New Yorker Magazine, Inc.)

probably be labeled obsessive-compulsive, if
not psychotic.

One of Matt R.'s behavior problems was
what clinicians call a *school phobia*. He would
often pretend that he was sick so he could
stay home, because he was afraid to leave his
mother and felt anxious about being in the
classroom. School-phobic behavior is one of
the common forms of neurotic behavior in
children. Lee Harvey Oswald, Charles Manson, and Jay Meredith were all school-phobic
during their first years of schooling.

Children who refuse to go to school because
of school phobia—because of their fears of the
school situation—should be distinguished from
the *truant* child, who avoids school as part of
a delinquent rather than a neurotic pattern of
behavior. Oswald and Manson were also
school truants during their early adolescent

years. The school phobia may show itself as
morbid fear of going to school, frequent somatic complaints, excessive dependence on the
mother, or a conflict between the child's parents and the school. The school phobia often
reflects a disruption in family relationships,
with the result that both a mother and child
share a mutual separation anxiety. Matt, for
example, feared that his mother would die as
his father had, while Mrs. R. was afraid of
what might happen to Matt once he went outside the home. While growing up involves
learning to separate from the mother, some
children become excessively anxious about
that separation. If the mother herself shares
this anxiety, she will probably reinforce the
child for clinging to her.

Conduct disorders. Conduct disorders are
acts against other people or things, rather
than acts against the actor like the neurotic
disorders. The conduct disorders provide a
child with clear and immediate reinforcement.
Acting up in class, stealing, cheating, or lying
are all "taboo" behaviors which nonetheless
possess immediate reward value. By contrast,
problems classified as neurotic have less obvious reward value besides creating more discomfort in the child. Neurotic behaviors often
serve a clear anxiety-reduction function; conduct disorders seem to be sustained by the
"pleasure" they yield. It is easier for a naïve
observer to understand the rewards which
maintain the conduct disorders.

The most common forms of conduct disorder among boys involve aggression. One
of the primary tasks of parents and teachers
is to train children in the rules that govern
aggression, and boys who are unable to learn
them make up a large group of the patients
treated in most child-guidance clinics. As
Robins's research indicated, boys who fail to
learn these rules are likely to continue to exhibit antisocial behavior as adults.

For some children, aggressive behavior is
consistent with the norms of their subculture.
The child may share the norms of his family,
gang, or community, but not those of the wider
society. As an adolescent Malcolm X made a

realistic and successful social adjustment to life in Boston's Roxbury ghetto, and that adjustment involved criminal behavior. The rules of the larger society finally resulted in his imprisonment. Mrs. R. was fearful precisely because she thought her children might imitate the illegal behaviors they saw around them in the Newark ghetto. The rewards for doing so were obvious: peer approval, money from stolen goods, and the euphoria of drugs, alcohol, and sex.

A considerable body of literature demonstrates that aggressive behavior can readily be taught and learned (Bandura, 1969). Once aggression is viewed as a learned response, the possibility of eliminating it through the very principles of learning by which it was acquired makes more sense. Many studies have shown that aggressive behavior in the classroom yields to the systematic application of behavioral procedures. Here is a case study in which tantrum behavior was extinguished:

Subject S-2 was an 11-year old boy who . . . had no apparent organic disorder and was also of normal intelligence. In initial class sessions, S-2 emitted behavior considered undesirable in the classroom context with high frequency. He displayed temper tantrums (kicking, screaming, etc.), spoke baby-talk, and incessantly made irrelevant comments or posed irrelevant questions.

Several times a week, [hospital] attendants dragged this boy down the hall to one of his classes as the boy screamed and buckled his knees. On several of these occasions, the boy threw himself on the floor in front of a classroom door. A crowd of staff members inevitably gathered around him. The group usually watched and commented as the boy sat or lay on the floor, kicking and screaming. Some members of the group hypothesized that such behavior seemed to appear after the boy was teased or frustrated in some way. However, the only observable in the situation was the consistent consequence of the behavior in terms of the formation of a group of staff members around the boy.

Observing one such situation which occurred before E's [the experimenter's] class, E asked the attendant to put the boy in the classroom at his desk and to leave the room. Then E closed the door. The boy sat at his desk, kicking and screaming; E proceeded to her desk and worked there, ignoring S-2. After 2 or 3 min. the boy, crying softly, looked up at E. Then E announced that she would be ready to work with him as soon as he indicated that he was ready to work. He continued to cry and scream with diminishing loudness for the next 4 or 5 min. Finally, he lifted his head and stated that he was ready. Immediately, E looked up at him, smiled, went to his desk, and said, "Good, now let's get to work." The boy worked quietly and cooperatively with E for the remainder of the class period.

[Zimmerman & Zimmerman, 1962, p. 60]

Although girls may also engage in aggressive acts, it is most often their sexual behavior that is a source of concern to family and wider society. For girls under the age of 18, sexual delinquency is a frequent source of clinic referral as well as legal action. Among young-

(Bacchus/DPI)

sters appearing in juvenile court, 9 percent of the girls and 2 percent of the boys are charged with sexual offenses (Hoover, 1965; Juvenile Court Statistics, 1964). This discrepancy, doubtless reflecting the double standard of our society, suggests that sexual behavior on the part of young girls is more closely regulated than that of young boys. Sexual promiscuity in boys is considered role-appropriate unless it involves forcible rape, while promiscuity in girls is more often viewed as delinquent.

Although promiscuous sexual behavior may be associated with serious forms of psychopathology like schizophrenia, mental retardation, or sociopathy, it is much more often a reflection of behavior modeled from parents (Scharfman & Clark, 1967), a response to peer-group pressure, or an attempt to determine one's attractiveness and sexual effectiveness. The majority of young girls who are sexually promiscuous eventually abandon this behavior for a more conventional marital relationship.

Organic brain disorders: Lead poisoning. Although the organic brain disorders are discussed in Chapter 17, this section will deal with one form of brain disorder—lead poisoning—that is particularly relevant to children, especially inner-city children. Lead poisoning is most often caused by eating lead-based paint. It is frequently the result of *pica,* meaning the craving for and ingestion of unnatural substances such as laundry starch, plaster, paint, crayons, paper, and wood. For reasons that are unclear, some children even prefer these substances to candy, cake, and cookies. Eating most of them will not do permanent harm, but eating others—like lead-based paint —can cause permanent brain damage.

Since flaking lead-based paint is more likely to be found on the crumbling walls of inner-city apartments than in more affluent suburban development homes, the ghetto child runs a much greater risk from pica than the suburban child. Lead poisoning from pica is a striking instance of the avoidable waste of human potential. Better housing and more effective

Children often eat things like PAINT CHIPS when you're not watching. They peel them from walls and window sills. Or pick them off the floor.

Muchas veces los niños comen cosas raras cuando usted no los observa, como pedacitos de pintura que despegan de las paredes y marcos de las ventanas, y que a veces caen al piso. O los recogen del piso.

Lots of times these paint chips contain LEAD. If your child eats them he can get very sick. Even a little bit is bad for him.

Muchas veces estos pedacitos de pintura contienen PLOMO. Si su niño los come se puede enfermar. La menor cantidad le puede enfermar.

From a bilingual pamphlet prepared and distributed by New York City in its campaign against lead poisoning. *(Health Services Administration, City of New York)*

community education on the dangers of eating nonnutritive substances would drastically reduce lead poisoning.

Mary R., who is now 8 years old, had pica when she was younger. Mr. R. was still alive at the time. Since he knew the dangers of lead poisoning from hearing public-service announcements on the radio, he became very upset when he realized that Mary was eating flakes of peeling paint from the walls of her room. He quickly took her to a doctor, and because she had only just discovered the paint flakes on her walls, she did not suffer permanent brain damage. Her father organized the tenants in his building to force the landlord to repaint the apartments with non-lead-based paint.

Deviant behaviors of unknown etiology

The following section focuses upon three childhood disorders—early infantile autism, childhood schizophrenia, and minimal brain injury—for which the etiology is unknown. While innumerable theories to account for them have been formulated, no theory has gained universal acceptance.

Early infantile autism.   One of the most devastating forms of childhood psychosis, early infantile autism is a relatively uncommon condition first described by the psychiatrist Leo Kanner (1943). It strikes 1 or 2 of 10,000 people; it is three to four times more common in males than in females. The cause—or causes—of this affliction and the proper treatment for it are still uncertain despite extensive research during the past two decades.

The autistic infant looks normal. He is often physically attractive, with an alert, thoughtful expression that belies his profound disability. His motor coordination is also good. But along with these attributes is the central behavioral deficit present from birth: the total failure to develop normal social, interpersonal responsivity. There is no social smiling, no cuddling in the mother's arms, no reaching out to be picked up. While the autistic child is sometimes described as "a good baby" since he rarely cries for attention, by the end of his first year of life his disability is evident to everyone, because he fails to show such social behaviors as waving "bye-bye," playing peek-aboo, or recognizing his parents with a smile. In fact, mothers of an autistic child will sometimes observe that he never seems to notice when they are in the room. Instead, the child seems content to play with the same toy, bottle top, or puzzle for endless weeks. He favors objects that are shiny and that he can spin, roll, or somehow manipulate.

Many of the behaviors of the autistic child

can also be observed in other forms of childhood psychosis. Its distinguishing features, however, are a profound lack of interpersonal relations from birth, an inability to tolerate change or novelty, failure to use speech for communication, and the absence of neurological or developmental dysfunctions (Ward, 1970).

Kanner's view of the etiology of early infantile autism came from his experiences with the parents. He described them as very bright, obsessive, and without emotional warmth—as "refrigerator parents" (1943). Kanner's conclusions may have been distorted by a sampling bias that brought only certain kinds of parents to the clinic where he worked. In fact, more recent research on the etiology of this disorder casts doubt on both the exceptional intellect and the "refrigerator" quality of the parents (Wolff & Morris, 1971). Further, DeMyer and her colleagues, who compared the infant-care behavior of parents of autistic, normal, and brain-injured children, found no data to support the notion that people with autistic children were unstimulating, cold, or defective as parents (1972). The psychologist who interviewed the parents of Roger G., whose case was described at the beginning of the chapter, found them neither cold nor exceptionally intelligent.

Three current major theories of the etiology of early infantile autism are Rimland's (1964), Bettelheim's (1967), and Ferster's (1961).

● RIMLAND'S THEORY OF AUTISM.   Rimland favors an organic view of the etiology of autism. He believes that damage to the reticular activating system causes the autistic child's inability to link together memories and sensations and to coordinate past experiences with new events (1964). As a result, the autistic child seems aware only of isolated sensations, never of the relationships among events. Unfortunately, Rimland's theory is largely untestable because procedures for exploring the reticular activating system in live human subjects do not yet exist.

Other researchers advocating the biological position on autism suggest that both autism

Bruno Bettelheim.

and childhood schizophrenia result from a neurophysiological deficit combined with a severe language disorder caused by central nervous system damage (Churchill, 1972; DeMyer et al., 1972). These children may fail to imitate and learn from the actions of others because they cannot integrate sensory and motor functions. The autistic child seems to be unable to observe the action of another person, retain the concept, and then transfer it to his own body.

● BETTELHEIM'S THEORY OF AUTISM. Bettelheim believes that early infantile autism is psychological in origin (1967). In his view the autistic child has chosen to shut out the world because of the frustration and lack of satisfaction he found in it during his infancy. One of the sources of this early frustration and dissatisfaction, in Bettelheim's opinion, is the autistic child's mother. Because of her own psychopathology, she creates an environment for the young child in which he learns that what he does—or tries to do—has no influence on events around him. He learns that he is best off when he behaves passively.

The severity of autism, according to Bettelheim's explanation, depends upon how early the child is frustrated in his attempts to respond to and change his environment, how extensive the frustration is, and how long it lasts. Treatment should consist of creating an atmosphere of permissiveness and acceptance in which the child can feel that the therapist has entered into his world rather than, as usual, forcing the child into the world of the adult. The existence of autistic symptoms from birth, and the presence of normal siblings in many families of autistic children, have been raised as objections to Bettelhiem's theory.

● FERSTER'S THEORY OF AUTISM. Ferster's theory of autism is based on learning theory (1961). At a result, it is not so much concerned with what causes autism but with the application of behavioral techniques to modify autistic behavior. To Ferster the autistic child differs from the normal child in his frequency of emitting behaviors, but not in his potential range, kind, or quality of behaviors. The autistic child is deficient in his repertoire of complex social behaviors and excessive in simple, asocial behaviors. This situation has come about, Ferster believes, because the autistic child has not received the kind of consistent reinforcement from his parents necessary for the development of appropriate social behavior.

While Ferster's theory is not inconsistent with Bettelheim's opinion that the autistic child's parents caused the development of autism, the two differ markedly so far as treatment is concerned. Bettelheim regards Ferster's operant conditioning techniques as inhuman and dehumanizing, while Ferster sees Bettelheim's broadly psychoanalytic approach as imprecise and undocumented.

● AUTISM: NO CONCLUSION. Despite these efforts, a satisfactory explanation for early infantile autism has yet to be put forth. We, the authors, suspect that biophysiological factors are important in the etiology of the disorder. But we acknowledge that its specific form and severity may depend in part upon the reaction of the autistic child's parents to his disability, especially to his social unresponsiveness.

Roger G., the autistic boy described at the beginning of the chapter, showed many of the classic characteristics of this disorder, including lack of social responsivity, failure to develop language, absence of neurological defects, and preference for the constant repetition of favorite activities. But as we have already pointed out, Roger's parents did not fit Kanner's stereotype of the parents of autistic children. Although intelligent, they were not exceptionally so. Most important, they were warm, loving people who were definitely not "refrigerator parents." Parents like Mr. and Mrs. G. lead the clinician to lean towards a biological explanation for Roger's autism. Case studies alone, however, cannot provide sufficient data to prove or disprove an etiologic theory.

(Joel Gordon)

Childhood schizophrenia. Although a wide range of behaviors—more than 100 (Boatman & Szurek, 1960)—have been suggested as characteristic of the schizophrenic child, the essential feature of this disorder is simpler. It is the child's lack of contact with external reality and his apparent focus upon his own internal world. Among the most striking behaviors of the schizophrenic child are his:

1 Bizarre and repetitive body movements (e.g., hand waving, robot-like or mechanical walking)
2 Disturbances in speech (e.g., peculiar tone, unusual content)
3 Inability to respond emotionally to people
4 Inappropriate affect (e.g., terror of dogs, indifference to self-injury)
5 Distortions of time (e.g., confusing the past and present)
6 Peculiar preoccupations (e.g., a fascination with air conditioners or railroad schedules)

On evaluating the speech of twenty-five schizophrenic and twenty-five normal children, Goldfarb and his co-workers found that while the schizophrenic children demonstrated more "speech faults," no specific cluster of faults was uniquely schizophrenic (1972). This finding is consistent with similar observations that have been made of adult schizophrenic speech (see Chapter 6).

Bender identified a set of prognostic signs in a follow-up study of 100 childhood-schizophrenic patients. The four signs that signaled a favorable prognosis were

1 Symbiotic behavior (a relationship, even if it is pathological, with another person)
2 Testable IQ of at least 70
3 Some responsiveness to treatment
4 Good home situation

Poor prognostic indicators included

1 The presence of organic brain disorder
2 Absence of language
3 Untestable IQ

Differential diagnosis of autism and schizophrenia. Discrimination between early infantile autism and childhood schizophrenia has long been a controversial issue, even though the pragmatic value of the distinction is small. That is, we cannot treat either condition with much success. Theorists who believe that the two are separate disorders point to specific differences that Rimland (1964) has identified, among which are these:

1 *Onset and course:* Early infantile autism is usually diagnosed in infancy. Childhood schizophrenia often develops after several years of apparently normal development.
2 *Health and appearance:* Autistic children are almost always described as attractive children who have been in excellent physical health. Schizophrenic children, by contrast, are frequently described as having been in poor health since birth.
3 *Physical responsiveness:* From infancy autistic children are described as physically withdrawn; schizophrenic children, on the other hand, are often responsive, sometimes overresponsive, to physical touch and bodily contact.
4 *Preservation of sameness:* The autistic child has difficulty tolerating novelty in the environment, while the schizophrenic child does not seem bothered by minor change.
5 *Motor performance:* Autistic children have excellent gross and fine motor coordination; schizophrenic children are poorly coordinated.
6 *Personal orientation:* The schizophrenic child is confused and disoriented about his relationship to his environment; the autistic child is completely detached and hence completely uninvolved.
7 *Familial mental disorder:* The families of autistic children have a lower than average incidence of mental disorders, while the families of schizophrenic children tend to have a higher than average rate of disorder.

The question of whether early infantile autism and childhood schizophrenia represent one, two, or more than two distinct disorders has not been answered. The importance of the question, which does not seem urgent now, will become critical when and if a successful treatment is discovered for one or the other condition.

Minimal brain damage. The child with minimal brain damage shows none of the signs of gross injury observable in the child with cerebral palsy, epilepsy, or brain tumor. His behavioral deficits are more subtle and difficult to define. Clements (1966) found that ten characteristics were most frequently cited in relation to children with diagnosed minimal brain injury:

1 Hyperactivity
2 Perceptual-motor impairments
3 Rapid emotional changes
4 General orientation defects
5 Disorders of attention
6 Impulsiveness
7 Disorders of memory and thinking
8 Specific learning disabilities in reading, arithmetic, writing, and spelling
9 Disorders of speech and hearing
10 Equivocal neurological signs and EEG irregularities

Chess compared eighty-eight brain-injured children with matched control children bearing other diagnostic labels (1972). She found that of all behaviors thought to be associated with minimal brain damage, only one—perseveration (repeating the same verbal or psychomotor behavior over and over)—differentiated the brain-injured children from the others. She reported that clusters of three or more of the most common characteristics of brain injury were also significant predictors of diagnosis.

Some clinicians regard the cues to minimal brain injury as so equivocal that they believe the diagnostic category is more of a "wastebasket" entity than a meaningful syndrome. It is true that the minimally brain-damaged child is often diagnosed by the process of elimination: if he has a learning disability but is not retarded, emotionally disturbed, or suffering from gross brain damage, he may be labeled minimally brain-damaged. Certainly there is not much evidence of overt physical lesions in the brains of these children. Many clinicians, however, continue to find the diagnostic label useful; they feel that it refers to a discrete syndrome characterized by hyperactivity, distractibility, and impulsiveness.

Compared with the reactions of normal adults, stimulants and sedatives have opposite effects on the central nervous systems of some hyperactive children. Stimulants tend to calm such children, while sedatives tend to increase their activity. For this reason stimulants are used to treat the hyperactivity of children with minimal brain damage. The most popular stimulant for the treatment of hyperactivity in children is best known by its brand name of Ritalin (Millichap, 1968).

The question of minimal brain damage was raised in connection with Matt R.'s behavioral problems when other more definitive labels could not be given them. While Matt was not retarded, he was not able to do schoolwork at his grade level. A neurological examination had failed to find clear evidence of brain injury, though there were tentative indicators of possible mild damage. These included hyperactivity, emotional lability (rapid emotional changes), and difficulty in reading and spelling. Although his school placed Matt in the special class for neurologically impaired children, the school psychologist who made this decision did not feel sure about the label he and his colleagues had conferred on Matt. His uncertainty stemmed from his awareness that Matt had recently lost his father and was excessively dependent upon his protective mother. Nonetheless, Matt did receive the "minimal brain dysfunction" label.

Prevalence and prognosis of behavioral disorders in childhood

Research has shown that some of the behavioral deviations of childhood predict later adult psychopathology, while others do not. This section reviews the prognostic significance of some common childhood behavior problems.

The normal child

As a moment of reminiscence may remind you, childhood and adolescence are not wholly carefree times free from emotional trauma, stress, or unhappiness. "Normal" children are also prone to the development of behavioral problems. A major survey of their problems, the California Growth Study, reported that more than 30 percent of a sample of normal children between 21 months and 14 years of age showed such behaviors as bed-wetting, bad dreams, nail-biting, overactivity, lying, oversensitivity, tantrums, and jealousy (MacFarlane et al., 1954). A more recent study found that the average child exhibits a few symptoms of many types of deviant behavior, but rarely shows a large number of symptoms from any one disorder (Miller et al., 1971). For example, the normal child may talk back to his mother but not also fight with smaller children, talk back to his teacher, and destroy property, whereas a seriously aggressive child is more likely to show all these behaviors. Normal children show more disordered behavior when they are younger; as a result, deviations from the norm are thought to have more serious consequences as the child grows older (Shechtman, 1970b).

In summary: The presence of problem behaviors does not automatically mean that a child has a serious emotional problem. As a normal part of the growth process, children do exhibit temporary psychological difficulties. These problems, though they are important to the child and his parents, either disappear with maturity or are resolved by the counsel and affection of the family. Such children rarely find their way to a clinic or other treatment facility.

The child in the clinic

MacFarlane and her associates reported that normal children generally outgrow their problems, although children with many problems in childhood are more likely to have difficulties during adolescence (1954). But these were normal children; what about children with special problems? Do the children who are referred to a psychological clinic or a private clinician for more or less serious reasons grow up to be psychopathological adults?

There are two ways to answer this question. One is to look back at the childhood of emotionally disturbed adults, a method called *retrospective study*. Another is to make a *longitudinal* (long-term) study of children seen in clinics to determine how they develop as adults. Attempts to retrace the histories of adult schizophrenics have generally found that their teachers in childhood did not think of them as having major emotional problems (Bower et al., 1960). Retrospective studies, however, are subject to serious forms of bias. First, they must rely upon the memories of teachers or other adults about children of the past. Second, the memories may well be influenced by the knowledge that the person in question is a mental patient.

To overcome these biases, follow-up studies of children seen for treatment are most often employed for prognostic research. In a major study designed to examine relationships between childhood and adult psychopathology, Robins and her colleagues followed 524 patients of a child-guidance clinic and 100 control children for as much as thirty years after their initial contact with the child-guidance clinic (1966). Robins's patient population contained a large number of children with records of delinquency.

One major conclusion from the study was that children who had been referred initially for antisocial behavior showed the highest rate of antisocial behavior as adults. The same individuals as adults were poorer, more alienated socially, and more likely to report symptoms of poor health. The prognosis for antisocial children was worse than for any other group seen at the clinic. At the other end of the prognostic continuum, for example, were the adults who had suffered from fearfulness, withdrawal, tics, hypersensitivity, restlessness, speech defects, insomnia, nightmares, or temper tantrums as children. They were not significantly different from the control subjects in frequency of adult psychopathology.

After reviewing the Robins study and related research, Clarizio and McCoy conclude that the stability of emotional problems over time depends upon their specific nature (1970). Thus, while neurotic behaviors in childhood are often unrelated to the development of adult neurosis, children with childhood schizophrenia and infantile autism usually retain their psychoses as adults (Bender, 1970; Kanner et al., 1972). Shy and withdrawn children, contrary to popular opinion, do not become schizophrenic adults. The children who are most likely to become adult schizophrenics are those who combine antisocial behavior with other serious behavioral deviations. It is interesting that adult psychotic depressives were generally not seen in child-guidance clinics, because they typically made good childhood school adjustments (Offord, 1971). In summary, the more severe a child's behavioral deviation, the more likely it is that he will continue to exhibit difficulties in adulthood.

Treatment of child psychopathology

Many of the theoretical principles underlying psychotherapy or behavior therapy for children are identical with those of adult treatment. But as Clarizio and McCoy (1970) point out, there are important differences between child and adult treatment approaches in several areas:

1 *Motivation for treatment:* The adult usually refers himself, while the child is usually referred by others.
2 *Insight into treatment objectives:* The adult is more likely to understand his role in therapy and to share many of the therapist's objectives than the child, who must be provided with an intrinsically interesting experience in order to sustain his motivation.
3 *Linguistic development:* The adult usually has adequate verbal ability for verbal psychotherapy, whereas children must often be reached on a nonverbal level. The child's behavior, including his play, are often the only guides to his difficulties. He cannot tell us "what hurts."

4 *Dependence upon environmental forces:* The adult can be more independent of his environmental circumstances than the child, who must rely upon his parents for sustenance and support.

5 *Plasticity of personality:* The adult has a more established, less flexible pattern of behavior than the child, who is more pliable and presumably more receptive to the benefits of therapy.

Play therapy

An important therapy technique makes use of childrens' pleasure in play. Play becomes a medium of communication with a child, allowing the therapist to build a relationship with him. The playroom provides a setting for therapy in which the child can express his feelings, even unacceptable or unpleasant ones, such as anger at his parents or fear of death. Toys commonly used in play therapy include dolls, doll furniture, sandboxes, crayons, finger paints, and running water. Complicated mechanical toys are avoided, since they may distract the child from more creative, more personal forms of expression.

Within the same playroom setting, however, therapists of different theoretical orientations take different approaches to treatment. Client-centered therapists will work for freedom of expression, using minimal interpretations and control (Axline, 1947). Client-centered play therapy encourages the child to express himself freely without fear of rejection. Psychoanalytic child therapists, by contrast, are much more concerned with interpreting the meaning of the child's play and the specifics of his past history (Freud, 1946). In essence, they aim to teach him the meaning of what he does.

Very little controlled research is available on the effectiveness of play therapy. The few studies that have been done have yielded equivocal results. Levitt, for example, found little evidence to support claims of the effectiveness of dynamically oriented play therapy (1957, 1963). However, many of the studies he reviewed had either no control groups or in-

Play therapy. *(Suzanne Szasz)*

appropriate control groups, and many utilized inexperienced therapists (Eisenberg & Gruenberg, 1961; Kessler, 1966).

In an important recent study, Love and her co-workers report data which strongly challenge the efficacy of child psychotherapy (1972). Their well-designed experiment evaluated the effectiveness of three approaches to child treatment: child psychotherapy, parent counseling, and an experimental technique they recently developed called *information feedback*. In the feedback technique, experts give parents information and some perspective about the problems their children are experiencing. The purpose is to provide the factual information that the parents need in order to make their own decisions about how they will raise their child. It is hoped that they will put their own problem-solving abilities to work to resolve the child's problems. Thus the expert does not suggest solutions; he simply supplies the kinds of data necessary for rational decision making.

Ninety-one children were randomly assigned to one of the three treatment groups. After they had completed treatment, ratings from unbiased observers showed that the two treatment methods which actively involved the child's parents—parent counseling and information feedback—were both significantly more effective than child therapy. Little or no clinical improvement was observed where the burden of change was placed almost entirely upon the child in his own therapy. Love and her colleagues also noted that parents of lower socioeconomic status utilized the parent-counseling procedures most effectively, while middle-class parents were able to benefit most from information feedback. The investigators concluded that middle-class parents may be better able to take advantage of situations which permit them to draw upon their own problem-solving ability and that lower-class parents can function more effectively when they have the direct advice of an expert.

Family therapy

Some therapists, recognizing the limitations inherent in treating only the child in what may be a troubled family situation, have turned to family therapy techniques. The philosophy of family therapy is that while the child may be the patient who is brought for treatment, it is probably the entire family which needs help. Family therapists believe that each member of the family plays a role in maintaining the family's pathology. There are no innocent victims and no villains—just a family that needs help and understanding. The following excerpt from a family therapy session guided by Dr. Nathan Ackerman, a leader in the movement, illustrates how a skilled family therapist is able to make family members aware of their influence upon one another.

Family therapy. *(Family Service Association of America)*

Dr. A.: Bill, you heaved a sigh as you sat down tonight.

Father: Just physical, not mental.

Dr. A.: Who are you kidding?

Father: Really not . . . Really physical. I'm tired because I put in a full day today.

Dr. A.: Well, I'm tired every day, and when I sigh it's never purely physical.

Father: Really?

Dr. A.: What's the matter?

Father: Nothing, really!

Dr. A.: Well, your own son doesn't believe that.

Father: Well, I mean, nothing . . . nothing could cause me to sigh especially today or tonight.

Dr. A.: Well, maybe it isn't so special, but . . . How about it, John?

Son: I wouldn't know.

Dr. A.: You wouldn't know? How come all of a sudden you put on a poker face? A moment ago you were grinning very knowingly.

Son: I really wouldn't know.

Dr. A.: You . . . do you know anything about your pop?

Son: Yeah.

Dr. A.: What do you know about him?

Son: Well, I don't know, except that I know some stuff.

Dr. A.: Well, let's hear.

Therapist instantly fastens on a piece of nonverbal behavior, the father's sigh.

Therapist challenges father's evasive response.

An example of therapist's use of his own emotions to counter an insincere denial.

Therapist now exploits son's gesture, a knowing grin, to penetrate father's denial and evoke a deeper sharing of feelings.

Therapist stirs son to unmask father.

Now son wipes grin off his face, and turns evasive, like father.
Therapist counters by challenging son, who took pot shot from sidelines and then backed away.

[Ackerman, 1966, pp. 3–4]

Increasing numbers of studies are investigating the interactions which occur within the family of a child who has been identified as disturbed (Alkire et al., 1971; Bugental et al., 1972; Mishler & Waxler, 1968; Schuham, 1970, 1972; Werner et al., 1970). In general they indicate that the interaction patterns within "disturbed families" are significantly different from those within "normal families." For example, the mother of a disturbed child may say, "That's not nice," in a sugary-sweet voice that attempts to negate her criticism (Bugental et al., 1971). Mothers of normal children show less tendency to give conflicting messages. The existence of a disturbed pattern does not prove that this pattern contributed to the development of a child's psychopathology; the distorted communication patterns may have evolved as a reaction to family stress rather than because of it. But investigations of disturbed patterns have provided empirical support for the prevailing view that families need to be treated as a whole rather than in parts.

Behavior therapy

Recent developments in behavior therapy have been extensively applied in the treatment of child psychopathology. Such childhood problems as phobias (Yates, 1970), stuttering (Jones,

1970), thumb-sucking (Davidson, 1970), enuresis (Lovibond & Coote, 1970; Yates, 1970), hyperactivity (Werry & Sprague, 1970), and childhood psychosis (Yates, 1970) are all being treated by behavioral means. Behavior therapy in many of these cases can be accomplished by parents with direction and guidance from professionals. The parents are taught the basic principles of reward and punishment in order to enable them to analyze their interactions with their children (Kozloff, 1973). Frequently they realize that they have been unintentionally rewarding behaviors which they really consider undesirable. For example, if a child has to nag repeatedly before gaining his mother's attention, he will be rewarded for nagging when she finally does listen to him. Once the mother becomes aware of her behavioral pattern, she can change it for the better by attending to the child when he is *not* nagging and ignoring him when he is.

The use of behavioral techniques need not be cold or impersonal, as some uninformed critics of behavior therapy believe them to be. Love and affection are powerful social reinforcers which a child must be given with great frequency and regularity. If they are provided with increased consistency and awareness, they can help to reinforce the child's appropriate behavior as well as the adult's view of his own competence as a parent.

The application of behavioral methods in therapy for psychotic children has increased rapidly over the past few years. One of the outstanding psychologists in this area is Ivar Lovaas, who has used operant techniques to develop speech (Lovaas et al., 1966), to encourage social interaction (Lovaas et al., 1965b) and to eliminate self-destructive behavior (Lovaas & Simmons, 1969), all in psychotic children.

In one such study Lovaas and his colleagues developed functional speech in two 6-year-old schizophrenic boys, Chuck and Billy (1966). At the beginning of training each boy's language was confined to an occasional vowel sound that had no apparent communication value. Both boys were withdrawn, spent much of their time rocking and twirling, and had temper tantrums when they were forced into social contacts.

Chuck and Billy were seen for treatment six days a week, seven hours a day, for twenty six-days; both received a short break from therapy once an hour. Rewards were small bites of the children's meals. Punishment—spanking and shouting—was delivered for failure to pay attention, for tantrums, and for self-destructive behavior. There were four steps in the training process:

Step 1. The child was rewarded for any vocalization. He was also rewarded for looking at the therapist's mouth.
Step 2. The therapist made a sound and the child was rewarded if he made any kind of vocal response to that sound within six seconds.
Step 3. The child's vocalization had to match (model) the adult's vocalization.
Step 4. New sounds were added. The child had to discriminate among the sounds and then correctly imitate them.

After twenty-six-days both children were learning new words at such a rapid pace that a new program, designed to teach them to use the words meaningfully rather than simply in imitation, was put into effect. After a slow and difficult beginning at this task, their learning accelerated until both boys could communicate their basic needs. Following treatment the two boys were returned to an institution. Without trained staff to provide continuing therapy, they lost some of their hard-won gains in speech. Nonetheless, Billy eventually made a marginal adjustment in a foster home, and at the time of the follow-up there was hope that Chuck's mother would take him home (Lovaas et al., 1973). These cases provide clear support for the necessity of continuing treatment if behavioral techniques are to have more than a fleeting impact upon a severely disturbed child.

Several behavioral techniques have also been developed to treat phobias in children. *Emotive imagery* is considered by its originator, Arnold Lazarus, to be most appropriate for children who cannot learn to relax. The principle is the same as that of systematic desensitization (Chapter 10): the child cannot feel anxious and relaxed at the same time. In emotive imagery therapy the patient is asked to construct an elaborate fantasy involving a favorite hero, activity, or ambition. Thoughts about the feared stimulus object are then woven into the fantasy.

For example, Lazarus and Abromovitz used emotive imagery to treat a 14-year-old boy who was intensely afraid of dogs (1962). Since the boy had a passionate desire to race an Alfa Romeo in the Indianapolis 500, he was asked to imagine scenes involving his sports car. Each scene was described in vivid detail by his therapist, who then casually introduced a dog into the picture. The boy imagined himself "in the pit" at Indianapolis, spotting a dog from a distance, watching the dog approach, finally seeing the dog next to the car. As the dog came progressively closer, the boy was able to experience the image without serious anxiety because he was also imagining the car, the pit, and the reinforcing sensations associated with being in the 500 race. This successful use of more powerful competing stimuli to inhibit anxiety ultimately permitted the boy to approach and then touch live dogs without feeling his former anxiety. Lazarus and Abromovitz used emotive imagery therapy with nine phobic children aged 7 to 14 and reported complete recovery for seven of the children in an average of 3.3 therapy sessions (1962).

Modeling has also become an important behavioral approach to the treatment of phobias in children within the past several years. One study by Bandura and his colleagues, whose use of modeling in therapy for adult phobic behavior was reviewed in Chapter 10, evaluated the treatment of dog phobia in children by modeling and other behavioral techniques (1967). Members of a group of preschool children who were afraid of dogs were assigned randomly to one of four treatment conditions. The first group, the *modeling-positive context* group, observed another child play with a dog in a "party-like" atmosphere. The second group, *modeling-neutral con-*text, saw the same model play with the same dog, but not in the party atmosphere. The third group of children, those in the *exposure-positive context* group, went to parties with the dog present, but they saw no fearless model interacting with the animal. The fourth group, *positive context*, went to parties where no dog was present. This final group was a control to ensure that simple "good times" would not by themselves reduce the fear. Bandura reported that the two groups who had observed another child play with the dog showed a stable decrease in their fear of dogs. The positive-context conditions, by contrast, failed to have an influence on fear greater than the neutral context, thus demonstrating that the model was the important part of the therapy.

So far, not much controlled research on behavior therapy with children in outpatient clinics has been reported. Case studies involving one child as his own control have reported success with behavioral techniques, but this design permits only a limited test of efficacy. There was one recent controlled study comparing reciprocal inhibition and play therapy in the reduction of children's phobias (Miller et al., 1972b). Both techniques proved equally effective with the sixty-seven young children who were the subjects. In another study that contrasted the effectiveness of operant conditioning and play therapy in altering the "schizophrenic behavior" of a group of schizophrenic boys, operant conditioning techniques were found to be more effective (Ney et al., 1971).

Institutional treatment

Some forms of psychopathology are so difficult to handle within the child's own home and community that it becomes necessary to place him or her in a special institution to continue proper care.

Residential psychoanalytic treatment. One of the pioneer figures in the residential psychoanalytic treatment of severely disturbed children is Bruno Bettelheim. Recognizing that the autistic or schizophrenic child is unable to adapt to his environment, Bettelheim suggests allowing the child to create a therapeutic environment of his own in which he can finally feel comfortable. The adults who work in the Chicago school organized by Bettelheim respond to the needs of the child, rather than insisting that he conform to their notions of appropriate behavior. The long-range goal, of course, is to help the child reach the point where he can comfortably accept the demands and rewards of a normal environment. This goal cannot be reached, Bettelheim contends, by forcing the child into a pattern for which he is not ready. It is Bettelheim's expectation that when the child realizes that the adults who give him loving care truly accept his world rather than demanding that he share theirs, he will gradually become able to look at and accept the realities of the external environment.

This form of treatment requires infinite patience and acceptance. The child who is fearful of bowel movements, for example, may be allowed to eliminate into the bathtub and play with his floating feces. Such activities, repulsive to the untrained adult, come to be accepted and understood by the therapists at Bettelheim's school. The goal is not to have a child who smears feces, but a child who is comfortable with his body and can consequently grow beyond this form of exploration.

Inside or outside the Bettelheim model, the psychoanalytic therapist who works with a disturbed child must be aware of his own needs so that they will not conflict with the disparate needs of the patient. The child will use the therapist as he begins to explore his world. He will touch, look, cuddle, urinate upon, bite, and fondle his therapist's body as he awakens to the world around him. The therapist must be sensitive enough to help the child understand these events and free enough to accept them in the child. A therapist who cannot accept them will, like the child's mother, be punishing some of the very activities which are vital to the child's normal growth and development.

How effective are Bettelheim's methods?

According to his report, results were excellent with 42 percent of a group of forty children (1967). Many of them were able to adjust to society to the point of holding jobs or going on to high school and college. These statistics, admittedly impressive in a field with more failures than successes, have been criticized because of questions about the severity of the initial disorders and the measures of change which were used to assess outcomes. Few other clinicians have been able to replicate Bettelheim's remarkable results with unequivocally psychotic children. At present it is difficult to know which components of his therapy actually cause change in the child's behavior. For example, the constant interpersonal and verbal contact which the child experiences within the intimacy of the school may be more important than other factors that Bettelheim views as significant. Until more objective pre- and posttreatment studies with adequate measurements are used, his treatment approach remains within the realm of the untested.

Token economies. Clinicians have also attempted to treat severely disturbed behaviors within institutional settings that employ techniques based upon learning-theory principles. For example, institutions for antisocial youths have begun to use token economies in which the children must earn tokens in order to buy things they want, like a comfortable bed instead of a cot, or a private room instead of a dormitory room.

Phillips and his associates report on a successful token economy at Achievement Place, their school in Kansas for young delinquent boys whom the courts have ruled are in danger of becoming habitual lawbreakers (1971). At Achievement Place the boys are consistently reinforced for appropriate behavior and punished for inappropriate acts. They carry small cards indicating the number of points they have accumulated. Token rewards are given for such behaviors as going to bed on time, arriving on time at school, cleaning their rooms, and saving allowance money. Tokens are deducted for antisocial behaviors (including fighting, swearing, truancy from school) like those which originally brought the boys to Achievement Place. The boys function under a semi-self-government arrangement which permits them to make many of their own rules, but also sets limits on their autonomy that research has shown are necessary (Fixen et al., 1973). Five years of research at Achievement Place demonstrates the value of this kind of "halfway" house for delinquent youth, built on behavioral principles designed to make explicit the consequences for both wanted and unwanted behavior.

Early detection and treatment

It is much better to prevent psychological problems than to treat them once they arise. Mental health workers have endorsed the ideal of prevention, early detection, and early treatment for a long time, and today more and more of them are taking steps to implement this goal.

A good example of a program focused on early detection and treatment is the work being done in Rochester, New York, by Zax, Cowen, and their colleagues (1969). These psychologists have two aims: first, to identify as early as possible the children who are most likely to become troubled, and second, to provide treatment for them in the beginning stages of their disorders. Consistent with the community mental health model, Zax and Cowen's team did not wait for the children and their parents to show up at a clinic. Instead, they went to a public school—the best possible place for studying large numbers of children. The particular school Zax and Cowen selected for their early research was "in a somewhat deteriorating neighborhood. Except for an underweighting with respect to Negro and Jewish children, its ethnic composition closely reflected the city of Rochester at large. Although a modest range of socioeconomic levels was represented, children came predominately from 'upper-lower' SES families" (p. 72).

A number of evaluative measures were obtained from each first-grade child: school grades, achievement test scores, attendance records, intelligence test scores, and several measures of self-concepts. In addition, the child's teacher, the school psychologist, and the research team's school social worker all made ratings of the child's adjustment. The social worker interviewed each child's mother concerning his health, eating, sleeping, toilet habits, and relations with family and peers. The social worker also asked mothers about parental attitudes toward various child-rearing issues.

After all these data had been gathered, the psychologist and the social worker made a joint decision about each child, attempting to identify children they felt were vulnerable to later emotional dysfunction. Their judgments were recorded but not revealed to anyone at the school, to avoid the possibility of self-fulfilling prophecy in which teachers might see trouble in a child because it had been predicted. All children were followed up through the years in an effort to determine the validity of the early predictions. The data gathered in the follow-ups provide support for the view that incipient emotional problems can be detected early in a child's school career.

Early detection is only half of this complex problem; prevention is the other half. Zax and Cowen have also developed a prevention program operated by teacher's aides and college student companions, who consult with school psychologists, school social workers, and teachers to identify and then work with children who are potentially disturbed. In a two- to five-year follow-up of thirty-six children who participated in the program, Cowan and his colleagues reported that the children, all "high-risk" youngsters, showed enduring positive changes which appeared to stem largely from their therapeutic contacts (1972).

If early detection of psychological problems in grade school children is good, early detection of vulnerability to disability in preschool children and infants ought to be better. For this reason a number of researchers are exploring means of testing newborn infants and very young children for early signs of developmental disabilities (Hellmuth, 1971). Many hospitals now make the Apgar ratings of newborn infants, developed by the pediatrician Virginia Apgar. The ratings deal with the infant's appearance, pulse, grimace, activity, and respiration. Each characteristic is graded on a ten-point scale by a nurse just after birth. The ratings permit prediction of future physical health as well as research into relationships between physical health at birth and later emotional functioning. Such research contributes to our knowledge of the influence that physical factors have on psychopathology. For example, although learning will affect the ways in which a physically defective child handles his deficits, he is handicapped at the start in interactions with the world.

The main hope of this movement, of course, is that early detection will be followed by development of effective early treatment methods. Thus if it turns out that hyperactive children do suffer from a congenital brain defect, as some data suggest (Waldrop & Halverson, 1971), then early detection might have a significant effect on the course of the disorder by changing the attitudes of both parents and child toward his behavior. Certainly everyone concerned would recognize that the child's hyperactivity was not the result of bad behavior but of physical defect.

In another instance of early detection applied to early treatment planning, Fish identified developmental abnormalities in children who were later diagnosed as childhood schizophrenics (1971). The abnormalities, taken together, suggested that these children cannot adequately integrate central nervous system functioning during infancy. Fish concluded that maternal care and the home environment can either intensify the disorder or compensate for it, depending upon the mother's approach to the child's disability and its severity. It is hoped that if such children can be identified early, their parents can be helped to provide the kind of environment which will prevent, postpone, or lessen the intensity of the disorder.

A child advocacy system

One step toward assuring the availability of mental health services for all children, regardless of socioeconomic class, was taken in 1971. Acting upon the recommendation of the Joint Commission on Mental Health of Children, President Nixon established a National Center for Child Advocacy. This center, a part of the Children's Bureau, provides information about the needs of children and coordinates services for children on state and local levels. One of its divisions, the Children's Concern Center, answers questions from anywhere in the United States about particular child problems.

What is child advocacy? Unfortunately, children are legal nonpeople: they are the property of their parents and cannot act to protect their own rights. The child advocate may be a parent, judge, doctor, minister, or any other member of the community who acts in the interests of a child. The advocate may plead for better physical, emotional, or educational care for a single child—or for millions of children. The fortunate child's best advocates are his parents. Other children, less fortunate, may need advocacy services from someone else in the community who is in a better financial, educational, or political position than his parents to provide protection.

The goal of a nationwide advocacy system, although not yet fulfilled, is not a hollow ideal. In addition to the coordination and informa-

(Bacchus/DPI)

tion services provided by the federal government, states from Alaska to West Virginia have been establishing local programs to provide adequate child representation.   Though it would be unrealistic to believe that an effort of this sort by the federal government will instantly correct ages-old abuses to children, a start has been made.

Summary

Serious consideration of psychological disorders in childhood is a recent phenomenon.   Earlier societies, preoccupied with survival, had little time to concern themselves with the psychological welfare of their young.   Only with the affluence of the twentieth century have we been able to afford this kind of sensitivity to our children's needs.

Behavioral deviations are more difficult to recognize in children than in adults, partly because children are in a state of change and development.   How does one identify the child who needs help? To begin with, it is important to be sensitive to the age-appropriateness of the child's behavior.   One must also be alert to the number and frequency of problems, the persistence of the problems, the extent to which they hamper the child's functioning, and the degree to which they make the child unhappy.

There have been several major attempts to categorize the behavioral deviations of childhood.   In DSM II the American Psychiatric Association has provided a seven-part system.   The Group for the Advancement of Psychiatry (GAP) has devised a more elaborate classification with over sixty categories and subcategories.   Both of these systems have been criticized because they fail to use one consistent classification principle.   Because diagnostic systems, unsatisfactory as they are for adult disorders, are even weaker in the area of child psychopathology, most clinicians do not use a diagnosis with children or else apply the vague term "adjustment reaction" to all their child patients.

This chapter categorized disorders by distinguishing between those for which we can make some meaningful statement about etiology and those for which the etiology remains obscure.   For example, enuresis (bed-wetting) is a disorder which can be explained relatively well within a learning-theory framework.   The neurotic behaviors of childhood also fall into the category of behaviors which are fairly well accounted for by learning theory.   Although the childhood neuroses resemble the adult neurosis in appearance, there are significant differences.   Normal children often exhibit many "neurotic" behaviors as transient features of their development.   One fairly common childhood neurosis is school phobia, in which the child, like Matt R., becomes anxious about going to school. Conduct disorders—acts against other people or things—appear to be motivated more by external rewards than by the anxiety reduction which is a factor in the neuroses.

Under the heading of behavioral deviations of unknown etiology, we include the severe deviations of childhood, such as infantile autism (Roger G., for example), childhood schizophrenia, and the nebulous but sometimes useful concept of minimal brain damage.

Some of the behavioral deviations of childhood predict later adjustment, while others do not. Many normal children have a variety of problems, including bed-wetting, bad dreams, and tantrums, but these behaviors generally diminish over time. The neurotic behaviors of childhood also generally appear unrelated to problems of adulthood. However, antisocial behavior in childhood does seem to be predictive of difficulties as an adult.

The treatment of childhood deviations is complicated by children's general lack of motivation for and understanding of treatment. Nevertheless, a variety of treatment procedures have been developed both from the psychoanalytic and from the behavioral models. Behavior modification procedures, in particular, appear to have substantial experimental support for their efficacy. Recent research on preventive care suggests that many childhood problems can be identified and treated before they grow into difficulties of major proportion.

CHAPTER SIXTEEN
Mental Retardation

Ralph J. ● Jonathan W. ● History ● Heredity, environment, and mental retardation ● Classification ● Treatment

RALPH J.:
GROWING UP
IN WATTS

Ralph J. is a 7-year-old black boy who has lived all his life in Watts, the black ghetto of Los Angeles. Ralph came to the attention of his school psychologist after referrals from both his first- and second-grade teachers. Both complained that he seemed unable to grasp the material being presented in class. The boy was tested with the Stanford-Binet, an individual intelligence test, after he was referred by his second-grade teacher. He made an IQ score of 67, placing him in the "mildly retarded" category of intelligence.

The psychologist who tested Ralph commented that the child had been quiet and cooperative during testing and that he had given up easily when confronted by more difficult tasks on the test. Ralph's teachers said that his history of poor schoolwork and his low IQ seemed inconsistent with his adequate social adjustment and his ability to cope with the challenges of Watts street life. Living in Watts is not easy. Ralph has to be quick with his hands and quick on his feet. He fights well with strangers and peers, runs fast when he's outnumbered. He knows and avoids a number of narcotic addicts who wouldn't hesitate to beat up a kid for a nickel or dime toward their next fix.

The school social worker talked with Mrs. J., Ralph's mother, and learned that he was the third of five surviving children. An older brother had died at the age of 9 by drowning, and a younger sister had died in infancy from lead poisoning. Lead-based paint continues to peel from the walls of the J. apartment, an enduring threat to any toddler in the household. Ralph's oldest brother, Johnny, has been in trouble with the police since he took part in the 1965 Watts race riots. Shortly after the riots Johnny dropped out of school, became addicted to heroin, was arrested for assaulting a police officer, and is now serving an indefinite term in a California correctional institution for young offenders. Ralph's older sister Jennie, a sweet, gentle girl of 14, helps her mother care for the younger children.

(Joel Gordon)

467

School records reveal that Jennie, like Ralph, has an IQ in the middle 60s. Ralph's mother is a weary-looking woman, old beyond her years, who feels that she no longer knows how to cope with the needs of her family.

Ralph's father left the family just after the riots, in which he too participated. He is still wanted by the police for his part in the attempted shooting of a National Guardsman. Ralph has not seen him since Mr. J. visited home briefly about a year after the riots. But Ralph remembers vividly that his father, who drank heavily, would often beat his mother and any of the children who were foolish enough to get in his way. The J.'s are currently supported by welfare.

Although his mother did not seek prenatal care until her seventh month of pregnancy, Ralph's birth was uneventful. He was a small baby, though he appeared healthy, with good motor development and coordination. His older brother died when Ralph was 3 months old, and for nearly a year afterwards Mrs. J. was too depressed to provide more than minimal care for the surviving children. Ralph often lay wet and hungry in his crib for several hours before anyone attended to him.

If Ralph has heard one command during his childhood it has been to show respect and keep a civil tongue. There is little room for questioning or curiosity in his home. Discipline, although often unpredictable, is harsh.

JONATHAN W: A CHILD OF MIDDLE AGE

Mr. and Mrs. W. had been married for approximately twelve years before they had their first child, a boy whom they named Jonathan. Mr. W. was a printer, and Mrs. W. worked as a secretary at the local high school until the third month of her pregnancy. Both had been in their middle twenties when they married—two mature people who had entered marriage with self-awareness and a realistic view of each other. And it was a good marriage; the one flaw was their inability to conceive a child. After a few years they went to a doctor for tests, which indicated that while Mr. W. was not sterile, he did have a low sperm count.

Ultimately the W.'s gave up hope of having a child and stopped bothering with birth control. Then, just before her thirty-eighth birthday, Mrs. W. discovered that she was pregnant. Both of them were ecstatic. Although they had stopped talking about children of their own, neither had given up the dream.

Mrs. W.'s pregnancy was smooth and uneventful. She followed her obstetrician's directions to the letter. She took vitamins, drank

(National Association for
Retarded Children)

milk, watched her weight, and got the right amount of exercise. She was in excellent health. Their son was a full-term baby born after an easy three-hour period of labor. But he was a Mongoloid.

It took a while for Mrs. and Mrs. W. to take it in. Then they both felt guilty because they had not asked for the test of amniotic fluid which would have revealed the baby's genetic defect before birth. But they also knew how depressed they would have felt about an abortion after the years of struggle to conceive. They met with their pediatrician several times to sort out their feelings about having a retarded child. He pointed out that while it was impossible to measure Jonathan's IQ so soon after birth, they could expect him to have an ultimate IQ in the 30s or 40s. They were, he said, fortunate that the baby had not been born with any of the serious physical difficulties, such as heart defects, which are so common among these children. He also told them that Mongoloid children are often very friendly and affectionate, a fact which gave them little comfort at the time.

Gradually over the next several months, the W.'s overcame their depression and began to understand the meaning of their son's retardation. It did help that Jonathan was a lovable, cuddly baby; even though they were disappointed by his disability, they could respond to him with affection. As they began to learn more about Mongolism, they realized that what they did for him would have a significant influence upon his development. They were determined to offer Jonathan every possible opportunity, without pushing him beyond his limits or setting goals which were too high for him.

When the baby was about 6 months old his parents joined a local group of parents of retarded children. It was there that they found out about an interesting research project at a nearby university. The psychology department had a preschool center for retarded children which was designed to facilitate their speech and social development and instruct parents in behavioral training techniques.

The W.'s enrolled in a parents' training group at the university shortly before Jonathan's first birthday. They were taught the basic principles of behavior modification and learned how to observe and record important components of their son's behavior. First they decided to try and increase the amount of time that the baby spent looking at them in order to condition him to pay attention to them. They began watching him for half an hour each day while he played with first one parent and then the other. When Mrs. W. was playing with him, Mr. W. would record the number of times that Jonathan looked at his mother's face. Then the father would play with the boy while the mother kept the record. This procedure gave them a baseline for assessing any subsequent changes in their son's behavior. Next they began trying to increase the time that he spent looking at his parents. For every second that he focused on his mother or his father's face, he was given a small amount of his favorite baby food. Then he had to look at his parents' face for progressively longer periods—ultimately for ten seconds—before he received the food. The W.'s found that there was a remarkable increase in the frequency with which the baby looked at them. Probably because he saw their pleasure in his accomplishment, he continued his new behavior even after they discontinued food reinforcement for it.

The parents' next project was to increase Jonathan's vocalizing. They began again by collecting baseline data, this time on the frequency of his spontaneous babbling. Then they began to reward him with bits of food, hugs, and praise whenever he made any kind of sound. Jonathan's rate of vocalization increased markedly with this technique. The psychologist who worked with the W.'s told them not to expect actual speech for a long while, but to continue to reward the child simply for looking at them and making sounds. The process of shaping those sounds into words and those glances into social intercourse would be a gradual one.

At the age of 4 Jonathan was ready for the university's preschool program. Thanks to the training his parents had given him at home, he was toilet-trained and able to say a few words. The time the W.'s had invested was paying off for him. Emphasis in the preschool sessions was upon teaching the children basic skills like playing together, following simple commands, learning new words, feeding themselves, and dressing themselves. These were taught through behavior-modification techniques. Each child had an undergraduate tutor who spent time every day working with him on special skills.

(National Association for Retarded Children)

470

For example, Jonathan's tutor taught him to put on his zipper jacket by breaking the operation down into small steps. First the tutor helped the boy into his jacket and did everything necessary but zip it up for him. Then he took Jonathan's hand and guided him in the zipping motion. Gradually the tutor gave him less and less guidance in zipping until Jonathan was able to do it on his own. Once the child had learned to zip the jacket, the tutor went back one step and had him insert his arm in the sleeve of the coat. Again the tutor provided guidance at first and then slowly faded out. After about three weeks Jonathan was able to put the jacket on alone. Each step had been accompanied by praise, hugs, and bits of sugar-coated cereal. He had learned a complex task without experiencing frustration or failure. Repeated success would teach him that he was capable of learning new tasks and that learning is fun. By the same process he gradually learned such skills as eating with a fork, holding a crayon, using new words, and discriminating colors.

Jonathan is a retarded child. He will never function in all the ways that a normal child will. Certain complex cognitive and motor skills such as algebra or driving a car will remain beyond his capacity, no matter how hard he should work to acquire them or how patient his tutors might be. But given the appropriate kinds of instruction, Jonathan can be trained to do many more things than was once thought possible. When he grows up he will probably be able to function in a semi-independent fashion. He should have the skills to look after his own toileting, washing, eating, and dressing. He should be able to get around in his neighborhood and make small purchases in a familiar store. Even if he needs to be institutionalized after his parents' death, he will be capable of doing simple jobs within the institution, such as folding laundry, washing vegetables, or mowing the lawn. Or he may be able to live in a halfway house and work in a sheltered workshop.

Without the training that his parents have provided for him, Jonathan would probably have become a totally dependent person. He might not have been able to talk, to go to the toilet by himself, or feed himself. While Jonathan will not develop the skills required to take a trip by himself, make major purchases, hold a complex job, or supervise other people's activities, he need not end up as one of hundreds of residents in a hopeless institution for the retarded.

On the determinants of intelligence

This chapter focuses upon an area of abnormal psychological development which was once regarded only with despair: mental retardation. The very term conjures up images of dark, foul-smelling rooms with dozens of half-naked inmates rocking, masturbating, and screaming, oblivious to the world around them.

The term *mental retardation* actually covers a variety of disorders and a wide range of intellectual functioning. Mental retardation may be environmental, genetic, infectious, or physically traumatic in origin. The retarded person may hold a job, have social contacts, and live in his own apartment—or he may lie on a bed in the ward of a state institution and be unable to bring a spoon to his mouth or sit on a toilet.

Cultural-familial mental retardation is the most common form of retardation in this country. It is not related to any obvious physical defect and typically occurs in more than one family member. Ralph J., the young boy described at the beginning of the chapter, comes from a family where mild mental retardation is common. His childhood raises a series of questions. Is he retarded because the genetic material he received from his parents gave him only limited intellectual potential? Is he retarded because he has grown up in poverty and has had little opportunity for books, conversation, and wide exposure to ideas? Is he retarded because his mother, depressed over the death of his brother, was unable to give him adequate care during infancy? We will attempt to explore the causes of cultural-familial retardation as well as to examine some of the more controversial issues swirling around the disorder.

This chapter also considers other aspects of mental retardation. Although cultural-familial retardation is most common, a wide variety of other forms are caused by specific, identifiable physical defects. The case of Jonathan W. illustrates one kind of genetically based retardation: Mongolism. His case further illustrates the fact that even though a child may be born with retardation caused by genetic defect, the environment to which he is exposed determines how he utilizes his remaining potential. Simply to label a child as Mongoloid and conclude that he cannot learn is to deny him the chance to become a productive person. The story of Jonathan W. gives the lie to the old view that the mentally retarded person must forever be society's burden.

Historical perspectives

Mentally retarded people, like psychotics, have always been with us, though there are fewer historical references to retardation than to psychosis. One reason may be that in less complex societies than ours a person could function adequately with less intellectual ability than Western society now demands. People who would be identified today as mentally deficient were once satisfactory farm or household workers. In those days, perhaps only the most severely retarded were recognized as such. And many of them probably died young from the physical defects which often accompany serious mental retardation.

Cretinism, a particularly dramatic kind of retardation because it is marked by a dwarfed body and an enlarged, misshapen head, was mentioned as early as 1220. It was thought that the disorder occurred especially among people living in the Alps. The physical changes associated with cretinism led some people to speculate that cretins might represent a separate race. But in the late nineteenth century a British physician named William Gull identified a thyroid disorder in adults called *myxedema* which was strikingly similar to cretinism. The step from this discovery to the realization that cretinism comes from a thyroid deficiency followed quickly. Cretinism became the first of a number of physically based forms of mental retardation to be recognized in the nineteenth century. Some others were tuberous sclerosis, Tay-Sachs disease, and Mongolism.

The history of treatment approaches to retardation is best begun with the "wild boy of Averon," a child of 11 or 12 who was found wandering in the woods of France shortly after the French Revolution. He was believed to have been abandoned in infancy and then raised by wild animals. His severe retardation was seen as an inevitable consequence of his total lack of social contact. Shortly after the boy was found, the scientist Jean Itard undertook his education, with the consent of the French government. After five years Itard gave up in failure; the boy's behavior remained primitive and undisciplined, and he had learned only a few words. In retrospect the boy's education seems more of a success than a failure. Although he had not learned to speak, he had learned a great variety of new social behaviors. One of Itard's students, Edouard Seguin, was convinced that other retarded individuals could learn as much if they were given the right kind of intensive educational experience. Seguin became a major influence behind the nineteenth-century movement for special schools for the retarded in the United States (Cranefield, 1966).

During the early part of the twentieth century, the eugenics movement began to influence what had become relatively enlightened views on retardation. Eugenics, the science of improving heredity by controlled breeding, provided an appealing solution to one of mankind's most troublesome problems. If mental retardation is inherited, enthusiasts reasoned, then the best solution is to prevent the retarded from reproducing. Although it was recognized by more thoughtful leaders in the field that sterilization was not the final solution to retardation (Goddard, 1913), others grasped at eugenics as a simple and "foolproof" way to relieve society of its burdensome responsibility for the retarded.

Two evil consequences came of this approach to defective human beings. The first, of course, was Nazi Germany's terrible "final solution" to the problem of the retarded, the aged, and the psychotic as well as to the problem of German animosity toward the Jews and the Slavs. Their means of solution was murder; their crime was mankind's most momentous. Another negative consequence of the eugenics movement was a decline in concern for special education for the retarded. It was argued that since retardation might ultimately be eliminated by controlling reproduction among retarded persons, there is nothing to be gained by educating them. As a result, in the early 1900s retarded persons were put into custodial institutions and forgotten. Only recently have they been rediscovered. Cranefield, commenting on this period in the history of mental retardation, writes, "Seldom in the history of medicine have so many intelligent and well-meaning men embarked on so vicious and brutal a program with so little scientific foundation for their actions" (1966, p. 13).

Heredity, environment, and mental retardation

Defining mental retardation

According to the *Diagnostic and Statistical Manual* (1968), mental retardation is "subnormal general intellectual functioning which originates during the developmental period and is associated with impairment of either learning and social adjustment or maturation, or both" (p. 15). On the basis of IQ the retarded can be divided into the five categories shown in Table 16-1.

Over the years a variety of different definitions of mental retardation have been proposed. Since the definition of intelligence itself has long been in dispute, it is hardly surprising that there is also disagreement about the meaning of intellectual deficit (Robinson & Robinson, 1965). For the severely or profoundly retarded child, who is likely to be deficient in almost every area of development,

TABLE 16-1 CATEGORIES OF RETARDATION ON STANDARD IQ TESTS

Category	Stanford-Binet IQ	Wechsler IQ
Borderline	68–83	70–84
Mild	52–67	55–69
Moderate	36–51	40–54
Severe	20–35	25–39
Profound	under 20	under 25

it is not terribly important whether his retardation is defined in terms of impaired learning, inability to handle his own affairs, or incapacity to think abstractly. But the definition may be very important in the case of a child of borderline intelligence. Such children, like normal children, vary in the skills commonly included under the general heading of intelligence. Some mildly retarded children (like Ralph J., for example) have good social skills but impaired academic performance; others who can read well may not be able to hold a job. So if retardation is seen as the lack of ability to manage one's own affairs, it will define a different group of people than it will if it is viewed more narrowly as the inability to meet minimal academic standards. Recognizing the importance of this issue, the American Association on Mental Deficiency (AAMD) designed a diagnostic classification system for retardation to be used by professionals who are approaching retardation from different perspectives (Heber, 1959, 1961). The diagnostic system given in DSM II was derived from the more extensive AAMD system.

Several terms appear often in discussions of intelligence. To begin with, intelligence is said to occur in the general population in a

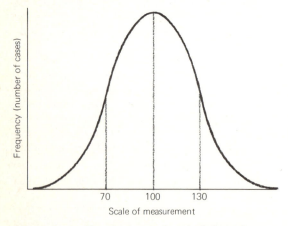

Figure 16-1. The ideal normal, or bell-shaped, curve. This curve describes the distribution of such characteristics as height, weight, and intelligence in the general population. It means simply that most people are in the middle of the distribution; few are at the extremes.

normal fashion—as a *bell-shaped* curve (Figure 16-1). This is the same kind of curve which describes the distribution of height and weight. It means, simply, that most people fall toward the middle of the distribution (they are "average in height, weight, and intelligence) and that relatively few people fall at the extremes (below 60 or above 77 inches, below 100 pounds or above 250, below an IQ of 70 or above an IQ of 130).

DSM II employs the term *subnormal* to refer specifically to IQ performance which falls 1 or more standard deviations below the population mean of 100 on the normal intelligence curve. *Standard deviation* is a statistical term referring to the spread of scores around the mean. In a normal distribution, 68 percent of the scores fall within 1 standard deviation of the mean, an additional 28 percent within 2 standard deviations, and another 3 percent within 3 standard deviations of the mean. See any statistics text for a discussion of this concept.

For diagnostic purposes, intelligence is almost always measured by giving the person an individual intelligence test. The intelligence tests most often used are the Stanford-Binet, the Wechsler Intelligence Scale for Children (WISC), and the Wechsler Adult Intelligence Scale (WAIS). All these tests are administered by one tester to one subject. Each test contains tasks designed to tap a variety of abilities, including short-term memory, vocabulary, abstract reasoning, general information, spatial reasoning, and practical judgment. Performance on the tasks yields a score which is then compared with scores made by a *normative sample*—a large group of people in the subject's age range who took the test while it was being developed. Mental retardation can be defined as performing significantly less well than people of the same age on an IQ test. On the Stanford-Binet, which has a standard deviation of 16, mental retardation is defined as an IQ below 68 (100 − 32 = 68, or 2 standard deviations below the test's mean). For the Wechsler tests of intelligence, which have a standard deviation of 15, mental retardation is an IQ below 70 (100 − 30 = 70).

Retardation, as DSM II uses the term, refers

to subnormal intellectual functioning which originates during the *developmental period.* While this period cannot be precisely defined, it is usually taken to mean the time from birth to the age of 16 (Robinson & Robinson, 1965). Most retarded people are either born retarded or become so at birth or during infancy. Another important component of the "official" definition of retardation is that the person's subnormal intellectual functioning must be reflected in *learning and social adjustment, or maturation, or both.* This means that the child who simply has a low IQ cannot be labeled retarded unless he also shows a deficiency in learning, in social adjustment, or in the maturation of his self-help and motor skills during infancy and childhood.

Classification of mental retardation

Retarded people have been classified in a number of ways. They have been grouped, for example, according to *the severity of their intellectual deficit.* This system depends upon accurate measurement of either IQ level or capacity to learn. Educators using the system refer to retarded persons as *educable* (IQ of 50 to 75), *trainable* (IQ of 25 to 49), or *custodial* (IQ below 25). A similar system, once popular but now obsolete, grouped the retarded as *idiot, imbecile,* and *moron.* Popular usage has debased these terms into meaningless insults. Alternatively, the retarded may be grouped according to their *physical stigmata, regardless of etiology.* All children whose retardation manifests itself in the physical symptoms of cretinism, for example, whether these come from genetic causes, a critical lack of iodine during gestation, or later thyroid damage, would be grouped together. Finally, the retarded have also been categorized by *etiologic* agent. In this classification system a distinction is sometimes made between the mentally retarded and the mentally deficient: Retarded persons are simply at the lower end of the normal distribution of intelligence, while the mentally deficient are persons whose retardation derives from organic causes.

The most common system for categorizing mentally retarded people is a variant of the etiologic classification system. It divides them into those whose retardation is the result of *cultural-familial factors* and those who are retarded because of *organic factors.*

Cultural-familial retardation

Cultural-familial retardates are those for whom no physiological basis can be identified. They often come from families like Ralph J.'s, in which other family members are also retarded. Retardation in such families presents diagnostic problems, since it may have both environmental and hereditary bases. The extent to which environment and heredity influence intellectual performance is a highly controversial issue which this chapter will explore.

Since mental retardation is usually defined as approximately 2 standard deviations below the average IQ of 100, the tendency has developed among some professionals to think that every one who falls below this arbitrary cutoff belongs to one big diagnostic group. Thus they lump all retarded people together, despite the tremendous variability there is in learning potential, capacity for independent existence, and physical condition in the retarded population. Psychologist Edward Zigler calls their attitude the "defect" orientation toward mental retardation (1967).

While it is certainly true that a number of retarded persons display obvious physical defects resulting from the genetic, infectious, or cerebral traumatic agents that caused their retardation, they are not in the majority of retardates. Zigler believes that it is important to distinguish between the cultural-familial retardates, who account for 75 percent of all retarded persons, and retardates who suffer from an associated physiological defect. Retardates whose IQs fall into the severe and profound categories (Stanford-Binet IQs below 36) are almost always victims of "physiological retardation," while cultural-familial retardates tend to have IQs in the borderline and mildly retarded categories (Stanford-Binet IQs above 50).

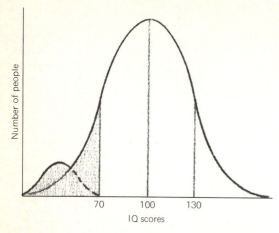

Figure 16-2. Distribution of intelligence test scores in the general population. Note that it departs from the "ideal" normal curve. The shaded areas show the range of scores that fall in the retarded group. More people than would be expected make scores below 50, which results in a "bump" in the curve. According to Zigler, this bump represents the group whose retardation is due to an organic defect. The much larger group of retarded people whose IQs are between 50 and 70 are cultural-familial retardates.

Support for this "two-group" approach to mental retardation comes from close examination of the distribution of intelligence test scores. When the scores are plotted on a graph they form a curve very like the ideal bell-shaped curve, with one striking difference. At the left-hand or lower end of the IQ continuum, in the area below the Stanford-Binet IQ level of 50, more persons than would be expected actually appear (see Figure 16-2). Zigler thinks that this "bump" in the actual distribution represents all the people who would have been much higher in the IQ distribution had it not been for a major physiological defect which interfered seriously with their intellectual development. Thus Zigler believes that there are two separate groups of retarded people: a small group whose low intelligence is the result of a physiological defect, and a much larger group with no obvious physiological defect whose low intelligence reflects normal variability in the distribution of IQ scores. It is these normal people of low intelligence who belong to the cultural-familial retardation group.

Physiological-organic retardation

The causes of cultural-familial retardation are very much open to question, but the etiology of retardation in the organic group is largely known. These are the persons who have suffered a physiological defect which prevented normal intellectual development.

Brain injury and mental retardation. Damage to the brain due to traumatic injury or to congenital or genetic defects sometimes results in mental retardation alone and sometimes in retardation accompanied by other symptoms of brain damage, such as loss of motor control and coordination, epileptic seizures or sensory losses.

Profoundly and severely retarded individuals often display physical abnormalities as well. These gross defects in body size or shape reflect the pervasive central nervous system damage these persons have sustained (Batchelor, 1969).

• CEREBRAL PALSY. This relatively common neurological disorder is often associated with some degree of mental retardation. The child with cerebral palsy shows motor symptoms ranging from clumsiness to total inability to voluntarily control muscular movement. Since cerebral palsy can arise from damage to many areas of the central nervous system, including the spinal cord, the exact kind of motor symptom shown depends upon the location and extent of the damage. It is difficult to test the intelligence of such children, because their motor and speech problems restrict their communication with the examiner. According to the best available evidence, it appears that approximately 75 percent of all cerebral palsied children have IQs below 90. And 50 percent of them probably have IQs below 70, in the retarded range (Heilbrun, 1956; Holden, 1956; Perlstein, 1955).

• EPILEPSY. While many epileptics have average or above-average intellectual ability, epilepsy exists among 10 to 15 percent of institutionalized retardates (Batchelor, 1969). The fact that epilepsy and mental retardation occur together does not explain the etiology of either condition. They may both result from the same brain injury, or the seizures may have caused damage to the brain, with subsequent retardation, or they may have interfered seriously with the child's learning by making school attendance difficult or impossible (Robinson & Robinson, 1965).

• MICROCEPHALY. This disorder, characterized by an abnormally small head circumference, is a major physical defect found in approximately 20 percent of severely retarded persons (Batchelor, 1969). It may result from a single recessive gene or it may derive from nongenetic prenatal causes, including maternal infection (Wesselhoeft, 1949) and birth injury (Heber, 1959). Plummer reports that microcephaly occurred in seven of eleven children whose mothers, during the first twenty weeks of their pregnancies, were within 1,200 meters of the center of the atomic blast at Hiroshima (1952). Microcephaly is frequently accompanied by other major physical defects such as epilepsy, cerebral palsy, and heart lesions.

• HYDROCEPHALY. The cranium is much larger than normal in hydrocephaly. The enlargement of the skull results from excessive reten-

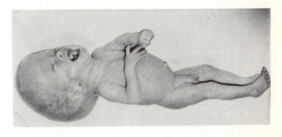

A marked case of hydrocephaly. This baby will almost certainly die before it reaches late childhood. *(Gamstorp, 1970)*

A microcephalic child whose small, pointed head is characteristic of this disorder. Like almost all such children, he is severely retarded. *(Gamstorp, 1970)*

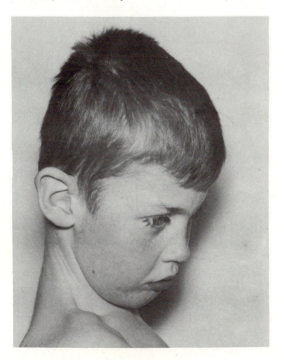

tion of cerebrospinal fluid, which is caused either by blockage of the canals which normally allow the flow of fluid from the skull to the spinal column or by an overproduction of the cerebrospinal fluid. In some cases surgery to relieve the pressure and provide proper drainage has proved useful (Giles & Rockett, 1971; Matson, 1956; Ransoheffet et al., 1960). Hydrocephaly may be accompanied by blindness, epilepsy, paralysis, and deafness.

Genetics and mental retardation. Although intelligence is probably determined by the interaction of a number of genes, there are a few instances where one dominant gene from a parent or a recessive gene from both parents may produce mental retardation.

• DOMINANT-GENE MENTAL RETARDATION. The inheritance of mental retardation through a *single dominant gene* is rare. Most people with the dominant-gene form of retardation are so severely retarded that they die during childhood and hence do not have children. Many such cases die before birth as badly defective fetuses. Two notable exceptions to this general role are tuberous sclerosis and Huntington's chorea.

Tuberous sclerosis, also known as epiloia, can be severe or mild. In its most dramatic form the first observable symptom is mental retardation. Later come characteristic physical cues including a butterfly-shaped rash on the cheeks, tumors of the internal organs, and small hardened areas in the cortex. The patient may also be epileptic. Mental retardation in epiloia is frequently degenerative: the patient grows worse with age. The development of tumors and of severe convulsions often leads to an early death. But not everyone who inherits the dominant gene for tuberous sclerosis exhibits these marked symptoms. Many victims of the disorder have milder symptomatology and normal intellectual ability, with the result that they are likely to marry and pass this destructive disorder on to their children.

Huntington's chorea is also transmitted through a dominant gene. Unfortunately, the symptoms do not usually appear until middle age, well after most victims have already married, had children, and achieved a portion of life's goals. The disease is an especially virulent one, marked by sensory, motor, and cognitive impairments that rapidly and inexorably progress to psychosis, then dementia, and only then death.

Genetic counseling for families in which one or more members have had tuberous sclerosis or Huntington's chorea could prevent much grief. The 50 percent probability of transmitting the dominant gene to one's children should lead many people to consider other alternatives to reproduction (Leonard et al., 1972).

● RECESSIVE-GENE MENTAL RETARDATION.

Forms of retardation caused by recessive genes are more common than dominant-gene disorders. In recessive-gene retardation the child receives a defective recessive gene from each parent. If one parent has the defective

gene but the other does not, the child will not be retarded—although he may acquire a recessive gene which he can then transmit to his own offspring. The chances for retardation under this genetic condition are only 1 in 4, as contrasted with 1 in 2 chances in the case of the dominant-gene defect. Still, a 1 in 4 risk is greater than many parents would willingly take. Genetic counseling is again advisable for parents who may be carriers of recessive genes for mental retardation.

Phenylketonuria (PKU) is a form of retardation caused by a recessive gene. The condition was discovered in 1934 by a Norwegian biochemist, Folling, who was struck by the musty odor of the urine of two young defective brothers he was studying. This characteristic of their urine led to a great deal of biochemical research that ultimately revealed a disease caused by the inadequate metabolic transformation of *phenylalanine.* Once this metabolic defect was discovered, it became possible to prevent the syndrome by utilizing a special diet low in phenylalanine.

PKU can be diagnosed easily during the first few weeks of life by a blood or urine test. The urine test has come into widespread use in many areas as a required screening device. Once the PKU child is identified, he is placed on the special diet which prevents the development of retardation. Ironically, when this treatment was first introduced, the diet itself created retardation in the PKU children by causing malnutrition (Hanley et al., 1970). The problem is now prevented by using a more carefully balanced diet.

Amaurotic familial idiocy is another form of retardation transmitted by a recessive gene. One variation, *Tay-Sachs disease,* is much more prevalent among Jewish than non-Jewish families (Aronson et al., 1960). Although he appears normal at birth, the infant with genes for amaurotic familial idiocy becomes apathetic to most stimuli in about 3 months. His previously normal motor development deteriorates and he loses the ability to hold his head steady or grasp objects. He becomes progressively blind; one of the distinguishing symptoms of Tay-Sachs disease is a *cherry-red spot* in the macular area of the retina. The child with these disorders usually dies before the age of 3.

Gargoylism, also called *Hurler's disease,* is transmitted through a recessive gene. This condition, named for the grotesque appearance of the victims, is characterized by a severely deformed body, an enlarged head, coarse facial features, and limited flexibility of the limbs. Although retardation is not inevitable, it is usually present in gargoylism, and it is severe.

Chromosomal defects and mental retardation. Some kinds of mental retardation are caused by a defect in chromosomal material. These defects, which occur during the process of cell division (meiosis) that results in the gametes, yield a gamete (egg or sperm) that has an abnormal chromosomal composition. Defects caused by such genetic errors can be detected before birth by a process known as *amniocentesis.* A sample of amniotic fluid is withdrawn from the mother and fetal cells in it are examined for evidence of diseases caused by chromosomal defects such as Mongolism (Down's Syndrome). Other biochemical defects can also be identified in the amniotic fluid; for example, analysis can establish the presence of genetically caused defects such as Tay-Sachs disease and Hurler's disease. Ideally, amniocentesis is done around the sixteenth week of gestation. The resultant risk to mother and child appears minimal (Friedman, 1971).

•MONGOLISM. The best-known example of mental retardation caused by chromosomal abnormality is Mongolism, also known as *Down's Syndrome* or *Trisomy-21.* It was first described by a British physician, Langdon Down, in 1896. The term "Mongolism" derives from the superficial resemblance of these retardates to the Mongoloid race. That is, to unobservant Westerners certain facial anomalies give the victims of Down's Syndrome an oriental appearance. Actually there are important physical differences between Mongoloids and orientals.

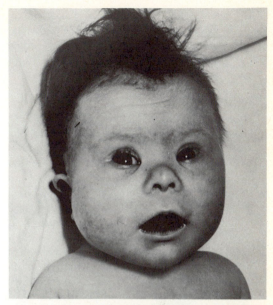

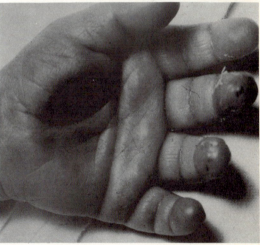

This Mongoloid child shows all the usual signs of the disorder, including the characteristic single palmar crease extending across the entire width of the hand. *(Gamstorp, 1970)*

In Mongolism the skull is small, there is a large protruding tongue with deep cracks in it, and the eyes are often narrow and slit-like, with a marked *epicanthal fold.* (This fold is quite different from the fold which is characteristic of people from the Far East.) Other abnormalities include a single crease in the palm, a shortened fifth finger, and short, broad square hands and feet. Both congenital heart defects and respiratory illnesses (caused by the mouth breathing which the enlarged tongue makes necessary) frequently lead to early death.

Most Mongoloids fall into the severely and moderately retarded range of intelligence, although there are reports of brighter children. In terms of personality, Mongoloids have often been described as happier and friendlier than other retardates. There are some data to support this impression, although the child's environment makes a difference in his behavior just as it does for children of normal intellectual ability (Silverstein, 1964).

Etiology of Down's Syndrome has been traced to a third chromosome attached to the pair of chromosomes labeled, by convention, as #21. There are at least three ways in which such a chromosomal abnormality might occur. The most common is *nondisjunction,* which takes place during meiosis when the two #21 chromosomes fail to separate prior to ovulation. The ovum that is produced has two rather than one #21 chromosomes, and when the ovum meets the sperm, which brings along a third #21 chromosome, the resultant embryo has an extra #21 chromosome. Of every 600 to 900 infants, one is a Mongoloid (Robinson & Robinson, 1965). A woman over 35 years of age runs a 1 in 150 risk of bearing a Mongoloid child, as contrasted with 1 chance in 2,000 for a woman in her twenties (Hamerton et al., 1961). A risk this great suggests that an older woman should consider adoption as an alternative to having a child of her own.

• TURNER'S SYNDROME. Several forms of retardation are transmitted as abnormalities in the sex chromosomes. The normal female has two X sex chromosomes (XX); the normal male has an X and a Y (XY). Variations in this normal chromosomal complement produce serious problems. Turner's syndrome is a disorder inherited by women only; it is characterized by a single X chromosome rather than the normal two (XX). Although the re-

tardation is recognized early, females with Turner's syndrome are most often given a specific diagnosis at puberty, when they fail to develop the usual secondary sex characteristics such as breasts and pubic hair. Mild to moderate retardation is present in about 20 percent of such women (Haddad & Wilkins, 1958).

• KLEINFELTER'S SYNDROME. This is a sex-chromosome abnormality restricted to males. The embryo has an extra X chromosome, forming an abnormal XXY pattern instead of the normal XY one. As in Turner's syndrome, the form of retardation becomes apparent at puberty, when the adolescent boy fails to develop the usual male secondary sex characteristics. While retardation is not inevitable, Kleinfelter's syndrome does occur more often among institutionalized retardates than among men in the general population.

Endocrine disorders and mental retardation. The most common form of retardation associated with endocrine disorder is *cretinism,* which results from inadequate thyroid secretion. The symptoms of cretinism include a placid and unaggressive personality, a dwarfed body, dry skin and coarse hair, and a large head. Cretinism can result from several causes. It may be inherited through a recessive gene. It may result from damage to the thyroid gland. Or it may develop in a fetus whose mother is living in a part of the world which has little natural iodine in the air, water, and soil. One way to compensate for low natural iodine is to use table salt containing iodine. This increased supply of iodine can prevent fetal damage and allow normal development. Regardless of cause, the symptoms of cretinism are the same. Early diagnosis is important, because adding thyroid to the infant's diet may modify or prevent severe mental retardation.

Intrauterine factors and mental retardation. The state of a mother's health during pregnancy affects her child's later intellectual and physical development. Women who are sick or malnourished may pass along their disorders to their children. Although the "placental barrier" protects the fetus from many maternal infections, certain bacterial and viral infections, as well as other conditions, can penetrate it.

• GERMAN MEASLES. German measles (rubella) is a relatively mild disease when contracted by a healthy child, but for a woman in her first three months of pregnancy the results can be disastrous. The earlier in pregnancy this infection occurs, the more likely it is that the embryo will develop enough defects to cause spontaneous abortion. If abortion does not occur, the infant may be born with cataracts, deafness, heart lesions, or varying degrees of retardation. The recent development of an effective rubella vaccine has, it is hoped, made this disorder one of the past (Schiff & Rauh, 1971).

• CONGENITAL SYPHILIS. Another illness which no modern mother need pass along to her child is congenital syphilis, a chronic maternal infection. Because of the widespread availability of blood tests for diagnosis and penicillin for treatment, syphilis is no longer a major source of retardation in the United States. It remains a problem mainly in poor areas of the country, where an illegitimate child might be born to a mother who didn't know she had syphilis because she didn't know that her child's father had it.

• RH FACTOR. Blood incompatibility between mother and fetus may also produce retardation in the child. The most common form of blood incompatibility results from the inherited Rhesus (Rh) factor. People who have the Rh factor in their blood are called *Rh positive;* those who lack it are *Rh negative.* If an Rh negative mother is carrying an Rh positive fetus, the blood cells from the fetus occasionally enter the mother's bloodstream via the placental juncture. In response to these cells, a sensitization process called *isoimmunization* occurs: the mother produces an antibody to fight the fetal blood cells as a foreign substance. While the process is harmless for the mother, her antibodies may enter the fetus's bloodstream and destroy its red blood cells. The likelihood that this sequence of events will occur is greater for later-born than for firstborn babies, since the mother has already accumulated a supply of antibodies in her blood after her first pregnancy. Because the circulatory systems of mothers and their fetuses are separate, the Rh reaction occurs in only 5 percent of Rh-negative mothers (Lyght, 1956). When it does, however, it can produce permanent brain damage or even kill the fetus. But if the incompatibility is relatively mild, the child can be protected from serious damage by testing before birth and by a series of blood transfusions during his first few days of life.

• MALNUTRITION. As noted earlier, maternal malnutrition is often associated with mental retardation. The food a mother eats—or more important, fails to eat—can influence the later intellectual development of her child. Mothers whose diet is poor in protein, vitamins, and minerals are more likely to bear children of low birth weight. And children who had exceptionally low birth weights are overrepresented in institutions for the retarded and in special education classes. Since poverty often necessitates an inadequate diet, it makes sense to assume that poor mothers are most likely to have children who are retarded because of maternal malnutrition. The assumption has been borne out empirically (Caputo & Mandell, 1970; Kaplan, 1972). Income level, not race, seems to be the crucial factor tying maternal malnutrition and infant intellectual deficit together (Naeye et al., 1971).

Malnutrition, then, is a prime example of an environmental factor which begins to act upon poor children from the moment of their conception to "stack the cards" against them. Maternal malnutrition means that from birth, the poor child may be several steps behind children from higher-income families.

The damaging consequences of inadequate diet extend beyond intellectual deficit in children of malnourished mothers. The following excerpt from the *Report of the Joint Commission on Mental Health of Children* (1970) illustrates the consequences on poor children of having to feel hungry all the time:

Children who are chronically sick and hungry may also come to question their own worth and the worth of their families. They may come to doubt any offer and to mistrust any favorable turn of events. As Dr. Robert Coles has noted, "These children learn to be 'tired, fearful, anxious, and suspicious' because they have experienced a kind of starvation in which 'the body is slowly consuming itself.' This bitter experience may breed potential recruits for riots in cities. . . . Federal food programs and public assistance measures have been inadequate to the challenge. In a land of abundance, children still suffer hunger. Many of these children belong to minority groups and are denied aid from federal food programs because of discriminatory practices." [1970, p. 238]

Treatment of mental retardation

Two broad areas will be considered in this discussion of treatment. First, how much can compensatory education do to boost the intellectual functioning of cultural-familial retardates? Second, is there any way to improve the functioning of more severely retarded people (which generally means those with clear biological defects)?

Cultural-familial retardation: Compensatory education

If intelligence is an inherited characteristic—like hair, skin, and eye color—is it, like them, relatively impervious to change? Or, does it make sense to provide children from deprived environments with compensatory educational experiences in order to upgrade their ultimate intellectual performance? These questions represent the "tip of the iceberg" of an extraordinarily important controversy among psychologists, educators, and public policy makers. Though the debate has smouldered for

years, it burst into flames with the publication in 1969 of the psychologist Arthur Jensen's article, "How Much Can We Boost IQ and Scholastic Achievement," in the prestigious *Harvard Educational Review.* Jensen's general subject was the degree to which intelligence is inherited, as well as the more specific and more emotionally laden question of racial differences in intelligence. Here we focus upon the broader question of the inheritance of intelligence and the value of compensatory education as these topics relate to cultural-familial retardation.

Assumptions of education. One of the assumptions made by people who favor an environmental view of retardation is that if the culturally deprived child were given an adequate environment, his intellectual functioning would be, on the average, equal to that of other children. An effort to provide this environment was made during the decade of the 1960s through a variety of federally funded compensatory education programs. Given this fact—and the enthusiasm with which many people supported the whole idea of compensatory education—it was inflammatory for Jensen to begin his paper with the statement that "Compensatory education has been tried and apparently has failed." Continuing in this vein, Jensen said that despite the great enthusiasm which greeted such endeavors as the federally financed Head Start programs, they did not manage to narrow the intellectual and academic discrepancies between poor children and those from the wider culture.

Jensen's explanation for this failure is complicated. To begin with, he points out, most compensatory education programs made two important assumptions: that most children are potentially capable of achieving at acceptable levels in school, and that culturally deprived children fail in school because they lack important experiences which are necessary building blocks for future education. As a result, most compensatory programs have aimed at raising either a child's IQ or his scholastic achievement. To evaluate these aims, Jensen turns to the basic issues concerning the function of intelligence tests and the "heritability" of intelligence.

Function of intelligence tests. Intelligence tests were originally devised for the pragmatic purpose of separating children likely to do well in school from those likely to have problems in learning. They are based, as Jensen points out, upon the educational traditions of Europe and are designed to measure performance in the narrow range of skills we have defined as necessary for education. They put heavy emphasis on abstract and verbal abilities. Had the tests been built to predict success in another kind of educational system, they would probably aim to assess a different range of behaviors.

Jensen believes that intelligence should not be equated with mental ability—that is, with a person's total mental capacities. Just because our society has picked out one particular group of skills to label as intelligence does not mean that other skills are not relevant to success in other societies or in subsocieties within our own. In short, it is a mistake to overlook the fact that there is a broader range of important abilities than those we have chosen to label as intelligence. Recognizing this opens the possibility that while a child may be low in intelligence as measured by the usual tests, he may have other mental capacities which could be utilized to increase his scholastic achievement.

Heritability of intelligence. Many studies, Jensen argues, support the view that intelligence is in large part an inherited characteristic. Most researchers who take this position believe that intelligence does not depend upon one gene but rather on many genes working in interaction, a mechanism called *polygenic*. The actual number of genes involved is unknown. After a complex discussion of the concept of heritability, which can be roughly defined as the proportion of variability in a trait which is due to genetic factors, Jensen concludes that the best estimate of the heritability of intelligence is about 80 percent. That is, environmental factors account for a relatively small proportion of intelligence as we measure and define it, while hereditary factors account for a very large proportion. Although profound environmental deprivation may produce children who respond dramatically to enrichment of their surroundings, Jensen does not feel that most children, even poor children, grow up under conditions involving such a marked degree of deprivation.

Jensen ends his article by returning to the question of compensatory education—why it has failed and how it might be changed to be more helpful. He concludes that these programs have generally produced only small changes in IQ. Jensen claims that while extreme environmental deprivation may keep a child from reaching his genetic IQ potential, even enriched experiences cannot push him beyond his intellectual potential once he is in an environment of minimal adequacy. But, Jensen adds, it may still be possible to increase the scholastic achievement of these children. To this end, he suggests utilizing other mental abilities in the children rather than trying and failing to train them in the ones we have traditionally defined as relevant to our society.

Replies to Jensen. The controversial nature of Jensen's article led a number of prominent scientists and laymen to respond to his position. Jerome Kagan, a psychologist, centered his criticism on the logic of Jensen's argument. Beginning his rejoinder with the thesis that "Ninety out of every 100 children, black, yellow or white, are capable of adequate mastery of the intellectual requirements of our schools" (1969, p. 277), Kagan questions Jensen's view that IQ differences are genetically determined. He maintains that Jensen ignored important data on the profound influence of the environment upon IQ test performance. Kagan also argues that compensatory education has not been tried long enough to justify being dismissed "out of hand."

Another psychologist, J. McV. Hunt, takes the position that poor children need to be given a more enriched and stimulating environment from birth onward, not simply from school age onward (1969). Hunt cites evidence from animal research which shows the importance of early stimulation upon later brain development. He points out that infants demonstrate a great deal of plasticity in their early behavioral development. Thus Hunt concludes that compensatory education should begin at this stage, when the organism is perhaps most receptive to change and growth.

In what is probably the most telling critique of Jensen, Professor Leon Kamin of Princeton University recently presented convincing data pointing to serious procedural flaws in a number of the studies upon which Jensen based his arguments about the heritability of IQ. Kamin states: "A critical review of the literature produces no evidence which would convince a reasonably prudent man to reject the hypothesis that intelligence test scores have zero heritability" (1973, p. 1). In Kamin's view, neither Jensen nor anyone else has demonstrated beyond question that intellectual level is not largely or entirely a function of environmental variables. Kamin's step-by-step evaluation of the data collection and reporting procedures which underlie the most important studies of the heritability of intelligence do indeed cast doubt upon their value.

The debate initiated by Jensen has not ended. For many it has become an inflammatory racial issue because of Jensen's suggestion that the lower IQ of black people as compared with whites is genetically based. For others it has become a major issue of scholarly concern. The arguments will not end without definitive facts—facts no one yet has. Nevertheless, the data that Jensen does present must also be evaluated on their scientific merit, not on the basis of emotional argument or wishful thinking. We cannot dismiss arguments because they make us feel good or bad. Society's most pressing problems are best confronted rationally, objectively, and above all, factually.

One recent development is that behavior-modification procedures have begun to be used with poor children for whom an enriched environment may mean the difference between normal intellectual development and cultural-familial retardation. Though Jensen believes

that compensatory education has failed, other psychologists believe that it has never really been tried. Both views may be wrong. Risley and his colleagues, for instance, have studied the learning problems most typical of preschool children in day-care and Head Start programs. By using behavioral procedures, they have been able to improve the correspondence between what a child says he does and what he actually does (Risley & Hart, 1968), increase the amount of time a child spends at various work-related tasks (Jacobson et al., 1969), and increase verbal imitation skills (Risley & Reynolds, 1970).

The severely retarded: Changing the environment

There once was an institution for the mentally retarded a part of which was described by a group of visitors as "a dimly lighted, foul-smelling room, where about 60 severely retarded boys, some partly clad and some moaning and drooling, sat crammed on wooden benches" (*New York Times,* January 13, 1972). The place? Willowbrook Hospital in New York State. The date? 1972. In a society that sends men to the moon, it is unbelievable that there should still be retarded children sitting neglected on wooden benches.

Things have improved at Willowbrook since that article was written. But the reality is that Willowbrooks abound in our country, and the saddest thing about them is that we have the knowledge and resources to make the lives of the retarded meaningful and productive.

Once a mentally retarded person has to be institutionalized, the prevailing attitude in our society has been one of hopelessness and resignation. The apathy is broken occasionally by sensational public disclosures of the filth, inhumane treatment, and indifference at one or another institution for the mentally retarded. But the public mainly sees its responsibility to the retarded as one of providing funds for custodial care, if possible, though always within the constraints of the public budget. For the retarded child in a public school, this attitude often results in the creation of a special class that is little more than a baby-sitting service run by well-intentioned but poorly trained persons.

Since the early 1960s, however, a good deal of research has been aimed at developing inexpensive and effective treatment programs for the retarded. Some of that research, described below, shows promise of paying off.

Motivation and readiness for change. Zigler and his colleagues have studied how motivation and environment influence the performance of institutionalized cultural-familial retardates (1967). They point out that these children often experience more failure in a day than brighter children do in a week. Since repeated failure is bound to influence any child's concept of himself as a person who can handle new challenges, the retarded child ends up learning to *expect* to fail. But if his environment were structured so that he failed less and succeeded more, he might well develop different expectations about his chances for success. As a result he might be more willing to tackle new problems.

Behavior modification. Thus, Zigler's conclusion is that retarded children need to be provided with environments in which they can experience frequent success rather than consistent failure. If they were enabled to take tiny steps that are correct rather than large, incorrect ones, their self-confidence would grow. The behavioral approach to retardation attempts to structure this kind of environment. It employs a series of *successive approximations* to *shape* the child's behavior to its desired form. Jonathan W. learned to zip his coat when the task was broken down into a sequence of small steps (units of behavior), for which he was reinforced if he performed them successfully. Essentially the same process is used to teach retarded children academic skills like reading, writing, and arithmetic.

The use of operant techniques to modify the behavior of retarded children has increased dramatically during the past few years. They have made it possible to teach institutionalized

Our society's prevailing attitude toward the institutionalized mentally retarded has been "one of hopelessness and resignation." But need it be so? *(President's Committee on Mental Retardation)*

children practical skills such as dressing and eating (Roos & Oliver, 1969). They have also proved useful for teaching more traditional classroom subjects. And token economies have been extremely successful in institutions for the retarded (Bricker et al., 1972; Musick & Luckey, 1970; Roberts & Perry, 1970).

Whitney and Barnard used operant conditioning techniques to change the behavior of a severely retarded adolescent (1966). Their patient, a 15-year-old girl, was unable to sit without support or to grasp objects—all behaviors necessary for self-feeding. The patient was trained by the technique of successive approximations to spoon-feed herself. The reinforcement for successively more correct spoon-handling behavior was food, and the food was withdrawn whenever she used the spoon inappropriately. In a similar fashion she was taught to hold and then drink from a cup. Eventually she learned to sit at a table and eat with other patients. The profound differences between what the girl had learned during fifteen years of traditional care and what she learned in the few weeks of treatment by Whitney and Barnard show the tremendous potential of operant conditioning.

Azrin and Foxx toilet-trained nine incontinent retardates who had a median IQ of 14 and an average age of 43 years (1971). The investigators used a moisture-sensitive pair of shorts that activated a buzzer whenever the patient urinated or defecated in his pants, as well as a specially designed toilet bowl that signaled the presence of urine or feces. With this equipment a trainer was able to keep close track of his patients' toilet behavior so that he could appropriately reinforce correct toileting acts. Training was effective and rapid: it took a median of only four days for each retardate. On a follow-up several weeks later, the patients were continuing their new toilet behavior.

Operant conditioning techniques have also been applied to far more complex behaviors than eating, drinking, and going to the toilet. They can, for example, be used to teach skills useful in industry. Clarke and Hermelin taught six retardates with IQs between 22 and 42 to perform the rather complicated sequence of behaviors needed to fold and glue cardboard boxes (1955). Their patients were initially much poorer at this task than normal persons—but by the end of the training period they were turning out a product which met industrial specifications.

Retarded people can learn to wire electrical components, assemble mechanical devices, count and sort money, do office filing, and use simple office machines (Neuhaus, 1967:

These residents of a home for the mentally retarded work on a jigsaw puzzle together. Clearly the attitude of those who administer and those who live in this institution is a far cry from "hopelessness and resignation." *(President's Committee on Mental Retardation)*

Tate & Baroff, 1967). Studies have found that performance by retarded persons in various simple jobs is influenced more by personality variables such as perseverance than by IQ (Sali & Amir, 1971). These studies indicate that vocational training programs can make young adult retardates self-supporting and independent.

A word of hope

We have tried to show you that the subject of mental retardation today is one of hope as well as sorrow. Improved prenatal diagnostic techniques like amniocentesis, and postnatal treatment techniques like behavior modification, are more effective approaches to the problems of retardation than anything available a decade ago. We have also tried to give you a sense of dissatisfaction and even anger about the present state of institutions for the retarded and about the benign neglect with which politicians and their communities continue to regard the malnourished poor child.

The words of, two retarded people speak better than any others can of how much the retarded can do for themselves—and for the rest of us.

My Job, by Lynn

I work at Briarcliff taking care of little babies.
We do a lot of things with them. We feed them,
we take them for their baths, play with them
and change their diapers, help dress them, Finally
after working five days there I am getting paid.
I like my job and I am getting along there pretty
well.

God Made, by Joseph

God made the stars
God made plants like flowers, and trees.
God made the animals like the Birds that fly
  through the sky.
God made planets like the Earth, Moon and
  others.
God made us people to.
God will love you, to pray for him.

[Anonymous, 1973, p. 291]

Summary

Mentally retarded persons have always existed. But they have only become a major problem—and a challenge—since the development of the complex technology of our times. This technology brought improved procedures for keeping damaged infants alive, as well as increased demands on all people for more complicated intellectual behavior.

Retardation is subnormal intellectual functioning originating in early life. It is associated with impairment of learning, social adjustment, and maturation. It can be measured along several different dimensions: level of intellectual functioning (whether the person is educable, trainable, or custodial), physical symptoms regardless of etiology (for example, cretinism arises from several different causes), or etiologic agent (say, organic damage or cultural-familial retardation).

Cultural-familial retardation, the most common form, is shown by persons who fall naturally at the lower end of the normal distribution of intelligence. These are the people whose IQs are in the borderline and mildly retarded categories. Often they come from families which have other retarded members. Ralph J., the boy whose case was described at the beginning of the chapter, may have been appropriately diagnosed as a cultural-familial retardate. The relative importance of genetic and environmental factors in this form of retardation has not yet been fully explored.

Mental retardation arising from organic damage is usually easier to recognize and diagnose than cultural-familial retardation. The most common forms of retardation in this category include disorders caused by dominant genes (e.g., tuberous sclerosis), recessive genes (e.g., phenylketonuria), chromosomal defects (e.g., Mongolism), endocrine disorders (e.g., cretinism), and intrauterine factors (e.g., congenital syphilis). Jonathan W. was a victim of Mongolism, a chromosomal defect.

To what extent do environmental factors as opposed to genetic factors influence intelligence? This question is a highly controversial one, especially because of the racial implications which Jensen raised when he argued that genetic factors are all-important. But the issue has implications far beyond racial ones, and it cannot be decided until more evidence has been gathered.

The extent to which special environments can be created to compensate for retardation, either mild or severe, is another important question. Regardless of the ultimate answer to the nature-nurture question, it is clear that the behavior of a person functioning at a retarded level can be significantly altered in the proper learning environment. Given a setting which stresses success rather than failure and which structures learning at a pace appropriate for the student, many retarded persons can learn to lead meaningful and productive lives. Behavior modification procedures have been especially helpful in creating such environments.

CHAPTER SEVENTEEN
The Organic Brain Disorders

Webster R. ● Mirian S. ● History: The story of syphilis ●
Cues ● Diagnosis ● Assessment ● Types of organic brain
disorders ● Treatment

WEBSTER R.:
ROUND TRIP
FROM NEWARK

Webster R. has been a patient on the neurological ward of the Veterans Administration hospital near Newark for several years.   Before that he lived in a tent at an Army camp near Da Nang in Vietnam. He wasn't happy about being in Vietnam and he hoped every day that he wouldn't have to kill anyone, but he also felt that someone had to fight the war and that it wasn't such a bad deal for him.   He had two stripes and hoped to earn another, he had made some good buddies in his outfit, and he liked the combat pay that Uncle sent home to his family every month.   Sometimes he even thought about making a career out of the Army, but not often; his real plan was to return home and go to college.   Then one day on patrol, he was hit in the head with fragments from a hand grenade thrown at his squad by "Charlie."

It was touch and go with Webster for three weeks.   Surgery to dislodge the fragments of bone and metal embedded in his brain had to

(UPI photo by Shunsuke Akatsuka)

489

be postponed for several days because of his weakened condition and an infection that set in almost immediately. When the neuro-surgeons finally did their work, they found that Webster had suffered extensive damage to sensory, motor, and cognitive areas of the brain. He remained in a coma for ten days after surgery. It was several weeks before he became fully aware of what was going on around him. As soon as possible he was airlifted back to a large East Coast Army hospital in the States. After treatment there, he was sent to the Veterans hospital near his home in Newark.

Webster had heard the sounds of gunfire long before he joined the Army, for he was a youngster in the Newark ghetto during the riots of 1967. Although their newfound sense of community and aware-ness of potential political power excited Webster's parents, like the other residents of Newark's central ward, and though they saw some value in this civil disobedience, they had not allowed Webster to join in the rioting. Even after the riots and after the election of a black as mayor of the city, the R.'s hoped that Webster would be able to leave Newark and the ghetto when he grew up. In fact, they hoped he would do well enough in life to take them along when he left.

Webster showed early promise of fulfilling his parents' dreams. He did well in school and took the college preparatory curriculum while many of his classmates were dropping out or electing vocational training. He spent three afternoons a week working in a local gro-cery store and gave his mother most of his wages. He even found time to go out for the track team. Webster's teachers and his minis-ter all described him as "a hardworking boy with a good head on his shoulders."

After he graduated from Newark's Central High School, Webster decided to enlist in the Army so that he could go to college after-wards on the GI bill. He did well in basic training. Mostly he kept to himself, but he worked at his job and people liked him for it. After basic and advanced infantry training, he was shipped to Vietnam. He had been there six months when the grenade exploded near his head.

Webster's parents visit him regularly at the hospital. It is not an easy trip for them, because they don't own a car and have to ask Mrs. R.'s nephew to drive them. It is usually a painful visit. Webster recognizes them, but he can only say a few words and they don't always make much sense. His frustration is obvious; he breaks down and cries, even though he knows how it upsets his mother.

The resident doctor who speaks to Mr. and Mrs. R. about Webster from time to time has never been very encouraging. Although Web-ster has regained his motor control to the point where he can walk, feed himself, and dress himself, he still shows many effects of brain damage nearly a year after the injury. When the ward attendant

(Rohn Engh/Photo Researchers, Inc.)

or the volunteer worker walks Webster down the hall from his bedroom to the recreation room, sometimes he cannot find his way back by himself. He also has difficulty thinking abstractly: while he can pick up a glass of water and take a drink, if a therapist asks him to pretend he is drinking from a glass, he can't. He no longer seems to have any imagination. And he is surprisingly indifferent to most of the events around him. At times he becomes so frustrated with himself that he grows tearful and depressed.

The hospital is doing its best to rehabilitate Webster through a number of different treatments. He gets an anticonvulsant drug to control the grand mal epileptic seizures he has experienced unpredictably since the injury. He regularly attends speech therapy classes to help improve his ability to find words to express himself. He had physical therapy to improve his motor coordination. In fact, Webster is probably getting the best care that can be provided for him, in a hospital dedicated to helping veterans recover from or adjust to the consequences of war.

Impressed by the hard work of Webster's doctors and nurses, his parents wrote the President of the United States to tell him how much the Veterans Administration means to them. They received a brief but courteous reply from one of his secretaries, acknowledging their letter and thanking them for it. The reply is framed and hangs on the wall in the R. family's living room.

However, there are limits to what else the hospital can do for Webster. A large area of his brain was damaged by the fragments which lodged in his head and by the bleeding which resulted from the injury. It is unlikely that he will ever recover sufficiently to lead an independent life.

MIRIAN S.: CONFUSION THAT GROWS

Jeffrey and Wilma S. brought their mother to the psychiatric outpatient clinic of a large medical school in downtown Chicago because they had become more and more worried about her behavior. They might have acted sooner, but they had been inclined to view her increasing oddness as part of the depression caused by the recent death of her husband. Finally, however, it became impossible for her children to ignore the way she was changing.

Mirian S. is 58 years old. Harold, her husband, died of a heart attack a little more than a year ago, shortly after his sixty-first birthday and their thirty-sixth year of marriage. Since then Mirian has lived alone in the large apartment on Chicago's near north side that she and Harold moved to many years ago. Harold, a stockbroker, earned a good living and invested his money carefully, so that Mirian has no financial worries. Her son Jeff, who is 32, works as a stockbroker in the firm that his father founded. He is married and has a

(Henry Monroe/DPI)

young son. Wilma, always the "brain" of the family, has nearly completed her Ph.D. in mathematics. She is 28 and much to her mother's distress, has never married; even now she seems to enjoy her books more than her boy friends. Both Jeff and Wilma visit their mother regularly, usually on Sundays.

About six months ago, Mirian began to complain that she felt confused and forgetful. She went to her doctor, who could find nothing wrong. Because she was still mourning Harold's death, the doctor suggested that the confusion might be related to her depression and gave her a mild mood-elevating drug. But as time went on, the confusion grew worse instead of better.

Mirian began to do other peculiar things which worried Jeff and Wilma even more. One day Jeff stopped on his way into the city to visit his mother. It was nearly time for lunch, and she invited him to eat with her. Jeff noticed that she seemed muddled as she set to work, and that she cooked and served in a sloppy way not at all like her. Strangest of all was the meal itself: mashed potatoes, boiled noodles, and tapioca pudding.

When Jeff called Wilma that night to tell her about it, she said that their mother had also stopped taking care of the apartment. Wilma had noticed on her last few visits that the living room table was dusty, the bathroom was dirty, and the floors hadn't been washed for weeks. Not only that, but their mother had taken to wearing the same shabby, stained housedress for weeks, though she was a woman whose person had always been as immaculate as her household.

A few weeks later Wilma made a date with her mother to go Christmas shopping. But when she arrived at the apartment Mirian was surprised; she had forgotten their plans. Wilma fixed lunch for them, and while she was washing the lunch dishes her mother came into the kitchen to ask when lunch would be ready.

Alarming as these events were for the S. children, it took another incident to convince them that their mother needed professional help. One Friday night at 11 o'clock, the Chicago police called Jeff to tell him that they had found his mother wandering in the street, apparently lost and unable to find her way home. When Jeff picked his mother up at the police station, he was amazed by her vagueness and bewilderment. The desk sergeant urged him to see a doctor about his mother. The next day Jeff made arrangements for Mrs. S. to have some tests at the hospital, and since the S.'s were able to pay the hospital's private fees, she was given an appointment within a week.

The psychiatrist who first saw Mirian found that her attention span was quite limited and that she was defective in coordination, especially in complex activities. When he tested her abstract ability

492

with the proverb, "A stitch in time saves nine," she replied, "You had better sew up the mattress cover or it will come apart." She was restless during the long evaluation session and several times got up and wandered around the room. On tests of visual-motor coordination given later in the day by a psychologist, she made striking errors without seeming to realize it. For example, she spontaneously rotated a set of geometric designs 45 degrees when she was asked to copy them from cards onto a sheet of paper. The psychologist who tested her felt that she was unmistakably suffering from some form of organic brain syndrome. Before reaching a diagnostic decision, however, he wanted her to have a complete physical and neurological examination. Those tests, done the next day, identified Mrs. S.'s disorder as Alzheimer's disease, a form of presenile dementia.

The doctor who met with Jeff and Wilma had to tell them that the prognosis for their mother was poor. While she might live for several more years, her physical and psychological condition was likely to show a steady downward course. The children decided to hire a private nurse and keep their mother at home for a while, but she will probably have to be placed in a nursing home before long. Probably within four years—by the time she is 62—Mrs. S. will reach a vegetative state of existence, from which only death (from infection, most likely) will free her.

(Henry Monroe/DPI)

Brain pathology and behavior

Webster R. and Mirian S., despite their very different early lives, will now lead tragically similar ones. Though Mirian has lived in material comfort and ease as the wife of an affluent businessman, she is now a woman in late middle age who is afflicted with a progressive brain disorder that will ultimately render her totally demented. Webster R., still a young man, a product of Newark's black ghetto, will also continue to suffer from a serious brain disorder which has left him permanently incapacitated. Both these people, so different in age, socioeconomic position, and educational level, share the enduring fact of permanent, irreversible damage to the brain. Each must continue to experience the physical and psychological stigmata of their conditions. While some of their symptoms are different, they also share some central problems. Both have suffered a marked loss in intellectual capacity; both have lost much of their ability to think in abstract terms; both are impaired in language skills. Furthermore, both have lost much of their capacity for appropriate emotional response.

A vast array of deficits can develop from damage to the central nervous system. Many of them bear no relationship to age, sex, race, or social class. Others do relate, at least indirectly, to sociological and personal factors such as diet and occupation. This chapter explores the consequences of physical damage to the central nervous system.

History: The story of syphilis and general paralysis

The scientific discovery of each organic disorder discussed in this chapter has its own interesting history. None, however, played a more significant role in our changing ideas about organic psychopathology than the discovery of the etiology of *general paralysis* (general paresis). Its story is a model of the pitfalls and successes connected with the study of organically based psychopathology.

Today we know that general paralysis is caused by syphilis, a venereal disease transmitted by sexual intercourse. But the symptoms, which may include paralysis, blindness, and psychosis, appear many years after the person is first infected by the spirochetal organism *Treponema pallidum.* As a result it took a long while before researchers associated the relatively minor physical symptoms of the early stages of syphilis, which appear shortly after infection, with the much more serious later ones of general paralysis.

"English pox." It is believed that syphilis was brought to Europe by sailors in Columbus's crew (Zilboorg & Henry, 1941). Some evidence indicates that Columbus himself suffered from the disease (Kemble, 1936). Regardless of how it got there, once it was introduced in Europe it spread with appalling speed. No nation wanted to take credit for it. The English called it the French pox, the French called it the English pox, and the Italians alternately labeled it the English *or* French Soldiers' Disease. The name *syphilis* became attached to the disorder when an Italian doctor wrote a plaintive love poem about an unfortunate shepherd named Syphillis who had become afflicted with it.

General paralysis is a form of syphilis which sometimes appears fifteen to twenty years after a person is infected. Soon there were a great many cases of general paralysis in Europe. Recognition that the disorder was connected with syphilis came gradually. Bayle, a Frenchman, identified it as a specific form of psychopathology in 1825, although

he did not trace its cause. Twenty years later, Esmarch and Jensen proposed in a German medical journal that the cause of general paralysis was syphilis.

Treponema pallidum. Esmarch and Jensen's etiologic views were rejected by medical authorities, who had concluded that general paralysis was due to too much drinking and smoking. At last a famous demonstration by Krafft-Ebing proved that Esmarch and Jensen had been right. In 1897 he injected nine victims of general paralysis with *Treponema pallidum,* the organism which was thought to be responsible for syphilis. Although none of the nine people had reported a history of syphilis, all failed to develop its symptoms after the injection. Their immunity led Krafft-Ebing to conclude that they must already have had the disease.

Shortly afterward, Schaudinn identified *Treponema pallidum* as the spirochete (bacterium) causing syphilis. Naguchi and Moore then demonstrated that this same spirochete

Treponema pallidum, the bacillus that causes syphilis. Its size is indicated by the one-micron scale shown at lower left; a micron is one-thousandth of a millimeter, or about .000039 inch. *(Center for Disease Control)*

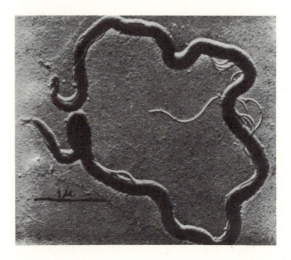

was present in the brains of general paralysis patients. The link between the two conditions was confirmed. Although the discovery of the etiology of general paralysis is one of the best-documented stories in the annals of the organic disorders, the etiologies of others have been traced in much the same way.

Cues to the organic disorders

According to the *Diagnostic and Statistical Manual* (1968) of the American Psychiatric Association, the organic brain syndromes are characterized by the following behavioral cues:

1 Impairment of orientation
2 Impairment of memory
3 Impairment of intellectual functions—including comprehension calculation, knowledge, and learning
4 Impairment of judgment (ability to make sound decisions)
5 Lability (rapid emotional change) and shallowness of affect.

The presence and severity of these cues form the basis for the diagnosis of organic brain syndromes. The syndromes can be further described by labeling the patient's condition as a state of either delirium or dementia.

Delirium

Delirium usually arises from agents acting outside the brain itself. High fever, poisons, accidents, cardiac failure, and intoxication from drugs or alcohol can all produce delirium. It may also accompany the final stages of a terminal illness. It is usually associated with fever, sweating, rapid heartbeat, and muscular tremors. In most cases delirium lasts a few hours or, at most, a few days and then disappears, often without a trace. Occasionally, as with Korsakov's psychosis (a brain disorder associated with long-term heavy drinking), the patient may continue to function in an impaired fashion after the *acute* (reversible) delirium has passed.

The severity of a delirious state varies a great deal. Some patients may show only minimal "clouding of consciousness," while others may be incoherent or unconscious. As you read through the following list of behaviors associated with delirium, keep in mind that each can be intense or mild, each can fluctuate in a given patient, and different patients may demonstrate their impairment along different dimensions.

Impairment of orientation and memory. The delirious patient is disoriented as to time and place. He may not be able to tell you that he's in a hospital, why he's there, or what time it is. He also shows temporary impairment of memory, including an inability to understand what is happening or to relate it to past experiences. On recovery, most patients have no memory of events that took place during the episodes of delirium.

Impairment of intellectual functions and judgment. The thoughts of the delirious patient are disconnected and often focused upon imaginary experiences. His perceptions are altered by hallucinations. Functions such as comprehension, problem solving, and judgment (decision making) are impaired, though the patient is usually not aware of it. He is markedly confused.

Impairment of affect. The mood of the delirious patient may swing between apathy or indifference, and rage or panic. He often appears fearful and anxious—not a surprising response to the frightening bodily sensations he may be experiencing.

Dementia

Dementia arises from actual structural damage to the brain. Though the damage is often irreversible, some conditions which cause dementia are reversible. The conditions which are not reversible are usually called *chronic* in contrast to the reversible disorders, which may be designated as *acute*. Typical causes of dementia include aging, cerebral arteriosclerosis, and degenerative brain diseases. Dementia reflects damage to the areas of the brain involved in higher mental processes (the temporal, parietal, and frontal lobes).

A firsthand description of the insidious onset of dementia is provided in the following anonymous excerpt:

Over the period that we worked together . . . I became gradually aware that the fine edge of his intellect was becoming dulled. He was less clear in discussion and less quick to make the jump from a new piece of evidence to its possible significance. He spent more time over his work and achieved less; and he found it increasingly difficult to get his results ready for publication. He tended also to become portentious and solemn about his subject, as though one small corner of knowledge nearly filled his world, and the wider horizons were narrowing in. The change was so slow as to be barely perceptible, and the signs vanished when I tried to pin them down: they were like those faint stars which are seen more easily when they are not in the direct line of vision. I was left with a feeling of uneasiness which I could not justify. [1950, p. 1012]

As with delirium, the severity of dementia can vary within wide limits; thus each of the following sets of cues is a continuum rather than a fixed point.

Impairment of orientation and memory. The memory and orientation of the demented patient are affected by his brain damage. His recent memory is generally worse than his remote memory, although both are disturbed. He pays attention with difficulty and may lose his train of thought in the middle of a sentence. At first the patient may simply appear absent-minded and careless, but eventually he may not be able to find his way around in a familiar setting or recognize people whom he once knew well. Both Mirian S. and Webster R. showed this kind of behavior from time to time, the difference being that Webster's behavioral deficit will stabilize while Mirian's will progress.

Impairment of intellectual functions and judgment. Dementia leads to impairment of intellectual functioning. The person's capacity for learning new material and ability to think in abstract terms are both reduced. Webster R's loss of abstract thinking skills was shown by his inability to pretend that he was drinking from a glass. Mirian S., when asked to explain a proverb, could not conceptualize it in its abstract sense; she interpreted it in concrete terms, using words that remained very close to the proverb's literal meaning.

A variety of other intellectual functions, including the abilities to learn new information, comprehend instructions, and reason problems through to a solution, deteriorate with dementia. The capacity for sound judgment rests in large part on such functions as well as on self-control and social awareness. As the patient's skills in these areas diminish his judgment suffers. He loses the ability to think about himself, to be sensitive to social interactions, and to create new concepts.

Language deficits, termed *aphasia,* often accompany the patient's intellectual impairment. Aphasia can take a variety of forms. Consider the book you are now reading; if you were asked to name the object in front of you, you would first recognize it and then call it a book. But if you were aphasic you might not recognize it, which would mean that your intellectual mechanism for storing or retrieving concepts—like "book"—was defective. Or you might recognize the object by its function but not be able to remember its name. Or, finally, you might recall the word "book" but find yourself unable to say the word.

Although mild language deficits often accompany diffuse organic conditions (disorders in which there is no single site of brain damage injury), severe deficits may be a sign that there is a specific area of damage, and in fact may prove useful in localizing the site of brain damage. A disruption of the ability to hear and understand spoken language—*auditory-receptive aphasia*—can often be traced to the dominant temporal lobe. *Anomia,* the inability to find the proper words to express oneself, arises from damage to the temporal-parietal areas of the brain. The inability to communicate through spoken or written language—*motor aphasia*—is usually traced to the frontal lobes. The inability to understand written language—*visual-receptive aphasia*—is often caused by parietal-occipital lobe damage. While these diagnostic clues are not infallible, they are extremely helpful to the clinician who is trying to localize an area of damage.

The topic of aphasia is a difficult and complex one. Interested readers will find a detailed discussion in Penfield and Roberts's *Speech and Brain Mechanisms* (1959).

Impairment of affect. The changes in intellectual functioning associated with dementia are also accompanied by significant personality changes. The patient first loses his most recently acquired behaviors: the mature, adult, and sophisticated part of his repertoire. Then there is a gradual decline in good manners, thoughtfulness, and self-control—the behaviors that he learned earlier in life. Eventually he becomes completely preoccupied with himself and insensitive to other people; in behavior he has returned to early childhood.

When they begin, these personality changes may appear to be more neurotic than "organic" (which usually ensures a delay in diagnosis). The person begins to show increasingly rapid emotional fluctuations. He may overreact to minor irritations and disappointments, or his mood may shift quickly, with anger instantly giving way to laughter, laughter to tears. Along with these changes the patient shows little insight and less control over his emotional behavior, and his frustration tolerance is diminished. Toward the end of his life his mood often becomes apathetic, though some demented patients may instead develop chronic depressive, manic, or paranoid behavioral patterns.

Differential diagnosis of the organic disorders

Distinguishing dementia from delirium

Most delirium is caused by agents acting outside the brain (for example, infections, poisons, high fever), while almost all dementias arise from actual physical damage to brain tissue. Distinguishing between them is vital in diagnosis, since treatment of the organic disorders is based on etiology.

The onset of delirium is usually sudden, whereas dementia comes on gradually. Delirium involves alterations in consciousness (varying from "cloudiness" to coma) and autonomic symptoms such as fever and sweating, none of which are usually found with dementia. In addition, the delirious patient's symptoms shift frequently, sometimes from hour to hour, while the demented patient's change much more gradually.

Distinguishing organic brain disorders from functional disorders

As you read the preceding section about behavioral cues to the organic brain disorders, you probably noticed that the cues are not specific to these disorders; they are found in many psychopathologic conditions that were discussed in other chapters. The problem of differentiating between the patient with an organic disorder and the patient with a functional (nonorganic) disorder can be a major challenge. Because this distinction, unlike many others among the psychopathological disorders, has a real impact on decisions about treatment, the differential diagnosis of the organic brain disorders and the functional psychoses (for example, schizophrenia) is an important one.

It is often possible to mistake the early stages of dementia for the behavior of the neurotic (Epstein et al., 1971). The clinician may be able to make a distinction on the basis of the patient's case history, but frequently only time permits this difficult judgment. Sometimes, though, the organic patient will exhibit a certain vagueness and uncertainty which are not characteristic of neurosis. Another clue which may be helpful is that the neurotic's mood is more likely to be one of anxiety or depression, while the organic patient's mood is marked by its lability (rapid change).

As dementia progresses, it becomes more difficult to distinguish from schizophrenia or from severe depression. One pointer for the diagnostician may be that the onset of psychotic depression is typically more abrupt than the onset of dementia. In addition, depression that is functional in etiology (so-called neurotic or psychotic depression) is apt to color the depressed patient's total existence, while depression in dementia may be one among several shifting moods.

Distinguishing between organic brain disorder and schizophrenia is one of the most common problems encountered by the clinical psychologist who specializes in psychodiagnostic testing. On entering the hospital, many psychiatric patients present signs which do not permit a clear distinction to be drawn between the two disorders. But besides showing differences in test performance, which will be discussed later in the chapter, schizophrenic and organic patients often behave differently in important ways.

For example, both groups experience a breakdown in reality testing. In the delirious patient, however, this breakdown fluctuates in intensity and is accompanied by disorientation as to time and place. Also, the resultant disorganization is on a primitive level. The schizophrenic, on the other hand, tends to show his breakdown in reality testing much more in terms of preoccupation with himself. His delusions are usually systematized and usually involve his special relationship to the world. In addition, the demented patient ultimately comes to show areas of permanent loss (say, in memory, abstract ability, and reasoning), while schizophrenic functioning is characterized more appropriately as distortion rather than loss.

Sometimes repeated observations of a patient over a long period are necessary before his disorder can be labeled organic or functional. Sometimes the distinction cannot be made at all. Often the clinician must arrive at a "best guess" about diagnosis and begin treatment, watching the patient's progress to see whether he responds.

Assessment of organic brain disorders

Level of consciousness

Confusion and *stupor* have been identified as two of the most prominent symptoms of organic brain disorder (Nathan, 1967). Both represent marked alterations from normal levels of consciousness. For this reason a clinician examining a person who may be suffering from an organic brain disorder looks for cues to consciousness: How alert does the patient appear? Does he listen attentively? Is he drowsy or stuporous? Are there times when he appears to "drift off" or lose contact with the environment? While the clinician watches for other behavioral cues to organicity —for hallucinations, delusions, or areas of peculiar preoccupation—he attends first to level of consciousness.

Neurological examination

An important part of any assessment procedure when there may be brain impairment is the neurological examination which evaluates the patient's perceptual and expressive functions. In addition, some or all of the following specialized tests may be performed. An *electroencephalographic* (EEG) recording of the brain's electrical activity can sometimes pinpoint areas of damage. A *spinal tap* makes it possible to test the spinal fluid for evidence of inflammation or tumor. And x-rays of the skull using *radioisotope tracer agents* can identify brain tumors. This relatively new procedure depends upon the fact that normal brain tissue does not allow radioactive material to penetrate to it through the blood-brain barrier, while brain lesions are protected by an imperfect blood-brain barrier and do permit the material to pass through. As a result, damaged brain tissue shows an increased concentration of the tracer on an x-ray film (Steegmann, 1970).

Psychological tests

Psychological tests provide another source of data regarding brain damage. Tests of intelligence, such as the Wechsler Adult Intelligence Scale, help differentiate chronic brain syndrome patients from schizophrenics (Davis et al., 1972; DeWolfe et al., 1971). They are also sometimes useful in localizing brain lesions. In one well-designed early study, Weinstein and Teuber compared pre- and postinjury intellectual functioning in a group of soldiers who had suffered known head injuries (1957). The scores made by the soldiers on tests of intellectual ability before they were injured were juxtaposed with their scores afterward. It was found that men who had sustained left hemispheric damage to the parietal or temporal lobes showed severe intellectual deficits, while those whose damage was to the right hemisphere did not lose nearly as much intellectual capacity.

In another study of soldiers with head injuries, Williams and his colleagues reported that verbal ability apparently suffered more than spatial judgment following the same gross amount of brain damage (1959). Parsons and his co-workers made a somewhat more sophisticated and detailed evaluation of pre- and postinjury intellectual performance in a group of veterans who had sustained brain damage to the right hemisphere, to the left hemisphere, or to both (1969). They found that patients with left hemispheric damage showed greater loss of language ability, while those with right hemispheric damage showed more difficulty with perceptual organization skills. More recent studies have reported conflicting results (Reiten & Fitzhugh, 1971; Russell, 1972). Thus before the earlier findings can be judged, additional research must be carried out that carefully matches subjects in replicated studies

for site, severity, and duration of brain damage as well as for age, sex, and premorbid functioning.

Some clinicians claim that the projective tests are sensitive to the particular kinds of personality changes which follow development of the organic brain syndromes and can thereby differentiate them from functional disorders (Dorken & Kral, 1952; Evans & Marmorston, 1964; Hughes, 1950; Piotrowski, 1937). But Goldfried and his colleagues caution that research of this sort has been so badly designed that the diagnostic value of the Rorschach test, at least, remains uncertain (1971).

A number of specialized psychological tests have also been developed to measure loss of specific sensory, motor, and cognitive functions following organic damage. The Halstead-Reitan Neuropsychological Battery (Russell et al., 1970), the Hunt-Minnesota Test (Hunt, 1943), and the Illinois Test of Psycholinguistic Abilities (Kirk et al., 1968) are all broad-spectrum instruments which tap a wide range of abilities that deteriorate in organic disorders. More specialized tests of visual-motor coordination and memory include the Bender Visual-Motor Test (Bender, 1938), the Benton Visual Retention Test (Benton, 1950), and the Memory-for-Designs Test (Graham & Kendall, 1960).

Types of organic brain disorders

Organic brain disorders related to aging

Many physical, psychological, and social stresses are involved in aging. Approximately 10 percent of the United States population (about 20 million people) is now 65 or older (Birren, 1970)—a percentage that will continue to grow as the birthrate slows. Study of the phenomena which accompany aging is obviously becoming more important to more Americans than ever.

The physical changes caused by aging are

the most obvious. The skin loses its elasticity; it wrinkles and sags. Freedom of movement decreases as muscle power wanes and the heart becomes less efficient. The digestive and eliminative processes do not function as well as they once did. The young—and some of the elderly themselves—often recoil at these "ravages" of aging. But it is important to remember that for most people such changes are normal at a certain age.

The elderly must also cope with the serious psychological problems that result from aging itself and from the changes in status that accompany aging. The realization that one is growing older and drawing inexorably closer to death is difficult for most people to accept. And the knowledge that one is aging brings very real fears about failing health and reduced financial circumstances. Finally—and often most difficult—an elderly person's friends and family also begin to die, so that many old people are almost completely alone. Brief "duty visits" once or twice a month from children and grandchildren are not enough to

In many other societies, the elderly have an honored place and perform valued work. Surely it is time for America to utilize the talents of its older citizens. *(Drawing by Val; Copyright 1969 by Saturday Review/World, Inc.)*

ward off the devastating feeling of no longer being needed by anyone.

Aging, of course, also involves unpleasant financial problems for many of the elderly. Of the 20 million people in the United States who were over 65 in 1971, 4.8 million were below the federal "poverty level," and an additional 2 million were too poor to pay for necessary medical expenses (Townsend, 1971). The median income for all persons 65 years old and over is half that for people who have not reached 65 (Kreps, 1969). Yet the older person must spend more than twice as much for his medical expenses as the person under 65 (Townsend, 1971). As a consequence the elderly must accept a standard of living much lower than the one they had before retirement. Not only does a smaller income put limits on the food, housing, and medical care one can buy; less money in our society also means less status and lower self-esteem.

These problems make the process of aging an extremely difficult one for Americans. Other societies, especially Eastern civilizations, do much better by their aged. The following discussion focuses upon the pathological processes that occur during aging, but remember as you read it that normal aging is not easy for many people either. In some ways "normal" problems are similar to the pathology of old age, although they usually have less serious consequences.

Senile and presenile dementia. The symptoms of senile and presenile dementia are similar; the two disorders differ primarily in age of onset. Presenile dementia first appears between the ages of 45 and 60, whereas the senile dementias develop after the age of 60. The growing number of older people in the population makes it increasingly important to learn about these conditions, their causes, and their proper treatment.

As a person ages, his or her entire body functions less efficiently than it did in youth. The central nervous system, which is better protected than the other organ systems, often shows fewer signs of deterioration than other systems. However, it too cannot escape the ravages of time. Thus the elderly become rigid in their ways—resistant to behavioral change. They are reluctant to try new approaches to new environmental problems brought on by the pressures of a changing society. They tend to focus on reliving the past rather than realistically confronting the present or the future—perhaps because the present and future seem to hold so little promise.

These patterns of behavior, which are integral components of normal aging, appear in exaggerated form in patients whose brains have begun to undergo pathological deterioration. But recent data suggest that the specific changes in intellectual functioning which accompany normal aging differ significantly from those which characterize the chronic brain syndromes (Ben-Yishay et al., 1971; Overall & Gorham, 1972).

• SENILE DEMENTIA. Typically, senile dementia develops after the age of 75 years. It occurs more often among women than among men (Batchelor, 1969). It begins as a gradual failure to recall names, dates, and recent events—confusional behavior which grows progressively worse over time. One of the most serious consequences is that life may become physically dangerous as the patient grows more disoriented.

Upon autopsy after death (which may or may not have been directly caused by the dementia), the patient's brain is often small and shrunken. There may also be a significant loss of brain tissue, associated with the growth of senile plaques (roundish areas of tissue degeneration). While the origin of senile plaques is uncertain, they are found only in the cortex of humans who have developed senile dementia. Some investigators say that there seems to be a relationship between the number of senile plaques and the severity of symptoms of senile dementia (Blessed et al., 1968).

The etiology of senile dementia itself remains obscure. Wang and Busse consider the condition to be a "sociopsychosomatic disorder"—a disorder in which the individual's

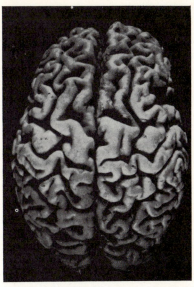

This picture of the brain of a person who had Alzheimer's disease shows the severe atrophy which occurs with this disorder. Is it any wonder that the patient suffered gross behavioral impairment? *(Adams & Sidman, 1968)*

external environment and personality interact with structural changes in the brain to produce pathological behavior (1971). Specifically, some older people, because of a more adaptive premorbid personality and a more supportive environment, show fewer signs of dysfunction than other less fortunate patients whose actual brain pathology may be no greater.

• PRESENILE DEMENTIA. Among the presenile dementias, which are senile disorders that occur in younger patients, the two most important are *Alzheimer's disease* and *Pick's disease.*

The average age of onset of Alzheimer's disease is 56 years. Like senile dementia, it occurs more often in women than in men. Alzheimer's disease accounts for about 7 percent of all psychoses of later life (Ferraro, 1959). As it was with Mirian S., the onset of this form of dementia is insidious; the disease usually runs its course from earliest symptoms to death in four to six years.

On autopsy, the brain of the Alzheimer's

patient appears even more atrophied than that of the senile dementia patient. Instead of the senile plaques in the senile dementia patient's brain, however, there is a deterioration of brain tissue called *Alzheimer's neurofibrillar degeneration*—a positive sign of Alzheimer's disease (Ferraro, 1959). The cause of the disease remains unknown, although genetic predisposition is thought to play a role in some cases.

Pick's disease is much rarer than Alzheimer's disease. Since the symptoms of the two are similar in the early stages, differential diagnosis is difficult. In fact, an autopsy is often the only way to distinguish between the two diseases. It reveals that patients suffering from Pick's disease have atrophied frontal and temporal lobes. The cause of Pick's disease, like those of the other dementias, is unknown.

There is no known treatment for either Alzheimer's or Pick's disease, which both run a course of 4 to 7 years. Consequently, differential diagnosis of the two disorders is not an urgent necessity.

Cerebral arteriosclerosis. One of the most common chronic brain syndromes associated with aging is *cerebral arteriosclerosis.* This condition, which occurs more often in men than in women, usually first shows itself when the patient is in his or her middle sixties. In some families where there is genetic predisposition, however, the symptoms of cerebral arteriosclerosis can appear in a person's thirties or forties (Batchelor, 1969). When it does occur in younger people, death from *heart failure* or a *cerebrovascular accident* (stroke) often follows within three or four years.

Arteriosclerosis causes the walls of the body's arteries to become thickened from fatty deposits, which dramatically reduce the diameter of the vessels. The arteries can no longer carry enough blood to provide all the food, minerals, vitamins, oxygen, and other substances necessary for good health. Since brain cells consume more oxygen and other nutritive materials than almost any other cells in the body, the harmful consequences of arteriosclerosis often affect them first and most seriously.

In addition, arteriosclerosis is often associated with high blood pressure (hypertension), since the heart must work harder to push the blood through narrow vessels than through unencumbered ones. Hypertension in turn puts pressure on the walls of arteries and veins that sometimes causes them to rupture or block. Blockage or rupture of a blood vessel in the brain is called a *cerebrovascular accident,* or stroke.

The immediate consequence of a stroke is often delirium in the form of acute confusion or coma. Frequently the patient dies during this acute stage; if he does not, some of his behavioral symptoms will remit, but he will be left with some amount of residual brain damage. Its precise nature depends upon the severity and location of the damage caused by the stroke.

By contrast, the mental symptoms which accompany cerebral arteriosclerosis may occur either gradually or abruptly. In slowly progressive cases of cerebral arteriosclerosis, the early psychological symptoms resemble senile dementia. In cases of acute onset, however, the central symptoms are confusion, lack of coherence, restlessness, and sometimes hallucinations. Marked physical symptoms, including paralysis, accompany acute cerebral arteriosclerosis.

Parkinson's disease. Although it is not exclusively an illness of old age, *Parkinson's disease* occurs more often in older people than younger ones. The average age of onset is 55 years (Calne, 1970). Recent research has clarified the nature of this neurological disorder. Approximately 40 percent of Parkinson patients show symptoms of dementia. Another 37 percent exhibit depressive symptoms (Celesia & Wanamaker, 1972). But the major symptoms of Parkinsonism are in the motor area. The patient develops an uncontrollable tremor in his hands, arms, and legs. His arms and legs become resistant to passive movement—that is, to being lifted or otherwise moved. And his voluntary motor activity declines, producing a mask-like facial expression which is one of the cardinal signs of Parkinson's disease.

The course of the untreated disease depends in part upon the patient's age and race. Blacks have a better prognosis than whites, and people who develop the disease later in life have a better prognosis than younger victims. The outcome varies from an essentially undisturbed life-span to premature death produced by a patient's weakened condition.

The majority of cases of Parkinsonism are of unknown etiology. Some Parkinson's patients are thought to have developed the disorder in association with encephalitis or arteriosclerosis (Calne, 1970; Pollock & Hornabrook, 1966). But recent research has suggested that there may be a defect in the neurotransmitter system of the brains of many Parkinsonism patients (see Chapter 3 for a review of the functions of neurotransmitters). This research indicates that the neurotransmitter *dopamine* may be important in Parkinsonism (McGeer, 1971).

Parkinson's disease has always puzzled the neuropathologist because, on autopsy, the brains of Parkinson's patients fail to show the amount of cellular damage which would be expected of persons with such debilitating symptoms. Abnormally low levels of dopamine in their brains could explain why extensive gross brain tissue damage was not necessary to produce their severe motor disability.

While the reasons for the apparently inadequate production of dopamine in this disease remain unknown, it has now become possible to compensate for the lack of naturally occurring dopamine with a drug called *levadopa* (L-dopa). L-dopa does produce significant positive changes in some Parkinson's patients: Cotzias and his co-workers report that among 28 patients treated with the drug, 10 showed dramatic improvement, 10 marked improvement, 4 moderate improvement, and 4 modest change (1969). The improvements were sustained over a two-year period (1971). But this study and others report serious side effects in some patients from the use of L-dopa (Nakano & Tyler, 1971). According to Goodwin, delirium and confusion, depression, overactivity, and delusions occur in

significant numbers of Parkinson's patients after being given L-dopa (1971). Parkinson's patients who are already demented seem especially prone to develop serious side effects (Sacks et al., 1972). Thus, despite its promise, L-dopa must be prescribed with great caution for Parkinson's patients.

Organic brain disorders caused by infection

Infections in the central nervous system produce a variety of psychological symptoms. Untreated infections can cause agitation, stupor, depression, hallucinations, delusions, and ultimately, dementia. Among the major forms of central nervous system infection with serious psychological aftereffects are brain abscesses and general paralysis.

Brain abscess. A brain abscess is simply an infection that occurs within the brain. The use of antibiotic drugs has made these abscesses quite rare, but at one time they were a very serious problem. The brain abscess usually develops from an ear or sinus infection, although occasionally an infection may be carried from another part of the body through the bloodstream to the brain.

Initial symptoms of an abscess may be little more than fever or a subnormal temperature and a general decrease in alertness, with few neurological signs. During the later stages the patient may suffer from delirium, chills, headaches, and abnormal neurological responses. In diagnosing this kind of infection one clue is the existence of infection elsewhere in the body. Laboratory tests can also help in diagnosis. Brain abscesses are treated by antibiotic drugs or, in more serious cases, by surgery.

General paralysis. The history of general paralysis and its relationship to syphilis were traced earlier in this chapter. Not everyone who contracts syphilis and fails to obtain treatment for it develops general paralysis. Only 1 to 2 percent of syphilis victims ultimately suffer central nervous system involvement (Batchelor, 1969). Why some people fall victim to general paralysis and others do not is unknown.

Untreated syphilis usually progresses through four stages. The first begins shortly after the spirochetes enter the body. Multiplying rapidly, they cause a hard chancre (sore) to appear at the site of infection—usually the penis or vagina—in ten to forty days. The syphilitic chancre takes the form of either a hard pimple or an open ulcerated sore. The victim may ignore it as a minor problem, with the result that the chancre obligingly disappears within a month to six weeks. The person may think that he is cured.

The second stage of syphilis is often more subtle. About three to six weeks after the stage 1 chancre has disappeared, the patient develops a copper-colored skin rash which is usually mild. He may also be feverish, have headaches, and experience a variety of other symptoms not solely associated with venereal disease. If he ignores the stage 2 symptoms also, he will enter stage 3. This period is a quiet one in terms of symptoms, but a good deal of pathological activity takes place within the body. It is in stage 3 that the spirochetes attack internal organs, especially the blood vessels and nerve cells, though the bone marrow, spleen, or other organs may be the site of attack.

As much as thirty years after the initial syphilitic infection, the fourth and most damaging stage of untreated syphilis begins. Heart disease, blindness, and psychosis may ravage the victim. When the spirochetes of syphilis attack the central nervous system, they produce the condition called general paralysis. Unless treated, general paralysis will kill within two to three years of onset. The very term *general paralysis* indicates how pervasively incapacitating it can be. The early clinicians who named it knew of no other mental disorder that produced such total disruption of mental and physical functioning. In fact, untreated patients could reach the point of total immobility from which improvement in functioning was impossible.

General paralysis patients have been divided into three categories: the *expansive* type, who is characterized by euphoria and delusions of affluence and power; the *depressed* type, who may also have somatic delusions centering on bodily deterioration; and the *simple* type, who is neither euphoric or depressed but shows instead a gradual constriction in his behavioral repertoire, along with an increasingly limited ability to respond cognitively and emotionally.

The diagnosis of syphilis can be made during any stage by a Wasserman test of the blood or spinal fluid. Once the diagnosis is confirmed, treatment with penicillin is begun. Penicillin given before stage 3 syphilis will prevent development of state 4—general paralysis. But once stage 3 has begun, ensuing damage to the central nervous system cannot be undone but only arrested.

Systemic infection. In addition to infectious diseases which attack the central nervous system directly, a number of diseases arising in other parts of the body, including pneumonia, typhoid fever, malaria, and acute rheumatic fever, can produce delirium as well as associated psychological symptoms. As a general rule, these symptoms remit when the patient recovers from the physical disease.

Organic brain disorders caused by intoxication

Not every drug addict or alcoholic suffers the symptoms of an organic brain disorder, but each is a potential victim.

Delirium tremens. Delirium tremens (DTs) is an acute (rapid-onset) brain syndrome which occurs when chronic alcoholics withdraw from long periods of drinking. It is characterized by delirium, tremors, and terrifying visual hallucinations. The patient is restless, sleepless, and acutely fearful. Even when he does manage to fall asleep, he is likely to be awakened by nightmares.

When he is awake, the patient misinterprets

events around him. He sees a shadow on the wall as a creeping monster and a spot on the sheet as an insect. "The visual hallucinations may be exceedingly bizarre; one patient stated that an octopus came out of the wall and climbed on her bed, another, that he saw chipmunks raise his window and sit on the window sill. He related that, when the nurse came into the room, they suddenly ran out of the window so that she could never see them" (Thompson, 1959, p. 1209). During his delirium the patient may try to escape from the terrifying creatures of his hallucinations and must be watched lest he hurt himself or other people in his panic.

The symptoms of DTs, which last from three to six days, are so distinctive that their presence is almost always definitive evidence of chronic alcoholism. Bill H., for example, remembered having experienced DTs at least three times. When each bout was finally over, Bill "swore off" drinking—until the next time.

Delirium tremens rarely occur in people under the age of 30, largely because the disorder develops only after many years of heavy drinking. Although the actual cause of DTs is unknown, they appear only after a heavy drinker abruptly stops drinking. Untreated delirium tremens has a 10 to 15 percent mortality (death) rate, a fact that makes this withdrawal consequence among the most dangerous of all drug withdrawal phenomena. Appropriate treatment includes massive sedation, vitamins, and an adequate intake of fluids.

Korsakov's psychosis. Although *Korsakov's psychosis* results from neglect of diet rather than from alcohol as such, it is usually alcoholics who eat so little that they develop this dietary disorder. Thus Korsakov's psychosis is traditionally classified as a disorder of alcoholism.

Victor, Adams, and Collins have devoted twenty years to the study of what they call the Wernicke-Korsakov syndrome (1971). One of their earliest observations was that both Wer-

A Drunkard's Dream.

"A Drunkard's Dream." *(New York Public Libary)*

nicke's disease and Korsakov's psychosis are two facets of the same disorder, a nutritional-deficiency disease resulting from the chronic alcoholic's preference for beverage alcohol over foods containing vitamins and minerals.

Patients first develop the symptoms of Wernicke's disease: poor balance, difficulty in controlling eye movement, and general confusion. These symptoms then begin to merge with the symptoms reflecting the dementia of Korsakov's psychosis: loss of memory, inability to acquire and retain new information, slight impairment of perceptual and conceptual abilities, and loss of spontaneity. The most dramatic symptom of Korsakov's psychosis is *con-fabulation*—"manufacture of memories" to fill gaps in one's own memory. Confabulated memories sometimes take absurd or bizarre forms. Thompson describes a Korsakov's patient confined to a hospital bed on a hot summer day who, when asked where she was and why she was there, claimed that she was on board a ship, that the physician was the ship's doctor, and the stench emanating from garbage outside her window was a delightful sea breeze (1959). No one really knows why Korsakov's patients feel compelled to fill the gaps in their memories with confabulated details, though the profound degree of memory loss associated with the condition may be one explanation.

Wernicke-Korsakov syndrome patients have poor prognoses. The disorder runs a long course in which the patients' physical health intermittently improves, but their cognitive and affective deficits remain. Virtually the only treatment consists of massive doses of vitamins, a high-calorie diet, and of course, withdrawal from alcohol. But this regimen does little more than halt further cognitive deterioration.

Drug intoxication. Though alcohol and the other commonly abused drugs present their greatest hazards to health in the acute brain disorders—the "highs" and "rushes" they bring on, with the resulting automobile accidents or accidental suicides—prolonged use of these drugs is associated with two other physical dangers. The first is the risk to health of withdrawal after a person has become physically addicted to the drug. This substantial risk was discussed in Chapter 11. The second danger is the possibility of developing an organic brain syndrome. For example, on a short-term basis morphine (or heroin) in excessive amounts causes motor difficulties, paralysis, ataxia (poor balance), and loss of bladder control, as well as personal negligence, selfishness, and apathy. Consequences of chronic morphinism include memory defects and loss of a sense of responsibility, as well as serious, sometimes permanent, physical damage.

The long-term effects of heroin use are discussed in Chapter 11. In addition to these, a heroin overdose may be fatal; the person may rapidly become unconscious, enter a coma, and die unless he or she is given immediate medical attention. Comparable effects of short- and long-term consumption of the other drugs of abuse have been reported.

Organic brain disorders caused by nutritional deficiency

After World War II the strikingly altered behavior of people who had been prisoners of war and concentration-camp internees led to a great deal of research on the physical and psychological effects of long-continued, profound dietary deficiency (Antonev, 1947; LaPorte, 1946; Montagu, 1972). In one such study Brozek and Grande reported extensive neurological and psychological change in people who had survived the wartime famines of Leningrad and other Russian cities (1960). Many of these victims, who were otherwise uninjured, felt the effects of poor nutrition long after the war had ended. They were apathetic, irritable, or both; they found it difficult to concentrate and they suffered from episodic depressions.

Dietary deficiencies are not confined to prisoners of war or inhabitants of cities under siege. Adults and children living in every part of the United States are afflicted with them, owing largely to a combination of poverty and ignorance. Higher-income United States families have both more varied and adequate as well as more expensive diets (Citizens' Board, 1968; Wilson et al., 1965). By way of contrast, consider the fact that Massachusetts residents on welfare in 1969 received approximately 30 cents per person per meal—a sum which guarantees dietary inadequacy (Massachusetts Welfare Rights Organization, 1969).

One of the gravest forms of nutritional deficiency is protein deficiency which, among other things, retards intellectual development. Protein malnourishment is a worldwide problem, especially in the tropics and subtropics (Pearson, 1968). Approximately 75 percent of preschool children in South America, Asia, and Africa are underweight, in part because of protein deficiency (Behar, 1968). Protein deficiency is also a problem in the Western world (Baird et al., 1954; Dieckmann et al., 1951; Kirkwood, 1955). Though the United States has one of the highest standards of living, and though its citizens consume more meat per capita than the citizens of almost any other country, many poor Americans cannot afford to buy enough meat to prevent protein deficiency.

The influence of a protein deficiency upon growth and development depends upon a child's age. Protein deficiency in pregnant women results in lower average birth weights for their infants (Kaplan, 1972; Montagu, 1962), an increase in physical defects (Kaplan, 1972), a higher rate of premature births, a higher mortality rate in the months after birth, and a greater likelihood of serious childhood diseases (Anderson et al., 1958; Montagu, 1962; Walker, 1955).

Monkeys fed a diet deficient in protein show a disordered pattern of social development similar to that found in animals deprived of all social contact (Zimmerman et al., 1972). Animals whose diet is deficient in these and other essential dietary elements suffer significant retardation in brain tissue development (Davison & Dobbing, 1966; Dickerson et al., 1967; Winick & Noble, 1966). Autopsies performed on children who have died of malnutrition likewise reveal that they developed a subnormal number of brain cells (Brown, 1966; Parekh et al., 1970; Winick et al., 1970).

In a thorough review of the research, Kaplan concluded that diet is most influential upon brain development from six months before to six months after birth (1972). The results of nutritional deprivation during this period may be irreversible. A dietary deficiency which occurs from six months after birth to the end of the second year of life is also potentially damaging because brain development is very rapid then, but an improved diet can often partly repair incipient damage.

Brain damage is especially likely to be reflected in retarded intellectual functioning.

This five-year-old Cheyenne Indian boy is impoverished; he is therefore probably malnourished as well. *(Rohn Engh/Photo Researchers, Inc.)*

The poor child, all other factors aside, often has a lower intellectual potential at birth because of his mother's lifelong history of inferior nutrition (see Chapter 16 for a discussion of diet and retardation).

Organic brain disorders caused by head injury

Head injuries most commonly result from falls, blows to the head, automobile accidents or, as with Webster R., penetration of foreign objects like bullets, hand grenades, or land-mine fragments. While most head injuries cause acute rather than chronic brain syndromes, some are severe enough to produce enduring changes in personality, physical functioning, or both

The brain is so well protected in its bony, cushioned enclosure, the skull, that it withstands numerous bumps and small blows with little or no damage. But major injuries can result in three degrees of acute brain trauma: cerebral concussion, cerebral contusion, or cerebral laceration.

Cerebral concussion, the mildest form of brain injury, is characterized by brief loss of consciousness. It may be accompanied by slight bewilderment, loss of memory concerning the accident, and a headache for a day or two. The victim of a cerebral concussion is unlikely to suffer residual effects of his injury. Because concussion by definition is not fatal, we do not have autopsy reports of the effects of these injuries on the brain.

Cerebral contusion occurs when the head is hit with enough force to cause the brain to bump the inside of the skull, thus compressing and then bruising it. The patient may remain unconscious for hours or days and may be delirious on regaining consciousness. For days or even weeks afterwards, he may experience headaches, dizziness, nausea, and muscular weakness. Once these acute symptoms remit, he may continue to show signs of impaired intellectual and motor functioning, depending upon the extent and location of the injured brain tissue. Boxers who suffer cerebral contusions frequently enough or intensely enough become permanently "punch-drunk."

Cerebral laceration occurs when brain tissue is actually torn or broken. Webster R. suffered severe cerebral lacerations from the hand grenade and bone fragments which penetrated his skull and entered his brain. The symptoms immediately following cerebral laceration are like those which follow cerebral contusion: At first the patient is unconscious; if he survives, he usually passes from coma to delirium to consciousness. If the injury is serious enough, however, he may remain comatose for months or years. Residual symptoms like headaches and motor and intellectual impairment almost always follow cerebral laceration.

Organic brain disorders caused by brain tumor

Brain tumors are abnormal growths within the brain. Some brain tumors are *malignant* and regrow even after attempts at removal. Others are *benign,* meaning that once they are removed, they do not return. Because the skull is bone, it allows little room for growth or expansion once it has become rigid during early childhood. Consequently, considerable pressure may be exerted on the brain by a tumor. It is usually the pressure on the brain caused by the expanding tumors that is responsible for the physical and psychological symptoms they produce.

Psychological symptoms depend upon the location and size of the tumor as well as on the patient's premorbid personality. Initially such symptoms are vague and nonspecific. The person may tire easily, have difficulty in concentrating and feel diffuse anxiety—problems which may be diagnosed as the result or overwork or a developing neurosis. As the tumor grows, however, the increased pressure on the brain produces headaches, vomiting, nausea, and visual problems (papilledema). The patient may become confused or irrational, and his condition will progress to dementia unless death intervenes or treatment is provided. Tumors can also cause symptoms specific to their location as well as these general symptoms. For example, a frontal lobe tumor may result in mild euphoria; temporal tumors may produce aphasia, depression and irritability; and occipital lobe tumors may cause visual defects.

Treatment of brain tumors is usually surgical, although radiation therapy and drugs may also be used. The effectiveness of treatment depends upon the type of tumor, its size, and its location. The prognosis is worst for malignant growths or very large tumors in critical areas of the brain.

Organic brain disorders caused by epilepsy

Epilepsy has the longest recorded history of any of the organic brain syndromes (Hoch & Knight, 1947). Hundreds of years ago it was considered a "sacred disease"; people believed that the fits resulted from a divine presence in the victim's body. Many figures in history suffered from it, including Julius Caesar, Napoleon, Van Gogh, and Dostoevsky. It occurs in both men and women, among all races, in all age groups, and throughout all strata of society.

The term *epilepsy* encompasses a heterogeneous group of disorders which share one defining feature: episodic disruption of normal electrical activity in the central nervous system. There are four common categories of epilepsy—grand mal, petit mal, psychomotor, and Jacksonian.

Grand mal epilepsy. Grand mal epilepsy is the most common and most dramatic of these disorders. There are five common stages in the usual grand mal seizure. The sequence begins when the patient experiences the *aura* during the first few seconds of the seizure. This is a set of distinct physical sensations which vary depending upon the locus of the abnormal brain discharge. Common varieties of aura include a sinking feeling in the stomach, a headache, dizziness, visual or auditory hallucinations, and involuntary muscular activity.

After the aura, which usually lasts only a few seconds, the seizure itself begins. First the patient falls to the ground unconscious. He may emit a loud cry due to muscular contractions of the chest and throat over which he has no control. During the second, or *tonic,* stage of the seizure (which lasts ten to thirty seconds),

every skeletal muscle becomes rigid. During the three to four minutes of the third, or *clonic,* stage, his arms and legs jerk up and down rapidly and repeatedly, his head may strike the ground again and again, his jaws open and close and open again—all without control or consciousness. The movements of his jaw and face muscles may cause the epileptic to bite his tongue or his lips; he may lose bladder or bowel control, or he may vomit. Finally, as the fourth stage is entered, the clonic movements end and the victim lapses into a coma lasting from a few minutes to several hours. When he wakes he is confused, tired, bruised, and sometimes bloody.

Grand mal seizures, untreated with drugs, may occur as often as several times a day or as rarely as once in several months. In an unusual and very dangerous variant of grand mal epilepsy, *status epilepticus,* seizures follow one another in a series without intervening intervals of consciousness. These seizures may be fatal if they are not interrupted immediately by treatment with anticonvulsant drugs.

Petit mal epilepsy. Petit mal seizures are brief losses of consciousness without accompanying convulsive movements. The petit mal patient does not experience auras. He or she may not even be aware of the seizures

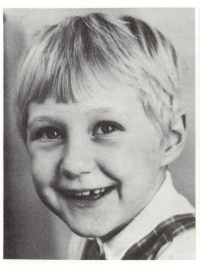 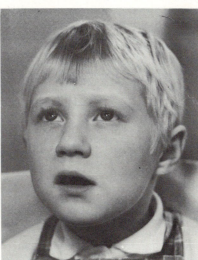

Left, a young girl before a petit mal seizure; she is fully conscious of her surroundings. Right, the girl during a momentary petit mal attack, during which she is impervious to her environment. *(Gamstorp, 1970)*

when they occur, largely because they last only a few seconds and rarely interrupt the activities in which the petit mal victim is engaged. Petit mal seizures may appear without warning during the first decade of life and then disappear as unexpectedly during adolescence. Though petit mal epilepsy may be a minor part of one child's life, another child may experience more than 100 seizures in a day and appear confused, inattentive, or demented as a result. Thus petit mal epilepsy can create school problems even though the majority of children who suffer from it are at least average in intelligence. For the adolescent or adult, uncontrollable petit mal seizures rule out activities like driving a car or operating machinery.

Psychomotor epilepsy. The patient who has psychomotor epilepsy engages in automatic behaviors which may seem purposeful to outside observers but which he is unaware of. Fortunately, most people who suffer from this disorder do nothing more ominous than mumble, grind their teeth, take off their clothes, or wander around harmlessly during their psychomotor seizures.

Clinicians have long been intrigued by the fact that some patients with psychomotor epilepsy also show psychotic behavior between seizures. At times their behavior is so similar to the behavior of schizophrenics that differential diagnosis is very difficult. Data available at present indicate that there is a significant correlation between incidence of psychomotor epilepsy and emission of schizophrenic-like behavior, though it is not clear whether the epilepsy causes the psychotic behavior or whether both are due to some other underlying cause (Heath, 1962; Slater & Beard, 1963; Stevens et al., 1969, Taylor & Falconer, 1968). Most important, these data raise questions about relationships between brain disorder and schizophrenia.

Jacksonian epilepsy. Jacksonian seizures were originally described by the famous British neurologist, J. Hughlings Jackson (1834 to 1911). A Jacksonian seizure is a localized convulsion that begins in one part of the body and then spreads to surrounding ones. For example, a Jacksonian seizure might start in the big toe, then spread to the foot, then the leg, and finally the thigh. There is usually no loss of consciousness with a Jacksonian seizure.

Etiology and treatment of epilepsy. Because there is no single cause of epilepsy, we should more accurately speak of its etiologies. It develops in association with brain tumors, cerebral arteriosclerosis, general paralysis, head injury, cerebral palsy, tuberous sclerosis, and presenile dementia. It also develops idiopathically—from unknown causes. While not all forms of epilepsy are inherited, a tendency toward cerebral dysrhythmia, or abnormal cerebral discharge, does appear to be hereditary in some cases. We do not yet have adequate diagnostic procedures to identify with certainty that percentage of cases in which heredity is the dominant factor.

Epilepsy can now be treated successfully with drugs. Phenobarbital and Dilantin are used to control grand mal seizures, Tridone is effective with petit mal seizures, and Phenurone reduces the frequency of psychomotor seizures. Though these drugs are taken for granted now, not so long ago they transformed the lives of a generation of epileptics who had been hopeless invalids.

Despite the enlightened age in which we live, a number of myths about epilepsy remain. One of the most popular is the "old wives' tale" that epileptics commit violent crimes. Research clearly indicates that epileptic prisoners are no more violent than nonepileptic prisoners (Gunn & Bonn, 1971). Other bits of folklore, equally questionable, portray the epileptic as personally unpredictable, sexually uncontrolled, and intellectually inferior. As a result of such holdovers from myth and magic, the epileptic often feels ashamed of his epilepsy and hides it from others for fear it will be held against him. In reality, epilepsy is neither a "sacred disease" nor a disgrace. It is a malfunction of the electrical activity of the brain, and it can often be so well controlled that it need not hamper any aspect of living. To view epilepsy as anything else is to join those medieval witch-hunters, Kraemer and Sprenger, in propagating the lies of *The Witches' Hammer.*

Treatment of organic brain disorders

Medical treatment

Treatment of most organic brain syndromes is primarily medical. In the case of brain tumors, abscesses, or head injuries, surgery may be necessary to remove a growth or repair the damage caused by injury. Anticonvulsant drugs to control seizures, antibiotics to treat brain abscesses, and the use of L-dopa to treat Parkinson's disease are also part of sound medical management. In addition, antipsychotic drugs and tranquilizers may be used to reduce the agitation and distress which accompany many forms of organic brain disorder.

Behavioral treatment

After the necessary medical steps have been taken to save a patient's life, treat some of his symptoms, or both, he often retains residual behaviors that may be psychological in origin and that can be treated nonmedically. Atthowe used behavioral techniques to control bed-wetting in severely disabled chronic brain syndrome patients (1972). Garber employed operant procedures to eliminate drooling in a 14-year-old boy with cerebral palsy (1971). Holland and Harris used operant procedures to restore speech in a 23-year-old doctoral student who had undergone surgery to remove a tumor on the parietal lobe (1968). A year after the onset of the aphasia which unfortunately resulted from the surgery, his speech skills had been restored to the point where he could read more than 300 words a minute with 100 percent comprehension. While he still had mild problems in finding words, he had improved so much that he could audit graduate courses and prepare to return to school fulltime.

The full potential of behavioral techniques for the brain-damaged patient has yet to be explored. Perhaps this unfortunate failure is due to the general social neglect of the elderly (Lindsley, 1964) and of the chronic brain syndrome patient. They may seem to many psychologists and psychiatrists to be less exciting and to show less potential than other patient populations which have traditionally been the targets of research.

Prosthetic environments

Modification of environments to meet the needs of the elderly has received thoughtful attention from Ogden Lindsley (1964). He proposes changing the environments of older persons to compensate for some of their failing physical abilities. Such modifications would lead to the design of *prosthetic environments,* just as glasses or a hearing aid are prosthetic devices that improve vision or hearing. For example, Lindsley suggests that the same kind of electronic device now used to open supermarket or garage doors could be installed in the doors of hospitals or residences for the elderly to make their lives easier and more comfortable. Similarly, older people with severe hand tremors could be given telephones and typewriters with buttons and keys spaced far enough apart so that shaking hands could still touch the correct key. And if the elderly prove to be less responsive to stimuli from the environment than necessary, these stimuli could be intensified, or additional signals could be added. If the ring of the phone is not enough, for example, a flashing red light could be an additional cue that the phone is ringing. To institute these changes, Lindsley noted, it is first necessary to observe the older person within his environment in order to analyze what gadgets would be helpful.

Changing the environment need not depend upon mechanical devices alone. A change in the social setting can also significantly alter an elderly person's perceptions of his environment. Chein describes a study in which male patients with an average age in the early seventies were exposed to one of four settings

(1971). Three groups were given a beverage (beer, fruit punch, or fruit punch with tranquilizer), while the fourth group had only a tranquilizer. The three drinking groups had their beverage in a "pub" on the ward. The patients who were given a daily glass of beer showed the greatest improvement and the highest degree of social interaction of all four groups. Since 70 percent of the subjects were chronic brain syndrome patients, it is particularly impressive that something as simple as having a glass of beer could alter their behavior. Chein suggests that the beer helped to provide a more congenial atmosphere in which the men felt less lonely and more comfortable. This approach may be communicating to the patient that he is a responsible adult who can hold a drink rather than a dependent "child" who should not be given alcohol. Such findings lend further support to the deceptively simple view expressed by Teuber (1960) and others more recently that motivation can play a major role in the adjustment of brain-injured patients.

These innovative suggestions and approaches stand in stark contrast to the way in which our society *really* treats its elderly people. The failure of the American system in this regard is scathingly documented in *Old Age: The Last Segregation,* a report by Ralph Nader's study group on nursing homes (Townsend, 1971).

Many of the elderly are also given psychiatric hospitalization, although for most of them a state psychiatric hospital is the worst place they could be sent. It is generally conceded that placement of the elderly in most institutional settings hastens their deaths. There is a painful need in our country for day-care centers, outpatient clinics, and a variety of other services which would allow the elderly to maintain themselves in society as long as possible (Markson et al., 1971).

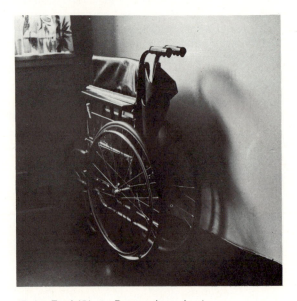

(Rohn Engh/Photo Researchers, Inc.)

Summary

It is inevitable in an organ as complex as the human brain that damage to various areas will be reflected in a wide range of behavioral deviations. The *Diagnostic and Statistical Manual* specifies impairment in orientation, memory, intellectual functioning, judgment, and affect as major behavioral cues to the identification of brain damage. Two broad organic syndromes, delirium and dementia, are also convenient in describing the essentials of organic impairment. Delirium is usually caused by an agent acting outside of the brain (fever or poison) and is generally transitory (although it may have some long-term residual effects). Dementia reflects a disease process taking place within the brain itself; it generally causes permanent brain damage, although its progress can sometimes be arrested or partially reversed. Both Mirian S. and Webster R. suffer from dementia. In Mirian's case, the disease will grow progressively worse; in Webster's, his functioning has stabilized, and he may even show some limited behavioral improvement as he adapts to his handicap. Because treatment for the organic brain disorders is different from treatment for the functional psychoses (like schizophrenia), it is very important to make an early diagnosis which accurately distinguishes between them.

Diagnosis of the organic brain syndromes is based largely upon neurological examination, though interviews and observations are also useful. Assessment of actual brain functioning by means of spinal taps, x-rays, and electroencephalograms are important aspects of the diagnostic sequence. Tests of intelligence as well as highly specialized psychological batteries to assess loss of specific sensory, motor, and cognitive functions may aid both diagnosis and treatment planning.

Many of the organic brain disorders are related to aging processes. As such they are a reflection of the generally deteriorating body functioning that accompanies age. Senile dementia, cerebral arteriosclerosis, and Parkinson's disease are all a reflection of aging. Presenile dementia, which is similar in appearance to senile dementia, occurs in somewhat younger patients, such as Mirian S. Brain disorders may also arise from infection (e.g., brain abscess, general paralysis) and intoxication (delirium tremens, Korsakov's psychosis, and drug intoxication). Nutritional deficiency at all ages, but especially in the fetus or young infant, can produce permanent brain damage. Damage to the brain by a head injury, such as Webster R.'s, or by the growth of brain tumors can cause irreversible harm. Finally, epilepsy in its several different forms reflects an abnormality in the electrical functioning of the brain. The causes of epilepsy are varied and not always known, but the disease can often be treated with appropriate drugs.

Treatment of organic brain syndromes is generally medical. Drugs and surgery can control, stop, or reverse many brain disorders. Because these syndromes often leave a permanent scar upon functioning, patients must frequently be retrained or provided with special environments in order to compensate for their handicap. Motivational and environmental factors are of critical importance in the recovery of functioning following brain damage.

Glossary

Abnormal behavior: Behavior deviating from usual adaptive behavior.

Abreaction: Expression of pent-up emotion.

Abstract: Thinking transcending the immediate qualities of a situation and examining its broader perspectives. Contrasts with *concrete*.

Accessory symptoms: From Bleuler. Symptoms found in some cases of schizophrenia, but not all. Contrasted with *fundamental symptoms*.

Acetylcholine: A neurotransmitter found within the sympathetic and parasympathetic nervous systems.

Acid: Slang term for LSD.

Acute: A condition of recent onset, usually (but not always) severe.

Acute brain syndrome: Organic brain syndrome of sudden onset.

Acute schizophrenic episode: A first psychotic episode of schizophrenic behavior. Acute onset of confusion, depression, agitation, and anxiety.

Adrenal cortex: Portion of adrenal gland which secretes cortisone and corticosterone, both of which are important in metabolism and the control of inflammation.

Adrenalin: Sympathetic nervous system stimulant secreted by the adrenal medulla. Also known as *epinephrine*.

Adrenal medulla: Portion of adrenal gland which secretes epinephrine and norepinephrine, both of which function as sympathetic nervous system stimulants.

Adrenochrome: Abnormal metabolite of epinephrine. Implicated in some theories of schizophrenia.

Adrenocorticotrophic hormone: (ACTH): A secretion of the pituitary gland. Acts upon adrenal gland.

Affect: Feeling, mood.

Agitated depression: Serious disorder marked by both anxiety and depression.

Agoraphobia: Fear of open spaces.

Alpha alcoholism: From Jellinek. Psychological dependence on alcohol, with resulting damage to the drinker's interpersonal relations.

Alpha suppression: Blocking of alpha wave activity in brain.

Alpha waves: Electrical brain activity with a frequency of 8 to 13 cycles per second. Occurs during periods of relaxed wakefulness.

Alzheimer's disease: A form of presenile dementia.

Ambivalence: Simultaneous experiencing of two conflicting emotions. One of Bleuler's "four A's," the four fundamental symptoms of schizophrenia.

Amnesia: Partial or total loss of recall for past experiences.

Amniocentesis: Test of amniotic fluid for chromosomal and genetic defects.

Amobarbital: A barbiturate (sedative) drug.

Amphetamine: Stimulant drug. Brand name *Benzedrine*.

Anal stage: Second stage of psychosexual development in psychoanalytic theory. Gratification is focused upon anal area.

Anesthesia: Form of hysterical neurosis involving loss of feeling in a portion or portions of body without accompanying physical damage to nervous system.

Anhedonia: Inability to experience pleasure.

Anorexia nervosa: Psychosomatic disorder characterized by severe loss of appetite with consequent weight loss.

Antabuse: Drug used in treatment of alcoholism. Generic name disulfiram.

Antecedent events: Activities preceding emission of a target behavior.

Antecedents: Events which precede a response.

Antisocial personality: See psychopathic personality.

Anxiety: Unrealistic fear which may or may not be connected to a particular object or situation.

Anxiety attack: Episode of acute anxiety.

Anxiety neurosis: Neurosis characterized chiefly by presence of pervasive anxiety.

Aphasia: Defect in ability to receive or express language.

Approach-approach conflict: A forced choice between two attractive options.

Approach-avoidance conflict: Situation in which goal has both attractive and aversive elements.

Arousal: Physiological response to a stimulus.

Assertive training: Form of behavior therapy in which patients are taught to make appropriate social responses.

Astasia abasia: Form of hysterical neurosis in which patient can move his lower extremities while sitting but not while standing.

Asthenic: One of Kretschmer's body types. Characterized by a lean, long, and relatively weak body.

Asthenic personality: A personality disorder characterized by low energy and lack of interest in the world.

Asthma: Respiratory disorder. May be psychosomatic.

Athletic: One of Kretschmer's body types. Characterized by muscular frame, wide shoulders, well-developed chest, and tapered trunk.

Aura: Warning stage of grand mal seizure.

Autistic: Excessive withdrawal from external reality and corresponding overdependence on one's own fantasy life.

Autonomic nervous system: Portion of nervous system which controls functioning of internal organs.

Aversive conditioning: The use of a noxious event (such as shock) to punish unwanted behavior.

Avoidance-avoidance conflict: Forced choice between two aversive options.

Bad trip: Slang term for unpleasant drug experience.

Barbiturate: Group of sedative drugs with addictive properties.

Behavioral repertoire: The range of behaviors of which a person is capable.

Behavior therapy: Psychological treatment based upon principles of learning.

Benactyzine: Minor tranquilizer. Brand name *Suavitil.*

Benzedrine: Stimulant drug. Generic name *amphetamine.*

Bestiality: Sexual gratification from contact with animals.

Beta alcoholism: From Jellinek. Neither physical nor psychological dependence on alcohol; primarily physical complaints from excessive use.

Beta waves: Electrical brain activity with frequency of 14 to 25 cycles per second. Occurs during states of alertness.

Biofeedback: Providing a person direct information on his physiological functioning.

Bisexuality: Willingness to experience sexual activity with persons of either sex.

Bizarre: Strange and unusual.

Blackout: Short-term memory loss in a drug user.

Blood-alcohol level: Measure of the concentration of alcohol in the blood.

Body concept: The image a person has of the size, shape, adequacy, etc., of his body.

Bufotenine: Derivative of serotonin, one of the neurotransmitters. Implicated in some theories of schizophrenia.

Butch: Slang term for female homosexual who takes aggressive sexual role.

Castration: Removal of the genitals or, more generally, threatening the masculinity or femininity of a person.

Catatonic schizophrenia: Form of schizophrenia marked by decreased motor activity, thought disorder, mutism, and posturing.

Catecholamines: Sympathetic nervous system stimulants, including adrenalin and nonadrenalin.

Catharsis: Psychoanalytic term referring to an outpouring of emotion that may yield temporary relief from psychological suffering.

Central nervous system: Portion of the nervous system comprising brain and spinal cord.

Cerebellum: Portion of hindbrain responsible for smooth, coordinated motor activity.

Cerebral arteriosclerosis: Chronic brain syndrome of old age. Hardening of cerebral arteries causing reduction in blood flow to brain.

Cerebral concussion: Mild brain injury.

Cerebral contusion: Brain injury severe enough to cause brain to bump against inside of skull.

Cerebral cortex: Outer covering of cerebrum.

Cerebral laceration: Tearing or breaking of brain tissue following severe head injury.

Cerebral palsy: Chronic brain injury with loss of motor control.

Cerebrum: Largest and most advanced part of human brain.

Childhood schizophrenia: Schizophrenic behavior which is observed in prepubertal children.

Chlordiazepoxide: Minor tranquilizer. Brand name *Librium.*

Chlorpromazine: First of the phenothiazines to come into major use. Brand name *Thorazine.*

Chromosomes: Groupings of genes. There are 46 chromosomes in each cell in the human body.

Chronic: Condition of long standing.

Chronic-acute: Dimension of schizophrenia based upon the duration of the disorder.

Chronic brain syndrome: Organic brain syndrome of long duration.

Chronic undifferentiated schizophrenia: Label given schizophrenic patients who fail to show clear-cut behaviors of other categories of schizophrenia.

Clang associations: Words associated with one another only on basis of sound (e.g., "long-song"); a behavior characteristic of schizophrenia.

Classical (Pavlovian) conditioning: Learning in which an unconditioned stimulus and a conditioned stimulus are paired often enough to form a conditioned reflex.

Claustrophobia: Fear of enclosed spaces.

Clinical psychologist: Person with M.A. or Ph.D. training in assessment, treatment, and research on psychological disorders.

Cocaine: Stimulant derived from coca leaves.

Codeine: Addictive drug derived from the poppy.

Cognition: Mental functions involved in knowing, thinking, planning, creating, etc.

Cognitive slippage: From Meehl. Refers to the loose associations of the schizophrenic.

Coitus: Sexual intercourse.

Coke: Slang for cocaine, a stimulant.

Cold turkey: Slang for abrupt withdrawal from an addictive drug.

Colitis: Inflammation of the colon. May be psychosomatic.

Compazine: Major tranquilizer. Generic name *prochlorperazine.*

Compensatory education: Academic programs aimed at making up for educational deficiencies. Have been used with children who show cultural-familial retardation.

Compulsion: Inability to avoid engaging in certain behaviors.

Concordance: In genetic studies, the occurrence of the same disorder in two subjects (who may be relatives).

Concrete: Thinking which focuses upon the immediate or literal meaning of an object or idea. Contrasts with *abstract*.

Conditioned response: Behavior that occurs in response to a conditioned stimulus after repeated pairing with an unconditioned stimulus.

Conditioned stimulus: An originally neutral stimulus which becomes capable of eliciting a conditioned response, after repeated pairing with an unconditioned stimulus.

Confabulation: Manufacture of memories to cover gaps in recall. Observed in certain organic brain syndromes, especially Korsakov's psychosis.

Conflict: Situation in which a subject must choose between two equally attractive or unattractive options.

Congenital: Condition existing at or before birth. Not necessarily hereditary.

Conscious: Material that is currently in a person's awareness.

Consequent events: Events which follow the emission of a target behavior and affect its future frequency. An operant conditioning term.

Contract: In behavior therapy, an agreement between two parties regarding obligations and rewards.

Control group: In research, subjects who are not given an experimental treatment. They are then compared with experimental subjects to judge the efficacy of the treatment.

Conversion hysteria: A neurosis involving loss of functioning of the senses or the voluntary nervous system.

Covert sensitization: A form of behavior therapy in which the patient imagines aversive consequences to his unwanted behavior in order to reduce the frequency of that behavior.

Crash: Slang for psychological and physical withdrawal from amphetamines.

Cretinism: Mental retardation resulting from thyroid deficiency.

Cunnilingus: Oral stimulation of female genitals.

Custodial: Mental retardation category for IQ below 25.

Cyclothymic personality: Personality disorder characterized by alterations in mood.

Defect orientation: The theory that all retarded persons suffer from a physical defect.

Defense mechanism: In psychoanalysis, behavior which protects the person from being aware of or overwhelmed by primitive sexual and aggressive impulses.

Delirium: Reduction in level of consciousness usually due to infection.

Delirium tremens: Acute brain syndrome occurring during alcohol withdrawal.

Delta alcoholism: From Jellinek. Physiological and psychological dependence, with loss of control over alcohol intake.

Delta waves: Electrical activity of the brain with a frequency of 0.5 to 3.5 cycles per second. Occurs during deep sleep.

Delusion: A false belief.

Dementia: Alteration in consciousness and cognition due to organic deterioration.

Dementia praecox: Early name for schizophrenia.

Demerol: Synthetic drug with addicting properties. Generic name *meperidine.*

Denial: Primitive defense mechanism leading the person to act as though a profound feeling did not exist.

Deoxyribonucleic acid (DNA): Chemical substance from which genes are made.

Depersonalization: The person feels that he is no longer himself.

Depersonalization neurosis: A neurosis in which the patient has a sense of unreality and estrangement from himself.

Depression: Mood state marked by sadness, lowered self-esteem, retarded motor activity.

Depressive neurosis: Depression triggered by a genuine loss. Eventual improvement almost always takes place.

Deserpidine: Rauwolfia compound; a major tranquilizer. Brand name *Harmonyl.*

Detoxification: Process of withdrawal from a drug.

Dexedrine: An addictive stimulant drug. Generic name *dextroamphetamine.*

Dextroamphetamine: An addictive stimulant drug. Brand name *Dexedrine.*

Diathesis: In theories of schizophrenia, inborn or constitutional factors (as contrasted with environmental factors).

Diazepam: Minor tranquilizer. Brand name *Valium.*

Dilantin: Drug used in treatment of epilepsy.

Discriminative stimulus: Cue in the environment indicating that a given behavior will be reinforced. An operant term.

Displacement: Primitive defense mechanism in which feelings experienced toward one person are redirected toward another.

Dissociation: Defense mechanism in which segments of behavior (for example, feelings) are separated from rest of functioning.

Dissociative hysteria: Hysterical neurosis in which patient experiences change in state of consciousness.

Disulfiram: Drug used in treatment of alcoholism. Brand name *Antabuse.*

Dizygotic twins: Fraternal twins, conceived at the same time from two different fertilized ova. Important in the study of heredity of certain mental disorders.

DMPEA: A derivative of dopamine, one of the neurotransmitters. Implicated in some theories of schizophrenia.

Dominant gene: A gene which always determines the heredity of a characteristic. Contrasted with *recessive.*

Dopamine: Neurotransmitter whose absence can bring on the symptoms of Parkinson's disease.

Doriden: Nonbarbiturate addictive sedative. Generic name *Glutethimide.*

Double approach-avoidance conflict: Forced choice between two options both having aversive and attractive elements.

Double bind: Situation in which a person receives conflicting verbal and nonverbal messages allowing him no comfortable answer. Implicated in some theories of schizophrenia.

Downer: Slang for sedative.

Drive: Impetus for behavior that arises from inside the organism (e.g., hunger, thirst, sex, etc.).

Durham decision: Legal definition of insanity stressing the notion that a person is not responsible for his or her crime if it was the product of mental disease or defect.

Dyspareunia: Painful intercourse in women; a sexual dysfunction.

Dyssocial personality: A person whose antisocial behavior is compatible with his subculture.

Early infantile autism: Childhood psychosis of unknown etiology.

Echolalia: Parrot-like repetition of words, usually in schizophrenia.

Ectomorph: One of Sheldon's body types. A fragile and slender body.

Educable: Retardation category for IQ between 50 and 75.

Ego: Psychoanalytic term for that aspect of the personality which copes with reality demands while attempting to permit instinctual gratification.

Ego-alien: A thought or idea which is not compatible with the individual's self-concept. Contrasted with *ego-syntonic.*

Ego-syntonic: A thought or idea which is compatible with the individual's self-concept. Contrasted with *ego-alien.*

Ejaculation: Male sexual response involving release of sperm.

Elavil: Tricyclic drug used in treatment of depression.

Electroconvulsive therapy (ECT): Use of electric shock for treatment of depression.

Electroencephalograph (EEG): Device which measures electrical activity of the brain. Used in study of brain function and for diagnosis of neurological impairment.

Electromyograph (EMG): Machine for measuring muscle tension.

Emotive imagery: Behavior therapy technique using pleasant fantasy to counter anxiety.

Endocrine glands: Ductless glands which produce hormones that stimulate a variety of physiological functions.

Endogenous: Resulting from internal causes.

Endomorph: One of Sheldon's body types. Characterized by a soft roundness in body.

Enuresis: Bed-wetting.

Epidemiology: Study of the occurrence of a disease or diseases within a given population.

Epilepsy: Neurological defect characterized by repeated seizure activity.

Epinephrine: See *adrenalin.*

Equanil: Minor tranquilizer. Generic name *meprobamate.*

Essential hypertension: High blood pressure of psychological etiology.

Ethanol: Ethyl alcohol—drinkable alcohol.

Etiology: Cause.

Exhibitionism: Sexual gratification derived from display of genitals.

Exogenous: Resulting from external causes.

Experimental neurosis: Condition resembling human neurosis created in animals that are forced to make impossible discriminations.

Explosive personality Personality disorder characterized by uncontrollable episodes of rage.

Extinction: Learning-theory term referring to process by which reinforcement is withdrawn from a behavior. The frequency of that behavior then almost always decreases.

Extrapyramidal symptoms: Side effects of phenothiazine therapy. They resemble symptoms of Parkinson's disease.

Fellatio: Oral stimulation of male genitals.

Femme: Slang term for female homosexual who takes passive sexual role.

Fetishism: Sexual gratification from inanimate objects.

Fixation: Psychoanalytic term referring to attachment of psychic energy to a particular level of psychosexual development.

Fixed-interval schedule: Operant schedule of reinforcement by which a subject's behavior is rewarded after a specific interval of time.

Fixed-ratio schedule: Operant schedule of reinforcement by which a subject's behavior is reinforced after he emits a given number of responses.

Flagellation: Whipping, often for sexual gratification.

Flashback: Slang for the return of a drug-like state in a person no longer taking the drug.

Flattening of affect: Inability to express a full range of emotional responses.

Flight of ideas: Rapid, involuntary movement from one thought to another.

Flooding: Form of behavior therapy in which patient is exposed to situations that produce intense anxiety.

Fluphenazine: Major tranquilizer. Brand name *Prolixin.*

Four A's: Bleuler's fundamental symptoms of schizophrenia: *loosening of associations, autism, inappropriate affect,* and *ambivalence.*

Free association: Basic psychoanalytic technique; patient is instructed to say everything he thinks without the usual censorship.

Free-floating anxiety: Anxiety which is not clearly attached to any particular object or situation.

Frigidity: Deficiency in female sexual responsiveness.

Frontal lobes: Portion of forebrain responsible for problem solving and abstract thought.

Fugue: Pervasive loss of memory, which may last for years.

Functional disorder: Disorder arising from psychological as opposed to physical causes.

Fundamental symptoms: From Bleuler. Symptoms found in every case of schizophrenia. Contrasted with *accessory symptoms.*

Galvanic skin response (GSR): A measure of anxiety derived from palmar sweating.

Gamete: Egg or sperm.

Gamma alcoholism: From Jellinek. Physiological and psychological dependence on alcohol, with loss of control of drinking.

Gargoylism: Recessive-gene form of mental retardation. Also called Hurler's disease.

Gay: Slang for homosexual.

Gene: Chemical unit which enables transmission of inherited characteristics.

General adaptation syndrome (GAS): From Selye. Bodily responses to physical and psychological stress.

General paralysis: Organic brain syndrome caused by late stage of syphilis. Also called *general paresis*.

Genetic counseling: Advice given by an expert to prospective parents about the possibility of transmitting hereditary defects to their offspring.

Genotype: Genetic characteristics inherited by an individual. See *phenotype*.

Gland: Body organ which secretes chemicals important for regulation of functioning.

Glutethimide: Nonbarbiturate addictive sedative. Brand name *Doriden*.

Grand mal epilepsy: Epilepsy marked by tonic and clonic seizures followed by a period of unconsciousness.

Grass: Slang for marijuana.

Hallucination: Perception of a sensory stimulus when there is no real external stimulation. A false visual, auditory, tactile, gustatory, olfactory, or kinesthetic perception.

Hallucinogen: Drug that produces hallucinations.

Harmonyl: Rauwolfia compound; a major tranquilizer. Generic name *deserpidine*.

Hash: Slang for hashish.

Hashish: Drug with marijuana-like effects. Derived from the hemp plant.

Hebephrenic schizophrenia: A form of schizophrenia characterized by grossly inappropriate affective responses and highly disorganized thinking.

Heritability: Extent to which a characteristic is genetically determined.

Heroin: Addictive narcotic drug derived from the poppy.

Heterosexuality: Preference for sexual activity with members of opposite sex. Contrasted with *homosexuality*.

Hierarchy: In behavior therapy, a list of scenes which create anxiety, arranged from least to most anxious.

Hindbrain: Most primitive part of man's brain. Composed of cerebellum, pons, and medulla.

Homosexuality: Preference for sexual gratification with members of one's own sex. Contrasted with heterosexuality.

Hormones: Chemicals released by endocrine glands which stimulate activity in various bodily organs.

Huntington's chorea: Dominant-gene form of terminal neurological deterioration.

Hydrocephaly: Form of mental retardation marked by abnormally large head and increased intercranial pressure.

Hypnosis: Trance-like state created through suggestion with cooperation of the subject.

Hypochrondriacal neurosis: Neurosis marked by unwarranted preoccupation with one's health.

Hypothalamus: Portion of the forebrain which regulates a number of bodily functions and influences appetite and wake-sleeping cycle. Presumed seat of emotional responsivity.

Hysterical neurosis: Neurosis characterized by physical symptoms which lack a somatic basis.

Hysterical personality: Personality disorder characterized by shallow affect and self-centeredness.

Id: Psychoanalytic term referring to that primitive aspect of the personality which is totally preoccupied with instinctual gratification.

Identification: Primitive defense mechanism in which the individual "takes on" aspects of the behavior of another person who is important to him.

Imipramine: Tricyclic drug used in treatment of depression. Brand name *Tofranil*.

Implicit reaction: Physiological events like heart rate and muscle tension.

Implosion therapy: Form of behavior therapy in which the subject is encouraged to experience intense anxiety about a phobic situation and in which psychoanalytic explanations are given for the source of the phobia.

Impotence: Inability by the male to obtain or maintain an erection suitable for sexual intercourse.

Inadequate personality: Personality disorder characterized by pervasive inability to cope.

Incest: Sexual activity between parent and child or among siblings.

Incidence: Number of people per 100,000 members of a population who are diagnosed as having acquired a disease within a given time interval (usually a year).

Index case: Subject in an epidemiological study who suffers from the disease or diseases under study.

Inferiority complex: Adler's term referring to the child's sense of inadequacy arising from his realization that he is small and helpless in comparison with adults.

Insanity: Legal term for severe behavioral deviation.

Insomnia: Difficulty in falling or staying asleep.

Insulin coma therapy: Form of treatment for schizophrenia in which insulin is given to induce coma. No longer widely used.

Interpretation: Explaining to the patient the meaning of his behavior or statements. A psychoanalytic technique.

Introjection: Primitive defense mechanism in which the individual symbolically takes in or incorporates characteristics of another person.

Introversion-extraversion: Dimension of psychological functioning used by Eysenck. Placement upon this dimension and several others replaces traditional diagnostic categorization.

In vivo: In the living organism.

Involutional melancholia: Depression of later middle age.

Isoimmunization: Production of antibodies.

Isolation: Defense mechanism in which a thought but not its associated affect is experienced.

Jacksonian epilepsy: Seizures taking the form of localized convulsions.

Joint: Slang for marijuana cigarette.

Kleinfelter's syndrome: Male sex chromosome abnormality.

Korsakov's psychosis: Acute and chronic brain syndrome due to vitamin deficiency associated with chronic alcoholism.

La belle indifférence: Attitude of indifference shown by some hysterical neurotics to their incapacitating physical disabilities.

Latent: Underlying meaning. Contrasted with *manifest*.

Latent schizophrenia: Patients who, while not overtly psychotic, show some schizophrenic behaviors. A controversial diagnostic label.

L-dopa: Drug used in treatment of Parkinson's disease. Replaces natural dopamine in brain.

Lesbian: Female homosexual.

Libido: Psychic energy derived from the sex drive.

Librium: Minor tranquilizer. Generic name *chlordiazepoxide*.

Lithium carbonate: Drug used in treatment of manic-depressive psychosis.

Loosening of associations: One of Bleuler's fundamental symptoms of schizophrenia. Marked by a tendency to tie together thoughts not usually connected with one another.

Loss of control (alcoholism): A person's inability to stop drinking once he has started, until he is forced to withdraw.

Lysergic acid diethylamide (LSD): Synthetic drug that produces hallucinations and other psychotic behaviors.

Mainlining: Injecting heroin directly into veins.

Major tranquilizers: Tranquilizers used to control psychotic behaviors. Contrasted with minor tranquilizers, used to alleviate mild anxiety.

Malignant: Tumor which regenerates, after surgical removal.

Malleus Maleficarum: *The Witches' Hammer*—a book published in 1487 which attributed mental illness to witchcraft.

Manic-depressive psychosis: Disorder characterized by alterations in affect—from elation to depression.

Manifest: Surface meaning. Contrasted with *latent*.

Marijuana: Nonaddicting drug derived from hemp plant.

Marplan: Drug used in treatment of depression.

Masochism: Sexual gratification derived from pain inflicted on oneself.

Masturbation: Genital self-stimulation.

Medical model: View of psychological deviations which explains them as the result of disease. Attempts to extrapolate from the medical view of physical illnesses to mental disorders.

Medulla: Portion of hindbrain responsible for such activities as regulation and control of respiration, heart rate, and gastrointestinal activity.

Meiosis: Cell division during reproduction.

Mellaril: Major tranquilizer. Generic name *thioridazine*.

Mental-status examination: Interview aimed at assessing patient's psychological functioning.

Meprobamate: Minor tranquilizer. Brand names *Miltown* and *Equanil*.

Mescaline: Hallucinogen derived from the buttons of certain mushrooms.

Mesomorph: One of Sheldon's body types. Muscle and bone predominate.

Methadone: Synthetic heroin substitute with addictive properties.

Methamphetamine: Addictive stimulant drug. Brand name *Methedrine*.

Methedrine: Addictive stimulant drug. Generic name *methamphetamine*.

Microcephaly: Form of mental retardation marked by abnormally small head size.

Miltown: Minor tranquilizer. Generic name *meprobamate*.

Minnesota Multiphasic Personality Inventory (MMPI): Objective paper-and-pencil test of psychological functioning.

Minor tranquilizer: Tranquilizing drug used largely to treat neurosis.

M'Naghten rules: Legal definition of insanity stressing that the criminally insane person did not know what he did, or did not know that what he did was wrong.

Modeling: Behavior learned through imitation of another person that is unaccompanied by explicit reinforcement.

Mongolism: Most common form of organic mental retardation. Caused by a chromosomal defect, this condition is also called Down's Syndrome and Trisomy-21.

Monoamine oxidase (MAO) inhibitors: A group of drugs used in the treatment of depression.

Monozygotic twins: Identical twins, who develop from the same fertilized ovum. Important subjects in the study of heredity of certain disorders.

Morphine: Addictive drug derived from the poppy that also has important medical uses.

Multiple personality: Form of hysterical neurosis in which the patient maintains two or more distinct personalities that alternate in consciousness.

Narcissism: Psychoanalytic term referring to preoccupation with one's self.

Nardil: Drug used in treatment of depression.

Neologism: A new word, often coined by persons considered schizophrenic.

Neurasthenic neurosis: Form of neurosis marked by chronic physical and mental fatigue.

Neurodermatitis: Skin disorder that can be psychosomatic in etiology.

Neurologist: Physician who specializes in treatment of neurological disorders.

Neuron: Cell which functions to receive sensory information or to transmit impulses from other neurons to muscle or gland cells.

Neurotic paradox: Persistence of neurotic behavior in spite of its unpleasant consequences and "stupidity."

Neurotransmitters: Chemical substances which transmit information from one neuron to another across synapses.

Nondisjunction: Form of chromosomal defect that sometimes results in retardation.

Noradrenalin: A sympathetic nervous system stimulant secreted by the adrenal medulla. Also known as *norepinephrine.*

Norepinephrine: See *noradrenalin.*

Normal distribution: Statistical term referring to the normal or "bell-shaped" curve.

Object: Psychoanalytic term referring to persons with whom one forms attachments.

Observational learning: Learning by watching (as against reinforcement-motivated learning).

Obsession: Preoccupation with certain thoughts or ideas.

Obsessive-compulsive neurosis: A disorder in which the patient's obsessive thoughts or compulsive rituals interfere with his everyday life.

Obsessive-compulsive personality: Personality disorder characterized by need for order and perfection.

Occipital lobes: Portion of forebrain responsible for visual perception.

Oedipus complex: Desire to displace same-sex parent in the affection of opposite-sex parent. Psychoanalysis gives the Oedipus complex a central place in the etiology of neurosis.

Opium: Addictive drug derived from the poppy seed.

Oral stage: First stage of psychosexual development in psychoanalytic theory. Gratification is focused upon activity surrounding the lips, tongue, and mouth.

Orgasm: Stage of peak sexual tension followed by relaxation brought on by intense sexual stimulation.

Outcome criteria: Measures used in treatment-outcome research to evaluate the effectiveness of a new treatment method.

Outcome research: Research aimed at evaluating the effectiveness of a new drug or treatment by examining the effect of that treatment upon the behavior in question.

Overarousal: Excessive physiological response to a stimulus.

Overinclusion: Thinking in which conceptual categories are too broad. A common schizophrenic accompaniment.

Oxazepam: Minor tranquilizer. Brand name *Serax.*

Paranoia: Rare form of psychosis characterized solely by well-formulated delusions.

Paranoid-nonparanoid: Dimension of schizophrenia based on the presence or absence of associated paranoid behaviors.

Paranoid personality: Personality disorder characterized by extreme and continuing suspiciousness.

Paranoid schizophrenia: Form of schizophrenia marked by delusions of a grandiose or persecutory nature as well as by other fundamental symptoms of schizophrenia. Delusions are well-organized and systematic.

Parasympathetic division: That portion of the autonomic nervous system which conserves energy and attends to bodily "housekeeping." Contrasts with *sympathetic division.*

Parietal lobes: Portion of forebrain responsible for sense of touch and for some aspects of symbolic speech.

Parkinson's disease: Organic brain syndrome now treatable with L-dopa.

Passive-agressive personality: Personality disorder characterized by continuing but always indirect expressions of anger.

Pedophilia: Sexual preference for young children.

Pentobarbital: A barbiturate.

Peripheral nervous system: That part of the nervous system which lies beyond the brain and spinal cord.

Perphenazine: Major tranquilizer. Brand name *Trilafon.*

Personality disorder: Deviation in which the individual suffers little if any anxiety. His disorder causes discomfort to people around him but little to the individual himself because his behavior is ego-syntonic.

Petit mal epilepsy: Seizure disorder characterized by very brief periods of unconsciousness unaccompanied by tonic or clonic movements.

Petting: Sexual stimulation that does not include sexual intercourse.

Phallic stage: Third stage of psychosexual development, according to psychoanalytic theory. Gratification is centered upon immature genital functioning. The oedipal situation occurs during this developmental stage.

Phenobarbital: A sedative drug.

Phenomenological: Referring to the individual's immediate experiencing of his environment.

Phenothiazines: Major tranquilizing drugs used primarily with psychotic patients.

Phenotype: Observable bodily and behavioral characteristics. They develop as an interaction between heredity and environment. See *genotype.*

Phenurone: Drug used to treat psychomotor epilepsy.

Phenylketonuria (PKU): Form of mental retardation caused by a recessive gene. The retardation can now be prevented if diagnosed and treated early enough.

Phobic neurosis: Intense fear of an object or situation which is not realistically dangerous. This fear interferes with effective normal functioning.

Pica: Craving for and ingestion of unnatural substances like dirt.

Pick's disease: A form of presenile dementia of organic origin.

Pituitary gland: "Master gland." Triggers activities of many other glands by release of hormones. Adrenocorticotropic hormone (ACTH) is one of the most important.

Placebo drug: Chemically inert substance used in drug experiments to control for expectancy effects.

Polygenic: Interactive effect of many genes.

Polygraph: Device which measures the electrical activity of a number of bodily functions, including heart rate, muscle activation, blood pressure, and galvanic skin response.

Pons: Portion of hindbrain which connects two halves of cerebellum.

Pot: Slang for marijuana.

Preconscious: In psychoanalysis, material readily available to awareness.

Prefrontal leucotomy: Form of brain surgery once popular for the treatment of schizophrenic behavior.

Premature ejaculation: Inability to postpone ejaculation in males.

Premorbid: Before the onset of illness.

Presenile dementia: Brain deterioration of middle age resembling deterioration of old age.

Prevalence: The total number of people within a given population who suffer from a particular disease.

Primary prevention: Creation of an environment which prevents an individual from developing a psychological dysfunction.

Process-reactive: Dimension of schizophrenia based upon gradual versus abrupt onset of symptoms.

Prochlorperazine: Major tranquilizer. Brand name *Compazine.*

Prognosis: The eventual consequence or outcome of a physical or mental disorder.

Projection: Primitive defense mechanism by which the individual attributes his own feelings or desires to another person.

Prolixin: Major tranquilizer. Generic name *fluphenazine.*

Psychiatrist: Physician who specializes in treatment of psychological disorders.

Psychic determinism: The view that no behavior happens by chance, that every psychic event is determined by events which preceded it.

Psychic energy: In psychoanalysis, the energy of mental life. Analogous to physical energy. Components are libido and mortido.

Psychoactive drug: Drug which has a marked effect on psychological functioning.

Psychoanalysis: Theory of personality and technique of treatment developed by Sigmund Freud.

Psychological dependence: Strong desire for a drug that is not based on physiological need.

Psychomotor epilepsy: Involuntary episodes in which the person engages in seemingly purposeful activity of which he is later totally unaware.

Psychomotor retardation: Slowing down of motor responses. A cue to depression.

Psychopathic personality: Personality disorder characterized by unsocial, impulsive behavior.

Psychosexual development: In psychoanalysis, the stages of development through which every child passes. They include the *oral, anal, phallic,* and *genital* stages of development.

Psychosis: Severe behavioral deviation involving loss of contact with reality. Includes schizophrenia, manic-depressive states, and organic conditions involving deterioration.

Psychosomatic illnesses: Disorders in which physical symptoms are caused by psychological phenomena.

Punishment: An event which follows a behavior and decreases the probability of recurrence of that behavior.

Pupillography: Technique for measuring changes in size of pupils of eyes. Thought to reflect emotional changes.

Pyknic: One of Kretschmer's body types. Characterized by pronounced body cavities, short, compact body, and short extremities.

Rationalization: Defense mechanism in which logical reasons are put forth to explain irrational behavior.

Rauwolfia compounds: Major tranquilizers used in the treatment of psychotic behavior.

Reaction formation: Defense mechanism in which one set of feelings is made unconscious by replacement with a contrasting set.

Recessive gene: Gene which predominates only if matched by both parents. Contrasted with *dominant.*

Reciprocal inhibition: Basic principle of Wolpe's system of behavioral treatment, namely, that an individual cannot experience two mutually incompatible feeling states (e.g., anxiety and relaxation) at the same time.

Reefer: Slang term for marijuana cigarette.

Regression: Defense mechanism in which one returns to a previous, less mature (but more comfortable) level of functioning.

Reinforcement: Event which follows the occurrence of a behavior and increases the probability of recurrence of that behavior.

Reliability: Ability of an assessment technique (test, interview, etc) to measure the same behavior in a consistent way.

REM: Rapid eye movement; thought to occur during dreaming.

Repetition compulsion: Form of neurosis in which patient feels he must repeat a ritual again and again.

Repression: Basic defense mechanism by which potentially dangerous thoughts are barred from conciousness.

Reserpine: Rauwolfia compound. Brand name *Serpasil.*

Resistance: A psychoanalytic construct referring to conscious and unconscious attempts by the patient to prevent psychoanalytic treatment from progressing.

Response specificity: Characteristic individual response patterns that people show to similar stressors.

Reticular activating system (RAS): Traverses the midbrain and hindbrain. Integral part of brain's "waking center."

Retrospective study: Research attempting to retrace earlier events in life of subject.

Rh factor: An incompatibility in the Rh factor in the blood between the fetus and the mother can cause brain damage or death to the fetus.

Ribonucleic acid (RNA): Chemical which acts as transmitter for DNA genetic code.

Ritalin: Drug used to treat childhood hyperactivity. Generic name *methylphenidate hydrochloride.*

Rorschach: Projective test of personality consisting of ten ambiguous inkblots to which the patient is to give meaning.

Rush: Slang for the sense of well-being that follows heroin injection.

Sadism: Sexual gratification derived from inflicting pain on others.

Schedule of reinforcement: Operant program according to which rewards are dispensed for requisite behavior.

Schizo-affective schizophrenia: Patients showing both the thought disorder characteristic of schizophrenia and the mood disturbance signaling an affective disorder.

Schizoid personality: Personality disorder characterized by interpersonal withdrawal and social isolation.

Schizophrenia: Severe psychological disorder characterized by the presence of certain "thought disorders," among other symptoms.

School phobia: Fear of attending school.

Secobarbital: A barbiturate.

Secondary gain: Indirect benefits from neurosis that may exempt a person from some unpleasant situations.

Secondary prevention: Minimizing the intensity and duration of a psychological deviation by early recognition and treatment.

Self-reinforcement: Rewards given to oneself for appropriate behavior.

Semantic dementia: Gap between words and deeds of the psychopathic personality.

Senile dementia: Organic brain syndrome of old age.

Sensate focus training: In Masters and Johnson's sex therapy, the process of concentrating on pleasure derived from touching and being touched preliminary to direct sexual stimulation.

Serax: Minor tranquilizer. Generic name *oxepam.*

Serotonin: Neurotransmitter which has also been linked to the etiology of schizophrenia.

Serpasil: Rauwolfia compound. Generic name *reserpine.*

Sex chromosomes: Chromosomes which transmit sexual characteristics. Females have two X chromosomes (XX), while males have an X and a Y (XY).

Shaping: Use of behavioral principles gradually to build in a new behavior.

Sign: Externally observable indicator of a disease. Opposed to symptom.

Simple schizophrenia: Form of schizophrenia characterized by gradual social withdrawal and an ultimate general state of apathy.

Skin popping: Injecting heroin under the skin.

Socioeconomic status (SES): A person's standing within his culture, based upon occupation, income, education, family background, etc.

Sociopathic personality: See *psychopathic personality.*

Sociosyntonic: Antisocial behavior compatible with one's subculture (as in organized crime, etc.).

Somatic delusions: False beliefs about the state of one's body or health.

Somnambulism: Sleepwalking.

Speed: Slang for the amphetamines.

Speed freak: Slang for amphetamine user.

Spontaneous remission: Recovery from a disorder without treatment.

Stage 1 sleep: Light sleep. Low-amplitude, high-frequency brain-wave activity.

Stage 2 sleep: Predominant level of sleep. Marked by short periods of exceptionally fast electrical brain activity.

Stage 3 sleep: Deep sleep. Marked by slow, high-amplitude brain-wave activity.

Stanford-Binet test: Intelligence test for persons of all ages.

Status epilepticus: Repeated grand mal seizures without intervening intervals of consciousness. Can cause death.

Stelazine: Major tranquilizer. Generic name *trifluperazine.*

Stereotype: Ritualized, repetitive behavior.

Stimulus generalization: In learning theory, responding to a group of related stimuli with a response initially learned to one stimulus.

Suavitil: Minor tranquilizer. Generic name *benactyzine.*

Sublimation: Defense mechanism by which an unwanted impulse is transformed into an acceptable act.

Substitution: Defense mechanism by which an unacceptable goal is replaced by an acceptable one.

Successive approximations: In behavior modification, repeated steps designed to bring the patient closer and closer to a target behavior.

Succinylcholine: Paralytic drug used in aversive conditioning research.

Suicide: Voluntary taking of one's own life.

Superego: Psychoanalytic term referring to that aspect of the personality which reflects the strong incorporation of society's rules through parental prohibitions.

Suppression: Basic defense mechanism of voluntary forgetting.

Symmetry compulsion: Form of neurosis in which patient feels each of his acts must be balanced out by another.

Sympathetic division: Portion of the autonomic nervous system which activates the body for emergency action.

Symptom: Internally experienced indicator of disease. Opposed to *sign.*

Symptom choice: The reason why one person develops one form of disability and another person a different disability.

Systematic desensitization: A form of reciprocal inhibition in which muscle relaxation is paired with anxiety stimuli.

Taraxein: A component of blood serum. Implicated in some theories of schizophrenia.

Taylor Manifest Anxiety Scale (TMAS): A paper-and-pencil test of anxiety.

Tay-Sachs disease: Recessive-gene form of mental retardation.

Temporal lobes: Portion of forebrain which processes visual information.

Tertiary prevention: Provision of treatment for an individual with serious psychological disturbance. Contrasts with *primary* and *secondary* prevention.

Tetrahydrocannabinol (THC). Generic name for the active component in marijuana and hashish.

Thalamus: Portion of forebrain which relays impulses to higher brain centers. Plays a role in emotional behavior and in sleep.

Thematic Apperception Test (TAT): Projective test of personality employing a set of pictures of ambiguous scenes.

Therapeutic community: Treatment setting in which staff and patients together create an environment conducive to improved functioning.

Thioridazine: Major tranquilizer. Brand name *Mellaril.*

Thorazine: Major tranquilizer. Generic name *chlorpromazine.*

Thought disorder: Cognitive dysfunction; a cue to schizophrenia.

Tofranil: Drug used in treatment of depression. Generic name *imipramine.* A tricyclic compound.

Token economy: A behavior-modification technique in which appropriate behaviors are rewarded with tokens, which may then be traded for desired items. Tokens function in the same way as money in the wider society.

Tolerance: Need for increasing the quantities of an addicting drug to maintain its effect.

Trainable: Mental retardation category for IQ between 25 and 49.

Transference: Psychoanalytic term referring to patient's displacement of childhood feelings (largely about his parents) onto the therapist.

Transsexual: Individual with a gender identification opposite to his biological gender.

Transvestism: Sexual gratification derived from wearing the clothes of the opposite sex.

Treponema pallidum: Spirochete which causes syphilis.

Tricyclic compounds: Group of drugs used to treat depression.

Tridone: Drug used to treat petit mal seizures.

Trifluperazine: Major tranquilizer. Brand name *Stelazine.*

Trilafon: Major tranquilizer. Generic name *perphenazine.*

Tuberous sclerosis: Dominant-gene form of mental retardation. Also called *epiloia.*

Turner's syndrome: Female sex-chromosome abnormality.

Ulcer: Open sore in mucosa of stomach or intestine. May be psychosomatic in origin.

Unconditioned response: In classical (Pavlovian) conditioning, a natural response to a stimulus (e.g., salivating to food).

Unconditioned stimulus: In classical (Pavlovian) conditioning, a stimulus which is naturally capable of eliciting a certain autonomic response (e.g., food elicits salivation).

Unconscious: In psychoanalytic theory, thoughts and feelings that are not in the individual's awareness.

Underarousal: Insufficient physiological response to a stimulus.

Underinclusion: Thinking in which the conceptual categories are too narrow. A cue to organic disorder. Contrasted with *overinclusion.*

Undoing: Defense mechanism in which an act is undertaken to counter another.

Vaginismus: Painful contraction of vagina during intercourse.

Validity: Ability of an assessment measure (test, interview, etc.) to provide the data it is supposed to provide.

Valium: Minor tranquilizer. Generic name *diazepam.*

Variable-interval schedule: Operant schedule of reinforcement in which subject is rewarded for a response given after differing intervals of time which cluster around a given average.

Variable-ratio schedule: Operant schedule of reinforcement in which subject is rewarded after differing number of responses which cluster around a given average.

Von Domarus principle: The idea that schizophrenic logic is based upon an assumption of identity when two things share the same adjective.

Voyeurism: Sexual gratification from watching others.

Waxy flexibility: A feature of catatonic schizophrenia marked by the patient's willingness to allow the observer to "mold" his limbs into any position.

Wechsler Adult Intelligence Scale (WAIS): Adult intelligence test.

Wechsler Intelligence Scale for Children (WISC): Child intelligence test.

Withdrawal: Physical symptoms experienced upon removal from an addicting drug.

Word salad: Schizophrenic language so disjointed that the observer cannot understand it.

Yellow Jacket: Slang for Nembutal, a barbiturate.

Acknowledgments

Quotations

In addition to the acknowledgments given in the text and in References (page 532), we also wish to give special credits and thanks to the following:

Page 3. Quotation from: Malcolm X with assistance of Alex Haley. *The Autobiography of Malcolm X.* New York: Grove Press, 1966. Reprinted by permission of Grove Press, Inc. Copyright © 1964 by Alex Haley and Malcolm X.

Page 4. Quotation from: Malcolm X with assistance of Alex Haley. *The Autobiography of Malcolm X.* New York: Grove Press, 1966. Reprinted by permission of Grove Press, Inc. Copyright © 1964 by Alex Haley and Malcolm X.

Page 4. Quotation from: Malcolm X with assistance of Alex Haley. *The Autobiography of Malcolm X.* New York: Grove Press, 1966. Reprinted by permission of Grove Press, Inc. Copyright © 1964 by Alex Haley and Malcolm X.

Page 4. Quotation from: Malcolm X with assistance of Alex Haley. *The Autobiography of Malcolm X.* New York: Grove Press, 1966. Reprinted by permission of Grove Press, Inc. Copyright © 1964 by Alex Haley and Malcolm X.

Page 5. Quotation from: Malcolm X with assistance of Alex Haley. *The Autobiography of Malcolm X.* New York: Grove Press, 1966. Reprinted by permission of Grove Press, Inc. Copyright © 1964 by Alex Haley and Malcolm X.

Page 7. Quotation from: Jahoda, M. In Senn, M. (Ed.), *Symposium on the Healthy Personality.* New York: Josiah Macy, Jr., Foundation, 1950.

By permission of the publisher.

Page 13. Quotation from: Summers, M. (Trans.), *Malleus Maleficarum.* New York: Benjamin Blom, Inc., 1970. By permission of the publisher.

Page 13. Quotation from: Zilboorg, H. *A History of Medical Psychology.* New York: W. W. Norton, 1941. By permission of the publisher.

Page 14. Quotation from: *Memoirs of My Nervous Illness.* By Schreber, D. P. Translated and edited by Macalpine, I. & Hunter, R. Kent, England: Wm. Dawson & Sons, 1955. Reprinted by permission of the publisher.

Page 20. Material from: Leonard P. Ullmann and Leonard Krasner, A PSYCHOLOGICAL APPROACH TO ABNORMAL BEHAVIOR, © 1969, pp. 382-383. By permission of Prentice-Hall, Inc., Englewood Cliffs, New Jersey.

Page 22. By permission from MAYER-GROSS, SLATER & ROTH: CLINICAL PSYCHIATRY, 3d ed. (1969), Bailliere Tindall & Cassell Ltd., London, published in the United States of America by the Williams & Wilkins Company, Baltimore.

Page 31. Quotation from: Ehrmann, F. (Ed.), *Terezin.* Prague: Council of Jewish Communities in the Czech Lands, 1965. By permission of the publisher.

Page 32. Quotation from: Feder, R. Religious life in Terezin. In Ehrmann, F. (Ed.), *Terezin.* Prague:

Council of Jewish Communities in the Czech Lands, 1965. By permission of the publisher.

Page 32. Quotation from: Fryd, N. Culture in the anteroom to hell. In Ehrmann, F. (Ed.), *Terezin.* Prague: Council of Jewish Communities in the Czech Lands, 1965. By permission of the publisher.

Page 33. Quotation from: Sedova, J. Theatre and cabaret in the ghetto of Terezin. In Ehrmann, F. (Ed.), *Terezin.* Prague: Council of Jewish Communities in the Czech Lands, 1965. By permission of the publisher.

Page 33. Quotation from: Iltis, R. Terezin—Its influence on Czechoslovak literature, music, plastic arts and film. In Ehrmann, F. (Ed.), *Terezin.* Prague: Council of Jewish Communities in the Czech Lands, 1965. By permission of the publisher.

Page 38. Quotation from: Srole, L., Langer, T., Michael, S., Opler, M., & Rennie, T., *The Midtown Manhattan Study,* Vol. I. New York: McGraw-Hill, 1962. By permission of the author.

Page 43. Quotation from: Cleaver, E. *Soul on Ice.* New York: McGraw-Hill, 1968. By permission of the publisher.

Page 44. Excerpted from "The other bodies in the river" by L. T. Delaney in PSYCHOLOGY TODAY Magazine, June, 1968. Copyright © Communications / Research / Machines, Inc.

Page 44. Excerpted from "A conversation with Kenneth B. Clark" by M. H. Hall in PSYCHOLOGY TODAY Magazine, June, 1968. Copyright © Communications/Research /Machines, Inc.

Pages 44-45. List based on: Lewis, O. A Puerto Rican boy. In Finney, J. C. (Ed.), *Culture Change, Mental Health and Poverty.* Lexington, Kentucky: University of Kentucky Press, 1969. By permission of the publisher.

Page 46. Quotation from: Thomas, A., & Sillen, S. *Racism and Psychiatry.* New York: Brunner/Mazel, 1972. By permission of the publisher.

Page 47. Quotation from: Grier, W. & Cobbs, P. *Black Rage.* New York: Basic Books, 1968. By permission of the publisher.

Pages 47-48. Quotation from: Thomas, A., & Sillen, S. *Racism and Psychiatry.* New York: Brunner /Mazel, 1972. By permission of the publisher.

Page 48. Quotation from: Kardiner, A., & Ovesey, L. *The Mark of Oppression.* New York: W. W. Norton, 1951. By permission of the author.

Page 49. Quotation from: Halleck, S. *The Politics of Therapy.* New York: Science House, 1971. By permission of the publisher.

Pages 55-57. Quotation from: DOWN THESE MEAN STREETS, by Piri Thomas. Copyright © 1967 by Piri Thomas. Reprinted by permission of Alfred A. Knopf, Inc.

Pages 57-60. Excerpt from Anne Frank: THE DIARY OF A YOUNG GIRL. Copyright 1952 by Otto H. Frank. Reprinted by permission of Doubleday & Company, Inc., New York: and Vallentine, Mitchell, & Co., Ltd., London.

Pages 81-86. Quotations from: Chapter II, "Analysis of a Phobia in a Five-Year Old Boy," in COLLECTED PAPERS OF SIGMUND FREUD, Vol. III, edited by Ernest Jones, M.D., translation by Alix and James Strachey, Published by Basic Books, Inc., by arrangement with The Hogarth Press Ltd. and the Institute of Psycho-Analysis, London.

Pages 86-88. Quotation from: Wolpe, J., & Rachman, S. Psychoanalytic "Evidence": A critique based on Freud's case of Little Hans. *Journal of Nervous and Mental Diseases,* 1960, 130. Copyright © 1960, The Williams & Wilkins Co., Baltimore. By permission of the publisher and the author.

Page 89. Quotation from: Eysenck, H. Psychoanalysis—Myth or science? *Inquiry,* 4 (1). Reprinted by permission of the author and *Inquiry.*

Page 89. Quotation from: Bandura, A. *Principles of Behavior Modification.* New York: Holt, Rinehart & Winston, Inc., 1969. By permission of the publisher.

Page 119. Quotation from: Kety, S. The heuristic aspect of psychiatry. *American Journal of Psychiatry,* 1961, 118, 385-397. Copyright © 1961, The American Psychiatric Association. By permission of the publisher and the author.

Page 119. Quotation from: Nathan, P., Andberg, M., Behan, P., & Patch, V. Thirty-two observers and one patient. A study of diagnostic reliability. *Journal of Clinical Psychology,* 1969, 25, 9-15. By permission of the publisher.

Page 120. Quotation from: Nathan, P., Andberg, M., Behan, P., & Patch, V. Thirty-two observers and one patient. A study of diagnostic reliability. *Journal of Clinical Psychology,* 1969, 25, 9-15. By permission of the publisher.

Page 124. Reproduced by special permission from The Inpatient Multidimensional Psychiatric Scale by Maurice Lorr. Copyright date 1966. Published by Consulting Psychologists Press, Inc.

Page 124. Quotation from: Wittenborn, J. R. *Wittenborn Psychiatric Rating Scales,* New York: Psychological Corporation, 1955. By permission of the author.

Page 140. Quotation from: Tharp, R., & Wetzel, R. *Behavior Modification in the Natural Environment.* New York: Academic Press, 1969. By permission of the publisher and the author.

Page 141. Quotation from: Kanfer, F., & Saslow, G. Behavioral diagnosis. In Franks, C. (Ed.), *Behavior Therapy: Appraisal and Status.* New York: McGraw-Hill, 1969. By permission of the publisher.

Page 145. Quotation from: Warren, E. *The President's Commission on the Assassination of President John F. Kennedy.* 1964. Superintendent of Documents, Washington, D.C.

Page 146. Quotation from: Warren, E. *The President's Commission on the Assassination of President John F. Kennedy.* 1964. Superintendent of Documents, Washington, D.C.

Page 146. Quotation from: Warren, E. *The President's Commission on the Assassination of President John F. Kennedy.* 1964. Superintendent of Documents, Washington, D.C.

Pages 147, 148. Quotations from: Warren, E. *The President's Commission on the Assassination of President John F. Kennedy.* 1964. Superintendent of Documents, Washington, D.C.

Pages 149-150. Quotations from: *The Case of Rudolph Hess* by Rees, J. New York: W. W. Norton, 1948. Copyright 1948 by J. R. Rees. By permission of A. Watkins, Inc.

Pages 152-153. Quotation from: *The Case of Rudolph Hess* by Rees, J. New York: W. W. Norton, 1948. Copyright 1948 by J. R. Rees. By permission of A. Watkins, Inc.

Page 160. Quotation from: *The Case of Rudolph Hess* by Rees, J. New York: W. W. Norton, 1948. Copyright 1948 by J. R. Rees. By permission of A. Watkins, Inc.

Page 160. Quotation from: *Memoirs of My Nervous Illness.* By Schreber, D. P. Translated and edited by Macalpine, I. & Hunter, R. Kent, England: Wm. Dawson & Sons, 1955. By permission of the publisher.

Table 6-1, page 167. Based on: Kantor, R., Wallner, J., & Windner, C. Process and reactive schizophrenia. *Journal of Consulting Psychology,* 1953, 17. Copyright 1953 by the American Psychological Association. Reprinted by permission of the publisher and the author.

Page 171. Quotation from: *Memoirs of my Nervous Illness.* By Schreber, D. P. Translated and edited by Macalpine, I., & Hunter, R. Kent, England: Wm. Dawson & Sons, 1955. By permission of the publisher.

Page 171. Quotation from: *The Case of Rudolph Hess* by Rees, J. New York: W. W. Norton, 1948. Copyright 1948 by J. R. Rees. By permission of A. Watkins, Inc.

Page 171. Quotation from: Warren, E. *The President's Commission on the Assassination of President John F. Kennedy.* 1964. Superintendent of Documents, Washington, D.C.

Page 173. Quotation from: Gregory, I. *Fundamentals of Psychiatry* (2d ed.) Philadelphia: W. B. Saunders, 1968. By permission of the author and the publisher.

Page 187. Quotation from: Rosenthal, D. A program of research on heredity in schizophrenia. *Behavioral Science,* 1971, 16, 3. By permission of the publisher and the author.

Pages 188-189. Quotations from: Schreber, D. P. *Memoirs of My Nervous Illness.* Translated and edited by Macalpine, I., & Hunter, R. Kent, England: Wm. Dawson & Sons, Ltd., 1955. By permission of the publisher.

Page 190. Quotation from: Bateson, G., Jackson, D., Haley, J., & Weakland, J. Double-bind hypothesis of schizophrenia. *Behavioral Science,* 1956, **1,** (4) (October 1956). By permission of the publisher.

Page 191. Quotation from: Lidtz, T., & Fleck, F. Schizophrenia, human integration and the role of the family. In Jackson, D. (Ed.), *The Etiology of Schizophrenia.* New York: Basic Books, 1960. By permission of the publisher.

Page 192. Quotation from: Laing, R. B. Is schizophrenia a disease? *International Journal of Social Psychology,* 1964, **10,** 184-193. By permission of the publisher.

Page 195. Quotations from: Bleuler, E. *Dementia Praecox or the Group of Schizophrenias.* New York: International Universities Press, 1950. By permission of the publisher.

Page 196. Quotation from: Epstein, S., & Coleman, M. Drive theories of schizophrenia. *Psychosomatic Medicine,* 1970, **32,** 113-140. By permission of the American Psychosomatic Society and the author.

Pages 197-198. Quotation from: Bateson, G. *Perceval's Narrative: A Patient's Account of His Psychosis.* Stanford: Stanford University Press, 1961. By permission of the publisher.

Page 198. Quotation from: Bandura, A. A social learning interpretation of psychological dysfunctions. In London, P., & Rosenhan, D. (Eds.), *Foundations of Abnormal Psychology.* New York: Holt, Rinehart and Winston, Inc., 1968. By permission of the publisher.

Page 202. Quotation from: Arieti, S. Schizophrenia: Other aspects; psychotherapy. In Arieti, S. (Ed.), *American Handbook of Psychiatry,* Vol. I. New York: Basic Books, 1959. By permission of the publisher.

Page 202. Quotation from: MAYER-GROSS, SLATER & ROTH: CLINICAL PSYCHIATRY, 3d ed. (1969), Bailliere Tindall & Cassell, Ltd., London. Published in the United States of America by the Williams & Wilkins Company, Balitmore. By permission of the publisher.

Page 206. Quotation from: Laing, R. D. *The Politics of Experience.* Middlesex, England: Penguin Books, Ltd., 1967. By permission of the publisher.

Page 207. Quotation from: Skinner, B. F. A new method for the experimental analysis of the behavior of psychotic patients. *Journal of Nervous and Mental Diseases,* 1954, **120,** 403-406. Copyright © 1954, The Williams & Wilkins Co., Baltimore. By permission of the publisher and the author.

Page 207. Quotation from: Lindsley, O. Operant conditioning methods applied to research in chronic schizophrenia. *Psychiatric Research Reports,* 1956. By permission of American Psychiatric Association.

Page 208. Quotation from: Ayllon, T., & Michael, J. The psychiatric nurse as a behavioral engineer. *Journal of Experimental Analysis of Behavior,* 1959, **2.** By permission of the publisher and the author.

Pages 217-218. Quotations from: Doestoevsky, F. *White Nights and Other Stories.* Translated by Constance Garnett. Reprinted with permission of Macmillan Publishing Company "Notes from the Underground" by F. Doestoevsky. Published in the United States by Macmillan Publishing Co., Inc. Published in Great Britian by William Heinemann, Ltd.

Pages 218-219. Excerpts from A MIND THAT FOUND ITSELF by Clifford Beers. Copyright 1907, 1917, 1921, 1923, 1931, 1932, 1934, 1935, 1939, 1940, 1942, 1944, 1948, 1953 by the American Foundation for Mental Hygiene, Inc. Reprinted by permission of Doubleday & Company, Inc.

Pages 220-223. Excerpts from A MIND THAT FOUND ITSELF by Clifford Beers. Copyright 1907, 1917, 1921, 1923, 1931, 1932, 1934, 1935, 1939, 1940, 1942, 1944, 1948, 1953 by the American Foundation for Mental Hygiene, Inc. Reprinted by permission of Doubleday & Company, Inc.

Page 224. Quotation from: Meier-Graefe, J. *Doestoevsky, The Man and His Work.* London: Routledge & Kegan Paul, Ltd., 1928. By permission of the publisher.

Page 339. Quotation from: Beck, A. *Depression.* Philadelphia: University of Pennsylvania Press, 1971. Published in Great Britian by The Granada Publishing Company, London. By permission of the University of Pennsylvania Press and the author.

Page 228. Quotation from: Beck, A. *Depression.* Philadelphia: University of Pennsylvania Press, 1971. Published in Great Britian by The Granada Publishing Company, London. By permission of the University of Pennsylvania Press and the author.

Page 233. Quotation from: Lazarus, A. Some reactions to Costello's paper on depression. *Behavior Therapy,* 1972, 3. By permission of Academic Press and the author.

Page 237. Quotation from: Kagan, J. Personality Development. In London, P., & Rosenhan, D. (Eds.), *Foundations of Abnormal Psychology.* New York: Holt, Rinehart & Winston, Inc., 1968. By permission of the publisher.

Page 239. Excerpted from "We're driving young blacks to suicide" by R. Seiden in PSYCHOLOGY TODAY Magazine, August 1970. Copyright © Communications/Research/Machines, Inc.

Page 239–240. Excerpted from "We're driving young blacks to suicide" by R. Seiden in PSYCHOLOGY TODAY Magazine, August 1970. Copyright © Communications/Research/Machines, Inc.

Page 240. Quotation from: Teicher, J., & Jacobs, J. Adolescents who attempt suicide: Preliminary findings. *American Journal of Psychiatry,* 1966, **122,** 1248–1257. Copyright © 1966, The American Psychiatric Association and the authors.

Page 244. Quotation from: Lazarus, A. Learning theory and the treatment of depression. *Behavior Research and Therapy,* 1968, **6**. With the permission of Microforms International Marketing Corporation exclusive copyright licensee of Pergamon Press back files.

Page 245. Quotation from: Todd, F. J. Conversant control of self-evaluative responses in the treatment of depression: A new use for an old principle. *Behavior Therapy,* 1972, **3.** By permission of Academic Press and the author.

Page 259. Quotation from: American Psychiatric Association. *Diagnostic and Statistical Manual of Mental Disorders.* Washington, D.C.: American Psychiatric Association, 1968. By permission of the publisher.

Page 262. Quotation from: Prince, M. *The Dissociation of a Personality.* New York: Doubleday & Co., 1925. By permission of David McKay Co.

Page 289. Quotation from: Dollard, J., & Miller, E. N. *Personality and Psychotherapy.* New York: McGraw-Hill, 1950. By permission of the publisher.

Page 290. Reprinted with permission from Wolpe, J. *The Practice of Behavior Therapy,* 1969, Pergamon Press, Ltd., and the author.

Page 291. Quotation from: Bandura, A. *Principles of Behavior Modification.* New York: Holt, Rinehart and Winston, Inc., 1969. By permission of the publisher.

Page 293. Quotation from: Chapter 7 of THE DISCOVERY OF THE UNCONSCIOUS: The History and evolution of dynamic psychiatry, by Henri F. Ellenberger, © 1970 by

Henri F. Ellenberger, Basic Books, Inc., Publishers, New York.

Page 295. Quotation from: Halleck, S. *The Politics of Therapy.* New York: Science House, Inc., 1971. By permission of the publisher.

Page 296. Quotation from: Freud, S. *A General Introduction to Psychoanalysis.* New York: Liveright, 1953. Reprinted by permission of Liveright, New York.

Pages 296–297. Quotation from Wolberg, L. *The Technique of Psychotherapy.* New York: Grune & Stratton, 1954. By permission from the publishers.

Pages 297–298. Quotation from: Menninger, K. *Theory of Psychoanalytic Technique.* New York: Basic Books, 1958. By permission of the publisher.

Page 298. Quotation from: Kenneth Mark Colby—A PRIMER FOR PSYCHOTHERAPISTS. Copyright 1951 The Ronald Press Company, New York. By permission of the publishers.

Page 299. Quotation from: Franz Alexander and Thomas Morton French — PSYCHOANALYTIC THERAPY Copyright 1946 The Ronald Press Company, New York.

Pages 302. Quotation from: Rogers, C. *On Becoming A Person.* Boston: Houghton Mifflin Co., 1961. By permission of the publisher.

Page 303. Quotation from: Rogers, C. *Client-Centered Therapy.* Boston: Houghton Mifflin Co., 1951. By permission of the publisher.

Pages 304–306. Quotation from Paul, N. L. Effects of playback on family members of their own previously recorded conjoint material. *Psychiatry Research Reports,* 1966, **20.** By permission of the American Psychiatric Association.

Page 307. Quotation from: Krasner, L. Behavior Therapy. In *Annual Review of Psychology.* Palo Alto, California: Annual Reviews, Inc., 1971. By permission of Annual Reviews, Inc. and the author.

Page 308. Reprinted with permission from Wolpe, J. *The Practice of Behavior Therapy,* 1969, Pergamon Press, Ltd., and the author.

Page 308. Quotation from: Jacobson, E. *Progressive Relaxation.* Chicago: University of Chicago Press, 1938.

Copyright 1938, University of Chicago Press. By permission of the publisher.

Pages 310–311. Quotation from: Baum, M., & Posner, E. Comparison of flooding procedures in animals and man. *Behaviour Research and Therapy,* 1971, **9.** With the permission of Microform International Marketing Corporation exclusive copyright licensee of Pergamon Press Journal back files.

Page 314. Quotation from: Rachman, S. Clinical applications of observational learning, imitation and modeling. *Behavior Therapy,* 1972, **3.** By permission of Academic Press and the author.

Pages 315–316. Quotation from: Lazarus, A. *Behavior Therapy and Beyond.* New York: McGraw-Hill, 1971. By permission of the publisher.

Page 317. Quotation from: Eysenck, H. *The Effects of Psychotherapy.* New York: The International Science Press, Inc. 1966. By permission of the author.

Pages 317–318. Quotations from: Bergin, A. The evaluation of therapeutic outcomes. In Bergin, A., & Garfield, S. (Eds.), *Handbook of Psychotherapy and Behavior Change.* New York: John Wiley & Sons, 1971. By permission of the publisher.

Page 318. Quotation from: May, P. Psychotherapy and ataraxic drugs. In Bergin, A., & Garfield, S. (Eds.), *Handbook of Psychotherapy and Behavior Change.* New York: John Wiley & Sons, 1971. By permission of the publisher.

Page 318. Quotation from: Paul, G. Outcome of systematic desensitization. I. Background, procedures, and uncontrolled reports of individual treatment. In Franks, C. *Behavior Therapy: Appraisal and Status.* New York: McGraw-Hill, 1969. By permission of the publisher.

Pages 325–326. From DOWN THESE MEAN STREETS, by Piri Thomas. Copyright © 1967 by Piri Thomas. Reprinted by permission of Alfred A. Knopf, Inc.

Page 339. Quotation from: Cautela, J. The treatment of alcoholism by covert sensitization. *Psychother-*

apy: Theory Research and Practice, 1970, 1. By permission of the publisher and the author.

Page 343. Quotation from: Malcolm X with assistance of Alex Haley. *The Autobiography of Malcolm X.* New York: Grove Press, 1966. Reprinted by permission of Grove Press, Inc. Copyright © 1964 by Alex Haley and Malcolm X.

Pages 344–345. Quotation from: Smith, L., Vine, M., & Hibbard, E. Changing drug patterns in the Haight-Ashbury. *California Medicine,* 1969, **110,** 151–157. By permission of the California Medical Association.

Page 345. Quotation from *Playboy* magazine. Copyright © 1963 by Alan Harrington. By permission of the author and the publisher.

Pages 347–348. Quotation from: The National Commission on Marihuana and drug abuse. *Marihuana.* New York: The New American Library, 1972. With credit to the New American Library, publisher.

Page 349. Quotation from: Canadian Government Commission of Inquiry. *The Non-Medical Use of Drugs.* Ottawa: Information Canada, 1971. Reproduced by permission of Information Canada.

Page 362. Quotation from: Feinbloom, D. H. *The heterosexual transvestite: An interactionist view.* Unpublished M. A. thesis. Boston University Department of Sociology, 1972, pp. 30–33. By permission of the author.

Page 364. Quotation from: *Sexual Behavior* by Ronald M. Holmes (Ed.). Berkeley: McCutchan Publishing Corp. Copyright © 1971 by Ronald M. Holmes. Reprinted by permission.

Pages 366–367. Quotation from: Green, R., & Money, J. *Transsexualism and Sex Reassignment.* Baltimore: The Johns Hopkins Press, 1969. By permission from the publisher.

Page 370. Quotation from: Perloff, W. Hormones and homosexuality. In Marmor, J. (Ed.), *Sexual Inversion.* New York: Basic Books, Inc., 1965. By permission of the publisher.

Page 372. Quotation from: Bieber, I. Sexual deviations II: Homosexuality. In Freedman, A., & Kaplan, H.

(Eds.), *Comprehensive Textbook of Psychiatry.* Baltimore: copyright © 1967. The Williams & Wilkins Co., Baltimore. By permission of the publisher and the author.

Page 373. Quotation from: McGuire, R., Carlisle, J., & Young, B. Sexual deviations as conditioned behavior. *Behavior Research and Therapy,* 1965, **2,** 185–190. With the permission of Microform International Marketing Corporation exclusive copyright licensee of Pergamon Press Journal back files.

Page 373. Quotation from: Bandura, A. *Principles of Behavior Modification.* New York: Holt, Rinehart & Winston, Inc., 1969. By permission of the publisher.

Page 377. Quotation from: Paige, J. Quest for sexual identity. *Douglass College Caellian,* 1973, **34,** No. 30;1. By permission of the *Caellian.*

Page 379. Quotation from: Ward, D. A., & Kassenbaum, G. C. *Women's Prison.* Chicago: Aldine Publishing Co., 1969. By permission of the publisher.

Page 380. Quotation from: Barber, D. *Pornography and Society.* London: Charles Skilton, Ltd., 1972. By permission of the publisher.

Page 381. Quotations from U.S. Commission on Obscenity and Pornography. *The Report of the U.S. Commission on Obscenity and Pornography.* Washington, D.C.: U.S. Government Printing Office. Public Document.

Page 387. Quotation from: Jones, E. *The Life and Work of Sigmund Freud, The Last Phase: 1919–1939.* Vol. 3. New York: Basic Books, 1957. By permission of the publisher.

Page 387. Quotation from: *Sexual Behavior* by Ronald M. Holmes (Ed.). Berkeley: McCutchan Publishing Corp. Copyright © 1971 by Ronald M. Holmes. Reprinted by permission.

Pages 389–390. Quotation from: Brady, J. Brevital-aided systematic desensitization. In Rubin, R., Fensterheim, H., Lazarus, A., & Franks, C. (Eds.), *Advances in Behavior Therapy.* New York: Academic Press, 1971. By permission of the publisher and the author.

Page 392. Quotation from: Masters,

W., & Johnson, V. *Human Sexual Inadequacy.* Boston: Little, Brown & Co., Copyright © 1970. By permission of the publisher.

Page 407. List based on Cleckley, H. *The Mask of Sanity,* 4th ed. St. Louis: C. V. Mosby Co., 1964. By permission of C. V. Mosby Co. and the author.

Page 409. Quotation from Schachter, S., & Latane, B. Crime, cognition and the autonomic nervous system. In Jones, M. (Ed.), *Nebraska Symposium on Motivation,* 1964. Lincoln: University of Nebraska Press. By permission of the publisher.

Page 411. Quotation from: Robins, L. *Deviant Children Grow Up.* Baltimore: Williams & Wilkins Co., 1966. Copyright © 1966 The Williams & Wilkins Co., Baltimore. By permission of the publisher and the author.

Page 420. Quotation from: Alexander, F., French, T., & Pollock, G. *Psychosomatic Specificity.* Vol. I. *Experimental Study and Results.* Chicago: University of Chicago Press, 1968. Copyright 1968, University of Chicago Press. By permission of the publisher.

Table 14-1, page 423. Based on Lachman, S. *Psychosomatic Disorders: A Behavioristic Interpretation.* New York: John Wiley & Sons, 1972. Reprinted by permission of the publisher.

Page 429. Quotation from: Neisworth, J., & Moore, F. Operant treatment of asthmatic responding with the parent as therapist, *Behavior Therapy,* 1972, **3,** 95–99. By permission of Academic Press and the author.

Pages 429–430. From "The Control of Eating Behavior in an Anorexic by Operant Conditioning Techniques" by Arthur J. Bachrach, William J. Erwin, and Jay P. Mohr, in CASE STUDIES IN BEHAVIOR MODIFICATION, edited by Leonard P. Ullmann and Leonard Krasner. Copyright © 1965 by Holt, Rinehart and Winston, Inc. Reproduced by permission of Holt, Rinehart and Winston, Inc.

Page 431. From "Behavior Therapy with a Case of Nervous Anorexia" by Peter Lang, in CASE STUDIES

IN BEHAVIOR MODIFICATION, edited by Leonard P. Ullmann and Leonard Krasner. Copyright © by Holt, Rinehart and Winston, Inc. Reproduced by permission of Holt, Rinehart and Winston, Inc.

Page 441. Quotation from CRISIS IN CHILD MENTAL HEALTH by Joint Commission on Mental Health of Children. Copyright © 1969, 1970 by the Joint Commission on Mental Health of Children, Inc. By permission of Harper & Row, Publishers, Inc.

Pages 441–442. Quotation from CRISIS IN CHILD MENTAL HEALTH by Joint Commission on Mental Health of Children. Copyright © 1969, 1970 by the Joint Commission on Mental Health of Children, Inc. By permission of Harper & Row, Publishers, Inc.

Pages 444–445. List based on: Group for the Advancement of Psychiatry, Committee on Child Psychiatry. *Psychopathological Disorders in Childhood: Theoretical Considera-* *tions and a Proposed Classification.* New York: Group for the Advancement of Psychiatry, 1966. Pp. 217–219. By permission Group for the Advancement of Psychiatry, Inc.

Page 449. Quotation from: Zimmerman, E., & Zimmerman, J. The alteration of behavior in a special classroom situation. *Journal of Experimental Analysis of Behavior,* 1962, **5,** 59–60. Copyright © 1962 by the Society for the Experimental Analysis of Behavior, Inc. By permission of the publisher and the author.

Page 459. Quotation from: Ackerman, N. *Treating the Troubled Family.* New York: Basic Books, Inc., 1966. By permission of the publisher.

Page 463. Quotation from: Zax, M., & Cowen, E. Research on early detection and prevention of emotional dysfunction in young school children. In Spielberger, C. (Ed.), *Current Topics in Clinical and Community Psychology.* Vol. I.

1969. New York: Academic Press, 1969. By permission of the publisher and the author.

Page 482. Quotation from CRISIS IN CHILD MENTAL HEALTH by Joint Commission on Mental Health of Children. Copyright © 1969, 1970 by the Joint Commission on Mental Health of Children, Inc. By permission of Harper & Row, publishers, Inc.

Page 487. Quotation from: Anonymous. Our voices. *Journal of Clinical Child Psychology,* 1973. By permission of *Journal of Clinical Child Psychology.*

Page 496. Quotation from: Anonymous. Death of a mind. A study in disintegration. *Lancet,* 1950, i, 1012–1015. By permission of *Lancet.*

Page 505. Quotation from: Thompson, G. Acute and chronic alcoholic conditions. In Arieti, S. (Ed.), *American Handbook of Psychiatry.* Vol II. New York: Basic Books, 1969. By permission of the publisher.

Figures

In addition to the credits listed below and cited in the text, the following people provided photographs of themselves: Hans Eysenck (page 9), B. F. Skinner (page 104), David Wechsler (page 131), Albert Bandura (page 197), Erich Fromm (page 287), John Dollard (page 288), J. Wolpe (page 289), Neal E. Miller (page 290), Carl C. Rogers (page 302), Arnold A. Lazarus (page 315), and Bruno Bettelheim (page 452).

Figure 1-1, page 10. From: Hildebrand, H. A factorial study of introversion-extraversion. *British Journal of Psychology,* 1958, **49,** 1–11. By permission of the publisher.

Figure 3-6, page 71. From: Selye, H. *The stress of life,* New York: McGraw-Hill, 1956. P. 187. Adapted by permission of the author.

Figure 5-1, page 125. From: Spitzer, R. L., & Endicott, J. Problem Appraisal Scales. MS 02 (7/69). Front page. By permission of the author.

Figure 5-2, page 126. From: Spitzer, R. L., & Endicott, J. Diagno II. Further Developments in a Computer program for psychiatric diagnosis. *American Journal of Psychiatry,* 1969, **125,** 12–21. Copyright © 1969, The American Psy-

chiatric Association. By permission of the publisher and the author.

Figure 5-3, page 127. From: Nathan, P. E., Samaraweera, A., Andberg, M. & Patch, V. Syndromes of psychosis and psychoneurosis. *Archives of General Psychiatry,* 1968, **19,** 706–716. Copyright 1968, American Medical Association. By permission of the publisher and the author.

Figure 5-4, page 130. From Wechsler, D. *Wechsler Adult Intelligence Scale.* Psychological Corporation, 1955. By permission of the publisher.

Figure 5-5, page 134. From: Hathaway, S. R., & McKinley, J. C. *The Minnesota Multiphasic Personality Inventory.* Psychological Corporation, 1948. By permission of the publisher.

Figure 5-8, page 138. From: Murray,

H. *Thematic Apperception Test.* Card 12F. Copyright, 1943, Harvard University Press, publisher. By permission of the publisher.

Figure 6-3, page 174. From: Fenz, W. B., & Velner, J. Physiological concomitants of behavioral indexes of schizophrenia. *Journal of Abnormal Psychology,* 1970, **76,** 27–35. Copyright 1970 by the American Psychological Association. Reprinted by permission of the publisher and the author.

Figure 7-1, page 204. From: Grinspoon, L., Ewalt, J. R., & Shader, R. Long-term treatment of chronic schizophrenia. *International Journal of Psychiatry,* 1967, **4,** 116–128. By permission of the author and the publisher.

Figure 7-2, page 208. Figure from: Lindsley, O. R. Free-operant conditioning and psychotherapy. In Masserman, J. H. (Ed.), *Current Psychiatric Therapies.* Vol. III. New York: Grune & Stratton, 1963. By permission of the author and the publisher.

Figure 7-3, page 210. From: Ayllon, T., & Azrin, N. H. The measurement and reinforcement of behavior of psychotics. *Journal of the Experimental Analysis of Behavior,* 1965, **8.** By permission of the author and the publisher.

Figure 8-1, page 225. By permission from MAYER-GROSS, SLATER & ROTH: CLINICAL PSYCHIATRY, 3d ed., 1969. Bailliere, Tindall & Cassell Ltd., London, published in the United States of America by the Williams & Wilkins Company, Baltimore.

Figure 10-1, page 312. From: Bandura, A., Blanchard, E., & Ritter, B. Relative efficacy of desensitization and modeling approaches for inducing behavioral, affective, and attitudinal changes. *Journal of Personality and Social Psychology,* 1969, **13,** 173–199. Copyright 1969 by the American Psychological Association. Reprinted by permis-

sion of the publisher and the author.

Figure 10-2, page 313. From: Bandura, A., Blanchard, E. & Ritter, B. Relative efficacy of desensitization and modeling approaches for inducing behavioral, affective, and attitudinal changes. *Journal of Personality and Social Psychology,* 1969, **13,** 173–199. Copyright 1969 by the American Psychological Association. Reprinted by permission of the publisher and the author.

Figure 11-1, page 335. From: Nathan, P. E., & O'Brien, J. Experimental analysis of the behavior of alcoholics and non-alcoholics during experimental drinking. *Behavior Therapy,* 1971, **2,** 455–476. By permission of the publisher.

Figure 11-2, page 337. Reprinted with permission of A.A. World Services, Inc., copyright owners, P.O. Box 459, Grand Central Station, New York, N.Y. 10017.

Figure 11-3, page 340. From: Lovibond, S., & Caddy, G. Discriminated aversive control in the moderation of alcoholic drinking behavior. *Behavior Therapy,* 1970, **1,** 437–444. By permission of the publisher and the author.

Figure 14-1, page 426. From: Schwartz, G., Shapiro, D., & Tursky, B. Learned control of cardiovascular integration in man through operant conditioning. *Psychosomatic Medicine,* 1971, 57–62. By permission of the American Psychosomatic Society and the author.

Figure 14-2, page 429. From: Moore, N. Behavior therapy in bronchial asthma: A controlled study. *Journal of Psychosomatic Research,* 1965, **9,** 257–276. By permission of the publisher.

Figure 14-3, page 430. From: Neisworth, J., & Moore, F. Operant treatment of asthmatic responding with the parent as therapist. *Behavior Therapy,* 1972, **3,** 95–99. By permission of the publisher and the author.

Figure 15-1, page 446. Based on: Bemporad, J., Pfeifer, C., & Bloom, W. Twelve months' experience with the GAP classification of childhood disorders. *American Journal of Psychiatry,* 1970, **127,** 658–664. Copyright © *American Journal of Psychiatry,* 1970. By permission of the publisher and the author.

Addenda

Table 2-1, page 39. From: Srole, L., Langer, T., Michael, S., Opler, M., & Rennie, T. *The Midtown Manhattan Study.* Vol. I. New York: McGraw-Hill, 1962. By permission of the author.

Table 7-1, page 209. From: Ayllon, T., & Azrin, N. H. The measurement and reinforcement of behavior of psychotics. *Journal of the Experimental Analysis of Behavior,* 1965, **8,** 357–383. By permission of the publisher and the author.

Page 211. Quotation from: Ayllon, T., & Azrin, N. H. The measurement and reinforcement of behavior of psychotics. *Journal of the Experimental Analysis of Behavior,* 1965, **8,** 357–383. By permission of the publisher and the author.

Table 8-2, page 235. From: Wittenborn, J. R. *Wittenborn Psychiatric Rating Scales.* New York: Psychological Corporation, 1955. By permission of the author.

NOTE: For work by T. Ayllon and his colleagues, additional information and related research can be found in *The token economy: A motivational system for therapy and rehabilitation,* by T. Ayllon and N. H. Azrin, published by Appleton-Century-Crofts, 1968.

References

The numbers in parentheses at the end of each reference indicate the pages in this text where the works are cited.

Abenson, M. EEGs in chronic schizophrenia. *British Journal of Psychiatry*, 1970, **116**, 421-425. *(174)*

Abraham, K. Notes on the psychoanalytic investigation and treatment of manic-depressive insanity and allied conditions (1911). In *Selected papers on psychoanalysis.* New York: Basic Books, 1960. *(230)*

Acker, B. Depersonalization. I: Aetiology and phenomenology. *Journal of Mental Science*, 1954, **100**, 838-853. *(266)*

Ackerman, N. *Treating the troubled family.* New York: Basic Books, 1966. *(459)*

Adler, A. *The neurotic constitution.* New York: Moffatt, Yard & Co., 1917. *(286-287, 300)*

Affleck, D. C., & Strider, F. D. Contribution of psychological reports to patient management, *Journal of Consulting and Clinical Psychology,* 1971, **37**, 177-179. *(129)*

Agras, W. S., Leitenberg, H., & Barlow, D. H. Social reinforcement in the modification of agoraphobia. *Archives of General Psychiatry,* 1968, **19**, 423-427. *(312)*

Alanen, Y. O. The families of schizophrenic patients. *Proceedings of the Royal Society of Medicine,* 1970, **63**, 227-230. *(192)*

Albee, G. W. Conceptual models and manpower requirements in psychology. *American Psychologist.* 1968, **23**, 317-324. *(16)*

Alcoholics Anonymous. *World directory,* New York: Alcoholics Anonymous, 1973. *(337)*

Alexander, F. The logic of emotions and its dynamic background. *International Journal of Psychoanalysis,* 1935, **16**, 339-413. *(420)*

Alexander, F. Emotional factors in essential hypertension. *Psychosomatic Medicine,* 1948, **1**, 173-179. *(420)*

Alexander, F. The development of psychosomatic medicine. *Psychosomatic Medicine,* 1962, **24**, 13-24. *(420)*

Alexander, F., & French, T. M. *Psychoanalytic therapy.* New York: Ronald, 1946. *(299)*

Alexander, F., French, T. M., & Pollock, G. H. (Eds.) *Psychosomatic specificity.* Vol. 1. *Experimental study and results.* Chicago: University of Chicago Press, 1968. *(420)*

Alkire, A., Goldstein, M., Rodnick, E., & Judd, L. Social influence and counterinfluence within families of four types of disturbed adolescents. *Journal of Abnormal Psychology,* 1971, **77**, 32-41. *(457)*

American Psychiatric Association. *Diagnostic and statistical manual of mental disorders.* Washington, D.C.: American Psychiatric Association, 1968. *(14, 117, 164, 259, 264, 326, 329, 364, 418, 443-445, 471-474, 495)*

Anastasi, A., & Foley, J. P. *Differential psychology: Individual and group differences in behavior.* New York: Macmillan, 1949. *(227)*

Andersen, P., & Andersson, S. A. *Physiological basis of the alpha rhythm.* New York: Appleton-Century, 1968. *(427)*

Anderson, W., Baird, D., & Thomson, A. Epidemiology of stillbirths and infant deaths due to congenital malformation. *Lancet,* 1958, **1**, 1304-1306. *(507)*

Anonymous. Death of a mind: A study in disintegration. *Lancet,* 1950, **258**, 1012-1015. *(496)*

Anonymous. Our voices. *Journal of Clinical Child Psychology,* 1973, **11**, 29. *(491)*

Anonymous. The twelve steps. *A. A. Grapevine,* 1973, **30**, cover page. *(337)*

Anthony, E. J. A clinical evaluation of children with psychotic parents. *American Journal of Psychiatry,* 1969, **126**, 177-184. *(192)*

Antonov, A. Children born during the siege of Leningrad in 1942. *Journal of Pediatrics,* 1947, **30**, 250-259. *(506)*

Arieti, S. *Interpretation of schizophrenia.* New York: Brunner, 1955. *(159, 188)*

Arieti, S. Schizophrenia: Other aspects; psychotherapy. In S. Arieti (Ed.), *American handbook of psychiatry.* Vol. 1. New York: Basic Books, 1959. *(202)*

Arnhoff, F., & Damianopoulos, E. Self-body recognition and schizophrenia. *Journal of Genetic Psychology,* 1964, **70,** 353-361. *(162)*

Aronson, S., Valsamis, M., & Volk, B. Infantile amaurotic familial idiocy. *Pediatrics,* 1960, **26,** 229-242. *(478)*

Arthur, B. Role perceptions of children with ulcerative colitis. *Archives of General Psychiatry,* 1963, **8,** 536-545. *(420)*

Arthur, T. S. *The sons of temperance offering.* New York: Nafis & Cornish, 1850. *(321-324)*

Arthurs, R., & Cahoon, E. A clinical and electroencephalographic survey of psychopathic personality. *American Journal of Psychiatry,* 1964, **120,** 875-882. *(409)*

Atthowe, J. M. Controlling nocturnal enuresis in severely disabled and chronic patients. *Behavior Therapy,* 1972, **3,** 232-239. *(511)*

Atthowe, J. M. Behavior innovation and persistence. *American Psychologist,* 1973, **28,** 34-41. *(213)*

Atthowe, J. M., & Krasner, L. Preliminary report on the application of contingent reinforcement procedures (token economy) on a "chronic" psychiatric ward. *Journal of Abnormal Psychology,* 1968, **73,** 37-43. *(210)*

Ax, A. The physiological differentiation between fear and anger in humans. *Psychosomatic Medicine,* 1953, **15,** 433-442. *(69)*

Axline, V. *Play therapy.* Boston: Houghton Mifflin, 1947. *(457)*

Ayllon, T. Intensive treatment of psychotic behaviour by stimulus satiation and food reinforcement. *Behaviour Research and Therapy,* 1963, **1,** 53-61. *(209)*

Ayllon, T., & Azrin, N. H. The measurement and reinforcement of behavior of psychotics. *Journal of the Experimental Analysis of Behavior,* 1965, **8,** 357-383. *(209, 210)*

Ayllon, T., & Haughton, E. Control of the behavior of schizophrenic patients by food. *Journal of the Experimental Analysis of Behavior,* 1962, **5,** 343-352. *(209)*

Ayllon, T., & Michael, J. The psychiatric nurse as a behavioral engineer. *Journal of the Experimental Analysis of Behavior,* 1959, **2,** 323-334. *(208)*

Azrin, N., & Foxx, R. A rapid method of toilet training the institution-alized retarded. *Journal of Applied Behavior Analysis,* 1971, **4,** 89-100. *(486)*

Azrin, N. H., & Holz, W. C. Punishment. In W. K. Honig (Ed.), *Operant behavior: Areas of research and application.* New York: Appleton-Century-Crofts, 1966. *(106)*

Bachrach, A. J., Erwin, W. J., & Mohr, J. P. The control of eating behavior in an anorexic by operant conditioning techniques. In L. P. Ullmann & L. Krasner (Eds.), *Case studies in behavior modification.* New York: Holt, 1965. *(429-431)*

Backner, B. Counseling black students: Any place for whitey? *Journal of Higher Education,* 1970, **41,** 630-637. *(46)*

Bagchi, B. K., & Wenger, M. A. Electrophysiological correlates of some Yogi exercises. In *EEG, clinical neurophysiology and epilepsy.* London: Pergamon, 1959. *(427)*

Baird, D., Walker, J., & Thomson, A. Causes and prevention of stillbirths and first week deaths. III: Classification of deaths by clinical cause: Effect of age, parity, and length of gestation on death rates by causes. *Journal of Obstetrics and Gynaecology of the British Empire,* 1954, **61,** 433-448. *(507)*

Ball, J. C., & Chambers, C. D. (Eds.) *The epidemiology of opiate addiction in the United States.* Springfield, Ill.: Charles C Thomas, 1970. *(341)*

Ban, T. A., & Lehmann, H. E. Nicotinic acid in the treatment of schizophrenia. *Canadian Psychiatric Association Journal,* 1970, **15,** 499-500. *(184)*

Bancroft, J. H. J. The application of psychophysiological measures to the assessment and treatment of sexual behavior. *Behaviour Research and Therapy,* 1971, **9,** 119-130. *(388)*

Bancroft, J. H. J., Jones, H. G., & Pullan, B. R. A simple transducer for measuring penile erection, with comments on its use in the treatment of sexual disorders. *Behaviour Research and Therapy,* 1966, **4,** 239-241. *(383)*

Bandura, A. A social learning interpretation of psychological dysfunctions. In P. London & D. Rosenhan (Eds.), *Foundations of abnormal psychology.* New York: Holt, 1968. *(197, 198)*

Bandura, A. *Principles of behavior modification.* New York: Holt, 1969. *(89, 290-292, 312-314, 373, 374, 449, 461)*

Bandura, A. Vicarious and self-reinforcement processes. In R. Glaser (Ed.), *The Nature of Reinforcement.* New York: Academic, 1971. *(314)*

Bandura, A., Blanchard, E. B., & Ritter, B. Relative efficacy of desensitization and modeling approaches for inducing behavioral, affective, and attitudinal changes. *Journal of Personality and Social Psychology,* 1969, **13,** 173-199. *(312-313)*

Bandura, A., Grusec, J. E., & Menlove, F. L. Observational learning as a function of symbolization and incentive set. *Child Development,* 1966, **37,** 499-506. *(100)*

Bandura, A., Grusec, J. E., & Menlove, F. L. Vicarious extinction of avoidance behavior. *Journal of Personality and Social Psychology,* 1967, **5,** 16-23. *(461)*

Bandura, A., & Mischel, W. Modification of self-imposed delay of reward through exposure to live and symbolic models. *Journal of Personality and Social Psychology,* 1965, **2,** 698-705. *(100)*

Bandura, A., Ross, D., & Ross, S. A. Transmission of aggression through imitation of aggressive models. *Journal of Abnormal and Social Psychology,* 1961, **63,** 575-582. *(99)*

Bandura, A., Ross, D., & Ross, S. A. Imitation of film-mediated aggressive models. *Journal of Abnormal and Social Psychology,* 1963, **66,** 3-11. *(99, 410)*

Bandura, A., & Walters, R. *Adolescent aggression: A study of the influence of child training practices and family interrelationships.* New York: Ronald, 1959. *(410)*

Bandura, A., & Walters, R. *Social learning and personality development.* New York: Holt, 1963. *(99, 410)*

Barber, D. F. *Pornography and*

society. London: Charles Skelton, Ltd., 1972. *(380)*

Barendregt, J. T. *Psychological studies: Research in psychodiagnostics.* Vol. 1. The Hague: Mouton, 1961. *(420)*

Barrett, B. H., & Lindsley, O. R. Deficits in acquisition of operant discrimination and differentiation shown by institutionalized retarded children. *American Journal of Mental Deficiency,* 1962, **67,** 424–436. *(207–208)*

Bartell, G. D. Group sex among the mid-Americans. *Journal of Sex Research,* 1970, **6,** 113–130. *(385)*

Basowitz, H., Persky, H., Korchin, S., & Grinker, R. *Anxiety and stress.* New York: McGraw-Hill, 1955. *(270)*

Batchelor, I. *Henderson and Gillespie's textbook of psychiatry.* New York: Oxford, 1969. *(476–477, 500, 502, 504)*

Bateson, G. (Ed.) *Perceval's narrative: A patient's account of his psychosis.* Stanford, Calif.: Stanford, 1961. *(197, 198)*

Bateson, G., Jackson, D. D., Haley, J., & Weakland, J. Double-bind hypothesis of schizophrenia. *Behavioral Science,* 1956, **1,** 251–264. *(190)*

Baughman, E. E. *Black Americans: A psychological analysis.* New York: Academic, 1971. *(48)*

Baum, M., & Poser, E. G. Comparison of flooding procedures in animals and man. *Behaviour Research and Therapy,* 1971, **9,** 249–254. *(310)*

Baxter, J., & Becker, J. Anxiety and avoidance behavior in schizophrenics in response to parental figures. *Journal of Abnormal and Social Psychology,* 1962, **64,** 432–437. *(168)*

Baynes, T. E. Continuing conjectural concepts concerning civil commitment criteria. *American Psychologist,* 1971, **26,** 489–495. *(214)*

Beck, A. T. *Depression.* Philadelphia: University of Pennsylvania, 1967. *(228, 231, 238, 241, 243)*

Beck, A. T., & Hurvich, M. S. Psychological correlates of depression. I: Frequency of "masochistic" dream content in a private practice sample. *Psychosomatic Medicine.* 1959, **21,** 50–55. *(231)*

Beck, A. T., Sethi, B., & Tuthill, R. Childhood bereavement and adult depression. *Archives of General Psychiatry,* 1963, **9,** 295–302. *(232)*

Beck, A. T., & Valins, S. Psychotic depressive reactions in soldiers who accidentally killed their buddies. *American Journal of Psychiatry,* 1953, **110,** 347–353. *(231)*

Beck, A. T., & Ward, C. H. Dreams of depressed patients: Characteristic themes in manifest content. *Archives of General Psychiatry,* 1961, **5,** 462–467. *(231, 232)*

Beck, A. T., Ward, C. H., Mendelson, M., Mock, J. E., & Erbaugh, J. K. Reliability of psychiatric diagnoses. II: A study of consistency of clinical judgments and ratings. *American Journal of Psychiatry,* 1962, **119,** 351–357. *(117, 119, 231)*

Beck, S. J. Personality structure in schizophrenia: A Rorschach investigation in eighty-one patients and sixty-four controls. *Nervous and Mental Diseases Monographs.* New York: Nervous and Mental Diseases Publishing Co., 1938. *(137)*

Beers, C. W. *A mind that found itself* (1905). New York: Longmans, Green, 1920. *(218–221, 223)*

Beier, E. G., Robinson, P., & Micheletti, G. Susanville: A community helps itself in mobilization of community resources for self-help in mental health. *Journal of Consulting and Clinical Psychology,* 1971, **36,** 142–150. *(53)*

Behar, M. Prevalence of malnutrition among pre-school children of developing countries. In N. Scrimshaw & J. Gordon (Eds.), *Malnutrition, Learning and Behavior.* Cambridge, Mass.: M.I.T., 1968. *(507)*

Bemporad, J., Pfeifer, C., & Bloom, W. Twelve months' experience with the GAP classification of childhood disorders. *American Journal of Psychiatry,* 1970, **127,** 658–664. *(444–446)*

Bender, L. A visual motor Gestalt test and its clinical use. *American Orthopsychiatric Association Monograph,* 1938, No. 3. *(499)*

Bender, L. Drug addiction in adolescence. *Comprehensive Psychiatry,* 1963, **4,** 131–134. *(347)*

Bender, L. The life course of schizophrenic children. *Biological Psychiatry,* 1970, **2,** 165–172. *(453, 455)*

Benedict, R. *Patterns of culture.* Boston: Houghton Mifflin, 1934. *(10)*

Benjamin, H. *The transsexual phenomenon.* New York: Julian Press, 1966. *(371)*

Benson, H., Shapiro, D., Tursky, B., & Schwartz, G. E. Decreased systolic blood pressure through operant conditioning techniques in patients with essential hypertension. *Science,* 1971, **173,** 740–742. *(426)*

Benton, A. A multiple choice type of the visual retention test. *Archives of Neurology and Psychiatry,* 1950, **64,** 699–707. *(499)*

Benton, A. The MMPI in clinical practice. In G. Welsh & W. Dahlstrom (Eds.), *Basic readings on the MMPI in psychology and medicine.* Minneapolis: University of Minnesota Press, 1963. *(408)*

Ben-Yishay, Y., Diller, L., Mandelberg, I., Gordon, W., & Gerstman, L. Similarities and differences in block design performance between older normal and brain-injured persons. *Journal of Abnormal Psychology,* 1971, **78,** 17–25. *(500)*

Berest, J. J. Fetishism: Three case histories. *Journal of Sex Research,* 1971, **7,** 237–239. *(366)*

Berger, A. A test of the double-bind hypothesis of schizophrenia. *Family Process,* 1965, **4,** 198–205. *(191)*

Berger, H. Über das Elektrenkephalogramm des Menschen. *Archiv der Psychiatrie und Nervenkranhen,* 1929, **87,** 527–570. *(427)*

Bergin, A. E. The evaluation of therapeutic outcomes. In A. E. Bergin & S. L. Garfield (Eds.), *Handbook of psychotherapy and behavior change.* New York: Wiley, 1971. *(317–318)*

Bergin, A. E., & Garfield, S. L. *Handbook of psychotherapy and behavior change: An empirical analysis.* New York, Wiley, 1971. *(316–317)*

Bergin, A. E., & Strupp, H. H. *Changing frontiers in the science of psychotherapy.* New York: Aldine-Atherton, 1972. *(316–317)*

Berkun, M., Bialek, H., Kern, R., & Yagi, K. Experimental studies of psychological stress in man. *Psychological Monographs,* 1962, **76,** 534. *(72)*

Bernard, J., & Eisenman, R. Verbal

conditioning in psychopaths with social and monetary reinforcement. *Journal of Personality and Social Psychology,* 1967, **6,** 203-206. *(409)*

Bernstein, D. A., & Beaty, W. E. The use of *in vivo* desensitization as part of a total therapeutic intervention. *Journal of Behavior Therapy and Experimental Psychiatry,* 1971, **2,** 259-266. *(309)*

Berzins, J. I., Dove, J. L., & Ross, W. F. Cross validational studies of the personality correlates of the A-B therapist "type" distinction among professionals and nonprofessionals. *Journal of Consulting and Clinical Psychology,* 1972, **39,** 388-395. *(300)*

Berzins, J. I., Ross, W. F., & Monroe, J. J. A multivariate study of the personality characteristics of hospitalized narcotic addicts on the MMPI. *Journal of Clinical Psychology,* 1971, **27,** 174-181. *(300, 349)*

Bettelheim, B. *The empty fortress.* New York: Free Press, 1967. *(451-453, 461-463)*

Betz, B. Validation of the differential treatment success of "A" and "B" therapists with schizophrenic patients. *American Journal of Psychiatry,* 1963, **119,** 883-884. *(300)*

Bibring, E. The mechanism of depression. In P. Greenacre (Ed.), *Affective disorders.* New York: International Universities Press, 1953. *(231)*

Bieber, B., Bieber, I., Dain, H. J., Prince, P. R., Drellich, M. C., Grand, H. C., Grundlach, R. H., Kremer, M. W., Wilbur, C. B., & Bieber, T. B. *Homosexuality,* New York: Basic Books, 1962. *(373, 388)*

Bieber, I. Sexual deviations. II: Homosexuality. In A. M. Freedman & H. I. Kaplan (Eds.), *Comprehensive textbook of psychiatry.* Baltimore: Williams & Wilkins, 1967. *(372, 385, 387)*

Bieber, I. Homosexuality. *American Journal of Nursing,* 1969, **69,** 2637-2641. *(387)*

Birk, L. Behavior therapy—Integration with dynamic psychiatry. *Behavior Therapy,* 1970, **1,** 522-526. *(291)*

Birk, L., Huddleston, W., Miller, E.. & Cohler, B. Avoidance conditioning for homosexuality. *Ar-*

chives of General Psychiatry. 1971, **25,** 314-323. *(388)*

Birren, J. The abuse of the urban aged. *Psychology Today,* 1970, **3,** 37-38. *(499)*

Black, S. Labeling and psychiatry: A comment. *Social Science and Medicine,* 1971, **5,** 391-392. *(124)*

Blanchard, E. B., & Young, L. D. Self-control of cardiac functioning: A promise as yet unfulfilled. *Psychological Bulletin,* 1973, **79,** 145-163. *(426)*

Blessed, G., Tomlinson, B., & Roth, M. The association between quantitative measures of dementia and of senile change in the cerebral grey matter of elderly subjects. *British Journal of Psychiatry,* 1968, **114,** 797-811. *(500)*

Bleuler, E. Autistic thinking. *American Journal of Insanity,* 1913, **69,** 873. *(159)*

Bleuler, E. *Dementia praecox or the group of schizophrenias.* New York: International Universities Press, 1950. *(155, 195)*

Blinder, J., Freeman, D. M. A., & Stunkard, A. J. Behavior therapy of anorexia nervosa: Effectiveness of activity as a reinforcer of weight gain. *American Journal of Psychiatry,* 1970, **126,** 1093-1098. *(428)*

Blum, D. MMPI characteristics of males in a private hospital population. *Psychological Reports,* 1970, **26,** 234. *(268)*

Blumer, D. Transsexualism, sexual dysfunction, and temporal lobe disorder. In R. Green & J. Money (Eds.), *Transsexualism and sex reassignment.* Baltimore: Johns Hopkins, 1969. *(371)*

Boatman, J. J., & Szurek, S. A. A clinical study of childhood schizophrenia. In D. D. Jackson (Ed.), *The etiology of schizophrenia.* New York: Basic Books, 1960. *(453)*

Bonner, D. & Mills, S. *Heredity.* Englewood Cliffs, N. J.: Prentice-Hall, 1964.

Boren, J. J. The study of drugs with operant techniques. In W. K. Honig (Ed.), *Operant behavior: Areas of research and application.* New York: Appleton-Century-Crofts, 1966. *(106)*

Boring, E. G. *A history of experimental psychology.* New York:

Appleton-Century-Crofts,   1950. *(418)*

Borkovec, T. D. Effects of expectancy on the outcome of systematic desensitization and implosive treatments for analogue anxiety. *Behavior Therapy,* 1972, **3,** 29-40. *(310)*

Boudewyns, P. A., & Wilson, A. E. Implosive therapy and desensitization therapy using free association in the treatment of inpatients. *Journal of Abnormal Psychology,* 1972, **79,** 259-268. *(310)*

Boudin, H. M. Contingency contracting as a therapeutic tool in the deceleration of amphetamine use. *Behavior Therapy,* 1972, **3,** 604-608. *(353)*

Bourdillon, R. E., Clarke, C. A., Ridges, A. P., Sheppard, P. M., Harper, P., & Leslie, S. A. "Pink spot" in the urine of schizophrenics. *Nature,* 1965, **208,** 453-455. *(184)*

Bower, E., Shellhammer, T., Daily, J., & Bower, M. *High school students who later become schizophrenic.* Sacramento: California State Department of Education, 1960. *(456)*

Braaten, L. J., & Darlin, C. D. Overt and covert homosexual problems among male college students. *Genetic Psychology Monographs,* 1965, **71,** 269-310. *(382)*

Brady, J. P. Brevital-relaxation treatment of frigidity. *Behaviour Research and Therapy,* 1966, **4,** 71-77. *(389)*

Brady, J. P. Brevital-aided systematic desensitization. In R. D. Rubin, H. Fensterheim, A. A. Lazarus, & C. M. Franks (Eds.), *Advances in behavior therapy.* New York: Academic, 1971. *(389)*

Brady, J. V. Ulcers in executive monkeys. *Scientific American,* 1958, **199,** 95-100. *(424, 425)*

Brady, J. V., Porter, R. W., Conrad, D. G., & Mason, J. W. Avoidance behavior and the development of gastroduodenal ulcers. *Journal of the Experimental Analysis of Behavior,* 1958, **1,** 69-72. *(425)*

Braucht, G. N., Brakarsh, D., Follingstad, D., & Berry, K. L. Deviant drug use in adolescence. *Psychological Bulletin,* 1973, **79,** 92-106. *(331, 348)*

Breger, L., & McGaugh, J. L. A critique and reformulation of "learning theory" approaches to psychotherapy and neurosis. *Psychological Bulletin,* 1965, **63,** 335-358. *(291)*

Breuer, J., & Freud, S. *Studies on hysteria (1905).* New York: Basic Books, 1957. *(249-251, 254-255, 257, 261, 293)*

Bricker, W., Morgan, D., & Grabowski, J. Development and maintenance of a behavior modification repertoire of cottage attendants through T.V. feedback. *American Journal of Mental Deficiency,* 1972, **77,** 128-136. *(485)*

Brodie, B. B., & Costa, E. Some current views on brain monoamines. *Psychopharmacology Service Center Bulletin,* 1962, **2,** 1. *(230)*

Brody, E. B., & Sata, L. S. Personality disorders. I: Trait and pattern disturbances. In A. Freedman & H. Kaplan (Eds.), *Comprehensive textbook of psychiatry.* Baltimore: Williams & Wilkins, 1967. *(403)*

Brostoff, P. K. The utility of quantified diagnostic interview information for a psychiatric treatment indication. *Dissertation Abstracts International,* 1972, **32,** 4202. *(124)*

Broverman, I. K., Broverman, D., Clarkson, F., Rosenkrantz, P., & Vogel, S. Sex-role stereotypes and clinical judgments of mental health. *Journal of Consulting and Clinical Psychology,* 1970, **34,** 1-7. *(49)*

Broverman, I. K., Vogel, S. R., Broverman, D. M., Clarkson, F. E., & Rosenkrantz, P. S. Sex-role stereotypes: A current appraisal. *Journal of Social Issues,* 1972, **28,** 59-78. *(50)*

Brown, B. Recognition of aspects of consciousness through association with EEG alpha activity represented by a light signal. *Psychophysiology,* 1970, **6,** 442-452. *(427)*

Brown, J., & Kosterlitz, N. Selection and treatment of psychiatric outpatients. *Archives of General Psychiatry,* 1964, **11,** 425-437. *(49)*

Brown, R. Organ weight in malnutrition with special reference to brain weight. *Developmental Medicine and Child Neurology,* 1966, **8,** 512-522. *(507)*

Brozek, J., & Grande, F. Abnormalities of neural function in the presence of inadequate nutrition. In J. Field (Ed.), *Handbook of Physiology.* Sec. 1: *Neurophysiology,* Vol. 3. Baltimore: Williams & Wilkins, 1960. *(506)*

Bugental, D., Love, L., & Kaswan, J. Videotaped family interaction: Differences reflecting presence and type of child disturbed. *Journal of Abnormal Psychology,* 1972, **79,** 285-290. *(459)*

Bugental, D., Love, L. Kaswan, J., & April, C. Verbal-nonverbal conflict in parental messages to normal and disturbed children. *Journal of Abnormal Psychology,* 1971, **77,** 6-10. *(459)*

Bunney, W. E., & Fawcett, J. A. Possibility of a biochemical test for suicidal potential: An analysis of endocrine findings prior to three suicides. *Archives of General Psychiatry,* 1965, **13,** 232-239. *(229)*

Burchard, J. D., & Barrera, F. An analysis of timeout and response cost in a programmed environment. *Journal of Applied Behavior Analysis,* 1972, **5,** 271-282. *(212)*

Burdock, E. I., & Hardesty, A. S. A multivariate analysis of the relations between intelligence and psychopathology. In M. Hammer, K. Salzinger, & S. Sutton (Eds.), *Psychopathology.* New York: Wiley, 1973, pp. 427-440. *(129)*

Burgess, E. P. The modification of depressive disorders. In R. D. Rubin & C. M. Franks (Eds.), *Advances in behavior therapy.* New York: Academic, 1969. *(245)*

Buss, A. H. Two anxiety factors in psychiatric patients. *Journal of Abnormal and Social Psychology,* 1962, **65,** 426-427. *(260)*

Buss, A. H. *Psychopathology.* New York: Wiley, 1966. *(265)*

Buss, A. H., Wiener, M., Durkee, A., & Baer, M. The measurement of anxiety in clinical situations. *Journal of Consulting Psychology,* 1955, **19,** 125-129. *(270)*

Cade, J. F. J. Lithium salts in treatment of psychotic excitement. *Medical Journal of Australia,* 1949, **2,** 349-352. *(242)*

Cahalan, D., Cisin, I. H., & Crossley, H. M. *American drinking practices: A national survey of drinking behavior and attitudes.* New Brunswick: Rutgers Center of Alcohol Studies, 1969. *(331)*

Caldwell, D., & Domino, E. Electroencephalographic and eye movement patterns during sleep in chronic schizophrenic patients. *Electroencephalography and Clinical Neurophysiology,* 1967, **22,** 414-420. *(174)*

Callahan, E. J., & Leitenberg, H. Reinforced practice as a treatment for acrophobia: A controlled outcome study. *Proceedings of the American Psychological Association,* 1970, **5,** 533-534. *(312)*

Callahan, E. J., & Leitenberg, H. Aversion therapy for sexual deviation: Contingent shock and covert sensitization. *Journal of Abnormal Psychology,* 1973, **81,** 60-73. *(388)*

Calne, D. *Parkinsonism: Physiology, pharmacology and treatment.* London: Edward Arnold, Ltd., 1970. *(501-503)*

Cameron, N. A. The place of mania among the depressions from a biological standpoint. *Journal of Psychology,* 1942, **14,** 181-195. *(228, 229)*

Cameron, N. A. *Personality development and psychopathology.* Boston: Houghton Mifflin, 1963. *(173, 224)*

Cameron, N. A. Paranoid reactions. In A. M. Freedman & H. I. Kaplan (Eds.), *Comprehensive textbook of psychiatry.* Baltimore: Williams & Wilkins, 1967. *(228)*

Canadian Government Commission of Inquiry. *The nonmedical use of drugs.* Baltimore, Md.: Penguin, 1971. *(349)*

Caplan, G. *Principles of preventive psychiatry.* New York: Basic Books, 1964. *(52)*

Caprio, F. S. *Female homosexuality.* New York: Grove Press, 1954. *(379)*

Caputo, D., & Mandell, W. Consequences of low birth weight. *Developmental Psychology,* 1970, **3,** 363-383. *(481)*

Carlin, A. S., Bakker, C. B., Halpern, L., & Post, R. D. Social facilitation of marijuana intoxication: Impact of social set and pharmacological activity. *Journal of Abnormal Psychology,* 1972, **80,** 132-140. *(350)*

Carson, R. C. Interpretive manual to the MMPI. In J. N. Butcher (Ed.), *MMPI: Research developments and clinical applications.* New York: McGraw-Hill, 1969. *(382)*

Catania, A. C. Self-inhibiting effects of reinforcement. *Journal of the Experimental Analysis of Behavior,* 1973, **19,** 517-526. *(106)*

Cattell, R. B., & Stice, G. F. *Handbook for the sixteen personality factor questionnaire.* Champaign, Ill.: Institute for Personality and Ability Testing, 1957. *(132)*

Cautela, J. R. The treatment of alcoholism by covert sensitization. *Psychotherapy: Theory, Research & Practice,* 1970, **7,** 83-90. *(339)*

Celesia, G., & Wanamaker, W. Psychiatric disturbances in Parkinson's disease. *Diseases of the Nervous System,* 1972, **33,** 577-583. *(502)*

Chapman, L. J. Illusory correlation in observational learning. *Journal of Verbal Learning and Verbal Behavior,* 1967, **6,** 151-155. *(383)*

Chapman, L. J., & Chapman, J. P. The genesis of popular but erroneous psychodiagnostic observations. *Journal of Abnormal Psychology,* 1967, **72,** 193-204. *(119, 383)*

Chapman, L. J., & Chapman, J. P. Illusory correlation as an obstacle to the use of valid psychodiagnostic signs. *Journal of Abnormal Psychology,* 1969, **74,** 271-280. *(119, 383)*

Chapman, L. J., & Chapman, J. P. Test results are what you think they are. *Psychology Today,* 1971, **5,** 18-22. *(119)*

Charalampous, K. D., & Tansey, L. W. Metabolic fate of B-(3,4-dimethoxyphenyl)-ethylamine in man. *Journal of Pharmacology and Experimental Therapy,* 1967, **155,** 318, 329. *(184)*

Chartier, G. M. A-B therapist variable: Real or imagined? *Psychological Bulletin,* 1971, **75,** 22-33. *(300)*

Chein, L., Gerard, D., Lee, R., & Rosenfeld, E. *The road to H.* New York: Basic Books, 1964. *(347, 350)*

Cherek, D. R., Thompson, T., & Heistad, G. T. Responding maintained by the opportunity to attack during an interval food reinforce-

ment schedule. *Journal of Experimental Analysis of Behavior,* 1973, **19,** 113-123. *(106)*

Chesler, P. Men drive women crazy. *Psychology Today,* 1971, **5,** 18-22, 26-27, 97-98. *(49)*

Chesler, P. *Women and Madness.* New York: Doubleday, 1972. *(49, 50)*

Chess, S. Neurological dysfunction and childhood behavioral pathology. *Journal of Autism and Childhood Schizophrenia,* 1972, **2,** 299-311. *(454)*

Chien, C. Psychiatric treatment for geriatric patients: "Pub" or drug? *American Journal of Psychiatry,* 1971, **127,** 1070-1075. *(511)*

Child, I. The relation of somatotype to self-ratings on Sheldon's temperament traits. *Journal of Personality,* 1950, **18,** 440. *(73)*

Churchill, D. The relation of infantile autism and early childhood schizophrenia to developmental language disorders of childhood. *Journal of Autism and Childhood Schizophrenia,* 1972, **2,** 182-197. *(452)*

Chynoweth, R. The problem of drug dependency. *Australian Occupational Therapy Journal,* 1969, **16,** 9-13. *(349)*

Cimbolic, P. Counselor race and experience effects on black clients. *Journal of Consulting & Clinical Psychology,* 1972, **39,** 328-332. *(46)*

Citizens' Board of Inquiry into Hunger and Malnutrition in the United States. *Hunger, U.S.A.* Boston: Beacon Press, 1968. *(506)*

Claghorn, J. The anxiety-depression syndrome. *Psychosomatics,* 1970, **11,** 438-441. *(267)*

Claridge, G. Psychosomatic relations in physical disease. In H. J. Eysenck (Ed.), *Handbook of abnormal psychology.* London: Pitman, 1973. *(421)*

Clarizio, H., & McCoy, G. *Behavior disorders in school-aged children.* Scranton: Chandler, 1970. *(456)*

Clark, J., & Mallett, B. A follow-up study of schizophrenia and depression in young adults. *British Journal of Psychiatry,* 1963, **109,** 491-499. *(166)*

Clark, L. D. Marijuana and human behavior. *Rocky Mt. Medical Journal,* 1972, **69,** 43-46. *(353)*

Clark, L. D., & Done, A. K. Drug abuse and dependence. In *Brennemann's practice of pediatrics.* Vol. 1. Hagerstown, Md.: Harper & Row, 1972. *(348)*

Clark, L. D., Hughes, R., & Nakashima, E. N. Behavioral effects of marijuana. *Archives of General Psychiatry,* 1970, **23,** 193-198. *(353)*

Clarke, A., & Hemerlin, B. Adult imbeciles: Their abilities and trainability. *Lancet,* 1955, **2,** 337-339. *(486)*

Cleaver, E. *Soul on Ice.* New York: McGraw-Hill, 1968. *(43)*

Cleckley, H. *The mask of sanity.* St. Louis: Mosby, 1964. *(400, 407, 411)*

Clements, S. Minimal brain dysfunction in children. *NINDB Monograph,* No. 3. Public Health Service Bulletin, No. 1415. Washington: United States Department of Health, Education, & Welfare, 1966. *(454)*

Cleveland, S. E., & Fisher, S. A comparison of psychological characteristics and physiological reactivity in ulcer and rheumatoid arthritis groups. I: Psychological measures. *Psychosomatic Medicine,* 1960, **22,** 283-289. *(424)*

Cohen, D. J. Justin and his peers: An experimental analysis of a child's social world. *Child Development,* 1962, **33,** 697-716. *(106)*

Cohen, H. L., Filipczak, J., Bis, J., Cohen, J., & Larkin, P. *Contingencies applicable to special education—Motivationally oriented design for an ecology of learning.* United States Department of Health, Education, & Welfare, 1968. *(212, 412-413)*

Cohen, M. B., Baker, G., Cohen, R. A., Fromm-Reichmann, F., & Weigert, E. V. An intensive study of twelve cases of manic-depressive psychosis. *Psychiatry,* 1954, **17,** 103-137. *(231)*

Cohen, S. Review of *The ethics of addiction. Psychotherapy & Social Science Review,* 1973, **7,** 19. *(18)*

Colby, K. M. *A primer for psychotherapists.* New York: Ronald, 1951. *(298)*

Cole, J. O., & Davis, J. M. American college of neuropsychopharmacology fifth annual meeting. *Psycho-*

pharmacological Bulletin, 1967, **4**, 28-31. *(230)*

Coleman, J. *Abnormal psychology and modern life.* Glenview, Ill.: Scott, Foresman, 1972. *(260, 264-267)*

Coles, R., & Piers, M. *Wages of neglect.* Chicago: Quadrangle, 1969. *(18)*

Cooper, A. J. A case of bronchial asthma treated by behavior therapy. *Behaviour Research and Therapy,* 1964, **1**, 351-356. *(428)*

Cooperman, M., & Child, I. L. Differential effects of positive and negative reinforcement on two psychoanalytic character types. *Journal of Consulting and Clinical Psychology,* 1971, **37**, 57-59. *(285)*

Coppen, A. J. The biochemistry of affective disorders. *British Journal of Psychiatry,* 1967, **113**, 1237-1264. *(229)*

Costa, E., Gessa, G. L., Hirsch, C., Kuntzman, R., & Brodie, B. B. On current status of serotonin as a brain neurohormone and in action of reserpine-like drugs. *Annals of New York Academy of Science,* 1962, **96**, 118-133. *(230)*

Costello, C. G. Depression: Loss of reinforcers or loss of reinforcer effectiveness. *Behavior Therapy,* 1972, **3**, 240-247. *(233)*

Costello, C. G., & Comrey, A. L. Scales for measuring depression and anxiety. *Journal of Psychology,* 1967, **66**, 303-313. *(234)*

Cotzias, G. Levodopa in the treatment of Parkinsonism. *Journal of the American Medical Association,* 1971, **128**, 1903-1908. *(503)*

Cotzias, G., Papavasilios, P., & Gellene, R. Modification of Parkinsonism—Chronic treatment with L-dopa. *New England Journal of Medicine,* 1969, **280**, 337-345. *(503)*

Cowen, E., Dorr, D., Trost, M., & Izzo, L. Follow-up study of maladapting school children seen by nonprofessionals. *Journal of Consulting and Clinical Psychology,* 1972, **39**, 235-238. *(463)*

Craddick, R. Wechsler-Bellevue I.Q. scores of psychopathic and non-psychopathic prisoners. *Journal of Psychological Studies,* 1961, **12**, 167-172. *(410)*

Craft, M., Stephenson, G., & Granger, C. A controlled trial of authoritar-

ian and self-governing regimes with adolescent psychopaths. *American Journal of Orthopsychiatry,* 1964, **34**, 543-554. *(414)*

Crammer, J. L. Water and sodium in two psychotics. *Lancet,* 1959, **1**, 1122-1126. *(229)*

Cranefield, P. Historical perspectives. In I. Philips (Ed.), *Prevention and treatment of mental retardation.* New York: Basic Books, 1966. *(473)*

Crumpton, E., Weinstein, A. D., Acker, C. W., & Annis, A. P. How patients and normals see the mental patient. *Journal of Clinical Psychology,* 1967, **23**, 46-49. *(14)*

Cumming, J., & Cumming, E. *Ego & Milieu.* New York: Atherton, 1962. *(205)*

Cushman, P. Methadone maintenance in hardcore criminal addicts: Economic effects. *New York State Journal of Medicine,* 1971, **71**, 1768-1774. *(351)*

Cushman, P. Addicts and methadone: A dilemma. *Wall Street Journal,* Jan. 10, 1973. *(351)*

Dahlstrom, W. G. Portfolio of profiles. *Contemporary Psychology,* 1970, **15**, 153-154. *(135)*

Dahlstrom, W. G., Welsh, G. S., & Dahlstrom, L. E. *An MMPI handbook,* Vols. I and II. Minneapolis: University of Minnesota Press, 1972. *(133)*

Dastur, D. K., Mann, J. D., & Pollin, W. Hippuric acid secretion, coffee, and schizophrenia. *Archives of General Psychiatry,* 1963, **9**, 79-82. *(183)*

Davidson, P. Thumbsucking. In C. G. Costello (Ed.), *Symptoms of psychopathology.* New York: Wiley, 1970. *(460)*

Davis, J. Efficacy of tranquilizing and antidepressant drugs. *Archives of General Psychiatry,* 1965, **13**, 552-572. *(242)*

Davis, J. M., Klerman, G. L., & Schildkraut, J. J. Drugs used in the treatment of depression. In Efron, D. H., Cole, J. D., Levine, J., & Wittenborn, J. R. (Eds.), *Psychopharmacology. A Review of Progress 1957-1967.* Washington, D.C.: U.S. Superintendent of Documents, 1968.

Davis, K. R., & Sine, J. O. An anti-

social behavior pattern associated with a specific MMPI profile. *Journal of Consulting and Clinical Psychology,* 1971, **36**, 229-234. *(349)*

Davis, W., DeWolfe, A., & Gustafson, R. Intellectual deficit in process and reactive schizophrenia and brain injury. *Journal of Consulting and Clinical Psychology,* 1972, **38**, 146. *(499)*

Davison, A., & Dobbing, J. Myelination as a vulnerable period in brain development. *British Medical Bulletin,* 1966, **22**, 40-44. *(507)*

Davison, G. C. Elimination of a sadistic fantasy by a client-controlled counterconditioning technique: A case study. *Journal of Abnormal Psychology,* 1968, **73**, 84-90. (a) *(389)*

Davison, G. C. Systematic desensitization as a counterconditioning process. *Journal of Abnormal Psychology,* 1968, **73**, 91-99. (b) *(291, 373)*

Davison, G. C., & Wilson, G. T. Processes of fear-reduction in systematic desensitization: Cognitive and social reinforcement factors in humans. *Behavior Therapy,* 1973, **4**, 1-21. *(291)*

Day, W. F. Review of *Beyond freedom and dignity. Contemporary Psychology,* 1972, **17**, 465-469. *(104)*

Delany, L. T. The other bodies in the river. *Psychology Today,* 1968, **2**, 26-31, 59. *(44)*

DeLeon, G., & Mandell, W. A comparison of conditioning and psychotherapy in the treatment of functional enuresis. *Journal of Clinical Psychology,* 1966, **22**, 326-330. *(447)*

DeLeon, G., & Sacks, S. Conditioning functional enuresis: A four-year follow-up. *Journal of Consulting and Clinical Psychology,* 1972, **39**, 299-300. *(451)*

DeLeon, G., & Wexler, H. K. Heroin addiction: Its relation to sexual behavior and sexual experience. *Journal of Abnormal Psychology,* 1973, **81**, 36-38. *(342)*

Dement, W. Dream recall and eye movement during sleep in schizophrenics and normals. *Journal of Nervous and Mental Disease,* 1955, **122**, 263-269. *(174)*

DeMyer, M., Alpern, G., Barton, S., DeMyer, W., Churchill, D., Hingtgen, J., Bryson, C., Pontius, W., &

Kimberlin, C. Imitation in autistic, early schizophrenic and non-psychotic subnormal children. *Journal of Autism and Childhood Schizophrenia*, 1972, **2**, 264–287. *(452)*

DeMyer, M., Pontius, W., Norton, J., Barton, S., Allen, J., & Steele, R. Parental practices and innate activity in normal, autistic and brain-damaged infants. *Journal of Autism and Childhood Schizophrenia*, 1972, **2**, 49–66. *(451)*

Denber, H. C. B. Tranquilizers in psychiatry. In A. M. Freedman & H. I. Kaplan (Eds.), *Comprehensive textbook of psychiatry*. Baltimore: 1262. *(202)*

Denber, H. C. B. Electroencephalographic findings during chlorpromazine-diethazine treatment. *Journal of Nervous and Mental Disease*, 1958, **126**, 392–398. *(235)*

Derogatis, L. R., Covi, L., Lipman, R. S., Davis, D. M., & Rickels, K. Social class and race as mediator variables in neurotic symptomatology. *Archives of General Psychiatry*, 1971, **25**, 31–40. *(46)*

Derogatis, L. R., Klerman, G., & Lipman, R. Anxiety states and depressive neuroses. *Journal of Nervous and Mental Diseases*, 1972, **155**, 392–403. *(267)*

Despert, J. L. *The emotionally disturbed child—Then and now.* New York: Brunner, 1965. *(439)*

Detre, T. P., & Jarecki, H. G. *Modern psychiatric treatment.* Philadelphia: Lippincott, 1971. *(236, 241, 242)*

DeVito, R. A., Flaherty, L. A., & Mozdzierz, G. J. Toward a psychodynamic theory of alcoholism. *Diseases of the Nervous System*, 1970, **31**, 43–49. *(331)*

DeWolfe, A., Barrell, R., Becker, B., & Spaner, F. Intellectual deficit in chronic schizophrenia and brain damage. *Journal of Consulting and Clinical Psychology*, 1971, **36**, 197–204. *(499)*

Diamond, D. R. Enhancement of creativity: A study of approach and personality. *Dissertation Abstracts International*, 1971, **32**, 2998–2999. *(135)*

DiCara, L. Learning in the autonomic nervous system. *Scientific American*, 1970, **222**, 30–39. *(425)*

Dickerson, J., Dobbing, J., & McCance, R. The effect of undernutrition on the postnatal development of the brain and cord in pigs. *Proceedings of the Royal Society of London*, 1967, **166**, 396. *(507)*

Dieckmann, W., Turner, D., Meiller, E., Savage, L., Hill, A., Straube, M., Pottinger, R., & Rynkiewicz, L. Observations of protein intake and the health of the mother and baby. I: Clinical and laboratory findings. *Journal of the American Dietetic Association*, 1951, **27**, 1046. *(507)*

DiGiusto, E., Cairncross, K., & King, M. Hormonal influences on fear-motivated responses. *Psychological Bulletin*, 1971, **6**, 432–444. *(69)*

DiLoreto, A. O. *Comparative psychotherapy: An experimental analysis.* Chicago: Aldine, 1971. *(316–317)*

DiScipio, W. J. Homosexuality and the deconditioning of fears of heterosexuality. *Behavior Therapy*, 1972, **3**, 150. *(387)*

Ditman, K. S. A controlled experiment on the use of court probation for drunk arrests. *American Journal of Psychiatry*, 1967, **124**, 160–163. *(338)*

Dixon, J. Depersonalization phenomena in a sample population of college students. *British Journal of Psychiatry*, 1963, **109**, 371–375. *(266)*

Dobbs, N. J. Predicting length of psychiatric hospitalization using demographic and psychological test data. *Dissertation Abstracts International*, 1970, **31**, 2276. *(135)*

Docter, R. F., Naitch, P., & Smith, J. C. Electroencephalographic changes and vigilance behavior during experimentally induced intoxication with alcoholic subjects. *Psychosomatic Medicine*, 1966, **28**, 605–615, *(332)*

Dodge, G., & Kolstoe, R. The MMPI in differentiating early multiple sclerosis and conversion hysteria. *Psychological Reports*, 1971, **29**, 155–159. *(268)*

Dohrenwend, B. P., & Chin, S. E. Social status and attitudes toward psychological disorder: The problem of tolerance of deviation. *American Sociological Review*, 1967, **32**, 417–433. *(5)*

Dole, V. P., Nyswander, M. E., &

Warner, A. Successful treatment of 750 criminal addicts. *Journal of the American Medical Association*, 1968, **206**, 2708–2711. *(351)*

Dollard, J., & Miller, E. *Personality and psychotherapy.* New York: McGraw-Hill, 1950. *(273, 282, 288–289)*

Dorfman, E., & Kleiner, R. Race of examiner and patient in psychiatric diagnosis and recommendations. *Journal of Consulting Psychology*, 1962, **26**, 393. *(45)*

Dorken, H., & Kral, L. The psychological differentiation of organic brain lesions and their localization by means of the Rorschach test. *American Journal of Psychiatry*, 1952, **108**, 764–770. *(499)*

Dostoevsky, F. *Notes from underground (1864).* In *The short novels of Dostoevsky.* New York: Dial, 1951. *(217, 218)*

Dreger, R. M., Reed, M., Lewis, P., Overlade, D., Rich, T., Taffel, C., Miller, K., & Flemming, E. Behavioral classification project. *Journal of Consulting Psychology*, 1964, **28**, 1–13. *(445)*

Dreikurs, R. Psychodynamic diagnosis in psychiatry. *American Journal of Psychiatry*, 1963, **119**, 1045–1048. *(139)*

Dunbar, F. *Emotions and bodily changes.* New York: Columbia, 1954. *(420)*

Dunn, B. A. Aggressive behavior of the Mongolian gerbil *Meriones unguiculatus* in relation to physiology and population dynamics. *Dissertation Abstracts International*, 1971, **36**, (6-B), 3190. *(385)*

DuPont, R. L., & Katon, R. N. Development of a heroin-addiction treatment program: Effect on urban crime. *Journal of the American Medical Association*, 1971, **216**, 1320–1324. *(350, 351)*

Eaton, J. W., & Weil, R. J. *Culture and mental disorders.* Glencoe, Ill.: Free Press, 1955. *(228)*

Edelman, R. I., & Snead, R. Self-disclosure in a simulated psychiatric interview. *Journal of Consulting Clinical Psychology*, 1972, **38**, 354–358. *(123)*

Edwards, A. L. *Edwards personal preference schedule.* New York: Psychological Corporation, 1959. *(132)*

Edwards, G. Diagnosis of schizophrenia: An Anglo-American comparison. *British Journal of Psychiatry,* 1972, **120**, 385–390. *(123)*

Edwards, N. B. Case conference: Assertive training in a case of homosexual pedophilia. *Journal of Behavior Therapy and Experimental Psychiatry,* 1972, **3**, 55–64. (a) *(309)*

Edwards, N. B. Review of *Behavior therapy and beyond. Journal of Behavior Therapy and Experimental Psychiatry,* 1972, **3**, 75. (b) *(315)*

Efron, V., & Keller, M. *Selected statistics on consumption of alcohol (1850–1968) and on alcoholism (1930–1968).* New Brunswick, N.J.: Rutgers Center of Alcohol Studies, 1970. *(334)*

Ehrmann, F. Introduction. In F. Ehrmann (Ed.), *Terezin.* Prague: Council of Jewish Communities in the Czech Lands, 1965. *(31)*

Eiduson, B. The two classes of information in psychiatry. *Achives of General Psychiatry,* 1968, **18**, 405–419. *(263)*

Eigenbrode, C. R., & Shipman, W. G. The body image barrier concept. *Journal of Abnormal & Social Psychology,* 1960, **60**, 450–452. *(424)*

Eisenberg, L., & Gruenberg, E. The current status of secondary prevention in child psychiatry. *American Journal of Orthopsychiatry,* 1961, **31**, 355–367. *(457)*

Eisenthal, S., Harford, T., & Solomon, L. Premorbid adjustment, paranoid-nonparanoid status, and chronicity in schizophrenic patients. *Journal of Nervous and Mental Diseases,* 1972, **155**, 227–231. *(169)*

Ellenberger, H. F. *The discovery of the unconscious.* New York: Basic Books, 1970. *(293)*

Ellenberger, H. F. The story of "Anna O": A critical review with new data. *Journal of the History of the Behavioral Sciences,* 1972, **13**, 267–279. *(255)*

Ellingson, R. J. Incidence of EEG abnormality among patients with mental disorders of apparently nonorganic origin: A critical review. *American Journal of Psychiatry,* 1954, **111**, 263–275. *(408)*

Ellingson, R. J. Brain waves and problems of psychology. *Psychological Bulletin,* 1956, **53**, 1–34. *(427)*

Ellis, A. *Reason and emotion in psychotherapy.* New York: Lyle Stuart, 1962. *(316)*

Ellis, A. *Growth through reason: Verbatim cases in rational emotive therapy.* Palo Alto, Calif.: Science and Behavior Books, 1971. *(316)*

Ellis, H. *Studies in the psychology of sex.* Philadelphia: F. A. Davis Co., 1915. *(379)*

Ellman, G. L., Jones, R. T., & Rychert, R. C. Mauve spot and schizophrenia. *American Journal of Psychiatry,* 1968, **125**, 849–851. *(184)*

Endore, G. *Synanon.* Garden City, N.Y.: Doubleday, 1968. *(352)*

Epstein, B., Epstein, J., & Postel, D. Tumors of spinal cord simulating psychiatric disorders. *Diseases of the Nervous System,* 1971, **32**, 741–743. *(497)*

Epstein, S. Toward a unified theory of anxiety. In B. Maher (Ed.), *Progress in Experimental Personality Research,* Vol. 4, New York: Academic, 1967. *(173, 196)*

Epstein, S., & Coleman, M. Drive theories of schizophrenia. In R. Cancro (Ed.), *The schizophrenic syndrome.* New York: Brunner/Mazel, 1971. *(196)*

Erickson, M. H., Hershman, S., & Sector, I. I. *The practical application of medical and dental hypnosis.* New York: Julian Press, 1961. *(425)*

Eriksen, C., & Davids, A. The meaning and clinical validity of the Taylor anxiety scale and the hysteria-psychasthenia scales from the MMPI. *Journal of Abnormal and Social Psychology,* 1955, **50**, 135–137. *(270)*

Erikson, E. H. *Childhood and society.* New York: Norton, 1950. *(93)*

Evans, R., & Marmorston, J. Rorschach signs of brain damage in cerebral thrombosis. *Perceptual and Motor Skills,* 1964, **18**, 977–988. *(499)*

Evans, R. B. Physical and biochemical characteristics of homosexual men, *Journal of Abnormal Psychology,* 1972, **39**, 140–147. *(371)*

Eysenck, H. J. The effects of psychotherapy: An evaluation. *Journal of Consulting Psychology,* 1952, **16**, 319–324. *(317)*

Eysenck, H. J. *The dynamics of anxiety and hysteria.* London: Routledge and Kegan Paul, 1957. *(132, 290)*

Eysenck, H. J. *The Maudsley personality inventory.* London: University of London Press, Ltd. 1959. *(270)*

Eysenck, H. J. (Ed.) *Handbook of abnormal psychology.* London: Pitman, 1960. (b) *(10)*

Eysenck, H. J. Classification and the problems of diagnosis. In H. J. Eysenck (Ed.), *Handbook of abnormal psychology.* New York: Basic Books, 1960. (c) *(73)*

Eysenck, H. J. The effects of psychotherapy. In H. J. Eysenck (Ed.), *Handbook of abnormal psychology.* New York: Basic Books, 1960. (d) *(260, 290, 317)*

Eysenck, H. J. Psychoanalysis—Myth of science. In S. Racjman (Ed.), *Critical essays on psychoanalysis.* New York: Macmillan, 1963. *(89)*

Eysenck, H. J. *Crime and personality.* London: Methuen, 1964. (a) *(411)*

Eysenck, H. J. Principles and methods of personality description, classification and diagnosis. *British Journal of Psychology,* 1964, **55**, 284–294. (b) *(9)*

Eysenck, H. J. *The effects of psychotherapy.* New York: International Scientific Press, 1966. *(317)*

Eysenck, H. J. The non-professional psychotherapist. *International Journal of Psychiatry,* 1967, **3**, 150–153. *(317)*

Eysenck, H. J. (Ed.) *Readings in extraversion-introversion.* Vol. 1. *Theoretical and methodological issues.* New York: Interscience-Wiley, 1970. *(9)*

Eysenck, H. J. (Ed.) *Readings in extraversion-introversion.* Vol. 2. *Fields of application.* New York: Interscience-Wiley, 1971. (a) *(9)*

Eysenck, H. J. (Ed.) *Readings in extraversion-introversion.* Vol. 3. *Bearings on basic psychological processes.* New York: Interscience-Wiley, 1971. (b) *(9)*

Eysenck, H. J. Counterconditioning and related methods in behavior therapy. In A. E. Bergin & S. L. Garfield (Ed.), *Handbook of psychotherapy and behavior change.* New York: Wiley, 1971. (c) *(318)*

Eysenck, H. J. The experimental

study of Freudian concepts. *Bulletin of the British Psychological Society*, 1972, **25**, 261-267. (b) *(285, 290)*

Eysenck, H. J. (Ed.) *Handbook of abnormal psychology.* (2d ed.) London: Pitman, 1973. *(318)*

Eysenck, H. J., Eysenck, S. B. G. *Eysenck personality inventory.* London: University of London Press, 1964. *(9)*

Fabine, H. D., & Hawkins, J. R. Intravenous bufotenine injection in the human being. *Science,* 1956, **123**, 886-887. *(184)*

Fairweather, G. W., Sanders, D. H., Crissler, D. L., & Maynard, H. *Community life for the mentally ill.* Chicago: Aldine, 1969. *(205, 212)*

Fancher, R. E., & Strahan, R. F. Galvanic skin response and the secondary revision of dreams. *Journal of Abnormal Psychology,* 1971, **77**, 308-312. *(285)*

Farber, I., & Spence, K. Complex learning and conditioning as a function of anxiety. *Journal of Experimental Psychology,* 1953, **45**, 120-125. *(270)*

Farrar, C. H., Powell, B. J., & Martin, K. L. Punishment of alcohol consumption by apneic paralyses. *Behaviour Research and Therapy,* 1968, **6**, 13-16. *(339)*

Faulk, M. Factors in the treatment of frigidity. *British Journal of Psychiatry,* 1971, **119**, 53-56. *(387)*

Favale, E., Seitun, A., Tartaglione, A., & Tondi, M. Studies on pyramidal-evoked activity during the sleep-wakefulness cycle. *Brain Research,* 1971, **28**, 573-575. *(64)*

Fazio, A. F. Treatment components in implosive therapy. *Journal of Abnormal Psychology,* 1970, **76**, 211-219. *(310)*

Feder, R. Religious life in Terezin. In F. Ehrmann (Ed.), *Terezin.* Prague: Council of Jewish Communities in the Czech Lands, 1965. *(32)*

Feinberg, I., Koresko, R., Gottlieb, F., & Wender, P. Sleep electroencephalographic and eye movement patterns in schizophrenic patients. *Comprehensive Psychiatry,* 1964, **5**, 44-53. *(174)*

Feinbloom, D. H. The heterosexual transvestite: An interactionist view. Unpublished M.A. thesis, Boston University, Department of Sociology, 1972. *(360-362)*

Feldman, M. P., & MacCulloch, M. J. The application of anticipatory avoidance learning to the treatment of homosexuality. I: Theory, technique and preliminary results. *Behaviour Research and Therapy,* 1965, **3**, 165-183. *(339, 388)*

Feldman, M. P., & MacCulloch, M. J. *Homosexual behaviour: Therapy and assessment.* Oxford: Pergamon Press, 1971. *(388)*

Fenton, G. W., & Scotton, L. Personality and the alpha rhythm. *British Journal of Psychiatry,* 1967, **113**, 1283-1289. *(427)*

Fenz, W., & Velner, J. Physiological concomitants of behavioral indexes in schizophrenia. *Journal of Abnormal Psychology,* 1970, **76**, 27-35. *(173, 174)*

Ferraro, A. Senile psychoses. In S. Arieti (Ed.), *American handbook of psychiatry.* Vol. II. New York: Basic Books, 1969. *(501-502)*

Ferster, C. B. Positive reinforcement and behavioral deficits of autistic children. *Child Development,* 1961, **32**, 437-456. *(451-453)*

Ferster, C. B., & Skinner, B. F. *Schedules of reinforcement.* New York: Appleton-Century-Crofts, 1957. *(105)*

Fish, B. Contributions of developmental research to a therapy of schizophrenia. In J. Hellmuth (Ed.), *Exceptional infant.* Vol. 2. *Studies in abnormalities.* New York: Brunner/Mazel, 1971. *(464)*

Fisher, G. M. Discrepancy in verbal-performance I.Q. in adolescent psychopaths. *Journals of Clinical Psychology,* 1961, **17**, 60-61. *(408)*

Fisher, S., & Cleveland, S. E. Relationship of body image to site of cancer. *Psychosomatic Medicine,* 1956, **18**, 304-309. *(424)*

Fisher, S., & Cleveland, S. E. A comparison of psychological characteristics and physiological reactivity in ulcer and rheumatoid arthritis groups. II: Differences in physiological reactivity. *Psychosomatic Medicine,* 1960, **22**, 290-293. *(424)*

Fitzgibbons, D. J., Berry, D. F., & Shearn, C. R. MMPI and diagnosis

among hospitalized drug abusers. *Journal of Community Psychology,* 1973, **1**, 79-81. *(135)*

Fixsen, D. L., Phillips, E. L., & Wolf, M. M. Achievement Place: The reliability of self-reporting and peer-reporting and their effects on behavior. *Journal of Applied Behavior Analysis,* 1972, **5**, 19-30. *(212)*

Fixsen, D. L., Phillips, E. L., & Wolf, M. M. Achievement Place: Experiments in self-government with predelinquents. *Journal of Applied Behavior Analysis,* 1973, **6**, 31-48, *(463)*

Flach, F. Calcium metabolism in states of depression. *British Journal of Psychiatry,* 1964, **110**, 588-593. *(229)*

Follman, J. Delinquency prediction scales and personality inventories. *Child Study Journal,* 1972, **2**, 99-103. *(135)*

Ford, C. S., & Beach, F. A. *Patterns of sexual behavior.* New York: Harper & Row, 1951. *(365, 366, 368, 385)*

Ford, H. Involutional psychotic reaction. In A. M. Freedman & H. I. Kaplan (Eds.), *Comprehensive textbook of psychiatry.* Baltimore: Williams & Wilkins, 1967. *(243)*

Fosberg, I. A. Rorschach reactions under varied instructions. *Rorschach Research Exchange,* 1938, **3**, 12-31. *(137)*

Foulds, G. A method of scoring the TAT applied to psychoneurotics. *Journal of Mental Science,* 1953, **99**, 235-246. *(268)*

Foulds, G. Attitudes toward self and others of psychopaths. *Journal of Individual Psychology,* 1960, **16**, 81-83. *(408)*

Fowler, R. D. Computer interpretation of personality tests: The automated psychologist. *Comprehensive Psychiatry,* 1967, **8**, 455-467. *(135)*

Fowler, R. S., Chawla, N. S., Lehmann, J. F., & Tindall, V. L. An application of behavior therapy to a program of debilitating vertigo. *Behavior Therapy,* 1971, **2**, 589-591. *(428)*

Frank, A. *The diary of a young girl.* New York: Doubleday, 1952. *(57-60, 70)*

Franks, C. M. Conditioning and abnormal behaviour. In H. J. Eysenck (Ed.), *Handbook of abnormal psychology.* New York: Basic Books, 1960. *(290)*

Franks, C. M. Alcoholism. In C. G. Costello (Ed.), *Symptoms of psychopathology,* New York: Wiley, 1970. *(331, 338)*

Frazier, S., & Carr, A. Phobic reaction. In A. Freedman & H. Kaplan (Eds.), *Comprehensive textbook of psychiatry.* Baltimore: Williams & Wilkins, 1967. *(264)*

Freedman, A. M., & Kaplan, H. I. *Comprehensive textbook of psychiatry.* Baltimore: Williams & Wilkins, 1967. *(242, 343, 368)*

Freedman, D. X. Implications for research. *Journal of the American Medical Association,* 1968, **206,** 1280-1284. *(352)*

Freeman, T. A psychoanalytic critique of behavior therapy. *British Journal of Medical Psychology,* 1968, **41,** 53-59. *(291)*

Freud, A. *Psychoanalytic treatment of children.* London: Imago, 1946. *(441, 457)*

Freud, S. Three essays on the theory of sexuality (1905). In *Standard edition.* Vol. VII. London: Hogarth, 1949. *(363)*

Freud, S. *Beyond the pleasure principle* (1920). In *Standard edition.* Vol. XVIII. London: Hogarth, 1950. (a) *(230)*

Freud, S. Mourning and melancholia (1917). In *Collected papers.* Vol. IV. London: Hogarth Press, 1950. (b) *(230)*

Freud, S. The ego and the id (1932). In *Standard edition.* Vol. XIX. London: Hogarth, 1950. (c) *(93, 293)*

Freud, S. *A general introduction to psychoanalysis (1924).* New York; Permabooks, 1953. *(296)*

Freud, S. The interpretation of dreams (1900). In *Standard edition.* Vols. IV-V. London: Hogarth, 1955. (a) *(296)*

Freud, S. Some neurotic mechanisms in jealousy, paranoia and homosexuality (1896). In *Standard edition.* Vol. XVIII. London: Hogarth, 1955. (b) *(224)*

Freud, S. Analysis of a phobia in a five-year-old boy (1909). In *Collected papers.* Vol. III. New York: Basic Books, 1959. (a) *(81-86)*

Freud, S. The dynamics of the transference (1912). In *Collected papers.* Vol. II. New York: Basic Books, 1959. (b) *(293)*

Freud, S. The employment of dream interpretation in psychoanalysis (1912). In *Collected papers.* Vol. II. New York: Basic Books, 1959. (c) *(293)*

Freud, S. Further recommendations in the technique of psychoanalysis, recollection, repetition and working through (1914). In *Collected papers.* Vol. II. New York: Basic Books, 1959. (d) *(293)*

Freud, S. Observations on "wild" psychoanalysis (1910). In *Collected papers.* Vol. II. New York: Basic Books, 1959. (e) *(293)*

Freud, S. Psycho-analytic notes upon an autobiographical account of a case of paranoia (Dementia paranoides) (1911). In *Collected papers.* Vol. III. New York: Basic Books, 1959. (f) *(21, 187, 224, 293)*

Freud, S. On Narcissism: An introduction (1914). In *Collected papers.* Vol. IV. 1959. (g) *(188, 293)*

Freud, S. Neurosis and psychosis (1924). In *Collected papers.* Vol. II. 1959. (h) *(188, 293)*

Freund, K. Some problems in the treatment of homosexuality. In H. J. Eysenck (Ed.), *Behaviour therapy and the neuroses.* London: Pergamon, 1960. *(388)*

Freund, K. A laboratory method for diagnosing predominance of homo- or hetero-erotic interest in the male. *Behaviour Research and Therapy,* 1963, **1,** 85-93. *(383)*

Freund, K. Diagnosing homo- or heterosexuality and erotic age-preference by means of a psychophysiological test. *Behaviour Research and Therapy,* 1967, **5,** 209-228. *(383)*

Freund, K. A note on the use of the phallometric method of measuring mild sexual arousal in the male. *Behavior Therapy,* 1971, **2,** 223-228. *(383)*

Fried, J. J. The bloody pressure on 22 million Americans. *The New York Times Magazine,* February 25, 1973, 14, 17, 19, 21, 23, 25, 27. *(419)*

Friedhoff, A. J., & Van Winkle, E. Isolation and characterization of a compound from the urine of schizophrenics. *Nature,* 1962, **194,** 897-898. *(184)*

Friedman, A. S., Granick, S., Cohen, H. W., & Cowitz, B. Imipramine (Tofranil) vs. placebo in hospitalized psychotic depressives. *Journal of Psychiatric Research,* 1966, **4,** 13-36. *(242)*

Friedman, D. E., & Lipsedge, M. S. Treatment of phobic anxiety and psychogenic impotence by systematic desensitization employing methohexitone-induced relaxation. *British Journal of Psychiatry,* 1971, **118,** 87-90. *(389)*

Friedman, T. Prenatal diagnosis of genetic disease. *Scientific American,* 1971, **225,** 34-42. *(479)*

Fromm, E. *Escape from freedom.* New York: Farrar & Rinehart, 1941. *(287-288, 301)*

Fromm-Reichmann, F. *Psychotherapy with schizophrenics.* New York: International Universities Press, 1952. *(203)*

Fryd, N. Culture in the anteroom to hell. In F. Ehrmann (Ed.), *Terezin.* Prague: Council of Jewish Communities in the Czech Lands, 1965. *(32)*

Gagnon, J. H. Sexuality and sexual learning in the child. *Psychiatry,* 1965, **28,** 212-228. *(374)*

Gagnon, J. H., & Simon, W. They're going to learn in the street anyway. *Psychology Today,* 1969, **3,** 46-71. *(374)*

Gagnon, J. H., & Simon, W. *Sexual conduct: The social origins of human sexuality.* Chicago: Aldine, 1973. *(374)*

Ganrot, P. O., Rosengren, E., & Gottfires, C. G. Effect of iproniazid on monoamines and monoamine-oxidase in human brain. *Experientia,* 1962, **18,** 260-261. *(230)*

Garber, N. Operant procedures to eliminate drooling behavior in a cerebral palsied adolescent. *Developmental Medicine and Child Neurology,* 1971, **13,** 641-644. *(511)*

Garfield, S. L., & Bergin, A. E. Therapeutic conditions and outcome. *Journal of Abnormal Psychology,* 1971, **77,** 108-114. *(302-303)*

Garfield, S. L., Prager, R. A., & Bergin, A. E. Evaluation of outcome in psychotherapy. *Journal of Con-*

sulting and Clinical Psychology. 1971, **37**, 307-313. *(135)*

Garlington, W. K., & Cotler, S. B. Systematic desensitization of test anxiety. *Behaviour Research & Therapy,* 1968, **6**, 247-256. *(310)*

Garmezy, N. R., Clarke, A. R., & Stockner, C. Child rearing attitudes of mothers and fathers as reported by schizophrenic and normal patients. *Journal of Abnormal and Social Psychology,* 1961, **63**, 176-182. *(168)*

Garside, R. F. Depressive syndromes and the classification of patients. *Psychological Medicine,* 1971, **1**, 333-338. *(234)*

Gazzaniga, M. S. *The bisected brain.* New York: Appleton, 1970. *(66)*

Getsinger, S. H., Kunce, J. T., Miller, D. E., & Weinberg, S. R. Self-esteem measures and cultural disadvantagement. *Journal of Consulting and Clinical Psychology,* 1972, **38**, 149. *(48)*

Gibbons, J. L. Electrolytes and depressive illness. *Postgraduate Medical Journal,* 1963, **39**, 19-25. *(229)*

Giddings, J. W., & Lanyon, R. I. Modification of refractive error through conditioning: An exploratory study. *Behavior Therapy,* 1971, **2**, 538-542. *(428)*

Giffin, M. W., Johnson, A. M., & Litin, E. M. Antisocial acting out. II. Specific factors determining antisocial acting out. *American Journal of Orthopsychiatry,* 1954, **24**, 668-684. *(373)*

Gilberstadt, H. *Comprehensive MMPI codebook for males.* Minneapolis: VA Hospital, 1970. *(133)*

Gilberstadt, H., & Duker, J. *A handbook for clinical and actuarial MMPI interpretation.* Philadelphia: Saunders, 1965. *(133)*

Gilbert, J. G., & Lombardi, D. N., Personality characteristics of young male narcotic addicts. *Journal of Consulting Psychology,* 1967, **31**, 536-538. *(346)*

Gilles, F., & Rockett, F. Infantile hydrocephalus: Retrocerebellar "arachnoidal" cyst. *Journal of Pediatrics,* 1971, **79**, 436-443. *(477)*

Glassman, A. H. Indoleamines and affective disorders. *Psychosomatic Medicine,* 1969, **2**, 107-114. *(230)*

Glatt, C. T. Some Rorschach corre-lates of change in clinical status: An investigation of ego regression in schizophrenia. *Dissertation Abstracts International,* 1972, **32**, 7309. *(137)*

Glickstein, M., Chevalier, J., Korchin, S., Basowitz, H., Sabshin, M., Hamburg, D., & Grinker, R. Temporal heart rate patterns in anxious patients. *Archives of Neurology and Psychiatry,* 1957, **78**, 101-106. *(268)*

Glover, E. The abnormality of prostitution. In A. M. Krich (Ed.), *Women: The variety and meaning of their sexual experience.* New York: Dell, 1953. *(380)*

Gluck, M., Tanner, M., Sullivan, D., & Erickson, P. Follow-up evaluation of 55 child guidance cases. *Behaviour Research and Therapy,* 1964, **2**, 131-134. *(49)*

Glynn, E. L. Classroom applications of self-determined reinforcement. *Journal of Applied Behavior Analysis,* 1970, **3**, 123-132. *(315)*

Goddard, H. *The Kallikak family.* New York: Macmillan, 1913. *(473)*

Goldberg, L. R. Diagnosticians vs. diagnostic signs: The diagnosis of psychosis vs. neurosis from the MMPI. *Psychological Monographs,* 1965, **79**, 9. *(135, 268)*

Goldberg, L. R. Simple models or simple processes? *American Psychologist,* 1968, **23**, 483-496. *(117, 119)*

Goldberg, L. R. Man vs. model of man: A rationale, plus some evidence for a method of improving on clinical inferences. *Psychological Bulletin,* 1970, **73**, 422-432. *(135)*

Goldberg, L. R. Man versus mean: The exploitation of group profiles for the construction of diagnostic classification systems. *Journal of Abnormal Psychology,* 1972, **79**, 121-131. *(135)*

Goldberg, S. C. Prediction of response to antipsychotic drugs. Paper presented at the meeting of the American College of Neuropsychopharmacology, San Juan, 1966. United States Government Printing Office, Washington, D.C. 1967. *(200)*

Goldfarb, W., Goldfarb, N., Braustein. P., & Scholl, H. Speech and language faults of schizophrenic chil-dren. *Journal of Autism and Childhood Schizophrenia,* 1972, **2**, 219-233. *(453)*

Goldfried, M. R., & Kent, R. N. Traditional versus behavioral personality assessment: A comparison of methodological and theoretical assumptions. *Psychological Bulletin,* 1972, **77**, 409-420. *(138, 285)*

Goldfried, M., Stricker, G., & Weiner, I. B. *Rorschach handbook of clinical and research applications.* Englewood Cliffs, N.J.: Prentice-Hall, 1971. *(171, 259, 268, 497)*

Golding, S. L., & Rorer, L. G. Illusory correlation and subjective judgment. *Journal of Abnormal Psychology,* 1972, **80**, 249-260. *(383)*

Goldstein, I. B. The relationship of muscle tension and autonomic activity to psychiatric disorders. *Psychosomatic Medicine,* 1965, **27**, 39-52. *(236)*

Goldstein, K. Methodological approach to the study of schizophrenic thought. In J. Kasanin (Ed.), *Language and thought in schizophrenia.* Berkeley: University of California Press, 1944. *(173)*

Goldstein, K. Prefrontal lobotomy: Analysis and warning. *Scientific American,* 1950, **182**, 44-47. *(66)*

Goldstone, S. Flicker fusion measurements and anxiety level. *Journal of Experimental Psychology,* 1955, **49**, 200-202. *(270)*

Goodman, D. Performance of good and poor premorbid male schizophrenics as a function of paternal versus maternal censure. *Journal of Abnormal and Social Psychology,* 1964, **69**, 550-555. *(168)*

Goodwin, D., Alderson, P., & Rosenthal, D. Clinical significance of hallucinations in psychiatric disorders. *Archives of General Psychiatry,* 1971, **24**, 76-80. *(160)*

Goodwin, D., Guze, S., & Robbins, E. Follow-up studies in obsessional neurosis. *Archives of General Psychiatry,* 1969, **20**, 182-187. *(264-265)*

Goodwin, F. Psychiatric side effects of levodopa in man. *Journal of the American Medical Association,* 1971, **218**, 1915-1920. *(503)*

Gottesman, I. I. Differential inheritance of the psychoneuroses. *Eugenics Quarterly,* 1962, 223-227. *(292)*

Gottesman, I. I. Heritability of personality: A demonstration. *Psychological Monographs,* 1963, 77, 9. *(297)*

Gottesman, L., & Chapman, L. Syllogistic reasoning errors in schizophrenia. *Journal of Consulting Psychology,* 1960, **24,** 250-255. *(159)*

Gottesman, L., & Shields, D. *Schizophrenia in twins.* New York: Academic, 1973. *(186)*

Gough, H. G. Diagnostic patterns on the MMPI. In G. Welsh & W. Dahlstrom (Eds.), *Basic readings on the MMPI in psychology and medicine.* Minneapolis: University of Minnesota Press, 1963. *(268)*

Gough, H. G. *California psychological inventory: manual.* (Rev. ed.) Palo Alto, Calif.: Consulting Psychologists Press, 1964. *(132)*

Gough, H. G. Some reflections on the meaning of psychodiagnosis. *American Psychologist,* 1971, **26,** 160-167. *(117, 119)*

Governor's Select Commission on Civil Disorder. *Report for action.* Trenton: State of New Jersey, 1969. *(27-30)*

Grace, W., Wolf, S., & Wolff, H. G. *The human colon: An experimental study based on four fistulous subjects.* New York: Harper & Row, 1951. *(420)*

Graham, F., & Kendall, B. Memory-for-designs test: Revised general manual. *Perceptual and Motor Skills,* 1960, **11,** 147-190. *(499)*

Graham, J. R., Lilly, R. S., Konick, D. S., Paolino, A. F., & Friedman, I. MMPI changes associated with short-term psychiatric hospitalization. *Journal of Clinical Psychology,* 1973, **29,** 69-73. *(135)*

Gray, K. C., & Hutchison, H. C. The psychopathic personality: A survey of Canadian psychiatrists' opinions. *Canadian Psychiatric Association Journal,* 1964, **9,** 452-461. *(407)*

Greaves, G. MMPI correlates of chronic drug abuse in hospitalized adolescents. *Psychological Reports,* 1971, **29,** 12-22. *(349)*

Green, R., & Money, J. *Transsexualism and sex reassignment.* Baltimore: Johns Hopkins, 1969. *(366, 367, 385, 386)*

Greenberg, I. Clinical correlates of fourteen- and six-cycles-per-second positive EEG spiking and family pathology. *Journal of Abnormal Psychology,* 1970, **76,** 403-412. *(408)*

Greenwald, H. *The elegant prostitute.* New York: Ballantine Books, 1970. *(379)*

Greer, S. Study of parental loss in neurotics and sociopaths. *Archives of General Psychiatry,* 1964, **11,** 177-180. *(410)*

Gregory, I. *Fundamentals of psychiatry* (2d ed.) Philadelphia: Saunders, 1968. *(173)*

Grier, W. H., & Cobbs, P. M. *Black rage.* New York: Basic Books, 1968. *(47)*

Grinspoon, L. Half a loaf: A reaction to the marihuana report. *Saturday Review of Literature,* 1972, 55. *(354)*

Grinspoon, L., Ewalt, J. R., & Shader, R. Long term treatment of chronic schizophrenia: A preliminary report. *International Journal of Psychiatry,* 1967, **4,** 116-128. *(204)*

Grinspoon, L., Ewalt, J. R., & Shader, R. Psychotherapy and pharmacotherapy in chronic schizophrenia. *American Journal of Psychiatry,* 1968, **124,** 1645-1652. *(204)*

Gross, H. S., Herbert, M. R., Knatterud, G. L., & Donner, L. The effect of race and sex on the variation of diagnosis and disposition in a psychiatric emergency room. *Journal of Nervous & Mental Disease,* 1969, **148,** 638-642. *(46)*

Group for the Advancement of Psychiatry. *Psychopathological disorders in childhood: Theoretical considerations and a proposed classification.* Vol. VI. GAP Report No. 62, 1966. *(444-446)*

Gruendel, A. D., & Arnold, W. J. Effects of early social deprivation on reproductive behavior of male rats. *Journal of Comparative and Physiological Psychology,* 1969, **67,** 123-128. *(385)*

Gruzelier, J., Lykken, D., & Venables, P. Schizophrenia and arousal revisited. *Archives of General Psychiatry,* 1972, **26,** 427-432. *(174)*

Guertin, W., Frank, G., & Rabin, A. Research with the Wechsler-Bellevue intelligence scale: 1950-1955. *Psychological Bulletin,* 1956, **53,** 235-257. *(408)*

Guertin, W., Rabin, A., Frank, G., & Ladd, C. Research with the Wechsler intelligence scales for adults, 1955-60. *Psychological Bulletin,* 1962, **59,** 1-28. *(170)*

Guilford, J. P., & Zimmerman, W. S. *The Guilford-Zimmerman temperament survey: Manual of instructions and interpretations.* Beverly Hills, Calif.: Sheridan Supply Co., 1949. *(132)*

Gullattee, A. C. Mental health planning and evaluation for the black and the poor. *Journal of the National Medical Association,* 1972, **64,** 134-138. *(46, 48)*

Gunn, J., & Bonn, J. Criminality and violence in epileptic prisoners. *British Journal of Psychiatry,* 1971, **118,** 337-343. *(510)*

Gurland, B. A flexible approach to psychiatric classification. In M. Hammer, K. Salzinger, & S. Sutton, (Eds.) *Psychopathology,* New York: Wiley-Interscience, 1973. *(120)*

Guthrie, G. Six MMPI diagnostic profile patterns. In G. Welsh & W. Dahlstrom, (Eds.), *Basic readings on the MMPI in psychology and medicine.* Minneapolis: University of Minnesota Press, 1963. *(268, 408)*

Guze, S., Woodruff, R., & Clayton, P. A study of conversion symptoms in psychiatric outpatients. *American Journal of Psychiatry,* 1971, **128,** 643-646. *(262, 268)*

Gynther, M. D. White norms and black MMPIs: A prescription for discrimination. *Psychological Bulletin,* 1972, **78,** 386-402. *(46, 47)*

Hacaen, H., Penfield, W., Bertrand, C., & Malmo, R. The syndrome of apractognosia due to lesions of the minor cerebral hemisphere. *Archives of Neurology and Psychiatry,* 1956, **75,** 400-434. *(66)*

Haddad, H., & Wilkins, L. Congenital anomalies associated with gonadal aplasia: Review of 55 cases. *Pediatrics,* 1959, **23,** 885. *(480)*

Haertzen, C. A. Subjective drug effects: A factorial representation of subjective drug effects on the Addiction Research Center Inventory. *Journal of Nervous and Mental Disease,* 1965, **40,** 280-289. *(349)*

Haertzen, C. A., & Hooks, N. T.

Changes in personality and subjective experience associated with the chronic administration and withdrawal of opiates. *Journal of Nervous and Mental Disease,* 1969, *148,* 606–614. *(349)*

Hain, J. D., & Linton, P. H. Physiological response to visual sexual stimuli. *Journal of Sex Research,* 1969, *5,* 292–302, *(383)*

Hake, D. F., Vukelich, R., & Kaplan, S. J. Audit responses: Responses maintained by access to existing self or coactor scores during nonsocial, parallel work, and cooperation procedures. *Journal of Experimental Analysis of Behavior,* 1973, *19,* 409–423. *(106)*

Hall, M. H. A conversation with Kenneth B. Clark. *Psychology Today,* 1968, *2,* 19–25. *(44)*

Halleck, S. L. *The politics of therapy.* New York: Science House, 1971. *(49, 295)*

Hamerton, J., Briggs, S., Giannelli, F., & Carter, C. Chromosome studies in detection of parents with high risk of second child with Down's syndrome. *Lancet,* 1961, *2,* 788–791. *(480)*

Hamilton, M. The assessment of anxiety states by rating. *British Journal of Medical Psychology,* 1959, *32,* 50–59. *(260)*

Hamlin, R. M., & Lorr, M. Differentiation of normals, neurotics, paranoids, and nonparanoids. *Journal of Abnormal Psychology,* 1971, *77,* 90–96. *(165)*

Hamlin, R. M., & Ward, W. D. Schizophrenic intelligence, symptoms, and release from the hospital. *Journal of Abnormal Psychology,* 1973, *81,* 11–16. *(129)*

Hammerman, S. Ego defect and depression. Paper presented at the meeting of the Philadelphia Psychoanalytic Society, 1962, *(231)*

Handlon, J. Hormonal activity and individual responses to stresses and easements in everyday living. In N. Greenfield & R. Roessler (Eds.), *Physiological Correlates of Psychological Disorders.* Madison: University of Wisconsin Press, 1962. *(72)*

Hanley, W., Linsao, L., Davidson, W., & Moes, C. Malnutrition with early treatment of phenylketonuria. *Pediatric Research,* 1970, *4,* 318–327. *(478)*

Hare, R. Acquisition and generalization of a conditioned-fear response in psychopathic and non-psychopathic criminals. *Journal of Psychology,* 1965, *59,* 367–370. (a) *(409)*

Hare, R. Temporal gradient of fear arousal in psychopaths. *Journal of Abnormal Psychology,* 1965, *70,* 442–445. (b) *(409)*

Hare, R. Psychopathy, autonomic functioning, and the orienting response. *Journal of Abnormal Psychology,* 1968, *73.* *(410)*

Hare, R. *Psychopathy: Theory and research.* New York: Wiley, 1970. *(408, 410, 412)*

Hare, R. Psychopathy and physiological responses to adrenalin. *Journal of Abnormal Psychology,* 1972, *79,* 138–147. *(410)*

Hare, R., & Quinn, M. Psychopathy and autonomic conditioning. *Journal of Abnormal Psychology,* 1971, *77,* 223–235. *(410)*

Harlow, H. F., Gluck, J. P., & Suomi, S. J. Generalization of behavioral data between nonhuman and human animals. *American Psychologist,* 1972, *27,* 709–716. *(237)*

Harris, S. L. The relationship between family income and number of parent-perceived problems. *International Journal of Social Psychiatry,* 1974, *20,* 109–112. *(443)*

Harrower-Erickson, M. R., & Steiner, M. E. *Large scale Rorschach techniques.* Springfield, Ill.: Charles C Thomas, 1945. *(137)*

Hart, J. T. Autocontrol of EEG alpha. Paper presented at the 7th annual meeting of the Society for Psychophysiological Research, San Diego, October, 1967. *(427)*

Harty, M. K. Studies of clinical judgement. Part II: Toward a new model for research. *Bulletin of the Menninger Clinic,* 1972, *36,* 279–301. *(183)*

Hawkins, D., & Mendels, J. Sleep disturbance in depressive syndromes. *American Journal of Psychiatry,* 1966, *123,* 682–690. *(266)*

Hawks, D. V. The dimensions of drug dependence in the United Kingdom. *International Journal of Addiction,* 1971, *6,* 135–160. *(345)*

Haynes, S. N., & Geddy, P. Suppression of psychotic hallucinations through time-out. *Behavior Therapy,* 1973, *4,* 123–127. *(212)*

Hearst, E., Munoz, R., & Tauson, V. Catatonia: Its diagnostic validity. *Diseases of the Nervous System,* 1971, *32,* 453–456. *(166)*

Heath, R. G. Common characteristics of epilepsy and schizophrenia: Clinical observation and depth electrode studies. *American Journal of Psychiatry,* 1962, *118,* 1013–1026. *(510)*

Heath, R. G. Schizophrenia: Biochemical and physiologic aberrations. *International Journal of Neuropsychiatry,* 1966, *2,* 597–610 *(184)*

Heath, R. G., & Krupp, I. M. Schizoprenia as an immunologic disorder. I: Demonstration of antibrain globulins by fluorescent antibody techniques. *Archives of General Psychiatry,* 1967, *16,* 1–9. *(185)*

Heath, R. G., Krupp, I. M., Byers, L. W., & Liljekvist, J. I. Schizophrenia as an immunologic disorder. II: Effects of serum protein fractions on brain function. *Archives of General Psychiatry,* 1967, *16,* 10–23. *(185)*

Heath, R. G., Martens, S., Leach, B. E., Cohen, M., & Feigley, C. A. Behavioral changes in nonpsychotic volunteers following administration of taraxein, a substance obtained from serum of schizophrenic patients. *American Journal of Psychiatry,* 1958, *114,* 917–920. *(184)*

Heber, R. A manual on terminology and classification in mental retardation. *American Journal of Mental Deficiency,* 1959, *64* (Monogr. Suppl.) Rev. ed., 1961. *(474, 477)*

Hecker, E. Die Hebephrenie (1877). Cited by O. Bumke, *Handbuch der Geisteskrankheiten.* Berlin: Springer, 1932. *(118)*

Heilbrun, A. Psychological test performance as a function of lateral localization of cerebral lesion. *Journal of Comparative and Physiological Psychology,* 1956, *49,* 10–14. *(476)*

Heilbrun, A., & Norbert, N. Sensitivity to material censure in paranoid and nonparanoid schizophrenics. *Journal of Nervous and*

Mental Disease, 1971, **152,** 45–49. *(169)*

Hellmuth, J. (Ed.) *Exceptional infant.* Vol. 2. *Studies in abnormalities.* New York: Brunner/Mazel, 1971. *(463)*

Helson, R. The changing image of the career woman. *Journal of Social Issues,* 1972, **28,** 33–46 *(50)*

Henderson, J. D., & Scoles, P. E. Conditioning techniques in a community-based operant environment for psychotic men. *Behavior Therapy,* 1970, **1,** 245–251. *(212)*

Herbert, E. W., & Baer, D. M. Training parents as behavior modifiers: Self-recording of contingent attention. *Journal of Applied Behavior Analysis,* 1972, **5,** 139–150. *(212)*

Hetherington, E., & Klinger, E. Psychopathy and punishment. *Journal of Abnormal and Social Psychology,* 1964, **69,** 113–115. *(409)*

Higgins, J. The concept of process-reactive schizophrenia: Criteria and related research. *Journal of Nervous and Mental Disease,* 1964, **138,** 9–25. *(168)*

Higgins, J., & Peterson, J. Concept of process-reactive schizophrenia: A critique. *Psychological Bulletin,* 1966, **66,** 201–206. *(167)*

Hill, M. J., & Blane, H. T. Evaluation of psychotherapy with alcoholics: A critical review. *Quarterly Journal of Studies on Alcohol,* 1967, **28,** 76–104. *(338)*

Hillarp, N. A., Fuxe, K., & Dahlstrom, A. Demonstration and mapping of central neurons containing dopamine, noradrenaline and 5-hydroxytryptamine and their reactions to psychopharmaca. *Pharmacological Review,* 1966, **18,** 727–741. *(230)*

Hinkle, L. E., & 14 others. Studies in human ecology: Factors relevant to the occurrence of bodily illness and disturbances in mood, thought and behavior in three homogeneous population groups. *American Journal of Psychiatry,* 1957, **114,** 212–220. *(422)*

Hoch, A. The problem of toxic-infectious psychoses. *N.Y. State Hospital Bulletin,* 1912, **5,** 384–392. *(118)*

Hoch, P., & Knight, R. *Epilepsy.* New York: Grune and Stratton, 1947. *(508)*

Hoffer, A. The effect of nicotinic acid on the frequency and duration of re-hospitalization of schizophrenic patients: A controlled comparison study. *International Journal of Neuropsychiatry,* 1966, **2,** 234–240. *(184)*

Hoffer, A., & Osmond, H. Malvaria: A new psychiatric disease. *Acta Psychiatrica Scandinavica,* 1963, **39,** 335–366. *(184)*

Hoffer, A., & Osmond, H. Nicotinamide adenine dinucleotide in the treatment of chronic schizophrenic patients. *British Journal of Psychiatry,* 1968, **114,** 915–917. *(184)*

Hoffer, A., Osmond, H., Callbeck, M. J., & Kahan, I. Treatment of schizophrenia with nicotinic acid and nicotinamide. *Journal of Clinical Experimental Psychopathology,* 1957, **18,** 131–158. *(183, 184)*

Hoffer, A., Osmond, H., & Smythies, J. Schizophrenia: New approach: Result of year's research. *Journal of Mental Science,* 1954, **100,** 29–45. *(184)*

Hoffman, M. Homosexual. *Psychology Today,* 1969, **3,** 43–45, 70. *(385)*

Hokanson, J. E., & Burgess, M. The effects of three types of aggression on vascular process. *Journal of Abnormal and Social Psychology,* 1962, **65,** 232–237. *(420)*

Holden, R. A review of psychological studies in cerebral palsy: 1947–1952. *American Journal of Mental Deficiency,* 1956, **49,** 10–14. *(476)*

Holland, A., & Harris, A. Aphasia rehabilitation using programmed instruction. In H. Solane & B. MacAulay (Eds.), *Operant procedures in remedial speech and language training.* Boston: Houghton Mifflin, 1968. *(511)*

Hollingshead, A. B., & Redlich, F. C. *Social class and mental illness: A community study.* New York: Wiley, 1958. *(42, 43)*

Hollister, L. E. Drug therapy: Mental disorders—antipsychotic and antimanic drugs. *New England Journal of Medicine,* 1972, **286,** 984–987. *(242)*

Holmes, F. B. An experimental investigation of a method of overcoming children's fears. *Child Development,* 1936, **7,** 6–30. *(308)*

Holmes, R. M. A college panel rap session on homosexuality. In R. M. Holmes (Ed.), *Sexual behavior.* Berkeley, Calif.: McCutchan Publ. Co., 1971. *(364, 387)*

Holt, R. R., & Havel, S. A method for assessing primary and secondary process in the Rorschach. In M. A. Rickers-Ovsiankina (Ed.), *Rorschach psychology.* New York: Wiley, 1960. *(137)*

Holzinger, R., Mortimer, R., & Van Dusen, W. Aversion conditioning treatment of alcoholism. *American Journal of Psychiatry,* 1967, **124,** 246–247. *(339)*

Hooker, E. Male homosexuality in the Rorschach. *Journal of Projective Techniques,* 1958, **22,** 33–54. *(365, 383)*

Hoover, J. E. *Uniform crime reports.* Washington, D.C.: U.S. Department of Justice, 1965, 116–121. *(450)*

Hopkinson, G. A genetic study of affective illness in patients over 50. *British Journal of Psychiatry,* 1964, **110,** 244–254. *(228)*

Hordern. A. The antidepressant drugs. *New England Journal of Medicine,* 1965, **272,** 1159–1169. *(241)*

Horney, K. *The neurotic personality of our time.* New York: Norton, 1937. *(287)*

Horney, K. *New ways in psychoanalysis.* New York: Norton, 1939. *(287, 301, 372)*

Hovey, H. Somatization and other neurotic reactions and MMPI profiles. In G. Welsh & W. Dahlstrom (Eds.), *Basic readings on the MMPI in psychology and medicine.* Minneapolis: University of Minnesota Press, 1963. *(268)*

Howe, E. GSR conditioning in anxiety states, normals, and chronic functional schizophrenic subjects. *Journal of Abnormal and Social Psychology,* 1958, **56,** 183–189. *(269)*

Hughes, J. A review of the positive spike phenomenon. In W. Wilson (Ed.), *Applications of electroencephalography in psychiatry.* Durham, N.C.: Duke, 1965. *(408)*

Hughes, R. A factor analysis of the Rorschach diagnostic signs. *Journal of General Psychology,* 1950, **43,** 85–103. *(499)*

Hull, C. L. *Principles of behavior,* New York: Appleton, 1943, *(195, 288–289)*

Hullen, R. P., McDonald, R., & Allsopp, M. N. Prophylactic lithium in recurrent affective disorders.

Lancet, 1972, **1,** 1044-1046. *(242)*

Humphrey, M. Functional impairment in psychiatric patients. *British Journal of Psychiatry,* 1967, **113,** 1141-1151. *(234)*

Hunt, H. F. A practical clinical test for organic brain damage. *Journal of Applied Psychology,* 1943, **27,** 375-386. *(497)*

Hunt, J. M. Has compensatory education failed? Has it been attempted? *Harvard Educational Review,* 1969, **39,** 278-300. *(483-484)*

Hunt, W. A., & Arnhoff, F. The repeat reliability of clinical judgment of test responses. *Journal of Clinical Psychology,* 1956, **12,** 289-290. *(172)*

Hunter, H. Kleinfelter's syndrome and delinquency. *British Journal of Criminology,* 1968, **8,** 203-207. *(410)*

Hyman, E. T., & Gale, E. N. Galvanic skin response and reported anxiety during systematic desensitization. *Journal of Consulting and Clinical Psychology,* 1973, **40,** 108-114. *(310)*

Hyman, H., & Barmack, J. E. Special review: *Sexual behavior in the human female. Psychological Bulletin,* 1954, **51,** 418-427. *(376)*

Ikemi, T., & Nakagawa, T. Irritable colon syndrome. *Naika,* 1965, **16,** 232-236. *(425)*

Iltis, R. Terezin—Its influence on Czechoslovak literature, music, plastic arts and film. In F. Ehrmann (Ed.), *Terezin.* Prague: Council of Jewish Communities in the Czech Lands, 1965. *(33)*

Jackman, N. R., O'Toole, R., & Geis, G. The self-image of the prostitute. *Sociological Quarterly,* 1964, **4,** 150-161. *(379)*

Jackson, B. The revised diagnostic and statistical manual of the American Psychiatric Association. *American Journal of Psychiatry,* 1970, **127,** 65-73. *(444)*

Jackson, B. Treatment of depression by self-reinforcement. *Behavior Therapy,* 1972, **3,** 298-307. *(245)*

Jackson, C. W., & Wohl, J. A. A survey of Rorschach teaching in the university. *Journal of Projective Techniques & Personality Assessment,* 1966, **30,** 115-134. *(129)*

Jackson, G. G. Racial self-referral and preference for a counselor. Unpublished manuscript, 1974. *(469)*

Jacobs, J. *Adolescent suicide.* New York: Wiley, 1971. *(240)*

Jacobs, J., & Teicher, J. D. Broken homes and social isolation in attempted suicides of adolescents. *International Journal of Social Psychiatry,* 1967, **13,** 140-148. *(240)*

Jacobs, L., Feldman, M., & Bender, M. B. Eye movements during sleep. I: The pattern in the normal human. *Archives of Neurology,* 1971, **25,** 151-159. *(236)*

Jacobson, E. *Progressive relaxation.* Chicago: Univ. of Chicago Press, 1938. *(308)*

Jacobson, E. Transference problems in the psychoanalytic treatment of severely depressive patients. *Journal of the American Psychoanalytic Association,* 1954, **2,** 595-606. *(231)*

Jacobson, J., Buschell, D., & Risley, T. Switching requirements in a Head Start classroom. *Journal of Applied Behavior Analysis,* 1969, **2,** 43-47. *(484)*

Jahoda, M. Toward a social psychology of mental health. In M. Senn (Ed.), *Symposium on the healthy personality.* New York: Josiah Macy, Jr., Foundation, 1950, 211-231. *(7, 8)*

Jahoda, M. *Current concepts of positive mental health.* New York: Basic Books, 1958. *(8)*

James, B. Homosexuality. In C. G. Costello (Ed.), *Symptoms of psychopathology.* New York: Wiley, 1970. *(383)*

Jansson, B. The prognostic significance of various types of hallucinations in young people. *Acta Psychiatrica Scandinavica,* 1968, **44,** 401-409. *(162)*

Jellinek, E. M. *The disease concept of alcoholism.* New Haven: College and University Press, 1960. *(329)*

Jensen, A. How much can we boost IQ and scholastic achievement? *Harvard Educational Review,* 1969, **39,** 1-123. *(482-484)*

Jensen, D. E., Prandoni, J. R., &

Abudabbeh, N. N. Figure drawings by sex offenders and a random sample of offenders. *Perceptual and Motor Skills,* 1971, **32,** 295-300. *(383)*

Jessor, R., Collins, M. I., & Jessor, S. L. On becoming a drinker: Social-psychological aspects of an adolescent transition. *Annals of the New York Academy of Science,* 1972, **197,** 199-213. *(331)*

Johannsen, W., Friedman, S., Leitschuh, T., & Ammons, H. A study of certain schizophrenic dimensions and their relationship to double alternation learnings. *Journal of Consulting Psychology,* 1963, **27,** 375-382. *(168)*

Johns, J., & Quay, H. The effect of social reward on verbal conditioning in psychopathic and neurotic military offenders. *Journal of Consulting Psychology,* 1962, **26,** 217-220. *(409)*

Johnson, M. H. Verbal abstracting ability and schizophrenia. *Journal of Consulting Psychology,* 1966, **30,** 275-277. *(173)*

Johnston, N., & Cooke, G. Relationship of MMPI alcoholism, prison escape, hostility control and recidivism scales to clinical judgments. *Journal of Clinical Psychology,* 1973, **29,** 32-34. *(135)*

Joint Commission on Mental Health of Children. *Crisis in child mental health.* New York: Harper & Row, 1970. *(441-442, 482)*

Jones, E. *The life and work of Sigmund Freud.* Garden City, N.Y.: Doubleday, 1963.

Jones, H. The behavioral treatment of enuresis nocturna. In H. Eysenck (Ed.), *Behavior therapy and the neuroses.* Oxford: Pergamon, 1960. *(447)*

Jones, H. Stuttering. In C. Costello (Ed.), *Symptoms of psychopathology.* New York: Wiley, 1970. *(459)*

Jones, H. E. The conditioning of overemotional responses. *Journal of Educational Psychology,* 1931, **22,** 127-130. *(308)*

Jones, M. *The therapeutic community.* New York: Basic Books, 1953. *(205)*

Jones, M. C. Elimination of children's fears. *Journal of Experimental Psychology,* 1924, **7,** 382-390. *(259)*

Jones, N. The validity of clinical judgment of schizophrenic pathology based upon verbal responses to intelligence test items. *Journal of Clinical Psychology,* 1959, **15,** 396–400. *(172)*

Jung, C. G. The theory of psychoanalysis. *Nervous and mental disease monograph series,* 1915, **19.** *(286, 300–301)*

Juvenile Court Statistics. Washington, D.C.: United States Department of Health, Education and Welfare, 1964, No. 83. *(450)*

Kagan, J. Personality development. In P. London, & D. Rosenhan (Eds.), *Foundations of abnormal psychology.* New York: Holt, 1968. *(237)*

Kagan, J. Inadequate evidence and illogical conclusions. *Harvard Educational Review,* 1969, **39,** 274–277, *(483)*

Kahlbaum, K. L. *Die Katatonie oder das Spannungsirresein.* Berlin: Hirschwald, 1874. *(118)*

Kaij, L. *Alcoholism in twins: Studies on the etiology and sequels of abuse of alcohol.* Stockholm: Alcuquist & Wiksell, 1960. *(330)*

Kales, A., Paulson, M., Jacobson, A., & Kales, J. Somnambulism: Psychophysiological correlates. *Archives of General Psychiatry,* 1966, **14,** 595–604. *(263)*

Kalinowsky, L. B. Problems of war neuroses in the light of experiences in other countries. *American Journal of Psychiatry,* 1950, **107,** 340–346. *(33)*

Kalinowsky, L. B. The convulsive therapies. In A. M. Freedman & H. I. Kaplan (Eds.), *Comprehensive textbook of psychiatry.* Baltimore: Williams & Wilkins, 1967. *(202)*

Kallmann, F. J. *The genetics of schizophrenia.* Locust Valley, N.Y.: J. J. Augustin, 1938. *(186)*

Kallmann, F. J. The genetic theory of schizophrenia. *American Journal of Psychiatry,* 1946, **103,** 309–322. *(186)*

Kallmann, F. J. A comparative twin study on the genetic aspects of male homosexuality. *Journal of Nervous and Mental Disease,* 1952, **115,** 283–298. (a) *(227, 370)*

Kamin, L. J. Heredity, intelligence, politics, and psychology. Paper

presented at the meeting of the Eastern Psychological Association, Washington, May, 1973. *(484)*

Kamiya, J. Conditional discrimination of the EEG alpha rhythm in humans. Paper presented at the meeting of the Western Psychological Association, April, 1962. *(426)*

Kamiya, J. Conscious control of brain waves. *Psychology Today,* 1968, **1,** 57–60. *(427)*

Kamiya, J. Operant control of the EEG alpha rhythm and some of its reported effects on consciousness. In C. Tart (Ed.), *Altered states of consciousness: A book of readings.* New York: Wiley, 1969. *(426)*

Kanfer, F. H. Self-monitoring: Methodological limitations and clinical applications. *Journal of Consulting and Clinical Psychology,* 1970, **35,** 148–152. (a) *(314)*

Kanfer, F. H. Self-regulation: Research issues and speculations. In C. Neuringer & J. L. Michael (Eds.), *Behavior modification in clinical psychology.* New York: Appleton-Century-Crofts, 1970. (b) *(314)*

Kanfer, F. H., & Karoly, P. Self-control: A behavioristic excursion into the lion's den. *Behavior Therapy,* 1972, **3,** 398–416. *(314)*

Kanfer, F. H., & Saslow, G. Behavioral diagnosis. *Archives of General Psychiatry,* 1965, **12,** 529–538. *(15, 140)*

Kanfer, F. H., & Saslow, G. Behavioral diagnosis. In C. M. Franks (Ed.), *Behavior therapy: Appraisal and status.* New York: McGraw-Hill, 1969. *(140–141)*

Kanner, L. Autistic disturbances of affective content. *Nervous Child,* 1943, **2,** 217–240. *(441, 451–453)*

Kanner, L., Rodrigues, A., & Ashden, B. How far can autistic children go in matters of social adaptation. *Journal of Autism and Childhood Schizophrenia,* 1972, **2,** 9–37. *(456)*

Kant, H. S. & Goldstein, M. J. Pornography. *Psychology Today,* 1970, **4,** 58–61. *(381, 382)*

Kantor, R., Wallner, J., & Windner, C. Process and reactive schizophrenia. *Journal of Consulting Psychology,* 1953, **17,** 157–162. *(167)*

Kaplan, B. Malnutrition and mental deficiency. *Psychological Bulletin,* 1972, **78,** 321–334. *(481, 507)*

Kaplan, H. S. Treatment of psychophysiological disorders. In A. M. Freedman & H. I. Kaplan (Eds.), *Comprehensive textbook of psychiatry.* Baltimore: William & Wilkins, 1967. *(428)*

Karacan, I., & Williams, R. L. The relationship of sleep to psychopathology. *International Psychiatry Clinics,* 1970, **7,** 85–92. *(236)*

Kardiner, A., & Ovesey, L. *The mark of oppression.* New York: Norton, 1951. *(48)*

Karlsson, J. L. *The biologic basis of schizophrenia.* Springfield, Ill.: Charles C Thomas, 1966. *(185)*

Karpman, B. Psychopathy in the scheme of human typology. *Journal of Nervous and Mental Disease,* 1946, **103,** 276–288. *(399–400)*

Kasamatsu, A., & Hirai, T. An electroencephalographic study on the Zen meditation (Zasen). *Folia Psychiatrica et Neurologica Japonica,* 1966, **20,** 315–336. *(427)*

Kasl, S., & Mahl, G. The relationship of disturbances and hesitations in spontaneous speech to anxiety. *Journal of Personality and Social Psychology,* 1965, **1,** 425–433. *(270)*

Katahn, M., & Lyda, L. Anxiety and learning of responses varying in initial rank in the response hierarchy. *Journal of Personality,* 1966, **34,** 287–299. *(270)*

Kaufman, I. C., & Rosenbloom, L. A. Depression in infant monkeys separated from their mothers. *Science,* 1957, **55,** 1030–1031. *(236)*

Kaufman, K. F., & O'Leary, K. D. Reward, cost, and self-evaluation procedures for disruptive adolescents in a psychiatric hospital school. *Journal of Applied Behavior Analysis,* 1972, **5,** 293–310. *(212)*

Kazansky, V. I. *Cancer.* Moscow: Foreign Languages Publishing House, 1955. *(425)*

Kazdin, A. E. Covert modeling and the reduction of avoidance behavior. *Journal of Abnormal Psychology,* 1973, **81,** 87–95. *(313)*

Kazdin, A. E., & Bootzin, R. R. The token economy: An evaluative review. *Journal of Applied Behavior Analysis,* 1972, **5,** 343–372. *(213)*

Kelman, H. *Helping people: Karen Horney's psychoanalytic approach.* New York: Science House, 1971. *(301)*

Kemble, J. *Idols and invalids.* New York: Doubleday, 1936. *(494)*

Kessler, J. *Psychopathology of childhood.* Englewood Cliffs, N.J.: Prentice-Hall, 1966. *(443, 457)*

Kessley, S., & Moos, R. The XYY karyotype and criminality: A review. *Journal of Psychiatric Research,* 1970, **7,** 153-170. *(410)*

Kety, S. S. The heuristic aspect of psychiatry. *American Journal of Psychiatry,* 1961, **118,** 385-397. *(119, 139)*

Kety, S. S. Toward hypotheses for a biochemical component in the vulnerability to schizophrenia. *Seminars in Psychiatry,* 1972, **4,** 233-238. *(183)*

Kety, S. S., Rosenthal, D., Wender, P. H., & Schulsinger, F. The types and prevalence of mental illness in the biological and adoptive families of adopted schizophrenics. In D. Rosenthal & S. S. Kety (Eds.), *The transmission of schizophrenia.* London: Pergamon, 1968. *(187)*

Kidder, L., & Campbell, D. T. The indirect testing of social attitudes. In G. F. Summers (Ed.), *Attitude measurement.* Chicago: Rand McNally, 1970.

Kiesler, D. J. Some myths of psychotherapy research and the search for a paradigm. *Psychological Bulletin,* 1966, **65,** 110-136. *(317)*

Kingsley, L. A comparative study of certain personality characteristics of psychopathic and non-psychopathic offenders. Unpublished doctoral dissertation. New York University, 1956. *(408)*

Kingsley, L., & Struening, E. Changes in intellectual performance of acute and chronic schizophrenics. *Psychological Reports,* 1966, **18,** 791-800. *(172)*

Kinsey, A. C., Pomeroy, W. B., & Martin, C. E. *Sexual behavior in the human male.* Philadelphia: Saunders, 1948. *(369, 374-376)*

Kinsey, A. C., Pomeroy, W. B., Martin, C. E., & Gebhard, P. H. *Sexual behavior in the human female.* Philadelphia: Saunders, 1953. *(374-376)*

Kirk, S., McCarthy, J., & Kirk, W. *Illinois test of psycholinguistic abilities.* Urbana, Ill.: University of Illinois Press, 1968. *(499)*

Kirkwood, W. Aspects of fetal environment. In H. Wolff (Ed.), *Mechanisms of congenital malformation.* New York: Association for the Aid of Crippled Children, 1955. *(507)*

Kissin, B., & Begleiter, H. *The biology of alcoholism.* New York: Plenum, 1972.

Kleeman, S. Psychophysiologic disorders. In P. Solomon & V. D. Patch (Eds.), *Handbook of psychiatry.* Los Altos, Calif.: Lange, 1971. *(428)*

Klein, M. A contribution to the psychogenesis of manic-depressive states (1934). In *Contributions to psycho-analysis 1921-1945.* London: Hogarth, 1948. *(230, 231)*

Klein, R., & Nunn, R. F. Clinical and biochemical analysis of a case of manic-depressive psychosis showing regular weekly cycles. *Journal of Mental Science,* 1945, **91,** 79-88. *(229)*

Kleinmuntz, B. Profile analysis revisited: A heuristic approach. *Journal of Consulting Psychology,* 1963, **10,** 315-324. *(135)*

Kleinmuntz, B., & McLean, R. S. Computers in behavioral science: Diagnostic interviewing by digital computer. *Behavioral Science,* 1968, **13,** 75-80. *(135)*

Klerman, G. L. Clinical research in depression. *Archives of General Psychiatry,* 1971, **24,** 305-319. *(234)*

Klerman, G. L., & Cole, J. O. Clinical pharmacology of imipramine and related antidepressant compounds. *Pharmacological Review,* 1965, **17,** 101-141. *(242)*

Klopfer, W. G. Current status of the Rorschach test. In P. McReynolds (Ed.), *Advances in psychological assessment.* Palo Alto, Calif.: Science and Behavior Books. 1968. *(137)*

Klopfer, W. G. The short history of projective techniques. *Journal of the History of the Behavioral Sciences,* 1973, **9,** 60-65. *(137)*

Knopf, I. J. Rorschach summary scores in differential diagnosis. In B. I. Murstein (Ed.), *Handbook of projective techniques.* New York: Basic Books, 1965. *(408)*

Knott, J., Platt, E., Ashby, M., & Gottlieb, J. A familial evaluation of the electroencephalogram of patients with primary behavior disorder and psychopathic personality. *EEG and Clinical Neurophysiology,* 1953, **5,** 363-370. *(410)*

Koegler, R. R., & Brill, N. Q. *Treatment of psychiatric outpatients.* New York: Appleton-Century-Crofts, 1967. *(318)*

Kokonis, N. D. Sex-role identification in neurosis: Psychoanalytic-development and role theory predictions compared. *Journal of Abnormal Psychology,* 1972, **80,** 52-57. *(285)*

Kolodny, R. C., Masters, W. H., Hendry, J., & Toro, G. Plasma testosterone and semen analysis in male homosexuals. *New England Journal of Medicine,* 1971, **285,** 1170-1174. *(370)*

Kondas, O., & Scetnicka, B. Systematic desensitization as a method of preparation for childbirth. *Journal of Behavior Therapy and Experimental Psychiatry,* 1972, **3,** 51-54. *(309)*

Koranyi, E., & Lehmann, H. Experimental sleep deprivation in schizophrenic patients. *Archives of General Psychiatry,* 1960, **2,** 534-544. *(174)*

Koscherak, S., & Masling, J. Noblesse oblige effect: The interpretation of Rorschach responses as a function of ascribed social class. *Journal of Consulting and Clinical Psychology,* 1972, **39,** 415-419. *(138)*

Kozloff, M. *Reaching the autistic child: A parent training program.* Champaign, Ill.: Research Press, 1973. *(460)*

Kraepelin, E. *Dementia praecox and paraphrenia.* (1st ed.), Edinburgh: Livingston, 1896. *(118, 224, 225)*

Kraepelin, E. *Psychiatry: A textbook.* Leipzig: Barth, 1913. *(225, 399)*

Kraft, T., & Al-Issa, I. The use of methohexitone sodium in the systematic desensitization of premature ejaculation. *British Journal of Psychiatry,* 1968, **114,** 351-352. *(389)*

Kraines, S. H. *Mental depressions and their treatment.* New York: Macmillan, 1957. *(238)*

Krasner, L. Behavior therapy. In *Annual review of psychology.* Palo Alto, Calif.: Annual Reviews, 1971. *(307, 318)*

Krauss, H. H., & Tesser, A. Social contexts of suicide. *Journal of*

Abnormal Psychology, 1971, **78,** 222-228. *(238)*

Kreitman, N., Pearce, K. I., & Ryle, A. The relationship of psychiatric, psychosomatic and organic illness in a general practice. *British Journal of Psychiatry,* 1966, **112,** 569-579. *(420)*

Kreps, J. Higher income for older Americans. In R. Boyd & G. Oakes (Eds.), *Foundations of practical gerentology.* Columbia: University of South Carolina Press, 1969. *(500)*

Kretschmer, E. *Physique and character* (Trans. by W. J. H. Sprout). New York: Harcourt, Brace, & World, 1925. *(118, 224, 227)*

Kris, A. O. Case studies in chronic hospitalization for functional psychosis. *Archives of General Psychiatry,* 1972, **26,** 326-333. *(189)*

Kubie, S. The fundamental nature of the distinction between normality and neurosis. *Psychoanalytical Quarterly,* 1954, **23,** 167-204. *(7)*

Kuehl, F. A., Hichens, M., Ormond, R. E., Meisinger, M. A. P., Gale, P. H., Cirillo, V. J., & Brink, N. G. *Para-O*-methylation of dopamine in schizophrenic and normal individuals. *Nature,* 1964, **203,** 154-155. *(184)*

Kuehn, J. L. Student drug user and his family. *Journal of College Student Personnel,* 1970, **11,** 404-413. *(348)*

Kurland, H. D. Steroid excretion in depressive disorders. *Archives of General Psychiatry,* 1964, **10,** 554-560. *(229)*

Kurland, H. D., Yeager, C., & Arthur, R. Psychophysiologic aspects of severe behavior disorders. *Archives of General Psychiatry,* 1963, **8,** 599-604. *(408)*

LaBrosse, E. H., Mann, J. D., & Kety, S. S. Physiological and psychological effects of intravenously administered epinephrine and its metabolism in normal and schizophrenic men. III: Metabolism of 7-H^3-epinephrine as determined in studies on blood and urine. *Journal of Psychiatric Research,* 1961, **1,** 68-75. *(184)*

Lacey, J. I., & Lacey, B. C. The law of initial value in the longitudinal study of autonomic constitution: Reproducibility of autonomic responses and response patterns over a four-year interval. *Annals of the New York Academy of Sciences,* 1962, **98,** 1257-1290. *(421)*

Lachman, S. J. A behavioristic rationale for the development of psychosomatic phenomena. *Journal of Psychology,* 1963, **56,** 239-248. *(421)*

Lachman, S. J. *Psychosomatic disorders: A behavioristic interpretation.* New York: Wiley, 1972. *(418, 420, 422)*

Lader, M. Palmar skin conductance measures in anxiety and phobic states. *Journal of Psychosomatic Research,* 1967, **11,** 271-281. *(268-269)*

Ladewig, D., & Battegay, R. Abuse of anorexics with special reference to newer substances. *International Journal of Addiction,* 1971, **6,** 167-172. *(345)*

Laing, R. D. Is schizophrenia a disease? *International Journal of Social Psychiatry,* 1964, **10,** 184-193. *(192)*

Laing, R. D. *The politics of experience.* New York: Ballantine Books, 1967. *(192, 206)*

Lancaster, E. The dreams of the traumatic neuroses. *American Journal of Psychoanalysis,* 1970, **30,** 13-18. *(285)*

Lane, E. A., & Albee, G. W. Intellectual antecedents of schizophrenia. In M. Roff & D. F. Ricks (Eds.), *Life history research in psychopathology.* Minneapolis: University of Minnesota Press, 1970, 189-207. *(129)*

Lang, P. J. Behavior therapy with a case of nervous anorexia. In L. P. Ullmann, & L. Krasner (Eds.), *Case studies in behavior modification.* New York: Holt, 1965. *(431)*

Lang, P. J. Stimulus control, response control, and the desensitization of fear. In D. J. Levis (Eds.), *Learning approaches to therapeutic behavior change.* Chicago: Aldine, 1970. *(310)*

Lang, P. J., & Buss, A. Psychological deficit in schizophrenia. II: Interference and activation. *Journal of Abnormal Psychology,* 1965, **70,** 77-106. *(196)*

Lange, J. *Crime and destiny.* New York: Boni, 1930. *(410)*

Lanyon, R. I. *A handbook of MMPI group profiles.* Minneapolis: University of Minnesota Press, 1968. *(133)*

LaPorte, M. The effect of war imposed dietary limitations on growth of Paris school children. *American Journal of Diseases in Children,* 1946, **71,** 244. *(506)*

Lawless, J. C., & Wake, F. R. Sex differences in pupillary responses to visual stimuli. Paper presented at the 8th annual meeting of the Society for Psychophysiological Research, Washington, October, 1968. *(383)*

Lazarus, A. A. The treatment of chronic frigidity by systematic desensitization. *Journal of Nervous and Mental Disease,* 1963, **136,** 272-278. *(389)*

Lazarus, A. A. Learning theory and the treatment of depression. *Behaviour Research and Therapy,* 1968, **6,** 83-90. *(232, 243, 244)*

Lazarus, A. A. *Behavior therapy and beyond.* New York: McGraw-Hill, 1971. *(245, 306, 309, 315-316, 389)*

Lazarus, A. A. Some reactions to Costello's paper on depression. *Behavior Therapy,* 1972, **3,** 248-250. *(233)*

Lazarus, A. A. Multimodal behavior therapy: Treating the "basic id." *Journal of Nervous and Mental Disease,* 1973, **156,** 404-411. *(245)*

Lazarus, A. A., & Abramovitz, A. The use of "emotive imagery" in the treatment of children's phobias. *Journal of Mental Science,* 1962, **108,** 191-195. *(460-461)*

Lehmann, H. Schizophrenia, IV: Clinical features. In A. Freedman & H. Kaplan (Eds.), *Comprehensive textbook of psychiatry.* Baltimore: Williams and Wilkins, 1967. *(157, 162, 164)*

Leitenberg, H. Positive reinforcement and extinction. In W. S. Agras (Ed.), *Behavior modification: Principles and clinical applications.* Boston: Little, Brown, 1972. *(311-312)*

Leitenberg, H., Agras, W. S., Butz, R., & Wincze, J. Relationship between heart rate and behavioral change during the treatment of phobias. *Journal of Abnormal Psychology,* 1971, **78,** 59-68. *(291, 312)*

Leitenberg, H., Agras, W. S., & Thomson, L. E. A sequential analysis of the effect of selective positive reinforcement in modifying anorexia nervosa. *Behaviour Research and Therapy,* 1968, **6,** 211-218. *(311-312, 428)*

Leitenberg, H., Agras, W. S., Thomson, L. E., & Wright, D. E. Feedback in behavior modification: An experimental analysis in two phobic cases. *Journal of Applied Behavior Analysis,* 1968, **1,** 131-137. *(311-312)*

Leonard, C., Chase, G., & Childs, B. Genetic counseling: A consumer's view. *New England Journal of Medicine,* 1972, **287,** 433-439. *(478)*

Lerner, J., & Shanan, J. Coping style of psychiatric patients with somatic complaints. *Journal of Personality Assessment,* 1972, **36,** 28-32. *(137)*

Lesse, S. Combined drug and psychotherapy of severely depressed ambulatory patients. *Canadian Psychiatric Association Journal,* 1966, **11,** 5123-5130. *(243)*

Lesser, E. Behavior therapy with a narcotics user: A case report. *Behaviour Research and Therapy,* 1967, **5,** 251-252. *(353)*

Levine, S., & Mullins, R. F., Jr. Hormonal influences on brain organization in infant rats. *Science,* 1966, **152,** 1585-1591. *(72)*

Levitt, E. Results of psychotherapy with children: An evaluation. *Journal of Consulting Psychology,* 1957, **21,** 189-196. *(457)*

Levitt, E. Psychotherapy with children: A further review. *Behaviour Research and Therapy,* 1963, **1,** 45-51. *(461)*

Levy, R. J. The Rorschach pattern in neurodermatitis. *Psychosomatic Medicine,* 1952, **14,** 41-49. *(422)*

Lewin, K. *A dynamic theory of personality: Selected papers.* (Trans. by K. Adams, & K. Zener) New York: McGraw-Hill, 1935. *(272)*

Lewinsohn, P. M., & Libet, J. Pleasant events, activity schedules, and depressions. *Journal of Abnormal Psychology,* 1972, **79,** 291-295. *(232)*

Lewinsohn, P. M., & Shaffer, M. Use of home observations as an integral part of the treatment of depression. *Journal of Consulting and Clinical Psychology,* 1971, **37,** 87-94. *(232)*

Lewinsohn, P. M., & Shaw, D. A. Feedback about interpersonal behavior as an agent of behavior change: A case study in the treatment of depression. *Psychotherapy and Psychosomatics,* 1969, **17,** 82-88. *(245)*

Lewis, O. *The children of Sanchez.* New York: Random House, 1961. *(44)*

Lewis, O. *La Vida.* New York: Random House, 1966. *(44)*

Lewis, O. A Puerto Rican boy. In J. C. Finney (Ed.), *Culture change, mental health, and poverty.* New York: Simon and Schuster, 1969. *(44, 45)*

Liberman, R. P. Aversive conditioning of drug addicts: A pilot study. *Behaviour Research and Therapy,* 1968, **6,** 229-231. *(353)*

Liberman, R. P., Teigen, J. R., Patterson, R., & Baker, V. Reducing delusional speech in chronic paranoid schizophrenics. *Journal of Applied Behavior Analysis,* 1973, **6,** 57-64. *(212)*

Lidz, T., Cornelison, A. R., Fleck, S., & Terry, D. The intrafamilial environment of the schizophrenic patient. I: The father. *Psychiatry,* 1957, **20,** 329-342. (a) *(191)*

Lidz, T., Cornelison, A. R., Fleck, S., & Terry, D. The intrafamilial environment of schizophrenic patients. II: Marital schism and marital skew. *American Journal of Psychiatry,* 1957, **114,** 241-248. (b) *(191)*

Lidz, T., & Fleck, S. Schizophrenia, human integration, and the role of the family. In D. D. Jackson (Ed.), *The etiology of schizophrenia.* New York: Basic Books, 1960. *(191)*

Lindsley, D. B. Attention, consciousness, sleep and wakefulness. In J. Field (Ed.), *Handbook of physiology.* Sec. 1. *Neurophysiology,* Washington, D.C.: American Physiological Society, 1960. *(427)*

Lindsley, O. R. Operant conditioning methods applied to research in chronic schizophrenia. *Psychiatric Research Report,* 1956, **5,** 118-139. *(207)*

Lindsley, O. R. Characteristics of the behavior of chronic psychotics as revealed by free-operant conditioning methods. *Diseases of the Nervous System,* 1960, **21,** 66-78. *(207)*

Lindsley, O. R. Operant conditioning techniques in the measurement of psychopharmacologic response. In *The first Hahnemann symposium on psychosomatic medicine,* 1962. *(207)*

Lindsley, O. R. Experimental analysis of social reinforcement. *American Journal of Orthopsychiatry,* 1963, **33,** 624-633. *(207)*

Lindsley, O. R. Geriatric behavioral prosthetics. In R. Kastenbaum (Ed.), *New thoughts on old age.* New York: Springer, 1964. *(511)*

Lippert, W., & Senter, R. Electrodermal responses in the sociopath. *Psychonomic Science,* 1966, **4,** 25-26. *(409)*

Lisman, S. A. Alcoholic "blackout": State-dependent learning? *Archives of General Psychiatry,* 1974, **30,** 46-53. *(331)*

Loeb, A., Feshback, S., Beck, A. T., & Wolf, A. Some effects of reward upon the social perception and motivation of psychiatric patients varying in depression. *Journal of Abnormal and Social Psychology,* 1964, **68,** 609-616. *(232)*

Logan, D. G., & Deodhar, S. D. Schizophrenia, an immunologic disorder? *Journal of the American Medical Association,* 1970, **212,** 1703-1704. *(185)*

Lolli, G., Serianni, E., Golden, G. M., & Luzzatto-Fegiz, P. Alcohol in Italian culture. *Monograph of the Rutgers Center of Alcohol Studies,* 1958, No. 3. *(331)*

Lomont, J. F., & Brock, L. Cognitive factors in systematic desensitization. *Behaviour Research and Therapy,* 1971, **9,** 187-196. *(310)*

London, P. The end of ideology in behavior modification. *American Psychologist,* 1972, **27,** 913-920. *(371)*

LoPiccolo, J. Case study: Systematic desensitization of homosexuality. *Behavior Therapy,* 1971, **2,** 394-399. *(387)*

Lorenz, M. Problems posed by schizophrenic language. *Archives of General Psychiatry,* 1961, **4,** 603-610. *(172)*

Lorion, R. P. Socioeconomic status and traditional treatment approaches reconsidered. *Psycho-*

logical Bulletin, 1973, **79,** 263–270. *(42)*

Lorr, M. A behavioral perspective on schizophrenia. *Diseases of the Nervous System,* 1968, **29,** 45–52. *(124, 139)*

Lorr, M., & Klett, C. J. *The inpatient multidimensional psychiatric scale manual.* Palo Alto, Calif.: Consulting Psychologists Press, 1966. *(124)*

Lorr, M., McNair, D. M., Klett, C. J., & Lasky, J. J. Evidence of ten psychotic syndromes. *Journal of Consulting Psychologists,* 1962, **26,** 185–189. *(124)*

Lorr, M., McNair, D. M., & Weinstein, G. J. Early effects of chlordiazepoxide used with psychotherapy. *Journal of Psychiatric Research,* 1962, **1,** 257–270. *(318)*

Louria, D. B. Medical complications of pleasure-giving drugs. *Archives of Internal Medicine,* 1969, **123,** 82–89. *(348)*

Lovaas, O. I., Berberich, J., Perloff, B., & Schaeffer, B. Acquisition of imitative speech by schizophrenic children. *Science,* 1966, **151,** 705–707. *(460)*

Lovaas, O. I., Koegel, R., Simmons, J. Q., & Long, J. S. Some generalization and follow-up measures on autistic children in behavior therapy. *Journal of Applied Behavior Analysis,* 1973, **6,** 131–166. *(460)*

Lovaas, O. I., Schaeffer, B., & Simmons, J. Building social behavior in autistic children by the use of electric shocks. *Journal of Experimental Research in Personality,* 1965, **1,** 99–109. *(460)*

Lovaas, O. I., & Simmons, J. Q. Manipulation of self-destruction in three retarded children. *Journal of Applied Behavior Analysis,* 1969, **2,** 143–157. *(460)*

Love, L., Kaswan, J., & Bugenthal, D. Differential effectiveness of three clinical interventions for different socioeconomic groupings. *Journal of Consulting and Clinical Psychology,* 1972, **39,** 347–360. *(457)*

Lovibond, S. H. *Conditioning and enuresis.* Oxford: Pergamon, 1964. *(447)*

Lovibond, S. H. Aversive control of behavior. *Behavior Therapy,* 1970, **1,** 80–91. *(388)*

Lovibond, S. H., & Caddy, G. Dis-

criminated aversive control in the moderation of alcoholic drinking behavior. *Behavior Therapy,* 1970, **1,** 437–444. *(339, 340)*

Lovibond, S. H., & Coote, M. Enuresis. In C. Costello (Ed.), *Symptoms of psychopathology.* New York: Wiley, 1970. *(460)*

Lovitt, T. C., & Curtiss, K. Academic response rate as a function of teacher- and self-imposed contingencies. *Journal of Applied Behavior Analysis,* 1969, **2,** 49–53. *(315)*

Lubetkin, B. S., Rivers, P. C., & Rosenberg, C. M. Difficulties of disulfiram therapy with alcoholics. *Quarterly Journal of Studies on Alcohol,* 1971, **32,** 168–171. *(337)*

Lubin, B., Dupres, V. A., & Lubin, A. W. Comparability and sensitivity of set 2 of the depression adjective check lists. *Psychological Report,* 1967, **20,** 756–758. *(234)*

Luborsky, L. A note on Eysenck's article, "The effects of psychotherapy: An evaluation." *British Journal of Psychiatry,* 1954, **45,** 129–131. *(317)*

Luborsky, L., Chandler, M., Auerbach, A. H., Cohen, J., & Bachrach, H. M. Factors influencing the outcome of psychotherapy: A review of quantitative research. *Psychological Bulletin,* 1971, **75,** 145–185. *(317)*

Lucas, C., Sansbury, P., & Collins, J. A social and clinical study of delusions in schizophrenia. *Journal of Mental Science,* 1962, **108,** 747–758. *(160)*

Lundquist, G. Prognosis and course in manic-depressive psychoses. *Acta Psychiatric Neurological* Supplement 35, 1945. *(238)*

Lutker, E. R. Treatment of migraine headache by conditioned relaxation: A case study. *Behavior Therapy,* 1971, **2,** 592–593. *(428)*

Lyght, C. (Ed.) *The Merck manual of diagnosis and therapy.* (9th Ed.). Rahway, N.J.: Merck & Co., 1956. *(481)*

Lykken, D. T. *A study of anxiety in the sociopathic personality.* (Doctoral dissertation, University of Minnesota) Ann Arbor, Michigan: University Microfilms, 1955, No. 55-944. *(408, 409)*

Lynch, J. J., & Paskewitz, D. A. On

the mechanisms of the feedback control of human brain wave activity. In J. Stoyva, T. Barber, L. V. DiCara, N. E. Miller, & D. Shapiro (Eds.), *Biofeedback & self-control.* Chicago: Aldine-Atherton, 1972. *(427)*

Lynd, R. S., & Lynd, H. *Middletown.* New York: Harcourt, Brace, 1929. *(36)*

MacAndrew, C. The differentiation of male alcoholic outpatients from nonalcoholic psychiatric outpatients by means of the MMPI. *Quarterly Journal of Studies on Alcohol,* 1965, **26,** 238–246. *(332)*

MacCulloch, M. J., Birtles, C. J., & Feldman, M. P. Anticipatory avoidance learning for the treatment of homosexuality: Recent developments and an automatic aversion therapy system. *Behavior Therapy,* 1971, **2,** 151–169. *(388)*

MacCulloch, M. J., & Feldman, M. P. Aversion therapy in the management of 43 homosexuals. *British Medical Journal,* 1967, **2,** 594–597. *(388)*

MacCulloch, M. J., Feldman, M. P. Orford, J. F., & MacCulloch, M. L. Anticipatory avoidance learning in the treatment of alcoholism: A record of therapeutic failure. *Behaviour Research and Therapy,* 1966, **4,** 187–196. *(339)*

MacDonough, T. S. A critique of the first Feldman and MacCulloch avoidance conditioning treatment for homosexuals. *Behavior Therapy,* 1972, **3,** 104–111. *(388)*

MacFarlane, J., Allen, L., & Honzik, M. A developmental study of the behavior problems of normal children between twenty-one months and fourteen years. Berkeley: University of California Press, 1954. *(455)*

Maher, B. *Principles of psychopathology.* New York: McGraw-Hill, 1966. *(159, 172, 271, 285)*

Maher, B., McKean, K., & McLaughlin, B. Studies in psychotic language. In P. Stone (Ed.), *The general inquirer: A computer approach to content analysis.* Cambridge, Mass.: M.I.T., 1966. *(172)*

Mahl, G., & Karpe, R. Emotions and

hydrochloric acid secretion during psychoanalytic hours. *Psychosomatic Medicine,* 1953, **15,** 312-327. *(269)*

Mahoney, M. J. The self-management of covert behavior: A case study. *Behavior Therapy,* 1971, **2,** 575-578. *(315)*

Mahoney, M. J. Research issues in self-management. *Behavior Therapy,* 1972, **3,** 45-63, *(314)*

Malmo, R. B. Anxiety and behavioral arousal. *Psychological Review,* 1957, **64,** 276-287. *(270, 292)*

Malmo, R. B. Studies of anxiety: Some clinical origins of the activation concept. In C. Spielberger (Ed.), *Anxiety and behavior.* New York: Academic, 1966. *(269)*

Malmo, R. B. Physiological concomitants of emotion. In A. M. Freedman & H. I. Kaplan (Eds.), *Comprehensive textbook of psychiatry.* Baltimore: Williams & Wilkins, 1967. *(419)*

Malmquist, C. P. Depression and object loss in acute psychiatric admissions. *American Journal of Psychiatry,* 1970, **126,** 1782-1787. *(234)*

Mann, J. D., & LaBrosse, E. H. Urinary excretion of phenolic acids by normal and schizophrenic male patients. *Archives of General Psychiatry,* 1959, **1,** 547-551. *(183)*

Manne, S. H., Kandel, A., & Rosenthal, D. Differences between performance I. Q. and verbal I. Q. in a severely psychopathic population. *Journal of Clinical Psychology,* 1962, **18,** 73-77. *(408)*

Manosevitz, M. Education and MMPI Mf scores in homosexual and heterosexual males. *Journal of Consulting and Clinical Psychology,* 1971, **36,** 395-399. *(382)*

Marks, I. M. Agoraphobic syndrome (phobic anxiety state). *Archives of General Psychiatry,* 1970, **23,** 538-553. (a) *(264)*

Marks, I. M. The classification of phobic disorders. *British Journal of Psychiatry,* 1970, **116,** 377-386. (b) *(264)*

Marks, I. M., & Gelder, M. G. Transvestism and fetishism: Clinical and psychological changes during faradic aversion. *British Journal of Psychiatry,* 1967, **113,** 711-729. *(383, 384)*

Marks, I. M., & Gelder, M. G. Controlled trials in behaviour therapy. In R. Porter (Ed.), *The role of learning in psychotherapy.* London: Churchill, 1968. *(318)*

Markson, E., Kwoh, A., Cumming, J., & Cumming, E. Alternatives to hospitalization for psychiatrically ill geriatric patients. *American Journal of Psychiatry,* 1971, **127,** 1055-1062. *(512)*

Marquis, J. N. Orgasmic reconditioning: Changing sexual object choice through controlling masturbation fantasies. *Journal of Behavior Therapy and Experimental Psychiatry,* 1970, **1,** 263-271. *(373)*

Martin, B., & Sroufe, L. Anxiety. In C. Costello (Ed.), *Symptoms of psychopathology.* New York: Wiley, 1970. *(270-271)*

Martin, W. R., & Fraser, H. F. A comparative study of physiological and subjective effects of heroin and morphine administered intravenously in post addicts. *Journal of Pharmacology and Experimental Therapy,* 1961, **133,** 388. *(341)*

Martorano, R. D., & Nathan, P. E. Syndromes of psychosis and non-psychosis: Factor analysis of a systems analysis. *Journal of Abnormal Psychology,* 1972, **80,** 1-10. *(234)*

Maslow, A. Toward a humanistic biology. *American Psychologist,* 1969, **24,** 724-735. *(427)*

Massachusetts Welfare Rights Organization. *Five lies about welfare.* Cambridge, Mass.: MWRO, 1969. *(506)*

Masters, W. H., & Johnson, V. E. *Human sexual response.* Boston: Little, Brown, 1966. *(375, 377)*

Masters, W. H., & Johnson, V. E. *Human sexual inadequacy.* Boston: Little, Brown, 1970. *(389-392)*

Matarazzo, J. D. *Wechsler's measurement and appraisal of adult intelligence* (5th ed.). Baltimore: Williams & Wilkins, 1972. *(268)*

Matson, D. Current treatment of infantile hydrocephalus. *New England Journal of Medicine,* 1956, **255,** 933-936. *(477)*

Matulef, N. J., Pottharst, K. E., & Rothenberg, P. J. *The revolution in professional training.* Washington, D.C.: National Council on Graduate Education in Psychology, 1972. *(129)*

Max, L. W. Breaking up a homosexual fixation by the conditional reaction technique: A case study. *Psychological Bulletin,* 1935, **32,** 734. *(387, 388)*

May, P. R. A. *Treatment of schizophrenia.* New York: Science House, 1968. *(204, 205)*

May, P. R. A. Psychotherapy and ataraxic drugs. In A. E. Bergin & S. L. Garfield (Eds.), *Handbook of psychotherapy and behavior change.* New York: Wiley, 1971. *(204, 318)*

May, P. R. A., & Tuma, A. H. Ataraxic drugs and psychotherapy. *Journal of Nervous and Mental Disease,* 1964, **139,** 362-369. *(203)*

May, P. R. A., & Tuma, A. H. Treatment of schizophrenia. *British Journal of Psychiatry,* 1965, **3,** 503-510. *(203)*

Mayerson, P., & Lief, H. I. Psychotherapy of homosexuals: A follow-up study of nineteen cases. In Marmor, J. (Ed.), *Sexual inversion.* New York: Basic Books, 1965. *(387)*

McCabe, M., Fowler, R., Cadoret, R., & Winokur, G. Symptom differences in schizophrenia with good and poor prognosis. *American Journal of Psychiatry,* 1972, **128,** 1239-1243. *(163)*

McCawley, A., Stroebel, C., & Glueck, B. Pupillary reactivity, psychologic disorder, and age. *Archives of General Psychiatry,* 1966, **14,** 415-418. *(269)*

McCord, W., & McCord, J. *The psychopath: An essay on the criminal mind.* Princeton: Van Nostrand, 1964. *(410-411)*

McCully, R. S. Current attitudes about projective techniques in APA approved internship centers. *Journal of Projective Techniques and Personality Assessment,* 1965, **27,** 271-280. *(129)*

McGeer, P. The chemistry of the mind. *American Scientist,* 1971, **59,** 221-229. *(66, 501)*

McGlothlin, W. H., Sparkes, R. S., & Arnold, D. O. Effect of LSD on human pregnancy. *Journal of the American Medical Association,* 1970, **212,** 1483-1487. *(345)*

McGrath, S. D., O'Brien, P. F., Power, P. J., & Shea, J. R. Nicotinimide treatment of schizophrenia. *Schizophrenia Bulletin,* 1972, **5,** 74-76. *(184)*

McGuire, R. J. Classification and the problem of diagnosis. In H. J. Eysenck (Ed.), *Handbook of abnormal psychology.* London: Pitman Medical, 1973. *(120)*

McGuire, R. J., Carlisle, J. M., & Young, B. G. Sexual deviations as conditioned behavior: A hypothesis. *Behaviour Research and Therapy,* 1965, **2**, 185-190. *(373)*

McKinney, W. T., Suomi, S. J., & Harlow, H. F. Repetitive peer separations of juvenile age rhesus monkeys. *Archives of General Psychiatry,* 1972, **27**, 200-203. *(236)*

McMillan, D. E. Drugs and punished responding. I: Rate dependent effects under multiple schedules. *Journal of Experimental Analysis of Behavior,* 1973, **19**, 133-145. *(106)*

McNamara, J. R., & MacDonough, T. S. Some methodological considerations in the design and implementation of behavior therapy research. *Behavior Therapy,* 1972, **3**, 361-378. *(310)*

Mead, M. *Sex and temperament in three primitive societies.* New York: Morrow, 1935. *(385)*

Mednick, M. S., & Tangri, S. S. New social psychological perspectives on women. *Journal of Social Issues,* 1972, **28**, 1-16. *(50, 51)*

Mednick, S. A. A learning theory approach to research in schizophrenia. *Psychological Bulletin,* 1958, **55**, 316-327. *(195)*

Mednick, S. A. Breakdown in individuals at high risk for schizophrenia: Possible predispositional perinatal factors. *Mental Hygiene,* 1970, **54**, 50-63. *(196)*

Mednick, S. A. Birth defects and schizophrenia. *Psychology Today,* 1971, **4**, 49-50. *(196)*

Mednick, S. A., & Wild, C. Reciprocal augmentation of generalization and anxiety. *Journal of Experimental Psychology,* 1962, **63**, 621-626. *(195)*

Meehl, P. E. A comparison of clinicians with five statistical methods of identifying psychotic MMPI profiles. *Journal of Counseling Psychology,* 1959, **6**, 102-109. *(135)*

Meehl, P. E. Schizotaxia, schizotypy, schizophrenia. *American Psychologist,* 1962, **17**, 827-838. *(157)*

Meehl, P. E. Profile analysis of the MMPI in differential diagnosis. In G. Welsh & W. G. Dahlstrom (Eds.), *Basic readings on the MMPI in psychology and medicine.* Minneapolis: University of Minnesota Press, 1963. *(268, 408)*

Meehl, P. E., & Dahlstrom, W. G. Objective configural rules for discriminating psychotic from neurotic MMPI profiles. *Journal of Consulting Psychology,* 1960, **24**, 375-387. *(135)*

Meier-Graefe, J. *Dostoevsky, the man and his work.* London: George Routledge and Sons, Ltd., 1928. *(224)*

Mello, N. K. Behavioral studies of alcoholism. In B. Kissin & H. Begleiter (Eds.), *The biology of alcoholism.* New York: Plenum, 1972. *(334, 335)*

Mello, N. K. Theoretical review: A review of methods to induce alcohol addiction in animals. *Pharmacology, Biochemistry and Behavior,* 1973, **1**, 89-101. *(332)*

Mendels, J. The prediction of response to electroconvulsive therapy. *American Journal of Psychiatry,* 1967, **124**, 153-159. *(241)*

Mendels, J. Urinary 17-ketosteroid fractionation in depression: A preliminary report. *British Journal of Psychiatry,* 1969, **115**, 581-585. *(230)*

Mendels, J., & Hawkins, D. R. Sleep studies in depression. In *Proceedings of the symposium on recent advances in the psychobiology of affective disorders.* Bethesda, Md.: National Institute of Mental Health, 1970. *(235, 236)*

Mendelson, J. H. (Ed.) Experimentally induced chronic intoxication and withdrawal in alcoholics. *Quarterly Journal of Studies on Alcohol,* Suppl. 2, 1964. *(334)*

Mendelson, J. H. Ethanol-1-C^{14} metabolism in alcoholics and non-alcoholics. *Science,* 1968, **159**, 319-320. *(330)*

Mendelson, J. H. Biological concomitants of alcoholism. *New England Journal of Medicine,* 1970, **283**, 24-32. *(330)*

Mendelson, J. H., Mello, N. K., & Solomon, P. Small group drinking behavior: An experimental study of chronic alcoholics. In A. Wikler (Ed.), *The addictive states,* Vol. 46, Research Publication of the Association of Nervous & Mental Diseases, Baltimore: Williams & Wilkins, 1968.

Menninger, K. Recording the findings of the psychological examination ("mental status"). *American Journal of Psychiatry,* 1952, **108**, 600-609. *(118)*

Menninger, K. *Theory of psychoanalytic technique.* New York: Basic Books, 1958. *(298)*

Meyer, A. Fundamental conceptions of dementia praecox. *British Medical Journal,* 1906, **2**, 757. *(118)*

Meyer, A. *The commonsense psychiatry of Dr. Adolf Meyer.* New York: McGraw-Hill, 1948. *(224)*

Michael, R. P., & Gibbons, J. L. Interrelationships between the endocrine system and neuropsychiatry. In C. Pfeifer & J. Smythies (Eds.), *International review of neurobiology.* New York: Academic, 1963. *(229)*

Migeon, C. J., Rivarola, M. A., & Forest, M. G. Studies of androgens in male transsexual subjects: Effects of estrogen therapy. In R. Green & J. Money (Eds.), *Transsexualism and sex reassignment.* Baltimore: Johns Hopkins, 1969. *(371)*

Miles, H. H. W., Waldfogel, S., Barrabee, E. L., & Cobb, S. Psychosomatic study of 45 young men with coronary artery disease. *Psychosomatic Medicine,* 1954, **16**, 455-477. *(422)*

Miller, L., Barrett, C., Hampe, E., & Noble, H. Comparison of reciprocal inhibition, psychotherapy, and waiting list control for phobic children. *Journal of Abnormal Psychology,* 1972, **79**, 269-279. (a) *(447)*

Miller, L., Barrett, C., Hampe, E., & Noble, H. Factor structure of childhood fears. *Journal of Consulting and Clinical Psychology,* 1972, **39**, 264-268. (b) *(461)*

Miller, L., Hampe, E., Barrett, C., & Noble, H. Children's deviant behavior within the general population. *Journal of Consulting and Clinical Psychology,* 1971, **37**, 16-22. *(129, 455)*

Miller, N. E. Liberalization of basic S-R concepts: Extensions to conflict behavior, motivation and social learning. In S. Koch (Ed.), *Psychology: A study of a science.*

Vol. II. New York: McGraw-Hill, 1959. *(272)*

Miller, N. E. Integration of neurophysiological and behavioral research. *Annals of the New York Academy of Science,* 1961, **92,** 830-839. *(425)*

Miller, N. E. Some implications of modern behavior theory for personality change and psychotherapy. In D. Byrne & P. Worchel (Eds.), *Personality change.* New York: Wiley, 1964. *(425)*

Miller, N. E. Learning of visceral and glandular responses. *Science,* 1969, **163,** 434-445. *(427)*

Miller, N. E. Autonomic learning: Clinical and physiological implications. In M. Hammer, K. Salzinger, & S. Sutton (Eds.), *Psychopathology.* New York: Wiley, 1973. *(427)*

Millichap, J. Drugs in management of hyperkinetic and perceptually handicapped children. *Journal of the American Medical Association,* 1968, **206,** 1527-1530. *(455)*

Milliken, R. Mathematical-verbal ability differentials of situational anxiety as measured by blood pressure change. *Journal of Experimental Education,* 1964, **32,** 309-311. *(268)*

Mills, K. C., Sobell, M. B., & Schaefer, H. H. Training social drinking as an alternative to abstinence for alcoholics. *Behavior Therapy,* 1971, **2,** 18-27. *(340)*

Milman, D. S., & Goldman, G. D. (Eds.) *Psychoanalytic contributions to community psychology.* Springfield, Ill.: Charles C Thomas, 1971. *(286)*

Milner, B. Some effects of frontal lobectomy in man. In J. Warren & K. Akert (Eds.), *The frontal granular cortex and behavior.* New York: McGraw-Hill, 1964. *(66)*

Mintz, N. L. Patient fees and psychotherapeutic transactions. *Journal of Consulting and Clinical Psychology,* 1971, **36,** 1-8. *(295)*

Mirsky, I. A. Physiologic, psychologic, and social determinants in the etiology of duodenal ulcer. *American Journal of Diagnosis and Disease,* 1958, **3,** 285-314. *(420)*

Mischel, W. *Personality and assessment.* New York: Wiley, 1968. *(98, 138, 140)*

Mischel, W. *Introduction to personality.* New York: Holt, 1971. *(98)*

Mischel, W. Towards a cognitive social learning reconceptualization of personality. *Psychological Review,* 1973, **80,** 252-283. *(98, 107, 108)*

Mischel, W., & Liebert, R. M. Effects of discrepancies between observed and imposed reward criteria on their acquisition and transmission. *Journal of Personality and Social Psychology,* 1966, **3,** 45-53. *(100)*

Mishler, E. G., & Waxler, N. E. *Interaction in families: An experimental study of family processes and schizophrenia.* New York: Wiley, 1968. *(459)*

Missakian, E. A. Effects of adult social experience on patterns of reproductive activity of socially deprived male rhesus monkeys (Macaca mulatta). *Journal of Personality and Social Psychology,* 1972, **21,** 131-134. *(384, 385)*

Modlin, H. A study of the MMPI in clinical practice. In G. Welsh & W. G. Dahlstrom (Eds.), *Basic readings on the MMPI in psychology and medicine.* Minneapolis: University of Minnesota Press, 1963. *(268, 408)*

Money, J. Prefatory remarks on outcome of sex reassignment in 24 cases of transsexualism. *Archives of Sexual Behavior,* 1971, **1,** 163-165. *(386)*

Montagu, M. *Prenatal influences.* Springfield, Ill.: Charles C Thomas, 1962. *(506-507)*

Moore, C. H., Boblitt, W. E., & Wildman, R. W. Psychiatric impressions of psychological reports. *Journal of Clinical Psychology,* 1968, **24,** 373-376. *(129)*

Moore, N. Behavior therapy in bronchial asthma: A controlled study. *Journal of Psychosomatic Research,* 1965, **9,** 257-276. *(428, 429)*

Mordkoff, A. M., & Parsons, O. A. The coronary personality: A critique. *Psychosomatic Medicine,* 1967, **29,** 1-14. *(420)*

Morgan, C. *Physiological psychology.* New York: McGraw-Hill, 1965. *(65)*

Morse, W. H. Intermittent reinforcement. In W. K. Honig (Ed.), *Operant behavior: Areas of research and application.* New York: Appleton-Century-Crofts, 1966. *(106)*

Mosher, L. R., & Feinsilver, D. *Special report on schizophrenia.* United States Department of Health, Education, & Welfare, April, 1970. *(185)*

Mosher, L. R., & Gunderson, J. G. Special report on schizophrenia: 1972. *Schizophrenia Bulletin,* 1973, **7,** 10-52. *(183)*

Motto, J. A. Suicide attempts: A longitudinal view. *Archives of General Psychiatry,* 1965, **13,** 516-520. *(239)*

Mouruzzi, G., & Magoun, H. Brainstem reticular formation and activation of the EEG. *Electroencephalography & Clinical Neurophysiology,* 1949, **1,** 455-473. *(64)*

Mowrer, O. H. 'Sin,' the lesser of two evils. *American Psychologist,* 1960, **15,** 301-304. *(14)*

Mowrer, O. H. Review of *Beyond freedom and dignity. Contemporary Psychology,* 1972, **17,** 469-472. *(104)*

Mowrer, O. H., & Mowrer, W. Enuresis: A method for its study and treatment. *American Journal of Orthopsychiatry,* 1938, **8,** 436-447. *(19, 447)*

Mowrer, O. H., & Ullman, A. Time as a determinant of integrative learning. *Psychological Review,* 1945, **52,** 61-90. *(273)*

Mucha, T., & Reinhardt, R. Conversion reactions in student aviators. *American Journal of Psychiatry,* 1970, **127,** 493-497. *(262)*

Mulholland, T. Variations in the response duration curve of successive cortical activation by a feedback stimulus. *Electroencephalography & Clinical Neurophysiology,* 1964, **16,** 394-395. *(426)*

Murray, H. A. *Explorations in personality.* New York: Oxford, 1938. *(138)*

Murray, J. B. Drug addiction. *Journal of General Psychology,* 1967, **77,** 41-68. *(347)*

Murstein, B. *Theory and research in projective techniques.* New York: Wiley, 1965. *(268)*

Musick, J., & Luckey, R. A token economy for moderately and severely retarded. *Mental Retardation,* 1970, **8,** 35-36. *(485)*

Myers, D., & Grant, G. A study of depersonalization in students. *British Journal of Psychiatry,* 1971, **121,** 59-65. *(266)*

Naeye, R., Diener, M., Harcke, H., & Blanc, W. Relation of poverty and race to birth weight and organ cell structure in the newborn. *Pediatric Research,* 1971, **5,** 17-22. *(481)*

Nakano, K., & Tyler, H. A double-blind study of the effects of levodopa in Parkinson's disease. *Neurology,* 1971, **21,** 1969-1974. *(503)*

Narasimhachari, N., Heller, B., Spaide, J., Haskovec, L., Fujimori, M., Tabushi, K., & Himwich, H. E. Comparative effects of tranylcypromine and cysteine on normal controls and schizophrenic patients. *Life Sciences,* 1970, **9,** 1021-1032. *(184)*

Nathan, P. E. *Cues, decisions and diagnoses.* New York: Academic, 1967. *(120, 127, 139, 496)*

Nathan, P. E. A systems analytic model of diagnosis V: The diagnostic validity of disordered consciousness. *Journal of Clinical Psychology,* 1969, **25,** 243-246. *(139, 332)*

Nathan, P. E., Andberg, M. M., Behan, P. O., & Patch, V. D. Thirty-two observers and one patient: A study of diagnostic reliability. *Journal of Clinical Psychology,* 1969, **25,** 9-15. *(119, 120)*

Nathan, P. E., Goldman, M. S. Lisman, S. A., & Taylor, H. A. Alcohol and alcoholics: A behavioral approach. *Transactions of the New York Academy of Science,* 1972, **34,** 602-627. *(331)*

Nathan, P. E., Gould, C., Zare, N., & Roth, M. A systems analytic model of diagnosis VI: Improved diagnostic validity from median data. *Journal of Clinical Psychology,* 1969, **25,** 370-375. *(169, 170, 259, 265, 267)*

Nathan, P. E., & O'Brien, J. S. An experimental analysis of the behavior of alcoholics and non-alcoholics during prolonged experimental drinking: A necessary precursor of behavior therapy? *Behavior Therapy,* 1971, **2,** 455-476. *(331, 335)*

Nathan, P. E., O'Brien, J. S., & Lowen-stein, I. M. Operant studies of chronic alcoholism: Interaction of alcohol and alcoholics. In P. J. Creaven, & M. K. Roach (Eds.), *Biological Aspects of Alcohol.* Austin: University of Texas Press, 1971. *(335)*

Nathan, P. E., Robertson, P., & Andberg, M. M. A systems analytic model of diagnosis IV: The diagnostic validity of abnormal affective behavior. *Journal of Clinical Psychology,* 1969, **25,** 235-242. *(156, 233)*

Nathan, P. E., Samaraweera, A., Andberg, M., & Patch, V. Syndromes of psychosis and psychoneurosis. *Archives of General Psychiatry,* 1968, **19,** 704-716. *(166, 400)*

Nathan, P. E., Schneller, P., & Lindsley, O. R. Direct measurement of communication during psychiatric admission interviews. *Behaviour Research and Therapy,* 1964, **2,** 49-57. *(208)*

Nathan, P. E., Simpson, H. F., Andberg, M. M., & Patch, V. D. A systems analytic model of diagnosis III: The diagnostic validity of abnormal cognitive behavior. *Journal of Clinical Psychology,* 1969, **25,** 120-130. *(156, 233)*

Nathan, P. E., Zare, N., Simpson, H. F., & Andberg, M. M. A systems analytic model of diagnosis I: The diagnostic validity of abnormal psychomotor behavior. *Journal of Clinical Psychology,* 1969, **25,** 3-9. *(169, 170, 233)*

National Clearinghouse for Mental Health Information. *Mental health directory.* Bethesda, Md.: National Institute of Mental Health, 1968. *(42)*

National Commission on Marihuana and Drug Abuse. *Marihuana: A signal of misunderstanding.* New York: New American Library, 1972. *(347, 348, 353, 354)*

Neisworth, J. T., & Moore, F. Operant treatment of asthmatic responding with the parent as therapist. *Behavior Therapy,* 1972, **3,** 95-99. *(429, 430)*

Nemiah, J. Obsessive-compulsive reaction. In A. Freedman & H. Kaplan (Eds.), *Comprehensive textbook of psychiatry.* Baltimore: Williams & Wilkins, 1967. *(265)*

Neuhaus, E. Training the mentally retarded for competitive employment. *Exceptional Children,* 1967, **33,** 625-628. *(486)*

Neuman, C. P., & Tamerin, J. S. The treatment of adult alcoholics and teen-age drug addicts in one hospital: A comparison and critical appraisal of factors related to outcome. *Quarterly Journal of Studies on Alcohol,* 1971, **32,** 82-93. *(352)*

Newman, H. H., Freeman, F. N., & Holzinger, K. J. *Twins: A study of heredity and environment.* Chicago: University of Chicago Press, 1937. *(292)*

Ney, P., Palvesky, A., & Markley, J. Relative effectiveness of operant conditioning and play therapy in childhood schizophrenia. *Journal of Autism and Childhood Schizophrenia,* 1971, **1,** 337-349. *(461)*

Nielsen, J. The XYY syndrome in a mental hospital. *British Journal of Criminology,* 1968, **8,** 186-203. *(410)*

Nielsen, J. Prevalence and a 2½ years incidence of chromosome abnormalities among all males in a forensic psychiatric clinic. *British Journal of Psychiatry,* 1971, **119,** 503-512. *(410)*

Nowacki, C. M., & Poe, C. A. The concept of mental health as related to sex of person perceived. *Journal of Consulting and Clinical Psychology,* 1973, **40,** 160. *(49)*

Nowlis, D. P., & Kamiya, J. The control of electroencephalographic alpha rhythm through auditory feedback and the associated mental activity. *Psychophysiology,* 1970, **6,** 476-484. *(426)*

O'Brien, J. S., Raynes, A. E., & Patch, V. D. Treatment of heroin addiction with aversion therapy, relaxation training and systematic desensitization. *Behaviour Research and Therapy,* 1972, **10,** 77-80. *(353)*

Offord, D. The natural histories of schizophrenia, depressive disorder and psychopathy: Current status. *Psychosomatics,* 1971, **12,** 179-185. *(456)*

Okulitch, P. V., & Marlatt, G. A. Effects of varied extinction conditions with alcoholics and social drinkers. *Journal of Abnormal Psychology,* 1972, **79,** 205-211. *(331)*

Olds, J., & Milner, R. Positive reinforcement produced by electrical stimulation of septal area and other regions of rat brain. *Journal of Comparative and Physiological Psychology,* 1954, **47,** 419-427. *(67-68)*

O'Leary, K. D. Behavior modification in the classroom: A rejoinder to Winett and Winkler. *Journal of Applied Behavior Analysis,* 1972, **5,** 505-510. *(212)*

O'Leary, K. D., Becker, W. C., Evans, M. B., & Saudargas, R. A. A token reinforcement program in a public school: A replication and systematic analysis. *Journal of Applied Behavior Analysis,* 1969, **2,** 2-13. *(212)*

O'Leary, K. D., & Drabman, R. Token reinforcement programs in the classroom: A review. *Psychological Bulletin,* 1971, **6,** 379-398. *(212)*

Olive, H. Psychoanalysts' opinions of psychologists' reports: 1952 and 1970. *Journal of Clinical Psychology,* 1972, **28,** 50-54. *(129)*

Oltman, J., & Friedman, S. Parental deprivation in psychiatric conditions, III. *Diseases of the Nervous System,* 1967, **28,** 298-303. *(410)*

Ortigues, M. C., Martino, P., & Collomb, H. Données culturelles et psychiatries de l'enfant dans la pratique clinique au Sénégal. *Acta Paedopsychiatrica,* 1969, **36,** 104-114. *(12)*

Osborne, T. R., & Sanders, W. B. Rorschach characteristics of duodenal ulcer patients. *Journal of Clinical Psychology,* 1950, **6,** 258-262. *(422)*

Osmond, H., & Smythies, J. Schizophrenia: A new approach. *Journal of Mental Science,* 1952, **98,** 309-315. *(183)*

Ostow, M. The complementary roles of psychoanalysis and drug therapy. In P. Solomon (Ed.), *Psychiatric drugs.* New York: Grune & Stratton, 1966. *(243)*

Outpatient Psychiatric Clinics. *Special Statistical Report, 1961.* Bethesda, Md.: National Institute of Mental Health, 1963. *(165, 169)*

Overall, J. E., & Gorham, D. Organicity versus old age in objective and projective test performance. *Journal of Consulting and Clinical Psychology,* 1972, **39,** 98-105. *(501)*

Overall, J. E., Henry, B. W., & Markett, J. R. Validity of an empirically derived phenomenonological typology. *Journal of Psychiatric Research,* 1972, **9,** 87-99. *(183)*

Overall, J. E., & Patrick, J. H. Unitary alcoholism factor and its personality correlates. *Journal of Abnormal Psychology,* 1972, **79,** 303-309. *(332)*

Owen, D. The 47, XYY male: A review. *Psychological Bulletin,* 1972, **78,** 209-233. *(410)*

Pahnke, W. N. The experimental use of psychedelic (LSD) psychotherapy. *International Journal of Clinical Pharmacology, Therapeutics & Toxicology,* 1971, **4,** 446-454. *(345)*

Paige, J. Quest for sexual identity. *Douglass College Caellian,* 1973, **34,** No. 30:1. *(377)*

Painting, D. The performance of psychopathic individuals under conditions of partial positive and negative reinforcement. *Journal of Abnormal and Social Psychology,* 1961, **62,** 353-358. *(409)*

Pare, C. M. B. Homosexuality and chromosomal sex. *Journal of Psychosomatic Research,* 1956, **1,** 247-251. *(370)*

Pare, C. M. B. Etiology of homosexuality: Genetic and chromosomal aspects. In J. Marmor (Ed.), *Sexual inversion.* New York: Basic Books, 1965. *(370)*

Parekh, U., Pherwani, A., Udani, P., & Mukherjee, S. Brain weight and head circumference in fetus, infant and children of different nutritional and socio-economic groups. *Indian Pediatrics,* 1970, **7,** 347-358. *(507)*

Parsons, O., Vega, A., & Burns, J. Different psychological effects of lateralized brain damage. *Journal of Consulting and Clinical Psychology,* 1969, **33,** 551-557. *(499)*

Pasamanick, B. On the neglect of diagnosis. *American Journal of Orthopsychiatry,* 1963, **33,** 397-398. *(139)*

Paul, G. L. Outcome of systematic desensitization. I: Background,

procedures, and uncontrolled reports of individual treatment. In C. M. Franks (Ed.), *Behavior therapy: Appraisal and status.* New York: McGraw-Hill 1969 (a). *(310, 318)*

Paul, G. L. Outcome of systematic desensitization. II: Controlled investigations of individual treatment, technique variations and current status. In C. M. Franks (Ed.), *Behavior therapy: Appraisal and status.* New York: McGraw-Hill, 1969. (b) *(310)*

Paul, N. L. Effects of playback on family members of their own previously recorded conjoint therapy material. *Psychiatric Research Report,* 1966, **20,** 175-185. *(304-306)*

Paulson, G. W., & Gottlieb, G. A longitudinal study of the electroencephalographic arousal response in depressed patients. *Journal of Nervous and Mental Disease,* 1961, **133,** 524-528. *(235)*

Pavlov, I. P. *Lectures on conditioned reflexes.* (Trans. by W. H. Gantt) New York: International Universities Press, 1928. *(194, 258)*

Pavlov, I. P. *Conditioned reflexes and psychiatry.* (Trans. by W. H. Gantt) New York: International Universities Press, 1941. *(194)*

Payne, R. Disorders of thinking. In C. Costello (Ed.), *Symptoms of psychopathology.* New York: Wiley, 1970. *(172, 173)*

Payne, R., Caird, W., & Laverty, S. Overinclusive thinking and delusions in schizophrenic patients. *Journal of Abnormal and Social Psychology,* 1964, **68,** 562-566. *(173)*

Payne, R. W., & Hewlett, J. H. G. Thought disorder in psychotic patients. In H. V. Eysenck (Ed.), *Experiments in personality,* Vol. II. London: Routledge and Kegan Paul, 1960. *(168)*

Pearson, P. Scientific and technical aims. In S. Scrimshaw & J. Gordon (Eds.), *Malnutrition, learning and behavior.* Cambridge, Mass.: M.I.T., 1968. *(506)*

Peck, M. L., & Schrut, A. *Suicidal behavior among college students.* Washington, D.C.: United States Government Printing Office, 1971. *(240)*

Pelicier, Y. La psychologie des peuples et la psychiatrie. *Revue de*

Psychologie des Peuples, 1968, **23,** 288–302. *(12)*

Penfield, W., & Roberts, L. *Speech and brain mechanisms.* Princeton, N.J.: Princeton, 1959. *(497)*

Penick, S. B., Carrier, R. N., & Sheldon, J. B. Metronidazole in the treatment of alcoholism. *American Journal of Psychiatry,* 1969, **125,** 1063–1066. *(336)*

Perloff, W. H. Hormones and homosexuality. In J. Marmor (Ed.), *Sexual inversion.* New York: Basic Books, 1965. *(370)*

Perlstein, M. Infantile cerebral palsy. *Advances in Pediatrics,* 1955, **7,** 209–248. *(476)*

Perrett, L. F. Immediate and background contextual effects in clinical judgment. *Dissertation Abstracts International,* 1972, **32,** 4224. *(123)*

Persons, R. W., & Marks, P. A. The violent 4-3 MMPI personality type. *Journal of Consulting and Clinical Psychology,* 1971, **36,** 189–196. *(349)*

Pervin, L. A. *Personality: Theory, assessment, and research.* New York: Wiley, 1970. *(139)*

Philip, R. J. An experimental investigation of suggestion and relaxation in asthmatics. Unpublished doctoral dissertation. Kingston, Ont.: Queens University, 1970. *(425)*

Phillips, E., Phillips, E., Fixen, D., & Wolf, M. Achievement place: Modification of the behaviors of pre-delinquent boys with a token economy. *Journal of Applied Behavior Analysis,* 1971, **4,** 45–59. *(462–463)*

Phillips, L., & Draguns, J. G. Classification of behavior disorders. In *Annual review of psychology.* Palo Alto, Calif.: Annual Reviews, 1971. *(120, 124)*

Piers, E. Parent prediction of children's self-concept. *Journal of Consulting and Clinical Psychology,* 1972, **38,** 428–433. *(443)*

Pilowsky, I. Dimensions of hypochondriasis. *British Journal of Psychiatry,* 1967, **113,** 89–93. *(267)*

Pincus, G., & Hoagland, H. Adrenal cortical responses to stress in normal men and in those with personality disorders. I: Some stress responses in normal and psychotic subjects. *American Journal of Psychiatry,* 1950, **106,** 641–650. *(174)*

Piotrowski, Z. The Rorschach inkblot method in organic disturbances of the central nervous system. *Journal of Nervous and Mental Disease,* 1937, **86,** 525–537. *(137, 499)*

Pitts, F. N. The biochemistry of anxiety. *Scientific American,* 1969, **220,** 69–75. *(293)*

Pitts, F. N. & McClure, J. N. Lactate metabolism in anxiety neurosis. *New England Journal of Medicine,* 1967, **277,** 1329–1336. *(270)*

Plummer, G. Anomalies occurring in children exposed *in utero* to the atomic bomb in Hiroshima. *Pediatrics,* 1952, **10,** 687–693. *(477)*

Pokorny, A. D. Suicide rates in various psychiatric disorders. *Journal of Nervous and Mental Diseases,* 1964, **139,** 499–506. *(238)*

Pollack, M., & Hornabrook, R. The prevalence, natural history and dementia of Parkinson's disease. *Brain,* 1966, **89,** 429–448. *(503)*

Pope, B., Blass, T., Siegman, A., & Raher, J. Anxiety and depression in speech. *Journal of Consulting and Clinical Psychology,* 1970, **35,** 128–133. *(270)*

Pope, B., Siegman, A., & Blass, T. Anxiety and speech in the initial interview. *Journal of Consulting and Clinical Psychology,* 1970, **35,** 233–238. *(260)*

Porter, R. W., Brady, J. V., Conrad, D., Mason, J. W., Galambos, R., & Rioch, D. M. Some experimental observations on gastrointestinal lesions in behaviorally conditioned monkeys. *Psychosomatic Medicine,* 1958, **20,** 379–394. *(420)*

Poser, E. G., & Lee, S. G. Thematic content associated with two gastrointestinal disorders. *Psychosomatic Medicine,* 1963, **25,** 162–173. *(422)*

Potkay, C. R., & Ward, E. F. Clinical judgment under varied informational conditions: Rorschach, personal data and best guess. *Journal of Consulting and Clinical Psychology,* 1972, **39,** 513. *(138)*

Poussaint, A. F. Emotional factors in psoriasis: Report of a case. *Psychosomatics,* 1963, **4,** 199–202. *(420)*

Prichard, J. C. *Treatise on insanity.* London: Gilbert & Piper, 1835. *(399)*

Prien, R. F., Klett, C. J., & Caffey, E. M. *A comparison of lithium carbonate and imipramine in the prevention of affective episodes in recurrent affective illness.* Perry Point, Md.: Central Neuropsychiatric Laboratory, Veterans Administration, 1973. *(200, 242)*

Prince, M. *The dissociation of a personality.* New York: Longmans, Green, 1925. *(262)*

Pritchard, M. Homosexuality and genetic sex. *Journal of Mental Science,* 1962, **108,** 616–123. *(370, 399)*

Quay, H. C., & Hunt, W. A. Psychopathy, neuroticism and verbal conditioning: A replication and extension. *Journal of Consulting Psychology,* 1965, **29,** 283. *(409)*

Quinlan, D., Harrow, M., Tucker, G., & Carlson, K. Varieties of disordered thinking on the Rorschach: Findings in schizophrenic and non-schizophrenic patients. *Journal of Abnormal Psychology,* 1972, **79,** 47–53. *(171)*

Rabin, A. I. Diagnostic use of intelligence tests. In B. B. Wolman (Ed.), *Handbook of clinical psychology.* New York: McGraw-Hill, 1965. *(129)*

Rabin, A. I., & Guertin, W. H. Research with the Wechsler-Bellevue Test 1945–1950. *Psychological Bulletin,* 1951, **48,** 211–248. *(129)*

Rachman, S. Sexual fetishism: An experimental analogue. *Psychological Record,* 1967, **16,** 293–296. *(374, 385)*

Rachman, S. *Phobias: Their nature and control.* Springfield, Ill.: Charles C Thomas, 1968. *(314, 385)*

Rachman, S. Clinical applications of observational learning, imitation and modeling. *Behavior Therapy,* 1972, **3,** 379–397. *(314)*

Rachman, S., & Hodgson, S. Experimentally-induced 'sexual fetishism': Replication and development. *Psychological Record,* 1968, **18,** 25–27. *(373)*

Rachman, S., Hodgson, R., & Marks, I. M. The treatment of chronic obsessive-compulsive neurosis. *Behaviour Research and Therapy,* 1971, **9,** 237–248. *(314)*

Rachman, S., & Teasdale, J. *Aversion therapy and behaviour disorders: An analysis.* Coral Gables, Fla.: University of Miami Press, 1969. *(388)*

Rackensperger, W., & Feinberg, A. M. Treatment of a severe hand-washing compulsion by systematic desensitization: A case report. *Journal of Behavior Therapy and Experimental Psychiatry,* 1972, **3,** 123–128. *(309)*

Rado, S. The problem of melancholia. *International Journal of Psycho-analysis,* 1928, **9,** 420–438. *(230)*

Rado, S. *Psychoanalysis of behavior.* New York: Grune & Stratton, 1956. *(372)*

Randell, J. Indications for sex reassignment surgery. *Archives of Sexual Behavior,* 1971, **1,** 153–161. *(383)*

Ransonhoff, J., Shulman, K., & Fishman, R. Hydrocephalus: A review of etiology and treatment. *Journal of Pediatrics,* 1960, **56,** 399–411. *(477)*

Rapaport, D., Gill, M., & Schafer, R. *Diagnostic psychological testing.* Vol. I. Chicago: Year Book Medical Publishers, 1945. *(129, 268)*

Rapaport, D., Gill, M., & Schafer, R. *Diagnostic psychological testing.* Vol. II. Chicago: Year Book Publishers, 1946. *(171)*

Rappaport, H. Modification of avoidance behavior: Expectancy, autonomic reactivity, and verbal report. *Journal of Consulting and Clinical Psychology,* 1972, **39,** 404–414. *(291)*

Rappaport, J., Gross, T., & Lepper, C. Modeling, sensitivity training, and instruction. *Journal of Consulting and Clinical Psychology,* 1973, **40,** 99–107. *(314)*

Rathus, S. A. An experimental investigation of assertive training in a group setting. *Journal of Behavior Therapy and Experimental Psychiatry,* 1972, **3,** 81–86. *(309)*

Ravensborg, M. R. An operant conditioning approach to increasing interpersonal awareness among chronic schizophrenics. *Journal of Clinical Psychology,* 1972, **28,** 411–413. *(212)*

Raymond, M. J. Case of fetishism treated by aversion therapy. *British Medical Journal,* 1956, **2,** 854–857. *(388)*

Razin, A. M. A-B variable in psychotherapy: A critical review. *Psychological Bulletin,* 1971, **75,** 1–21. *(300)*

Rees, J. (Ed.) *The case of Rudolph Hess.* New York: Norton, 1948. *(160, 171)*

Rees, W. L. Constitutional factors and abnormal behavior. In H. J. Eysenck (Ed.), *Handbook of abnormal psychology.* New York: Basic Books, 1960. *(227)*

Rehm, L. P., & Marston, A. R. Reduction of social anxiety through modification of self-reinforcement. *Journal of Consulting and Clinical Psychology,* 1968, **32,** 565–574. *(315)*

Reid, L. D. Processes of fear reduction in systematic desensitization: An addendum to Wilson and Davison (1971). *Psychological Bulletin,* 1973, **79,** 107–109. *(290)*

Reiss, I. L. *The social context of premarital sexual permissiveness.* New York: Holt, 1967. *(376)*

Reitan, R., & Fitzhugh, K. Behavioral deficits in groups with cerebral vascular lesions. *Journal of Consulting and Clinical Psychology,* 1971, **37,** 215–223. *(499)*

Renik, O. Awareness of the back of the body and homosexual impulses. *Perceptual and Motor Skills,* 1971, **33,** 1268. *(285)*

Rennie, T. Prognosis in manic-depressive psychoses. *American Journal of Psychiatry,* 1942, **98,** 801–814. *(238)*

Resnick, J. H., & Kendra, J. M. Predictive value of the "Scale for assessing suicide risk" (SASR) with hospitalized psychiatric patients. *Journal of Clinical Psychology,* 1973, **29,** 187–190. *(238)*

Rice, L. N., & Gaylin, N. L. Personality processes reflected in client vocal style and Rorschach performance. *Journal of Consulting and Clinical Psychology,* 1973, **40,** 133–138. *(137)*

Richardson, E. L. *Marihuana and health: 2nd Annual report to Congress from the Secretary of HEW.* Washington, D.C.: Department of Health, Education, and Welfare, 1972. *(354)*

Rickels, K., Cattell, R. S., Weise, C., Gray, B., Yee, R., Mallin, A., & Aaronson, H. G. Controlled psychopharmacological research in private psychiatric practice. *Psychopharmacology,* 1966, **9,** 228–306. *(318)*

Rimland, B. *Infantile autism.* New York: Appleton, 1964. *(451–453)*

Rimon, R., Steinback, A., & Huhmar, E. Electromyographic findings in depressive patients. *Journal of Psychosomatic Research,* 1966, **10,** 159–170. *(236)*

Risley, T., & Hart, B. Developing correspondence between the nonverbal and verbal behavior of preschool children. *Journal of Applied Behavior Analysis,* 1968, **1,** 267–281. *(484)*

Risley, T., & Reynolds, N. Emphasis as a prompt for verbal imitation. *Journal of Applied Behavior Analysis,* 1970, **3,** 221–222 *(484)*

Ritter, A. & Eron, L. The use of the TAT to differentiate normal from abnormal groups. *Journal of Abnormal and Social Psychology,* 1952, **47,** 147–158. *(268)*

Roberts, C., & Perry, R. A total token economy. *Mental Retardation,* 1970, **8,** 15–18. *(485)*

Roberts, S. V. Charlie Manson: One man's family. *New York Times Biographical Edition* 7 Ja. New York: The New York Times Company, 1970. *(396–397)*

Roberts, W. Normal and abnormal depersonalization. *Journal of Mental Science,* 1960, **106,** 478–493. *(266)*

Robins, E. Antisocial and dysocial personality disorders. In A. Freedman & H. Kaplan (Eds.), *Comprehensive textbook of psychiatry.* Baltimore: Williams & Wilkins, 1967. *(407)*

Robins, E., Gassner, S., Kayes, J., Wilkinson, R. H., & Murphy, G. E. The communication of suicidal intent: A study of 134 consecutive cases of successful (completed) suicide. *American Journal of Psychiatry,* 1959, **115,** 724–733. *(239)*

Robins, E., Smith, K., & Lowe, I. P. Discussion of clinical studies with taraxein. In H. A. Abramson (Ed.), *Neuropharmacology: Transactions of the fourth conference.* New York: Josiah Macy Jr. Foundation, 1957. *(185)*

Robins, L. N. *Deviant children grown up.* Baltimore: Williams & Wilkins, 1966. *(409, 410–411, 456)*

Robins, L. N., Murphy, G., Woodruff, R., & King, L. Adult psychiatric status of black school boys. *Archives of General Psychiatry,* 1971, **24,** 338–345. *(46)*

Robinson, H., & Robinson, N. *The mentally retarded child.* New York: McGraw-Hill, 1965. *(473, 475, 477, 479)*

Robinson, J. C., & Lewinsohn, P. M. Behavior modification of speech characteristics in a chronically depressed man. *Behavior Therapy,* 1973, **4,** 150–152. *(245)*

Rodgers, D. A., & McClearn, G. E. Mouse strain differences in preference for various concentrations of alcohol. *Quarterly Journal of Studies on Alcohol,* 1962, **23,** 26–33. *(331)*

Roe, A. Children of alcoholic parentage raised in foster homes. In *Alcoholism, science and society.* New Haven: Yale Summer School of Alcohol Studies, 1945. *(187)*

Roebuck, J., & Spray, S. L. The cocktail lounge: A study of heterosexual relations in a public organization. *American Journal of Sociology,* 1967, **72,** 388–398. *(385)*

Rogers, C. R. *Client-centered therapy.* Boston: Houghton Mifflin, 1951. *(303)*

Rogers, C. R. *On becoming a person.* Boston: Houghton Mifflin, 1961. *(301–302)*

Rogers, C. R., Gendlin, G. T., Kiesler, D. V., & Traux, C. B. *The therapeutic relationship and its impact. A study of psychotherapy with schizophrenics.* Madison: University of Wisconsin Press, 1967. *(302)*

Rohan, W. P. MMPI changes in hospitalized alcoholics: A second study. *Quarterly Journal of Studies on Alcohol,* 1972, **33,** 65–76. *(332)*

Rohan, W. P., Tatro, R. L., & Rotman, S. R. MMPI changes in alcoholics during hospitalization. *Quarterly Journal of Studies on Alcohol,* 1969, **30,** 389–400. *(332)*

Roos, P., & Oliver, M. Evaluation of operant conditioning with institutionalized retarded children. *American Journal of Mental Deficiency,* 1969, **74,** 325–330. *(485)*

Rorschach, H. *Psychodiagnostik.* Bern and Leipzig: Ernst Bircher Verlag, 1921. *(135)*

Rosanoff, A., Handy, L. M., & Plesett, I. R. The etiology of child behavior difficulties, juvenile delinquency, and adult criminality, with special reference to their occurrence in twins. *Psychiatric Monographs,* 1941, No. 1. *(410)*

Rose, J. T., Leahy, M. R., Martin, I. C. A., & Westhead, T. T. A comparison of nortriptyline and amitriptyline in depression. *British Journal of Psychiatry,* 1965, **111,** 1101–1103. *(234)*

Rosen, B., Barn, A., & Cramer, M. Demographic and diagnostic characteristics of psychiatric out-patient clinics in the U.S.A. *American Journal of Orthopsychiatry,* 1964, **34,** 455–468. *(445)*

Rosen, G., Rosen, E., & Reid, J. Cognitive desensitization and avoidance behavior: A reevaluation. *Journal of Abnormal Psychology,* 1972, **80,** 176–182. *(291)*

Rosencrans, C., & Schaeffer, H. Bender-Gestalt time and score differences between matched groups of hospitalized psychiatric and brain damaged patients. *Journal of Clinical Psychology,* 1969, **25,** 409–410. *(268)*

Rosengarten, H., Piotrowski, A., Romaszewska, K., Szemis, A., Jus, A., & Matsumoto, H. The occurrence of N,N-dimenthyltryptamine and bufotenine in schizophrenic patients without MAO blockage and methionine loading. Paper presented at the meeting of the International Congress of Neuropharmacology, 1970. *(184)*

Rosenhan, D. L. On being sane in insane places. *Science,* 1973, **179,** 250–258. *(16)*

Rosenthal, D. An historical and methodological review of genetic studies of schizophrenia. In *The origins of schizophrenia,* Excerpta Medica International Congress Series No. 151, 1967. *(186)*

Rosenthal, D. *Genetic theory and abnormal behavior.* New York: McGraw-Hill, 1970. *(187)*

Rosenthal, D. A program of research on heredity in schizophrenia. *Behavioral Science,* 1971, **16,** 191–201. (b) *(187)*

Rosenthal, D., Wender, P. H., Kety, S. S., Welner, J. & Schulsinger, F. The adopted-away offspring of schizophrenics. *American Journal of Psychiatry,* 1971, **128,** 307–311. *(187)*

Rosenwald, G. C. Effectiveness of defenses against anal impulse arousal. *Journal of Consulting and Clinical Psychology,* 1972, **39,** 292–298. *(285)*

Rosenzweig, S. A transvaluation of psychotherapy—A reply to Hans Eysenck. *Journal of Abnormal and Social Psychology,* 1954, **49,** 298–304. *(317)*

Ross, D. M., Ross, S. A., & Evans, T. A. The modification of extreme social withdrawal by modeling with guided participation. *Journal of Behavior Therapy and Experimental Psychiatry,* 1971, **2,** 273–280. *(314)*

Rotenberg, M., & Diamond, B. The biblical conception of psychopathy: The law of the stubborn and rebellious son. *Journal of the History of the Behavioral Sciences,* 1972, **12,** 29–38. *(399)*

Routh, D. K., & King, K. M. Social class bias in clinical judgement. *Journal of Consulting and Clinical Psychology,* 1972, **38,** 202–207. *(123)*

Rubin, R. T., & Mandell, A. J. Adrenal cortical activity in pathological emotional states: A review. *American Journal of Psychiatry,* 1966, **123,** 387–400. *(229)*

Rudestam, K. E. Stockholm and Los Angeles: A cross-cultural study of the communication of suicidal intent. *Journal of Consulting and Clinical Psychology,* 1971, **36,** 82–90. *(238)*

Russell, E. WAIS factor analysis with brain-damaged subjects using criterion measures. *Journal of Consulting and Clinical Psychology,* 1972, **39,** 133–139. *(499)*

Russell, E., Neuringer, C., & Goldstein, G. *Assessment of brain damage.* New York: Interscience-Wiley, 1970. *(499)*

Russell, G. F. M. Body weight and balance of water, sodium, and potassium in depressed patients given electroconvulsive therapy. *Clinical Science,* 1960, **19,** 327–336. *(229)*

Ryan, E., & Lakie, W. Competitive and noncompetitive performance in relation to achievement motive and manifest anxiety. *Journal of Personality and Social Psychology,* 1965, **1**, 342-345. *(270)*

Sachar, E. J. Corticosteroid responses to psychotherapy of depressions. *Archives of General Psychiatry,* 1967, **16**, 461-470. *(229)*

Sacks, O., Kohl, M., Messeloff, C., & Schwartz, W. Effects of levodopa in Parkinsonian patients with dementia. *Neurology,* 1972, **22**, 516-519. *(503)*

Sajwaj, T., Twardosz, S., & Burke, M. Side effects of extinction procedures in a remedial preschool. *Journal of Applied Behavior Analysis,* 1972, **5**, 163-176. *(212)*

Sali, J. & Amir, M. Personal factors influencing the retarded person's success at work: A report from Israel. *American Journal of Mental Deficiency,* 1971, **76**, 42-47. *(484)*

Sand, P. L. Performance of medical patient groups with and without brain damage on the Hovey(O) and Watson(Sc-O) MMPI scales. *Journal of Clinical Psychology,* 1973, **29**, 235-237. *(135)*

Sanderson, R. E., Campbell, D., & Laverty, S. G. An investigation of a new aversive conditioning treatment for alcoholism. *Quarterly Journal of Studies on Alcohol,* 1963, **24**, 261-275. *(338)*

Sandifer, M. G. Science and set in treatment decisions. *American Journal of Psychiatry,* 1972, **128**, 1140-1145. *(123)*

Sanes, J., & Zigler, E. Premorbid social competence in schizophrenia. *Journal of Abnormal Psychology,* 1971, **78**, 140-144. *(169)*

Sarbin, T. E., & Mancuso, J. C. Failure of a moral enterprise: Attitudes of the public toward mental illness. *Journal of Consulting and Clinical Psychology,* 1970, **35**, 159-173. *(5)*

Sarbin, T. E., & Mancuso, J. C. Paradigms and moral judgements: Improper conduct is not a disease. *Journal of Consulting and Clinical Psychology,* 1972, **39**, 6-8. *(15)*

Sarnoff, I. *Testing Freudian concepts: An experimental social approach.* New York: Springer, 1971. *(285)*

Sawrey, W. L., & Weiss, J. D. An experimental method of producing gastric ulcers. *Journal of Comparative and Physiological Psychology,* 1956, **49**, 269-270. *(425)*

Schachter, S. The interaction of cognitive and physiological determinants of emotional states. In L. Berkowitz (Ed.), *Advances in experimental social psychology.* New York: Academic, 1964. *(237, 291)*

Schachter, S., & Latane, B. Crime, cognition and the autonomic nervous system. In M. Jones (Ed.), *Nebraska symposium on motivation, 1964.* Lincoln: University of Nebraska Press, 1964. *(409-410)*

Schachter, S., & Singer, J. E. Cognitive, social, and physiological determinants of emotional state. *Psychological Review,* 1962, **69**, 379-399. *(237)*

Schachter, S., & Wheeler, L. Epinephrine, chlorpromazine, and amusement. *Journal of Abnormal and Social Psychology,* 1962, **65**, 121-128. *(237)*

Schaefer, H. H. Twelve-month follow-up of behaviorally trained ex-alcoholic social drinkers. *Behavior Therapy,* 1972, **3**, 286-289. *(340)*

Schafer, R. *The clinical application of psychological tests.* New York: International Universities Press, 1948. *(268)*

Schapira, K., Roth, M., Kerr, T., & Gurney, C. The prognosis of affective disorders: The differentiation of anxiety states from depressive illness. *British Journal of Psychiatry,* 1972, **121**, 175-181. *(267)*

Sharfman, M., & Clark, R. Delinquent adolescent girls. *Archives of General Psychiatry,* 1967, **17**, 441-447. *(450)*

Sheckel, C. L., & Boff, E. Behavioral effects of interacting imipramine and other drugs with d-amphetamine, cocaine, and tetrabenazine. *Psychopharmacology,* 1964, **5**, 198-208, *(230)*

Schiff, G., & Rauh, J. Rubella control. *American Journal of Diseases of Children,* 1971, **122**, 112-116. *(481)*

Schildkraut, J. J. The catecholamine hypothesis of affective disorders: A review of supporting evidence. *American Journal of Psychiatry,* 1965, **122**, 509-522. *(230)*

Schmidt, H. Test profiles as a diagnostic aid. In G. Welsh & W. Dahlstrom (Eds.), *Basic readings on the MMPI in psychology and medicine.* Minneapolis: University of Minnesota Press, 1963. *(268, 408)*

Schönfelder, T. Sexual trauma in childhood and its consequences. *Praxis Psychotherapie,* 1970, **15**, 12-20. *(368)*

Schreber, D. P. *Memoirs of my nervous illness.* (Trans. by J. Macalpine & R. Hunter) London: Dawson & Sons, 1955. *(2, 14, 160, 171, 188, 189)*

Schuham, A. Power relations in emotionally disturbed and normal family triads. *Journal of Abnormal Psychology,* 1970, **75**, 30-37. *(459)*

Schuham, A. Activity, talking time, and spontaneous agreement in disturbed and normal family interaction. *Journal of Abnormal Psychology,* 1972, **79**, 68-75. *(459)*

Schwab, J. J., Bialow, F., Holzer. C. E., Brown, J. M., & Stevenson, B. E. Sociocultural aspects of depression in medical inpatients. *Archives of General Psychiatry,* 1967, **17**, 533-538. *(235)*

Schwade, E. D., & Geiger, S. G. Abnormal electroencephalographic findings in severe behavior disorders. *Diseases of the Nervous System,* 1965, **17**, 307-317. *(408)*

Schwartz, G. E., Shapiro, D., & Tursky, B. Learned control of cardiovascular integration in man through operant conditioning. *Psychosomatic Medicine,* 1971, **33**, 57-62. *(426)*

Schwitzgebel, R. *Streetcorner research: An experimental approach to the juvenile deliquent.* Cambridge, Mass.: Harvard, 1965. *(412)*

Scott, W. A., & Johnson, R. C. Comparative validities of direct and indirect personality tests. *Journal of Consulting and Clinical Psychology,* 1972, **38**, 301-318. *(132)*

Scrignar, C. B. Food as the reinforcer in the outpatient treatment of anorexia nervosa. *Journal of Behavior Therapy and Experimental Psychiatry,* 1971, **2**, 31-36. *(428)*

Sears, R. R. Experimental studies of projection I: Attribution of traits. *Journal of Social Psychology,* 1936, **7**, 151-163. *(285)*

Seay, B., Hansen, E., & Harlow, H. F. Mother-infant separation in monkeys. *Journal of Child Psychology and Psychiatry,* 1962, **3**, 123-132. *(236, 384)*

Seay, B., & Harlow, H. F. Maternal separation in the rhesus monkey. *Journal of Nervous and Mental Disease,* 1965, **140,** 434-441. *(384)*

Secretary of Health, Education, and Welfare. *First special report to the U.S. Congress on alcohol and health.* Washington, D.C.: National Institute of Alcohol Abuse and Alcoholism, 1971. *(331)*

Sedman, G. Theories of depersonalization: A re-appraisal. *British Journal of Psychiatry,* 1970, **117,** 1-14. *(266)*

Sedova, J. Theatre and cabaret in the ghetto of Terezin. In F. Ehrmann (Ed.), *Terezin.* Prague: Council of Jewish Communities in the Czech Lands, 1965. *(33)*

Seiden, R. We're driving young blacks to suicide. *Psychology Today,* 1970, **4,** 24-28. *(239, 240)*

Seitz, F. C. Behavior modification techniques for treating depression: A survey and analysis. Paper presented at the Rocky Mountain Psychological Association Meeting, 1970. *(243)*

Seligman, M. E. For helplessness: Can we immunize the weak? *Psychology Today,* 1969, **3,** 42-44. *(237)*

Seligman, M. E. Learned helplessness. *Annual Review of Medicine,* 1972, **23,** 207-412. *(237)*

Selye, H. The physiology and pathology of exposure to stress. Montreal: ACTA, 1950. *(70-71)*

Selye, H. *The stress of life.* New York: McGraw-Hill, 1956. *(70-71, 292, 425)*

Sewell, W. H. Review of *Sexual behavior in the human female. American Sociological Review,* 1955, **20,** 584-587. *(376)*

Shagass, C., & Schwartz, M. Cerebral cortical reactivity in psychotic depressions. *Archives of General Psychiatry,* 1962, **6,** 235-242. *(235)*

Shakow, D. Psychological deficit in schizophrenia. *Behavioral Sciences,* 1963, **8,** 275-305. *(169)*

Shakow, D. On doing research in schizophrenia. *Archives of General Psychiatry,* 1969, **20,** 618-642. *(166)*

Shakow, D., & Rapaport, D. *The influence of Freud on American psychology.* New York: International Universities Press, 1964. *(285)*

Shapiro, D., Tursky, B., Gershon, E., & Stern, M. Effect of feedback and reinforcement on the control of human systolic blood pressure. *Science,* 1969, **163,** 588-590. *(425)*

Shapiro, D., Tursky, B., & Schwartz, G. E. Control of blood pressure in man by operant conditioning. *Circulation Research,* 1970, **271,** 27-32. (a) *(425)*

Shapiro, D., Tursky, B., & Schwartz, G. E. Differentiation of heart rate and blood pressure in man by operant conditioning. *Psychosomatic Medicine,* 1970, **32,** 417-423. (b) *(425)*

Shaw, D. M. Mineral metabolism, mania, and melancholia. *British Medical Journal,* 1966, **2,** 262-267. *(229)*

Shechtmen, A. Age patterns in children's psychiatric symptoms. *Child Development,* 1970, **41,** 683-693. (a) *(443)*

Shechtmen, A. Psychiatric symptoms observed in normal and disturbed children. *Journal of Clinical Psychology,* 1970, **26,** 38-41. *(455)*

Shechtmen, A. Psychiatric symptoms observed in normal and disturbed black children. *Journal of Clinical Psychology,* 1971, **27,** 445-447. *(443)*

Sheldon, W. H. The New York study of physical constitution and psychotic pattern. *Journal of the History of the Behavioral Sciences,* 1971, **7,** 115-126. *(72-73)*

Sheldon, W. H., Stevens, S., & Tucker, W. *The varieties of human physique.* New York: Harper, 1940. *(72-73)*

Shemberg, K., & Keeley, S. Psychodiagnostic training in the academic setting: Past and present. *Journal of Consulting and Clinical Psychology,* 1970, **34,** 205-211. *(129)*

Shentoub, S. A., & Mijolla, A. Note sur la particularité de "l'agir" dans la relation psychoanalytique avec la patient alcoolique chronique. *French Review of Psychoanalysis,* 1968, **32,** 1049-1053. *(338)*

Shields, J. Monozygotic twins brought up apart and brought up together. London: Oxford, 1962. *(292)*

Shields, J., & Gottesman, I. I. (Eds.) *Man, mind, and heredity: Selected papers of Eliot Slater on psychiatry and genetics.* Baltimore, Md.: Johns Hopkins, 1971. *(185)*

Shoben, E. Toward a concept of normal personality. *American Psychologist,* 1957, **12,** 183-189. *(7)*

Siegler, H., Osmond, H., & Man, H. Laing's models of madness. *British Journal of Psychiatry,* 1969, **115,** 947-958. *(193)*

Silber, A. An addendum to the technique of psychotherapy with alcoholics. *Journal of Nervous and Mental Disease,* 1970, **150,** 423-437. *(338)*

Silver, A. W. TAT and MMPI psychopathic deviate scale differences between delinquent and nondelinquent adolescents. *Journal of Consulting Psychology,* 1963, **27,** 370. *(408)*

Silverstein, A. An empirical test of the mongoloid stereotype. *American Journal of Mental Deficiency,* 1964, **68,** 493-497. *(480)*

Singer, B. D. Some implications of differential psychiatric treatment of Negro and white patients. *Social Science and Medicine,* 1967, **1,** 77-83. *(45)*

Skinner, B. F. *The behavior of organisms.* New York: Appleton-Century-Crofts, 1938. *(104)*

Skinner, B. F. A new method for the experimental analysis of the behavior of psychotic patients. *Journal of Nervous and Mental Disease,* 1954, **120,** 403-406. *(104, 207)*

Skinner, B. F. *Beyond freedom and dignity.* New York: Knopf, 1971. *(104)*

Skodak, M., & Skeels, H. M. A final follow-up study of one hundred adopted children. *Journal of Genetic Psychology,* 1949, **75,** 85-125. *(187)*

Slack, C. Experimenter-subject psychotherapy: A new method of introducing intensive office treatment in unreachable cases. *Mental Hygiene,* 1960, **44,** 238-256. *(412)*

Slater, E. Psychiatric and neurotic illness in twins. *Medical Research Council Special Report.* Series No. 278. London: Her Majesty's Stationery Office, 1953. *(227)*

Slater, E., & Beard, A. The schizophrenia-like psychoses of epilepsy. *British Journal of Psychiatry,* 1963, **109,** 95-150. *(510)*

Slater, E., & Roth, M. *Mayer-Gross clinical psychiatry.* Baltimore:

Williams & Wilkins, 1969. *(22, 202, 225)*

Slawson, P. F., Flynn, W. R., & Kollar, E. J. Psychological factors associated with the onset of diabetes mellitus. *Journal of the American Medical Association,* 1963, **185,** 166–170. *(422)*

Slosarska, M. & Zernicki, B. Synchronized sleep in the chronic pretrigeminal cat. *Acta Biologae Experimentalis,* 1969, **29,** 175. *(64)*

Small, I., Small, J., Alig, V., & Moore, D. Passive-aggressive personality disorder: A search for a syndrome. *American Journal of Psychiatry,* 1970, **126,** 973–983. *(405)*

Smart, R. G., & Fejer, D. Drug use among adolescents and their parents: Closing the generation gap in mood modification. *Journal of Abnormal Psychology,* 1972, **79,** 153–160. *(347)*

Smart, R. G., & Jones, D. Illicit LSD users: Their personality characteristics and psychopathology. *Journal of Abnormal Psychology,* 1970, **75,** 286–292. *(348)*

Smith, C. G. Alcoholics: Their treatment and their wives. *British Journal of Psychiatry,* 1969, **115,** 1039–1042. *(338)*

Smith, D. E. Killing in the rat: Its chemical basis in the lateral hypothalamus. *Dissertation Abstracts International,* 1971, **31,** 7648. *(55)*

Smith, L. H., Cline, M. J. & Hibbard, E. W. Changing drug patterns in the Haight-Ashbury, California. *Medicine,* 1969, **110,** 151–157. *(345)*

Smith, R. C. Item ambiguity in the 16 PF and MMPI: An assessment and comparison. *Journal of Consulting and Clinical Psychology,* 1972, **38,** 460. *(135)*

Snyder, F. Dynamic aspects of sleep disturbance in relation to mental illness. *Biological Psychiatry,* 1969, **1,** 119–130. *(235)*

Snyder, S. H., & Pert, C. B. Opiate receptor: Demonstration in nervous tissue. *Science,* 1973, **179,** 1011–1014. *(346)*

Sobell, M. B., & Sobell, L. C. Individualized behavior therapy for alcoholics. *Behavior Therapy,* 1973, **4,** 49–72. *(340)*

Socarides, C. W. A psychoanalytic study of the desire for sexual transformation ("transsexualism"): The plaster-of-paris man. *International Journal of Psychoanalysis,* 1970, **51,** 341–349. *(372)*

Sohler, A., Beck, R., & Novel, J. M. Mauve factor re-identified as 2,4-dimethyl-3-ethylpyrrole and its sedative effect on the CNS. *Nature,* 1970, **228,** 1318–1320. *(184)*

Sohler, A., Renz, R. H., Smith, S., & Kaufman, J. Significance of hydroxyskatole and mauve factor excretion in schizophrenia. *International Journal of Neuropsychiatry,* 1967, **3,** 327–331. *(184)*

Solomon, P., & Patch, V. D. *Handbook of psychiatry.* Los Altos, Calif.: Lange, 1971. *(202, 340, 343, 365, 426)*

Solomon, S. The neurological evaluation. In A. Freedman & H. Kaplan (Eds.), *Comprehensive textbook of psychiatry.* Baltimore: Williams & Wilkins, 1967. *(408)*

Sommer, R., & Witney, G. The chain of chronicity. *American Journal of Psychiatry,* 1961, **118,** 111–117. *(168)*

Sperry, R. W. Hemisphere deconnection and unity in conscious experience. *American Psychologist,* 1968, **23,** 723–733. *(66)*

Spielberger, C. D., Parker, J. B., & Becker, J. Conformity and achievement in remitted manic-depressive patients. *Journal of Nervous and Mental Disease,* 1963, **137,** 162–172. *(231)*

Spitzer, R. L., & Endicott, J. DIAGNO II: Further developments in a computer program for psychiatric diagnosis. *American Journal of Psychiatry,* 1969, **125,** (Suppl.), 12–20. *(124–127, 139)*

Spitzer, R. L., & Endicott, J. An integrated group of forms for automated psychiatric case records. *Archives of General Psychiatry,* 1971, **24,** 540–547. *(126)*

Sprenger, J., & Kraemer, H. *Malleus maleficarum.* (Trans. by M. Summers) New York: Benjamin Bloom, Inc., 1970. *(13)*

Srole, L., Langner, T. S., Michael, S. T., Opler, M. K., & Rennie, T. A. C. *Mental health in the metropolis: The midtown Manhattan study.* Vol. 1. New York: McGraw-Hill, 1962. *(36, 38, 39, 40)*

Stabenau, J. R., Creveling, C. R., & Daly, J. Common tea as a source for 3,4-dimethoxyphenylethyl-amine, or "pink spot" in the urine of schizophrenics and normals. Paper presented at the meeting of the International Congress of Neuropharmacology, 1970. *(184)*

Stachnik, T. J. The case against criminal penalties for illicit drug use. *American Psychologist,* 1972, **27,** 637–642. *(351)*

Stampfl, T. G., & Levis, D. J. Essentials of implosive therapy: A learning-theory-based psychodynamic behavioral therapy. *Journal of Abnormal Psychology,* 1967, **72,** 496–503. *(310–311)*

Stampfl, T. G., & Levis, D. J. Implosive therapy: A behavioral therapy? *Behaviour Research and Therapy,* 1968, **6,** 31–36. *(310–311)*

Staub, E. The effects of persuasion, modeling, and related influence procedures on delay of reward choices and attitudes. Unpublished doctoral dissertation, Stanford University, 1965. *(100)*

Steegman, A. T. *Examination of the nervous system.* Chicago: Year Book, 1970. *(499)*

Stekel, W. *Sexual aberrations: The phenomena of fetishism in relation to sex.* New York: Liveright, 1971. *(366)*

Stengel, E. Recent research into suicide and attempted suicide. *American Journal of Psychiatry,* 1962, **118,** 725–727. *(238)*

Stenstedt, A. Involutional melancholia: An etiologic, clinical and social study of endogenous depression in later life, with special reference to genetic factors. *Acta Psychiatrica Scandinavica,* Suppl. 1959, **127.** *(228)*

Stephens, J., & Kamp, M. On some aspects of hysteria: A clinical study. *Journal of Nervous and Mental Disease,* 1962, **134,** 305–315. *(261)*

Stevens, J., Mark, V., Erwin, F., Pacheco, P., & Suematsu, K. Deep temporal stimulation in man. *Archives of Neurology,* 1969, **21,** 157–169. *(510)*

Stoller, R. J. Transvestites' women. *American Journal of Psychiatry,* 1967, **129,** 333–339. *(373)*

Stoller, R. J., & Newman, L. E. The bisexual identity of transsexuals: Two case examples. *Archives of Sexual Behavior,* 1971, **1,** 17–28. *(383)*

Stone, Alan D. Psychiatry and the law. *Psychiatric Annals,* 1971, **1,** 19-43. *(22)*

Strauss, M. Behavioral differences between acute and chronic schizophrenics: Course of psychosis, effects of institutionalization, or sampling bias? *Psychological Bulletin,* 1973, **79,** 271-279. *(168)*

Stricker, L. J., Messick, S., & Jackson, D. N. Desirability judgments and self-reports as predictors of social behavior. *Journal of Experimental Research & Personality,* 1968, **3,** 151-167. *(132)*

Strupp, H. H. The outcome problem in psychotherapy: A rejoinder. *Psychotherapy,* 1964, **1,** 101. *(317)*

Sue, D. The role of relaxation in systematic desensitization. *Behaviour Research and Therapy,* 1972, **10,** 153-158. *(310)*

Sullivan, H. S. *Conceptions of modern psychiatry.* Washington, D.C.: William A. White Psychiatric Foundation, 1946. *(190)*

Sullivan, H. S. *The interpersonal theory of psychiatry.* New York: Norton, 1953. *(203, 372)*

Suomi, S. J. Repetitive peer separation of young monkeys: Effects of vertical chamber confinement during separations. *Journal of Abnormal Psychology,* 1973, **81,** 1-10. *(384)*

Suomi, S. J., Harlow, H. F., & Domek, C. J. Effect of repetitive infant-infant separation of young monkeys. *Journal of Abnormal Psychology,* 1970, **76,** 161-172. *(384)*

Sushinsky, L., & Bootzin, R. Cognitive desensitization as a model of systematic desensitization. *Behaviour Research and Therapy,* 1970, **8,** 29-33, *(291)*

Sutker, R. B. Personality differences and sociopathy in heroin addicts and nonaddict prisoners. *Journal of Abnormal Psychology,* 1971, **78,** 247-251. *(346)*

Szasz, T. S. The myth of mental illness. *American Psychologist,* 1960, **15,** 113-118. *(13, 17)*

Szasz, T. S. *Law, liberty, and psychiatry,* New York: Collier, 1968. *(18)*

Szasz, T. S. *The manufacture of madness: A comparative study of the inquisition and the mental health movement.* New York: Harper & Row, 1970. *(18)*

Takesada, M., Kakimoto, Y., Sano, I., & Kaneko, Z. 3,4 Dimethyoxyphenylethylamine and other amines in the urine of schizophrenic patients. *Nature,* 1963, **199,** 203-204. *(184)*

Talland, G. A. Effects of alcohol on performance in continuous attention tasks, *Psychosomatic Medicine,* 1966, **28,** 596. *(334)*

Talland, G. A., Mendelson, J. H., & Ryack, P. Experimentally induced chronic intoxication and withdrawal in alcoholics. Part 5: Tests of attention. *Quarterly Journal of Studies on Alcohol,* 1964, Suppl. **2,** 74-86. *(334)*

Tanner, B. A. A case report on the use of relaxation and systematic desensitization to control multiple compulsive behaviors. *Journal of Behavior Therapy and Experimental Psychiatry,* 1971, **2,** 267-272. *(309)*

Tate, B., & Baroff, G. Training the mentally retarded in the production of a complex product: A demonstration of work potential. *Exceptional Children,* 1967, **33,** 405-408. *(486)*

Taulbee, E., & Sisson, B. Configurational analysis of MMPI profiles of psychiatric groups. *Journal of Consulting Psychology,* 1957, **21,** 413-417. *(170)*

Taves, I. Is there a sleep walker in the house? *Today's Health,* 1969, **47,** 76. *(262-263)*

Taylor, D., & Falconer, M. Clinical, socio-economic, and psychological changes after temporal lobectomy for epilepsy. *British Journal of Psychiatry,* 1968, **114,** 1247-1261. *(510)*

Taylor, J. The relationship of anxiety to the conditioned eyelid response. *Journal of Experimental Psychology,* 1951, **41,** 81-92. *(270)*

Taylor, J. A personality scale of manifest anxiety. *Journal of Abnormal and Social Psychology,* 1953, **48,** 285-290. *(270)*

Taylor, J., & Spence, K. The motivational components of manifest anxiety: Drive and drive stimuli. In C. Spielberger (Ed.), *Anxiety and behavior.* New York: Academic, 1966. *(270)*

Taylor, W. J. History and pharmacology of psychedelic drugs. *International Journal of Clinical Pharmacology, Therapeutics, and Toxicology,* 1971, **5,** 51. *(345)*

Teicher, J. D. Why adolescents kill themselves. In *Mental health program reports,* No. 4. Washington, D.C.: National Institute of Mental Health, 1970. *(240)*

Teicher, J. D., & Jacobs, J. Adolescents who attempt suicide: Preliminary findings. *American Journal of Psychiatry,* 1966, **122,** 1248-1257. *(240)*

Telfer, M., Clark, G., Baker, D., & Richardson, C. Incidence of gross chromosomal errors among tall, criminal American males. *Science,* 1968, **159,** 1249-1250. *(410)*

Temoche, A., Pugh, T. F., & MacMahon, B. Suicide rates among current and former mental institution patients. *Journal of Nervous and Mental Disease,* 1964, 136, 124-130. *(238)*

Terhune, W. B. Phobic syndrome: Study of 86 patients with phobic reactions. *Archives of Neurology and Psychiatry,* 1949, **62,** 162-172. *(308)*

Terman, L. M. Kinsey's *Sexual behavior in the human male:* Some comments and criticisms. *Psychological Bulletin,* 1948, **45,** 443-459. *(376)*

Teuber, H. L. The premorbid personality and reaction to brain damage. *American Journal of Orthopsychiatry,* 1960, **30,** 322-329. *(512)*

Tharp, R. G., & Wetzel, R. J. *Behavior modification in the natural environment.* New York: Academic, 1969. *(140)*

Thelen, M. H., Varble, D. L., & Johnson, J. Attitudes of academic clinical psychologists toward projective techniques, *American Psychologist,* 1968, **23,** 517-521. *(129)*

Thigpen, C., & Cleckley, H. *Three faces of Eve.* New York: McGraw-Hill, 1957. *(262)*

Thomas, A., Chess, S., & Birch, H. *Temperament and behavior disorders in children.* New York: New York University Press, 1968. *(73-74)*

Thomas, A., & Sillen, S. *Racism and psychiatry.* New York: Brunner/Mazel, 1972. *(46, 47, 48)*

Thomas, C. B. Pathogenetic interrelations in hypertension and coronary artery disease. *Diseases of the Nervous System,* 1961, **22,** Monogr. Suppl. 39-45. *(422)*

Thomas, P. *Down these mean streets.* New York: New American Library, 1967. *(55-57, 60, 70, 325-326)*

Thompson, C. *Psychoanalysis: Evolution and development.* New York: Grove Press, 1950. *(301)*

Thompson, G. Acute and chronic alcholic conditions. In S. Arieti (Ed.), *American handbook of psychiatry. Vol. II.* New York: Basic Books, 1959. *(505-506)*

Thompson, N. L., McCandless, B. R., & Strickland, B. R. Personal adjustment of male and female homosexuals and heterosexuals. *Journal of Abnormal Psychology,* 1971, **78,** 237-240. *(365, 382)*

Thompson, R. *Foundations of physiological psychology.* New York: Harper & Row, 1967. *(67)*

Thompson, I. G., & Rathod, N. H. Aversion therapy for heroin dependence. *Lancet,* 1968, **2,** 382-384. *(353)*

Thorne, F. C. The etiology of sociopathic reactions. *American Journal of Psychotherapy,* 1959, **13,** 319-330. *(44)*

Thorne, F. C. Diagnostic classification and nomenclature for existential state reactions. *Journal of Clinical Psychology,* 1970, **26,** 401-420. *(400)*

Thorne, F. C. The existential study. *Journal of Clinical Psychology,* 1973, **29,** 387-391. *(400)*

Thorpe, J. G., Schmidt, E., Brown, P. T., & Castell, D. Aversion-relief therapy: A new method for general application. *Behaviour Research and Therapy,* 1964, **2,** 71-82. *(388)*

Todd, F. J. Coverant control of self-evaluative responses in the treatment of depression: A new use for an old principle. *Behavior Therapy,* 1972, **3,** 91-94. *(245)*

Tooth, G. C., & Newton, M. P. *Leucotomy in England and Wales, 1942-1954.* Ministry of Health Reports on Public Health and Medical Subjects, No. 104. London: Her Majesty's Stationary Office, 1961. *(199)*

Townsend, C. *Old age: The last segregation.* New York: Grossman Publishers, 1971. *(500, 512)*

Tremper, M. Dependency in alco-
holics: A sociological view. *Quarterly Journal of Studies on Alcohol,* 1972, **33,** 186-190. *(332)*

Truax, C. B., & Carkhuff, R. R. *Toward effective counseling and psychotherapy.* Chicago: Aldine, 1967. *(302)*

Turnbull, J. W. Asthma conceived as a learned response. *Journal of Psychosomatic Research,* 1962, **6,** 59-70. *(425)*

Tyhurst, J. S. Paranoid patterns. In A. H. Leighton, J. A. Clausen, & R. N. Wilson (Eds.), *Explorations in social psychiatry.* New York: Basic Books, 1957. *(228)*

Tyler, V., & Brown, G. The use of swift, brief isolation as a group control device for institutionalized delinquents. *Behaviour Research and Therapy,* 1967, **5,** 1-9. *(412)*

Uhlenhuth, E. H., Lipman, R. S., & Covi, L. Combined pharmacotherapy and psychotherapy: Controlled studies. *Journal of Nervous and Mental Disease,* 1969, **148,** 52-64. *(318)*

Ullmann, L. P., & Krasner, L. *A psychological approach to abnormal behavior.* Englewood Cliffs, N.J.: Prentice-Hall, 1969. *(20, 198, 291)*

United States Commission on Obscenity and Pornography. *The report of the commission of obscenity and pornography.* Washington, D.C.: United States Government Printing Office, 1970. *(381, 382)*

Vaernet, K., & Madsen, A. Stereotaxic amygdalotomy and basofrontal tractotomy in psychotics with aggressive behaviour. *Journal of Neurology, Neurosurgery, & Psychiatry,* 1970, **33,** 858-863. *(199)*

Valins, S., & Ray, A. Effects of cognitive desensitization on avoidance behavior. *Journal of Personality and Social Psychology,* 1967, **7,** 345-350. *(291)*

Valliant, G. E. The natural history of narcotic drug addition. *Seminars in Psychiatry,* 1970, **2,** 486-498. *(350)*
Van Hemel, S. B. Pup retrieving as a reinforcer in nulliparous mice. *Journal of Experimental Analysis of Behavior,* 1973, **19,** 233-238. *(106)*

Van Zoost, B., & McNulty, J. Autonomic functioning in process and reactive schizophrenia. *Canadian Journal of Behavioral Science,* 1971, **3,** 307-323. *(168)*

Venables, P. H. Input dysfunction in schizophrenia. In B. A. Maher (Ed.), *Progress in experimental personality research.* New York: Academic, 1964. *(194)*

Victor, M., Adams, R., & Collins, G. *The Wernicke-Korsakoff syndrome.* Philadelphia: Davis, 1971. *(505)*

Vogler, R. E., Lunde, S. E., Johnson, G. R., & Martin, P. L. Electrical aversion conditioning with chronic alcoholics. *Journal of Consulting and Clinical Psychology,* 1970, **34,** 302-307. *(339)*

Volkman, R., & Cressey, D. R. Differential association and the rehabilitation of drug addicts. *American Journal of Sociology,* 1963, **64,** 129-142. *(352)*

Von Domarus, E. The specific laws of logic in schizophrenia. In J. Kasanin (Ed.), *Language and thought in schizophrenia.* Berkeley: University of California Press, 1944. *(159)*

W., Bill et. al. *Alcoholics anonymous: The story of how many thousands of men and women have recovered from alcoholism.* New York: Works Publishing Company, 1955. *(337)*

Wagner, N. N., Fujita, B. N., & Pion, R. J. Sexual behavior in high school. *Journal of Sex Research,* 1973, **9,** 150-155. *(376)*

Waldrop, M. & Halverson, C. Minor physical anomalies and hyperactive behavior in young children. In J. Hellmuth (Ed.), *Exceptional infant. Vol. 2, Studies in abnormalities.* New York: Brunner/Mazel, 1971. *(464)*

Walinder, J. Transsexuals: Physical characteristics, parental age, and birth order. In R. Green & J. Money (Eds.), *Transsexualism and sex reassignment.* Baltimore: Johns Hopkins, 1969. *(371)*

Walker, J. Aspects of fetal environment. In H. Wolff (Ed.), *Mechanisms of congenital malformation.* New York: Association for the Aid of Crippled Children, 1955. *(507)*

Wallin, P. An appraisal of some methodological aspects of the Kinsey report. *American Sociological Review,* 1949, **14,** 197–210. *(376)*

Walter, W. G. Intrinsic rhythms of the brain. In I. Field (Ed.), *Handbook of physiology.* Sect. I. *Neurophysiology.* Washington, D.C.: American Physiological Society, 1959. *(427)*

Walton, D. The application of learning theory to the treatment of a case of bronchial asthma. In H. J. Eysenck (Ed.), *Behavior therapy and the neuroses.* Oxford: Pergamon, 1960. (a) *(428)*

Walton, D. The application of learning theory to the treatment of a case of neurodermatitis. In H. J. Eysenck (Ed.), *Behavior therapy and the neuroses.* Oxford: Pergamon, 1960. (b) *(428)*

Wanderer, Z. W. Existential depression treated by desensitization of phobias: Strategy and transcript. *Journal of Behavior Therapy and Experimental Psychiatry,* 1972, **3,** 111–116. *(245)*

Wang, H., & Busse, E. Dementia in old age. In C. Wells (Ed.), *Dementia.* Philadelphia: Davis, 1971. *(501)*

Ward, A. Early infantile autism: Diagnosis, etiology, and treatment. *Psychological Bulletin,* 1970, **73,** 350–362. *(501)*

Ward, C. H., Beck, A. T., Mendelson, M., Mock, J. E., & Erbaugh, J. K. The psychiatric nomenclature: Reasons for diagnostic disagreement. *Archives of General Psychiatry,* 1962, **7,** 198–205. *(231)*

Ward, D. A., & Kassebaum, G. G. *Women's prison.* Chicago: Aldine, 1965. *(379)*

Warner, L. K., & Lunt, C. G. *The social life of a modern community.* New Haven: Yale, 1941. *(36)*

Warren, E. (Ch.) *Report of the President's commission on the assassination of President John F. Kennedy.* Washington: United States Government Printing Office, 1964. *(145–149)*

Watson, C. G. Intratest scatter in hospitalized brain-damaged and schizophrenic patients. *Journal of Consulting Psychology,* 1965, **29,** 596. *(129)*

Watson, C. G. An MMPI scale to separate brain-damaged from schizophrenic men. *Journal of Consulting and Clinical Psychology,* 1971, **36,** 121–125. *(170)*

Watson, J. B., & Rayner, P. Conditioned emotional reactions. *Journal of Experimental Psychology,* 1920, **3,** 1–14. *(103, 258–259, 419)*

Weakland, J. H. The "double-bind" hypothesis of schizophrenia and three-party interaction. In D. D. Jackson (Ed.), *The etiology of schizophrenia.* New York: Basic Books, 1960. *(190)*

Webb, J. T., Miller, M. I., & Fowler, R. D. Extending professional time: A computerized MMPI interpretive service. *Journal of Clinical Psychology,* 1970, **26,** 210–214. *(135)*

Weckowicz, T. Depersonalization. In C. Costello (Ed.), *Symptoms of psychopathology.* New York: Wiley, 1970. *(266)*

Wegrocki, H. J. A critique of cultural and statistical concepts of abnormality. *Journal of Abnormal and Social Psychology,* 1939, **34,** 166–178. *(11)*

Weiner, H., Singer, M. T., & Reiser, M. F. Cardiovascular responses and their psychological correlates. I: A study in healthy young adults and patients with peptic ulcer and hypertension. *Psychosomatic Medicine,* 1962, **24,** 477–498. *(422)*

Weingaertner, A. H. Self-administered aversive stimulation with hallucinating hospitalized schizophrenics. *Journal of Consulting and Clinical Psychology,* 1971, **36,** 422–429. *(212)*

Weinman, B., Gelbart, P., Wallace, M., & Post, M. Inducing assertive behavior in chronic schizophrenics: A comparison of socioenvironmental, desensitization, and relaxation therapies. *Journal of Consulting and Clinical Psychology,* 1972, **39,** 246–252. *(212)*

Weinstein, S., & Teuber, H. L. Effects of penetrating brain injury on intelligence test scores. *Science,* 1957, **105,** 1036–1037. *(499)*

Weiss, L., & Masling, J. Further validation of a Rorschach measure of oral imagery: A study of six clinical groups. *Journal of Abnormal Psychology,* 1970, **76,** 83–87. *(422)*

Welner, A., Liss, J. L., Robins, E., & Richardson, M. Undiagnosed psychiatric patients. I: Record study. *British Journal of Psychiatry,* 1972, **120,** 315–319. *(120)*

Welsh, G. An anxiety index and an internalization ratio for the MMPI. *Journal of Consulting Psychology,* 1952, **16,** 65–72. *(270)*

Wender, P. H., Rosenthal, D., Zahn, T. P., & Kety, S. S. The psychiatric adjustment of the adopting parents of schizophrenics. *American Journal of Psychiatry,* 1971, **127,** 1013–1018. *(187)*

Wenger, M. A., Averill, J. R., & Smith, D. D. B. Autonomic activity during sexual arousal. *Psychophysiology,* 1968, **4,** 468–478. *(383)*

Wenger, M. A., Clemens, T. L., Coleman, D. R., Cullen, T. D., & Engel, B. T. Autonomic response specificity. *Psychosomatic Medicine,* 1961, **23,** 185–193. *(420)*

Werry, J., & Cohrssen, J. Enuresis—An etiologic and therapeutic study. *Journal of Pediatrics,* 1965, **67,** 423–431. *(447)*

Werry, J., & Sprague, R. Hyperactivity. In C. Costello (Ed.), *Symptoms of psychopathology.* New York: Wiley, 1970. *(460)*

Wesselhoeft, C. Rubella (German measles) and congenital deformities. *New England Journal of Medicine,* 1949, **240,** 258–261. *(477)*

Whatmore, G. B., & Ellis, R. M., Jr. Some neurophysiologic aspects of depressive states: An electromyographic study. *Archives of General Psychiatry,* 1959, **1,** 70–80. *(236)*

Whatmore, G. B., & Ellis, R. M., Jr. Further neurophysiologic aspects of depressed states: An electromyographic study. *Archives of General Psychiatry,* 1962, **6,** 243–253. *(236)*

Wheeler, W. M. An analysis of Rorschach indices of male homosexuality. *Rorschach Research Exchange,* 1949, **13,** 97–126. *(383)*

Whitehorn, J. C., & Betz, B. Further studies of the doctor as a crucial variable in the outcome of treatment of schizophrenic patients. *American Journal of Psychiatry,* 1960, **117,** 215–223. *(300)*

Whitelock, P. R., Patrick, J. H., &

Overall, J. E. Personality patterns and alcohol abuse in a state hospital population. *Journal of Abnormal Psychology*, 1971, **78**, 9–16. *(332)*

Whitlock, F. A. The syndrome of barbiturate dependence. *Medical Journal of Australia*, 1970, **2**, 391–396. *(349)*

Whitney, L., & Barnard, L. Implications of operant learning theory for nursing care of the retarded child. *Mental Retardation*, 1966, **4**, 26–29. *(485–486)*

Whittingham, S., Mackay, I. R., Jones, I. H., & Davies, B. Absence of brain antibodies in patients with schizophrenia. *British Medical Journal*, 1968, **1**, 347–348. *(185)*

Whybrow, R. C., & Mendels, J. Toward a biology of depression: Some suggestions from neurophysiology. *American Journal of Psychiatry*, 1969, **125**, 1491–1500. *(236)*

Wikler, A. Conditioning factors in opiate addiction and relapse. In D. M. Wilner & G. G. Kassebaum (Eds.), *Narcotics*. New York: McGraw-Hill, 1965. *(346)*

Wikler, A. Opioid addiction. In A. M. Freedman & H. I. Kaplan (Eds.). *Comprehensive textbook of psychiatry*. Baltimore: Williams & Wilkins, 1967. *(349)*

Williams, E. Deductive reasoning in schizophrenia. *Journal of Abnormal and Social Psychology*, 1964, **69**, 47–61. *(159)*

Williams, H., Lubin, A., & Gieseking, C. Direct measurement of cognitive deficit in brain injured patients. *Journal of Consulting Psychology*, 1959, **23**, 300–305. *(499)*

Williams, J., Dudley, H., & Overall, J. E. Validity of the 16 PF and the MMPI in a mental hospital setting. *Journal of Abnormal Psychology*, 1972, **80**, 261–270. *(268)*

Willie, C. V., & Levy, J. D. Black is lonely. *Psychology Today*, 1972, **5**, 50–52, 76, 78, 80. *(48)*

Wilner, D. M., & Kassebaum, G. G. *Narcotics*. New York: McGraw-Hill, 1965. *(342)*

Wilson, E., Fisher, K., & Fuqua, M. *Principles of nutrition*. New York: Wiley, 1965. *(506)*

Wilson, G. T. Behavior therapy and homosexuality: A critical perspective. Unpublished manuscript, Rutgers University, 1972. *(388)*

Wilson, G. T. Counterconditioning versus forced exposure in the extinction of avoidance responding and conditioned fear in rats. *Journal of Comparative and Physiological Psychology*, 1973, **82**, 105–114. *(290)*

Wilson, G. T., & Davison, G. C. Processes of fear reduction in systematic desensitization: Animal studies. *Psychological Bulletin*, 1971, **76**, 1–14. *(290)*

Wilson, W., & Mishkin, M. Comparison of the effects of inferotemporal and lateral occipital lesions on visually guided behavior in monkeys. *Journal of Comparative and Physiological Psychology*, 1959, **52**, 1–17. *(66)*

Winett, R. A., & Winkler, R. C. Current behavior modification in the classroom: Be still, be quiet, be docile. *Journal of Applied Behavioral Analysis*, 1972, **5**, 499–504. *(212)*

Wing, L. Physiological effects of performing a difficult task in patients with anxiety states. *Journal of Psychosomatic Research*, 1964, **7**, 283–294. *(270)*

Winick, M., & Noble, A. Cellular response in rats during malnutrition at various ages. *Journal of Nutrition*, 1966, **89**, 300–306. *(507)*

Winick, M., Rosso, P., & Waterlow, J. Cellular growth of cerebrum, cerebellum, and brain stem in normal and marasmic children. *Experimental Neurology*, 1970, **26**, 393–400. *(507)*

Winnicott, D. W. *The child and the outside world: Studies in developing relationships*. New York: Basic Books, 1957. *(33)*

Winter, A. *The surgical control of behavior: A symposium*. Springfield, Ill.: Charles C Thomas, 1971. *(199)*

Winter, W., & Salcines, R. The validity of the objective Rorschach and the MMPI. *Journal of Consulting Psychology*, 1958, **22**, 199–202. *(170)*

Wittenborn, J. R. *Wittenborn psychiatric rating scales*. New York: Psychological Corporation, 1955. *(124)*

Wittenborn, J. R. Depression. In B. B. Wolman (Ed.), *Handbook of clinical psychology*. New York: McGraw-Hill, 1965. *(235)*

Wittenborn, J. R. Do rating scales objectify clinical impressions? *Comprehensive Psychiatry*, 1967, **8**, 386–392. *(124)*

Wittkower, E. D., & Lipowski, Z. J. Recent developments in psychosomatic medicine. *Psychosomatic Medicine*, 1966, **28**, 722–737. *(420)*

Wittman, P., Sheldon, W. H., & Katz, C. J. A study of the relationship between constitutional variations and fundamental psychotic behavior reactions. *Journal of Nervous and Mental Disease*, 1948, **108**, 470–476. *(72–73, 227)*

Wolberg, L. R. *The technique of psychotherapy*. New York: Grune & Stratton, 1954. *(296–297)*

Wolf, M. M., Giles, D. K., & Hall, R. V. Experiments with token reinforcement in a remedial classroom. *Behaviour Research and Therapy*, 1968, **6**, 51–64. *(212)*

Wolff, W. H., & Morris, L. A. Intellectual and personality characteristics of parents of autistic children. *Journal of Abnormal Psychology*, 1971, **77**, 155–161. *(451)*

Wolpe, J. Experimental neuroses as learned behavior. *British Journal of Psychology*, 1952, **43**, 243–268. *(290–292)*

Wolpe, J. *Psychotherapy by reciprocal inhibition*. Stanford, Calif.: Stanford, 1958. *(19, 290–292, 389)*

Wolpe, J. *The practice of behavior therapy*. New York: Pergamon, 1969. *(19, 20, 260, 290–292, 306–310, 315)*

Wolpe, J., & Rachman, S. Psychoanalytic "evidence": A critique based on Freud's case of little Hans. *Journal of Nervous and Mental Diseases*, 1960, **130**, 135–148. *(86–88)*

Woodruff, R., Clayton, P., & Guze, S. Hysteria: Studies of diagnosis, outcome, and prevalence. *Journal of the American Medical Association*, 1971, **215**, 425–428. *(261, 262)*

Woods, J. H., Ikomi, F., & Winger, G. The reinforcing property of ethanol. In P. J. Creaven & M. K. Roach (Eds.), *Biological aspects of alcohol*. Austin: University of Texas Press, 1971. *(332)*

Woodward J. Emotional disturbances of burned children. *British Medical Journal*, 1959, **1**, 1009–1013. *(441)*

Woodworth, C. H. Attack elicited in

rats by electrical stimulation of the lateral hypothalamus. *Dissertation Abstracts International. 1971.* **32,** 602. *(65)*

World Health Organization. Cannibus sativa. *WHO Chronicle,* 1972, **26,** 20–28. *(344)*

Wyatt, R. J., Termini, B. A., & Davis, J. Biochemical and sleep studies of schizophrenia: A review of the literature 1960–1970. Pt. I: Biochemical studies. *Schizophrenia Bulletin,* 1971, **4,** 10–44. *(183)*

X, Malcolm. *The autobiography of Malcolm X.* New York: Grove Press, 1966. *(3, 4, 5)*

Yamamoto, K., & Dizney, H. F. Rejection of the mentally ill: A study of attitudes of student teachers. *Journal of Counseling Psychology,* 1967, **14,** 264–268. *(5)*

Yates, A. J. *Behavior therapy.* New York: Wiley, 1970. *(309, 447, 459, 460)*

Yates, A. J., & Poole, A. D. Behavioral analysis in a case of excessive frequency of micturition. *Behavior therapy,* 1972, **3,** 449–453. *(428)*

Young, R. C. Clinical judgment as a means of improving actuarial prediction from the MMPI. *Journal*

of Consulting and Clinical Psycology, 1972, **38,** 457–459. *(135)*

Zax, M., & Cowen, E. Research on early detection and prevention of emotional dysfunction in young school children. In C. Spielberger (Ed.), *Current topics in clinical and community psychology,* Vol. 1. New York: Academic, 1969, *(463)*

Zechnich, R. Exhibitionism: Dynamics and treatment. *Psychiatric Quarterly,* 1971, **45,** 70–75. *(387)*

Zelin, M. L. Validity of the MMPI scales for measuring twenty psychiatric dimensions. *Journal of Consulting and Clinical Psychology,* 1971, **37,** 286–290. *(135)*

Zetzel, E. R. The predisposition to depression. *Canadian Psychiatric Association Journal,* 1966, **11,** Suppl. 236–249. *(231)*

Zigler, E. Familial mental retardation: A continuing dilemma. *Science,* 1967, **155,** 292–298. *(475–476, 485)*

Zigler, E., Imboden, J., & Meyer, E. Contemporary conversion reactions: A clinical study. *American Journal of Psychiatry,* 1960, **116,** 901–910. *(261)*

Zigler, E., & Phillips, L. Psychiatric diagnosis: A critique. *Journal of Abnormal and Social Psychology.* 1961, **63,** 607–618. *(445)*

Zilboorg, G., & Henry, G. *A history of medical psychology.* New York: Norton, 1941. *(7, 13, 154, 256, 494)*

Zimmerman, E., & Zimmerman, J. The alteration of behavior in a special classroom situation. *Journal of Experimental Analysis of Behavior,* 1962, **5,** 59–60. *(449)*

Zimmerman, R., Steere, R., Strobel, D., & Hom, H. Abnormal social development of protein-malnourished rhesus monkeys. *Journal of Psychology,* 1972, **80,** 125–131. *(507)*

Zubin, J., Eron, L. D., & Schumer, F. *An experimental approach to projective techniques.* New York: Wiley, 1965. *(139)*

Zucker, R. A., & Manosevitz, M. MMPI patterns of overt male homosexuals. Reinterpretation and comment on Dean and Richardson's study. *Journal of Consulting Psychology,* 1966, **30,** 555–557. *(382)*

Zucker, R. A., & Van Horn, H. Sibling social structure and oral behavior: Drinking and smoking in adolescence. *Quarterly Journal of Studies on Alcohol,* 1972, **33,** 193–197. *(332)*

Zung, W. W. K. A self-rating depression scale. *Archives of General Psychiatry,* 1965, **12,** 63–70. *(234)*

zur Nieden, M. The influence of constitution and environment upon the development of adopted children. *Journal of Psychology,* 1951, **31,** 91–95. *(187)*

Index